JOURNALISM AND THE PERIO
IN NINETEENTH-CENTUR\

C000045514

Newly commissioned essays by leading scholars offer a comprehensive and authoritative overview of the diversity, range and impact of the newspaper and periodical press in nineteenth-century Britain. Essays range from studies of periodical formats in the nineteenth century – reviews, magazines and newspapers – to accounts of individual journalists, many of them eminent writers of the day. The uneasy relationship between the new 'profession' of journalism and the evolving profession of authorship is investigated, as is the impact of technological innovations, such as the telegraph, the typewriter and new processes of illustration; contributors go on to consider the transnational and global dimensions of the British press and its impact in the rest of the world. As digitisation of historical media opens up new avenues of research, the collection reveals the centrality of the press to our understanding of the nineteenth century.

JOANNE SHATTOCK is Emeritus Professor of Victorian Literature at the University of Leicester. Her books include *Politics and Reviewers: the* Edinburgh *and the* Quarterly *in the Early Victorian Age* (1989); the *Oxford Guide to British Women Writers* (1993); and as editor, *The Cambridge Bibliography of English Literature 1800–1900* (Cambridge, 1999), *Women and Literature in Britain* (Cambridge, 2001), and *The Cambridge Companion to English Literature* (Cambridge, 2010). She is the editor of *The Works of Elizabeth Gaskell*, 10 vols. (2005–06), and co-editor with Elisabeth Jay of *Selected Works of Margaret Oliphant*, 25 vols. (2011–16). She is Past President of the Research Society for Victorian Periodicals and was Founding President of the British Association for Victorian Studies (2000–03).

JOURNALISM AND THE PERIODICAL PRESS IN NINETEENTH-CENTURY BRITAIN

EDITED BY

JOANNE SHATTOCK

University of Leicester

CAMBRIDGE
UNIVERSITY PRESS

CAMBRIDGE
UNIVERSITY PRESS

University Printing House, Cambridge CB2 8BS, United Kingdom

One Liberty Plaza, 20th Floor, New York, NY 10006, USA

477 Williamstown Road, Port Melbourne, VIC 3207, Australia

314-321, 3rd Floor, Plot 3, Splendor Forum, Jasola District Centre, New Delhi - 110025, India

79 Anson Road, #06-04/06, Singapore 079906

Cambridge University Press is part of the University of Cambridge.

It furthers the University's mission by disseminating knowledge in the pursuit of education, learning and research at the highest international levels of excellence.

www.cambridge.org
Information on this title: www.cambridge.org/9781107449961
10.1017/9781316084403

First published 2017
First paperback edition 2019

A catalogue record for this publication is available from the British Library

ISBN 978-1-107-08573-2 Hardback
ISBN 978-1-107-44996-1 Paperback

Contents

v

Illustrations

Tables

Notes on Contributors

JULIETTE ATKINSON is Lecturer in English at University College London. She is the author of *Victorian Biography Reconsidered: A Study of Nineteenth-Century 'Hidden' Lives* (2010). Other publications include articles on the Victorian reception of Dumas *père*, the London Library's stock of French fiction and the activities of the Burlington Arcade foreign bookseller William Jeffs. Her book *French Novels and the Victorians* is forthcoming in 2017.

LAUREL BRAKE is Professor Emerita of Literature and Print Culture at Birkbeck, University of London. Author of *Print in Transition* (2000) and *Subjugated Knowledges* (1994), she has co-edited the *Nineteenth-Century Serials Edition*, www.ncse.ac.uk/, a digital edition of six nineteenth-century periodicals; the *Dictionary of Nineteenth-Century Journalism* (2009) with Marysa Demoor; and *W. T. Stead: Newspaper Revolutionary* (2012) and a special issue on Stead in *19*. www.19.bbk.ac .uk/. In 2015, she co-edited *The News of the World and the British Press, 1843–2011*, with Chandrika Kaul and Mark Turner. She is now writing *Ink Work* on Walter and Clara Pater and editing an edition of Walter Pater's journalism.

GEOFFREY CANTOR is Professor Emeritus of the History of Science at the University of Leeds and Senior Honorary Research Fellow in the Department of Science and Technology Studies, University College London. Between 1999 and 2006, he co-directed, with Sally Shuttleworth, the SciPer (Science in the Nineteenth-Century Periodical) Project. His publications include *Religion and the Great Exhibition of 1851* (2010); he co-authored *Science in the Nineteenth-Century Periodical: Reading the Magazine of Nature* (2004) and edited *The Great Exhibition: A Documentary History*, 4 vols. (2013).

IAIN CRAWFORD is Associate Professor of English and Faculty Director of Undergraduate Research and Experiential Learning at the University of

Delaware. His current book project examines the relationship between Charles Dickens and Harriet Martineau and its implications for the formation of Victorian journalism and the emergence of the professional woman author. Work from this project has appeared in *Nineteenth-Century Literature* and the collections *Charles Dickens and the Mid-Victorian Press 1850–1870* (2012) and *Dickens and Massachusetts: The Other America* (2015). He is President of the Dickens Society.

FIONNUALA DILLANE is Lecturer in Nineteenth-Century Literature at the School of English, Drama and Film, University College Dublin. She publishes in the fields of Victorian print culture, genre history, memory studies and gender. Recent work is forthcoming in *Researching the Nineteenth-Century Periodical Press: Case Studies* (2017), and in the *Journal of European Periodical Studies* (2016). Her monograph *Before George Eliot: Marian Evans and the Periodical Press* (2013), joint winner of the Robert and Vineta Colby Prize for 2014, was published in paperback in 2016.

JOHN DREW is Professor of English Literature at the University of Buckingham, where he has taught since 1998. He is the author of *Dickens the Journalist* (2003); the editor, with Michael Slater, of *The Uncommercial Traveller and Other Papers, 1859–1870* (2000); and director of the *Dickens Journals Online* project (www.djo.org.uk). He has published numerous articles and book chapters on aspects of Victorian journalism and Dickens's connections with the mid-Victorian press. He is editing *Hard Times* for Oxford University Press's relaunched Clarendon Press edition of the novels of Charles Dickens and sits on its editorial advisory board.

ABHIJIT GUPTA is Professor of English at Jadavpur University, and Director, Jadavpur University Press. He is co-editor, along with Swapan Chakravorty, of the Book History in India series, of which four volumes have been published: *Print Areas* (2004), *Moveable Types* (2008), *New Word Order* (2011) and *Founts of Knowledge* (2016). He was associate editor for South Asia for the *Oxford Companion to the Book* (2010). He has completed an electronic database and location register of all books printed in Bengali from 1801 to 1867 and is currently at work on the 1868–1914 period. His other research areas include science fiction and fandom, graphic novels, crime fiction and physical cultures.

MARTIN HEWITT is Pro Vice Chancellor and Dean, Faculty of Arts, Law and Social Sciences at Anglia Ruskin University. He has published widely on mid-Victorian urban culture, Victorian culture institutions (including lectures and libraries) and on the historiography of Victorian Studies. He has served as editor of the *Journal of Victorian Culture* and as Hon. Secretary of the British Association for Victorian Studies. His most recent study is *The Dawn of the Cheap Press in Victorian Britain. The End of the 'Taxes on Knowledge', 1849–1869* (2014). He is currently developing a project on Victorian generations.

LORRAINE JANZEN KOOISTRA is Professor of English and Co-Director of the Centre for Digital Humanities at Ryerson University in Toronto, Canada. A specialist in Victorian illustration, her publications include *The Artist as Critic: Bitextuality in Fin-de-Siècle Illustrated Books* (1995), *Christina Rossetti and Illustration: A Publishing History* (2002) and *Poetry, Pictures, and Popular Publishing: The Illustrated Gift Book and Victorian Visual Culture* (2011). She is co-editor of the electronic resource *The Yellow Nineties Online* (www.1890s.ca), which publishes searchable editions of fin-de-siècle aesthetic magazines.

GRAHAM LAW is Professor in Media Studies at the Graduate School of Culture and Communication Studies, Waseda University, Tokyo. He is one of the editors of *The Public Face of Wilkie Collins: The Collected Letters*, 4 vols. (2005); among his publications on Victorian literature and media are *Serializing Fiction in the Victorian Press* (2000) and (with Andrew Maunder) *Wilkie Collins: A Literary Life* (2008).

BRIAN MAIDMENT is Professor of the History of Print at Liverpool John Moores University and President of the Research Society for Victorian Periodicals. His most recent book is *Comedy, Caricature and the Social Order 1820–1850* (2013). He is currently completing a study of Robert Seymour and Regency print culture.

JAMES MUSSELL is Associate Professor of Victorian Literature at the University of Leeds. He is the author of *Science, Time and Space in the Late Nineteenth-Century Periodical Press* (2007) and *The Nineteenth-Century Press in the Digital Age* (2012). He is one of the editors of the *Nineteenth-Century Serials Edition* and *W.T. Stead: Newspaper Revolutionary* (2012).

BARBARA ONSLOW was educated at Oxford and Manchester Universities. Although most of her career has been spent in higher education, lately at Reading University, her first job was as a journalist on a regional evening newspaper. She is the author of *Women of the Press in Nineteenth Century*

Britain (2000) and has published widely on the work of women journalists. Her blog *Victorian Page* includes material on annuals (www.victorianpage.com).

LINDA H. PETERSON (1948–2015) was Niel Gray Jr. Professor of English at Yale University. Her books include *Victorian Autobiography* (1986), *Traditions of Victorian Women's Autobiography* (1999) and *Becoming a Woman of Letters: Myths of Authorship and Facts of the Victorian Market* (2009). She edited the *Cambridge Companion to Victorian Women's Writing* (2016).

SIMON J. POTTER is Reader in Modern History at the University of Bristol. He is the author of *News and the British World: The Emergence of an Imperial Press System, 1876–1922* (2003) and editor of *Newspapers and Empire in Ireland and Britain* (2004). He has written articles on the relationship between the media, empire and 'globalisation': on British popular imperialism and the press: and on the interface between imperial history and global history. His published work on broadcasting history includes *Broadcasting Empire: The BBC and the British World, 1922–1970* (2012).

DEEPTANIL RAY received his Phd from Jadavpur University, Kolkata, and is currently Assistant Professor in the Department of English, The Neotia University, India. He is working on the history of newspapers and periodicals in colonial and postcolonial India. His broader interests are in the interplay of politics, economics, technology, colonialism and culture in non-Western encounters with the medium of print.

MARY L. SHANNON is Lecturer in the English Department at the University of Roehampton, London. She is a graduate of the University of Cambridge and holds a PhD from King's College London. Her book *Dickens, Reynolds and Mayhew on Wellington Street: The Print Culture of a Victorian Street* was published in 2015 and won the Robert and Vineta Colby Prize for 2015. Her current project is on sound in nineteenth-century print culture and visual culture.

JOANNE SHATTOCK is Emeritus Professor of Victorian Literature at the University of Leicester. Her books include *Politics and Literature: The* Edinburgh *and the* Quarterly *in the Early Victorian Age* (1989); the *Oxford Guide to British Women Writers* (1993); and as editor, *The Cambridge Bibliography of English Literature 1800–1900* (1999), *Women and Literature in Britain 1800–1900* (2001) and the *Cambridge Companion to English Literature 1830–1914* (2010). She edited *The Works of Elizabeth Gaskell* (2005–6) and is general editor with Elisabeth Jay of the *Selected Works of Margaret Oliphant*, 25 vols. (2011–16).

DAVID STEWART is Senior Lecturer in Romantic Literature, Northumbria University. He has published widely on Romantic-period literature and culture, with articles in *Essays in Criticism*, the *Keats-Shelley Journal*, *Romanticism*, *Studies in English Literature* and the *Review of English Studies*. His work focuses on the intersections between literary and popular culture in the early nineteenth century, with a particular focus on periodicals. His monograph *Romantic Magazines and Metropolitan Literary Culture* was published in 2011.

JOHN STOKES is Emeritus Professor of Modern British Literature at King's College London and Honorary Professor of English and Drama at the University of Nottingham. Together with Mark W. Turner, he has edited two volumes of Oscar Wilde's journalism for Oxford English Texts (2013).

MARK W. TURNER is Professor of English at King's College London. His publications include *Trollope and the Magazines* (2000), *Backward Glances* (2003) and two volumes of Oscar Wilde's journalism for the Oxford English Texts complete works series, co-edited with John Stokes in 2013. Recently he has co-edited, with Laurel Brake and Chandrika Kaul, *News of the World, 1843–2011: Journalism for the Rich, Journalism for the Poor* (2015), and he is one of the editors of the journal *Media History*.

CATHERINE WATERS is Professor of Victorian Literature and Print Culture at the University of Kent. She is the author of *Dickens and the Politics of the Family* (1997) and *Commodity Culture in Dickens's Household Words: The Social Life of Goods* (2008). The latter monograph was awarded the 2009 Robert and Vineta Colby Prize by the Research Society for Victorian Periodicals. She has been working on an Arts and Humanities Research Council-funded project investigating the writing of the Victorian special correspondent, 'Journalism on the Move: The Special Correspondent and Victorian Print Culture'.

JOEL H. WIENER is Emeritus Professor of History at The City University of New York. He has written widely on aspects of modern press history. His books include *The War of the Unstamped* (1969), *Papers for the People* (1988) and *The Americanization of the British Press, 1830s–1914* (2011).

Acknowledgements

I would like to thank my fellow contributors to this volume for sharing their expertise and enthusiasm for their subjects and for their professionalism and good humour at all times. At Cambridge University Press, Linda Bree first proposed the project and has been enthusiastic throughout. I am grateful to Anna Bond, Chloe Harries and Lisa Sinclair for guiding the book through the production process. Various libraries have made available original copies of newspapers and periodicals from which the illustrations are taken. These include the library of the Institute of Historical Research, University of London; the University of Toronto Library; and the State Library of Victoria. For specialist advice relating to individual chapters, thanks are due to Barbara Cantor, Ann Donahue, Michael Lobban and Jonathan Topham.

Chronology of Publications and Events

1802   *Edinburgh Review*, quarterly, Whig, published by Archibald
Constable
Political Register founded by William Cobbett, weekly, initially
Tory
1803   The *Globe*, evening newspaper, daily
1805   *Eclectic Review*, monthly
1806   *Monthly Repository*, radical, nonconformist, closely associated
with the Unitarian movement
La Belle Assemblée, women's magazine, monthly
1808   *Examiner*, weekly, Leigh Hunt first editor
1809   *Quarterly Review*, founded in response to *Edinburgh Review*,
published by John Murray, Tory
1811   *Reflector*, edited by Leigh Hunt
1814   *New Monthly Magazine*, published by Henry Colburn
Steam-powered Koenig presses installed at *The Times*
1815   Newspaper Stamp Duty increased to 4d per sheet
British Lady's Magazine
1817   *Blackwood's Edinburgh Magazine* established by publisher
William Blackwood, Tory, monthly
Black Dwarf, radical, reformist weekly published by
T. J. Woolner
The Scotsman, weekly newspaper, Whig, published in
Edinburgh, daily from 1855
Literary Gazette and Journal of Belles Lettres, Arts, Sciences etc,
launched by Henry Colburn, weekly, edited by William Jerdan
1818   *Kaleidoscope*, weekly literary magazine
Dig-darshan, first Bengali periodical, launched by Joshua
Marshman
Samachar Darpan, first Bengali newspaper, weekly

L'Echo britannique, translated articles from English periodicals, competitor of *Revue britannique*

1825   *The Glasgow Looking Glass*, later the *Northern Looking Glass*, caricature magazine, folio

Revue britannique, monthly, published translations from English periodicals

1826   *Amulet: A Christian and Literary Remembrancer*, annual

1827   *Foreign Quarterly Review*

1828   *Athenaeum*, literary weekly

Spectator, weekly

Keepsake, annual, published by Charles Heath

1829   *London Review*, quarterly, only 2 issues

Revue de Paris (April), weekly

Revue des deux mondes (July), published twice monthly

1830   *Fraser's Magazine for Town and Country*, monthly

The Looking Glass, monthly, almost entirely graphic content

1831   *Poor Man's Guardian*, radical, unstamped weekly newspaper

Figaro in London, radical comic weekly, illustrated, edited by Gilbert À Beckett

The Caricaturist, illustrated satirical magazine, edited by C. J. Grant

Revue des deux mondes, French, published twice monthly

Drawing-Room Scrap-Book, annual, published by Henry Fisher

Englishman's Magazine, illustrated monthly, April–October only

Journal des connaissances utiles, monthly

1832   *Chambers's Edinburgh Journal*, weekly, included fiction

Sambad Prabhakar, Bengali daily newspaper, conservative

Penny Magazine, weekly, edited by Charles Knight for Society for the Diffusion of Useful Knowledge, illustrated

Tait's Edinburgh Magazine, monthly

1833   *Magasin pittoresque*, and *Musée des familles*, cheap weeklies, modelled on the *Penny Magazine*

Dublin University Magazine, monthly

Book of Beauty, annual, published by Charles Heath

1834   *Everybody's Album and Caricature Magazine*, edited by C. J. Grant

Political Drama, illustrated weekly, radical

1835   *British and Foreign Review*, quarterly

Comic Almanack, illustrated, published annually

1836   *Dublin Review*, monthly
        Newspaper Stamp Act cut stamp from 4d to 1d
        La Presse and *Le Siècle*, French daily newspapers, published some
        fiction
1837   *Northern Star*, Chartist, weekly
        Penny Satirist, radical, weekly, illustrated
        Cleave's London Satirist and Gazette of Variety, radical weekly
        paper
        Finden's Tableaux, annual
        Le Commerce, liberal newspaper, published literary criticism
        Bentley's Miscellany, illustrated, monthly, founded by publisher
        Richard Bentley, edited by Dickens, serialised fiction
1838   *Era*, Sunday paper, included sport, theatre, music hall reports as
        well as news
1839   *Art Journal*, illustrated monthly, initially the *Art-Union*,
        renamed *Art-Journal*
1840   Newspapers obtain right to report Parliamentary debates
1841   *Punch*, comic miscellany, weekly
1842   *Illustrated London News*, weekly
        Lloyd's Weekly Newspaper, Sunday newspaper
        Builder, illustrated weekly magazine
        Family Herald, penny weekly, featured fiction and poetry
1843   *Illuminated Magazine*, monthly, contained coloured woodcuts
        Tattwabodhini Patrika, radical Bengali monthly, reformist
        agenda
        News of the World, weekly Sunday newspaper
1844   Telegraph first used in Britain (to report the birth of the Prince
        of Wales)
        North British Review, quarterly
        Hood's Magazine and Comic Miscellany, monthly, published
        poetry and fiction
1845   *Douglas Jerrold's Shilling Magazine*, monthly
        British Quarterly Review
        Prospective Review, quarterly
        London Journal and Weekly Record of Literature, Science and Art,
        weekly, edited by G. W. M. Reynolds
1846   *Daily News*, Dickens first editor
        Mitchell's Newspaper Press Directory issued, appeared annually
        from 1856

Reynold's Magazine, changed title from fifth issue to *Reynold's Miscellany*. Edited by G. W. M. Reynolds. Illustrated penny fiction weekly
Douglas Jerrold's Weekly Newspaper

1847 *Howitt's Journal*, monthly, founded by William and Mary Howitt from the *People's Journal*

1848 *Rambler*, Catholic weekly, monthly from 1848, bi-monthly from 1859
New York Press Association established

1849 Association for the Repeal of the Taxes on Knowledge (ARTK) formed
Henry Mayhew reports on 'London Labour and the London Poor' in the *Morning Chronicle*
Eliza Cook's Journal, weekly, some signed articles

1850 *Reynolds's Weekly Newspaper*. Sunday newspaper
Leader, radical weekly paper founded by Thornton Hunt and G. H. Lewes
Household Words, weekly miscellany founded by Charles Dickens, published by Bradbury and Evans
Germ, illustrated magazine founded by Pre-Raphaelite brotherhood, 4 issues
Expositor: A Weekly Illustrated Recorder of Inventions, Designs, and Art-Manufactures, illustrated, weekly

1851 Paul Julius Reuter sends financial information by telegraph between London and the Continent
Illustrated Exhibitor, weekly, published by Cassell
Bibidhartha-sangraha, Bengali monthly, modelled on cheap British miscellanies, printed in colour

1852 *Englishwoman's Domestic Magazine* established by Samuel and Isabella Beeton, illustrated, monthly

1853 Repeal of advertisement duty
London Quarterly Review

1854 William Howard Russell dispatched to the Crimea to cover the war as a 'special correspondent' for *The Times*

1855 Repeal of newspaper stamp duty
National Review, quarterly, successor to *Prospective Review*, edited by Walter Bagehot and R. H. Hutton
Saturday Review, weekly
Journal pour tous, serialised French and English fiction

Daily Telegraph, first London morning newspaper
Saturday Review, weekly, acerbic style prompted the name 'Saturday Reviler'

1856   High-speed Hoe press introduced by *Lloyd's Newspaper*

1857   Obscene Publications Act

1858   *Bookseller*, monthly (to 1908)
English Woman's Journal, monthly, promoted by Langham Place women's group

1859   *All the Year Round*, successor to *Household Words*, weekly miscellany, 'conducted' by Dickens
Once a Week, miscellany, published by Bradbury & Evans
Macmillan's Magazine, monthly, house magazine of Macmillan publishers, first of the 'shilling' monthly magazines, signed contributions
Bentley's Quarterly Review (4 issues only)

1860   *Cornhill Magazine*, monthly, priced at one shilling, house magazine of Smith, Elder and Co.; emphasis on serialised fiction, illustrated, edited by W. M. Thackeray.
Temple Bar, shilling monthly, focus on serial fiction in response to *Cornhill*, edited by G. A. Sala
Good Words, weekly, monthly from 1861, published by Alexander Strahan, serialised fiction
National Reformer, founded by Charles Bradlaugh, weekly, radical

1861   Repeal of excise duty on paper, the last of the so-called Taxes on Knowledge
Sixpenny Magazine: A Miscellany for All Classes and All Seasons, published translations of French serial fiction

1862   *Home and Foreign Review*, quarterly, derived from *Rambler*
Bow Bells, penny weekly magazine aimed at lower-middle-class readers; absorbed *Reynold's Weekly Newspaper* in 1869

1863   *Reader*, weekly, published by Macmillan
Literary Times, literary weekly, 11 issues only
Bamabodhini Patrika, Bengali periodical directed to women readers

1865   *Pall Mall Gazette*, London evening newspaper, instrumental in developing 'new journalism'
Fortnightly Review, frequency changed to monthly, published by Chapman and Hall, signed articles

1866   Atlantic cable laid, facilitating transatlantic journalism
        Contemporary Review, monthly, published by Alexander
        Strahan, edited by James Knowles
        Belgravia, shilling monthly, edited by Mary Elizabeth Braddon
1867   *Saint Paul's Magazine*, shilling monthly, edited by Anthony
        Trollope
        Tinsley's Magazine, shilling monthly, illustrated, house magazine
        of Tinsley Brothers, publishers, edited by Edmund Yates
        New York Evening Telegram founded
1868   Press Association (UK) founded
        Walter (Hoe) Web Rotary Presses introduced at *The Times*
        Amritabazar Patrika, Bengali weekly newspaper, later bilingual
        and then daily English language publication
1869   Newspapers, Printers, and Reading Room Act abandoned
        registration and sureties for newspapers
        Academy, monthly, specialist academic journal
        Nature, general scientific weekly
        Graphic, weekly (daily from 1890), illustrated, rival of *Illustrated
        London News*
1870   Post Office Act required registration of newspapers intended for
        transmission through the post
1871   May's *British and Irish Press Guide* issued
1872   *Bangadarshan*, Bengali literary periodical, serialised fiction,
        political articles
1873   Tillotson's Newspaper Literature Syndicate established,
        syndicated fiction in newspapers in Britain and Europe
1874   *World*, weekly newspaper founded by Edmund Yates, featured
        celebrity interviews and society gossip
1876   *Chicago Daily News* founded
1877   *Nineteenth Century* founded, edited by James Knowles, monthly,
        advocated signature
        Truth founded, 6d weekly, edited by Henry Labouchère
1880   *St James's Gazette*, daily evening paper, rival of *Pall Mall Gazette*,
        edited by Frederick Greenwood
1881   Newspaper Libel and Registration Act transferred
        responsibility for registration to the registrar of Joint Stock
        Companies
        Evening News, London evening newspaper selling for ½ d,
        intensive reporting, purchased by Harmsworth brothers in 1894

Tit-Bits, penny paper consisting of extracts from other publications, published by George Newnes

1882   *Scottish Review*, quarterly

1883   *National Review* (II), quarterly

1884   Society of Authors founded

National Association of Journalists (later the Institute of Journalists) founded

Sell's *Dictionary of the World's Press* founded

1885   W. T. Stead publishes 'Maiden Tribute of Modern Babylon' in *Pall Mall Gazette*

1886   *Lady's World*, monthly, launched by Cassell, retitled *Woman's World* (1887) with Oscar Wilde as editor

1887   Matthew Arnold uses the term 'New Journalism' in his essay 'Up to Easter' in the *Nineteenth Century* (May 1887)

1888   Institute of Journalists founded (formerly National Association of Journalists)

Observer, later *National Observer* (1890), weekly, edited by W. E. Henley

Financial Times, initially titled *London Financial Guide*, thrice weekly, then six days per week, printed on pink paper from 1893

Star, daily evening newspaper, edited by T. P. O'Connor, first daily to include regular political cartoons

1889   *New Review*, monthly

1890   *Speaker*, weekly review, Liberal

1891   *Daily Graphic*, first daily illustrated paper

1892   *Review of Reviews*, monthly, founded by W. T. Stead

Strand Magazine, monthly, illustrated, published by George Newnes

1893   *Westminster Gazette*, evening daily founded by George Newnes

Sketch, first weekly illustrated entirely by photographic processes, edited by C. K. Shorter

1894   Society of Women Journalists founded

Yellow Book, quarterly, illustrated, edited by Henry Harland and Aubrey Beardsley (1894–5), published by John Lane and Elkin Matthews

1896   *Daily Mail* founded by Harold and Alfred Harmsworth, selling for 1/2d

Cosmopolis, monthly, contributions in French, German and English

CHAPTER I

Introduction

Joanne Shattock

> Journalism is a plant of slow and gradual growth . . . And taken in its
> history, position, and relations, it is unquestionably the most grave,
> noticeable, formidable phenomenon – the greatest FACT of our
> times.[1]

W. R. Greg's assessment of newspaper press in 1855, written in the wake of
the repeal of two of the so-called Taxes on Knowledge levied on newspapers, was one of several articles on the current state of the press and on
the emergent profession of journalism at mid-century. 'Journalism is now
truly an estate of the realm; more powerful than any of the other estates;
more powerful than all of them combined if it could ever be brought to act
as a united and concentrated whole', the anonymous article continued.
Writers for the press could be classed under three heads: barristers waiting
to practice, young and promising politicians, and 'men of trained and
cultivated minds who have chosen literature as a profession and politics as
a favourite pursuit' and who have been driven into journalism by 'acci-
dental connexions' or by the attractions of an income and an audience.[2]

   Greg himself was a good example of the last category of recruits to the
new profession. So too was E. S. Dallas, a prolific contributor to the
periodical press, who was similarly buoyant about its present condition
in a two-part article on 'Popular Literature – the Periodical Press' in
Blackwood's Magazine in 1859:

> The rise of the periodical press is the great event of modern history. It has
> completely altered the game of politics; it has rendered obsolete more than
> half the State maxims of European Cabinets; it represents the triumph of
> moral over physical force; it gives every one of us a new sense – a sort of
> omniscience as well as a new power – a sort of ubiquity.[3]

---

[1] [W. R. Greg], 'The Newspaper Press', *Edinburgh Review* 102 (October 1855), 470–98, 470.
[2] 'The Newspaper Press', 477, 484.
[3] [E. S. Dallas], 'Popular Literature – the Periodical Press', *Blackwood's Magazine* (January 1859),
96–112, 100.

Dallas's focus was on the growth of the press, the explosion of print which reached out to all sectors of society:

> The newspaper is the elemental form of modern literature. Who is not interested in it? Who is not reached by it? The railway, the steamboat, and the telegraph, all add to its importance. Every improvement that is made in the art of communication and travel contributes to its dignity and increases its utility. No class is beyond its influence. There is not a man, there is hardly a woman, who is not more or less dependent on it.[4]

The periodical press was a material presence on the streets of villages, towns and cities, its readers numbering in hundreds of thousands:

> The most vivid idea of the enormous diffusion of periodical literature will be obtained by a visit to any flourishing newsvender: by seeing how his shop is loaded with periodicals of all sorts and sizes, and at prices from a halfpenny up to a shilling; by noting the rapidity with which he disposes of all these, each transaction being for the most part limited to the value of a penny and by considering how many hundreds of such shops and stands there are in London alone, not to speak of the country, where we find every shire, every town, almost every village, with its local newspaper, strong in itself, and stimulating the absorption of the metropolitan literature. It is out of such an organisation, which is continually spreading its influence, that we obtain journals whose daily or weekly circulation is to be measured by tens and hundreds of thousands.[5]

Both Greg and Dallas emphasised the representative power of the press; it reflected the views of a far broader cross section of society than Parliament, given the limits of the franchise. Both argued vigorously in support of anonymous versus signed articles, the subject of an ongoing debate in the late 1850s as new publications such as *Macmillan's Magazine* adopted signature as a matter of policy.[6] Dallas pointed to an aspect of periodical literature that had long been a subject for comment – its ephemerality:

> A periodical differs from a book in being calculated for rapid sale and for immediate effect. A book may at first fall dead upon the market, and yet may endure for ages, a wellspring of life to all mankind. A periodical, on the other hand – be it a daily paper, a weekly journal, a monthly magazine, or

---

[4] [E. S. Dallas], 'Popular Literature – the Periodical Press', *Blackwood's Magazine* (February 1859), 180–95, 180–81.
[5] 'Popular Literature' (January 1859), 101.
[6] See Dallas Liddle, 'Salesmen, Sportsmen, Mentors: Anonymity and Mid-Victorian Theories of Journalism', *Victorian Studies* 41:1 (Autumn 1997), 31–68.

a quarterly review – is a creature of the day: if each successive number does not attain its object in the short span of existence allotted to it, then it fails for ever – it has no future ... It is necessary, therefore, to the success of a periodical, that it should attain an instant popularity – in other words, that it should be calculated for the appreciation, not of a few, but of the many.[7]

The popularity of the press and the vast increase in the number of titles published had not resulted in a deterioration in quality, he argued. Rather, the press had become increasingly specialised. Every interest group had its own organ, every profession its own journal. Periodical literature was 'essentially a classified literature':

> There is the *Builder* for architects, there is the *Art Journal* for artists, there is the *Mechanics' Journal* for artisans; there is the *Economist* for merchants. Lawyers have the *Law Times*; medical men have the *Medical Times* and the *Lancet*; chemists and druggists have the *Pharmaceutical Journal*; Churchmen of every shade – high, low and broad, have their papers; Dissenters have theirs; Catholics have theirs; the licensed victuallers have a daily paper ... And then there is an Agricultural Journal, a Shipping Gazette, a Bankers' Magazine, a Statistical Journal, a Photographic Journal, a Stereoscopic Magazine.[8]

Writing in the year in which the stamp duty on newspapers was repealed, Greg was cautious about the predicted expansion of the newspaper press, noting the number of new provincial papers that had begun and quickly folded, and prophesying the reinvigoration and expansion of existing titles as a more likely outcome of the removal of restrictions on the press. Wilkie Collins, writing in Dickens's weekly miscellany *Household Words* in 1858 was more pessimistic, despairing of the quality of the 'penny fiction weeklies' that were catering to a vastly increased readership, the 'Unknown Public' of the title of his now famous article.[9] But whether they were optimistic like Dallas or cautious like Greg and Collins, the mid-Victorian generation of writers for the press articulated a sense of a historic moment, an awareness that they were part of a modern phenomenon at a crucial point in its development. Greg's article was ostensibly a review of F. Knight Hunt's *The Fourth Estate: Contributions towards a History of Newspapers, and of the Liberty of the Press*, the first of several contemporary histories of the newspaper press, many of them written by newspaper men.

---

[7] 'Popular Literature' (January 1859), 101. Greg argued that articles were 'written to be read hastily and to be read only once', 'The Newspaper Press', 483.

[8] Ibid., 103.

[9] [Wilkie Collins], 'The Unknown Public', *Household Words* 21 (August 1858). See Chapter 19, this volume, pp. 328–40.

The following year the journalist Francis Espinasse, writing under the pseudonym 'Herodotus Smith', published a series of articles on 'The Periodical and Newspaper Press' in the literary weekly the *Critic*, which he described as 'biographies' of reviews, magazines and newspapers, together with sketches of their contributors past and present. As he later observed in his *Literary Recollections* (1893), several histories of the British newspaper press had been published since he wrote the articles, among them James Grant's *The Newspaper Press. Its Origin, Progress and Present Position* (1871) and H. R. Fox Bourne's *English Newspapers. Chapters in the History of Journalism* (1887), but apart from his series there was still no history of the periodical, as distinct from the newspaper, press.[10]

Espinasse's articles identified many individuals who were currently writing anonymously for reviews, magazines and newspapers. This was the first occasion on which this information had been in the public domain. The world of metropolitan journalism was an intimate one, however, and gossip was rife, so the authorship of controversial articles or those by high-profile contributors was often an open secret. Equally, for those in a journal's inner circle the authorship of recent articles and reviews was common knowledge; this too became a channel for information.[11]

More information about the identity of writers for the periodical press emerged from an unexpected quarter in 1862. Edward Walford, an experienced compiler of biographical dictionaries and other reference works took over an edition of *Men of the Time*, a dictionary of living persons first published by David Bogue in 1852. Walford was determined to enlarge his subject base by including members of what he termed 'the aristocracy of intellect', members of newer professions such as authorship and those involved in the creative arts. As a result, writers, many of whom earned a living by writing for the periodical press, were given entries that named the journals to which they contributed. Similarly lawyers, dons, clergymen and other professionals who wrote intermittently for periodicals were credited with writing for specific publications.[12] For the first time,

---

[10] James Grant, *The Newspaper Press. Its Origin, Progress and Present Position*. 2 vols. London: Tinsley Brothers, 1871; H. R. Fox Bourne, *English Newspapers. Chapters in the History of Journalism*. 2 vols. London: Chatto & Windus, 1887; Francis Espinasse, *Literary Recollections and Sketches*. London: Hodder and Stoughton, 1893, p. 368.

[11] Authors of articles were sometimes named in reviews and monthly summaries of periodical contents, and also in advertisements. See Chapter 22, this volume, p. 374. For a historical overview of anonymous publication see John Mullan, *Anonymity: A Secret History of English Literature*. London: Faber, 2007.

[12] *Men of the Time. A Biographical Dictionary of Eminent Living Characters (Including Women)*. A New Edition by Edward Walford. London: Routledge Warne and Routledge, 1862.

information about periodical networks was made public or could be deduced. The focus was now on professional authors, and on the portfolio careers of other professionals who were also part-time journalists. For the first time, too, there was evidence of the vital link between the profession of authorship and the world of journalism. They were not two distinct professions, but different facets of the same profession. That at least was the theory.

The 1850s were an obvious point at which to take stock of the press and to look to the future, as two of the restrictions on newspapers had been removed, and the repeal of a third was imminent.[13] At the same time, the number of cheap periodicals aimed at a new reading public increased. The 1880s were another such moment, as technological advances in newspaper production demanded large capital investment, a mass market for newspapers emerged, and anxieties about the so-called New Journalism were vented.[14] By the 1880s, journalism was acknowledged as a profession. The National Association of Journalists, later renamed the Institute of Journalists, was founded in 1884, the same year as the Society of Authors. Guides and handbooks to a career in journalism proliferated, among them A. A. Reade's *Literary Success: Being a Guide to Practical Journalism* (1880), E. P. Davies's *The Reporter's Handbook* (1884), and John Dawson's *Practical Journalism* (1885).[15] More would follow in the 1890s. H. R. Fox Bourne's *English Newspapers. Chapters in the History of Journalism* (1887) was an account of the development of newspapers from the seventeenth century onwards, designed according to the preface 'to show the connection of journalism in its several stages with the literary and the political history of our country'.[16] The last chapter offered some reflections on the present day. There was now a demand that newspapers contain something besides news, Fox Bourne observed. There were no longer clear lines separating news and criticism; journalists could be both reporters and commentators. This was enabling for prospective journalists, but there were still disadvantages in a profession that had neither entrance examinations nor requisite qualifications. Talent and ambition often counted for more

---

[13] The excise duty on paper was removed in 1861.

[14] For discussions of the 'new journalism' on both sides of the Atlantic, see Chapter 15, this volume, pp. 263–80 and for Oscar Wilde as a 'new journalist', Chapter 22, this volume, pp. 370–82.

[15] John Dawson, *Practical Journalism, How to Enter Thereon and Succeed. A Manual for Beginners and Amateurs*. London: L. Upcott Gill, 1885; E. P. Davies, *The Reporter's Hand-Book, and Vade Mecum. With Appendix ... Affording comprehensive instructions for reporting all kinds of events*. London: Guilbert Pitman, S. W. Partridge, 1884, rev. edn 1910; A. A. Reade, *Literary Success: Being a Guide to Practical Journalism*. London: Wyman & Sons, 1885.

[16] Fox Bourne, *English Newspapers* vol. 1, p. v.

than experience, allowing the gifted and determined outsider to leap ahead
of those working their way up in the profession:

> A smart member of parliament, a successful barrister, a versatile clergyman,
> a retired schoolmaster, a popular novelist or anyone else with enough
> influence or intellect, or with a name likely to prove useful, may slip into
> an editorship or be made a principal leader writer in preference to men of
> long standing in the office, who perhaps have to teach him his duties and
> correct his blunders.[17]

Moreover journalism required a particular temperament that often made
other occupations unattractive. It was not unusual for a journalist, seeing
that chances of promotion were slim, to regret having taken it up and yet
be unable to turn successfully to another career. Modern Fleet Street was in
many ways an improvement on eighteenth-century Grub Street, Fox
Bourne concluded, but some of the 'traditions and infirmities' of Grub
Street remained.[18]

His appraisal of present conditions was not an unqualified endorsement
for journalism as a career. An ambivalence about the status of journalism
lingered well into the twentieth century. However much discussions about
careers in journalism mapped on to discussions about authorship as
a profession, there remained an unspoken distinction between the two.
When it came to prestige, in many eyes the designation 'journalist' was
definitely not the equivalent of 'author' or 'writer'.[19]

In the various reflections on the press at mid-century and in the 1880s,
there was one aspect of the expansion of the press that was not alluded to.
What Greg, Dallas and their colleagues possibly did not foresee in the 1850s
and what historians such as Grant and Fox Bourne did not consider was the
extent of the influence of the British press abroad – the intricate connections between British periodicals and their counterparts on the Continent,
the reciprocal influences on the production of mass market newspapers
between Britain and America, and the export or 'migration' of British titles
to major centres of print culture in the Empire. Most of these relationships
existed in embryonic form at mid-century and were obvious by the 1880s,
but their significance was ignored by contemporary observers.

* * *

---

[17] Fox Bourne, vol. 2, p. 371.   [18] Fox Bourne, vol. 2, p. 372.
[19] The *Dictionary of National Biography* often used the designation 'author' or 'writer' rather than
'journalist' for biographical subjects. See the entries on Douglas Jerrold, G. H. Lewes and Harriet
Martineau in the *Dictionary of National Biography*, ed. Leslie Stephen and Sir Sidney Lee. London:
Smith Elder, 1885–1901.

The emergence in the first decade of the twenty-first century of a number of digital resources, among them *19th Century British Library Newspapers, 19th Century UK Periodicals* and *19th Century U. S. Newspapers* published by Gale Cengage, and Pro Quest's *British Periodicals*, has not only made the nineteenth-century newspaper and periodical press more accessible; it has also changed the way nineteenth-century print media is perceived. As one scholar has recently observed, 'it has never been so easy to consult the nineteenth-century press'.[20] In addition, a number of projects such as the *Nineteenth Century Serials Edition* and *Dickens Journals Online*[21] are freely available. All of these resources have enabled scholars to make use of the nineteenth-century press in new ways. This volume of newly commissioned essays offers a series of perspectives on nineteenth-century newspapers and periodicals, enabled and enhanced by these new digital resources.

Each of the scholars contributing to the volume has been engaged in innovative work on nineteenth-century print media, although not all would see themselves primarily as periodical scholars or students of book history. One of the purposes of the volume is to show the ways in which the periodical and newspaper press is central to an understanding of the long nineteenth century, whether one is a social historian or a historian of art or of science or engaged in media or literary studies. The nineteenth century rather than the Victorian period marks the chronological boundaries of the book, even though by far the greatest number of periodicals and news-papers were inaugurated during the Queen's reign. Several of the chapters, particularly those dealing with innovations in methods of illustration or issues of genre, look back to the eighteenth century; others that concentrate on developments of the newspaper press from the 1870s onwards take the discussion forward into the twentieth.

The book does not purport to be a comprehensive history of the nineteenth-century newspaper and periodical press. The twenty-one essays discuss the nineteenth-century press from a variety of positions, ranging from a focus on an individual journalist or periodical format through to the networks of editors, journalists and proprietors who produced print media and the influence of that media on public opinion. One section of the book looks beyond Britain to the intersection of the British press with its transatlantic and Continental counterparts and the 'globalisation' of print culture that the nineteenth century inaugurated.

---

[20] James Mussell, *The Nineteenth-Century Press in the Digital Age*. London: Palgrave Macmillan 2012, p. xiii

[21] See the 'Guide to Further Reading', pp. 383–4 for details.

The volume is divided into four parts. The chapters in Part I, 'Periodicals, Genres and the Production of Print', consider periodical formats and their evolution over the nineteenth century, as new readerships emerged and patterns of consumption changed. They also look at aspects of the production of print that influenced the content of particular formats. The opening essay by James Mussell examines the relationship between the new digital resources and the newspapers and periodicals on library shelves. He suggests that readers need to become more critically aware of the materiality of the resources they use, both the historic newspapers and periodicals and their digital counterparts, and argues that the 'discursive space' opened up by digitisation enables scholars to see print anew. David Stewart looks at the magazine culture of the early nineteenth century, a culture that was in continual flux, and argues that magazines were not simply reflectors of literary culture but active participants in it. Laurel Brake emphasises the importance of genre in understanding the periodical press and traces the evolution of the review from its origins in the eighteenth century through to the *Yellow Book* at the end of the nineteenth. She analyses the impetus behind the changes that occurred in content and frequency and shows how the phenomenon of sensation impacted reviews in the 1860s and beyond. Barbara Onslow's study of the annuals, or 'picture books for grown children',[22] as they were described by a contemporary commentator, shows how the genre flourished between 1820 and 1850, a discrete period determined by the technology that underpinned its engraved illustrations. Brian Maidment's chapter on graphic satire and the radical press focuses on the period 1820 to 1845, in which political caricature and other forms of graphic social commentary maintained a significant cultural presence. He then traces the reinvention of caricature through the development of wood engraving, which produced the political cartoon, a major feature of the Victorian periodical press. Lorraine Janzen Kooistra's chapter on illustration links the era of annuals and political caricature with the development of industrial processes of illustration later in the century, when speed became essential in producing and transmitting images. She shows how readers of the newspaper and periodical press developed a visual literacy and a sophisticated graphic vocabulary. The story of the pictorial press owes as much to its readers, she suggests, as to its 'multiple makers'.[23] Linda H. Peterson's chapter on 'Periodical Poetry' emphasises the ubiquity of poetry in Victorian print culture and points to the crucial role periodicals played in launching a poet's career. The symbiotic relationship between literature and journalism

---

[22] See Chapter 5, this volume, p. 68.   [23] See Chapter 7, p. 125.

was particularly striking in the case of poets, where publication of individual poems in periodicals was followed by collection into a book, the success of which was in turn determined by reviews in periodicals.

The essays in the second part on 'The Press and the Public' look primarily but not exclusively at the newspaper press, and at the way issues of public interest and concern were interrogated and presented to a rapidly expanding readership from the 1830s onwards. Nothing more fundamentally defined the British press in the nineteenth century than its freedom, Martin Hewitt points out in his essay 'The Press and the Law'. It was a mutually constitutive relationship; the law could protect as well as constrain, which was why many established papers welcomed the penny stamp as protection against competition. By the late 1860s, however, there was a clear transformation of the press as the removal of restrictions was felt. Catherine Waters, in '"Doing the Graphic": Victorian Special Correspondence', highlights a new kind of reporter who emerged in the 1850s, the 'special correspondent', who became vital to newspapers in need of authoritative reports from all parts of the country as well as from remote corners of the world. The 'specials' were often colourful and idiosyncratic writers whose work was ambiguously positioned between literature and journalism. In a richly detailed account of the press coverage and response to the Great Exhibition of 1851, Geoffrey Cantor argues that the exhibition could be seen as a creation of the newspaper and periodical press.

The essays in the third part of the book, under the heading 'The "Globalisation" of the Nineteenth-Century Press' are examples of the transformation of the study of print media that has been enabled by the extensive digitisation of archives. The periodicals and newspapers discussed in this section emanated from Melbourne, Sydney, New York, Chicago, Paris, Calcutta and Serampore. In his chapter 'Journalism and Empire in an English-Reading World: The *Review of Reviews*', Simon Potter warns against making simplistic comparisons between the mass media in 'our own hyper-connected age' and what was at most was a 'semi-globalised world' in which British models of journalistic practice were highly influential. The nineteenth century saw an unprecedented degree of 'transnational interconnectivity' which fell short of near-total interdependence. As Potter demonstrates, W. T. Stead's transnational publishing strategy with regard to the *Review of Reviews* was an attempt to unite English-speaking readers across the world, but due to clashes of personality, differences in management policy and the constraints imposed by contemporary technology, the experiment had only limited success.

Joel Wiener, in his comparative study of British and American newspapers, shows how the transformation of newspaper journalism followed a similar trajectory in both countries. The differences were owing to cultural factors including the strength of class feeling, levels of education and the impact of technological developments. Other than in visual technology, most of the stimuli came from America. In her study of 'Colonial Networks and the Periodical Marketplace', Mary Shannon points to the family relationships between periodicals and shows how through the efforts of two emigrant journalists, *Punch* 'migrated' first to Melbourne and then to Sydney, the two new publications demonstrating a healthy independence from the parent periodical. Juliette Atkinson's chapter 'Continental Currents: Paris and London' makes the point that whereas in England the journal was celebrated in contrast to the writers, who were unknown, in France 'writers were everything' and the journal merely 'the frame to the picture he paints'.[24] Atkinson points to a number of influential French critics who wrote for English periodicals, often under their own names, one of many cultural exchanges that bound European and British communities of print. The world of cosmopolitan periodicals, as she demonstrates, was often a remarkably intimate one. Deeptanil Ray and Abhijit Gupta's discussion of the newspaper and periodical press in colonial India begins with the manuscript newspaper culture of the eighteenth century. They trace its evolution through to a burgeoning native language newspaper press in Calcutta in the 1830s and from there to a vibrant print culture that included both English- and native-language newspapers and periodicals.

The fourth part on 'Journalists and Journalism' offers six case studies of well-known writers who were also highly productive journalists. Journalism played a different role in the careers of each of the three women journalists included. As Iain Crawford shows, Harriet Martineau became a model and also a mentor to the next generation of women authors, proving that women could earn a living by writing for the press provided they could negotiate the gender politics involved. Marian Evans's and Margaret Oliphant's careers initially intersected through their connection with the firm of William Blackwood and Sons and the benign oversight of John Blackwood. Their paths then diverged as Evans withdrew from journalism to pursue her career as a novelist. Oliphant in contrast kept up a steady pace of reviewing along with a prolific output of fiction for more than four decades. Joanne Shattock traces her long-standing

---

[24] Chapter 13, this volume, p. 230.

association with the House of Blackwood, a relationship not without its tensions, but one from which both parties ultimately benefitted. Fionnuala Dillane argues that despite Marian Evans's ambivalence about her journalism, it is impossible to imagine had she not become famous as George Eliot that the journalism would never be of interest. Rather than seeing it in terms of her later development as a novelist, she explores Evans's own selection of her journalism for republication and then considers the scope and rigour of the reviews she left out.

Writing about Dickens's 'conducting' of his two weekly miscellanies *Household Words* and its successor *All the Year Round,* John Drew suggests that Victorian readers embraced a more collective notion of authorship in which anonymity could provide strategic freedoms. There were, however, as he demonstrates, tensions between authorial and corporate identity in the operation of the two weeklies. He also offers some reflections on the reading experience provided by the *Dickens Journals Online* project, in which it is possible to read the digital version of the original publications in parallel with a modern corrected text. Graham Law writes about Wilkie Collins, one of Dickens's most valued contributors, who, he argues, developed a new mode of personalised journalism, which ultimately blurred the boundaries between fact and fiction. In the final chapter, John Stokes and Mark Turner discuss the journalism of Oscar Wilde, an author who found difficulty in accepting that he was a journalist. He began to write for newspapers at a point when the boundaries between the so-called higher journalism, the quarterlies, monthlies and weekly literary papers and the newspaper press were breaking down, when writing reviews for 'the press' as opposed to publishing in a prestigious review no longer carried a stigma. Wilde was, as they point out, a member of 'an admittedly factional literary community' in the 1880s, the decade which produced the controversial new journalism.

* * *

Of the various themes which connect the essays in this volume – the impact of technological developments in printing, illustration and communications; the growth and segmentation of reading audiences; the consequences of the repeal of the Taxes on Knowledge; the advantages and limitations of anonymous publication; the variety of genres that comprise nineteenth-century journalism; the emergence of a mass market for newspapers; the importance of speed; the dominance of the metropolitan press; the transnational connections between the British press and its counterparts in Europe, America and the Empire – most, apart from the last, were alluded to by nineteenth-century commentators and press historians. One further topic links contemporary discussions about the periodical press and those of modern scholars – the relationship between literature and journalism. That authorship had become a profession by the mid-nineteenth century and that this was enabled by the expansion of the periodical press was generally acknowledged. G. H. Lewes's article 'The Condition of Authors in England, Germany and France' in *Fraser's Magazine* for March 1847 set out the differential in journalists' earnings between England and its two Continental neighbours, making the point that in England a middle-class income could be earned by writing for the press:

> It is by our reviews, magazines, and journals, that the vast majority of professional authors earn their bread; and the astonishing mass of talent and energy which is thus thrown into periodical literature is not only quite unexampled abroad, but is, of course, owing to the certainty of moderate yet, on the whole, sufficient remuneration.[25]

He responded to the long-running argument that anything published in the press was ephemeral and that writers courted popularity and immediate effect:

> We are not deaf to the loud wailings set up (by periodical writers too!) against periodical literature. We have heard – not patiently, indeed but silently – the declamations uttered against this so-called disease of our age; how it fosters superficiality – how it ruins all earnestness – how it substitutes brilliancy for solidity and wantonly sacrifices truth to effect.

As was to be expected from a writer whom Carlyle had dubbed 'the prince of journalists' his defence of his profession was robust:

> Periodical literature is a great thing. It is a potent instrument for the education of a people. It is the only decisive means of rescuing authorship from the badge of servility. Those who talk so magniloquently about serious works, who despise the essay-like and fragmentary nature of periodical literature, forget that while there are many men who can produce a good essay, there has at all times been a scarcity of those who can produce good works. A brilliant essay, or a thoughtful fragment, is not the less brilliant, is not the less thoughtful, because it is brief, because it does not exhaust the subject.[26]

As many of the chapters in this collection demonstrate, the debate about literature and journalism persisted throughout the second half of the

---

[25] [G. H. Lewes], 'The Condition of Authors in England, Germany and France', *Fraser's Magazine* 35 (March 1847), 285–5, 289.

[26] 'The Condition of Authors', 289. For Carlyle's epithet, see Chapter 10, this volume, p. 174.

nineteenth century and into the twentieth. Martin Hewitt notes that in the 1880s, Oxford undergraduates were warned off journalism as an 'impossible profession' and 'fatal to good manners and honest thought'.[27] And as John Stokes and Mark Turner point out, Oscar Wilde's quip 'I write only on questions of literature and art – am hardly a journalist' was disingenuous in the extreme, given that he was a prolific contributor to newspapers and periodicals. The debate has continued up to the present. Journalism, as Laurel Brake observes, is not a topic that fits comfortably within the discourse of modern literary studies.[28]

Many of the chapters in this volume contribute to the ongoing discussion about the relationship of journalism and literature. As a collection, they illustrate the variety of approaches, the richness and the scope of current research on the nineteenth-century newspaper and periodical press, and the potential for future research in this dynamic field of study. Collectively, too, they underline the importance of the press in all its formats to our understanding of the nineteenth century.

[27] See Chapter 9, this volume, p. 149.
[28] See Chapter 22, this volume, p. 370 and Chapter 4, this volume, p. 65.

PART I

Periodicals, Genres and the Production of Print

Beyond the 'Great Index': Digital Resources and Actual Copies

James Mussell

In August 1886, W. T. Stead published an interview with Samuel Palmer, the compiler of *Palmer's Index to the Times Newspaper*, in the *Pall Mall Gazette*.[1] Stead, who had begun his own half-yearly index to the *Pall Mall Gazette* in 1884, was deeply interested in the archival status of old newspapers and periodicals. Stead recognised the value of the newspaper as the record of the moment but also understood the difficulties in recovering the information in its pages. In the preface to the interview, he acknowledged the importance of Palmer's ongoing index to *The Times*, remarking that 'the materials for a great part of our history lie embodied in its columns'. However, using an image he would later draw upon when setting out the case for both his *Review of Reviews* (1890–1936) and *Annual Index to the Periodical Literature of the World* (1891–1900), Stead claimed that without an index such as *Palmer's* the 'future historian . . . would be as helpless as a Theseus wanting his clue to the Labyrinth'.

Like *Palmer's Index*, digital resources provide just such a clue. However, whereas previous attempts to address the field's bibliographical complexity, whether published in the nineteenth century like *Palmer's Index* and Stead's various endeavours or more recent projects such as the *Wellesley Index to Victorian Periodicals* and the *Waterloo Directory of Victorian Periodicals*,[2] have produced discrete publications that have stood outside of the archive to describe its contents, digitisation has exerted an unprecedented degree of bibliographic control by changing paper and ink into bits

---

[1] Anonymous, 'A Great Index', *Pall Mall Gazette*, 14 August 1886, 11.
[2] *The Wellesley Index to Victorian Periodicals, 1824–1900*, Walter E. Houghton et al. (eds.), 5 vols. Toronto: University of Toronto Press; London: Routledge, 1966–89; *The Waterloo Directory of Victorian Periodicals, 1824–1900*. Phase 1, Michael Wolff, John S. North and Dorothy Deering (eds.). Waterloo, ON: Wilfrid Laurier University Press, 1977; *The Waterloo Directory of English Newspapers and Periodicals 1800–1900*, John S. North (ed.). Waterloo, ON: North Waterloo Academic Press, 1997; *The Waterloo Directory of English Newspapers and Periodicals 1800–1900*. Series 2. John S. North (ed.). Waterloo, ON: North Waterloo Academic Press, 2003.

and bytes. This transformation allows digital resources to serve as indices in which every word might be searched. With sufficient metadata, they can also become catalogues, enumerating articles, issues, volumes and publications.[3] Finally, they are also a kind of edition, reproducing aspects of the printed material in digital form.[4] Since at least the appearance of Gale Cengage's *Times Digital Archive* in 2003, the study of newspapers and periodicals has been structured by digital resources that combine all three of these functions at an unprecedented scale.[5]

As I will go on to argue, searchable digital resources offering access to page facsimiles are not the only digital projects relevant to the study of the press; equally, not all resources are the same. Nonetheless, it is this type of digital resource – in which a textual transcript is used to index content – that has come to dominate research into historical newspapers and periodicals. Never before has the nineteenth-century press been so accessible: with a few taps on the keyboard, millions of pages of newspapers and periodicals can be viewed on the desktop over the web (depending, of course, on hardware, software and the relevant subscriptions). The challenge is to place digital resources in longer traditions of indexing, cataloguing and editing while recognising what makes them distinctive. After explaining his methods, Palmer took Stead's reporter upstairs, 'leading the way to a large, light room, surrounded by unvarnished deal shelves, giving shelter to a good many hundred volumes, while at one end, occupying the whole space, stood a great array of *Times* volumes, looking appallingly large and bulky beside the octavos and duode-cimos surrounding them'.[6] Here, the forbidding bulky volumes represent the pure source, the raw authentic material of history. Palmer's indices leave these 'actual copies' untouched, referring readers back to the newspaper and so reinforcing the iconic solidity of *The Times*'s bound volumes. Digital resources, however, transform the actual copies into something else, referring readers to new digital images rather than old printed pages. In what follows, I consider how digital resources stand in relation to the copies of newspapers

[3] For a nineteenth-century account of the distinction between indices and catalogues, see Andrea Crestadoro, *The Art of Making Catalogues of Libraries* (London: The Literary, Scientific and Artistic Reference Office, 1856).

[4] For editions and archives, see Kenneth M. Price, 'Edition, Project, Database, Archive, Thematic Research Collection: What's in a Name?' *Digital Humanities Quarterly*, 3 (2009), 1–40; James Mussell and Suzanne Paylor, 'Editions and Archives', in *The Nineteenth-Century Press in the Digital Age*. Basingstoke: Palgrave, 2012, pp. 114–48.

[5] Important predecessors are *Making of America* (1995), *Internet Library of Early Journals* (*ILEJ*, 1999), Heritage Newspapers' *newspaperARCHIVE* (1999), ProQuest's *Historical Newspapers* (1999), *Periodicals Contents Index* (1995) and *Periodicals Contents Index Full Text* (2000).

[6] 'A Great Index', 11.

and periodicals in the archive. Predicated on a radical transformation, digitisation will always fail to reproduce print; however, such transformations make evident that what we think constitutes print and print culture is more complex than it appears. It is in the discursive space opened up by digitisation that we can see print anew.

Margins

Indices such as Palmer's were necessary because the very thing that made newspapers so valuable also made them difficult to use. Attuned to the moment with space to fill, newspapers combine disparate materials in timely fashion. Not only do they record major public affairs – the news as commonly understood – but set them alongside other content thought interesting to their readers. As serials, this content is always provisional, relevant only to the period before the appearance of the next number. As a result, old newspapers record moments intended to be superseded and forgotten, allowing readers in the present to revisit a past that has passed.

Stead, whose archival imagination complemented his journalistic instinct, recognised the value of an index to *The Times* but was reluctant to accord the newspaper any special status. Imagine, he asks, 'How many people would welcome an index to "Hansard" or the "Annual Register?"'[7] A few months previously, Stead had argued that the newspaper's claim to be a democratic instrument rested on more than its coverage of politics or public affairs. In his well-known essay 'Government by Journalism', published in the *Contemporary Review* in May 1886, Stead argued the newspaper better expressed the public will because it was closer to the people. This was partly a function of its periodicity, with 'the editor's mandate' renewed 'day by day' and the franchise extended to all who could make 'a voluntary payment of the daily pence'. But it was also because the newspaper better represented the interests of its readers. The editor must, 'often sorely against his will, write on topics about which he cares nothing, because if he does not, the public will desert him for his rival across the street'. A successful newspaper 'must "palpitate with actuality"', a kind of realism that binds the publication into the lives of its readers.[8]

In many ways, the newspaper's importance is the result of its supplementarity. Palmer, certainly, understood that the appeal of *The Times* lay in its compendious sweep of information as much as its lauded leading

---

[7] 'A Great Index', 11.

[8] Stead, W. T., 'Government by Journalism', *Contemporary Review*, 49 (1886), 653–74, 655.

articles. In his interview with the *Pall Mall Gazette*, he recounted a visit
from a policeman who needed to consult back issues of the paper to
determine whether or not a prisoner in his custody had prior convictions.
'It will be a matter of surprise to many', remarks Stead's reporter, 'that
Palmer's Index contains the only register of criminal cases in existence, the
same applying to "Suicides", "Inquests", and "Accidents."'[9] Coverage of
the courts was a staple of all sectors of the newspaper press in the period,
guaranteeing regular content that was reliably sensational and *Palmer's
Index* was the only record because it indexed a long-running newspaper,
not *The Times* in particular. Newspapers needed to fill white space, often
already organised into predetermined departments, and they attuned
themselves to newsworthy sources, whether formal such as the courts or
Parliament (when in session), or informal such as society gossip or the
queries of their readers. Not quite records of the everyday, the need to
provide copy of interest to their readers meant that newspapers nonetheless
recorded information that escaped more formalised documentary practices, even the otherwise impressive Victorian civic bureaucracy.

The Times might have supplemented more formal modes of record
keeping, but this supplementarity did not make it marginal. In his landmark essay 'Charting the Golden Stream', Michael Wolff argued that the
Victorian press – newspapers and periodicals – constitute 'repositories of
the general life of Victorian England'.[10] The word 'repository' might make
the newspaper appear passive, simply documenting what was going on, but
archiving is an intentional act (one must choose what gets put in the
repository, and how) and so too is the production of newspapers and
periodicals. While they do have a documentary function, the content of
newspapers and periodicals results from a number of authorial, editorial
and publishing decisions calibrated for a complex and changing market.
As Wolff argues, it is the dynamism of that market that makes the press
such an important resource. Not only was this, as Linda K. Hughes has
argued, the 'first mass media era', but the market was diverse and fluid,
allowing publications to target particular niches or, more commonly, to try
and maintain an appeal to multiple readerships simultaneously.[11] Wolff's
claim that the individual issue is 'the basic unit for the study of Victorian
cultural history' is quite correct – no other cultural documents from the

---

[9] 'A Great Index', p. 11.
[10] Michael Wolff, 'Charting the Golden Stream: Thoughts on a Directory of Victorian Periodicals',
Victorian Periodicals Newsletter, 4 (1971), 23–38, 26.
[11] Linda K. Hughes, 'SIDEWAYS!: Navigating the Material(ity) of Print Culture', *Victorian Periodicals
Review*, 47 (2014), 1–30, 1, 3.

period represent its diversity quite so fully – but such a history will always be inflected by that issue's mediating function.[12] The nineteenth-century press is not a simple reflection of nineteenth-century society, but rather one of its products.

Digitisation brings the press in from the margins. As Stead's account of *Palmer's Index* makes clear, the bibliographical condition of the newspaper archive was unwieldy even in the nineteenth century. Today, it is even more so. Not only is the archive incomplete (some publications were more likely to be kept than others), but it is also widely and unevenly dispersed. Of what survives, both newspapers and periodicals are likely to be in the form of bound volumes, with supplementary material and, in the case of periodicals (and many weekly newspapers), advertisements removed. Although consolidated online library catalogues help readers find runs, access is increasingly restricted to special collections rather than available on the shelves, and to readers one at a time during library hours.[13] The great bibliographic achievements of the twentieth century, the *Wellesley Index* and *Waterloo Directory*, serve as a checklist of periodical titles and a guide to some of their contents, and these can be supplemented with earlier works such as the press directories, Stead's *Annual Index to Periodical Literature* and *Poole's Index*.[14] Digital resources, however, provide access to anyone, anywhere, with access to the web and the relevant credentials. They usually provide sufficient metadata to generate lists of titles and articles. Finally, the use of textual transcripts provides an index that makes content recoverable, regardless of the size of the archive. None of these processes are perfect, and they frequently lack the scholarly rigour that characterises earlier bibliographic projects; however, whereas research into the newspaper and periodical press required access to well-stocked libraries, bibliographical tools (and the skills to use them) and sufficient experience to make sense of the engrossing but complex texts in their pages, digital resources bring newspapers and periodicals readily to hand.

Margins are important in another sense, too. The white space that surrounds the printed text, the margins mark the page rather than what is written upon it. If what makes newspapers and periodicals so valuable is

---

[12] Wolff, 'Charting the Golden Stream', 27.
[13] For more on access to periodicals, including the decline of material on open shelves, see Laurel Brake, 'London Letter: Researching the Historical Press, Now and Here', *Victorian Periodicals Review*, 48 (2015), 245–53.
[14] W. T. Stead and Eliza Hetherington, eds., *Index to the Periodical Literature of the World*. 11 vols. London: Review of Reviews, 1891–1900; William Frederick Poole et al., *Poole's Index to Periodical Literature*, 7 vols. London: Kegan Paul, Tench, Trübner and Co., 1882–1908.

their participation in a vibrant print culture, then their material facets are crucial for understanding how they were produced, distributed and consumed. To make sense of the press is to take materiality seriously, and this applies to encounters with newspapers and periodicals in digital resources as well as in print. The language of the virtual that still clings to digital objects elides their materiality; for digital representations of nondigital objects, this is even more pronounced, with the nondigital appearing as the substantial source for its ethereal digital other. Yet this is not a case of the digital being less material than the nondigital: each has its own distinct materiality and, in the case of digital representations of nondigital objects, these different materialities inform each other, shaping the way each is experienced.

Digitisation draws attention to the importance of materiality even as it is apparently imperilled. When material aspects of print such as weight of the volume, the size of the page or the colour of paper and ink are transformed, we become reminded of their importance. The print objects are unchanged, of course, but when compared with digital representations, certain aspects of their material form become enhanced. The nondigital world also structures our experience of digital materiality. Digital objects are often designed to act like nondigital counterparts, allowing users to turn pages or open folders, but they can only do this because of our readiness to read depth, structure and texture into the two-dimensional space of the screen. Materiality is not just a matter of fixed properties, associated with an object in advance of whatever is done with it; it also, as our experiences with digital media make clear, emerges in the context of a particular encounter.[15] Just as typography and layout lend print pages texture in addition to that bestowed by the impression of type on paper, so the behaviour of digital objects onscreen lends a further layer of materiality to that of drives and chips, screens and keyboards.[16] Only a richer understanding of materiality can make sense of the way we regularly interact with objects, treating articles as distinct entities on the page, for instance, or interacting with complex simulated worlds online. In other words, there is more to say about the 'hardness' of hard copy than the fact it is 'harder' than digital representations onscreen. It sounds counterintuitive, but materiality is culturally contingent and situated in the moment: the weight

---

[15] See, for instance, N. Katherine Hayles's arguments in *Writing Machines*. Cambridge, MA: MIT Press, 2002; and 'Translating Media: Why We Should Rethink Textuality', *The Yale Journal of Criticism*, 16 (2003), 263–90.

[16] For an account of this difference, see Matthew G. Kirschenbaum, *Mechanisms: New Media and the Forensic Imagination*. Cambridge, MA: MIT Press, 2008.

of the volume might stay the same, but its cultural heft changes. The challenge for scholars of the nineteenth-century press is to recover the material meanings of the past.

The material form of newspapers and periodicals is the key to understanding the place of these publications in society. Designed primarily to be read, print publications had all kinds of uses at different times of their lives.[17] One characteristic usually shared by those that survive is a large part of their cultural life: at some point they found themselves part of a library collection and were treated accordingly. As a result, the material forms that newspapers and periodicals took in the past can often only be imagined on the basis of the quite different forms in which they exist today. It is a commonplace in scholarship, for instance, to write about individual issues even if the scholar has only ever seen one copy in a bound volume. Just as we would be rightly sceptical of an account of the press that neglected aspects of material form, so too should we expect researchers to think about the materiality of the digital resources they use. Not only do the forms in which digital representations of nineteenth-century print affect the way we conceive the nondigital publications, but the material facets of the digital resource shape how it functions, determining what we see and how. Newspapers and periodicals are not passive bearers of textual content, neither are the digital resources that remediate them.[18]

By the Numbers

Palmer's method was to work through each article of *The Times* (except for advertisements) and assign relevant headings from the index. Some articles took longer to index than others: according to Palmer, sometimes a short article "'requires as many entries in the Index as lines in the paragraph, where again perhaps an article of a couple of columns require but one entry'".[19] The transcripts that underpin digital resources are more like the former than the latter. Generated through a process called optical character recognition (OCR) in which a programme attempts to identify verbal information on page images, the resulting transcripts can then be processed further to create searchable indices. Unlike Palmer's team (his four sons and 'but three strangers'[20]), who scanned articles for content to be indexed,

---

[17] See, for instance, Leah Price, *How to Do Things with Books in Victorian Britain*. Princeton, NJ: Princeton University Press, 2012.
[18] For a fuller account, see James Mussell, *The Nineteenth-Century Press in the Digital Age*. Basingstoke: Palgrave, 2012.
[19] 'A Great Index', 11.   [20] 'A Great Index', 11.

OCR programmes have to first identify which marks on an image constitute glyphs and then ascribe them correct alphanumeric values. Although some OCR programmes work at the level of words and the accuracy can be improved in various ways by using natural language processing, a semantic element to the process is rare. The transcripts might be machine readable; but as far as the machine is concerned, they are just strings of characters.

The shortcomings of OCR transcripts are well known. Despite the increasing sophistication of OCR technologies, producing transcripts from historical material will never be perfect, and the closely printed columns of nineteenth-century newspapers, especially when scanned from tightly bound volumes, are notoriously challenging to process. While even inaccurate transcripts can be used as the basis for search, accurate metadata is needed for browsing. Anyone who has tried to work with digitised periodicals published in resources designed for books – *Google Books* (2004–) for instance, or the *Internet Archive* (1996–) – can attest to the difficulties in locating the right volume in a list where each has the same title. The bibliographical complexity of periodicals makes such metadata quite complicated: titles change over the course of a run, volume sequences restart with a new series, and issues might appear in multiple editions. As some metadata will require addition by hand, it can be expensive to carry out at scale; however, as this metadata is used to label search results, helping users browse lists of hits, commercial publishers prefer to devote resources here rather than correct transcripts.

The limitations of free-text searching are also well known. As the transcripts lack semantic information, the assumption that underpins search is that if a particular search term appears in an article, then that article is likely to be about that search term. This works well for named entities (people, places, events, objects, etc.), especially when terms are sufficiently distinct, but less well for concepts, themes or topics. As Patrick Leary has argued, effective free-text searching requires a combination of precision and inclusiveness (to get just the right amount of detail in the search term) and 'a close prior acquaintance with nine-teenth-century prose' (to be able to predict terms likely to appear).[21] If done well, such searches can be extremely powerful, allowing scholars to map people, texts and events across the diverse terrain of nineteenth-century print. Familiar figures are encountered in new settings, predictable cultural narratives can be unsettled by alternative interpretations, and

---

[21] Patrick Leary, 'Googling the Victorians', *Journal of Victorian Culture*, 10 (2005), 2–86.

Victorian culture emerges in all its diversity.[22] However, if done with a lack of methodological rigour, free-text searching can reproduce many of the limitations of the archive. For instance, reading might usually be performed on page images, but free-text searching relies on verbal information, making form subsidiary to content. As search results return articles out of context, resources encourage what Mark Turner has called the 'smash-and-grab' approach whereby articles are studied in isolation while publications are forced back into the margins.[23] Finally, as most searches result in an abundance of hits and the diversity of the press makes it likely a range of views will be found, broad generalisations can be made to rest on individual articles, themselves part of an ongoing conversation. The uncritical use of these powerful resources can make scholarship little more than descriptive accounts of what people wrote in the past.

It is easy to blame digital resources for encouraging methodological bad habits, but these resources are designed in such a way because this is what users know and want. Habituated to Google, we are used to navigating an unknown mass of material on the basis of a few speculative search terms, confident that there will nearly always be something of relevance. I have argued previously that whenever nondigital material is encountered in digital form, researchers need to establish two things: first, what it is they are looking at (What type of article is this? What is its print context? Who produced it? In what genres is it situated?); second, why it appears as it does (Why does it behave this way? Why has it been returned in this search? How might its appearance be shaped by its production and display?).[24] Pursuing these lines of enquiry requires what Paul Fyfe has recently called 'curatorial intelligence', the need to 'assess and recontextualize digital objects' according to broader interpretive frameworks.[25] Both nondigital and digital objects must be put in context, recognised as cultural products that are produced under specific conditions for specific purposes. Only then can the relationship between them – the way the digital resource mediates the printed material – be fully understood. Without this critical engagement, digital resources are reduced to delivery mechanisms for page

---

[22] For more on search, see Catherine Robson, 'How We Search Now: New Ways of Digging Up Wolfe's "Sir John Moore"', in Veronica Alfano and Andrew Stauffer (eds.), *Virtual Victorians*. Basingstoke: Palgrave Macmillan, 2015, pp. 11–28.

[23] Mark W. Turner, 'Time, Periodicals, and Literary Studies', *Victorian Periodicals Review*, 39.4 (2006), 309–16, 309.

[24] See Mussell, *Nineteenth-Century Press*, chap. 1.

[25] Paul Fyfe, 'Technologies of Serendipity', *Victorian Periodicals Review*, 48 (2015), 261–66, 262. Fyfe credits the phrase to an audience member at the annual conference of the Research Society for Victorian Periodicals in Delaware, 2014.

scans, with access dependent on an incomplete index that is often undisclosed.

Despite the shortcomings of OCR transcripts, there is considerable scope for doing other things with structured data than simply free-text searching. Over the past few years, projects have emerged that leverage the digital difference to ask new questions of archive material and what it represents. Many adopt what has become known as 'distant reading', using techniques from corpus linguistics to map cultural trends.[26] Perhaps the most well-known example of this in Victorian studies is Dan Cohen and Fred Gibbs's project to test the conclusions of Walter Houghton's *The Victorian Frame of Mind* using the titles of the 1,681,161 books within *Google Books*.[27] Although such projects look beyond the specificities of individual texts to detect patterns within the wider corpus, there are ways to make print culture the object of analysis. Anne DeWitt's recent work, for instance, uses network analysis to explore the way reviews published in periodicals associated novels with one another: focusing on an important facet of the periodical, the review, DeWitt can challenge genealogical and evolutionary constructions of literary genre by presenting those delineated by reviewers instead.[28] Network analysis can also reveal the relationships between those clustered around particular publications. Susan Brown, for example, has shown how the data in the long-running *Orlando Project*, whose aim is to produce a digital history of women's writing, can be used to visualise the personal, social and political connections between contributors to particular publications. By mapping such relationships, it becomes easy to see what certain contributors might have in common, or otherwise unsuspected points of connection between people and publications.[29] Ryan Cordell's *Viral Texts* project also uses network analysis, but this time to trace content as it is reprinted across the press. As newspapers are

---

[26] 'Distant reading' was coined by Franco Moretti, 'Conjectures on World Literature', *New Left Review*, 1 (2000), 57–58. See also Franco Moretti, *Graphs, Maps, Trees*. London: Verso, 2005. For a good account of the possibilities of distant reading the nineteenth-century press, see Bob Nicholson, 'Counting Culture; Or, How to Read Victorian Newspapers from a Distance', *Journal of Victorian Culture*, 17 (2012), 238–46.

[27] See Dan Cohen, 'Searching for the Victorians', *Dan Cohen* (4 October 2010) www.dancohen.org /2010/10/04/searching-for-the-victorians [accessed 30 July 2015]; Frederick W. Gibbs and Daniel J. Cohen, 'A Conversation with Data: Prospecting Victorian Words and Ideas', *Victorian Studies*, 54 (2011), 69–77. Further details about the project and access to the underlying data are at *Victorian Books* (2010) www.victorianbook.org [accessed 30 July 2015].

[28] Anne Dewitt, 'Advances in the Visualization of Data: The Network of Genre in the Victorian Periodical Press', *Victorian Periodicals Review*, 48 (2015), 161–82.

[29] See Susan Brown, 'Networking Feminist Literary History: Recovering Eliza Meteyard's Web', in Veronica Alfano and Andrew Stauffer (eds.), *Virtual Victorians*. Basingstoke: Palgrave Macmillan, 2015, pp. 57–82.

date stamped, the project shows lines of influence between publications, but it also reveals the longevity of certain articles, as they reappear again and again over time, subject to different degrees of modification.[30] Some projects use metadata to study form. Tim Sherratt's *The Front Page*, for instance, uses genre labels from the National Library of Australia's digital library, *Trove*, to graph the changing types of articles on the front pages of Australian newspapers from the nineteenth century onwards.[31] Dallas Liddle's work on *The Times* focuses on technical metadata, using the file sizes to work out the number of characters in a particular issue. Such calculations allow Liddle to establish the density of the newspaper over time, linking digital information to decisions made in the print room.[32] Finally, Natalie Houston and Neal Audenaert's project *The Visual Page as Interface* explores various ways of representing the graphic dimensions of the printed page. Taking layout information from the OCR process, rather than the character strings, the project directs attention to the poetics of surface, allowing researchers to systematically examine presentational trends both within and between publications at scales that would be impossible in print.[33]

What unites these disparate projects is the recognition that digital objects have properties of their own. Although obtaining raw data presents difficulties, especially for British publications, most of which have been digitised as part of commercial resources, such projects make clear that digital research can do more for print than simply broaden access.[34] These data-driven projects are not a step towards a more objective analysis of the press, but a series of creative transformations that need interpretation. The graphs and visualisations produced by projects are neither objective representations of Victorian print culture nor the final

[30] *Viral Texts* (2013–) http://viraltexts.org [accessed 30 July 2015]. See Ryan Cordell, 'Viral Textuality in Nineteenth-Century US Newspaper Exchanges', in Veronica Alfano and Andrew Stauffer (eds.), *Virtual Victorians*. Basingstoke: Palgrave Macmillan, 2015, pp. 29–56; Ryan Cordell, 'Reprinting, Circulation, and the Network Author in Antebellum Newspapers', *American Literary History* 27 (2015) and David Smith, Ryan Cordell and Abby Mullen, 'Computational Methods for Uncovering Reprinted Texts in Antebellum Newspapers', *American Literary History* 27 (2015).

[31] Tim Sherratt, *The Front Page* (2012) http://dhistory.org/frontpages. For more information see '4 Million Articles Later . . .' *Discontents: Working for the Triumph of Content over Form, Ideas over Control, People over Systems* (29 June 2012) http://discontents.com.au/shed/experiments/4-million-articles-later [accessed 30 July 2015].

[32] See Dallas Liddle, 'Reflections on 20,000 Victorian Newspapers: "Distant Reading" The Times Using the Times Digital Archive', *Journal of Victorian Culture*, 17 (2012), 230–37.

[33] Natalie M. Houston, 'Toward a Computational Analysis of Victorian Poetics', *Victorian Studies*, 56 (2014), 498–510.

[34] For more on the availability of data, see Bob Nicholson, 'Tweeting the Victorians', *Victorian Periodicals Review*, 48 (2015), 254–60, 258–59.

word about them; rather, they are provocations that force us to return to the archive and look at its contents more closely.[35]

Clockwork

When Stead's reporter asked how long it took to index an issue of *The Times*, Palmer answered "'The best part of a day.'"[36] Given that Palmer was working backwards through the published volumes of *The Times* while, at the same, trying to keep up with the paper as published, this rate of work – one day per issue of a daily newspaper – suggests a Sisyphean nightmare of eternal indexing. Palmer told Stead's reporter it would take him forty years to reach the beginning of *The Times*, and this turned out to be more or less correct. The volume for 1790 appeared in 1925, the final five years completed under the supervision of *The Times* newspaper after it took over the index in 1941.[37]

A serial work indexing an ongoing serial, the material form of *Palmer's Index* is marked by its temporality. The same is true for digital resources. An iterative component remains, as resources move from closed to open beta and then to a full launch, but most resources tend to be cumulative, aggregating more data within a fairly stable interface.[38] Resources and their contents have a cultural life: interfaces are refreshed, new features are added, and sometimes they are withdrawn or cease functioning, their contents repurposed as part of another resource. *Palmer's Index* has itself been caught up in the temporality imposed by digital form. Computers began to assist compilation in 1973, but the first digital publication of the index was as a CD-ROM published by Chadwyck-Healey in 1995, then online as part of *Historical Newspapers* in 1999. Its data has been incorporated as part of *C19: The Nineteenth-Century Index* (2005–), and volumes have been incorporated in the large, free-to-access collections *Internet Archive, Google Books* and *Hathi Trust Digital Library* (2008–). These

---

[35] There is plenty of scope for more traditional quantitative work, too. Data could be harvested from periodicals such as the *Publishers' Circular* or the newspaper press directories. Equally, secondary sources such as the *Wellesley, Waterloo* and *Dictionary of Nineteenth-Century Journalism* contain information that, if fully encoded and made available, could support much important quantitative work.

[36] 'A Great Index', 11.

[37] See Barbara James, 'Indexing *The Times*', *The Indexer*, 11 (1979), 209–11.

[38] A good example of this is the *British Newspaper Archive*, which launched in November 2011 with 4 million pages; in July 2015 it had more than 11 million. See Anonymous, 'The British Newspaper Archive – Launch Press Release', *The British Newspaper Archive* (29 November 2011) http://blog .britishnewspaperarchive.co.uk/2011/11/29/221 [accessed 30 July 2015].

digital remediations, whether of data or full-text facsimiles, are more like different editions of the index: even if its contents are unchanged, the way they are situated within new digital contexts changes the terms under which they can be discovered and used. Even so-called new media can have complex bibliographical lives.

In her important recent article, Linda K. Hughes has argued that scholars need to move 'sideways', making 'lateral moves' that include 'analysis across genres; texts opening out into each other dialogically in and out of periodicals; sequential rather than "data mining" approaches to reading periodicals; and spatio-temporal convergences in print culture'.[39] Hughes offers two analogies to help conceptualise 'the mass circulation of Victorian print': the city, which captures the concurrent heterogeneity of print culture, a complex system known only through local knottings and connections, and the discursive web, the way texts responded to and perpetuated common ways of knowing.[40] Hughes does not argue for one analogy over the other but stresses how each illuminates a dimension of print culture. The urban metaphor 'attunes us to the materiality of print, the need to find routes or pathways through it, and the meaning to be found within its local formations, its "neighbourhoods" so to speak'. The discursive web, on the other hand, makes evident 'what is produced by materiality but often cannot be seen on a given page'.[41] Moving sideways allows the researcher to keep both in play, recognising the correspondences, whether continuous or contiguous, that constitute print culture.

Hughes recognises that moving sideways can be done online as well as with the surviving print archive. After all, even when 'drilling down' into search results, we are really following the recurrence of search terms across the corpus. For Hughes, free-text searching makes evident the discursive web but, for now, turning the pages of printed newspapers and periodicals is necessary to understand 'how print organizes itself locally, materially, and temporally'.[42] There is no substitute for turning pages: even the richest digital simulation cannot capture the haptic experience of an encounter with printed paper. Yet we should be as cautious of ossifying the current dominant trends in digitisation as we are of privileging existing research methodologies. For Hughes, page turning through successive issues 'constructs horizons of expectations that makes legible an array of temporal and material cruxes in print culture'.[43] The way the majority of

[39] Hughes, 'SIDEWAYS!' 1–2.   [40] Hughes, 'SIDEWAYS!' 2–4.   [41] Hughes, 'SIDEWAYS!' 5.
[42] Hughes, 'SIDEWAYS!' 20.   [43] Hughes, 'SIDEWAYS!' 21.

digitised newspapers and periodicals are presented makes this next to impossible, but this genre of resource is not the only way of doing digital research. Using some of the techniques currently being developed, it is possible to imagine resources that are attuned to the emergence of unexpected features or that are capable of detecting new configurations of content. And, because they leverage computational power, such resources can work at a much larger scale than the lone researcher, turning pages one by one. This is not to argue machines are better readers, or that more can be done working with data than with print; rather, we might learn more when we turn to print if we complement our reading with that of the machine.

In conclusion, I recommend one further analogy for the nineteenth-century press. In addition to the city and the discursive web, I would add the heart. Not only does this remind us that encounters with print necessarily involve feeling, but it also provides a way to think about repetition. Newspapers and periodicals are defined by their open-ended seriality, every issue published with the expectation of another to follow. Repetition is built into the logic of print, and no genres more fully embody this logic than newspapers and periodicals. Yet repetition also captures the various remediations that occur when historical print is digitised. Palmer's was one type of object while it was in progress, another once the sequence was completed, and then something else again when digitised and incorporated within larger resources. As readers, the repetitive becomes tiresome or, worse, invisible, our attention drawn to the novel or exceptional. When material is remediated in digital form, we tend to only notice the differences that are introduced through digitisation, overlooking the discontinuities upon which such processes depend. If digital research is, as Houston has argued, about moving 'beyond human limitations of vision, memory, and attention', then computers can help us see print in ways that otherwise escape our recognition.[44] The paradox of periodicals scholarship in the digital age is that although the print objects are closer to the past, it is by doing things to them – reading them, of course, but also transforming, translating, processing and reformatting them – that we bring the past closer to us.

---

[44] Houston, 'Toward a Computational Analysis of Victorian Poetics', 499.

CHAPTER 3

The Magazine and Literary Culture

David Stewart

Magazines sprang up everywhere in the first three decades of the nineteenth century, and they did so with a curious self-consciousness about their place in literary culture. Thomas De Quincey, in an unpublished editorial intended for the *London Magazine* in 1821, proposed that 'the literature of a nation' is not simply 'the total amount of its books' but is one of 'the Fine Arts'.[1] In 1823, he expanded on the idea, offering his influential distinction between the literatures of 'knowledge' and 'power'.[2] The literature of knowledge is useful but ephemeral because it, like scientific or industrial knowledge, is progressive; the literature of power possesses a permanent value and is not replaced by the latest development. It is a crucial idea for nineteenth-century cultural criticism, and its formulation in a magazine is at once appropriate and slightly odd. Magazines have tended to be placed in the former category by scholars of Romantic culture: they possess, that is, a historical or contextual, but not a literary interest. De Quincey's unpublished editorial suggests he was not quite sure on which side to place magazines. As magazines, he says, are *'vehicles of liberal amusement'*, they are *'themselves part of the literature'* in that they include writing in *'every* department of composition'; they might be considered to be 'literary' in a way that other periodicals (such as reviews) are not.[3] Magazines are miscellanies and do not simply review new books: they also include short stories, sketches, essays and poetry. But De Quincey's claims are larger: the magazine might be considered an *elevated* cultural form, capable of standing alongside *Paradise Lost* or *Macbeth* among the 'Fine Arts'. Magazines, as Mark Parker claims in his pioneering study of the

---

[1] Thomas De Quincey, 'On the London Magazine', in Grevel Lindop (gen. ed.), *The Works of Thomas De Quincey*, 21 vols. London: Pickering and Chatto, 2003, 3: pp. 350–59 (pp. 351–52).

[2] De Quincey, 'Letters to a Young Man Whose Education Has Been Neglected, No. 3', in Lindop (ed.), *The Works*, 3: pp. 59–74 (p. 70). He expanded on the distinction in a more famous article on Pope in 1848.

[3] De Quincey, 'London Magazine', p. 351.

form, have some claim to be the 'preeminent literary form' of the late Romantic period.[4] Yet if magazines attained a new prominence, they did so in tentative, uncertain and even volatile ways. De Quincey, in a magazine, draws the way magazines might be read into question. This suggests the ways magazines tested out, examined and challenged the constitution of 'literary culture'.

Scholars of Romanticism were once familiar with magazines only because they seemed to be something that 'literary' Romantic writers overcame. Wordsworth was opposed to the 'rapid communication of intelligence' enabled by an enhanced periodical press, and that press returned his disdain in parodies and tough reviews. Although few believe that Keats, as Byron joked, was really 'snuffed out by an article', the aggressive articles about him in *Blackwood's Magazine* and elsewhere are frequently cited as evidence of a politically and culturally reactionary climate for new writing. Even those writers who made their way principally through magazine publication, such as De Quincey, William Hazlitt, Leigh Hunt and Charles Lamb, were once celebrated only insofar as their work transcended its context in *Blackwood's*, the *New Monthly Magazine, The Indicator* or the *London Magazine*.[5]

A richer and more appreciative understanding of Romantic magazine culture began to develop in the 1980s. New Historicist accounts influenced by Jürgen Habermas's theory of the print public sphere by the likes of Jon Klancher, Kevin Gilmartin and Paul Keen began to consider magazine writing alongside the rest of the expanding periodical press as worthy of study on its own terms.[6] As Romantic scholars began to extend the definition of the 'literary' beyond novels, plays and poems, periodicals became important as, in Marilyn Butler's phrase, 'culture's medium': a reflection of the formation of Romanticism, and perhaps also a form of Romanticism itself.[7] Reviews and newspapers are significant in this story, but magazines began to seem increasingly so. They were, in the later

---

[4] Mark Parker, *Literary Magazines and British Romanticism*. Cambridge University Press, 2000, p. 1.
[5] For more favourable criticism of the influence of the magazines on Romantic writers, see Mark Schoenfield, *British Periodicals and Romantic Identity: The 'Literary Lower Empire'*. New York: Palgrave Macmillan, 2009; Simon P. Hull, *Charles Lamb, Elia and the London Magazine: Metropolitan Muse*. London: Pickering and Chatto, 2010; Kim Wheatley, *Romantic Feuds: Transcending the 'Age of Personality'*. Farnham: Ashgate, 2013.
[6] Jon P. Klancher, *The Making of English Reading Audiences, 1790–1832*. University of Wisconsin Press, 1987; Kevin Gilmartin, *Print Politics: The Press and Radical Opposition in Early Nineteenth-Century England*. Cambridge University Press, 1996; Paul Keen, *The Crisis of Literature in the 1790s: Print Culture and the Public Sphere*. Cambridge University Press, 1999.
[7] Marilyn Butler, 'Culture's Medium: The Role of the Review', in Stuart Curran (ed.), *The Cambridge Companion to British Romanticism*. Cambridge University Press, 1993, pp. 120–47.

Romantic period, more popular, but they also took on a new role. Magazines combined the capacity to reflect the contemporary field offered by other periodicals with a curious capacity to become something far closer to the kind of culture offered by the novels of Scott and Austen or the poetry of Wordsworth and Byron. As David Higgins has shown, magazines were one of the most important sources for new ideas such as De Quincey's about the sanctified separateness of 'literary' culture from a debased commercial context.[8] If magazines offered themselves as literary they did so, as I have argued elsewhere, with knowing irony.[9] In this chapter, I will track the subtle and suggestive ways in which magazines tested out what 'literary culture' might be.

The New School of Magazines

An account in the *New Monthly Magazine* in January 1824 of the previous year's activity notes the latest phenomena: 'Only ninety-nine new magazines, two of which do *not* promise to outstrip all their predecessors'.[10] There were not 'ninety-nine new magazines' launched in 1823, though the contributor to the *New Monthly* can be forgiven for feeling swamped. Accurate figures for the number of magazines and their sales are hard to establish. Alvin Sullivan's (incomplete) list of magazines from the eighteenth century to the end of the nineteenth records a considerable increase in the number of new magazines during the first three decades of the century, especially after 1815, as compared to the years since the birth of the form in 1731.[11] Eighteenth-century magazines should not be dismissed as unworldly, as if they existed in a pre-commercial hinterland, but there is, nonetheless, something in the comment of a *Blackwood's Magazine* writer in 1824 that in the early nineteenth century, 'this business has *progressed* in the most astonishing ratio'.[12] *Blackwood's* joked about vast sales of 20,000 per month: it was likely selling around 6,000 copies shortly after its launch in 1817.[13] This is impressive, if not spectacular, even taking

[8] David Higgins, *Romantic Genius and the Literary Magazine: Biography, Celebrity, Politics*. London: Routledge, 2005.

[9] David Stewart, *Romantic Magazines and Metropolitan Literary Culture*. Basingstoke: Palgrave Macmillan, 2011.

[10] James Smith, 'Annus Mirabilis! Or a Parthian Glance at 1823', *New Monthly Magazine*, 10 (January 1824), 10–16 (11).

[11] *British Literary Magazines*, Alvin Sullivan (ed.), 4 vols. London: Greenwood Press, 1983.

[12] 'Noctes Ambrosianae No. XVI', *Blackwood's Magazine*, 16 (August 1824), 231–50 (234).

[13] Letter from J. G. Lockhart to Rev. Williams, late 1817, in Margaret Oliphant, *Annals of a Publishing House: William Blackwood and His Sons*, 3 vols. Edinburgh: William Blackwood and Sons, 1897, 1:

into account the fact that each copy of the magazine was likely read by many readers: the magazines of the eighteenth century sold not much less than this.[14] The 'progression' is a matter of character, and it occurred in the 1810s.

Contemporaries were quick to claim that magazine writing changed in the early nineteenth century, and that it did so in or about October 1817. Scholars of the field have tended to agree.[15] This was the date when *Blackwood's Edinburgh Magazine* was launched, or rather relaunched following a failed first attempt as the *Edinburgh Monthly Magazine*. There are earlier precedents – notably the periodicals of Leigh Hunt – but *Blackwood's* startled the public and encouraged other publishers to follow its lead. *Blackwood's* has tended to be caricatured as a virulent Tory scandal rag, but it offered a model of magazine writing which influenced writers and publishers across a wide political, social and cultural spectrum. In a review of the periodical press in 1823, William Hazlitt noticed the huge number of new magazines and the 'antipathy' with which they held one another, and not without reason: perhaps the most celebrated anecdote of this period is the fatal duel between representatives of *Blackwood's* and the *London Magazine*.[16] Yet the *London* was set up very deliberately on the *Blackwood's* model, so much so that *Blackwood's* accused it, lightheartedly, of theft. The *New Monthly Magazine* was relaunched in 1821 to bring it in line with the new style. *Blackwood's*, the *London* and the *New Monthly* were the acknowledged market leaders. Each tried to maintain a distinctive style. *Blackwood's* was riotous, silly, inventive, aggressive, politically reactionary, up to the minute on literary culture and delightfully inconsistent. The *London* began on the same model: it was witty if less silly and far more muted in politics and became best known for the quality of its individual contributors, including Charles Lamb, William Hazlitt, Thomas Hood and Thomas De Quincey. The *New Monthly* was almost wholly apolitical, light, gentle, inoffensive and the home of many of the best writers in part

---

p. 191. For the extravagant claim, see 'On the Late Rumour of a Change of Administration', *Blackwood's*, 10 (December 1821, Part 2), 743–56 (753).

[14] Precise circulation figures are difficult to determine because full publishing records do not exist for most firms. William St Clair's comprehensive survey of recent research quotes figures of between 3,500 and 10,000 copies for the *Gentleman's Magazine*, the best-selling of the eighteenth-century magazines: *The Reading Nation in the Romantic Period*. Cambridge University Press, 2004, pp. 572–73.

[15] See, for example, Robert Morrison and Daniel S. Roberts, eds., *Romanticism and Blackwood's Magazine: 'An Unprecedented Phenomenon'*. Basingstoke: Palgrave Macmillan, 2013.

[16] William Hazlitt, 'The Periodical Press', *Edinburgh Review*, 38 (May 1823), 349–78 (369). On the duel, see Richard Cronin, *Paper Pellets: British Literary Culture After Waterloo*. Oxford University Press, 2010, pp. 1–6.

because it paid contributors so well. Descriptions such as these are possible, though it is worth remembering that a magazine is a miscellany, and no single description fits all of its contents; indeed, magazines in this period made a point of being various. Individual magazines had their differences, but together their production of a new kind of miscellany pushed the form into cultural prominence.

These three magazines may have dominated the public discussion, but to catch the tenor of the magazine culture one must appreciate the sheer range of magazines established in this period. Gold's *London Magazine* (a rival to the more famous *London* published by Baldwin) claimed to be overwhelmed by 'Literary placards of Indicators, Talismens, Londoners, Gazettes, Honeycombs, Bees, and Déjeunés', a little disingenuously, perhaps, given that the publishers Gold and Northhouse were responsible for both a 'Londoner' and the *Déjeuné*.[17] *Knight's Quarterly Magazine* appeared in Cambridge, *The Kaleidoscope* in Liverpool and *The Liberal* in Pisa. Most magazines were produced in the two main publishing centres, Edinburgh and London, but the culture was characterised by the rapid efflorescence of magazines right across Britain and Ireland. These included religious magazines, magazines of useful knowledge such as the *Glasgow Mechanics Magazine*, magazines which maintained the older style such as the *Monthly Magazine* and the still-popular *Gentleman's Magazine*, and many more. No city believed it could be without a magazine, but publications such as the *Newcastle Magazine* and *McPhun's Glasgow Magazine* did not assume an exclusively provincial audience. *The Leodiensian, or, Leeds Grammar School Magazine*, rather surprisingly at first sight, asserted confidently its 'hope of success'.[18] The success envisaged was financial, and even though, as it happened, the magazine made little impact, the idea was not fanciful: another school magazine, *The Etonian*, was so popular in the early 1820s that it went through four editions and was reviewed favourably by the *Quarterly Review*. Some magazines came out weekly, some monthly, some quarterly; some enjoyed very poor sales, and many folded after a few issues. This sense of a culture in continual flux and renewal is crucial. Scholars are increasingly investigating this range, and a student of any individual magazine must be conscious of its place in a rowdy magazine market.

Readers and commerce drove that market, and magazine writers knew it. A poem by James Harley in the *London* was typical in the open way it

---

[17] '*The Déjeuné*' (review), [Gold's] *London Magazine*, 3 (January 1821), 51–62 (51).
[18] 'Preface', *Leodiensian, or, Leeds Grammar School Magazine*, 1 (October 1827), iii–vi (vi).

addressed the point: 'Reader, I ask but little – being shy – / Abuse me if you please – but pray first buy'.[19] A magazine could not be sustained without regular readers, and the fact that so many readers were willing to buy magazines was the principal reason that publishers printed them. Scholars have tended to assume that magazines addressed discrete audiences (that male Tories read *Blackwood's*, aristocratic women *La Belle Assemblée*, while the *New Monthly* addressed the domesticated middle classes), though magazine writers assumed that their readership was far less clearly defined. The weekly *Déjeuné* hoped to appeal at once to 'the lady of fifty' drinking tea and the 'volatile youth' sipping his breakfast chocolate.[20] Magazines reached such diverse consumers by being themselves diverse. *Blackwood's* claimed to produce 'papers fit for every sort of folks: / For young and old, male, female, grave, and giddy'.[21] The *London* and *Blackwood's* cost half a crown for a monthly issue, placing them largely as a middle-class commodity, though many readers would have accessed copies through reading societies, libraries and other means. Female and middle-class readers played a significant role in shaping magazine culture, but the diversity *Blackwood's* identifies is the crucial point. That such a miscellaneous crowd of customers might come together to buy a miscellany was what made the format so appealing to publishers. No one article would appeal to every reader, but perhaps every reader would find something for him or her. Magazines do not provide unmediated access to reading communities: when they were so pointedly miscellaneous, it is hard to say that any magazine shaped the mentalities of its readers into unity. The difficult act of mediation between periodicals and readership became in these years a point for anxious discussion.

Many magazine articles puzzled over the nature of crowds, and when they did so they offered a disconcerting reflection of their readers. John Galt, in a characteristically experimental serial called 'The Steam-boat', has his narrator Thomas Duffle arrive in London from Glasgow for the coronation of George IV. In his lodgings, Duffle hears 'a great tooting of horns in the street' occasioned by the newly published newspapers. He heads down into the crowd and is swallowed up: 'I had nothing to do but flow in the stream of people'.[22] In a later instalment, he describes the people of the crowd as a new species, 'effigies': 'They resemble man in

[19] James Harley, 'Letter from John O'Groats to the Editor', *London Magazine*, 3 (January 1821), 48–50 (50).
[20] 'Preface', *Déjeuné*, 1 (21 October 1820), 1–2 (2).
[21] 'The Notices', *Blackwood's Magazine*, 3 (June 1818), unpaginated.
[22] John Galt, 'The Steam-Boat VI', *Blackwood's Magazine*, 10 (August 1821), 4–26 (9).

action and external bearing; but they have neither passions, appetites, nor affections'.[23] Magazines often point towards the sense of alienation and disconnection that a media-saturated society fosters. Galt hints at the dislocated, hollowed-out condition of the magazine consumer, but his narrator also registers the excitements of a crowd brought into being by the press and feels oddly at home in it. 'Thomas Duffle' is, after all, a kind of effigy – he is a 'phantom-cloud', a journalistic semi-reality like Charles Lamb's 'Elia' – but an effigy drawn with such warmth that his crowds of readers in *Blackwood's* might start to feel a bond of connection with him, and by extension with one another.[24] The crowd of readers, in conscious recognition of its status as a mixed collection of individuals, is offered by magazines the opportunity to test out feelings of belonging and new ideas of community.

Thomas De Quincey, in drawing into question the status of the magazines that he spent his whole career writing for, indicates that writing for this crowd of consumers produces oddly conflicted feelings. Many contributors remained anonymous, but increasingly readers bought magazines because the writers were famous and reading magazines was fashionable. Charles Lamb's essays as 'Elia' prompted poems of praise by readers of the *London Magazine*, and the essays also helped push up sales. At the beginning of the century, magazines consisted to a large extent of contributions volunteered by readers. There were certainly many famous contributors: the July 1800 edition of the *Monthly Magazine*, for example, contains contributions by the novelist Mary Hays and poetry by Mary Robinson, but it also contains a 'Receipt for Yeast'. Thirty years later, *Fraser's Magazine* made a pitch for its new readers partly by virtue of a new style (yeast recipes replaced by the exceptionally self-conscious 'Election of Editor for Fraser's Magazine', an event that ends with William Blackwood violently assaulting William Hazlitt), but also by virtue of its celebrated contributors. The July 1830 number has articles by acknowledged stars such as Letitia Elizabeth Landon, James Hogg, Robert Southey and Samuel Taylor Coleridge. Writers, in turn, were paid far more handsomely. William Maginn, who wrote for *Blackwood's* and *Fraser's* as well as setting up his own monthly magazine *John Bull*, was offered twenty guineas a sheet by Henry Colburn, proprietor of the *New Monthly*, and Lamb made the substantial sum of sixteen guineas a sheet at the *London*. Not every

---

[23] John Galt, 'The Steam-Boat VII', *Blackwood's Magazine*, 10 (September 1821), 166–71 (168).
[24] Lamb uses the phrase 'phantom-cloud', in 'New Year's Eve', *London Magazine*, 3 (January 1821), 5–8 (6).

magazine could afford to pay its writers so well, and some continued to solicit unpaid contributions, but this new professionalism affected the standing of the magazines.

Magazine writing was not quite respectable, but it ceased to seem like hack work and moved to the verge, as Richard Cronin has shown, of being 'gentlemanly'.[25] Most writers (even for magazines aimed exclusively at women) were male, but magazine writing moved closer to being a respectable occupation for women too. The fact that magazines paid well was one source of this unsettled status. 'Peter Morris', a character who began life as a magazine joke, a 'quiz', claims that 'I look upon periodical writing as by far the most agreeable species of authorship'. That he does so because magazines *pay* so much better than any others' suggests a lingering dubiety.[26] Magazines brought writers into contact with a substantial commercial apparatus, but in doing so writers began to seem like the purveyors of commodities. Being thrust into notice was tempting, but also worrying. The possibility of becoming a journalistic celebrity through the magazines was palpable, but this was always shadowed by De Quincey's ambiguity. One writer 'thought of my triumph, when, sauntering up to some friend, I should stroke my chin, adjust my cravat – "Ah! how d'ye do, Will? – how are you? – seen the Magazines? – What d'ye think? – Tell you a secret – I have – ha – give me a pinch of snuff – I – I write for "The Edinburgh"'.[27] This is a rather tender joke: the writer ironises ambitions this article nonetheless sets out to achieve. He or she did not succeed, though some writers achieved both fame and respectability. But the uncertainly 'literary' quality of articles like this also offered creative possibilities.

There were in these decades many more magazines, sales were up, and writers were more ready to advertise the fact that they wrote for magazines. It was a bustling, confident culture, and yet this uncertain self-consciousness bubbled under the surface. A poem in the *London* celebrated the vivid mix of 'Slang, scandal, gospel, quiz, and party squibs', yet that makes the 'new school' of magazines hard to categorise: ''tis a rum one!'[28] In an editorial, the *London* informed its readers that 'these are days of exertion, – of patronage, – of popularity, – of liberality, – and every fine quality besides! The LONDON MAGAZINE, therefore, must play its part, as occupying a distinguished place amongst the noise and bustle. *We apprehend that Magazines will soon form the only literature of the*

[25] Cronin, *Paper Pellets*, pp. 136–53.
[26] J. G. Lockhart, *Peter's Letters to his Kinsfolk*, 3 vols. Edinburgh: Blackwood, 1819, II, pp. 192, 193.
[27] 'What Shall I Write?', *Edinburgh [Scots] Magazine and Literary Miscellany*, II (July 1822), 38–40.
[28] 'The New Schools', *London Magazine*, I (May 1820), 543.

country![29] One thing that marks the 'new school' is bravura assertions like this one, undercut as it is with a knowing unease: a triumph for magazines might be seen as a defeat for literary culture.

Magazines on Literary Culture

Magazines changed their character in the first decades of the century because the culture they were so bound up in was changing. Magazines were, in fact, one of the primary sources for the complaint that the press was churning out too much. An article in the *New Monthly* declared that the future may outstrip the present age 'in every various science and every art but *one*: – in that of making and multiplying books we must ever hold our superiority'.[30] *La Belle Assemblée* (a fashionable women's magazine) included a letter from London to the country which reflected that 'every hour we find something new issuing from the press ... really the daily teeming of the British press is like the explosion of Mount Vesuvius'.[31] It might well be objected that the latest issue of *La Belle Assemblée* was not helping matters, but one purpose of these jeremiads was to justify a new kind of cultural criticism. Magazines, if they were to track literary culture, would do so in a new way.

The literary culture of the late Romantic period experienced, as book historians have shown, an acceleration in literary production.[32] Magazines offer an especially valuable guide to the age because their contents indicate just how various that culture was, and because they showed such an interest in dividing that range of works into categories. When *Blackwood's* was launched in October 1817, its contents page listed a huge number of articles that it promised to publish in future issues. These included 'Dialogues over a Punch-bowl, I, II, III, IV', 'On the Egotism of the Lake Poets, more especially Wordsworth' and a great many more, some apparently serious, some not. The sheer number of articles promised (118 of them) is a fitting embodiment of the effect the culture of the early nineteenth century had on writers. Writers encountered an age that seemed too large to map in detail; instead, we are left with lists that will be swallowed up by the progress of events as they pass. A few months later, a correspondent, P. P., complained that many of these promised articles had not appeared.

---

[29] 'The Lion's Head', *London Magazine*, 3 (February 1821), 123–24 (124).
[30] Eliza Walker, 'Book-Makers', *New Monthly Magazine*, 10 (April 1824), 342–47 (342).
[31] 'Letter from a Country Lady to her Sister', *La Belle Assemblée*, 22 (October 1820), 154–56 (154).
[32] For example, James Raven, *The Business of Books: Booksellers and the English Book Trade, 1450–1850*. New Haven: Yale University Press, 2007 and St Clair, *Reading Nation*.

P. P. was informed that 'We must overtake the [articles] as the press of new matter will permit', though the editor doubted whether P.P., 'who seems in his dotage', would live to see their completion.[33] *Blackwood's* finally ceased publication in 1980, but even at that the hope was unlikely to be fulfilled because the 'press of new matter' was relentless, and it was in that atmosphere which magazines thrived. When William Maginn, a regular contributor, was in London, William Blackwood urged him to pay attention: 'You are on the spot, and know how the pulse of the public beats. All depends on catching the thing at the right moment'.[34] His magazine, like the others, endeavoured to do just that, and the public pulse was increasingly rapid.

The *London Magazine* sought to mirror *Blackwood's* most particularly in its capacity to register the pulse of the present. John Scott, its editor, distinguished himself in his prospectus from the older magazines: 'opinion now busies itself with more venturous themes than of yore; discussion must start fleeter and subtler game; excitements must be stronger; the stakes of all sorts higher; the game more complicated and hazardous'.[35] The *London* set out its stall in its first issue with a review of *A Sicilian Story* by 'Barry Cornwall'. Cornwall was the pseudonym of Bryan Waller Procter, and he had begun to establish himself as a popular poet capable of appealing to a substantial audience, but also as a promising poet distinguished from the crowd of competitors by especially discerning commentators. The *London* wishes to show its new readers how closely it follows this culture. 'Cornwall' is, they assert, a pseudonym, and the reviewer also says confidently that the writer is unlike notable poets such as Leigh Hunt, Robert Southey, Charles Lamb, Lord Byron, Percy Shelley and John Keats. The inclusion of Shelley and Keats is especially telling: they are canonical now, but in 1820 they had a reputation only among a select few, and it was an important function of a magazine to be part of that select, discerning group. The *London* wishes to alert its readers to the fact that it can offer a guide not just to best sellers such as Byron and Scott but also to those writers who were establishing a reputation among the cultural elite.

At the heart of these surveys of literary culture is the capacity to make cultural distinctions like those De Quincey made between 'knowledge' and 'power': that which would become canonical, and that which would be forgotten. The *London* is keen to show it can place Cornwall securely: 'His

---

[33] Notices to correspondents, *Blackwood's*, 3 (January 1818), unpaginated.
[34] Letter to Maginn, 23 February 1825, Oliphant, *Annals*, 1, p. 403.
[35] 'Prospectus of the London Magazine', reprinted *London Magazine* 1 (1820), iv–viii (v).

poetry is in the true and natural class, in opposition to the false and artificial'. The *London* does not simply describe the latest developments; it divides them up for a readership struggling to cope with an overly abundant literary culture. These acts of taste making suggest an authoritative aloofness from popular culture. But the account of literary developments that magazines offer is constantly attuned to the fast-moving culture in which the *London* and Barry Cornwall jostle for space. 'We would like,' the reviewer says, 'to have written [these poems]: but we cannot do every thing. We have been fully occupied lately in correcting proofs, and arranging prices of cow-hides and molasses'.[36] Poetry seems to place itself above a tawdry commercial context, and the magazine seems happy to endorse the view, but it does not forget the world around it. Reviews of books are followed, eleven pages later, by the 'Commercial Report' (including discussion of molasses; meat prices follow on page 118). The 120-page issue of the *London* for January 1820 came wrapped in two sixteen-page advertising supplements. 'Literariness' is wrapped up in, and unable to extricate itself from, a miscellaneous culture of commercial transactions and uncertain speculations.

The *London*'s initial issue also contained the first in a series of articles on 'The Living Authors'. Discussion of the 'living poets' was common in these years, especially in magazines. In 1812, Leigh Hunt had imagined Apollo coming to a London pub to discuss their merits in the pages of *The Reflector* (a quarterly magazine); the *British Ladies Magazine* offered a series of essays on the living poets, as did the *Examiner*; even the *Leodiensian* joined in, and Gold's *London Magazine* offered an account of the 'living magazines'. In its opening issue, *Blackwood's* promised 'Lectures on the Living Poets of Britain, No. 1, Crabbe'. This did not appear, but *Blackwood's* shared with most magazines in this period an interest in tracking a culture which seemed still 'living', yet to be settled. The *New Monthly Magazine* was crucial in the development of this perception. The magazine seemed often obsessed with attempting to trace a culture that would not stay still. Horace Smith contributed frequently to the *New Monthly*, and his articles (part sketch, part fiction, part cultural critique) on topics such as dining with a self-regarding minor author, or John Huggins the barber poet, offer a map by which readers can attempt to navigate an overstocked age. Another piece by Smith reflected, as did many of his colleagues, on that 'overgorged vomitory *the Row*', though Smith is more forgiving than some and offers an account of all of 'these unembodied outlines, these dim and

---

[36] 'A Sicilian Story' (review), *London Magazine*, 1 (January 1820), 84–86 (85).

visionary configurations of uncomposed works', those books planned but never written.[37] Articles like these show a sympathetic fascination with an ephemeral age, surely because the writers believed themselves to be part of it. The particular feature of literary culture that magazines mirror is precisely the fact that it is so hard to ascribe it a stable character. 'Not only do more write, but each writes more' said another *New Monthly* writer, Eliza Walker, but magazine articles like these do not so much attempt to de-clutter the age, to categorise it securely for readers, as to provide a mode of appreciating it as it passes. 'Forgotten, *sooner or later*, will be the Breakwater and the Pavilion, Scotch novels and English hexameters, Congreve's rockets and Gill's copper caps, the splendour of our military fame and the brightness of Warren's blacking', and our task is to enjoy these fleeting colours.[38] After all, it is hard to tell whether a sketch in the *New Monthly* is more like *Waverley* or Gill's copper caps, or whether any one item can be separated from the rest. The whole culture seemed as miscellaneous as a magazine, and just as difficult to categorise. Rather than condemn it, magazine articles like these played along.

A distinguishing feature of the magazines was the pleasure they took in this uncertainty. The most famous and most brilliant way *Blackwood's* found was the *Noctes Ambrosianae*, a series of semi-fictional 'conversations' (begun in 1822) supposed to have occurred while the contributors met in an Edinburgh pub. A great many magazines adopted a similar forum. *McPhun's Glasgow Magazine* had 'The Supper Table', the Paisley *Wayfarer* had 'The Club Room', *Knight's Quarterly Magazine* had 'Castle Vernon', the *Newcastle Magazine* had the dialogues of 'Bob Tickler' and the *Scots Magazine* beat *Blackwood's* to it with 'The Modern Decameron' (begun in 1820). Conversational writing allows writers to disagree with themselves, to test out ideas, to hazard opinions that they are not quite sure about, and to bring together all the various aspects of a teeming culture. *Blackwood's* has tended to be considered a narrow-minded, violent defender of high literary tradition, but it exemplified this sympathetic embrace of a miscellaneous culture. As Mark Parker suggests, the *Noctes* offer a dialogic spirit of criticism that suggests the mutual interdependence of high and low cultures.[39] The semi-fictional 'Christopher North' put it this way: 'Our spirits are very unequal. We look on this world with many thousand eyes. On Monday, a man seems to us to shew some talent – on Tuesday, we find him feeble – and

[37] Horace Smith, 'A Lecture upon Heads and Unwritten Works', *New Monthly Magazine*, 10 (May 1824), 418–21, 419, 420.

[38] Eliza Walker, 'Book-Makers', *New Monthly Magazine*, 10 (April 1824), 342–47, 344, 342.

[39] Parker, *Literary Magazines*, p. 113.

on Wednesday, weep to acknowledge him a Macvey. Thus are we sometime led into inconsistencies'.[40] Magazines, by virtue of their miscellaneous but also their periodical nature, were able to track and reflect a culture that seemed to present new facets with each passing day. As scholars begin to explore the further reaches of magazine writing, this spirit of openness may prove instructive. A cultivated inconsistency was one way in which the magazines embraced and celebrated a diverse and endlessly proliferating literary culture.

Magazines as Literary Culture

The move from Keats to cow-hides in the *London* and the characterful 'quizzing' of the *Noctes* indicates the way that magazines toyed with their readers' expectations. They were not simply mirrors of literary culture, but creative participants in it. The first number of *Knight's Quarterly Magazine* has an article in which a correspondent offers to the editor a 'New Depository for Literary Manufactures': a *'factory for the exhibition and sale of original manuscripts'*. The editor, for twenty guineas a sheet, can buy poetry and 'descriptive pieces': 'On Pokers', 'On British Wines', or 'an elegant Dissertation on Razors'.[41] These are affectionate parodies of writers for the *London* and the *New Monthly* such as Hazlitt, Lamb and Hunt. The article, and it was one of many to take the same conceit, mocks the assumption of literary status by such brazenly commercial products as magazines. Yet in unveiling the commercial motivations that underpin magazine selling, the article also presents its readers with an enjoyable joke, one to be enjoyed principally for the pleasure it produces, rather than as a satire with some corrective purpose. After all, *Knight's* attempted to sustain itself on just the same wares. Articles like this at once assert the primacy which the truly 'literary' maintains over magazine writing and undermine the assumptions by which such claims are made. *Blackwood's* identified Wordsworth, Byron and Scott as the 'master-spirits' of the age in July 1818, separating the canonical wheat from the ephemeral chaff; but in the same issue, it numbered itself among the master-spirits. A brilliant poem (written in the Byronic ottava rima stanza) called *The Mad Banker of Amsterdam* asked 'Scott, Byron, Wordsworth, Wilson – why not I?'[42] One way in which magazines confused and delighted readers was the readiness

---

[40] 'Postscript to the Public', *Blackwood's*, 12 (July 1822), 53–55, 55. Macvey Napier was an Edinburgh lawyer and periodical writer, and a frequent target in *Blackwood's*.
[41] 'New Depository for Literary Manufactures', *Knight's Quarterly Magazine*, 1 (October 1823), 96–102.
[42] J. G. Lockhart, 'Mad Banker of Amsterdam', *Blackwood's*, 3 (July 1818), 402–7, 405. Wilson is John Wilson, a Wordsworthian poet and, with Lockhart, one of the principal contributors to

with which they crossed the apparent divide between critical commentator and creative writer. Yet the question that 'William Wastle', the fictional author of *The Mad Banker*, asks does not simply or unthinkingly offer magazine writing as equivalent to poetry or 'high art'. The magazines' distinctive contribution was to leave questions such as Wastle's open.

John Hamilton Reynolds's article 'Exmouth Wrestling', published in the *London Magazine* in December 1820, opens up that question in thoughtful ways. Reynolds was a close friend of Keats and had attempted to establish himself as a poet in the 1810s. By 1820, he was on the verge of giving up his literary ambitions: his collection *The Fancy*, published that year, offers a slightly rueful, if vigorous and comic, valediction to the literary world. This appears a familiar story: a minor poet fired by literary enthusiasm subsiding finally into ephemeral prose. His friend Keats's poems are securely 'literary' and are remembered by a grateful posterity; Reynolds's prose has at most a historical interest. The first is the literature of power, the second, of knowledge. But 'Exmouth Wrestling', like much else in the magazines, at once supports such ideas and draws them into doubt. The article describes a holiday in Exmouth and a trip to watch a wrestling match. Sport was a common magazine topic, and Reynolds's essay foreshadows closely the most famous example, Hazlitt's 'The Fight', published two years later in the *New Monthly Magazine*. The article moves between modes: travel writing, light satire of social mores, a historical account of the development of the sport, witty sports journalism in the manner of the boxing writer Pierce Egan (a wrestler keeps his feet 'like a cat in walnut shells'), and something of the spirit of literary antiquarianism associated with eighteenth-century magazines (a discussion of an early eighteenth-century pamphlet on 'The Art of Wrestling').[43] Reynolds's article approximates the miscellaneous nature of the magazine, and in doing so it poses a challenge to the reader: how should such an article be read?

'Exmouth Wrestling' adopts many generic modes, but it is pointedly literary. The article is scattered with quotations. He opens by considering the pleasures of a holiday. These exist in anticipation: 'To go, is something; but how much more is it, to enlarge, – to dwell, – to feed upon the promise! The core of the enjoyment is, in short, to "*stand* upon the *order* of your going"'.[44] The phrase is Lady Macbeth's, but Reynolds does not simply assume the equivalence of an anonymous article in the *London* and

---

Blackwood's. He contributed the essay on 'master spirits': 'Essays on the Lake School of Poets', *Blackwood's*, 3 (July 1818), 369–81, 369.
[43] John Hamilton Reynolds, 'Exmouth Wrestling', *London Magazine*, 2 (December 1820), 608–18, 613.
[44] Reynolds, 'Exmouth', 608.

Shakespeare's play. Reynolds's reflection is occasioned by the fact that holidays mean so much more to the clerks, lawyers and other 'city labourers' who have little leisure (pointedly, Reynolds says that all London knows this pleasure but hackney coachmen and 'Editors of newspapers').[45] This was precisely the social range from which magazines drew their writers and readers, a class for whom Shakespeare was an excursion from daily life (Reynolds gave up poetry to practise law).[46] The article describes an excursion from everyday cares, and its references to literary matters suggest a similar desire to escape a working context, but it maintains a difficult balance between the literary and magazine worlds. An allusion to Keats (interestingly to the then unpublished verse letter 'To J. H. Reynolds, Esq.' of 24 March 1818) brought a response in the *London* a few months later.[47] This intra-magazine dialogue is appropriate because 'Exmouth Wrestling' reflects continuously on its place in a magazine: literature is always in contact with other forms of culture, even as it pushes against them.

The allusion to Keats takes Reynolds back to a time when his aspirations as an artist were considerably loftier. His description of the local wrestling favourites, the Canns, might suggest bitterness in the contrast it draws between wrestling writing and higher artistic callings: 'one of the names which were in the mouths of women and domestics as synonyms for prowess and valour, and which at the onset had sounded to me like fame'.[48] Fame is unlikely, perhaps, to record the names of the Canns, or anonymous authors of articles about them. Yet this habit of linking literary aspiration to its context in the magazine also has its pleasures. A footnote tells us that 'Mr Wilson, the Plague-Poet, and *Moral Professor*, is very fond of running about the Highlands, wrestling and leaping'.[49] He refers to *Blackwood's Magazine* which took a lead in writing articles which mingled sport and poetry, and it links 'Exmouth Wrestling' to those articles as well as to the contest between *Blackwood's* and the *London* (which was not always as playful as this). Reynolds demands of his readers knowledge of Shakespeare and Keats, but also of a whole range of far more ephemeral sources, including his own articles about boxing in the *London*.[50] It is hard,

---

[45] Reynolds, 'Exmouth', 608.
[46] On class and magazines, see Gregory Dart, *Metropolitan Art and Literature 1810–1840: Cockney Adventures*. Cambridge University Press, 2012.
[47] 'Letter from Mr Humphrey Nixon', *London Magazine*, 3 (June 1821), 628–32.
[48] Reynolds, 'Exmouth', 613.   [49] Reynolds, 'Exmouth', 617.
[50] See Reynolds, 'On Fighting', *London Magazine*, 1 (May 1820), 519–22, or 'Jewels of the Book', *London Magazine*, 2 (August 1820), 155–61, which contains a reference to *Blackwood's* sporting articles.

therefore, to read or to categorise: is this a context-dependent article interesting in historical terms, or a literary article able to transcend that context? It is both, and in being so asks us to think through that distinction.

The magazines of this period contain much that remains untouched or undervalued by scholarship. The short fiction by the likes of Horace Smith, Caroline Bowles and Allan Cunningham deserves much closer attention, perhaps especially because it is so hard, as Tim Killick has shown, to separate the stories from their place in the magazines.[51] The same is true of many other articles that are just as hard to categorise. 'There is a pleasure in this waywardness of pleasure which only holiday hearts know' as Reynolds says in 'Exmouth Wrestling', and such articles formulate wayward pleasures by offering themselves as temporary holidays from the commercial and historical business of a magazine, business to which their readers must inevitably return.[52] Magazines are especially valuable to the student of Romantic literary culture because they were so keen to offer innovations in cultural forms, from unclassifiable essays like Reynolds's, to unclassifiable sketches like Smith's, to the wholly unclassifiable, like *Blackwood's* series of *Noctes Ambrosianae* and its many imitators. These innovations offer fruitful ground for further investigation both for the literary pleasures they offer and for the pressure they put on the nature of the literary in a period when that term was beginning, through writers such as De Quincey, to assume its modern form. As an article in *Blackwood's* put it: 'In short, nobody can well tell what to make of us, farther than that we are a set of delightful Incomprehensibles that keep the whole world in hot water, or the tepid bath; and then all of a sudden, down comes the shower bath upon our readers, making them hurry off *in puris naturalibus*'.[53] Readers of Romantic magazines, then and now, have often felt disconcerted, bemused and even upset by the astonishing mixture the magazines pour forth. Perhaps the trick is to let yourself be immersed.

[51] Tim Killick, '*Blackwood's* and the Boundaries of the Short Story', in Morrison and Roberts (eds.), *Romanticism and Blackwood's Magazine*, pp. 163–74.
[52] Reynolds, 'Exmouth', 610.
[53] John Wilson, 'An Hour's Tête-à-Tête with the Public', *Blackwood's*, 8 (October 1820), 78–105 (96).

CHAPTER 4

Periodical Formats: The Changing Review

Laurel Brake

This chapter will focus on the genre of the review in the 1860s and 1870s and explore the impact on it of 'sensation' in two forms, its fictional guise in the late 1850s and its 'new journalism' mode in the 1860s. There are three sections: the first interrogates the review as a genre in its own right. Is it justified conceptually to separate it from magazines? Are reviews, variable and hybrid as they are, sufficiently similar to each other to be distinct from other periodical genres? Can generations of reviews be discerned? If so, what characterises them? Do they retain an identity as a review, irrespective of whether it is the same identity across generations?

Second, I want to consider the effect, if any, of these new reviews' greater independence from the vagaries of the book trade, to which early nineteenth-century reviews were closely related. How has news entered the domain of these reviews which, once again[1] are frequent enough to be responsive to the news cycle? How does the new economy of the free-standing article compare with the tied book review economy of the early titles? How has competition with publications other than the limited field of quarterlies – to wit the entire monthly magazine market, and monthly issue of books – affected the distinctive nature of the contents of the new reviews, for example, the possibility of the addition of fiction or the presence of timely music reviews? And what about the shift from a subscriber economy to one-off sales from newsstand or bookseller? Do these or other characteristics mark their participation in the sensational new journalism? Under these pressures – from magazines and monthly frequency – can and do the reviews remain distinctive?

Third, does a search for sensation in the material, formal and paratextual elements of the mid-century reviews produce any results of significance that might distinguish one generation from another? The implication of evolving press formats among the vicissitudes of the print of the day is the larger point, illustrated by the symbiosis of sensation and this new generation of reviews.

---

[1] See Table 4.1. Most reviews in the eighteenth century were monthly.

We need to remember how slippery, ungainly, dynamic, competitive and resistant to categorisation periodicals and newspapers are. Mark Schoenfield, in *British Periodicals and Romantic Identity*, memorably invokes the kaleido-scopic contingent identities of periodicals and their contributors: 'Although committed to a cultural cohesiveness rooted in the habitual circulation of print, periodicals were rife with internal fissures, among journals, authors, publishing houses, and political parties.' Expanding on this, he notes:

> The industry required both cooperation and competition. The former included monopolistic cartels and puffing practices, while the latter ranged from ... gentle condescension ... to duels of words and occasionally bullets ... Individual writers ... were voices labouring together, at times in alliance and at times at war. Sometimes their proximity was deliberate, sometimes institutional, sometimes accidental; they were yoked together by editors or readers or critics, impersonating one another or were accused of doing so, admiring, hating, copying, and parodying.[2]

The Review: A Genre?

If I now offer a model for 'generations' of the review as a genre, it is a larger framework in which generations accommodate dissonance and variety, as Schoenfield leads us to expect. Apparently 'core' qualities found in early nineteenth-century reviews – including quarterly fre-quency, lengthy articles and issues, high price, anonymity, male orienta-tion and vituperative language – emerge as no such thing, but as characteristic of reviews in a fixed span of history. The generations in the Tables 4.1–4.4 are largely that of nineteenth-century reviews, with an indication of the main eighteenth-century titles out of which they emerged. Even allowing for dynamics within each generation, I still perceive in the nineteenth century alone, three fresh-start nodes, and continuity into the twentieth century, when the review becomes identi-fied with the so-called little magazines, some of which were called 'reviews'. So, the first five generations might be the eighteenth century (1749–98), the early nineteenth century (1802–54)[3], mid-century (1855–64), later nineteenth century (1865–99) and early twentieth century (1900–14). The point of this trope of generations of the review is not to map 'progress'

---

[2] Mark Schoenfield, *British Periodicals and Romantic Identity*. Basingstoke: Palgrave Macmillan, 2009, pp. 4–5.

[3] See Joanne Shattock, 'Contexts and Conditions of Criticism 1830–1914', in M. A. R. Habib (ed.), *The Cambridge History of Literary Criticism*. Vol 6. *The Nineteenth Century*. Cambridge University Press, 2013, pp. 21–45.

Table 4.1 *Generations of Reviews: First Generation*

• 1749–1844 *Monthly Review*	Whig, includes *belles lettres* and criticism
• 1756–1817 *Critical Review*	Tory until 1793, pro-reform, alternative to *Monthly Review*
• 1783–96 *English Review*	National affairs supplement, merged with *Analytical Review*
• 1788–99 *Analytical Review*	Quarterly, partial signature
• 1793–1843 *British Critic*	Monthly to 1825, then quarterly, High Church/ Tractarian
• 1798–1821 *Anti-Jacobin Review*	Anti-Catholic, ultra conservative
• All monthly except *Analytical*, which is quarterly	
• Tied to book trade and review format	
• Encyclopaedic coverage	
• Largely anonymous or pseudonymous	

but to note major and significant alterations in the general understanding of a review at any given time. What if anything do these generations add to our understanding of the review, and of its collision with sensation in the 1860s and 1870s? According to Derek Roper, in *Reviewing before the Edinburgh*, the eighteenth-century reviews were inspired by the Encyclopaedia model of the Enlightenment and initially attempted to comprise catalogues of all printed books. He singles out the *Monthly Review* as the model that was imitated, for its early innovative inclusion of belles lettres, learned works and pamphlets.[4] It is notable that most of the eighteenth-century reviews were monthlies, and shorter, cheaper and more timely than their nineteenth-century successors, gaining their authority from their breadth of coverage and eventually criticism and analysis of titles reviewed.

The second generation of reviews in the early nineteenth century – the *Edinburgh*, the *Quarterly* and the *Westminster* – included lengthy reviews of current titles, often between thirty and forty pages apiece. The articles' authority was enhanced by anonymity or pseudonymity that bastioned the 'brand' of the journal title as guarantor of quality. That the reviews selected titles for review, rather than undertaking to include the entire output of the quarter was a manifestation of their arguably superior taste that contributed to their status. This review discourse and format defined the genre of the review in this period, as did their stately, quarterly, (in)frequency, high

---

[4] Derek Roper, *Reviewing before the Edinburgh 1788–1802*. Newark: University of Delaware Press, 1978, p. 20.

Table 4.2 *Generations of Reviews: Second Generation*

• 1802–1900 ff	*Edinburgh Review*	Whig, selective coverage
• 1805–68	*Eclectic Review* monthly, nonconformist	
• 1809–1900 ff	*Quarterly Review*	Tory, rivalry with *Edinburgh Review*
• 1824–1900 ff	*Westminster Review*	Benthamite
• 1827–46	*Foreign Quarterly*	Foreign literature, merged with *Westminster Review*
• 1829	*London Review*	No political party affiliation (2 issues only)
• 1835–36	*London Review*	Broke away from *Westminster Review*, then merged with it
• 1836–1968	*Dublin Review*	Monthly, Roman Catholic
• 1844–71	*North British Review*	Free Church of Scotland
• 1844–53	*English Review*	High Church, replaced *British Critic*
• 1845–86	*British Quarterly Review*	Nonconformist, offshoot of *Eclectic Review*
• 1845–55	*Prospective Review*	Unitarian, emerged from *Christian Teacher* (1835), merged with *National Review* (1855)
• 1852–62	*New Quarterly Review*	Short reviews, encyclopaedic
• 1853–1968	*London Quarterly Review*	Methodist

- Mainly quarterly, lengthy, and highly priced, average 6/
- Articles largely anonymous or pseudonymous
- Survival directly related to target group, religious or party political
- Survival and format often due to earlier titles from which these titles sprang

price (six shillings) and the length and bulk of single issues that made them resemble books. Although an issue often extended to more than 225 pages, it normally included only eight to ten articles. Nor did the reviews ever stoop to the frippery of publishing fiction, although they did review it – sometimes in large batches that indicated its light weight.[5]

The infrequency of these reviews and the technic of distancing all topical material through the filter and trope of the book review meant that they maintained the appearance of keeping an hygienic distance from the

---

[5] Marian Evans's anonymous review of multiple titles in 'Silly Novels by Lady Novelists' in the *Westminster Review* in October 1856 exemplifies the affinity of a large number of titles with disdain on the part of a journal.

vulgarity of 'news' and 'journalism'. Complainants did note what Walter Bagehot, among others, retrospectively claimed in 1855 that book reviews in the early quarterlies often meandered into topical essays, or articles, rather than remaining reviews of current titles. This generation of reviews became a byword of seriousness and weight. They also had a male gender profile, which we are more attuned to detecting than nineteenth-century readers. Seldom if ever carrying fiction, and given their pronounced political orientation, they probably had few women readers, and in these early years few women contributors. This is borne out by author attributions in the *Wellesley Index to Victorian Periodicals*, and the permeation of party politics and detailed political analysis throughout the editorial matter, both of which largely excluded women.[6]

As may be seen in Tables 4.1 and 4.3, there were two reviews in different generations thirty years apart that attempted to go it alone without a political or organisational affiliation or orientation, and they both failed, and quickly – the *London Review*, launched in 1829 at the height of the success of the original quarterlies, and which failed after two issues, and *Bentley's Quarterly Review*, established in 1859 at the end of their reign, which went to four numbers before Bentley pulled it. The disinterested posture of the *London Review* lies behind the concept of the press laid out in its first article, which lists as its publications for review '*The Times, the Morning Chronicle, &c.&c. The Edinburgh Review, The Quarterly Review &c. &c*'. Its running head, which serves as its title, is 'Journals and Reviews', and its premiss is that journals and reviews of the present day were like the ancient Greek agora:

> These square pieces of paper are the Agoras of modern life ... In the centre of this square, where you observe the larger character, a public orator ... takes his daily stand. One makes his speeches in the morning, another reserves his for the evening; a third class, either disposed to take less trouble, or finding it convenient to construct their speeches from fragments of the daily orations, harangue (stet) once in two or three days; while a fourth way-lay the people in their road to visit the temples on our hebdomadal festivals.

The author goes on to distinguish the reviews from the dailies by their select readership, *and* by their potential for enhanced interest through variety of copy. This visionary version of reviews sounds magazine-like.

[6] W. E. Houghton, et al., *The Wellesley Index to Victorian Periodicals* 5 vols. University of Toronto Press, 1966–89. See Vol. 5; Joanne Shattock, *Politics and Reviewers: The* Edinburgh *and the* Quarterly *in the Early Victorian Age*. Leicester University Press, 1989, pp. 1–22; 'Reviews' and 'Reviewing', in Laurel Brake and Marysa Demoor (eds.), *Dictionary of Nineteenth Century Journalism*. London and Brussels: British Library and Academia Press, 2009, pp. 538–39.

Table 4.3 *Generations of Reviews: Third Generation*

• 1855–64	*National Review*	Quarterly, from *Prospective Review*, became *Theological Review*, March 1864
• 1855	*Saturday Review*	Weekly, acerbic, combination of politics and arts
• 1859–60	*Bentley's Quarterly Review*	4 issues. Same editor as the editor of weekly *Saturday Review*, anonymous articles non party political
• 1862–64	*Home and Foreign Review*	Quarterly, derived from *Rambler*; independent Catholic, literary

- Product of Stamp Duty repeal, cheaper newspapers result in new reviews
- Some experiments with frequency (e.g. *Saturday Review*) and price
- Some experiments with departure from exclusive review format
- Renewed and late attempts at quarterly review format
- Overlap with launch of 'shilling' monthlies, and pressure of monthly frequency, cheaper price, contained fiction; cf. demise of *Bentley's Quarterly Review*

However, the *London Review* was succeeded by a number of affiliated reviews that survive:

> The reviews are lounging places as well as the daily journals; but they are not open to the mob, and rank rather as the select porticos, set apart for the better sort of people. But, like the bazaars or coffee-houses of the East, they would not prosper without the occasional help of a storyteller, or a poet. A fiery speaker must also now and then be allowed to strut and fret his hour on the political stage, succeeded, according to approved custom, by an overture from some popular professor of music; and a doctor of physic should be at hand to correct the dyspepsy engendered by metaphysics or controversial matter.[7]

In Table 4.3, I have separated out four titles that call themselves reviews, which flourish after the repeal of the first of the newspaper taxes in 1855 but before the advent of the next generation of monthly reviews. They are

---

[7] Anon., 'Journals and Reviews', *London Review*, 1(1829), 4–5. Compare this with three influential articles on 'Periodical Literature' five years earlier in the new *Westminster Review*, 1-2 (Jan, April and July 1824), 206–49; 505–4; 194–212, which sought to distinguish itself from its predecessors. The preamble of the January piece on the *Edinburgh Review* begins ominously: 'If periodical criticism is good for anything, it cannot be less needed in the case of periodical literature ... It is indeed a subject of wonder, that periodical publications should have existed so long, and have come at last to occupy so great a portion of the time and attention of the largest class of readers, without having become subject to a regular and systematic course of criticism.'

clearly responding to the freedom from taxes, and the viability of discussing politics without attracting duty, so it is not altogether surprising to see a weekly, the *Saturday Review*, referencing the status of the review by its title. It made an immediate niche for itself, at once refreshing the weekly press and rethinking it. Challenging the concept of the review by ditching most of its identity marks, the *Saturday Review* adopted the early reviews' vituperative language, high spirits and assumption of authority. Aligning itself editorially with *The Times* and simultaneously invoking the early nineteenth-century review in its title, the new title remediated two genres – the quarterly review and long-established weeklies such as the *Spectator*, the *Examiner* and the *Athenaeum*.

So, as early as 1855, the review form was being extended and reimagined, in an arena and period when journalism proliferated and cultivated hybridity, an aspect of its characteristic alacrity to change shape as required. In this generation in Table 4.3, the *National Review* loosened its religious ties to claim the secular 'nation' as its defining identity, while *Bentley's Quarterly Review* was regarded as a welcome fresh start for the genre. At this moment at the end of the reign of the old quarterlies, *Bentley's* notices provide fascinating estimates of new and old quarterlies. Several of these contemporary notices hail *Bentley's* as a new departure, including that of *The Times* and the *Saturday Review*.[8] Reading their remarks, which *Bentley's* promulgated in its first and second numbers, one can see plainly that the time was ripe for a renewal of the review genre:

> We are not blind, we hope, to the merits of our established 'Quarterlies'; the glories of the past still hover invisibly over them, and many an article even now contains most useful information . . . [etc] But a deficiency – we make the remark as candid, but not unfriendly, critics – on two serious points may be observed in them – *thought* and *style*.
>
> It can be no matter of surprise, then, if the opinion is very openly and frankly expressed in many quarters that our old-established 'Quarterlies' are not showing themselves altogether equal to the intellectual wants of the present day. Whatever be its faults and errors, this age has undoubtedly been an age of thought . . . Can it fairly be said that this whole growth of mind has an echo or response in the quarter mentioned? Does any one

---

[8] Anon., 'Bentley's Quarterly Review', *Saturday Review* (16 July 1859), 81–82. In reading this review, which *Bentley's* printed repeatedly, it is important to bear in mind that it is not disinterested: the two journals shared a number of staff, including J. Douglas Cook, director of the *Saturday Review* and editor of *Bentley's*, and William Scott, leader writer for the *Saturday Review* and literary editor of *Bentley's*. Thanks to Joanne Shattock for pointing out the overlap of reviewers and the personnel of *Bentley's* and the *Saturday Review*.

expect on opening a number to meet with a single original idea in it from
beginning to end? Nobody does; that is not the purpose for which it is
consulted. We get a useful abrege of some Blue-book ... or we get
a review of some book of the season which shows a knowledge of
literature and quotes this author and that author. But information,
a knack at quotation, and *verbal* criticism cannot disguise the inherent
poverty of thought ... they no longer lead the thought of the day ...
People now really do want something more than this effete compound of
the dry and the trifling.[9]

In May 1863, the *Literary Times*, a short-lived weekly,[10] similarly charges
the *Quarterly Review* with obsolescence – referring to it as 'the dear old-
fashioned "Quarterly Review"', and suggesting that the *Quarterly's* usage of
the term 'sensation' was itself a sensational ploy to 'enliven ... its super-
annuated pages'.[11]

The second and third generations of reviews were also defined by what
they were not: slimmer, sprightly, lighter and cheaper contemporary monthlies such as the *Monthly Magazine* and *New Monthly Magazine*. As miscellanies, the monthly magazines were freer to lure readers with diverse topics of
the day not only because of their timeliness but also because they were not
obliged to select their contents through the limiting filter of reviews of new
books and other forms of already printed material, such as blue books,
pamphlets and part-issues. It was largely after the establishment of
Blackwood's in 1817 that monthly magazines as a genre spawned imitators
(e.g. *Fraser's*) and alternatives (*Tait's Edinburgh Magazine*), to such effect
that by 1859–60, when a new generation of even cheaper (shilling) monthlies
was launched – the *Cornhill* and *Macmillan's* – the combination of the less
circumscribed selection of their contents, comprising a true miscellany, the
low price, and the monthly frequency displaced the quarterly review model
decisively. The monthly magazines, first at a shilling and then at six pence,
swept all before them for the remainder of the century. The new reviews of
the fourth generation appeared monthly. So quarterly frequency was not
synonymous with the review as a genre.

---

[9] Anon. [William Scott?], 'The Quarterlies', *The Times* (20 August 1859), 7. While this piece was
anonymous, the *Wellesley Index* attributes it directly or indirectly to William Scott (Vol. 2, p. 5),
literary editor of *Bentley's*.

[10] The *Literary Times: A Critical Journal of Modern Literature*, a penny weekly, survived for eleven
numbers, from 14 March to 23 May 1863. It was a specialist title before its time, announcing in its
first issue, on page one among the adverts, it was to be 'a purely literary journal' and, it continues,
'The time has now arrived when literature should have a journal of its own'.

[11] Anon., 'Sensation' (9 May 1863), *Literary Times* (9 May 1863), 102, quoted in Laurie Garrison,
Science, Sexuality and Sensation Novels. Basingstoke: Palgrave Macmillan, 2011, p. 29.

Table 4.4 *Generations of Reviews: Fourth Generation*

• 1865	*Fortnightly Review*	Fortnightly then monthly, party political (liberal), fiction, poetry, signature
• 1866	*Contemporary Review*	Monthly, religious, some signature, no fiction
• 1877	*Nineteenth Century*	Monthly, emerged from *Contemporary Review*, symposia, poetry, no fiction, affiliated with Metaphysical Society, no advertising
• 1882–1900	*Scottish Review*	Quarterly, supported Scottish home rule, reviews of foreign literature, anonymous
• 1883–1960	*National Review* II	Monthly, Tory, fiction and poetry from 1890s, signature
• 1889–97	*New Review*	Monthly, priced at 6d, fiction, drama, poetry, signature
• 1890	*Review of Reviews*	Monthly, priced at 6d, digest and reviewed reviews, included Stead's version of fiction fit for the press, evangelical, illustrated
• 1896–98	*Cosmopolis.*	Monthly, fiction, drama, poetry, contributions in French, German, English, signature

- With one exception, monthly
- Shorter issues and articles, though reviews still included
- signature attached to most articles and literature
- All in competition with 1/0 monthlies that included fiction
- All cheaper than earlier quarterlies – price shift from 6/0 to 2/0 or 6d
- Fiction, poetry and occasionally drama in 5 of 8 titles
- Absence of fiction in *Contemporary Review, Scottish Review* and *Nineteenth Century* signals more serious reviews targeted at male interests
- Fewer reviews tied to political party and religious groups
- Reviews from earlier generations continue to appear: *Edinburgh, Quarterly, Westminster, Dublin Reviews*

An examination of individual numbers of *Edinburgh Review* and *Quarterly Review* in 1860–61, just after the launch of the shilling monthly magazines and before the new reviews, shows them to retain their bulk, their anonymity, their exclusive review contents, their infrequency and their long articles, often prefaced by a daunting list of the titles reviewed. These 1860s issues have additionally thick 'Advertisers' inside their covers that tout products that still do not suggest that women readers make up a significant portion of the readership. For example, the issue of July 1861 of the *Quarterly Review* opens with a 'Quarterly Literary Advertiser' of fifty-four pages supplemented by a sixteen-page catalogue of Murray's list of

New Books. Amidst many titles and topics unlikely to appeal to women readers – on classics, technical science, law, railway guides – is a Hurst and Blackett two-page spread, at the end of which are 'New and Popular Novels', and another smaller advert with more titles of their Standard Library of Cheap Editions of Popular Modern Works', which are 'elegantly bound and illustrated'.[12] Nevertheless, the orientation of most adverts seems directed to male readers and consumers. Nor are any of the eight articles – spanning 622 pages – apparently addressed to women readers.[13] Another 'old journalism' characteristic of the *Quarterly Review* in 1861 is its plain, drab buff cover, the front dominated by text providing its title, number, date and place of publication dispersed sparsely over the space of a rectangular box, which stands in for design. The back cover tersely lists the contents by topic, with little attempt to attract readers. The October 1860 issue of the *Edinburgh Review* is similarly structured: a bulky advertiser, nine articles, all anonymous, each prefaced by multiple new titles under review. Like the *Quarterly*, none of the articles are titled, but only numbered; the working titles remain located in the running heads only.

Comparison of the format of these second-generation reviews with that of the fourth generation seems to me to suggest that an element of 'sensation' resides in the latter's new format, layout, signature and display adverts, as well as in their contents. It is apparent that the new titles imitated British *magazines*, which routinely included some 'original papers' or freestanding articles commissioned especially by the journal, some of which were signed, and always provided their articles with titles. But the *Fortnightly Review* also drew on French feuilletons – parts of newspapers from 1800 onwards, which contained non-political copy, such as gossip; features on culture; reviews of books, music, theatre; and sometimes fiction. In its prospectus, the *Fortnightly* prominently cited the up-market fortnightly, the *Revue des deux mondes*, which published fiction as a regular part of its review contents, as well as occasional roundups of music or art. Another stylish aspect of the French Revue was its attempt to link itself with American journalism, the two 'mondes' being France and

---

[12] Advert, *Quarterly Review*, 110 (July 1861), 32.
[13] This is not to say that no women read the old quarterlies, but that few did. The quarterlies have a long history that includes over their life span women editors and writers such as George Eliot, Harriet Martineau, Harriet Taylor and others who intermittently appear in their pages. However, the *Yellow Book*, dating from 1894 and among the last generation of nineteenth-century reviews, is perhaps alone notable among quarterlies for publishing a number of signed pieces by women during its short run. This reflected the notably higher participation of women in literary work by the 1890s than before 1860.

the United States. Designed to maximise its topicality, this alliance reinforced its claim to speed and news that its fortnightly frequency denoted.
Thus, Chapman and Hall's new *Fortnightly Review*, edited by George
Henry Lewes, was fortnightly (an unusual frequency for a magazine, let
alone a review); contained serial fiction in its early numbers; and devoted
one of its eight articles in the first issue to Abraham Lincoln who had been
assassinated in April 1865, making it a newsy piece for the first number on
15 May. Lewes himself was a journalist oriented to the international press,
through his specialist knowledge of European languages and the
Continental press; the publisher's imprint includes, from the first, a list
of agents in Leipzig and Rotterdam, where it might be purchased.
Moreover, the cover clearly envisages its potential for circulation abroad
in its statement 'The Right of Translation is reserved.'

The focus on the United States is recurrent in succeeding numbers of
the *Fortnightly*, both in individual pieces and in the discussion on public
affairs. Its front cover, buff like the *Quarterly*'s, is similarly confined to type,
but it immediately signalled that it was adding names or signature to its
identity, with all the interest that names can carry for a readership possessed by the curiosity that decades of anonymity stimulated. The front
cover of the first of the new generation of reviews listed the nine pieces in its
first number with their authors, many of whom were well-known 'stars',
including Bagehot; Trollope, whose novel instalment is the second item;
Sir John Herschel, the renowned mathematician and astronomer; and the
Positivist Frederic Harrison. The titles of the articles, which were not
reviews of recent works, were original and topical, selected primarily
with the interest of readers in mind. They included the lead piece on the
Cabinet in Bagehot's series on the English Constitution; the scoop,
'Personal Recollections of Lincoln'; a review of Swinburne's dramatic
poem 'Atalanta in Calydon' that had scandalised and astonished its first
readers earlier in the year; two pieces on science, one on 'the Heart and the
Brain' and the other on 'Atoms'; and a final paper on a controversial topic,
'The Iron Masters' Trade Union'. It was an impressive, even sensationalist
line-up, both the contributors and their topics, a kind of double whammy.
These nine individual contributions were followed by two more generic
'Departments', one newsy ('Public Affairs'), and the other literary
('Notices of New Books'). A second novelist besides Trollope contributed
to the new review, a female author with a male pseudonym, the appearance
of her first book having eventually disclosed her gender, and whose second
novel in 1860 had been acclaimed. Here George Eliot wrote on rationalism
which, together with the other pieces on physical science, Swinburne and

trade unions indicated the materialist tenor of the journal, suggesting that
the old quarterly that it might challenge, if not acclaim was the progressive
Westminster Review. George Eliot, along with Francis Palgrave and Lewes
were named contributors to the review section, giving the whole as strong
a literary profile as one of scientific materialism.[14] Lewes added to this with
the first of his series on 'Principles of Success in Literature', a gesture to
light, popular writing, Such a fortnightly title faced competition from both
shilling monthlies such as the literary *Cornhill*, still glittering with fiction in
1865 and non-controversial feature articles, and the more muscular, socio-
political *Macmillan's Magazine*, which also offered a lively intellectual
range of robust masculine topics, unlike the *Cornhill*, plus signature. The
Fortnightly was also competing with the weeklies, with their political fronts
and arts backs, such as the *Saturday Review*, with its capacity to be topical
and acerbic and yet, as a weekly, remain firmly in the news stream. The
last alluring information on the cover of the *Fortnightly* was its price – a
cheap two-shilling review, with relatively short and readable-in-one-sitting
articles – ranging from six to twenty-four pages. The whole number was
a trim, digestible and readable 128 pages. Its physical size and layout were
also gracious, but not tome-like. In format, it resembled the rectangular
shape of the old quarterlies, but its page was slightly taller (at 9½ inches to
their 8½ inches) and wider (the *Fortnightly* was 6 inches wide and the
Edinburgh just short of 5½ inches wide). Moreover, the *Fortnightly's* block
of type on the page was slightly wider (4 inches in the *Fortnightly* and 3¾
inches in the *Edinburgh*), *and* one line shorter in the *Fortnightly* (44 to 45*)*,
and the bottom margin higher by ¼ inch (1¼ inch to 1 inch). The overall
effect was that the new review's pages, which were slightly larger, with
a taller bottom margin, and a line shorter than the old quarterly pages,
appeared lighter, brighter and more leaded.

'Sensation' in this formal sense is also found in the third new review.
Some nine months later in January 1866, the new *Contemporary Review*
followed the *Fortnightly*, to which it was a riposte. Like the *Fortnightly
Review*, the *Contemporary's* cover included its title, date, contents, with
only *some* named authors, and its publisher (Alexander Strahan) with
a similarly international location, but London *and New York* (rather than
Europe), and the price. At 184 pages, the first issue is nearly 60 pages longer
than the *Fortnightly's* 128, and its price is two shillings six pence, six pence
more. Also unlike the *Fortnightly*, the first editor Henry Alford, who was

---

[14] That George Eliot signed the article on Rationalism is doubly notable: it is one of few articles she
signed, and she signed it as 'George Eliot'.

Dean of Canterbury, was not named. So, although the *Contemporary* was chronologically among the new generation, and monthly, its break with the old model is less marked than that of the *Fortnightly*'s.

However, both journals were formally reader oriented. If its predecessor announced its liberal colours in its cover and contents, so did the *Contemporary* editorially stake out its ground and claim to attention as a meaningful, Christian alternative. Materially, its cover was an attention-getting garish orange, and the listed articles were immediately identifiable as theological and topical, the first picking up on one of the most divisive issues of the day, 'Ritualism and Ecclesiastical Law'. The contents list as a whole located all of the individual pieces in a theological environment, even when some titles did not suggest it: the religious import of the titles 'The Philosophy of the Conditioned', 'Modern Greece', 'Education and School' and 'Indian Questions' was signified by the adjacent 'Ancilla Domini. Thoughts on Christian Art', 'Mr Pusey on Daniel the Prophet' and 'Sunday'; the books noticed at the end of the number were a similar mixture of outright religious and apparently secular titles. This short section began with two theological 'Charges' by an archbishop and a bishop, but it also included reviews of Ruskin's *Sesame and Lilies* and of Mozart's letters. Of six titles reviewed, four were religious, and of sixteen pages, ten pages treated theology, and six pages Ruskin and Mozart. Unlike the *Fortnightly* book reviews, these were anonymous, perhaps because religious differences remained toxic in this period; the intensity of religious controversy was also perhaps reflected in its signature policy for its main contents. Only five out of its eight articles listed on the cover were signed. The vulnerability of clerics was indicated by the generic signature by one of them, who signed his piece on 'The Freest Church in Christendom', 'By a Clergyman of that Church' (1:3). However, the *Contemporary*'s deployment of names was no less eye-catching than the *Fortnightly*'s. These included Richard St John Tyrwhitt, a Ruskinian vicar who attacked 'The Greek Spirit in Modern Literature' (1877); Reverend Edward Plumptre; Reverend John James Perowne; and Edward Herbert Bunbury and Benjamin Shaw, all well-known authors and scholars at the time. Its address to its liberal, materialist rivals was made explicit in its reference to John Stuart Mill in the title of one of its secular pieces, on the 'Conditioned', and it did not hesitate to use sensational titles, such as 'The Fleshly School of Poetry' (October 1871), an open attack on D. G. Rossetti's works.

Among the distinctions of this review was its long-term exclusion of fiction, now potential content for the new generation of monthly reviews.

The absence of fiction signalled its seriousness and weight, and its decision not to court female readers through fiction, both of which aligned it with the established quarterlies. Another characteristic similarly indicated its continuities with the old reviews: some of the main articles were still attached to current book titles, a list of which preceded the review. So, it was a mixture of free-standing articles and reviews. Among the former were topical pieces such as Thomas Markby's 'The Education of Women' in the third number, a subject that indicated that it was appealing to women readers through means other than the inclusion of fiction. This article, which began historically, moved to contemporary detail and analysis. It was informed and alive to the need for improved education for women. Although positioned chronologically before the founding of women's halls in Cambridge (from 1869), this controversial topical piece ended with an upbeat account of the launch of secondary school–level examinations for women, which produced a qualification that allowed them to proceed to various forms of higher education.

In 1870 there was a change of editor, and James Knowles, editor from 1870 to 1877, pursued another strategy of topicality, cultivating a format of staged and controlled conflict enhanced by famous named combatants that exploited a robust policy of signature. This exploitation of signature, fame and controversy provided the *Contemporary* with a sensational edge. Regarding theology as a catholic category, Knowles daringly favoured what he termed an 'open platform', a symposium format for the juxtaposition of divergent points of view that he devised for the *Contemporary*. The symposia were rehearsed prior to publication in a debating forum, the secular Metaphysical Society, which Knowles founded to run concurrently with the journal. This structure of organised diversity – a kind of customised agora model – sat uneasily in a journal that was ideologically based, albeit in Christianity, rather than a political party. Expelling Knowles in 1877 as too inclusive in his selection of contents, Strahan and Company, the newly constituted publishers, steered the *Contemporary* to more narrowly religious material.

With Alexander Strahan himself stepping into the editorship until 1882, the *Contemporary* returned immediately to controversial religious topics by tried obstreperous contributors, such as Tyrwhitt on Arnold's and J. A. Symonds's Hellenism.[15] From 1882, it was edited by Percy Bunting,

---

[15] Richard St John Tyrwhitt, 'The Greek Spirit in Modern Literature', *Contemporary Review*, 29 (March 1877), 552–66

a Christian activist, and three years later one of the founders of the National Vigilance Association, an intellectual vigilante group, which stemmed from the revelations of W. T. Stead's 'Maiden Tribute of Modern Babylon' article in the *Pall Mall Gazette*. Publishing both of Stead's rousing claims to 'Government by Journalism' and 'The Future of Journalism' in 1886, Bunting linked the *Contemporary* explicitly with one of the main proponents and practitioners of 'new journalism' and replaced the Metaphysical Society with the National Vigilance Association as the journal's institutional affiliate. Retaining some book reviews, some anonymity, a broad adherence to a 'party' (a religious one), an address to serious largely male readers, the exclusion of fiction and a relatively high price, the *Contemporary* was more weighty and longer than its new generation rivals. Less radically divergent from its predecessors, it was able intellectually to compete with them as well as its more immediate rival the liberal *Fortnightly*.

Taking his symposia format with him, and many of the *Contemporary Review* staff, Knowles left in 1877 to form the *Nineteenth Century*, a more comfortably secular title. Having little reason now to shelter religiously vulnerable writers, Knowles made names work for the newest review. The eminence of the contributors and some of the controversies to which he lent the review were clearly designed to keep his readers interested. Knowles endorsed, for example, the anti-suffrage petition, which appeared in the *Nineteenth Century* in 1889. Nevertheless, it is perhaps one of the few examples of a durable review that relied on ingenuity of format and content to survive, rather than political affiliation and a core of politically sympathetic subscribers. Between them, the three new reviews of the 1860s and 1870s, all of which flourished for the remainder of the century, successfully re-thought the genre and availed themselves of the sensation zeitgeist.

Sensation and the Reviews

What about the relationship – if any – between the contemporary phenomenon of sensation and this new generation of the press? Scholars argue – Patrick Brantlinger, P. D. Edwards, Lyn Pykett, Laurie Garrison among them – that manifestations of sensation fiction, including melodrama, realism, romance, madness, bigamy and social disruption – were part of a more ubiquitous permeation of the 1860s by sensation, which extended to culture more generally: 'It was the age of " 'sensational' advertisements, products, journals, crimes, and scandals" … "poetry, art, auction sales, sport, popular science, diplomacy and preaching" '[16]. Similar claims appeared in the nineteenth-century press. In an anonymous article on 'Sensation Novels' in *Blackwood's* in May 1862, increased frequency itself was cited as allegedly sensational: 'The violent stimulant of serial publication – of weekly publication, with its necessity for frequent and rapid recurrence of piquant situation and startling incident – is the thing of all others most likely to develop the germ and bring it to fuller and darker bearing.'[17] The *Literary Times* was similarly insistent in 1863 that sensation was pervasive, claiming that in the press, *anything* could be sensational: ' "sensational" sermons, "sensational" novels, "sensational" histories, "sensational" magazines, "sensational" pictures ... in fact, sensational amusements of every kind are the only intellectual food upon which the British public now fatten.'[18]

Had sensation in this broader sense, by the mid-1860s, reached the weighty reviews? As for the magazines, the verdict is clear, as Katie Lanning shows.[19]

Initially my inquiry into reviews was prompted by my observation that in the 1860s and 1870s, reviews published radical 'sensation' writing by two young men, A. C. Swinburne and Walter Pater – each an intellectual tearaway at this period.[20] Their poems and articles in the *Fortnightly* and *Westminster Review* were characterised by dissident, disruptive and violent representations of affect, akin to those found in sensation narratives. Arguably this work was part of the sensation phenomenon, as was its location in the reviews. The reading that the perspective of sensation offers here is *male* sensation writing in the predominantly male space of reviews. Moreover, from the 1860s, that a review such as the *Fortnightly* rather than simply reviewing new fiction, published it – the principal literary genre associated with sensation – signalled their

---

[16] Lyn Pykett, *The Sensation Novel*. Plymouth: Northcote House, 1994, pp. 1–2. Pykett is quoting Patrick Brantlinger, 'What Is Sensational about the Sensation Novel?' *Nineteenth-Century Fiction*, 37 (1982), 1–28 (4–5) and P. D Edwards, *Some Mid-Victorian Thrillers*. University of Queensland Press, 1971, p. 4.

[17] [Margaret Oliphant,], 'Sensation Novels', *Blackwood's Magazine*, 91(May 1862), 564–84 (568), in Joanne Shattock (ed.), *Selected Works of Margaret Oliphant*, Vol. 1. London: Pickering and Chatto, 2011), pp. 251–2. Quoted in Garrison, *Science, Sexuality and Sensation Novels*, p. 13.

[18] Anon., 'Sensation', *Literary Times* (9 May 1863), 102 Quoted in Garrison, *Science, Sexuality and Sensation Novels*, p. 27.

[19] Katie Lanning, 'Tessellating Texts: Reading The Moonstone in All the Year Round', *Victorian Periodicals Review*, 45.1 (Spring, 2012), 1–22.

[20] Laurel Brake, 'The "Wicked *Westminster*", the *Fortnightly*, and Walter Pater's *Renaissance*', in John O. Jordan and Robert L. Patten (eds.), *Literature in the Marketplace: Nineteenth-Century Publishing and Reading Practices*. Cambridge University Press, 1995, pp. 289–305; '"A juggler's trick"? Swinburne and Journalism', in Catherine Maxwell and S. Evangelista (eds.), *Charles Swinburne: Unofficial Laureate*. Manchester University Press, 2013, pp. 69–92.

openness to the phenomenon of sensation. It also signalled their attempt to compete with the new shilling monthlies on this count, their glance at the possibility of attracting a new female readership to the new review, and their acknowledgement of the irresistible power of fiction by this date to attract readers.

The material, formal, paratextual and textual elements of this new generation of reviews suggest other manifestations of sensation are to be found even at the 'top' in the high culture market. Aspects of these reviews of the 1860s and 1870s might even be counted among the foothills of the new journalism. The move towards signature and personal journalism, for example, is marked in the new reviews. So is the general attempt to democratise or broaden readership through a number of new features. These include their severance from affiliation with narrow interest groups, such as political parties, and an attempt to attract a more inclusive, if not 'popular', readership base. Their frequency is more popular, bearing a closer relation to news, and topicality was fostered by monthly publication. So was their drop in price, shorter and stand-alone articles, and their brighter design of page and cover. Moreover, new formats such as the symposium stimulated interest across the sectarian, political, philosophical or literary spectrum, and these reviews generally made a virtue of their avowed dearth of affiliation to any one specific group.[21]

The phenomenon of sensation helps us understand the 'outbreak' of the aesthetic style by Pater and Swinburne, and the sensuous crenelated poetry of Swinburne. Moreover, it makes the appearance of Swinburne and Pater in the reviews understandable – the anonymous publication by the *Westminster Review* of Pater's 'Winckelmann' (1867) and 'Poetry by William Morris' (1868), and the generous space given by John Morley to Swinburne and Pater in the *Fortnightly*. Gender and sexuality figure significantly both in sensation writing and its critique by contemporaries; Pater and Swinburne follow suit, producing and publishing male discourse of sensation, in the largely male reviews, not in fiction but in genres more commonly found in the reviews, poetry and criticism. Thus, Winckelmann fingering Greek sculpture, the ecstasy Pater locates in 'The Poetry of William Morris' which ended with what we now know as the 'Conclusion' to his later book *Studies in the History of the Renaissance* (1873), and Swinburne's Sapphism together take their place

---

[21] Such protestations to independence were not always credible. The *Fortnightly* became closely allied with the liberals, while the *Nineteenth Century* aligned itself with conservative positions such as anti-suffrage.

amid the sensation discourse in the reviews. The path from this generation of reviews to the *Yellow Book* is short.

When in 1894 the *Yellow Book* opted for the quarterly frequency of the
early nineteenth-century reviews and the format of a hardcover book, one
of its messages was to insist on its weight and 'distinction' from the now
ubiquitous and popular 'new journalism', through its resistance to the
capitulation of the reviews in the 1860s and after to the monthly rhythms of
the magazines. That the *Yellow Book* combined formal claims to high
culture, the hard-covered book and the slow print frequency of the old
quarterlies with the sensational design and contents of an illustrated
monthly magazine, or an elaborate late Victorian annual gift book,
prompted contemporaries immediately to unmask it as yet another form
of new, sensational and cheap, if decadent, journalism. Arguably, it was
a late hybrid from the seeds of reform that generated the new press of the
1860s and 1870s.

Conclusion

Genre then is a manifestly persistent element of nineteenth-century print,
just as it is in writing and criticism in the West from Dryden and Pope to
Plato and Aristotle. Debates abound in different historical periods and
cultural conditions about the nature of specific genres and their respective
rules – drama, poetry, fiction, literature, history, philosophy, news and
biblical exegesis. Why do distinctions and overlaps among genres of
historical serials still matter? What does a consideration of genre add to
our understanding of what we have begun routinely to discuss in our
digital times as the history of print? How does genre figure in contemporary criticism?

As a point of entry to the study of a cultural field, genre figures equally
with 'author' studies. Thus, the primary categories might be 'fiction'/the
novel and an author – Dickens, Thackeray, Trollope or George Eliot and,
by implication, *not* their journalism, criticism, drama or poetry. Thus,
given the propensity for the primacy of the novel for more than150 years, it
is a natural choice for a scholar such as Graham Law to write a foundational
book on the periodical press and the novel; or for the Dickens scholar John
Drew to attempt to populate a truly neglected field in 2003, with *Dickens
the Journalist.*[22] Some scholars look at poetry and the press, others

---

[22] Graham Law, *Serialising Fiction in the Victorian Press.* Basingstoke: Palgrave, 2000; John Drew,
    Dickens the Journalist. Basingstoke: Palgrave, 2003.

illustration. A recent intervention bravely tries to theorise the unspoken assumptions about genre – its definitions and borders: Dallas Liddle's *The Dynamics of Genre* nails down a hard and fast border between literature and journalism, which are strenuously defined as mutually incompatible in a map delineated by Bakhtin.[23] However untenable this appears for nineteenth-century print culture, it is indicative of the generic anxiety literary studies has suffered historically and still possesses about journalism, a word that is seldom used in literature environments, where reviews become 'criticism' and articles 'essays'.

Within arguably more open fields such as media history or print culture, an orientation to genre can be a useful methodological tool. Information about genre helps readers assess more reliably 'evidence' for arguments based on material from historical serials. For writers and critics, alertness to genre can be part of a defence against the temptation to isolate an article or even sentences from a collective serial source. Otherwise, it might be deployed by the critic with no reference to the content of the issue in which it appears or the 'brand' of the periodical in which it is published – its politics, its genre, market niche and price all unavailable to help produce meaning.

While the isolation of serial text in the concept of 'sources' has been in evidence since scholarly citation was instituted, its incidence has been routinized by the practice of searching the Internet or digitised archives, hits of which can comprise isolated sentences or phrases, whose sources are distanced, encapsulated in verbal and numerical labels of bibliographical annotation rather than an accessible and equally present image. While the article or issue or run may be unobtainable at source, even its bibliographical trace may be dropped by the user altogether.

Genre may be thought of as always already comparative. The matrix of relations of genres of print comprises print culture. It encourages a critical practice that probes within issues and runs of a single title, and across titles and genres. It is not enough to identify 'X' as a novel or fiction by 'Y' but as a novel appearing in a named review, in monthly parts, over a time span of nineteen months, and in different miscellanies that made up successive issues.

---

[23] Dallas Liddle, *The Dynamics of Genre. Journalism and the Practice of Literature in Mid-Victorian Britain*. Charlottesville and London: University of Virginia Press, 2009; M. M. Bakhtin, *The Dialogic Imagination. Four Essays*, Michael Holquist (ed.). Austin: University of Texas Press, 1981.

CHAPTER 5

Gendered Production: Annuals and Gift Books

Barbara Onslow

The early illustrated annuals, characterised by the archetypal *Keepsake* and *Book of Beauty*, lavishly produced and marketed primarily to a female audience, constitute one of most intriguing, if short-lived, periodical phenomena of the nineteenth century; one which, though treated with disdain by many contemporary writers and artists, left a lasting legacy to nineteenth-century publishing and often provided the first openings into print for contributors and editors. The genre emerged from the technical advances in printing, and the introduction of steel mezzotints in 1820, enabling a single plate to produce many more copies than could be obtained from copper plates. These advances were allied to changes in the book trade and a burgeoning middle-class market eager to acquire affordable art in the form of prints and illustrated books, the latter being made more affordable by the practice of initial publishing in parts.[1]

Rudolf Ackermann, inspired by the German Taschenbuch (pocket-book), issued the first British literary annual, the *Forget Me Not* for 1823, in November 1822, astutely timed to catch the Christmas and New Year market.[2] The following year *Friendship's Offering* and the *Literary Souvenir* appeared, and the popularity of this new genre sparked a frenzy of annual publishing. Samuel Carter Hall, editor of the *Amulet, a Christian and Literary Remembrancer*, first published in 1826, claimed that by 1829 'no fewer than seventeen' titles were issued, estimating that 'in their zenith as to cost and beauty' the public 'paid for the elegant works in question . . . £100,000 per annum.'[3] By 1850, when the craze was over, publishers had spent, made, – and in some cases, Hall amongst them, lost – fortunes.

Whilst the original *Forget Me Not* was described as suffering from relatively poor-quality images and letterpress, some prints being 'coarsely

---

[1] See B. Hunnisett, *Steel-Engraved Book Illustration in England*. London: Scolar Press, 1980, pp. 1–3.
[2] Early volumes of the *Forget Me Not* were said to have a circulation of 15–20,000 copies. Anon, 'The Annuals of Former Days', *The Bookseller*, (1858), 496.
[3] S. C. Hall, *Retrospect of a Long Life: From 1815 to 1883*. London: Richard Bentley, 1883, p. 307.

stippled vignettes, emblematical of the Seasons, from wretched designs by Burney' and 'the literature . . . little better than the plates', by 1837 it had been transformed, physically and in the appeal of its content.[4] Influenced by rival annual publishers, the gilt-edged pages were now bound in blind-[5] and gilt-stamped morocco, engravings were of greater clarity, and names familiar to annual readers appeared among the contributors – such as Samuel Prout, Edmund Thomas (known as E.T.) Parris, Edwin Landseer, George Cattermole, Letitia Landon, Mary Howitt, Agnes Strickland and Henry Chorley along with the poet James Montgomery. In his Preface, Frederic Shoberl reflected sadly upon the changes in the fortunes of the genre since the twenties when they 'flourished for a time in the warm sunshine of the public favour.' Yet by 1836, of those modelled on the *Forget Me Not* format 'scarcely one survives . . . What a few years since it was the fashion to commend and to extol, it appears now to be the fashion to sneer at and to decry.'[6]

As early as 1829, the *Gem*, the *Bijou* and the *Literary Souvenir* had emulated Frederic Mansel Reynold's and Charles Heath's innovation of crimson watered silk as a covering for the boards of the 1828 *Keepsake*, by 1832 inspiring even Ackermann to change his paper pasteboards to silk, as Katherine Harris puts it, 'in solidarity' with this feminised garb.[7] The *Keepsake* was available in two sizes, the popular small silk-bound edition selling at thirteen shillings and the larger royal octavo available by special order for £2. 12s. 6d., its delicate, tasteful binding clearly part of its attraction for female readers.[8] In the early thirties, even more ostentatious annuals, in terms of the size of the plates, appeared.

In his memoir, Hall recalled his personal losses when his contract for editing the *Amulet* made him liable for losses incurred following the publishers' bankruptcy. He noted that celebrity contributors to annuals, in contrast, were lavishly rewarded. Walter Scott received 500 pounds for one issue of the *Keepsake*; artists lending a picture for copying were paid between 20 and 150 guineas, and engravers 150 guineas for the production of a single plate. Ruefully he noted that the total cost of the twelve plates for

[4] See *The Bookseller*, 495–96.
[5] Blind-stamping refers to the stamping of lettering or designs on the bindings which are neither gilded nor painted.
[6] F. Shoberl, *Forget Me Not, a Christmas, New Year's, and Birthday Present*. London: Ackermann and Co., 1836 (for 1837), 3–4.
[7] K. D. Harris, 'Feminizing the Textual Body: Women and the Literary Annuals in Nineteenth Century Britain', *Publications of the Bibliographical Society of America*, 99 (2005), 604.
[8] See 'Introduction' to T. Hoagwood, K. Ledbetter, Martin Jacobsen, 'L.E.L.'s "Verses" and *the Keepsake* for 1829'. www.rc.umd.edu/editions/lel/ksintro.htm

one issue of his own annual was 260 guineas, including payment for the drawings from which engravers worked, yet that was the only volume of the *Amulet* which made a profit.[9]

Celebrity authors were wooed with 'preposterous' sums, although not all authors were handsomely rewarded. As Robert Southey complained in a letter to Allan Cunningham: 'The literary department, make what exertions you will, must be as inferior in its effect upon the sale to the pictorial one, as it is in its cost. At the best, Allan, these Annuals are picture-books for grown children. They are good things for the artists and engravers.'[10] Alongside the portraits of royalty, the aristocracy, historical figures and contemporary celebrities such as writers, artists and politicians, there were landscapes and narrative scenes. These latter had often originally illustrated novels or books of poetry. The importance of engravings is exemplified in the *Spectator*'s decision to review the genre in a series entitled 'Illustrations of the Annuals'. This series spent relatively little time on the written 'illustrations', focusing instead on the original image, its interpretation for reproduction, and the skills of the artist and engraver. It offered a glowing critique[11] of the *Keepsake* for 1831, praising the high quality of the engravings and the choice of subjects, and crediting Charles Heath with his 'vigilant superintendence' of the work of other engravers as well as the excellence of his own. A Cornish coastal scene by Richard Parkes Bonington, prints of whose work had become very popular, was admired 'without any misgivings'. Charles Eastlake's 'Haidee', engraved by Heath himself, was so successful on all counts that it enabled the periodical 'justly to praise a work of modern art without any qualification.' This adulation of Heath's managerial skills as publisher was not always evident in the *Spectator*'s annual reviews; the 'Illustrations' article covering his *Picturesque Annual* for 1836 found much to complain of in the images of Russia by Alfred Vickers, though the engravings under Heath's direction were executed with their usual 'finish and brilliance'.

The Heath and Finden families had been successful copper engravers in the eighteenth century, and both were important producers in the nineteenth. Charles Heath made a major contribution to the effective development of steel line engraving for large-scale illustrated book publishing, seizing on the commercial opportunity offered by the new genre. Henry Fisher's firm, alongside that of George Virtue, was a leading publisher of

[9] S. C. Hall, *Retrospect*, pp. 307, 309.

[10] Quoted in A. Renier, *Friendship's Offering. An Essay on the Annuals and Gift Books of the 19th Century*. London: Private Libraries Association, 1964, pp. 12–13

[11] *Spectator*, 6 November 1830.

topographical works. Heath, too, originally specialised in topographical engravings but soon branched into portrait and figure work. Having successfully supplied plates for early annuals, including the *Forget Me Not* and the *Amulet*, he eventually turned publisher with what became a relatively long-lived title, the *Keepsake*. Although unable to persuade Walter Scott, with whom he co-operated professionally over many years, to edit an annual, he did elicit some contributions from him.[12] Towards the end of his career, Heath was forced by the failure of major debtors to sell his large collection of engravings, but his own annuals had enjoyed considerable success. The Preface to his 1833 *Picturesque Annual* could boast that 'the public last year contributed from ten to twelve thousand guineas' in its support. When the *Drawing-Room Scrap-Book* was founded in 1831, Fisher had already successfully produced a lavishly illustrated topographical volume, *Lancashire Illustrated*,[13] originally issued in relatively cheap part issues. By 1835, the firm was advertising five such works covering India and the East, as well as regions of Britain, with some titles also being available in French and German editions.

Among illustrators, from whose designs engravers worked, were those almost exclusively employed on book illustration, men such as Thomas Stothard, William Bartlett and Henry Corbould. The architect Thomas Allom, a founding member of the [Royal] Institute of British Architects, however, was also a prolific contributor to books, including annuals, notably the *Scrap-Book*. Other established artists with work appearing in annuals included William Turner, Samuel Prout, David Roberts and William Stanfield. When an existing painting was reproduced, its owner, who could be the artist himself, might for a fee lend it for an illustrator to draw prior to engraving – a complicated process.

The complexity of producing good-quality steel plates is the subject of a satirical account, 'Engraved in Steel', which appeared in Dickens's *All the Year Round* in 1866. Constructed on the lines of the informative, but accessible 'process articles', it traced the labourious process by which a portrait, stipple-etched on steel, and pleasing to the sitter, was produced from a photograph on a *carte de visite*.[14] At the last moment, as the twenty-second edition of the best-selling book on the 'great Coal

[12] 'The Walter Scott Digital Archive', Centre for Research Collections, Edinburgh University Library. Edinburgh: Paul Barnaby. See 'Image Database' for page on Charles Heath and his illustrations for Scott's works. www.walterscott.lib.ed.ac.uk/imdata.

[13] *Lancashire Illustrated*. London: H. Fisher Son & Jackson, 1831. Original drawings by S. Austin, J. Harwood, and G. and C. Pyne, with letterpress by W. H. Pyne and D. Wylie.

[14] 'Engraved in Steel', *All the Year Round*, 27 October 1866, 372–76.

Question' by the member of Parliament and 'great manufacturer'
Bunglebutt is going to press, someone has the brilliant idea that it should
be further embellished by Bunglebutt's portrait 'beautifully engraved
upon steel, in the highest style of art'.[15] References to the marketing of
the images as high art, and the repetitive nature of the poor journeyman's
labour echo some of the criticisms of stippling in contemporary reviews
of steel plates.

The narrator's derogatory tone in chap. 27 of George Eliot's
Middlemarch, where Ned Plymdale attempts to woo Rosamund Vincy
with 'the very best thing in art and literature', echoes the objections of the
sneerers and decriers that so irritated Shoberl: 'He had brought the last
Keepsake, the gorgeous watered-silk publication which marked modern
progress at that time' with its images of 'the ladies and gentlemen with
shiny copper-plate cheeks and copper-plate smiles' and its 'comic verses
and capital and sentimental stories'.[16]

Shoberl's conclusion to the 1837 Preface emphasised that his aims for the
Forget Me Not had never wavered from his belief that he had 'a higher duty
to perform than merely to minister to the amusement of the frivolous . . .
[his aim was] to mingle with lighter matters as much information and as
many a sound moral lesson as our opportunities and limits enable us to
do.'[17] Other annual editors, such as Cunningham and Alaric Watts, subscribed to similar ideals. Despite this, as the broadly sympathetic article in
the *Bookseller*, seeking to rehabilitate the genre's reputation, explained, in
its heyday a number of poets and writers refused to contribute to annuals.
Moreover, some who did were concerned about its adverse effect upon
their own careers:

> [Thomas] Moore seems to have cherished a rooted prejudice against the
> whole race, because he found that they interfered with the Christmas sale of
> his poetical volumes. This perfectly intelligible hostility was not confined to
> him; Southey complains with more bitterness than dignity, that these
> Annuals have grievously hurt the sale of all such books as used to be bought
> for presents . . . Charles Lamb was absolutely rabid in the expression of his
> aversion to them.

---

[15] See Hunnisett, pp. 53–54 on the introduction of this process. 'Engraved in Steel' is reproduced in an
     appendix. 'The Coal Question', fear that the supply of the fuel would soon run out, with devastating
     effect on manufacturing, and domestic heating, was a hot topic in the contemporary press. See
     B. Onslow, 'Sensationalising Science: Braddon's Marketing of Science in *Belgravia*', *Victorian
     Periodicals Review* 35:2 (2002), 160–77.

[16] G. Eliot, *Middlemarch*, Book III, chap. 27, 'Waiting for Death'. The actual engravings were not
     copper plate, but steel.

[17] Shoberl, p. 4.

James Montgomery is listed as worried about the effect on his cheap book sales, and John Gibson Lockhart described as one of the bitterest revilers of annuals because his own attempt at publishing one had failed.[18]

Mary Howitt's correspondence reveals her ambiguous attitude to publishing in the genre, though it was not solely the adverse effect on family income she feared. Her criticism was more high minded. 'I think, upon the whole, *The Winter Wreath* is as good a book as most of the annuals, for they are a chaffy, frivolous, and unsatisfactory species of publication, and are only valuable as works of art. How little, how very, very little good writing there is in the whole mass of them!' she wrote in 1828 when William Howitt's chapter 'Woods' appeared there in advance of his book *The Book of the Seasons; or the Calendar of Nature* (1831). Pragmatically she added, 'But that they serve to keep a young author alive in the mind of the public, and often draw upon him the favourable notice of reviewers, and bring in a little cash, I would forswear the whole community of them.'[19]

The most famous contemporary attacks on annuals came from Thackeray. He mocked the genre in his novel *Pendennis*[20] in the chapter where the impecunious hero is tempted to contribute a poem on 'The Church Porch' to the *Spring Annual*, a beautiful gilt volume edited by the Lady Violet Lebas. Far more savage was his earlier article 'A Word on the Annuals' in *Fraser's Magazine*.[21] He exempted just two works from his accusation that 'nothing can be more trumpery' than the images as 'works of art', and of the letterpress, than 'such a display of miserable mediocrity, such a collection of feeble verse, such a gathering of small wit'. He mocked the 'large weak plate, done in what we believe is called the stipple style of engraving', the artist, 'a woman badly drawn, with enormous eyes – a tear, perhaps, upon each cheek – and an exceedingly low-cut dress' and parodied the poetry: 'water-lily, chilly, stilly, shivering beside a streamlet, plighted, blighted, love-benighted'. He presumes that Miss Landon and Miss Mitford had not personally chosen the subjects

---

[18] *The Bookseller*, ibid., 494.

[19] Margaret Howitt, ed., *Mary Howitt: An Autobiography*, 2 vols. London: Wm.Isbister ltd, 1889, Vol. 2 pp. 205–7. William Howitt's book was a great success, running to seventeen editions.

[20] W. M. Thackeray, *The History of Pendennis* (1849–50). See chap. 32 'In which the Printer's Devil comes to the Door'.

[21] W. M. Thackeray, 'A Word on the Annuals', *Fraser's Magazine* (December 1837), vol .16, 757–63. See also V. Warne, 'Thackeray among the Annuals: Morality, Cultural Authority and the Literary Annual Genre', *Victorian Periodicals Review* 39 (2006), 158–78. *The Book of Gems* and *Jennings's Landscape Annual* for 1838 were exempted from Thackeray's scorn of the genre, to which, notwithstanding his criticism, most of *Fraser's* 'Regina's Handmaids' contributed.

they wrote on, sternly admonishing Landon for wasting her great talent: 'A *genius* has higher duties.' His main target, however, is the relationship of plate to letterpress. The *Keepsake*'s 'very good engraving from a clever picture by Mr. Herbert [in which a] fierce Persian significantly touches his sword; a melancholy girl in front, looks timidly and imploringly at the spectator' is accompanied by the tale 'A Turkish Visit'. Thackeray's summary ridicules some of its absurdities, and his footnote mocks the choice of image: 'We fancy the figure to be neither Turk nor Persian. There is a Jew model about town, who waits upon artists, and is very like Mr. Herbert's Sooliman.'

Equally he exposed Fisher's *Drawing-Room Scrap-Book* for its publisher's impertinence in reusing drawings that probably originally served 'some profane purpose before they were converted to pious use' and is now used 'to puff off old prints, and enhance publishers' profits'. Bindings were noted with disdain. The *Keepsake* in its new larger royal octavo size was 'in pink calico this year, having discarded its old skin of watered crimson silk', and as for the *Book of Beauty* – 'The binding of this book, by the way, is perfectly hideous – it looks like one of Lord Palmerston's cast-off waistcoats.' Despite his considerable reservations, Thackeray in later years contributed one poem to the 1847 *Scrap-Book* and to the *Keepsake*, prose in 1849 and 1851, and poetry in 1853 and 1854.[22]

Letitia Landon, according to Mary Howitt, once in conversation referred to the annuals as the 'butterflies of literature', an apt metaphor for these visually beautiful but lightweight collections. Their physical format, as much as their content, was designed to appeal to women, although some of the experiments with bindings, in particular the use of silk, proved to share the ephemeral quality of the butterfly rather than the sturdiness of the steel plates crucial to the internal embellishment. Intricate blind stamping, gilding and embossing applied to more humble cloth,[23] from surviving examples, appear to have been more practical.

The addition of decorative front matter – vignettes on title pages as well as a frontispiece, dedication pages to celebrities occasionally even royalty, and presentation plates – on pages designed to be inscribed to the recipient – all implied something valuable to be treasured. So elaborate was one of the two presentation plates in Allan Cunningham's *The Anniversary* for 1829 – intricate, illuminated letters, each representing

---

[22] *Scrap-Book*, 'The Anglers', 38. *Keepsake*, 1849, 'An Interesting Event', 207; 1851, 'Voltigeur', 238; 1853, 'The Pen and the Album', 48; 1854, 'Lucy's Birthday', 18.

[23] Cloth, as used for *Fisher's Drawing-Room Scrap-Book* was glazed, embossed and stamped. Quarter-binding (viz. spine and corners) in leather gave further protection.

a month, spelling 'ANNIVERSARIE', and circling the space for an inscription – that another page advised purchasers that 'the design, of the conundrum class, sometimes causes a momentary misconception or perplexity'. It gave advice on completing the design with recipient's and donor's names and occasion of the anniversary, warning (probably wisely) 'to use the pencil, rather than the pen' when inserting the details.

Reversing Traditional Roles: Writing to Illustrate the Image

Of the varied nineteenth-century publishing genres, few match the annuals as sites over which different media and individual creators battle for authority. Because they were sold on their luxury of presentation, the popular appeal of their engravings and the *cachet* of famous names, as more publishers competed in the market, the balance between illustration and text shifted further so that writers found themselves perforce 'illustrating' the images, and writing to order. Thackeray's assumption, however, that publishers were cheating the public by re-using plates is scarcely fair. *Heath's Book of Beauty* (1833) clearly acknowledged the re-use of those plates that had previously illustrated Byron's poems or Scott's novels. Moreover, the whole point of using steel was that it permitted large-scale print runs, and all plates were expensive to produce. There were precedents. When Henry Fisher brought out part issues of *Lancashire Illustrated*, one of the many illustrated topographical works the Fishers were to publish,[24] according to the Preface of its bound volume version (1831), the accompanying letterpress had been 'purposely adapted [in order] to elucidate, explain, and describe these superb graphic Illustrations'. However, it went on, 'to the expense incurred in sending this publication into the world, the price at which it has been, and still continues to be sold, bears but a very inadequate proportion'. The proprietors, it was clear, were looking to an extended sale (via the complete volume) to recoup their capital.

In her 'Introduction' to the 1831 *Scrap-Book*, Letitia Landon admits that 'it is not an easy thing to write illustrations to prints, selected rather for their pictorial excellence than their poetic composition.' Then, having listed her various strategies for providing as much variety as possible, including prevailing upon a friend to provide two poems, and accompanying three portraits with 'only brief prose notices', she openly presents the

---

[24] See note 13. For an account of Fisher's skill and enterprise in using the part-issue formula to market steel engravings see J. M'Kenzie Hall, 'The Peculiarities of Our Business', *Quadrat* issue 25 Autumn 2013, www.bookhistory.org.uk/publications/quadrat/.

case for republishing 'old' engravings in this new setting as marketing them
to a new audience. 'A book like this is a literary luxury, addressed chiefly to
a young and gentler class of readers', explaining in her final paragraph that
'the voluminous and expensive works from which they [the embellish-
ments] are selected,' were 'fountains sealed' to the many.[25]

The Bookseller, defending the genre, argued the economic case from its
success in providing employment within the publishing and printing
industries, and giving book wholesalers and retailers a welcome boost to
trade at a time of the year 'when business is proverbially dull'. Quoting
Samuel Carter Hall's estimate of the proceeds from annual sales in 1829 at
£90,000, the author claimed to have 'satisfactory grounds for the conviction that he has very much understated it'. On the *Keepsake* of the
preceding year £10,500 was expended; and we may fairly infer that its sale
realised a much larger sum.[26] The way this figure was arrived at was then
demonstrated in a breakdown of production costs for that year (Table 5.1)

Hall's remarks in his memoir on relatively high payments to artists and
engravers are vindicated here, although authors as well as editors appear to
suffer in comparison. The publisher's profits also appear relatively modest
compared with those of the retail booksellers.

Landon's argument that the annuals were introducing expensive art-
work to a new readership is little different from that of modern-day

Table 5.1 *Production Costs for 1829*

Authors and Editors	6,000
Painters for Pictures or Copyrights	3,000
Engravers	12,000
Copper-plate Printers	5,000
Letterpress Printers	5,000
Paper Manufacturers	6,000
Book Binders	9,000
Silk Manufacturers and Leather Sellers	500
Advertisements	2,000
Incidental Expenses	1,500
	50,000
Publisher's Profits	10,000
Retail Booksellers' Profits	30,000
	90,000

[25] The annual also included several views of India and Asia.   [26] *The Bookseller*, 493.

producers and arts administrators when rebutting certain objections to changes: that they are attracting and engaging a new audience. Within the *Scrap-Book*, engraved landscapes – commercial Liverpool, ancient Indian temples, the Lake District, eastern mosques – were being presented to new readers, where the visual context and the interpretation via accompanying text were quite different. The letterpress in Fisher's topographical works, focusing on geographical, historical, geological and cultural aspects of the images, was aimed at a different audience. In the annual, the emphasis was rather upon the emotions and associations aroused in the heart and mind of the beholder. Despite its relatively high number of topographical pictures, the annual was quite unlike the style of, say, Thomas Roscoe's landscape series.[27] Nor was there any overt attempt to market a theme, such as one gets with *Finden's Tableaux*, when the full title of the 1839 volume is *Finden's tableaux of the affections; a series of picturesque illustrations of the womanly virtues.*

In dedicating several images in Fisher's *Lancashire Illustrated* (1831) – cotton mills, factories, hospitals and other public buildings, as well as historic houses – to their owners or public authorities, the publisher indicated the market he sought. Lancashire's enterprising and commercial people would be bound to approve (and pay for) a work that illustrated and gave a history of the 'rise and progress of its trade'.[28] The 'great manufacturer' Bunglebutt, in Dickens's *All the Year Round* satire might require a flattering portrait of himself, but Fisher had judged that his readers would be delighted enough by an engraving of their factory chimney, or the street housing their business.

Despite some rural locations and historical information in accompanying essays, the book emphasises the vigour and enterprise of industrial and commercial cities. The letterpress accompanying *Liverpool from the Mersey No. II* (from Princes Parade) presents the buildings illustrated as testimony to the importance of 'Ships, Colonies and Commerce' for Liverpool's prosperity, derived from its port.[29] Landon's poem 'Liverpool' for the same engraving, celebrates instead, in a romantic and optimistic vein, the 1832 Macgregor Laird Expedition. Funded by Liverpool merchants, this first venture seeking to establish, via the Niger, a trade route to the interior of Africa, accompanied by Richard Lander, the explorer of that course of the river. Landon lauds these modern sailors because

---

[27] See section covering landscape annuals later in chapter.
[28] *Lancashire Illustrated* (1831), Preface, p. iii.   [29] *Lancashire Illustrated*, pp. 32, 34.

In peace they go, with pure intent,
And with this noble aim;
Barbaric hordes to civilize,
By traffic to reclaim,

Not as they went in former days,
To bear the wretched slave.
. . . .

A deep and ardent sympathy,
The heart has with the bold;
The cheek is flushed, the eye is bright,
Whene'er their deeds are told.[30]

Writing for the Annuals: Motives, Networking and Rewards

A prime motive that led contributors to engage with the annuals was undoubtedly money. A publisher's offer to a celebrity artist or poet could be so handsome for such a relatively small outlay that it was irresistible. For many others, it might be essential to pay the bills as it was for Mary Russell Mitford; the Howitts; Lady Blessington, despite her apparently glamorous life; and other nineteenth-century women.[31] Also, as Mary Howitt recognised, it gave a young writer or artist useful exposure.

Networking was crucial to working on the annuals, whether as an editor or a contributor. There were interlocking circles, of family and close friends, of co-religionists and literary acquaintances. The Howitts, brought up as Quakers, had connections through the Society of Friends, but also through various publishing ventures, so they knew the Carter Halls, the Leigh Smiths and the Pre-Raphaelites.[32] The salons, which played an important part in giving women opportunities to begin and develop writing and artistic careers, also provided models, later adapted by Victorian successors until by the end of the century women could belong to professional societies and clubs. One example was George Eliot's famous Sunday 'At Homes', which whilst not as aristocratic as Blessington's, operated successfully to support her own as well as the careers of new writers she encouraged.[33]

---

[30] *Scrap-Book*, 1833, 14.
[31] See B. Onslow, *Women of the Press in Nineteenth Century Britain*. Basingstoke and London: Macmillan, 2000, pp. 17–18 and 90–91.
[32] Onslow, pp. 27–30.
[33] Onslow, pp. 30–31. For a short account of the style of Eliot's 'Sundays', see W. S. Williams, *George Eliot, Poetess*. Farnham: Ashgate, 2014, pp. 23–4.

Blessington's journalism was partly necessitated by the financial demands made upon her by various dependents. Her extensive, influential social circle enabled her to use her patronage to find employment for impoverished female relatives. Thus, her favourite niece Louisa Fairlie, having contributed to the *Keepsake*, eventually became an editor. When visiting Italy in the 1820s, Blessington operated what has been called 'a fairly informal "traveling" salon' to be succeeded later with more formal ones when back in England. Bracketing Blessington with Elizabeth Vassall Fox and Lady Holland, Susanne Schmid argues that in varying degrees, as 'veritable hothouses of political and cultural agitation, often cosmopolitan in their outlook [British salons mirrored] earlier, similar formations like the bluestocking circles and the French aristocratic salons'.[34] Lady Blessington, the former Marguerite Power, was well paid for her work on annuals. William Jerdan claimed her literary earnings reached £2–£3,000 a year. Nevertheless, the expense of entertaining to secure the contributors and literary influence essential to her editorial role eventually meant her overall income was insufficient to cover the £4,000 per annum running costs of Gore House. Its contents were auctioned in a dramatic sale shortly before her death.[35] One function of annual editors was attracting 'celebrity' contributors, deemed valuable in generating commercial success. The 1830 *Forget Me Not* denigrated the practice in rival annuals: the 'merit of such contributions has generally been in an inverse ratio to the fame of the writers. This observation is more particularly applicable to poetical compositions' (p. iv). In response, its editor had reduced the space 'allotted to poetry'. It did not, however, prevent him from trumpeting his acquisition of a piece by one of the most striking literary celebrities – Lord Byron. It was, naturally, a poem of unique value:

> one which can scarcely fail to excite a very lively interest. It is the first attempt of the late Lord Byron's that is known to be extant; and we consider this piece as being the more curious, inasmuch as it displays no dawning of that genius which soon afterwards burst forth with such overpowering splendour.[36]

Additionally, the complexity of the mass production of steel engravings could make for a stressful editorial life, although there were striking

---

[34] S. Schmid, *British Literary Salons of the Late Eighteenth and Nineteenth Centuries.* New York: Palgrave Macmillan, 2013, pp. 1, 3.
[35] R. R. Madden, *The Literary Life and Correspondence of the Countess of Blessington*, 2nd edn. London: T.C. Newby, 1855, pp. 229, 273. Also W. H. Scheuerle, *Oxford Dictionary of National Biography.* Oxford University Press, 2004.
[36] *Forget Me Not*, 1830, Preface.

differences in the roles and powers of those accredited as editors. Letitia
Landon's was largely that of a poet/author providing letterpress for
the engravings. When after her death in 1839 the letterpress for 1840
was incomplete, and Mary Howitt took over Fisher's *Drawing-Room
Scrap-Book*, she found it daunting. The tone of her Preface suggests
only her friendship with Landon induced her to take on the task. She
resorted to adapting German poems or twisting the overt subject matter
of the image to extremes in order to reconcile her artistic integrity
with the demeaning task of writing to order. Faced with a 'Street in
Smyrna', presenting exotic architecture and a mysterious camel train,
Mary chose something well within her capabilities, and the verse opens
as follows:

> A street in Smyrna! let me think –
> Of Smyrna nought I know,
> Except that Homer was a child
> In Smyrna long ago.[37]

Poems on Homer's childhood were probably not what the fair young
readers of the *Scrap-Book* quite expected, and Christian Johnstone's review
for *Tait's Edinburgh Magazine* noticed that the new editor's poetic strain
had hitherto been pitched more to the 'cottage hearth' and predicted her
Scrap-Book would be 'widely different from what it has been'.[38] In contrast,
Mary Russell Mitford seems to have relished her opportunities for patronage, even soliciting a prominent position for Elizabeth Barrett Browning's
contribution to *Finden's Tableaux*.[39]

Despite the adverse views of the literary quality of annuals earlier in the
century, by the late eighties and nineties there was something of a revival of
the genre, albeit in more modest style.[40] Moreover, retrospective judgements were more generous. Austin Dobson reminded readers that the early
annuals 'are now so completely forgotten and out of date, that one scarcely
expects to find that Wordsworth, Coleridge, Macaulay, and Southey were
among the occasional contributors'. Camilla Toulmin, reflecting on the
annuals decades after their heyday, endorsed his view and that of the *Forget
Me Not*, on the value of publishing the work of the famous, modest though

---

[37] *Scrap-Book*, 1840, 35
[38] Christian Johnstone, 'The Annuals for 1840', *Tait's Edinburgh Magazine*(1839), Vol. 6, 812.
[39] Onslow, p. 115
[40] Examples include W. T. Stead's *Review of Reviews* Christmas annuals during the 1890s, *The House Annual* with popular contributors such as Marie Corelli and Max Pemberton, published at the turn of the twentieth century, and Mrs F. Harcourt-Williamson's revived *Book of Beauty*. London: Hutchinson, 1896, which, like the *House Annual*, was bound in a decorative cover.

it may be, and noted that Mr Ruskin had not disdained *Friendship's Offering* for his early work.[41]

For much of the twentieth century, there was little critical interest in the annual genre from literature specialists or art historians, although bibliographical work was carried out[42] and annuals lived on in the form of children's books, a 'must-have' on many a child's letter to Father Christmas. The developing scholarly interest in nineteenth-century periodicals in the 1960s, alongside encouragement from the feminist movement to study women's periodicals and women writers, led to new approaches to the annuals. The poet Thomas Campbell, addressing the students of Glasgow on the 'Epochs of Literature' in 1827, reminded them that they should be 'acquainted with the form and pressure of their times, and should know the moral atmosphere and light of their age and country, in order to judge their size by the shadows of their reputation'.[43] It is somewhat ironic that much of the recent critical attention paid to the annual as a genre is conducted precisely in the spirit urged by Campbell, whose own shadow of reputation has shrunk so dramatically since its peak in his lifetime. Katherine Harris has sought to distinguish the 'literary annual' from other earlier and contemporary formats, which share some of the annual's defining characteristics,[44] and both Linda Peterson and Kathryn Ledbetter[45] have encouraged new readings of the poetry of the period on its own terms.

Illustrated gift books, like many nineteenth-century anthologies, are in format superficially difficult to distinguish from examples of the annual. They were also marketed like annuals as gifts for Christmas, birthdays and other anniversaries. The distinguishing feature is that the gift books and anthologies are not periodicals, though several annual titles only survived for a couple of years. Allan Cunningham's *The Anniversary*, an attractive

---

[41] A. Dobson, 'Illustrated Books', in Andrew Lang (ed.), *The Library*. London: Macmillan and Co., 1881, pp. 122–78. Camilla Toulmin [Mrs Newton Crosland], *Landmarks of a Literary Life 1820–92*. New York: Charles Scribner's Sons, 1893, p. 96.

[42] A major work was F. W. Faxon, *Literary Annuals and Gift Books, 1823–1903*. Pinner, Middlesex: Private Libraries Association, 1973 (first pub. 1912).

[43] A. D. Harvey, *English Poetry in a Changing Society 1780–1825*. London: Allison and Busby, 1980, quoted p. iii.

[44] K. D. Harris, 'Borrowing, Altering, and Perfecting the Literary Annual Form – or What It Is Not: Emblems, Almanacs, Pocket-Books, Albums, Scrapbooks, and Gift Books', *The Poetess Archive*, 1 (2007) http://idhmc.tamu.edu/poetess/index.html.

[45] Linda H. Peterson, *Becoming a Woman of Letters: Myths of Authorship and Facts of the Victorian Market*. Princeton: Princeton University Press, 2009, particularly chap. 1. See also K. Ledbetter, *British Victorian Women's Periodicals: Beauty, Civilization, and Poetry*. Basingstoke: Palgrave Macmillan, 2009, particularly chap. 4, 'Editors and Magazine Poets'.

and promising example of an annual, only managed one issue. The gift
book, however, was part of the lasting legacy of the annuals, characterised,
as Lorraine Janzen Kooistra demonstrates, not by its seasonal content, but
by the material features of ornamental binding and wood-engraved illustrations to be presented and then displayed – in sum, an attractive manifestation of conspicuous consumption.[46]

Landscape, Comic, Religious and Children's Annuals

There were also several annual sub-genres: landscape annuals, comic
annuals, religious annuals and children's annuals. The popularity of topographical prints, and their versatility for subsequent re-use, encouraged the
development of landscape annuals. The first, entitled *The Tourist in
Switzerland and Italy*, appeared in 1830, published by Robert Jennings,
with 'Plates from originals by Samuel Prout, engraved under the direction
of Mr Charles Heath', its list of plates indicating a close relationship with
Thomas Roscoe's letterpress.[47] His 'To The Reader' begins by distancing
itself from the very genre with which its title appears to associate it.
Typically landscape annuals gained more praise from reviewers than the
average 'book of beauty'. In 1832, Heath split from Jennings, launching his
own landscape annual *The Picturesque*, with letterpress by the well-
travelled Leitch Ritchie whose overall strategy was to recount a personal
tour, and its attendant events and adventures, in contrast to Roscoe's more
academic approach.

The annual genre was not an insular one. It became popular in Europe,
and amongst the British working overseas. Not only were there versions of
the *Continental Annual* in other languages, and a number of American
titles but a *Bengal Annual* published in Calcutta flourished for several years.
Publishing in India presented an unusual problem for an annual editor –
there were no professional engravers in India at that time. The first
'embellishments' were therefore the contributions of amateurs whose first
efforts they were. The contents reflected both home and abroad. For the
1834 volume, some engravings had come from London, giving the publishers an additional 'very serious expense', although it was admitted that they
were not exclusively for this annual. For 1836, there was a further problem –
'delayed embellishments from England' held up publication.

---

[46] L. J. Kooistra, *Poetry, Pictures, and Popular Publishing: The Illustrated Gift Book and Victorian Visual
Culture 1855–75*. Athens: Ohio University Press, 2011.

[47] The series covering tours in different European countries ran from 1830 to 1839.

Annuals and gift books of a religious nature might seem particularly appropriate to many at Christmas, and a number were published, with different emphases. Tilt and David Bogue's *The Christian Souvenir*, edited by Reverend Charles B. Tayler included such articles as 'The Autobiography of a Young Polish Jew, now a Christian' and 'On Duelling' which ended with a proposed petition to the Queen for its abolition. The *Sacred Offering, a Poetical Annual* edited by Mary Jevons (nee Roscoe) published in Liverpool and London, ran from 1831 to 1838 with contents chiefly written by herself and family members. Pocketbook size, with gilt edges and bound in watered silk, it boasted an engraved frontispiece, and the advertisement section of the third volume testified to its success, containing glowing reviews of previous issues. The Fishers published (in London, Paris and America) *The Christian Keepsake and Missionary Annual* edited by Reverend William Ellis. Presumably in response to complaints about an earlier issue, the Preface to the 1837 volume boasted a favourable response to improvements including the 'importance of the subjects' treated, the writers who furnished them, and the number of portraits it contained. In other words, readers had wanted their religious annual to be more like the *Keepsakes*. They now had sixteen plates and contributors included James Montgomery (who wrote several pieces) and Sarah Stickney, later Mrs Ellis. The subtitle of Hall's *Amulet* for 1828 includes a 'Christian Remembrancer' because his publishers wanted it to have a religious dimension. As a result, the Howitts contributed poems on 'Thoughts of Heaven' and 'The Missionary', and, alongside contributions by Mary Russell Mitford, L. E. L. and John Clare, readers encountered ten pages of 'Thoughts on British Colonial Slavery'. This article by Reverend Daniel Wilson, later Bishop of Calcutta for twenty-six years, was republished in pamphlet form, but one suspects it had a more powerful effect between the covers of a 'butterfly of literature' than in a solemn pamphlet.[48]

John Murray never went ahead with Heath's suggestion that he publish an annual. He did, however, produce *The Biblical Keepsake* which came out in three consecutive years, containing pictures of the Holy Land and letter-press by Thomas Hartwell Horne, the biblical scholar and bibliographer. This was not designed as an annual, though; it was simply an alternative way of marketing a work, first issued in parts, as three yearly volumes.

Tom Hood's *Comic Annual* and Louisa Sheridan's *Comic Offering* are rebels against the ubiquitous steel engravings of the standard annuals.[49]

---

[48] See www.britannualsinfo.com/esi.html.

[49] Both were illustrated by the authors, wood engraving was much cheaper than steel plates, and the cartoon style of illustration was well suited to it.

The *Comic Annual* was a long-lived one, continuing late into the century, initially by Hood's son. *The Comic Offering* created something of a stir when it first appeared. Sheridan marketed it as designed specifically for women by a woman, who could best recognise the 'boundaries of delicacies and taste'. The first issue was entirely her own work. She wrote the text, produced the illustrations and edited the book, but it turned out to be controversial because some thought it unseemly for a woman to produce a humorous work.

Competing publishers produced children's annuals, including a *Juvenile Forget Me Not*, *Keepsake* and *Scrap-Book*, but in many cases the plates, sometimes even letterpress, were simply material that had appeared in adult volumes; although editors like Anna Maria Hall, wife of Samuel Carter Hall, were probably careful, as they claimed, to ensure the material was suitable for family viewing. One long-running title, *Peter Parley's Annual*, had a curious history. British publishers first imported copies of Samuel Griswood Goodrich's *Peter Parley* magazines from America, which provided interesting information about foreign countries. In the absence of copyright agreements, publishers were soon producing their own 'Parley' magazines and annuals, and the title lasted late into the nineteenth century.[50]

Changing Technologies, Changing Tastes: the End of the 'Annual Era'

What caused the collapse of the genre? Though Hunisett describes the adverse effects of the development of chromolithography on the viability of steel engraving, overall he considers wood engraving the more serious rival in bringing the heyday of the annuals to a close. When, in 1848, Henry Bohn produced a second edition of the *Picturesque Annual for 1840*, Leitch Ritchie's *Windsor and its Environs*, he was able to add as many as thirty-six wood engravings to the original fifteen steel plates.[51] This increase in 'embellishments' he thought would be a considerable attraction to the general public, at a cost with which the steel process could not possibly compete. Nineteenth-century commentators appeared to concur. Austin Dobson attributed the demise of both copper and steel plate engravings, which would have had a major adverse effect upon annual publishing, to

[50] K. Drotner, *English Children and Their Magazines 1751–1945*. New Haven and London: Yale University Press, 1988, p. 64
[51] Hunnisett, pp. 206–8.

modern methods of wood engraving, although there were some examples of the use of metal plates up to 'the present' (the 1880s), a notable case being their use in what he termed 'that mine of modern art-books – the *Art Journal*'. Metal engraving, he considered, was 'badly injured by modern wood-engraving; it has since been crippled for life by photography; and it is more than probable that the present rise of modern etching will give it the *coup de grace*'.[52] In the early thirties, Christian Johnstone had predicted that the economics of new technology and the development of a new reading public would lead to 'a new era' of 'cheap periodicals'. Camilla Toulmin, a notable contributor to the genre over many decades, reinforced these views in her memoir, blaming the 'era of cheap literature', when publishers could not afford to pay distinguished authors liberally, and engravers such as the Findens and Heath, the high prices they demanded in order to compete with 'five-shilling Christmas Books' soon to be replaced by cheaper 'holiday numbers' of magazines.[53]

For the scholar today the annuals still provide an underrated source in which to explore a range of dynamics: text/illustration, editor/publisher, editor/writer, publisher/artist/engraver and text/reader and, finally, the value of the book as decorative object.

[52] Dobson, p. 138.   [53] Mrs Newton Crosland, *Landmarks of a Literary Life*, p. 95.

CHAPTER 6

Graphic Satire, Caricature, Comic Illustration and the Radical Press, 1820–1845

Brian Maidment

Illustration, Satire and the Late Regency Periodical Press

This chapter is centrally concerned with mapping the ways in which, through an innovative and transformative engagement with the periodical press, the political caricature and other forms of humorous graphic social commentary maintained a significant cultural presence in the period between 1820 and 1845. The presence of a graphic tradition of political satire at this time has been significantly understated in the work of historians of British radicalism for a number of reasons which will become clear later in this chapter. In reconstructing an account of the importance of the political image in late Regency and early Victorian magazines and journals, it is important to understand something of ways in which comic and satirical illustration was being assimilated more broadly into a wide variety of periodicals at this time. Perhaps 'assimilation' is too passive a term for this process – 'invasion' is perhaps more accurate given the capacity of lithography and, especially, wood engraving to situate images within a circumambient or contiguous printed text, something that could only be accomplished with a considerable outlay of time and expense with etched or engraved caricatures.

The following discussion has two elements. The first section offers a largely descriptive and chronological account of the passage of the humorous and satirical image from a moment of an apparent decline in the caricature tradition in the 1820s towards a widespread presence in the early Victorian press most obviously represented by *Punch* and its many imitators in the 1840s. But even this ostensibly straightforward project of charting the transition of an important visual category from its roots in single-plate etched and engraved caricature into the cartoons or wood-engraved political 'big cuts' or 'pencillings' that so ostentatiously inhabited the early issues of *Punch* requires an acknowledgement of the changed reprographic modes through which such images were constructed and produced. As well as changes in reprographic processes, major changes in the distribution of satirical images took place in the 1820s and 1830s, with the specialist print shop, its windows freighted with rows of caricatures that attracted crowds of viewers, giving way to stationers, magazine stalls and bookshops where illustrated magazines as well as single prints were more widely available for purchase. The widespread use of wood engraving and lithography for the production of magazine illustrations from 1820 on brought different reprographic traditions into play that interacted with the graphic legacy of etched and engraved caricature. Accordingly, the following discussion draws its structure from a separate consideration of wood-engraved and lithographed political illustrations published in the periodical press.

The second section begins to consider the traditional reading of what happens to caricature as it becomes 'Victorian' – the view that caricature had in the 1820s and 1830s mislaid both its splenetic pleasure in the personal abuse of public figures and its energy and power as a politically engaged oppositional force, and that such qualities were only partially recovered in *Punch* and its contemporaries.[1] Such a sense of loss is usually situated within a more general narrative of comic art in this period that regards the decline in the aesthetic quality and the crudity of the social analysis offered in such images as the inevitable and depressing consequence of attempts to broaden and/or democratise the market for caricature. A detailed study of the satirical and comic images issued right across print culture and published between 1820 and 1845 does nonetheless largely confirm that outspoken or radical graphic topical commentary on political issues of the kind to be found in such late eighteenth-century caricaturists as Gillray or Rowlandson became less common, and that oppositional critiques of politics and politicians were frequently sheltered within more hybridised print cultural formations. Of these new cultural formations, the periodical is perhaps the most significant, especially if considered in rela-tion to other forms of serial publication such as the almanac or the song-book which were particularly active in associating comic modes with political and socio-cultural critique. Thus the sense of the continuity and

---

[1] For accounts of these shifts see M. D. George, *Hogarth to Cruikshank: Social Change in Graphic Satire*, rev. edn. London: Viking, 1987; D. Kunzle, *The History of Comic Strip – the Nineteenth Century*. Berkeley: University of California Press, 1990; B. Maidment, *Comedy, Caricature and the Social Order*. Manchester: Manchester University Press, 2013; F. G. Stephens and M. D. George, *British Museum Catalogue of Political and Personal Satires*, 11 vols. London: British Museum 1870–1954, Vol. 11, pp. xiii–xvii.

re-invention suggested in the first section of this chapter as a way of charting the emergence of the cartoon as a major presence in Victorian periodicals is, in the second section, submitted to a more nuanced account of the generic and cultural history of the satirical image that acknowledges, but is not constrained by, narratives of decline and loss of political energy.

Importing Images: Comic Illustration in Periodicals, 1820–1845

A range of publishing practices were invoked in the 1820s and early 1830s in an attempt to exploit the possibilities offered by emergent modes of serial-ity for the publication of satirical and comic images. Most of these formulations, despite their sometimes making use of the term, fell short of anything that would now be recognised as a 'magazine'. Thomas Tegg's *Caricature Magazine*, for example, was composed of a massive accumula-tion of reprinted caricatures by artists such as Rowlandson, Woodward and the Cruikshanks and was published in several volumes during the first two decades of the nineteenth century. But 'magazine' in this instance was a term drawn as much from military terminology meaning 'depot', 'repo-sitory' or 'storehouse' as from literary taxonomy.

By the 1820s, caricaturists had begun extensively to use small images to fill larger plates with panels of thematically related or, increasingly, gather-ings of miscellaneous jokes and jottings, many of which were directed at the widening market for graphic scraps to fill albums or cover screens. Additionally, many caricaturists began to use short series (usually com-posed of six, eight or twelve plates) of oblong folio sheets, published in paper covers and usually focused round a single theme, as a method of publication rather than adhering to the single comic idea that usually structured late eighteenth-century political caricature. All these formats offer evidence of a changing marketplace, and a recognition that caricature needed to be reinvented to remain commercially successful. Additionally, some magazines drew on precedents from other areas of print culture to suggest how larger etched or engraved images might be integrated into serial forms. Perhaps the most persuasive example of ways in which tradi-tional caricature used the central mechanism for such integration – the folding plate – comes from *The Attic Miscellany*, a periodical that was published between 1789 and 1792.[2] Each issue was prefaced by a folded

---

[2] *The Attic Miscellany; and Characteristic Mirror of Men and Things.* London: Bentley, 1789–1792. The use of 'mirror' in the title is an interesting foretaste of the widespread use of this term in later caricature magazines to suggest the ways in which caricature reflected back human folly to its consumers.

engraved caricature by Samuel Collings to augment the smaller, separate page copper engravings, usually of theatrical subjects, that were laid into the text of the magazine. Yet even here, where Collings's contributions were formulated to retain some semblance of the caricature tradition in terms of content, size and graphic vocabulary, the plates contained reprints of previously published work rather than newly commissioned illustrations that showed an interest in the potential of the periodical format.

The use of reprinted caricatures, however well adapted to their new serial context to give visual energy to magazines, hardly established something that might properly be called a 'caricature magazine'. By the 1820s, however, a magazine centred on caricature which might help to re-configure a declining tradition of graphic satire for a widening base of readers began to seem possible. A number of issues needed to be addressed if such a magazine were to be successful. The first concerned scale – caricatures had traditionally occupied relatively large single sheets and depended on the visual impact of their size, their simplified linearity and, in many cases, their bright colouring as much as their political commentary for their success. The second concerned price – caricatures were expensive, and their makers and sellers had to some extent positioned themselves as the producers of an exclusive commodity that belonged in the high end of the market-place for print. How could such bold, substantial and expensive images be reimagined for the constraints of scale and price imposed by magazine publication? And was there still a commercial case for engraved images that offered complex and sometimes trenchant commentary on passing political and social events drawn using the traditional graphic vocabulary and comic tropes of eighteenth-century caricature?

Duncombe's Miniature Caricature Magazine, which began publication in 1821, provides an interesting gloss on these issues. John Duncombe was a relatively down-market publisher with a broad interest in popular genres such as 'songsters' or anthologies of popular songs, children's books and primers, and serialised songbooks illustrated with wood-engraved vignettes or foldout engraved frontispieces. The title of his *Miniature Caricature Magazine* immediately addressed issues about scale, although in practice the fifty or so issues were still made up of quite large engravings. Duncombe's advertisements similarly focussed on scale – the *Magazine* was 'highly coloured in the best style: the size is nine inches long and eight wide'.[3] The work also offered 'one of the best collections of caricatures ever published' and was issued in single numbers at three pence each or in one shilling

---

[3] Advertisement published in *The Portfolio*, Vol. 6 (1828), p. 384.

parts 'in a neat printed wrapper' composed of four issues both 'at a lower price than ever before offered to the public'.[4] Duncombe, unsurprisingly, given his experience of the potential rewards of a burgeoning mass market for print gathered from elsewhere in his list, also understood that caricatures were beginning to be viewed and consumed in new contexts away from the genteel spaces of wealthy male conviviality. His advertisements begin by stating that the *Miniature Caricature Magazine* was offering 'Small caricature – Elegantly coloured, adapted for Scrap-Books, Comic Illustrations or Screens'.[5] *Duncombe's Miniature Caricature Magazine* lasted for at least forty-nine issues, thus offering evidence for a continuing fondness for engraved single-plate caricatures however adapted and reconfigured to fit the demands of a new commercial context. Nonetheless, the magazine remained an assembly or repository of single plates, published on an occasional or topical basis rather than as a regular serial. While it in many ways prefigured the idea of a 'caricature magazine', it still belonged largely to the commercial world of the single-plate caricature.[6]

The seventeen folio issues of the *Glasgow Looking Glass*, which were published between 1825 and 1826 and became the *Northern Looking Glass* after five issues, form perhaps the first recognisable caricature magazine.[7] The large folio pages that formed the magazine were produced lithographically, a relatively new medium that offered several key characteristics to its producer, William Heath, who was already a relatively well-established caricaturist.[8] Lithography allowed for rapid free-hand drawing on the stone that was used for printing off the image while retaining the linear facility of etching or metal engraving. Lithography also permitted long runs of copies and could accommodate a drawn text on the same plate as the image. The process also worked well for large-scale images. Despite the crayon-like textures and sometimes indecisive linearity of lithography, the technique gave images qualities comparable to those produced by etching or engraving but in a more durable, cheaper and more easily produced form. The Glasgow University website notes of the *Northern Looking Glass* that

---

[4] *Portfolio*, p. 384.   [5] *Portfolio*, p. 384.

[6] Wald's definition of a periodical – 'a nonlinear assemblage of text, the unity of which derives from a common program cumulatively implemented through repetition' – makes no mention of graphic elements, furthering the frequently expressed sense of illustration as a secondary characteristic. James Wald 'Periodicals and Periodicity', in S. Eliot and J. Rose (Eds.), *A Companion to the History of the Book*. Oxford: Wiley-Blackwell, 2007, pp. 421–23.

[7] A well-illustrated and extensive account of *The Glasgow/Northern Looking Glass* can be found at special.lib.gla.ac.uk/exhibns/month/june2005.html (accessed 17 April 17 2015).

[8] For an account of Heath as a magazine artist, see Richard Pound's unpublished 2002 University of London PhD thesis 'Serial Journalism and the Transformation of English Graphic Satire 1830–36'.

'each issue is laid out to imitate the make-up and contents of a contemporary newspaper. The usual elements – such as advertisements and regular features, including digests of domestic and foreign news – are pictorially and punningly illustrated.' Yet the effect is more one of a pastiche or even travesty of a newspaper rather than an imitation. The *Glasgow Looking Glass* was clearly a hybrid venture, more newspaper than magazine, more local than national, more socio-cultural than political, and composed as much of comic illustrations as something that is recognisably a caricature. Of particular interest is the way that Heath used the characteristics of lithography to allow himself to combine freehand script, rather than typeset text, with illustration, thus permitting the construction of a complex page in which images of differing size and scale could be assimilated into the overall design. Even though the venture was short lived and limited by its localness, the *Northern Looking Glass*, by making clever use of a new reprographic medium, provided a formula through which the traditional forms, size and graphic vocabulary of single-plate engraved political caricature might be assimilated into a periodical mode.

Thomas McLean, a well-established publisher of prints and caricatures, first found a way of translating the experimentation of the *Northern Looking Glass*, which had been expensive and localised, into something approaching a sustainable commercial venture. He again made use of William Heath's experience with lithography in establishing the *Looking Glass* in 1830. It ran under a number of titles as a monthly until 1836, Heath giving way to Robert Seymour, and Seymour to Henry Heath as the magazine's artist.[9] The *Looking Glass* concentrated almost entirely on graphic content, much of it drawn using the graphic iconography and the gestural vocabulary of political caricature. Both of the large double-sided pages that formed each issue were built entirely out of visual material with only the speech bubbles and captions of traditional caricature by way of textual accompaniment. The originality of the *Looking Glass* lay in bringing together political and social commentary to form a single issue or even a single page of the magazine, thus clearly acknowledging the increasing focus of caricature, widely visible across a range of contemporary print genres, on class tension, urban interaction and social pretension rather than on individual politicians and their public presence.

The nature of the caricaturist's role in magazines such as the *Looking Glass* needs clarification but still remains somewhat muddy. The *Looking*

---

[9] R. Pound, *Serial Journalism*, pp. 126–40.

Glass did not really have an editor. The publisher, as Pound's account makes clear, performed many of the editorial roles and wielded considerable power through his control of the title and, presumably, through suggesting subjects for his artists and making decisions about what each issue of the magazine should contain. But the comic inventiveness of the artist must also have been a central force in defining the nature of the magazine, and presumably McLean gave his draughtsmen scope to develop their own ideas. Such a division of responsibilities leaves unresolved the issue of who, if anyone, shaped the magazine's political stance and its response to current events. Such ambiguities are deeply embedded in the history of satirical magazine illustration – is it ever possible to say that an illustrator was able to hold and express a consistent individual sociopolitical point of view without bowing to the demands of publisher and editor even in magazines such as the *Looking Glass* where the draughtsman was the sole author of the journal's content? This is a question that complicates the entire issue of whether 'radical illustration', as opposed to 'illustrations for radical magazines', has any value as a distinct category. Seymour, the longest-lasting draughtsman who worked on the *Looking Glass* and who drew many images for it that, for example, satirised the reactionary and self-interested forces that both opposed and supported parliamentary reform, at the same time that he was producing work for the distinctly more progressive *Figaro in London*. If the editorial commentary contained within *Figaro in London* is to be believed, Gilbert À Beckett, its editor, involved Seymour closely in developing editorial policy.[10] Was Seymour then a moderate reformer or an outspoken radical? Is it possible at all to deduce his political opinions from his published work or was he always subject to the wishes of those who paid for his work?

Such questions are of particular importance in relation to the most important and protean figure in the development of satirical periodical illustration in the 1830s, the still obscure and little appreciated Charles Jameson Grant.[11] Grant worked extensively and with extraordinary productivity in both lithography and wood engraving, seeming to be led more by commercial potential than any sense of aesthetic preference. Restlessly

[10] See, for example, the editorial for issue 213 of *Figaro in London* (2 January 1836) p. 1 – 'we had a long consultation with Seymour, who knows, better than anyone else in the world, how these fellows deserve to be treated. The result of our consultation was to this effect, that Seymour should prepare for them something in the shape of a Christmas pudding.'

[11] For Grant see R. Pound's *ODNB* entry and B. Maidment, 'Student Grant – Caricature and Politics in the 1830s', *Journal of Victorian Culture* 3:2 (Autumn 1998), 339–48. There is a considerable amount of informative material about Grant posted on THEPRINTSHOPWINDOW website.

entrepreneurial, Grant produced a number of lithographed periodicals built entirely from graphic content in which he combined the role of editor and sole contributor and used the publisher just for the production and distribution of his magazine (*The Caricaturist* (1831) (Figure 6.1), *Everybody's Album and Caricature Magazine* (1834–5)). In the *Political Drama* (1833–5) he inaugurated and sustained a series of gigantic, crudely drawn and outspoken wood-engraved plates. But he also worked as an illustrator, mainly through wood engraving, for a range of magazines edited and published by others (*John Bull's Picture Gallery* 1831–2; the *Penny Satirist* 1837–46 (Figure 6.2); Cleave's *London Satirist and Gazette of Variety* 1837–44). He also inaugurated a series of satirical single-plate lithographs lampooning the introduction of 'information' magazines aimed at transforming the lives of the lower classes through literacy and the spread of knowledge.[12] In these as yet still largely unexplored illustrations and prints, Grant does seem to suggest a coherently radical social perspective based on a vehement critique of the forces of 'old corruption' – the law, the professions, the church as well as Parliament. Grant's work is so diverse in its character, so post-modern in its disassembling and reformulating the very forms and genres that he adopts, so experimental with issues of size and scale, and so ambiguous in its depiction of the urban poor as a carnival of grotesques that it remains elusively incoherent even as it seems to offer the most coherent and deeply felt progressive and oppositional graphic commentary on England in the 1830s. A detailed assessment of his work is much needed.

Grant's management of the lithographed page as a key element in a caricature magazine formed an original and important contribution to the development of the illustrated periodical. Large-page, multi-panelled, lithographed and seemingly miscellaneous caricature magazines of the early 1830s such as *Everybody's Album* formed a way of preserving as much of a tradition of political caricature as possible while acknowledging the changed circumstances of the market for comic visual culture. The evolution of wood engraving in the early 1830s into what would quickly become the dominant mechanism for illustrating humorous periodicals derived from quite different sources, and it depended largely on the importation and imitation of comic and satirical illustrations published in a wide range of publications which had, in the late 1820s and 1830s, reinvented the wood-engraved vignette as a sophisticated comic medium.

---

[12] B. Maidment, 'Subversive Supplements – Satirical Magazine Title Pages in the 1830s', *Victorian Periodicals Review*, 43.2 (Summer 2010), 133–45.

Figure 6.1 Charles Jameson Grant, lithographed page of the *Caricaturist — A Monthly Show Up* (London: Steill, 1 August 1832).
Author's personal collection.

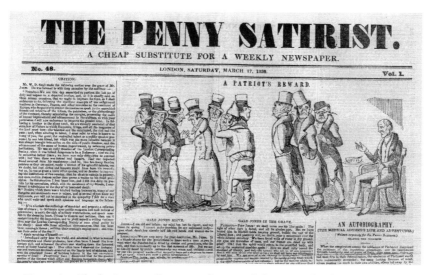

Figure 6.2 Charles Jameson Grant, wood-engraved illustration for the *Penny Satirist*,
Vol. 1, No. 48 (London: B. D. Cousins, 17 March 1838).
Author's personal collection.

Drawing on the respectability that Thomas Bewick and his followers had
given to small-scale wood engraving as both a precisely naturalistic and
expressive medium, the 1820s had seen the widespread adoption of the
medium for periodical illustration, thus underpinning the emergence of
a mass of cheap informative and entertaining miscellanies.[13] Comic artists,
most obviously George Cruikshank, began to make wide use of vignette
wood engravings to enrich pamphlet re-publication of classic comic texts
(often published under the generic heading of 'Jeux d'esprit'), serialised
songbooks, extended runs of play texts and children's literature, thus
offering an increasing gentility to an artistic medium that had been long
associated with the vulgar and the vernacular.[14] The assimilation of these
new sources and influences, none immediately or specifically derived from
political caricature, into a wide variety of wood-engraved illustrated comic

[13] For accounts of the development of cheap miscellanies, see: J. Klancher, *The Making of the English
Reading Audience 1790–1832*. Madison: University of Wisconsin Press, 1987; and A. Rauch, *Useful
Knowledge – The Victorians, Morality and the March of Intellect*. Durham, NC, and London: Duke
University Press, 2001. For illustration, see B. Maidment, 'Dinners or Desserts? – Miscellaneity,
Knowledge and Illustration in Magazines of the 1820s and 1830s', *Victorian Periodicals Review*, 43,4
(Winter 2010), 353–87.
[14] Maidment, *Comedy, Caricature*, pp. 47–110.

Figure 6.3   Charles Jameson Grant, wood-engraved print for the *Political Drama*,
No. 2 (London: Drake, n.d. [?1833]).
Author's personal collection.

periodical literature in the early 1830s suggests something of the ability of
comic draughtsmen such as Grant to re-formulate and re-energise political
imagery. The *Penny Satirist*, for example, inscribed a relatively small image
using the graphic codes of traditional caricature adapted for the cruder if
vigorous linearity of wood engraving into a large multi-columned page that
derived from the newspaper on the one hand and the vernacular broadside
on the other. In a different mode, Grant's extensive series of the *Political
Drama*, published by G. Drake in 1834 and 1835, played off the brash
linearity of the woodcut's vernacular energy, traditionally associated with
broadsides, against the more genteel scale and mode of the wood engraving, which used the end grain of boxwood blocks to produce more delicate
images. In doing so, he invented a form appropriate to his withering
critique of the old corruption and parliamentary privilege (Figure 6.3).

    The history of *Bell's Life in London*, primarily a journal for sporting and
theatrical interests, offers an exemplary account of the ways in which the
small-scale comic wood engraving was successfully recruited into a periodical
from other publications and then re-formulated and re-marketed to meet the

magazine's editorial and commercial strategy.[15] *Bell's Life in London* introduced its 'Gallery of Comicalities' on 9 September 1828 (issue 289) by inserting a small wood-engraved illustration drawn from one of George Cruikshank's engravings for *Illustrations of Time* into the top right-hand corner of its vast broadsheet five-column front page.[16] It continued to publish this feature reasonably consistently in each weekly issue until 7 May 1837, initially drawing its content from Cruikshank's published work,[17] but fairly rapidly changing to commissioning illustrations from relatively young and little-known artists such as Robert Seymour, Kenny Meadows and John Leech, often organised into series that paid homage to Hogarth's well-known graphic progresses or which showed an emergent interest in urban characters or 'types'. Short comic verses were often added to the images.

The commercial potential offered by the success of the 'Gallery of Comicalities' was quickly understood, and the magazine began to publish 'Recapitulations' or gatherings of the images used in the 'Gallery' as separate issues that assembled the illustrations into a striking broadside format that was as suitable for public display as for private scrutiny. By issue 481, the magazine boasted that in putting together the fourth 'Recapitulation', it had spent 265 guineas on the fifty-three illustrations that had been gathered together, thus ascribing a cost of 5 guineas to each illustration.[18] It is not clear if this amount included production costs, or even if it was a truthful claim, but it does suggest the magazine's wish to stress its commitment to its comic illustrations. Announced sales figures found elsewhere in the magazine, if true, suggest that the republication of magazine illustrations in separate form was an entirely sound commercial proposition. 'As furniture for the Scrap Book, and Portfolio, table-talk for the Club-House, and every other public and private house in Great Britain, as well as a cure for the Blue Devils

---

[15] Mason Jackson, *The Pictorial Press: Its Origin and Progress*. London, 1885, pp. 244–7; D. Kunzle, 'Between Broadsheet Caricature and "Punch": Cheap Newspaper Cuts for the Lower Classes in the 1830s', *Art Journal* (Winter 1983), 339–46.

[16] *Illustrations of Time* had appeared in May 1827 as six oblong folio sheets published by James Robins in paper wrappers. Each sheet consisted of a number of small vignettes, and it is one of these that was re-drawn on wood for the 'Gallery of Comicalities'. See A. M. Cohn, *George Cruikshank – A Catalogue Raisonne*. London: Bookman's Journal, 1924, p. 57.

[17] The use of Cruikshank's illustrations by *Bell's Life* is described in detail in Robert Patten's *George Cruikshank's Life, Times and Art*. London: The Lutterworth Press, 1992, vol. 1, pp. 300–1. Originally offered a few illustrations by Cruikshank as a favour to its editor Vincent Dowling, the magazine continued to publish other Cruikshank illustrations, thereby evoking the artist's fury. Eventually, *Bell's* turned to commissioning less-established artists. Patten notes that the introduction of the 'Gallery of Comicalities' increased the circulation of the magazine by 4,000 copies.

[18] *Bell's Life in London* 481 (12 June 1831).

and low spirits in the sick chamber, there has been nothing equal from the debarkation of Noah and his comical family down to the present period', *Bell's Life* insisted of its 'Recapitulations',[19] thus giving an interesting view on the reading habits of its purchasers. The business practices of *Bell's Life in London* in relation to the commercial potential of its illustrations provides an important guide to the ways in which comic images were both drawn into and spread beyond the serial rhythm of periodical publication.

The practice of drawing comic images across from previously published sources was relatively well understood in the late 1820s and 1830s. There was a widespread recognition that given the costs involved in their production, periodical illustrations might be cheaply and successfully imported from already published sources. Not only did such a process reduce costs, but it also gave magazine illustrations a significant status as images that had already formed part of more ambitious volume publications generally aimed at a more sophisticated readership. And it brought a lighter humorous tone into play to offset the typeset content. James Robins was one significant publisher who drew on other areas of his list, and especially books illustrated by George Cruikshank, to introduce comic illustrations, including coloured plates, into modestly priced magazines such as the *Pocket Magazine*.[20] Another long-running miscellany that was published in a number of series, the *Casket*, introduced a feature in 1832 called 'The Songster's Cabinet' that printed popular songs alongside small-scale comic engravings by Robert Seymour which were being drawn across from another serial publication, the *Cabinet Songster or Melodist's Popular Companion*.

If comic images were being increasingly drawn across from other publications to give a new diversionary lightness to serialised miscellanies, there was a simultaneous recognition that illustrations could be as easily exported as imported to form new ways of commodifying visual culture. Thus, the Seymour images and their associated texts derived from the *Cabinet Songster* but also serving their term as a feature in the *Casket* were subsequently republished in a tiny revised format as another serial, the *Vocal Library*, published in four series by F. J. Mason, and offering 'a thousand

---

[19] *Bell's Life in London* 481 (12 June 1831).
[20] Volume 1 of Robins's series of the *Pocket Magazine* (January–December 1827) has images by George Cruikshank drawn from works such as *More Mornings at Bow Street* and *German Popular Stories* and from Crowquill's *Eccentric Tales*. It also featured a long review of Hood's *Whims and Oddities* suggesting the extent to which Robins was investing in wood-engraved graphic comedy as a central strand in his business.

songs and recitations, the flowers of the lyric literature'.[21] The publisher of *Figaro in London*, William Strange, working with his editor, Gilbert À Beckett, was one publisher who understood both the commercial value and political potential of Seymour's wood engravings for the magazine. Among the many re-packaged assemblies of Seymour's illustrations published by Strange were *Figaro's Comic Almanack for 1836* and *1837* and four issues of *Seymour's Comic Scrap Sheets* issued in 1837 after Seymour's death. In these instances, the publisher shrewdly allied topical illustrations to widely popular print genres to sustain their appeal beyond their immediate political contexts.

These emerging modes for the commercial re-publication of comic graphic images suggest a widely diffused understanding that they constituted an autonomous commodity that could be exploited outside the confines of the original host magazine. Certainly, by the time that *Punch* was founded in 1841, the commercial value of its large-scale illustrations was quickly exploited by the separate publication of a series of 'Punch's Pencillings', a 'portfolio' costing one shilling that was composed of eight of the 'larger caricatures' which had been previously published in the magazine. It is interesting that *Punch* was still describing its full-page illustrations at this time as 'caricatures' despite the continuing simultaneous use of the term 'pencillings'. *Punch* was clearly trying to find a term that would encapsulate the modernity of its illustrations. In describing itself in early advertisements printed on the covers of its monthly issues as 'a work of wit and whim, embellished with cuts and caricatures', the magazine suggested its forward-looking policy of harnessing an inheritance of engraved single-plate political caricature to the more demotic attractions of the 'cut' (usually in fact by this time a wood engraving rather than a woodcut) to form the graphic content of its pages. The idea of the 'cartoon' is nowhere present at this moment, and it is interesting that *Punch* went on to call its 'larger caricatures' 'big cuts' rather than cartoons. In this way, *Punch* is suggesting that the democratic availability of the wood engraving, as well as its ability to combine 'wit' with 'whim', has within its pages transformed caricature from an elite form of cultural production into a popular one that primarily evokes the vernacular past of the 'cut', however highly mediated through the 'pencillings' of its artists, against the sophistication of the 'caricature'. Additionally, astutely learning a lesson from *Bell's Life in London* and *Figaro in London* about the market

[21] *The Vocal Library; containing nearly a thousand songs and recitations; the flowers of the lyric literature of England Scotland and Ireland.* London: F. J. Mason, n.d., 4 series.

value of the comic and satirical wood engraving even when detached from
its host publication, 'Punch's Pencillings' proved merely the first in a
continuing sequence of re-publications of images drawn from its pages
and marketed using the brand identity and imprimatur of 'The Punch
Office'.

Despite all these mechanisms for the wider diffusion of comic images,
which included politically motivated satirical and caricature periodical illustrations, it is probably fair to say that by 1840 the concept of a magazine
principally devoted to, or structured by, the publication of caricature had run
its course. The launch of *Punch* in 1841 led to the introduction of the full-page
wood-engraved cartoon as the mode of graphic political commentary. These
'big cuts' seem in retrospect an inevitable development of the caricature idiom
into new forms. Nonetheless, the presence of periodicals that gave a central
role to graphic political satire throughout the 1830s and on into the 1840s is
a considerable one, and there remains a pressing need for detailed study of the
illustrations that gave such visual energy to, among others, *Figaro in London*,
the *Penny Satirist* and the *Political Drama*.

Hybridity, Politics and the Satirical Image

The first part of this chapter has been primarily concerned with describing
the trajectory of the comic and satirical image from its origins in eighteenth-century caricature towards its eventual role as a major element in
periodical illustration in the decade before the founding of *Punch* in 1841,
thus forming an account of how the caricature tradition was assimilated
into and largely re-invented as a form of humorous and satirical illustration
for a broad range of differing periodicals in the 1830s and 1840s.
The processes through which such assimilation was managed established
a range of possible spaces for satirical images to occupy. Some periodicals,
such as *Figaro in London*, used comic and satirical images with a sense of
a necessary spatial and intellectual dialogue between text and image, so that
the visual content of the magazine fulfils a traditional definition of 'illustration'. Other periodicals, such as the *Penny Satirist* or *Bell's Life in
London*, maintained an autonomous or highly defended space for visual
socio-political commentary within a large and complex typeset page.
In a number of instances, most obviously Grant's *Everybody's Album*, the
images defined the entire structure of the periodical, with words and other
textual elements forming a framework within which the graphic content
could advertise and spread itself. All the periodicals from the two decades
between 1820 and 1840 that gave status to the satirical or comic image as

Figure 6.4 William Heath(?), wood-engraved masthead for the *New Figaro*, No. 3 (London: Berger, Steill and Purkiss, 31 March 1832). Author's personal collection.

a key element of their content showed an awareness of the emblematic and graphic potential that could be expressed most obviously by paratextual elements such as mastheads (Figure 6.4), but also through a pastiche of the layouts used by established forms such as the almanac. The sly visual irreverence of pastiche was of course central to the early success of such publications as the *Comic Almanack* (1835–53) and *Punch*, and it suggests a more subtle and subversive form of social commentary than the startling directness of caricature.

Scholarly understanding of the visual qualities and political effects of the graphic elements of late Regency and early Victorian periodicals has been to a considerable extent limited by the quest to construct a distinctively 'radical' and oppositional political tradition that expressed itself within print culture largely through the printed word.[22] These studies have given relatively little space to the visual content of the radical press except as a means of confirming attitudes largely derived from textual study. For

[22] P. Hollis, *The Pauper Press*. Oxford: Oxford University Press, 1970; J. Wiener, *The War of the Unstamped*. Ithaca and London: Cornell University Press, 1969.

many historians, the re-making of the caricature tradition at this time
represented a moment of profound loss, with the outspoken topicality,
linear energy and political irreverence of the caricature giving way to what
Kunzle has characterised as 'graphic bric-a brac'.[23] Broader studies of the
politics of literacy that acknowledge the centrality of the image to the
development of periodicals have largely relegated caricature to the periphery of the Regency visual experience.[24]

A number of cultural historians have been eager to publicise the
demise of caricature as a political force by the 1830s. Vic Gatrell, in the
first of his two lively studies that celebrate the rumbustious male-centred
culture that evolved around the making and consuming of caricature in
early nineteenth-century London,[25] lists the 'many reasons why satire
got tamer in the 1820s', among them 'the rise of new sensibilities and of
a new pietism, and by the increasing cultural presence and idealization
of women' and 'the final comeuppance of London's extreme radicalism'
on the deaths of the Cato Street conspirators in 1820.[26] He also points to
the increased hopes of parliamentary reform in the 1820s which contributed to a loss of radical energy in caricature. He concludes that
'we're faced with such abrupt capitulations to the new order that some
scepticism about the depth of such people's earlier disaffection may be
called for.'[27]

Such a loss of direct political energy and engagement with the topical
within graphic satire has been differently theorised by John Marriott in the
Introduction to his extensive anthology *Unknown London*,[28] a project
which offers visual culture a full and eloquent place within the textual
corpus devoted to urban exploration and analysis:

> No graphic satirist, author or publisher working with this literary subculture
> could pursue the radical cause without serious risk to their livelihood ...
> The risk was not merely from state repression; more important was the
> uncomfortable fact that the 'common tradition' in the post-war metropolis
> was replete with seeming ambiguity. Radicalism cohabited with the bawdy

---

[23] D. Kunzle, *History of the Comic Strip*, p. 20.
[24] P. Anderson, *The Printed Image and the Transformation of Popular Culture 1790–1860*. Oxford: Clarendon Press, 1991; C. Fox, *Graphic Journalism in England during the 1830s and 1840s*. New York and London: Garland Publishing, 1988; L. James, *Print and the People*. London: Allen Lane, 1976.
[25] V. Gatrell, *City of Laughter: Sex and Satire in Eighteenth-Century London*. London: Atlantic Books, 2006; V. Gatrell, *The First Bohemians: Life and Art in London's Golden Age*. London: Allen Lane, 2013.
[26] V. Gatrell, *City of Laughter*, p. 575.   [27] V. Gatrell, *City of Laughter*, p. 576.
[28] J. Marriott (Ed.), *Unknown London: Early Modernist Visions of the Metropolis, 1815–1845*. London: Pickering and Chatto, 6 vols., 2000.

and the trivial inherited from a pre-industrial plebeian culture, and publishers ignored this at their cost . . . With the decline in radicalism . . . publishers turned increasingly to these other forms, so carrying into the Victorian era a populist, carnivalesque, anti-establishment culture which found expression in virtually all aspects of urban working class life.[29]

In foregrounding the 'ambiguity' to be found in vernacular print culture formed by the dialogue between radicalism and traditional popular delight in 'the bawdy and the trivial', Marriott accurately describes the reading experience of magazines such as *Figaro in London* or the *Penny Satirist*. If for Gatrell bawdiness was a quality that essentially belonged to Regency genteel male sociability and to caricature, for Marriott it formed part of a lived 'carnivalesque, anti-establishment' culture that was happy to combine the political with the low-brow traditional pleasures of illustrated vernacular printed texts. Marriott's anthology offers sustained evidence of ways in which the radical 'co-habited' with the 'trivial' and the diversionary.

The hybridity of late Regency and early Victorian comic illustrations in periodicals that willingly accommodated 'the bawdy and the trivial' within the 'radical' has certainly been uncomfortable to commentators such as Gatrell and George, who have suggested that the consequence of appealing to mass readership in the making of oppositional or satirical images at this time was a disastrous dilution of the aesthetic and political power of the caricature tradition.[30] As Marriott's account of the repressive forces faced by graphic artists and journalists suggests, it is necessary to resist Gatrell's narrative of the 'abrupt capitulation' of caricature in the 1820s, and to think rather in terms of the shifting taxonomies of the comic image between 1820 and 1840. The most interesting commentary that partially brings together the historians of radicalism and the historians of illustrated journalism is David Kunzle's article 'Between Broadsheet Caricature and "Punch"'. One of very few studies of the visual content of magazines of this period, Kunzle identifies ways in which magazines such as *Bell's Life in London* found ways of offering the visual pleasures to be found in the depiction of the energy and vitality of 'trivial' vernacular urban experiences alongside some sense of social dissent and protest. Nonetheless, he concludes, the increasingly generalised nature of the depiction of the lived urban experience ultimately served to rob the images of their satirical and oppositional elements:

[29] J. Marriott, *Unknown London*, I, pp. xxix–xl.
[30] V. Gatrell, *City of Laughter*, pp. 574–80; M. D. George, *British Museum Catalogue*, II, pp. xi–xiv.

> Political caricature specified, localized, and personalized social and political issues. The illustrated magazine generalized and universalized them. The concept of universalization allied to a pseudo democratic 'equalization' (i.e. elimination) of class consciousness was dear to the new illustrated magazines . . . These magazines . . . sought to neutralise the radical potential of comic cuts and to educate the lower classes into more "respectable" looking and reading. They were very successful in this effort.[31]

Along with Gatrell and Marriott, Kunzle ultimately sees the graphic content of satirical and humorous illustrated magazines of the 1820s and 1830s, even those that declared themselves to be radical and oppositional, as showing increasing concessions to the respectable, the diversionary and the trivial, invoking the pleasures of low social comedy to satisfy a readership that might otherwise have engaged more directly with the political.

It is hard to dispute the conclusion of Marriott, Gatrell and Kunzle that the satirical and comic visual elements published in magazines between 1820 and 1845 were generally less topical and less politically focussed than the caricatures of the late Georgian period that preceded it. Nor is it straightforward to identify in these years a new or sustained tradition in periodical illustration defined entirely through radical or politically oppositional graphic satire. But instead of offering an elegy for lost satirical energy or embarking on the attempt to build a distinctively or even vestigially radical tradition out of relatively scanty evidence, it may be more useful to acknowledge the hybridity, entrepreneurial energy and commercial opportunism of late Regency and early Victorian satirical and comic art. The lines between the diversionary, the comic, the satirical and the political at this time, especially as manifested in graphic and visual elements, are extremely hard to maintain. Thus 'hybridity' in this context is constructed out of a dialogue between social and political satire (often manifested through pastiche and travesty of 'establishment' elements), 'fun' (a new term that is beginning to supersede 'the comic' as a way of describing the diversionary) and social observation (to use Kunzle's terms), a way of 'localizing' the political to the circumstances of individuals.

The title of this chapter suggests something of the overlaps, elisions and complexities involved in studying the illustrated political press in the years between 1820 and the increasingly dominant presence of *Punch* in the 1840s. With regard to illustration, the 'radical press' is not a self-evident category in the late Regency and early Victorian periods. In practice, while

---

[31] D. Kunzle, 'Between Broadsheet Caricature', p. 346.

'radical' may be a useful shorthand adjective for a variety of oppositional, dissident or progressive magazines, it fails to suggest the blurred edges and contradictory categories widely evident in the periodical press at this time which mediate between the political and the diversionary, the informative and the exhortatory, the angry and the conciliatory.

CHAPTER 7

Illustration

Lorraine Janzen Kooistra

The development of the nineteenth-century pictorial press is central to the history of media and modernity in Britain. Enabled by new technologies that dramatically reduced costs while increasing the speed of reproducing and disseminating multiple copies, illustrated letterpress became part of everyday life for the first mass readership. At the beginning of the century, crude woodcuts were a staple of popular culture; for the more middlebrow, satirical prints flourished and comic images embellished all kinds of ephemera in the commercial market.[1] Periodicals, however, typically presented readers with columns of unadorned text; illustrations only appeared to mark significant national occasions. By the end of the Victorian period, thanks to improved technologies, enlarged readerships and the ongoing commodification of the press, visual material dominated the papers read by people of all ages and walks of life. Commenting on 'the abundance of pictures illustrative of news that marks the termination of the century, as compared to their paucity at its commencement', Clement K. Shorter, editor of the *Illustrated London News* (*ILN*), observed in 1899 that in the history of pictorial journalism, 'ten years is a lifetime, and to write in detail the story of the last decade would be to make a book'.[2]

Shorter's observation highlights the complexity of the topic of nineteenth-century illustrated journalism, particularly in the century's closing years, when photomechanical modes of reproduction replaced the wood-engraving industry that had first made affordable pictures possible on a large scale. This chapter aims to give a selective overview of the pictorial press, highlighting its significant developments and titles and mapping how changing conditions affected the ways in which visual images were produced and received. In a competitive marketplace, illustrations helped sell papers; their number,

---

[1] Brian Maidment, *Comedy, Caricature and the Social Order, 1820–50* (Manchester University Press, 2013), pp. 30–34.

[2] Clement K. Shorter, 'Illustrated Journalism: Its Past and Its Future', *Contemporary Review* 75 (April 1899), 481.

Illustration 105

kind, size and placement were crucial to a title's identity and its creation of continuity across numbers. Visual coverage of war, crime, royalty and disaster reliably boosted sales. Stylistic registers and visual rhetoric varied to accommodate topics and readerships. Realistic depictions of foreign and domestic life, sporting and theatrical events, popular science, fashion, travel and celebrities jockeyed for readers' attention with satiric political cartoons and aesthetic illustrations of poetry and fiction. By the end of the century, pictorial advertising was integrated within the periodical's systems of communication, sharing the printed page with editorial matter. Visualising and producing consumer desire became central to selling illustrated periodicals to a mass audience.

Whether documenting current events, lampooning topical issues or illustrating literature, pictures were highly mediated representations, typically produced by multiple makers and a combination of manual and mechanical means. Despite their multiple mediations, however, these images communicated a rhetoric of authenticity and immediacy; their visual language shaped nineteenth-century readers' ways of seeing and understanding the world and contributed to their notions of self and other. Illustrations can pose interpretive challenges for students of periodicals today, not only because their technologies of reproduction do not realistically represent the world for us but also because their communication depends on a broad range of artistic conventions, alludes to both visual and literary culture and engages topical issues. Contemporary readers, in contrast, were schooled in the kind of interactive, intertextual, up-to-the-minute reading demanded by illustrated periodicals. The history of the pictorial press in nineteenth-century Britain maps the increasingly commodified, transnational and transmedia world of the image in the age of mechanical reproduction, rapid communication and mass readership.

The Artist as Journalist and the Pictorial Press

Writing in 1863, Charles Baudelaire identified 'the painter of modern life' not as an easel artist creating a unique artefact but as a pictorial journalist producing commercial drawings for large-scale reproduction in the periodical press. His example was the anonymous 'CG': Constantin Guys, a Dutch artist based in France who covered the Crimean War for the *ILN*. The graphic journalist, Baudelaire claimed, 'wants to know, understand, and appreciate everything that happens on the face of the globe'; in his visualised observations, he 'distills modernity' for periodical readers.[3] Baudelaire's essay highlights some significant features of the period's illustrated journalism, including its emphasis on 'on-the-spot' sketches, a growing internationalism, and a concern with modernity, defined by Baudelaire as 'the ephemeral, the fugitive, the contingent'[4] – terms equally applicable to illustrated periodicals themselves.

The on-the-spot documenter of the topical and everyday emerged as a vital element of the press only after decades of development in pictorial journalism. In the early 1800s, news illustration was reserved for solemn occasions such as coronations and state funerals or stories of criminal activities and executions. Launched in 1791 as a middle-class Sunday weekly, the *Observer* pioneered the use of wood-engraved illustration in reporting current events.[5] Like all dailies, *The Times* (1785–) lacked the technical capacity to produce pictures that could be printed within a twenty-four-hour publishing schedule. However, the paper did use wood-engraved images to mark national events, such as Nelson's funeral in 1806. Despite its steep price of 14 pence – about twice the cost of an ordinary issue – the *Observer*'s illustrated edition of George IV's coronation in 1821 sold 60,000 copies.[6] Working-class audiences, unable to afford the *Observer* or *The Times*, accessed popular broadsides – cheap single sheets illustrated with woodcuts of topical events – hawked in the streets.

In 1822, *The Mirror of Literature, Amusement, and Instruction* (1822–47) began to combine a miscellaneous content, cut and pasted from other publications, with the regular inclusion of one or two illustrations each week; this proved to be a popular formula for respectable readerships.[7] Pioneering the use of wood engraving to reproduce images, the *Mechanics' Magazine* (1823–73) provided scientific information at a low price for a quickly growing readership, the literate artisanal class.[8] Meanwhile, *Bell's Life in London, and Sporting Chronicle* (1822–86) was the first to focus on sport and entertainment, as well as notable crimes and 'interesting

[3] Charles Baudelaire, *The Painter of Modern Life and Other Essays*, trans. Jonathan Mayne. London: Phaidon Press, 1964, pp. 7, 14.

[4] Ibid., p. 13.

[5] John Richard Wood, '*The Observer (1791–)*', in Laurel Brake and Marysa Demoor (eds.), *Dictionary of Nineteenth-Century Journalism*. Brussels and London: The British Library, 2009, p. 466. Hereafter *DNCJ*.

[6] Richard Altick, *The English Common Reader: A Social History of the Mass Reading Public 1800–1900*. University of Chicago Press, 1957, p. 343.

[7] Ibid., pp. 320–1.

[8] David Magee and Brian Maidment, '*Mechanics' Magazine* (1823–1873)', in Brake and Demoor, eds., *DNCJ*, pp. 405–6.

Illustration 107

incidents of high and low life'; priced for a working-class audience, it enjoyed a wide readership that cut across classes.[9] Profusely illustrated in a range of pictorial styles, *Bell's Life* included caricatures in a popular series entitled 'A Gallery of Comicalities', featuring illustrations by George Cruikshank, Robert Seymour and Kenny Meadows. The visualisation of comic types and the method of the sketch became staples of graphic journalism throughout the century.

It was not until the 1830s and 1840s, however, that wood-engraved illustrations began to appear in any great number as the distinguishing feature of new titles. In the *Penny Magazine* (1832–45), an educational journal directed at the working and artisanal classes by the Society for the Diffusion of Useful Knowledge, these were often stock images. Edited by Charles Knight, the magazine was distinguished by its affordability, high-quality content and profitability.[10] As Knight explained to his readers in 'The Commercial History of a Penny Magazine', profit depended on large-scale printing and mass sales: 'a work like the "Penny Magazine," which requires a sale of 60,000 or 70,000 copies, before any profit can accrue, may be undertaken with a reliance alone upon the general demand arising out of the extended desire of knowledge'.[11] With increased competition in an expanding market, the *Penny Magazine* could not maintain profitability. Other cheap illustrated serials, directed at entertaining more than educating the new mass readership, vied for their pennies on Saturdays.[12]

It was in the long-lasting weeklies that illustration as a mode of visual reportage and entertainment developed on a large scale. *Punch* (1841–2002), with its political cartoons and satiric commentary on topical issues, and the *Illustrated London News* (1842–1989), the first newspaper to make pictorial reportage its dominant feature, are particularly important. According to Richard Altick, the *ILN* formula of subordinating word to image made 'a generous supply of pictures . . . an almost indispensable adjunct to text in the journals that sought to exploit the working-class market'.[13] The *London Journal; and Weekly Record of Literature, Science and Art* (1845–1928), a penny magazine aimed at a wide readership keen to read serialised fiction,

[9] Leah Richards and Maurice Milne, '*Bell's Life in London, and Sporting Chronicle* (1822–86)', in Brake and Demoor, eds., *DNCJ*, pp. 46–47.
[10] Patricia Anderson, *The Printed Image and the Transformation of Popular Culture 1790–1860*. Oxford: Clarendon Press, 1991, p. 72.
[11] Charles Knight, 'The Commercial History of a Penny Magazine', *Penny Magazine* 2 (Supplement for August 1833), 378.
[12] Anderson, *The Printed Image*, p. 138.   [13] Altick, *English Common Reader*, p. 344.

marks an important development in the cheap press and the illustration of literature.[14]

Although distinct in the purpose and style of their images, these weeklies led the way in establishing in-house artists, draftsmen and engravers, all under the supervision of an art editor. When the newspaper tax was abolished in 1855 and the paper duty lifted in 1861, the infrastructure was in place for the rapid expansion of the pictorial press: a cohort of professional artists and engravers and a literate mass readership. Working within the industrialised conditions of a mechanised, deadline-driven and highly competitive periodical press, illustrators developed graphic conventions ably read by a visually literate public.

Together with pictorial journalism of current events, literary illustration of serialised novels and poetry added visual interest and shaped readers' everyday experience. After the pioneering example of magazines such as the *Mirror of Literature* and the *London Journal*, the illustrated periodicals of the 1860s – led by *Once a Week* (1859–80), the *Cornhill* (1860–1975) and *Good Words* (1860–1911) – developed a sophisticated graphic vocabulary for literary illustration, drawing on some of the most noted artists of the period. In addition to serialised novels, *Good Words* and *Once a Week* made illustrated poetry central to their titles, setting up pictures and poems in intimate proximity on the printed page.[15] The *Cornhill* used full-page illustrations and pictorial initials to generate ongoing interest in the high-quality fiction that was synonymous with its brand.[16] The distinctive rhetorics of the two dominant modes of illustration, literary (accompanying poems and fiction) and journalistic (accompanying news stories), were in constant interaction and mutually informed each other.[17] And just as both modes drew on, and contributed to, the wider cultural field, they also shaped, and were shaped by, dominant notions of gender, class, race and nation. Notably, the identities and reading communities constructed by the illustrated press had international reach, as pictures that first appeared in British periodicals were reproduced in papers around the globe.

[14] Andrew King, '*The London Journal* (1845–1928)', in Brake and Demoor, eds., *DNCJ*, pp. 374–5.
[15] Linda K. Hughes, 'Inventing Poetry and Pictorialism in *Once a Week*: A Magazine of Visual Effects', *Victorian Poetry* 48.1 (Spring 2010), 41–72; and Lorraine Janzen Kooistra, '"Making Poetry" in *Good Words*: Why Illustration Matters to Periodical Poetry Studies', *Victorian Poetry* 52.1 (Spring 2014), 111–39.
[16] For an excellent overview, see Simon Cooke, *Illustrated Periodicals of the 1860s: Contexts and Collaborations*. New Castle, DE: Oak Knoll Press, 2010.
[17] Laurel Brake and Marysa Demoor, eds., *The Lure of Illustration in the Nineteenth Century: Picture and Press*. Basingstoke: Palgrave Macmillan, 2009, p. 5; and James Mussell, *The Nineteenth-Century Press in the Digital Age*. New York: Palgrave Macmillan, 2012, p. 74.

Illustration 109

International events established a new position for the graphic journalist at mid-century: the 'special artist' who travelled to record events as they happened.[18] When it began publishing in the 1840s, the *ILN* relied on local artists and amateurs for visual reportage outside the metropolis; John Gilbert, their own principal illustrator, depicted distant events based on written reports, printed copy from the dailies and stock images. During the revolution in Paris in 1848, the *ILN* drew on both methods: Guys produced some images on location in Paris, and Gilbert drew other scenes in his London studio. Thus, the illustrated news was a mix of on-the-spot coverage and imaginative composition.

The special artist emerged as a professional category when the *ILN* (which coined the term) and other papers began sending their own graphic journalists to the front during the Crimean War (1854–56).[19] The international arena rapidly expanded the professional opportunities and impact of special artists: the British *ILN*, for example, sent the Paris-based Guys to cover the battlefield. It was through the engravings of these 'drawings, sketched hastily on the spot' that Baudelaire claimed he had 'been able to *read*, so to speak, a detailed account of the Crimean campaign'.[20] As Michèle Martin points out, war journalism depends on its ability to create '*images vérité*', or pictures read as representations of the real.[21] By the time of the Franco-Prussian War (1870–71), the need for this kind of visual reportage had been firmly established, and national newspapers sent special artists to cover both sides of the conflict.

At the first signs of impending war, the recently launched *Graphic* (1869–1932) recalled its special artist Arthur Boyd Houghton from the other side of the Atlantic. Here he was engaged as another kind of 'special', recording his impressions of American life from the eastern seaboard to the western frontier after the Pacific Railway opened the West for immigration. Though stylistically very different, Houghton's *Graphic America* (1870–3), like Gustave Doré's *London: A Pilgrimage* (1872–3), indicates the growing demand for artists to provide visual reportage on a rapidly changing modern world.[22] In intense visualisations of American daily life in various locations – as diverse as a Shaker community, a New York prison and

---

[18] On the 'special' correspondent, see Chapter 10.
[19] Paul Hogarth, *The Artist as Reporter*. London: Gordon Fraser, 1986, p. 30.
[20] Baudelaire, *Painter of Modern Life*, p. 60.
[21] Michèle Martin, *Images at War: Illustrated Periodicals and Constructed Nations*. University of Toronto Press, 2006, p. 43.
[22] Arthur Boyd Houghton, *Graphic America, The Graphic* (March 1870–February 1873); Gustave Doré and Blanchard Jerrold, *London: A Pilgrimage*, 1st vol. ed. London: Grant, 1872.

a Pawnee settlement – Houghton's *America* combined social realism with the grotesque and the critical. Doré's London scenes, produced from notes he took on his nightly sojourns with journalist Blanchard Jerrold, drew on the picturesque and the Gothic, putting social realism into active dialogue with the fantastic.[23] Special artists producing visual documentation in war zones used a similar combination of subjective methods and artistic conventions in their reportage.

The Franco-Prussian War marks the first time that readers could follow a conflict in the press with daily reports and weekly images from the front. In a competitive market-place, graphic pictures of war predictably increased sales, and the special artist became a crucial component in the commodification of the news. Just as the *Graphic* recalled Houghton from America to Paris, the *ILN* recalled its top special William Simpson, from the East, where he was covering the opening of the Suez Canal.[24] Once on location, special artists produced drawings of dramatic events as well as depictions of the daily life of the troops. Subjects were determined by the artist's ability to get himself and his drawings expeditiously in and out of sites of conflict and his compositional decisions about the selection and arrangement of details.

Seeing and interpreting sites of conflict through the sketches of a graphic journalist had become such an entrenched representational code by the end of the century that the new technologies of the portable camera and photomechanical relief processes did not displace the special artist. Newspapers sent artists as well as photographers to South Africa to cover the Boer War (1899–1902) and printed both kinds of visual reportage. With both professional journalists and troops on each side using Kodak cameras to take pictures for publication, the Boer War is aptly named 'the first media war' by Gerry Beegan. The war in South Africa, Beegan notes, also marks another milestone in media history: the first time a periodical – the newly established *King* (launched January 1900) – relied solely on photographic imagery for its war coverage, on the grounds of its supposed documentary truthfulness.[25]

An ongoing discussion in the press about the relative merits of on-the-spot drawings versus photographs and the decision by most papers to combine the two in their Boer War coverage highlight the degree to

[23] Brian Maidment, *Reading Popular Prints 1790–1870*, 2nd ed. Manchester University Press, 2001, p. II.

[24] Paul Hogarth, *Arthur Boyd Houghton*. London: Gordon Fraser, 1981. p. 61

[25] Gerry Beegan, *The Mass Image: A Social History of Photomechanical Reproduction in Victorian London*. Basingstoke: Palgrave Macmillan, 2008, p. 171.

Illustration III

which publishers and their readers relied on readable visual codes as much as technological capacity. As Beegan demonstrates, the public needed to be educated in reading the halftone print before its widespread use could be accepted; thus, a hybridity of manual and mechanical means of reproducing images persisted into the early years of the twentieth century.[26] In 1899, Shorter was convinced that 'the future of illustrated journalism' would require an editor who could adequately judge 'the limits of the artist' – whose drawings he expected to remain in demand – and 'the limits of the photographer' – whose pictures he anticipated would play a larger role in the years ahead.[27] In the long view, Shorter seems to have been right: even in the digital age, when news is dominated by photographic and videographic images, artists continue to produce political cartoons, story illustrations and fashion drawings. Now, as then, the technology of the image conveys a rhetoric integral to its purpose and meaning.

Technologies and Rhetorics of the Periodical Image

In 1842, Charles Knight was taken aback when he saw a sketch artist in the Central Criminal Court taking on-the-spot visual notes for a news story about the two Lascars (Indian or Southeast Asian sailors) on trial. Surprised as he was by the choice of such a subject for special treatment, Knight was equally perplexed by the logistics of production, given his knowledge of the current state of wood-engraving technology. 'How', he wondered, 'could artists and journalists so work concurrently that the news and the appropriate illustrations should both be fresh? How could such things be managed with any approach to fidelity of representation unless all the essential characteristics of a newspaper were sacrificed in the attempt to render it pictorial?' The following Saturday, the mystery was apparently explained when he saw, in the first number of the *ILN*, 'the wretched foreigners standing at the bar'.[28]

Knight's anecdote highlights a critically important disjunction in the nineteenth-century illustrated press. Despite the prominence of the visual and the crucial interdependence of picture and word, there was always a gap between the two modes of reportage, papered over by the rhetoric of documentary and shaped by adjacency on the printed page. From the 1820s

---

[26] Beegan, *The Mass Image*, pp. 134, 16.   [27] Shorter, 'Illustrated Journalism', p. 492.
[28] Mason Jackson, *The Pictorial Press: Its Origin and Progress*. London: Hurst and Blackett, 1885, pp. 280–1.

to the 1890s, when photomechanical processes became the norm, wood engraving was the dominant mode of image reproduction. Since the size of the woodblock conformed to the width of the column or page, image and text built up a modular modernity out of moveable parts, and readers grew accustomed to reading the news as a composite of visual/verbal fragments, homogenised by black ink on paper. Nevertheless, the systems of communication differed considerably for image and text. The process of preparing pictures for the press was more time consuming than converting manuscript to letterpress because it required the transportation of material objects and involved multiple levels of mediation.

The expansion of the pictorial press into mass media was made possible when artisanal wood-engraving methods were converted to industrial processes dependent on the division of labour and assembly-line structures of organisation.[29] Relying on a hierarchy in which the artist provided the intellectual and creative labour while the engraver supplied its manual realisation, this head-versus-hand division became entrenched with the demand for facsimile reproduction. The critical need for speed drove other innovations in the division of labour. The master engraver became responsible for heads and faces, while others in the workshop were allotted specialised tasks. One would engrave animals, another figures, another only backgrounds. The latter would be given to the least accomplished apprentice. As Walter Crane recalled of his time in W. J. Linton's shop, 'there was a good deal of more or less meaningless scribble and crosshatching to fill up, or to balance, or to give a little relief and colour to the subject'.[30] Engravers could be taught to reproduce a particular kind of work rapidly and consistently, without knowing how to draw on the block or engrave complete pictures. The large engraving firms of Swain and the Dalziel Brothers, as well as the in-house engraving office of the *ILN*, were using this kind of factory system to produce facsimile illustration at top speed by the 1860s.[31]

Since blocks of boxwood are small, large illustrations required other kinds of division and fragmentation. To produce a large picture, a number of blocks had to be bolted together. After the draftsman drew the picture on this combined surface, the blocks would be taken apart and distributed to a number of engravers, each of whom only cut one portion of the image.

[29] Beegan, *Mass Image*, pp. 58–59; and Michèle Martin, 'Nineteenth-century Wood Engravers at Work: Mass Production of Illustrated Periodicals (1840–1880)', *Journal of Historical Sociology* 27.1 (March 2014), 133.
[30] Walter Crane, *An Artist's Reminiscences*. New York: Macmillan, 1907, p. 49.
[31] Beegan, *Mass Image*, p. 59.

Illustration 113

THE BRITISH LION'S VENGEANCE ON THE BENGAL TIGER.

Figure 7.1 John Tenniel. 'The British Lion's Vengeance on the Bengal Tiger'. *Punch*
33 (22 August 1857), pp. 76–77.
Wikimedia Commons.

Later, the blocks would be reassembled and the master engraver would complete the finishing touches. This would have been the production method for John Tenniel's double-page foldout for *Punch* during the so-called Indian Mutiny of 1857, 'The British Lion's Vengeance on the Bengal Tiger' (Figure 7.1). Janice Carlisle aptly describes wood engravers as the 'true heroes' of the nineteenth-century pictorial press, whose 'unheralded and underpaid labor was responsible for the images published in *Punch* and the *ILN*.[32] The mass production of illustrated periodicals each week made wood engravers 'one of the first classes of proletariats of the media industry'.[33]

While working to deadline was important for all artists preparing pictures for periodicals, the layers of mediation varied with the kind of image required. Until photographic transfer became the norm in the 1860s, illustrators of periodical poetry and fiction typically drew their images directly onto the woodblock with a pencil, pen, brush or some combination of these implements. In most cases, a single engraver would be responsible for cutting the lines; often, both artist and engraver would

---

[32] Janice Carlisle, *Picturing Reform in Great Britain*. Cambridge University Press, 2012, p. 23.
[33] Martin, 'Nineteenth-century Wood Engravers', p. 132.

sign the block. The presence of signatures is a significant rhetorical convention of literary illustration, invoking a long historical art tradition. An illustration in the *Cornhill* for Margaret Oliphant's *Carità*, 'Carry in her White Frock, Erect as a Little Pillar', shows George Du Maurier's signature in the lower right, while the engraver's signature, Swain, appears in the lower left (Figure 7.2).[34] In contrast to this artistic convention, and in keeping with nineteenth-century journalism's tradition of anonymity, artists and engravers seldom signed news illustration, whether in *Punch* (Figure 7.1) or the *ILN* (Figure 7.3). Notably, Baudelaire celebrated the anonymous journalist as the spectator who 'rejoices in his incognito', as it allowed him to melt into the crowd.[35] As Martin observes, the anonymity of news drawings applied not only to their producers but also to their subjects and readers: journalistic images produced a vocabulary 'of symbols, myths, and cultural icons that formed the collective imaginary of a large anonymous public'.[36]

Throughout the period, mixed manual and mechanical methods of reproduction were used for both literary and news illustrations. However, pictorial journalism typically involved even more mediation than literary illustration. Often hasty visual notes made on location augmented with written directions, the special artist's sketches served as the basis for a drawing made by the periodical's in-house draftsman, who produced the design in accordance with the size specifications determined by the editor. Necessarily, the draftsman's illustration also had to meet the requirements of both wood-engraving reproduction technology and a highly conventional language for representing war.

Comparing a front-page illustration for the *ILN* of 17 September 1870 showing 'The War: The Surrender of Sedan' (see Figure 7.3) with a facsimile of the special artist's sketch from which it was produced (Figure 7.4) illuminates the remediations required to produce so-called eye-witness reportage in the nineteenth century. Art editor Mason Jackson recalled that he received the sketch, which had evidently been made rapidly while the artist was 'under fire', within hours of the time 'the engravings for the current week were to be ready for the printer'.[37] The in-house draftsman translated the special artist's sketch, including his scrawled verbal explications, into a readable visual narrative by foregrounding the dramatic story of surrender. Ignoring virtually all details of the battlefield in the

---

[34] Margaret Oliphant, 'Carità, illustrated by George Du Maurier', *Cornhill Magazine* 34.7 (July 1876), 11–22.
[35] Baudelaire, *Painter of Modern Life*, p. 9.   [36] Martin, *Images at War*, p. 63.
[37] Jackson, *Pictorial Press*, p. 320.

Illustration 115

CARRY IN HER WHITE FROCK, ERECT AS A LITTLE PILLAR.

Figure 7.2 George Du Maurier. 'Carry in Her White Frock, Erect as a Little Pillar', for *Carità*, by Margaret Oliphant. *Cornhill Magazine* 34 (July 1876). Full-page illustration, facing p. 1.
Courtesy of Toronto Public Library.

Figure 7.3 'The War: The Surrender of Sedan', *Illustrated London News*
(17 September 1870), 285.
Courtesy of Toronto Public Library.

Illustration 117

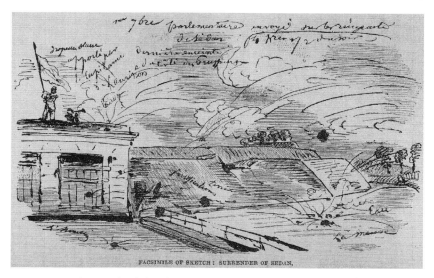

FACSIMILE OF SKETCH : SURRENDER OF SEDAN.

Figure 7.4 'Facsimile of Sketch: Surrender of Sedan'. *The Pictorial Press: Its Origin and Progress*, by Mason Jackson. London: Hurst and Blackett, 1885, p. 318. Courtesy of Toronto Public Library.

sketch, the draftsman reorganised the composition to focus on the French soldier waving a white flag, with a bugler behind him. The draftsman could count on readers to recognise the white flag as a symbol of truce, but he also asked them to make an associative leap by referencing a familiar portrait from the wider cultural field. In depicting the surrendering figure, the artist drew on the features of Emperor Napoleon III.[38] While this visual citation enhanced the romance of the scene, changing the image's orientation from landscape to portrait subtly deployed another graphic convention. As Carlisle points out, 'a picture in portrait generally celebrates individuality.'[39] Coupled with the suggestive features of the French soldier, the portrait orientation of the image encouraged readers to identify the surrendering figure with the defeated emperor himself. Additional visual tropes added further colour to the dramatised story. The broken wall on which the soldier stands – another non-empirical embellishment – suggests the crumbling edifice of the French Empire, while the lightening sky implies hope for the new day to come. Such graphic conventions were so well established that the draftsman was able to produce the drawing for

[38] Martin, *Images at War*, p. 213.   [39] Carlisle, *Picturing Reform*, p. 12.

engraving quickly enough, Jackson notes, that the illustration 'was ready for the press at the usual time'.[40]

Jackson offers this story to show 'the way in which hurried sketches are sometimes adapted to the purposes of a newspaper without at all imparting their original truth'.[41] From the start, the *ILN* had presented its brand of graphic journalism as unmediated images 'of the very form and presence of events as they transpire, in all their substantial reality'.[42] As Peter Sinnema observes, the *ILN* was adept in 'implicat[ing] the reader as a willing receiver of the world(s) pictorially configured'. Sinnema explains that 'an image is acceptable to the reader, or makes sense as a valid representation, when it aligns itself with the reader's own assumptions about the "way things are."'[43] Truth in nineteenth-century pictorial journalism was always a composite collage produced out of on-the-spot sketches, visual conventions and assumed legibility for the reader, all informed by the ideological position of the paper and the audience it cultivated. A pro-Napoleon newspaper, after all, would represent this event very differently.

While the image dominates the *ILN*'s front page and is to an extent self-explanatory, both its caption – 'The War: The Surrender of Sedan' – and the accompanying news item interact with the visual to shape its meaning. The proximity of image and text imply a simultaneity contradicted by their actual production schedule, however. Communication technologies such as the telegraph allowed the rapid transfer of verbal messages across great distances, but artist's sketches could not be translated in this way. Before being redrawn by draftsmen and engraved for printing, artists' sketches had to travel to London periodical offices as physical objects. During the Franco-Prussian War, artists used cameras to take images of their sketches and then sent multiple copies across the Channel by hot-air balloons, in the hope that at least one would make it safely to their editor. Newspaper inscriptions such as 'by balloon post' or 'on-the-spot' conveyed to readers a sense of up-to-the-minute reportage and authenticity.[44]

The lag time between publishing news stories and images, however, had at least two important consequences for the nineteenth-century illustrated press. The first is that the printed word provided copy for the pictorial image to mediate. In other words, pictures were often remediated verbal descriptions, rather than eye-witness reportage. Henry Vizetelly recalled

---

[40] Jackson, *Pictorial Press*, p. 320.   [41] Jackson, *Pictorial Press*, p. 320.
[42] 'Our Address', *Illustrated London News* 1 (14 May 1842), p. 1.
[43] Peter Sinnema, *Dynamics of the Pictured Page: Representing the Nation in the Illustrated London News*. Aldershot: Ashgate, 1998, p. 40.
[44] Martin, *Images at War*, p. 92.

Illustration 119

that the typical modus operandi for editors of illustrated weeklies 'was to scan the morning papers carefully, cut out such paragraphs as furnished good subjects for illustration, and send them with the necessary boxwood blocks to the draughtsman employed'.[45] The second consequence of the temporal disjunction in producing words and images is that, until the development of the photomechanical relief processes, a daily illustrated press was not technologically possible. In 1890, the *Daily Graphic* (1890–1928) led the way as the first successful pictorial daily, combining hand-drawn illustrations reproduced by line blocks and photographs reproduced by halftone engraving. Daily papers did not regularly use photographs until World War I.[46]

The non-documentary pictorial journalism of *Punch* provides an excellent example of the ways in which the visual image mediated both oral and print culture in the nineteenth-century periodical press, as Patrick Leary's work has shown. Artists visualised news items through literary allusions and nursery rhymes; recognisable symbols and pictures; and social situations such as the dinner party, the doctor's office, the street and so on. Individually and recursively, these *Punch* visualisations created, as Leary notes, 'a common rhetoric for the cartoon that would bind readers, writers, artists, and proprietors in a public conversation'. The *Punch* staff constantly tried to work within the perceived 'limits of the imagined reader's understanding'.[47] This imagined reader was, like the *Punch* staff, white, male, middle class and British. In keeping with periodical illustrations in general, the pictures in *Punch* should be viewed, in Brian Maidment's words, as 'essentially ideological formations which, whether consciously or unconsciously, are shaped by the cultural values and social aspirations of both make[r] and audience'.[48]

The size and centrality of the *Punch* Large Cut – the full-page illustration identified with the title – attested to the importance of the selected news subject. The technology of reproduction, however, also significantly contributed to the way in which that subject was represented. Because of the time necessary to draw and engrave the Large Cut for Saturday publication, the *Punch* staff had to imagine the outcome on Wednesday of an event still underway. When the news was being conveyed from far-flung parts of the empire, predictive drawing became even more complicated. For example, because of the time required to

[45] Sinnema, *Dynamics of the Pictured Page*, p. 69.   [46] Beegan, *Mass Image*, p. 40.
[47] Patrick Leary, *The* Punch *Brotherhood: Table Talk and Print Culture in Mid-Victorian England.* London: British Library, 2010, p. 41.
[48] Maidment, *Reading Popular Prints*, p. 11.

convey news from the Indian subcontinent to London, Tenniel's famous cartoon of the Sepoy rebellion, published on 22 August 1857, represented *Punch*'s patriotic response to news just received of the massacre that had taken place in Cawnpore in July. With the outcome still unknown, the resulting Large Cut visualises this news event through emotional content (see Figure 7.1). While the caption 'The British Lion's Vengeance Upon the Bengal Tiger' implicitly encouraged readers to anticipate victory, the dramatic picture itself focused on the two ferocious animals engaged in a violent allegorical battle. If the outcome remained uncertain, what was at stake was clear: British mothers and children were being mauled by savage foreign beasts. The Cut's imperialistic rhetoric was so powerful that the cartoon was rapidly incorporated into the wider visual field of Victorian everyday life, appearing on banners, in pantomimes and in engravings displayed on parlour walls.[49]

In addition to the Large Cut, *Punch* utilised a number of visual genres adapted by pictorial magazines of all kinds – from miscellanies to juvenile publications to fashion magazines – throughout the period. These visual genres included the use of cover designs, graphics and banners to promote title identity and consistency, and the development of pictorial initial letters, inset vignettes, half-page illustrations, 'blackies' (silhouette illustrations) and 'socials'. Small sketches of manners in the English tradition of caricature, *Punch*'s social cuts articulated the weekly's middle-class perspective by ridiculing upper-class pretensions (Du Maurier excelled at this) and finding a reliable source of humour in working-class 'types'.[50] Charles Keene made the latter a specialisation in his *Punch* contributions; at the end of the century, Phil May's line drawings for 'The Lighter Side' in the *Sketch* (1893–1959) became associated with the new journalism's graphic vocabulary of modernity. A lavishly illustrated sixpenny weekly of 'art and actuality', the aptly named *Sketch* focused on the individual personality, from the shoeblack to the glamorous celebrity. The determined focus of the *Sketch* was social rather than political: almost all the magazine's pictorial coverage was devoted to images of people, and social caricatures became worthy of full-scale reproduction.[51]

Punch's influence is also evident in the literary miscellanies that emerged in the 1860s. While magazines such as *Once a Week*, *Good Words* and the

---

[49] Frankie Morris, *Artist of Wonderland: The Life, Political Cartoons, and Illustrations of Tenniel*. Charlottesville: University of Virginia Press, 2005, p. 63.
[50] Beegan, *Mass Image*, p. 123; and Maidment, *Comedy, Caricature, and the Social Order*, p. 21.
[51] Beegan, *Mass Image*, p. 123.

Illustration 121

Cornhill have little in common with *Punch* in style or subject matter, their adaptation of particular visual genres such as the pictorial initial letter and their interest in the fleeting details of modern life records their debt. Aiming to give educated readers high-quality essays and illustrated literature, the *Cornhill* is one of the most important of these magazines. Rather than an abundance of images, the *Cornhill* focused on selective quality, publishing one or two illustrations per number by the best artists, almost exclusively for its literary contents. The *Punch* connection is evident in the cross-over of the two magazines' illustrators, including William Makepeace Thackeray (who was also the *Cornhill*'s founding editor) and Du Maurier. Both perfected the pictorial initial as a miniature commentary on a narrative's thematic concerns, and the full-page illustration as a visualisation of its principal characters. Du Maurier recalled that for many years he had enjoyed a regular commission from the *Cornhill* to produce 'every month a page-drawing and an initial letter'. Du Maurier celebrated the magazine's illustrators – including Luke Fildes, Frederick Leighton, John Everett Millais, Frederick Sandys and Fred Walker, among others – for treating 'the life of our time, which had been illustrated humorously by Leech, Doyle, and Keene in *Punch* . . . from quite a serious point of view'. As members of 'the modern school of illustration', these literary artists captured the fashion of the everyday: 'the chimney-pot hat and the trousers, the crinoline and the spoon-bonnet' became 'invested with artistic merit'. Echoing Baudelaire, Du Maurier hails these graphic artists as modern painters of 'the life of to-day'.[52]

In *Ariadne Florentine* (1876), art critic John Ruskin drew a comparison between *Punch* and the *Cornhill*, the graphic rhetoric of 'the modern school of illustration' and the industrialised technologies of wood engraving for nineteenth-century periodicals. Examining Du Maurier's social cuts for *Punch* and his illustrations of Margaret Oliphant's *Carità* for the *Cornhill*, Ruskin declared that they were 'representative of the entire illustrative art industry of the modern press'.[53] In a lengthy analysis of Du Maurier's 'Carry in her White Frock, Erect as a little Pillar' (see Figure 7.2), Ruskin calls attention to the wood engraving's sketchy rhetoric, from the minimally drawn faces, hands and feet to the creation of a foliage effect through the 'scrabble' technique of using many squiggled lines to create an impression of landscape. Developed out of the pressure to

---

[52] George Du Maurier, 'The Illustrating of Books from the Serious Artist's Point of View – I', *Magazine of Art* (January 1890), pp. 352, 351.
[53] John Ruskin, *Ariadne Florentine: Six Lectures on Wood and Metal Engraving*, in *The Complete Works of Ruskin*. New York: National Library Association, 2008, p. 151.

produce wood-engraved illustrations for periodical deadlines, the visual rhetoric of scrabble expressed, for Ruskin, the ugliness and speed of an increasingly mechanised and industrial world. 'It is just such a landscape', he declared, 'as the public sees out of its railroad window at sixty miles of it in an hour – and good enough for such a public'.[54]

While Ruskin objected to the social and moral problems he saw in wood-engraved illustrations as much as to their aesthetic value, his assessment of how changing conditions were affecting pictorial representation was accurate. As the century wore to a close, periodical images became increasingly sketchy and unfinished looking, expressive of the speed and fragmentation of modern urban society. They also became integrally linked to consumer desire within commodity culture. Notably, Ruskin himself participated in this discourse when he drew attention to Carry's white frock, 'in cheap white and black cutting', which he complained was executed 'with considerably less skill than that of an ordinary tailor's or milliner's shop-book pattern drawing' (see Figure 7.4).[55] The reciprocal influence of illustration and fashion is, in fact, a crucial aspect of representing the everyday in the periodical press. Anthony Trollope, for example, believed that Millais's drawing of Lucy Roberts's crinoline in 'Was it not a lie?' for *Framley Parsonage* (*Cornhill* 1860)[56] served readers as a fashion plate.[57] By the fin de siècle, publishers were actively bringing together the discourses of fashion, consumerism and modernity, strategically deploying pictures to sell their magazines and the commodities they advertised, particularly to women readers now increasingly targeted as shoppers.[58]

Image, Text and Reader at the Fin-de-siècle

Enabled by the development of photomechanical processes of reproduction and the snapshot, the discourse of the new journalism in the closing decade of the nineteenth century confirmed the dominance of the image. While the line block mimicked the linear qualities of the familiar wood engraving, the halftone print, which created tonal qualities through a cross-line grid of screens, was capable of reproducing the effect of a photograph. Because these reproduction methods were largely mechanical, they

---

[54] Ibid., p. 150.   [55] Ibid.
[56] Anthony Trollope, 'Framley Parsonage, illustrated by John Everett Millais', *Cornhill Magazine* 1.6 (June 1860), 691–715.
[57] David Skilton, 'The Centrality of Literary Illustration in Victorian Visual Culture: The Example of Millais and Trollope 1860 to 1864', *The Journal of Illustration Studies* (December 2007), 8.
[58] Margaret Beetham, 'Women's Periodicals', in Brake and Demoor, eds., *DNCJ*, pp. 683–4.

Illustration 123

brought with them a heightened discourse of actuality and the real: even more than wood engravings, process engravings were seen as virtually unmediated representations of the artist's hand or camera's lens. The rapidity with which they could be produced far exceeded the speed of any image reproduction method to date. In a word, process engraving was up to date and modern. The decrease in reproduction costs coincided with an increase in the use of advertising by commercial enterprises, and new illustrated titles, catering to a variety of demographics, sprang up. At the end of the century, Shorter boasted that with the launch of the *Sketch* in 1893 as the first middle-class weekly entirely illustrated by photographic processes, he had 'started a new era in journalism which is in evidence to-day in the picture page of every newspaper'.[59] The *Sketch* and its peers aimed to portray modern life in all its variety of personalities and ephemerality of interests. Specialising in coverage of music halls and theatres, and focusing on celebrities and style, the illustrated magazines at the fin-de-siècle showed readers how to define themselves through consumption and leisure.[60]

As Beegan notes, images of women predominated in the *Sketch* and other magazines of the period.[61] This was certainly true of the fin-de-siècle's most notorious journal *The Yellow Book* (1894–97), whose bold cover designs and many illustrations took women as their subject in ways that provoked critiques in the press but sales in the shop. Availing itself of the latest techniques in photomechanical reproduction, *The Yellow Book* was able to reproduce art of all kinds, from oil paintings to pencil sketches to painted fans. In setting out to make their modern illustrated magazine as different as possible 'from the bad old traditions of periodical literature', its founding editors, Aubrey Beardsley and Henry Harland, insisted on a complete separation of verbal and visual contents: 'the pictures will in no case serve as illustrations to the letter-press, but each will stand by itself as an independent contribution.'[62] *The Yellow Book* also eschewed advertisements, but its publisher, John Lane, was adept at branding his title by linking the magazine to his illustrated *belles lettres* list and cultivating an international readership that, by virtue of its subscription, felt knowing, avant-garde and aesthetic.

A painting by Gertrude Hammond, entitled *The Yellow Book* and reproduced in volume 6 (July 1895), mirrored ideal readers to themselves,

---

[59] Beegan, *Mass Image*, p. 27.   [60] Ibid., p. 99.   [61] Ibid., p. 119.
[62] *Prospectus: The Yellow Book* 1 (1894), in Dennis Denisoff and Lorraine Janzen Kooistra (eds.), *The Yellow Nineties Online*. Ryerson University, 2011.

Figure 7.5 Gertrude D. Hammond, *The Yellow Book. The Yellow Book* 6
(July 1895), 119. *The Yellow Nineties Online.* Ed. Dennis Denisoff and Lorraine
Janzen Kooistra.
Ryerson University.

Illustration 125

while also engaging in the modern marketing practice of product placement (Figure 7.5). Like Du Maurier's 'Carry in her White Frock' (see Figure 7.2), Hammond's *The Yellow Book* focuses on a fashionably dressed young woman with an air of innocence. Hammond's young woman, however, is placed within an aesthetic interior rather than outside under the trees; instead of a female chaperone, an ardent young man is her sole companion. Together, they are looking at an early volume of the *Yellow Book* – representing, for the consumers holding the current volume, aesthetic sensibility, erotic charge and a *beau ideal* of consumption and leisure.

While technologies of reproduction changed at the end of the century, the dominant rhetoric of the real, the actual and the now continued to shape readers' sense of themselves as consumers of print culture and the world of objects it depicted. At the same time, the partial and incomplete nature of pictures reproduced in the pictorial press, and their fragmentary status in an ephemeral, heterogeneous and hybrid form, invited modern readers to finish the visual story themselves – to 'poach' it, as Michel de Certeau says, for their own purposes.[63] The story of the pictorial press in nineteenth-century Britain, therefore, belongs as much to its readers as to its multiple makers.

---

[63] Michel De Certeau, *The Practice of Everyday Life*, trans. Steven Rendall. Berkeley: University of California Press, 1998, p. 165.

CHAPTER 8

Periodical Poetry

Linda H. Peterson

If a scholar today consults the *Wellesley Index to Victorian Periodicals* for entries on the poetry of Felicia Hemans or Alfred Tennyson, Christina Rossetti or Algernon Swinburne, the results will be disappointing.[1] No entries appear for Hemans's lyrical contributions to *Blackwood's Edinburgh Magazine* in the 1820s and 1830s, or for Tennyson's patriotic poetry in the *Nineteenth Century* in the 1870s and 1880s. Rossetti's 1861 debut in *Macmillan's Magazine* with 'Up-Hill' is unrecorded, and Swinburne's contributions to various numbers of the *Fortnightly Review* in the 1860s are missing. This gap in the original 1966 edition and the current online database reveals the secondary importance of poetry to the *Wellesley* editors. As Walter E. Houghton, the general editor, stated in the 'Introduction' to the second volume, 'To have included verse would have added an enormous number of worthless items to Part A [the title index] and a large number of obscure authors to be identified and then described in Part B [the author index].'[2] This editorial decision, as Linda K. Hughes has noted, presumed a predominance of sentimental verse in newspapers and magazines and an 'association of poetry with "filler"'.[3] It failed to account for major poems first published in periodicals and for the significance of occasional verse in which poets engaged the questions of their day. Even more, it underestimated the importance of poetry for the prestige of the periodical, the career of the poet and the aesthetic pleasure of the reader.

[1] *Wellesley Index to Victorian Periodicals, 1824–1900*, ed. Walter E. Houghton. 5 vols. (Toronto: University of Toronto Press, 1966–89).
[2] Walter E. Houghton, 'Introduction', *Wellesley Index*, Vol. 2 (Toronto: University of Toronto Press, 1972), pp. xvi–xvii. Houghton elaborates this point in 'A Bulletin from the "Wellesley Index,"' *Victorian Periodicals Newsletter* 8 (June 1975), 68, by arguing that the editors excluded poetry because it was too difficult to decide where to 'draw the line' for inclusion or exclusion based on the 'calibre of the poet'.
[3] Linda K. Hughes, 'What the *Wellesley Index* Left Out: Why Poetry Matters to Periodical Studies', *Victorian Periodicals Review* 40 (Summer 2007), 92.

Fifty years after the original publication of the *Wellesley Index*, the view has changed, and scholars now recognise the enormous importance of poetry in periodicals of all sorts – literary annuals, monthly and bi-weekly magazines, weekly and daily newspapers. Some nineteenth-century magazines featured a regular poetry column (as did the *Literary Gazette*), whereas others interspersed poetry throughout (as in *Blackwood's Edinburgh Magazine*, the *Examiner*, the *Cornhill* and *Macmillan's*). Local, regional and national newspapers were, moreover, important sites for popular poetry; as Andrew Hobbs and Claire Januszewski estimate, 'at least 3,600 poems were published in about 100 provincial newspapers in 1800, rising to 123,430 in nearly 1,500 papers in 1900'.[4] Poetry was everywhere in Victorian print culture, some enduring, some ephemeral. Periodical specialists have begun to fill in the gaps in the *Wellesley's* records, most notably in the *Periodical Poetry Index* online.[5] But our understanding of the interconnections among poets, poetry and periodicals has only begun to take shape. This chapter explores some of these interconnections as they reveal why poets needed periodicals, why periodicals included poetry, and what Victorian periodical poetry hoped to achieve.

Making a Poetic Debut

For many aspiring young poets, a newspaper, magazine or literary annual offered an opportunity to submit verse, test the editor's response and make a debut. As an adolescent, for example, Mary Howitt submitted two poems to a 'pocketbook' (an early form of literary annual) signing herself 'Mary of Uttoxeter'; later, she and her sister Anna published verse in the *Kaleidoscope*, a weekly Liverpool paper.[6] Appearance in these small publications confirmed Mary's talents (to herself at least) and spurred her on to a literary career. Similarly, as aspiring writers, Anne and Branwell Brontë submitted verses to periodicals – Anne modestly yet successfully to *Fraser's Magazine*; Branwell successfully to local organs such as the *Halifax Guardian*, *Bradford Herald*, *Leeds Intelligencer* and *Yorkshire Gazette*, but unsuccessfully to *Blackwood's Magazine*, the periodical he most admired.[7]

---

[4] Andrew Hobbs and Claire Januszewski, 'How Local Newspapers Came to Dominate Victorian Poetry Publishing', *Victorian Poetry* 52:1 (Spring 2014), 71–72, 77–79.

[5] Founded by Natalie Houston, Lindsey Lawrence and April Patrick, this index can be found at www.periodicalpoetry.org.

[6] Mary Howitt, *An Autobiography*, ed. Margaret Howitt (London: Ibister, [1889]), p. 100.

[7] For Branwell's early publications, see Victor A. Neufeldt, *Oxford Dictionary of National Biography* online, s.v. 'Branwell Brontë'; as Acton Bell, Anne published 'The Three Guides', *Fraser's Magazine* 38 (August 1848), 193–95, and 'The Narrow Way', *Fraser's Magazine* 38 (December 1848), 712.

Taking a jaundiced view of such early trials, William Makepeace
Thackeray satirised his own youthful submissions to the *Flindell's
Western Luminary and Family Magazine* by having his pseudo-hero
Arthur Pendennis 'br[ea]k out in the Poets' Corner of the Country
Chronicle'.[8] Thackeray's descriptions of Pendennis's tactics – the signature
'NEP' and verses titled 'To a Tear', 'On the Anniversary of the Battle of
Waterloo' and 'To Madame Caradori singing at the Assize Meetings' –
capture the custom of semi-anonymous publication and the sentimental
and occasional poems that dominated poetry columns of magazines, news-
papers and literary gazettes in the early Victorian period.

Although most such submissions probably came to naught, the case of
Letitia Landon reveals the crucial role that periodicals could play in
launching a poet's career. Landon's mother sent samples of her daughter's
poetry to their neighbour William Jerdan, editor of the *Literary Gazette*.
The *Gazette* regularly featured an 'Original Poetry' column, with some
verses by known authors, but most by amateur and aspiring poets like
Landon. In his *Autobiography*, Jerdan recalls that he was 'struck with the
innate genius they [Landon's poems] displayed, and the unmistakeable
proofs that the writer possessed the great essential elements of taste, feeling,
warmth, and imagination'.[9] He published her first poem, 'Rome', in the
Gazette on 11 March 1820 – not with the initials 'L.E.L.', by which she
would become known, but signed simply 'L', not as a featured poet but as a
'correspondent'. Later that year, the *Gazette* published other verse: 'To a
Michaelmas Daisy' (18 March 1820), 'A West Indian Anecdote' (5 August
1820), and a 'Fragment' (19 August 1820). In this fourth poem, which
Jerdan notes held the 'germ of the future' Landon found the subject matter
that would make her popular (the joys and woes of love) and a successful
mode of self-presentation (as a modern-day Sappho).

To make a successful debut, however, Landon also needed a distinctive
signature to distinguish her from other contributors and a regular appearance not merely as a 'correspondent' but as one of the *Gazette's* acknowledged poets. These she found in the initials 'L.E.L.' (to signal Letitia
Elizabeth Landon, the name on her books) and in a series of 'Poetic
Sketches' she launched in January 1822. The 'Sketches' announced as
their subject – 'A Woman's whole life is a history of the affections. The

---

[8] See Edgar F. Harden, *A Checklist of Contributions by William Makepeace Thackeray to Newspapers,
     Periodicals, Books, and Serial Part Issues, 1828–1864*. Victoria: English Literary Studies, University of
     Victoria, 1996), p. 13, for these early poems, and William Makepeace Thackeray, *The History of
     Pendennis*. Chicago and New York: Bedford, Clarke, n.d., p. 31.
[9] William Jerdan, *Autobiography* (London: Arthur Hall, Virtue, & Co., 1853), vol. 3, p. 176.

heart is her world' – a crystallisation of her sentiments in the earlier 'Fragment'.[10] In her rise to fame as a poetess, the periodical, with its regular poetry column, was crucial to her success. Bulwer Lytton later recalled his undergraduate fascination with her verse; along with other students, he would

> rush every Saturday afternoon for the 'Literary Gazette', [with] an impatient anxiety to hasten at once to that corner of the sheet which contained the three magical letters L.E.L. And all of us praised the verse, and all of us guessed at the author. We soon learned it was a female, and our admiration was doubled, and our conjectures tripled.[11]

That 'corner of the sheet' was an inner right-hand page of the weekly paper. Quite soon, Landon's poems became the featured verse of the 'Original Poetry' – with additional 'Poetical Sketches', 'Dramatic Scenes', 'Fragments', 'Metrical Tales' and other series. Landon's case represents a poet's shrewd use of periodical spaces to aid her career.

Although perhaps not as dramatic in their rise to fame, other poets used periodicals to launch or relaunch their careers. When Swinburne decided to pursue a career as a professional man of letters, he placed poems in the *Spectator* and reviews of poetry in the *Fortnightly Review*. In the *Spectator* of 1862, for instance, he published 'Faustine', 'Before Parting', 'A Song in Time of Order', 'A Song in Time of Revolution' and three other lyrics (all reprinted, without alteration, in his soon-to-be notorious *Poems and Ballads*).[12] In 1862, Swinburne also published a review of Charles Baudelaire's *Les Fleurs du Mal* in the *Spectator*, and followed with reviews of William Morris's *Life and Death of Jason* and Matthew Arnold's *New Poems* in the *Fortnightly* in 1867. Periodicals offered a venue not only to test the reception of his poetry but also to demonstrate his knowledge as a critic, while earning fees for his work.

Christina Rossetti, Swinburne's contemporary, turned to periodicals to relaunch her public career as a poet. Rossetti had published verse, under the pseudonym Ellen Alleyn, in the Pre-Raphaelite *Germ*, but that journal folded after only a few numbers in 1850. In the 1850s, despite the composition of some of her finest lyrics – 'A Birthday', 'Song' ('When I am dead,

---

[10] L.E.L., 'Poetic Sketches', *Literary Gazette* No. 260 (12 January 1822), 27–28.

[11] [Edward Bulwer Lytton], *New Monthly Magazine* 32 (December 1831), 546; rpt. in Jerome L. McGann and Daniel Riess, eds., Letitia Elizabeth Landon: *Selected Writings*. Peterborough, Ontario: Broadview, 1997, pp. 328–35. Edward Bulwer entered Trinity College, Cambridge, in 1822, so presumably he read the 'Poetic Sketches' as a freshman.

[12] See Richard Herne Shepherd, *The Bibliography of Swinburne* (London: George Redway, 1887), pp. 7–11, for these and other publications discussed in this paragraph.

my dearest'), 'Up-Hill' and 'Passing Away' – Rossetti lacked an outlet for her work and was reduced to almost amateur status when she directed her creative energy to a London ladies' magazine, *The Bouquet*. Her career changed sharply for the better when in January 1861, after her thirtieth birthday and a 'lost decade', she submitted poems to David Masson, editor of the newly founded *Macmillan's Magazine*. Masson responded positively, publishing 'Up-Hill' in February, followed by 'A Birthday' in April and 'An Apple-Gathering' in August. These successes led to an offer from Alexander Macmillan to publish a volume of her poetry – what became *Goblin Market and Other Poems*. For both poet and publisher, the success of Rossetti's verse in *Macmillan's* confirmed her standing as an important Victorian poet. Her brother praised her achievement, writing that Macmillan 'has been congratulated by some of his contributors on having got a poet at last in your person'.[13]

At the fin-de-siècle, Alice Meynell's case presents a variation on Rossetti's. As Alice Thompson, her name before marriage, Meynell had published *Preludes* in 1875; despite the optimistic title of this book of poetry, she turned (out of financial necessity) to journalism, art criticism and co-editorship with her husband of two Catholic magazines, the *Weekly Register* and *Merry England*. Meynell kept writing verse in the 1880s, though less frequently and only occasionally publishing it. In the 1890s, however, she submitted aesthetic essays – beautifully compact, lyrically expressive – to the *Scots* later the *National Observer*, where she also published a few new lyrics.[14] The essays, more than the poetry, led to an offer from John Lane of the Bodley Head Press, then the most important publisher of aesthetic literature, to gather her prose into a book, *The Rhythm of Life and Other Essays* (1892). Meynell negotiated for simultaneous release of a new edition of her poetry, *Poems* (1892), which included most of the verse from *Preludes* as well as the newer lyrics. This double launch secured Meynell's status as a significant fin-de-siècle woman of letters. *Poems* also turned out to provide a steady, if modest, source of income to both the poet and the press.

As these examples suggest, poets often initially turned to periodicals to publish their verse – not only expressive lyrics, though these were important, but also poems of religious, political and historical significance. Thereafter, most poets hoped to collect their periodical work into books – still the

---

[13] Quoted by Antony H. Harrison in *The Letters of Christina Rossetti*, Vol. 1, ed. Antony H. Harrison. Charlottesville: University of Virginia Press, 1997, p. 144, n. 1.
[14] The notes to *The Poems of Alice Meynell: Complete Edition*. London: Humphrey Milford, Oxford University Press, 1940, give original periodical publication where relevant.

symbol of cultural permanence – as in Rossetti's *Goblin Market and Other Poems* (1862), Swinburne's *Poems and Ballads* (1866) and Meynell's *Poems* (1892), all of which included poetry that had previously appeared in magazines. Even after book publication, periodicals played an important role in confirming (or negating) literary success, for reviews of poetry had an established place in many monthly, weekly and daily publications. A review of Rossetti's *Goblin Market* in the *Eclectic Magazine*, for instance, confirmed her gifts: 'We have ever been of the number of those who speak of the rare delight and refreshment', the reviewer began, 'with which they have read some volumes of poems by a new or unknown hand . . . Here, in Miss Rossetti's volume is a volume of really true poetry'.[15] Swinburne's early poetry received more mixed reviews – from the positive responses to *Atalanta in Calydon* (1865), his neo-Greek tragedy which, as the *Saturday Review* noted, revealed 'a poet of great grace, flexibility and power of expression', to the attack the next year on *Poems and Ballads* in the same periodical, which questioned whether the poet was 'the vindictive and scornful apostle of a crushing iron-shod despair' or 'the libidinous laureate of a pack of satyrs'.[16]

Although most Victorian poets sought periodical publication, it must be acknowledged that some disliked the format and preferred moving directly to the book. Robert Browning, whose early career is notable for its long poems – *Pauline* (1833), *Paracelsus* (1835) and *Sordello* (1840) – placed short poems in magazines only occasionally and usually at the request of the editor. Even some of his now-famous dramatic monologues – 'Porphyria's Lover' in the *Monthly Repository* (1836), 'The Tomb at St. Praxed's' (later titled 'The Bishop Orders His Tomb') in *Hood's Magazine* (1844) – made little or no impact within the magazine format. Although he experimented with serially issued pamphlets in the 1840s, a mode popular with novelists, these failed too. Almost all of Browning's famous dramatic lyrics and dramatic monologues appeared solely in books – *Men and Women* (1855), *Dramatis Personae* (1864) and *The Ring and the Book* (1868–69). Only later in his career, during a rift with his American publisher James R. Osgood over payment, did Browning deliberately turn to a periodical, the *New York Times*, to serialise *The Inn Album* (1875). As Linda K. Hughes speculates,

[15] [Edwin Paxton Hood], 'Miss Rossetti's Goblin Market', *Eclectic Review* 115 (June 1862), 493.
[16] Anonymous, 'Atalanta in Calydon', *Saturday Review* 19 (6 May 1865), 542, and [John Morley], 'Review of Swinburne, *Poems and Ballads*', *Saturday Review* 22 (4 August 1866), 145–47.

Browning was likely motivated 'by the pleasures of profits and retaliation'.[17]

Alfred Tennyson had a pronounced aversion to periodicals, especially literary annuals. In 1831, his college friend Arthur Henry Hallam urged him not to 'disdain a mode of publication which Schiller and Goethe chose for their best compositions'; on the sly Hallam sent Tennyson's 'Check Every Outflash' to Edward Moxon for inclusion in the new *Englishman's Magazine*, explaining that Alfred 'will contribute to your publication, although I know the periodical mode of writing is no favorite with him'.[18] (The magazine ceased publication almost immediately, so Tennyson was off the hook.) It was more difficult to convince Tennyson to contribute to literary giftbooks, issued annually for the Christmas market. Nonetheless, several early poems appeared in *The Gem, The Tribute, Friendship's Offering* and *The Keepsake* – the last two known to pay solid fees to the poets who contributed. After Tennyson became poet laureate in 1850, he felt inclined, if not obliged, to comment on English politics in verse form. During the Crimean War, he sent a series of poems to the *Examiner*, including 'The Charge of the Light Brigade', inspired by reading dispatches from the war front printed in *The Times*. Later, as Queen Victoria's children married or died, he published memorial verses in the *The Times*, including 'A Welcome to Alexandra' and 'To H.R.H. Princess Beatrice'. Although his predecessor, William Wordsworth, 'did not write a single official poem during his seven years as Laureate',[19] as Kathryn Ledbetter points out, Tennyson wrote ten – not to mention the twenty or thirty unofficial poems on political subjects that he placed in the *Examiner, Macmillan's Magazine* and the *Nineteenth Century*.

Making Money

'Poetry don't sell', lamented Mary Howitt to her sister Anna in 1834.[20] Howitt was referring primarily to the book market of the early 1830s, which took a downturn after the bank crash of 1826, cholera epidemic of 1831 and political instability during the agitation for the First Reform Bill of 1832. As

[17] Linda K. Hughes, '"Between Politics and Deer-Stalking": Browning's Periodical Poetry', *Victorian Poetry* 52 (Spring 2014), 170.
[18] Quoted in Kathryn Ledbetter, *Tennyson and Victorian Periodicals: Commodities in Context*. Aldershot: Ashgate, 2007, p. 28.
[19] Ledbetter, p. 145.
[20] Mary Howitt to Anna Harrison, 26 February 1834, in Manuscripts and Special Collections, The University of Nottingham; quoted in Linda H. Peterson, *Becoming a Woman of Letters: Myths of Authorship and Facts of the Victorian Market*. Princeton University Press, 2009, p. 106.

book historian Lee Erickson has shown, 'the market for individual volumes of poetry collapsed in the late 1820s', and as Mary and her husband William would learn, 'the literary Annuals were coming to monopolize the giftbook market, which individual volumes of poetry had previously dominated.'[21] Mary contributed poetry to several lesser annuals, including the *Literary Souvenir, Winter's Wreath* and *Juvenile Forget-Me-Not*, presumably for small fees. But in writing to her sister, Howitt was also thinking of the low fees paid for poetry by regional newspapers and magazines, where she placed much of her work. Her letters to Anna frequently remark on her failure to earn money as a poet and, despite praise for her work in reviews, the difficulty of placing work in prestigious magazines that might offer higher payment: 'Were I to send the most beautiful poem to any of the first magazines, the chances are a hundred to one it would never sell.'[22]

There were, of course, notable exceptions to this problem of earning money for periodical poetry, especially among established poets. Felicia Hemans, Howitt's contemporary but already a famous poetess in the 1820s, earned substantial income from her periodical poetry. According to Paula Feldman, between 1823 until her death in 1835 Hemans earned £280.16s.1d for poetry published in the *New Monthly Magazine* and £227.1s.6d for poetry in *Blackwood's Magazine*, together representing more than twenty per cent of her income for this period.[23]

Blackwood's began to feature Hemans's verse in 1827 when she submitted 'The Homes of England':

> The stately Homes of England,
> How beautiful they stand!
> Amidst their tall ancestral trees,
> O'er all the pleasant land!
> The deer across their green-sward bound
> Through shade and sunny gleam;
> And the swan glides past them with the sound
> Of some rejoicing stream.[24]   (1–8)

In what would become one of her most reprinted pieces, Hemans celebrates the 'stately', 'blessed', 'merry', 'cottage' and 'fair, free' homes of England. In offering this poem to *Blackwood's*, she chose work that would

---

[21] Lee Erickson, 'The Market', in Richard Cronin, Alison Chapman and Antony H. Harrison (eds.), *A Companion to Victorian Poetry*. Oxford: Blackwell, 2002, pp. 345–46.

[22] Mary Howitt to Anna Harrison, November 1826, quoted in Peterson, p. 107.

[23] Paula R. Feldman, 'The Poet and the Profits: Felicia Hemans', in Isobel Armstrong and Virginia Blain (eds.), *Women's Poetry, Late Romantic to Late Victorian*. London: Macmillan, 1999, p. 73.

[24] F. H., 'The Homes of England', *Blackwood's Magazine* 21 (April 1827), 392.

appeal to the magazine's readers and engage current topics of interest. For example, Hemans likely knew that the magazine had recently covered questions of surplus population and emigration.[25] 'The Homes of England' does not recommend emigration per se; it celebrates various kinds of *English* homes. By implication, though, such model homes might be re-created in the colonies. The topic – and the poet's treatment of it – appealed to William Blackwood, for he soon invited her to become a regular contributor and even agreed to pay the high rate of twenty-four guineas a sheet for her poetry (more than he paid Walter Scott).[26] Hemans followed with a 'Song of Emigration' as her next submission, a poem directly responding to the lead article for April 1827, 'The Surplus Population of the United Kingdom'.[27]

From 1827 until her death, Hemans appeared regularly in 'Maga' (as *Blackwood's* was called in-house). Further boosting her income, in 1828 the firm of William Blackwood became the publisher of her poetry volumes, beginning with *Records of Woman* (1828) and continuing with *The Forest Sanctuary* (1829), *Songs of the Affections* (1830) and *Scenes and Hymns of Life, with Other Religious Poems* (1834). As with his other authors, Blackwood featured Hemans's verse in the magazine before it appeared within a book – thus increasing his writers' incomes, implicitly advertising his books and overturning Howitt's generalisation that 'poetry don't sell.' Hemans earned profits from both periodical and book formats.

As Erickson's history of the market suggests, another exception to the generalisation that 'poetry don't sell' involved literary annuals. These gift-books, issued late in the year for the Christmas market, featured lavish engravings and stories or poems to accompany them. As luxury items selling for substantial fees (*The Keepsake* sold for a guinea, (£1.1s)), they tended to pay their contributors well, though payment varied according to the prestige of the author. For the 1829 *Keepsake*, for example, Landon contributed verses to accompany the society portrait of Georgiana, Duchess of Bedford, and Hemans contributed 'The Broken Chain' (payment unknown). William Wordsworth received 100 guineas for five poems, two sonnets, two lyrics and a longer work entitled 'The Triad'; one of the lyrics, 'The Country Girl', ran next to a painting of the same title by James Holmes, president of

---

[25] See [John Galt], 'Bandana on Emigration', *Blackwood's Magazine* 15 (April 1824), 433–40, and 20 (September 1826), 470–78.
[26] F. Hemans to William Blackwood, letter of 13 June 1827, in Susan J. Wolfson (ed.), *Felicia Hemans: Selected Poems, Letters, Reception Materials*. University Press, 2000, pp. 494–97.
[27] [David Robinson], 'The Surplus Population of the United Kingdom', *Blackwood's Magazine*, 21 (April 1827), 377–91, and F. H., 'Song of Emigration', *Blackwood's Magazine* 22 (July 1827), 32.

the Society of British Artists. Robert Southey, then poet laureate, wrote 'Lucy and her Bird' to accompany J. M. Wright's scene of a young girl's discovery of a cat killing her pet skylark; he received fifty guineas. Samuel Taylor Coleridge also received fifty guineas for four short epigrams and one longer poem, 'The Garden of Boccacio'. Coleridge remarked that this payment was 'more than all, *I* ever made by all my publications, my week's Salary of 5£ as Writer of the Leading Articles in the Morning Post during the Peace of Amiens excepted'.[28] If writers such as William Wordsworth dismissed the annuals as 'picture-books for grown Children',[29] they nonetheless appreciated the profits that this form of long-interval periodical publication rendered.

Literary annuals peaked in the 1830s, and most died out by the 1850s, leaving poets without this substantial if unesteemed source of income. Later Victorian poets relied on magazines and newspapers for a supplementary source of non-book income. Typical fees for short lyrics in magazines were modest. For example, in 1861 Christina Rossetti received a guinea each (£3.3s total) for 'Up-Hill', 'A Birthday' and 'An Apple-Gathering' in *Macmillan's*; the *Athenaeum* paid her ten pounds for 'Mirrors of Life and Death' in 1877.[30] In 1866, Matthew Arnold received twenty-five pounds for 'Thyrsis', his pastoral elegy for Arthur Hugh Clough, published in *Macmillan's* and the American magazine *Every Saturday*; Arnold noted that this was 'the best pay I have yet had'. More famous authors could garner higher fees. As Alexander Macmillan was sending Rossetti and Arnold modest guineas, he bargained with Tennyson for an original poem, 'Seaside Idyll', and paid £250.[31] In 1869, James Fields of the *Atlantic Monthly* offered George Eliot £300 for 'Agatha', what her biographer Rosemary Ashton calls a 'slight poem', further commenting that *Blackwood's* fee of fifty pounds for 'How Lisa Loved the King' was 'more realistic'.[32] Kipling scholars sometimes claim that the poet's 1899 poem 'The Absent-Minded Beggar' was the most expensive poem of the century. Written for an appeal by the *Daily Mail* to raise money for soldiers

---

[28] Quoted in Paula R. Feldman, 'Introduction', *The Keepsake for 1829*. Petersborough, ON: Broadview, 2006, p. 21. I have relied on Feldman's figures for payments to authors for the 1829 *Keepsake*.

[29] Feldman, *Keepsake*, p. 24.

[30] Marianne van Remoortel, posting on VICTORIA, 1 October 2010; see also Rossetti's letters to Alexander Macmillan, 5 February 1861 and 5 April 1861, acknowledging receipt of post-office-orders for £1-1-0, in *The Letters of Christina Rossetti*, ed. Antony H. Harrison. Charlottesville: University of Virginia Press, 1997, vol. 1, pp. 143, 146, 148.

[31] See Ledbetter, p. 57, for the fees Macmillan paid to Arnold and Tennyson.

[32] Rosemary Ashton, *George Eliot: A Life*. London: Penguin Books, 1997, p. 297.

fighting in the Boer War, it was sold for £250 on publication, its manuscript then sold for £525, and the appeal fund raised £250,000.[33]

Although high fees were the exception rather than the rule, the biographies of nineteenth-century poets suggest that periodical publication was
valued both for its payment and its prestige. And periodicals valued poems
by prestigious poets. Although it may have garnered only twenty-five
pounds, Arnold's 'Thyrsis' opened the April 1866 issue of *Macmillan's*. In
Tennyson's case, Macmillan held back 'Sea Dreams. An Idyll', as the poem
was eventually titled, for several weeks so that it would appear in January
1860 just as the *Cornhill Magazine* was making its debut.[34] Yet even for a
Tennyson or a Kipling, poets could not rely solely on periodicals for their
income. As Elizabeth Barrett Browning's poet-heroine Aurora Leigh dis-
covers, 'no one lives by verse that lives'; to survive in the nineteenth-
century literary marketplace, poets needed multiple sources. So Aurora
writes prose 'for cyclopaedias, magazines, and weekly papers'.[35] In this
diversification, she is typical: in addition to poetry, Landon wrote novels
and reviews; Howitt became a translator of Scandinavian literature; Arnold
wrote learned articles for magazines; Swinburne published reviews, biographies and literary criticism; Eliot wrote essays and novels, turning to
poetry only late in life; Meynell produced art criticism, book introductions
and short essays for periodicals. Only poets with independent incomes or
benevolent grants could afford to avoid periodicals or contribute only
poetry.

Making a Statement

In 1936, the American poet Archibald MacLeish ended his 'Ars Poetica'
with the lines 'A poem should not mean / But be.' The notion that poetry
does not contain a message, advocate a course of action or espouse political
or social causes is not just American or modernist, but it has its roots in late
nineteenth-century British aestheticism. In an 1868 review of William
Morris's poetry, later revised to become the conclusion to *The
Renaissance* (1873), Walter Pater insisted that readers should not pursue
knowledge from literature, but 'the poetic passion, the desire of beauty, the

---

[33] John Lee, posting on VICTORIA, 1 October 2010, provides these figures and queries, Was the *Daily
Mail* correct to claim that this was the most expensive poem of the era? As the sales figures for poems
by Tennyson and Eliot suggest, probably not.
[34] Ledbetter, p. 57.
[35] Elizabeth Barrett Browning, *Aurora Leigh*, ed. Kerry McSweeney. Oxford: World's Classics, 1993,
Book 3, ll. 307, 310–11.

love of art for its own sake'.[36] In 1890, Oscar Wilde famously prefaced *A Picture of Dorian Gray* with these aphorisms: 'The artist is the creator of beautiful things ... No artist desires to prove anything ... All art is quite useless.'[37] Even earlier in the century, literary critics distinguished rhetoric (in prose) from expression (in poetry) – as in John Stuart Mill's famous comment that 'eloquence is *heard*, poetry is *overheard*.'[38]

Despite this critical tradition of separating poetry from rhetoric, much Victorian poetry addressed serious moral, social and political questions, and eloquently expressed the poet's perspective or position. This was especially true for newspaper poetry. As Natalie M. Houston demonstrates for *The Times* of the 1860s, poetry printed in the newspaper 'participated in the larger shared public discourse of current events', offering 'emotional responses to current events in different language than that of the daily news'.[39] These responses might be humorous or nostalgic, patriotic or elegiac – as Houston illustrates with verse about St James's in past eras, patriotic lines about the London Volunteers who trained to defend Britain from invasion, and an elegy about mountaineers who died in an accident on the Matterhorn. Regional newspapers similarly included poetry that engaged with current events, as Kirstie Blair's study of working-class papers in Dundee suggests. Working-class poets were as likely to address international questions (the Risorgimento) as local concerns ('industrial development and its effect on the Scottish countryside') or personal matters ('love unreturned').[40]

Magazine poetry reveals a greater range in the *modes* of response to current events and greater *originality* in an attempt to make news. Whereas the typical newspaper poem was twenty-five to forty lines,[41] magazines allowed poets more scope. The examples in the remainder of this section focus on two broad issues that provoked poets into print: the conditions of the working-class poor in the 1830s and 1840s and Louis Napoleon's erratic, often threatening career as president, then emperor of France in the 1850s and 1860s.

---

[36] Walter Pater, *The Renaissance: Studies in Art and Poetry*, ed. Adam Phillips. Oxford University Press, 1986, p. 153.

[37] Oscar Wilde, *The Picture of Dorian Gray*, ed. Richard Ellmann. New York: Bantam Classic, 2005, pp. 3–4.

[38] Antiquus [John Stuart Mill], 'What Is Poetry?' *Monthly Repository* n.s. 7 (January 1833), 64.

[39] Natalie M. Houston, 'Newspaper Poems: Material Texts in the Public Sphere', *Victorian Studies* 50.2 (Winter 2008), 239.

[40] Kirstie Blair, '"A Very Poetical Town": Newspaper Poetry and the Working-Class Poet in Victorian Dundee', *Victorian Poetry* 52.1 (Spring 2014), 98, 103.

[41] Hobbs and Januszewski, p. 73.

When, for example, Elizabeth Gaskell and her husband William published 'Sketches among the Poor' in *Blackwood's Magazine* (January 1837), they chose to narrate the life story of single, working-class woman whose deeds of kindness enrich the lives of her neighbours:

> A call upon her tenderness whene'er
> The friends around her had a grief to share;
> And if in joy the kind one they forgot,
> She still rejoiced, and more was wanted not.[42]

In this sketch, the Gaskells show the complexity of urban workers' lives, their love of home and family and their ability to perform acts of goodness even in impoverished conditions. Like the industrial novels Gaskell would later write, *Mary Barton* (1848) and *North and South* (1854–5), the narrative mode aims to reveal a class unknown to middle-class readers and to bring the classes into dialogue based on common experience (familial love, neighbourly affection) and emotions (charity, pity, benevolence). Although the Gaskells were not the only authors to write about industrial workers, their poem (and their series, had they completed it) helped make those workers visible to *Blackwood's* readers; they did not state a moral, but their readers understood that they should not homogenise the working poor.

Other poets used different modes to reveal the plight of industrial workers. Elizabeth Barrett combines protest, proclamation and prophecy in 'The Cry of the Children', written after reading Richard Hengist Horne's 'Report of the Royal Commission on the Employment of Children and Very Young People in Mines and Factories' published in *Blackwood's Magazine* in August 1843. In a scathing exposé of the working conditions of child labourers, Horne and his fellow commissioners describe children who work below ground for twelve hours a day, never seeing sunlight until their Sunday off; girls clad in rags who stand in water all day; seven-year-old boys apprenticed until age twenty-one who receive nothing in return for their work but food, clothing and lodging; and unsafe working conditions for children and adult workers alike. In the first line of 'The Cry', Barrett addresses a male audience:

> Do you hear the children weeping, O my brothers,
> Ere the sorrow comes with years?

---

[42] [William and Elizabeth Gaskell], 'Sketches Among the Poor, No. 1', *Blackwood's Edinburgh Magazine* 41 (January 1837), 48–50, in *Journalism, Early Fiction and Personal Writings*, vol. 1, ed. Joanne Shattock, in *The Works of Elizabeth Gaskell*, ed. Joanne Shattock. London: Pickering & Chatto, 2005, pp. 33–35.

> They are leaning their young heads against their mothers, –
> And *that* cannot stop their tears.[43]

The distinction between men responsible for the mistreatment of working children and women who cannot intervene to save them acknowledges, even as it challenges, the doctrine of 'separate spheres': women who are limited to providing emotional support cannot alter the appalling working conditions in England's mines and factories. By confronting her 'brothers' and publishing their misdemeanours in a major magazine, Barrett breaks out of her designated sphere. Further, she voices the children's grief and weariness from long days working and their desire for sleep in death, death as sleep:

> Alas, the wretched children! they are seeking
> Death in life, as best to have!
> They are binding up their hearts away from breaking,
> With a cerement from the grave.[44]

By the final lines of the poem, the children turn from weeping to cursing the 'tyrants' whose 'mailed heel' treads on and crushes them. Although the final curse is voiced as the children's, it is also the poet's aligning herself with the Hebrew prophets:

> 'How long', they say, 'how long, O cruel nation,
> Will you stand, to move the world, on a child's heart?'[45]

This curse, now directed to the 'nation', requires every reader to respond, and men in power to take action. According to Julia Holloway Bolton, with this poem composed on 'her sickbed, EBB influenced legislation in Parliament'.[46]

Thomas Hood's 'Song of a Shirt', published anonymously in *Punch* on 16 December 1843, similarly addresses a problem of industrial work, in this case 'sweated labour' in textile manufacturing. Hood wrote the poem after reading a police report in *The Times* on 26 October 1843, which described 'a wretched-looking woman named Biddell, with a squalid-half starved infant at her breast'. A seamstress who sewed shirts and trousers from materials provided by her employer, Biddell had pawned the garments she had made to feed herself and her children and was arrested for doing so. *The Times* followed with an article called 'The White Slaves of London'

---

[43] Elizabeth B. Barrett, 'The Cry of the Children', *Blackwood's Magazine* 54 (August 1843), 260–62.
[44] Barrett, p. 261.   [45] Barrett, p. 262.
[46] Elizabeth Barrett Browning, *Aurora Leigh and Other Poems*, ed. John Robert Glorney Bolton and Julia Bolton Holloway. London: Penguin, 1995, p. 495.

and an editorial stating that the London seamstress was 'as much a slave as any negro who ever toiled under as cruel taskmasters in the West Indies'.[47]

Hood uses a popular meter (three stresses per line) to introduce the plight of the seamstress:

> With fingers weary and worn,
> With eyelids heavy and red,
> A woman sat in unwomanly rags,
> Plying her needle and thread –
> Stitch! Stitch! Stitch!
> In poverty, hunger, and dirt,
> And still with a voice of dolorous pitch
> She sang 'The Song of the Shirt!'[48]

With the refrains 'Work! work! work!' and 'Stitch! Stitch! Stitch', the seamstress describes the repetitive labour, the poverty of her life and the ever-present vision of death. Like the Gaskells' sketch of a Manchester labourer, Hood's poem contrasts conditions of urban life ('A bed of straw, / A crust of bread – and rags. / That shatter'd roof – and this naked floor – / A table – a broken chair') with memories of a country childhood ('the cowslip and primrose sweet – / With the sky above my head, / And the grass beneath my feet'). Hood's 'Song' inspired paintings of the weary seamstress by Richard Redgrave, George Frederick Watts and Anna Blunden, and it was set to music in Britain and America.

Periodical poetry not only addressed issues at home; it was also thoroughly international. Poets wrote about slavery in America, uprisings in India, settlements in Australia, exploration of Africa and European politics. In the latter category, one figure who provoked almost every major poet to a response was Louis Napoleon (1808–73), president of the Second French Republic and then, as Napoleon III, emperor of the Second French Empire. Louis Napoleon's actions throughout life seemed ambivalent if not downright contradictory. Early in life, he had fought with the Carbonari against Austrian domination of Italy, but as president, he deployed French troops to restore Pope Pius IX as ruler of the Papal States after the Italian revolutionaries Mazzini and Garibaldi overthrew him. In 1851, as his legal term as president came to an end, he staged a *coup d'état*, dissolved the national assembly, imposed press censorship, rewrote the constitution to allow the president to serve an unlimited number of terms, and arrested opponents or sent them into exile (Victor Hugo among

---

[47] *The Times*, 27 October 1843, 4.
[48] [Thomas Hood], 'The Song of the Shirt', *Punch, or the London Charivari*, 16 December 1843, 260.

them). In the late 1850s, Louis Napoleon, now Napoleon III, sent French troops to northern Italy to drive out the Austrians. An avid supporter of Il Risorgimento, Barrett Browning praised this act on behalf of Italian freedom, but when Italy was then asked (or forced) to cede Nice and Savoy to France, she was dismayed at his duplicity; to John Forster she wrote: 'Savoy has given me pain . . . I would rather not hear Robert say, for instance: "It was a great action; but he has taken eighteenpence for it, which is a pity."'[49]

For Tennyson, Louis Napoleon represented a threat of continental war and a challenge to Britain's military power. As poet laureate, he was among the first to publish periodical verse in response to Louis Napoleon's *coup d'ètat*, staged on the anniversary of the coronation of Napoleon I. Tennyson supported the concept of a voluntary rifleman's corps to protect British coasts against French invasion and submitted 'Britons, Guard Your Own' to the *Examiner* (31 January 1852), followed by 'The Third of February, 1852' (7 February 1852) and 'Hands All Round!' (7 February 1852). The first calls on British citizens to defend their coasts:

> Rise, Britons, rise, if manhood be not dead;
> The world's last tempest darkens overhead;
>   The Pope has blessed him;
>   The Church caressed him;
> He triumphs; may be, we shall stand alone:
>   Britons, guard your own.[50]   (ll. 1–6)

The second poem chastises the House of Lords for applauding an attack on the British press 'for antagonising Napoleon':

> My Lords, we heard you speak; you told us all
>   That England's honest censure went too far;
> That our free press should cease to brawl
>   Not sting the fiery Frenchman into war.[51]   (ll. 1–4)

The third drinks health to the Englishman 'who loves his native country best' and curses 'the crimes of southern kings, / The Russian whips and Austrians' rods' and, in the case of modern France, prays God 'the tyrant's cause confound'.[52] These poems, signed 'Merlin', addressed an immediate political situation that Tennyson believed to be dangerous. Composed in

[49] Quoted in Allan C. and Susan E. Dooley, eds., *Prince Hohenstiel-Schwangau, The Complete Works of Robert Browning*. Athens: Ohio University Press, 1999, Vol. 10, p. 244.
[50] 'Britons, Guard Your Own', in Christopher Ricks (ed.), *The Poems of Tennyson*. New York: Norton, 1969, p. 998.
[51] 'The Third of February, 1852', in Ricks, ed., p. 1000.
[52] 'Hands All Round!' in Ricks, ed., p. 1002.

rousing verse and some set to music by his wife Emily, Tennyson intended that the poems should capture the reader's patriotic imagination.

Two decades later, Swinburne's periodical verse on Louis Napoleon focuses on the betrayal of republican principles that the man's early career had promised. In November 1869, during the Franco-Prussian War, Swinburne published four sonnets in the *Fortnightly Review* under the ironic title 'Intercession'; although the poet does not name Louis Napoleon, it is clear that the prayer for torments to overtake this man and the curse that ends the sonnets –

> A name, a dream, a less thing than the least,
> Hover awhile above him with closed wings,
> Till the coiled soul, an evil snake-shaped beast,
> Eat its base bodily lair of flesh away.[53]

– are intended for the French emperor. As William Michael Rossetti commented in his diary: 'Swinburne sent round to me, for my perusal and opinion on one or two alternative expressions, his ruthless sonnets for the not-too-speedy death of Louis Napoleon. They are very forcible.'[54] In 1870, after Napoleon III's defeat at the battle of Sedan and the announcement of a new French government, Swinburne quickly composed an 'Ode of the Proclamation of the French Republic, September 4th, 1870'. 'I could not wait and let it miss the nick of time to appear in', Swinburne wrote to Charles Howell,[55] so the 'Ode' appeared as a pamphlet rather than in a periodical. When Louis Napoleon finally died in January 1873, Swinburne returned to the periodical format with a series of sonnets in the *Examiner*, steadily appearing from 22 March to 14 June 1873. Under the rubric 'Dirae' (the Furies), the sonnets begin: 'Go down to hell. This end is good to see.'[56] In the final poem, 'Apologia', the poet justifies his 'wrath', which has 'embitter[ed] the sweet mouth of song'[57] by citing the sufferings human beings had endured under Louis Napoleon's misguided reign.

In thinking about periodical versus book formats for political poetry, it is useful to consider the poet's immediate and long-term intentions. Tennyson wanted to rouse Britons to military readiness. A committed

---

[53] Algernon Charles Swinburne, 'Intercession, IV', *Fortnightly Review* 6 (November 1869), ' 510.

[54] William Michael Rossetti, comp. *Rossetti Papers, 1862 to 1870*. London: Sands & Co., 1913, entry for 18 October 1869, p. 411.

[55] Thomas J. Wise, ed., *A Bibliography of the Writings in Prose and Verse of Algernon Charles Swinburne*. London: Richard Clay & Sons, 1919, p. 196.

[56] A. C. Swinburne, 'Dirae', *Examiner*, No. 3399 (22 March 1873), 307.

[57] A. C. Swinburne, 'Dirae', *Examiner*, No. 3411 (14 June 1873), 615.

republican, Swinburne wanted to comment forcefully on, and intervene in, political events. Robert Browning's musings on Louis Napoleon's failures in *Prince Hohenstiel-Schwangau, Saviour of Society* (1871) link to political debates widely conducted in magazines and newspapers, but the poet's intention was not direct political engagement. Instead, *Prince Hohenstiel-Schwangau*, a poem of 2,146 lines published as a book, anatomises its subject and reflects on motives. As a reviewer in the *Examiner* of 23 December 1871 noted, Browning does not use poetry 'for working on the sentiments of [his] hearers concerning patriotism or religion, sexual passion and the like'; rather, his forte is 'to analyse the minds of men as deftly as a surgeon can dissect their bodies' – hence his achievement as 'a practiced soul-anatomist' in *Prince Hohenstiel-Schwangau*.[58]

Perhaps these different modes of political engagement simply reflect the poets' inclinations rather than the publishing formats. Swinburne would be Swinburne (cursing the despotism of Louis Napoleon), and Browning would be Browning (analysing a political despot's psychological self-justifications), no matter the forms in which they circulated their political views. Yet the poets seem to have considered print culture as they shaped their poems and used periodicals when their goals were immediate. If some of their periodical poems have become classic or canonical, that may reveal that the common distinction between 'journalism' and 'literature' simply does not hold.

[58] Anon, 'Mr. Browning's Saviour of Society', *Examiner*, No. 3334 (23 December 1871), 1267.

PART II

The Press and the Public

CHAPTER 9

The Press and the Law

Martin Hewitt

'A newspaper proprietor lately remarked to me that all the profits of an honest journal were destined to find their way into the pockets of the lawyers.'[1]

Nothing more fundamentally defined the identity of the British press in the nineteenth century than its 'freedom'. In contrast to the press of continental Europe,[2] it was free from direct state censorship. On the other hand, unlike America, where liberty of expression was constitutionally enshrined, the formal legal sanction of British press freedom was meagre, merely, in the words of Lord Chief Justice Mansfield, 'consist[ing] in printing without any previous licence, subject to the consequences of the law'.[3]

The 'consequences of the law', as nineteenth-century proprietors, printers, editors, journalists and newsagents were all too aware, were legion. Although legal guides for the press naturally focused on the laws relating to copyright and libel, the reality was that newspapers needed to accommodate themselves to all sorts of legal requirements. Employing staff, publishing advertisements, using printing machinery,[4] all created legal liabilities, and the idiosyncrasies of Victorian legislation left many traps for the careless or the ignorant, such as conviction for advertising a reward for the return of stolen property, made potentially illegal by the 1861 Larceny Act. William Lucy, later editor of the *Daily News*, characteristically recalled carefully studying 'a handy little volume of the "Law of Partnership"' before entering into his first editorial

---

[1] John B. Hopkins, 'Liberty and Libel', *Gentleman's Magazine* 9 (August 1872), 185–95, 185. My thanks to Michael Lobban for his suggestions.

[2] R. J. Goldstein, *Political Censorship of the Arts and the Press in Nineteenth Century Europe*. Basingstoke: Macmillan, 1989.

[3] Quoted in C. Kent, 'The Editor and the Law', in Joel Wiener (ed.), *Innovators and Preachers. The Role of the Editor in Victorian England*. Westport, CT: Greenwood Press, 1985, pp. 99–119, 100.

[4] See Arthur Powell's *The Law Specially Affecting Printers, Publishers and Newspaper Proprietors*. London: Stevens and Sons, 1887.

responsibilities.[5] Given the number of insolvencies, perhaps bankruptcy law and its courts were the most significant legal processes for the nineteenth-century press.

The law was also, of course, a staple of nineteenth-century newsprint, only eclipsed by politics in the number of column inches it generated. Legal obligations to publish and announce created valuable revenue, threats to which were fiercely resisted. A paper such as *The Times*, which saw the quality of its law reports as integral to its reputation, might maintain a substantial cadre of expert reporters. But for the most part, reporting the law courts was the unglamorous end of Victorian journalism, part of the 'bitter sorrow' of a journalistic apprenticeship, or the home of penny-a-liners scavenging for a profitable murder.[6] While the metropolitan dailies provided detailed coverage of the London courts, provincial papers devoted considerable space to magistrates', coroners' and assize courts. Through their 'Answers to Correspondents' columns, working-class papers acted as legal advisors to their readers.[7] Beneath this was a substratum of the press, most enduringly the *Illustrated Police News* (1864–1938), providing lurid details of criminal life drawn from the police courts.[8] Although the evolution was not straightforward, from the 1850s the new cheap papers increasingly imported the styles of popular sensation journalism into the mainstream press.[9] Murders were already generating prurient attention in the 1820s and 1830s, when the press still competed with broadsides. In the early 1840s, the *Illustrated London News* was initially conceived as entirely a record of crime.[10] A good murder trial could triple or quadruple sales and even persuade weekly papers to publish daily. The 'Ardlamont Mystery' trial in Edinburgh in 1893 attracted twenty feature writers, fifteen artists and more than seventy reporters.

In this context, it is perhaps not surprising that socially and culturally the connections between press and law were strong, especially in London,

[5] H. W. Lucy, *Sixty Years in the Wilderness*. London: Smith, Elder, 1911, pp. 42–43.

[6] 'Advice to a Young Journalist, by An Old Hand', *Bookman* (January 1892), 140–42.

[7] Thomas Catling recalls that Jonas Levy, founder of *Lloyds*, trained as a barrister and wrote the Answers to Correspondents for more than fifty years, *My Life's Pilgrimage*. London: John Murray, 1911, pp. 228–29.

[8] See Linda Stratmann, *Cruel Deeds and Dreadful Calamities: The Illustrated Police News 1864–1938*. London: British Library, 2011.

[9] Thomas Boyle, *Black Swine in the Sewers of Hampstead. Beneath the Surface of Victorian Sensationalism*. London: Hodder and Stoughton, 1989, *passim*.

[10] R. D. Altick, *Victorian Studies in Scarlet*. New York: Norton, 1970, p. 60 for this and subsequent material.

where in and around Fleet Street, newspapers jostled for space with the inns of court,[11] the rooms of journalists and barristers existing cheek by jowl.[12] Neophyte lawyers frequently supplemented their fees with journalistic work, just as many of the literary journalists of the London press initially trained for the law. In his youth, Frederick Knight Hunt, founder of the *Medical Times* and later editor of the *Daily News*, worked in the printing office of the *Morning Herald* at night, and as a barrister's clerk during the day.[13] The law also provided its fair share of prominent journalists, editors and proprietors, perhaps most notably Edward William Cox, proprietor of *The Field* and *The Queen*, founder of *Exchange and Mart* and the *Law Times*, a barrister who rose to be deputy assistant judge at Middlesex sessions while establishing himself as one the century's most vigorous newspaper entrepreneurs.

Despite these connections, relations between the law and the press were fractious through much of the century. The suspicion long persisted that the judiciary had a jaundiced view of the press. In the mid-1840s, moves to ban barristers in the Oxford and Western Circuits from reporting for newspapers created a fierce controversy about legal prejudice against journalism, especially newspaper journalism.[14] But judging by the autobiographical writings of William Jerdan, editor of the *Literary Gazette*, press prejudice against the law could be equally virulent.[15] There was intermittent debate as to whether newspaper editors or proprietors were fit persons for the magistracy; in 1869 the Provincial Newspaper Society protested when the nomination of F. W. Cutbush of the *South Eastern Gazette* was vetoed.[16] Although the status of journalism steadily improved as the century progressed, notwithstanding the emergence of the 'higher journalism', undergraduates at Oxford in the 1880s were still directed to the bar and warned off journalism as an 'impossible profession' 'fatal to good manners and honest thought'.[17]

---

[11] E. Beresford Chancellor, *The Annals of Fleet Street*. London: Chapman & Hall, 1912.
[12] [Thomas Wemyss Reid and William Henry Cooke], *Briefs and Papers. Sketches of the Bar and the Press*. London: H. S. King, 1872, p. 6.
[13] J. L. Hunt, 'Dr Frederick Knight Hunt (1814–54) Revisited: Medical Man and Journalist', *Journal of Medical Biography* 14.3 (August 2006), 129–35.
[14] J.-M. Schramm, 'The Anatomy of a Barrister's Tongue: Rhetoric, Satire and the Victorian Bar in England', *Victorian Literature and Culture*, 32.2, (2004), 295–97.
[15] *The Autobiography of William Jerdan, with his Literary, Political and Social Reminiscences* 4 vols. London, 1852.
[16] *Huddersfield Chronicle*, 2 October 1869.
[17] J. A. Spender, *Life, Journalism and Politics*. London: Cassell, 1927, p. 22, quoting Benjamin Jowett.

Repression

The first third of the century produced an especially hostile environment for the press. As William St Clair has suggested, 'during the Romantic period and later, the British state mounted the last sustained attempt in the country's history to control the minds of citizens by controlling their access to print.'[18] Lord Sidmouth, home secretary, 1812–22, described the press as the 'most malignant and formidable enemy to the constitution'.[19] Newspaper proprietors, printers and newsvendors were subjected both to new legislation and the weight of common law. The 1799 Seditious Societies Act made the registration of all presses and printing types compulsory and required the printer's name on all printed matter and the retention of a file of all printing for inspection. Extensive use was made of the three categories of 'disorderly libel', under which newspapers were subject to state prosecution for printing material deemed seditious, blasphemous or obscene. Judicial pronouncements propagated a broad compass for disorderly libels: the press could point out to the government its errors, but to appeal to the passions of the lower orders was sedition, and 'prosecuting societies' such as the Society for the Suppression of Vice (1802–) searched vigilantly for any sign of licentiousness.[20] Efforts were made to try to drive newspapers beyond the purchasing power of the poor. The newspaper stamp was increased from the 1d of 1776 to 4d by 1815. Excise duties were imposed on newspaper advertisements and on paper. The proliferation of radical journals, such as Cobbett's *Twopenny Trash* and Wooler's *Black Dwarf* after 1815 prompted further legislation, including the Blasphemous and Seditious Libels Act and the Newspaper Stamp Duties Act (1819) which required proprietors to find sureties against fines for libel, forced publications appearing more frequently than monthly to be stamped as newspapers, and according to Philip Harling had a 'devastating effect on the radical press'.[21]

During these years, press prosecutions were endemic, and not just for the radical press: in 1813 Leigh and John Hunt, editor and printer of the

[18] W. St Clair, *The Reading Nation in the Romantic Period*. Cambridge University Press, 2004, p. 309.
[19] Quoted in R. J. Goldstein, 'A Land of Relative Freedom: Censorship of the Press and the Arts in the Nineteenth Century (1815–1914)', in Paul Hyland and Neil Sammels, *Writing and Censorship in Britain*. New York: Routledge, 1992, pp. 125–40, 129.
[20] Judgement of Mr Justice Best, quoted W. H. Wickwar, *The Struggle for the Freedom of the Press*. London: Allen and Unwin, 1928, pp. 118–19.
[21] Philip Harling, 'The Law of Libel and the Limits of Repression, 1790–1832', *Historical Journal* (2001), 107–34, which informs much of the following material (quote at 131).

Examiner, were convicted for publishing a 'scandalous and defamatory' libel on the Prince Regent.[22] During 1817–20, it is possible to identify as many as 175 politically inspired libel prosecutions.[23] Defendants were denied information about the nature of the charges they faced. Judges were biased, juries often deliberately packed. But this was only the heavy artillery. Legal pressure operated pervasively through 'informations'. Technically, these were merely expedited prosecutions instituted by the attorney general. But because they often required the posting of substantial sureties, allowed months of imprisonment without trial and were open ended, they could be left hanging over journalists for years.[24] By later standards, sentences were savage: Daniel Lovell, proprietor and editor of the *Statesman*, spent more than four years in Newgate prison (1812–16), because having served his initial eighteen-month sentence, he was unable to find the securities for good behaviour required for his release.

Paradoxically, radical editors used the constraints of the libel laws to constitute spaces of opposition, both textual and physical. As Kevin Gilmartin comments, 'trials for seditious and blasphemous libel became a key forum for radical assembly and verbal expression'; they were 'intensely combative and dialectical, spilling from the courtroom to the press and back again'.[25] Fox's Libel Act of 1792 made it the responsibility of juries to determine both the fact of publication and whether it amounted to sedition; thereafter, libel trials were, as Harling has noted, 'a perilous gamble for the government'.[26] Editors and journalists used the latitude given them in court to draw out the absurdities and prejudices of 'judge-made law' and persuade jurors, notwithstanding direct judicial instruction, to find in their favour.[27] When Richard Carlile was prosecuted for selling Paine's *Age of Reason*, he was not only able to sell all his stock of the book but also increased the circulation of his *Republican* by 5,000 to 15,000. Prison did not always deter or restrain: several of Carlile's shopmen spent two years in Newgate publishing the

---

[22] For details of prosecutions, see *Return of Individuals Prosecuted for Political Libel and Seditious Conduct . . .*, *British Parliamentary Papers* (1821), p. 379.

[23] See Wickwar, *Struggle*, 97–114; Donald Thomas, 'Press Prosecutions of the Eighteenth and Nineteenth Centuries: The Evidence of King's Bench Indictments', *The Library* 32 (1977), 315–32, 327–28.

[24] Harling, 'Limits of Repression', p. 113.

[25] Kevin Gilmartin, *Print Politics. The Press and Radical Opposition in Early Nineteenth Century England*. Cambridge University Press, 1996, p. 115.

[26] Harling, 'Limits of Repression', p. 110.

[27] See A. Prentice, *Historical Sketches and Personal Recollections of Manchester*. London, 1851, pp. 386–91.

anti-Christian *Newgate Monthly Magazine.*[28] Equally it is clear that successive bouts of imprisonment could blunt oppositional journalism. T. J. Evans, editor of the *Manchester Observer*, imprisoned for eighteen months in 1820, resumed his journalistic career, but in the markedly more respectable and moderate guise of parliamentary reporter with the *British Press.*[29]

This assault on the press gradually ebbed in the 1820s and 1830s. not because the state sought to relax its grip, or because of any legislative change, but rather because direct assault came to be seen as counter-productive.[30] Aled Jones suggests that two landmark cases, the failure of the Duke of Wellington to prosecute the *Morning Chronicle* in 1829 and the acquittal in 1831 of William Cobbett in a case brought by government ministers, heralded the abandonment of any widespread application of the libel laws for political purposes.[31] At the same time, the press was gradually obtaining some limited legal recognition of its rights to publish. In 1840, newspapers formally obtained the right to report parliamentary debates. By a series of legal judgements, the press also acquired qualified privilege to report on proceedings in the law courts, initially in the London Courts of Justice, but by mid-century extending to local magistrates' courts on the same terms.[32] Nonetheless, press liberty remained a matter of toleration not right, of 'popular sympathy rather than . . . legislative enactment' as the *Morning Star* put it in 1860.[33]

Political Prosecutions in the Final Two-thirds of the Century

As the government abandoned repression, state prosecution theoretically became something that marked the subjugation of the foreign press. Even so, the overhaul of the libel laws in 1843 left prohibitions of 'disorderly libel' essentially untouched, and indeed at times sedition laws were not only used but reinforced. Political prosecutions waned, but they did not cease entirely.[34] Chartist editors including Bronterre O'Brien and Feargus

---

[28] Harling, 'Limits of Repression', p. 119.

[29] Iain McCalman, *Radical Underworld: Prophets, Revolutionaries and Pornographers in London, 1795–1840.* Cambridge University Press, 1993, pp. 183–84.

[30] For the background, and replacement of libel prosecutions with those for unlawful assembly, see M. J. Lobban, 'From Seditious Libel to Unlawful Assembly: Peterloo and the Changing Face of Political Crime, c.1770–1820', *Oxford Journal of Legal Studies*, 10.2 (1990), 307–52.

[31] Aled Jones, *Powers of the Press. Newspapers, Power and the Public in Nineteenth Century England.* Aldershot: Ashgate, 1996, p. 13.

[32] Kent, 'Editor and the Law', p. 109.   [33] Quoted *Belfast News*, 15 December 1860.

[34] Various instances detailed in Wickwar, *Struggle*, especially in the early 1820s, inc. pp. 221–38.

O'Connor in the 1840s, and Irish nationalist editors including John Mitchell, editor of the *United Irishman* in 1848, were imprisoned or transported for seditious speeches or articles. In the late 1880s, Irish newspaper proprietors were imprisoned under the Coercion Act merely for reporting meetings of the suppressed National League, and shopkeepers for selling the *United Irishman*.[35] *Reynolds's Weekly News* observed in 1866 that 'in Ireland the press is under a more crushing and remorseless censorship than that which prevails in France.'[36]

In Britain, obscenity was of more enduring significance than sedition. Prior to the 1868 'Hicklin ruling', which broadened the definition of obscenity to that which 'has the tendency to deprave and corrupt', obscenity had been governed by the common law of obscene libel, given statutory authority and enhanced police powers but not fundamentally altered by the 1857 Obscene Publications Act. In proposing the 1857 act, Lord Campbell had called attention to 'periodical papers of the most licentious and disgusting description'.[37] In fact, the law was more usually applied to pornographic pamphlets and novels of dubious morality than to the press. Even in the early decades of the century, when the links between radicalism and pornography had been particularly strong, although prosecutions and imprisonments occurred, a figure such as Henry Vizetelly, editor of the *Satirist* (1831–49), 'a ferocious anti-Tory scandal rag' which supposedly earned him substantial blackmail fees, was as likely to be horsewhipped as prosecuted.[38]

There were occasional prosecutions. The London publisher William Strange was convicted in the mid-1850s for selling two penny magazines, *Women of London* and *Paul Pry*, and in 1870 Charles Grieves endured a year's hard labour for publishing an illustration of bare-legged dancing girls on the cover of his weekly, *The Ferret*.[39] But at the same time from the 1840s, the risqué narratives characteristic of the penny fiction papers spread to popular journalism which, especially after the creation of the Divorce Court in 1857, dwelt increasingly on what the *Saturday Review* called 'a whole class of cases the discussion of which, though not

---

[35] J. J. Clancy, *Mr Balfour as a Lover of Truth*. London: Irish Press Agency, 1888, pp. 4–5.

[36] *Reynolds's Weekly News*, 12 January 1866.

[37] Quoted in Katherine Mullin, 'Poison More Deadly than Prussic Acid: Defining Obscenity after the 1857 Obscene Publications Act (1850–1885)', in David Bradshaw and Rachel Potter (eds.), *Prudes on the Prowl: Fiction and Obscenity in England, 1850 to the Present Day*. Oxford University Press, 2013, p. 13.

[38] McCalman, *Radical Underworld*, pp. 219–37, quote at p. 225.

[39] Donald Thomas, *Freedom's Frontier. Censorship in Modern Britain*. London: John Murray, 2008, p. 44.

necessarily obscene' was 'always hovering on the verges of the prurient'.[40]
The Yelverton bigamy trials of 1857, whose influence on the sensation
fiction of the 1860s has been widely acknowledged, was only one of
a series of similar *causes célèbres*.[41] This sort of journalism was increasingly central to attempts to construct mass reading audiences in the final
third of the century.[42] In the 1880s, lobbying of the Home Office to take
action against vulgar, vile and pernicious periodicals prompted informal
pressure on the press to self-censor coverage of divorce cases and criminal trials.[43] In 1879, Adolphus Rosenberg, editor of *Town Talk*, was
sentenced to eighteen months in prison for reporting that the actress
Lillie Langtry had had an affair with Prince Albert.[44] In normal circumstances, however, there was little legal restraint on coverage of this sort.
Significantly, the imprisonment of W. T. Stead, editor of the *Pall Mall
Gazette*, in the notorious 'Maiden Tribute of Modern Babylon' case of
1885, with its lurid accounts of rape and abduction, was for child
abduction not obscenity.

In the case of blasphemy, too, a common law offence constituted in
the sixteenth and seventeenth centuries, reinforced by statute in the
1830s, but imprecise as to the boundaries of acceptable criticism of
religion, was generally applied, if at all, to books rather than periodicals,
and as in the prosecution of Henry Hetherington, champion of the
unstamped press, largely touched on the press only indirectly. Although
prosecutions were rare, as Joss Marsh has suggested, blasphemy laws
provided weapons which could be used as surrogates for more general
hostility to the press. From this perspective, the prosecution of
G. W. Foote, editor of the *Freethinker*, who was sentenced
in March 1883 to a year in prison, reflected intensified anxieties at the
'new tabloid press, and the expansion and dumbing down of the journalistic public sphere'.[45]

---

[40] Allison Pease, *Modernism, Mass Culture and the Aesthetics of Obscenity*. Cambridge University Press,
2000; 'A Month in the Divorce Court', *Saturday Review*, 8 January 1859, 36.

[41] Lauren Harmsen Kiehna, 'Sensation and the Fourth Estate: *The Times* and the Yelverton Bigamy
Trials', *Victorian Periodicals Review*, 47.1 (Spring 2014); Richard D. Altick, *Deadly Encounters. Two
Victorian Sensations* Philadelphia: Pennsylvania University Press, 1986.

[42] J. Walkowitz, *City of Dreadful Delight. Narratives of Sexual Danger in Late Victorian London*.
University of Chicago Press, 1992.

[43] Joss Marsh, *Word Crimes: Blasphemy, Culture and Literature in Nineteenth Century England*.
University of Chicago Press, 1998, pp. 208–10; John B. Hopkins, 'The Liberty of the Press',
Tinsley's Magazine 40 (1887), 120–35.

[44] Allison Lee, 'A Secret Censorship', in A. D. Pionke and D. D. Millstein (eds.), *Victorian Secrecy:
Economies of Knowledge and Concealment*. Farnham: Ashgate, 2010, p. 184.

[45] Marsh, *Word Crimes*, p. 155.

The 'Liberalisation' of Press Control

As the significance of political libel ebbed from the 1820s, the burden of state attempts to control the press shifted to the fiscal exactions which became known as 'the taxes on knowledge', the advertising duty, the paper excise and in particular the newspaper stamp duty, which emerged from the relaxations of state pressure unscathed. The constraints were not merely financial. The necessity to print on stamped paper involved presses in considerable labour; it was not unknown for the lack of stamped paper to involve the cancellation of an entire edition.[46] Before 1848 when the loophole was closed, a number of titles were printed in Jersey and the Isle of Man to circumvent stamp legislation.

In the early 1830s, government attempts to suppress those radical papers, such as Cobbett's *Political Register*, which had survived the enforcement of the legislation of 1819, turned primarily to the stamp regulations, initiating what became known as the 'war of the unstamped'. The Stamp Office warned and then prosecuted editors of unstamped newspapers. Printers were tracked down and their presses confiscated. Stocks of unstamped papers were seized. Patricia Hollis notes that between 1830 and 1836, at least 1,130 cases of selling unstamped papers were considered by the London magistrates, and by 1836 almost 800 people had been imprisoned.[47] None of this prevented the most successful of the unstamped papers achieving large sales: by 1836 the combined sales of the *Poor Man's Guardian* and the *Weekly Police Gazette* exceeded that of *The Times*. Faced with threats from the owners of the stamped press of evasion of the duty, the 1836 Newspaper Stamp Act cut the stamp from 4d to 1d while toughening the police's powers to confiscate printing presses, and increasing the securities required by newspaper proprietors.

The settlement of the 1830s was a carefully calculated compromise. The rug of public sympathy was pulled out from under the promoters of the unstamped press. The advertising duty, although reduced from 3/6 to 1/6, encouraged substantial weekly publication, rather than smaller more frequent issues, because this retained maximum currency for expensive advertisements. This and the effectively enforced penny stamp helped shore up the established press, *The Times* in London, and the leading county weeklies in the provinces, and for twenty years entrenched

---

[46] For this and following paragraphs see my *The Dawn of the Cheap Press* (London: Bloomsbury Academic, 2014).
[47] P. Hollis, *The Pauper Press* (1970).

a newspaper culture which promoted public reading in clubs, pubs and newsrooms, rather than the purchase of personal copies for private reading.

It was only in the 1850s that effective resistance was renewed by the Association for the Promotion of the Repeal of the Taxes on Knowledge. The newspaper interest was far from united. Many of the established papers welcomed the penny stamp as a protection against unfettered competition and argued that the right to free and unlimited postage which it furnished was more than sufficient recompense. Opponents contended that the stamp, by preventing the publication of penny papers, effectively stymied the development of a popular daily press and handed a dominant position to *The Times*. Ultimately, a carefully orchestrated demonstration of the inconsistencies and absurdities of the regulations encouraged the abandonment of the advertising duty in 1853, the removal of the compulsory newspaper stamp in 1855 and finally the abolition of the paper duties in 1861. As the established papers had feared, several years of frantic instability ensued, especially in the provinces. By the later 1860s, there had been a clear transformation of the press: new metropolitan rivals to *The Times* such as the *Daily Telegraph*, a significant cadre of provincial dailies such as the *Manchester Guardian*, the proliferation of local titles, and a comprehensive cheapening of prices which greatly increased sales and encouraged new modes of private reading.

Registration

Briefly in the mid-1850s, it had appeared that the removal of the compulsory stamp would be accompanied by the abandonment of the requirements for registration and sureties. Since the eighteenth century, registration had been fundamental to the operation of legal pressure on the press, providing the means to identify those responsible for what newspapers published. The forms of registration, which for even a minor change of title, publishing arrangement or proprietorship, could involve co-ordinating as many as eighteen parties, were generally irritating rather than onerous but were yet another obstacle to prospective publishers.[48] In the run up to 1855, large sections of the existing press successfully resisted calls for this repeal.[49]

---

[48] See complaints of William Pressey of the *Luton Weekly Recorder*, 22 November [1858] in IR56/45, National Archives (NA), and discussion in Hewitt, *Dawn of the Cheap Press*, chap. 8.

[49] 'Newspaper Reform', reprinted *Dundee Courier*, 18 April 1855.

In reality, the registration laws were never efficiently enforced. More often than not, where action was taken, it was prompted by local rivalries. In 1865, it was suggested that there were 361 unregistered papers nationally, more than a quarter of the total.[50] After 1855, attempts to enforce the rules were intermittent and uneven. Although only a handful of actual prosecutions occurred, because papers eventually complied, the new penny press was especially resentful of what the *Luton Times* called 'this absurd system' with its 'unnecessary harassment of newspaper proprietors'.[51]

Matters were brought to a head by attempts to enforce the registration of the *National Reformer*, a secularist paper edited by Charles Bradlaugh. Not least because in his case the necessity of finding securities against blasphemy struck at the very core of the paper's identity and purpose, Bradlaugh defied the Inland Revenue to prosecute. Faced with the uncomfortable prospect of creating a press martyr, in 1869 the government dropped the case and speedily passed the Newspapers, Printers and Reading Rooms Act which abandoned both registration and sureties.

In practice, the break was only temporary. The desire for cheap newspaper postage brought partial reinstatement in 1870 when the Post Office Act required the registration of newspapers intended for transmission through the post. Over time successive postmasters-general constructed an elaborate series of rules which were rather arbitrarily enforced.[52] And almost as soon as registration was abolished, there were second thoughts; the Law Society expressed anxiety that it would be more difficult to enforce the libel laws if newspapers proprietors were not officially recorded.[53] An 1876 bill requiring registration was successfully opposed, but many provincial proprietors continued to advocate registration and sureties as a defence against irresponsibility,[54] and more formal registration requirements for England and Wales and Ireland were reimposed by the Newspaper Libel and Registration Act (1881), which transferred responsibility to the registrar of joint stock companies. Once again the law operated unevenly. It was acknowledged in 1893 that the official *Labour Gazette* was not registered, giving rise to some dry comments about ministers believing themselves above the law.[55]

---

[50] J. Fisher to the Board of Inland Revenue, 8 September 1866 [copy], IR 56/41, NA.
[51] *Luton Times*, 23 May 1857.
[52] J. Fisher and J. A. Strahan, *The Law of the Press. A Digest of the Law Specially Affecting Newspapers.* London: W. Clowes 1892, p. 12.
[53] *Law Times*, 20 August 1870.
[54] See evidence of Flux, solicitor and proprietor of the *Wilts Standard* to the *House of Commons Select Committee on Libel* (1879).
[55] 'Notes from Fleet Street', *Newcastle Weekly Courant*, 27 May 1893.

Libel

Acceptance of the reimposition of registration reflected renewed anxieties about the law of libel, a reminder that after the removal of fiscal constraints in the mid-century, even though political trials were largely a thing of the past, the law of libel remained by far the most important legal entanglement of the newspaper press.

Lucky indeed was the Victorian editor or newspaper proprietor who survived a career without being dragged into at least one libel case. Joseph Soames, solicitor to *The Times*, noted in 1889 that over the previous seven years he had assisted in more than 100 newspaper defences against libel actions.[56] The practice of extracting meant that a single libel could be quickly re-published widely, drawing multiple titles into the maw of legal action. In one notorious case of the 1880s, Joseph Chicken Colledge, a minor diplomatic official in the Crimea, successfully sued the *Globe*, the Central News agency, and more than thirty provincial papers, being awarded in total nearly £5,000 and costs.[57] Even where fines were negligible, costs could be substantial. A libel case in 1857 cost the editor of the *Durham Advertiser* £400, although damages were assessed at only one farthing.[58] Given the precarious finances of many nineteenth-century papers, such losses could easily be fatal. And the court cases were only the tip of the iceberg. The history of the engagement of the press with the laws of libel is largely hidden, resting in the daily practices of self-policing and literary restraint operated by journalists and editors. As Sir John Robinson recalled in 1904, newspaper coverage was produced with a keen regard to the dangers of libel.[59]

The avoidance of potential libels was one of the crucial tasks of the subeditor. The task was not easy, because libel remained a legal minefield. Advice on libel was a staple of the trade press and the guides to newspaper law. The inadequacies of the law were widely accepted, but the sanctity Victorians accorded to personal reputations meant solutions were elusive. Libel law remained in essence common law, constituted by the shifting sands of precedent, uncertain and unstable. There was no fixed definition. Except in Scotland, libel could be either a criminal or a civil offence, with different legal procedures, definitions and defences. The 1843 Libel Act

---

[56] *Pall Mall Gazette*, 9 May 1889.
[57] William Hunt, *Then and Now: or Fifty Years of Newspaper Work*. London: Hamilton & Adams, 1887, pp. 191–92.
[58] 'Libel Law Reform', *Macmillan's Magazine*, 47 (April 1883), 439.
[59] Quoted in F. M. Thomas, *Fifty Years of Fleet Street*. London: Macmillan, 1904, pp. 40–41.

allowed a defence of truth in civil cases, but not in criminal ones unless a public interest could be proved. Liability extended almost indiscriminately across proprietors, printers, editors, even agents and newsvendors. Nor was there any consistent understanding of what might be appropriate damages when libels were proved: this was the province of the jury and was constrained only by the power of the appeals courts to set aside obviously unreasonable awards. The tendency of the courts to award prosecution costs in all cases of conviction, even when the damages awarded indicated that the offence was merely technical, left the press open not only to the adventurer, hoping to extort a compromise, but also to all sorts of shady practices, such as attempts to place libellous items with the deliberate intent of then threatening prosecution.[60]

Above all, the press remained bitterly resentful of the fact that it could find itself liable to conviction merely for accurately reporting the proceedings of properly constituted public meetings or public bodies. Advocates for the press urged without success the argument that a newspaper was not merely a private commercial speculation but 'a trustee for the public, the self-appointed guardian of its worthiest interests', as the Sydney *Empire* put it in 1863.[61] Offset against this ideal, however, must be set the tendency of nineteenth-century journalism to indulge in often reckless vituperation of political opponents, only to be nonplussed when a summons for libel ensued. Some late century pioneers of society journalism such as Henry Labouchere, the owner of *Truth*, actively courted the notoriety of the libel courts.[62] Indeed William Hunt, editor of the *Eastern Morning News*, acknowledged that his conviction for libel in 1866 'did the paper good': his costs were reimbursed by public subscription, and public sympathy was engendered.[63]

For all this, almost as soon as the newspaper industry had seen off the advertising and stamp duties, the attention of bodies such as the Newspaper Society turned to reform of the libel laws. A House of Lords Select Committee investigated the privilege of reports in 1857, and a Commons Select Committee in 1879–80 examined the libel laws and the press more broadly. Here again newspaper opinion was not unanimous; from the conservative standpoint, the libel laws helped ensure

---

[60] See case of Oliver J. Prince, newspaper correspondent, against the *Maidstone and Kentish Journal, Lancaster Evening Post*, 16 January 1890.

[61] For example, Sir E. R. Russell at the Institute of Journalists, *Morning Post*, 31 August 1899.

[62] Kent, 'Editor and the Law', 116–17; A. L. Thorold, *Life of Henry Labouchere*. London: Constable, 1913, pp. 496–503.

[63] Hunt, *Then and Now*, 104–8.

that the press was 'more free from scurrility, scandal and slander of private character than any Press in the world'.[64] Bills in 1858, 1865, 1867 and 1878 attempted variously to limit the press's liability for prosecution costs when the damages levied were less than 20/-, to define appropriate restitution for libels published without malice or gross negligence, and above all to establish the principle of a press privilege to report in full public meetings without liability for libel.

Eventually, in 1881 the Newspaper Libel and Registration Act appeared to offer privilege to any report of a public meeting convened for a legal purpose if it was fair, published without malice and for the public benefit. Unfortunately, uncertainties remained, and prosecutions continued.[65] A Libel Law Reform Committee, in which Henry Whorlow, secretary of the Newspaper Society, was prominent, pressed for further reform. The Libel Act of 1888 required the consolidation of libel proceedings, in the hope of avoiding repeats of the Colledge affair, and transferred responsibility for proving malice to the plaintiff. But the act did not extend privilege to any sort of commentary, even headlines, and did not remove liability for costs in the case of conviction, even when damages were purely nominal, and newspapers continued to need to prove their reporting was in the public good. During the 1890s, the Newspaper Society unsuccessfully promoted an almost annual libel bill which allowed judges to require plaintiffs to give security for costs.[66] Unfortunately, the increasing sensationalism of the press served only to reinforce legal suspicion: papers, it was observed, 'publish libellous statements ... because they find that it pays: many of their readers prefer to read and believe the worst of everybody, and the newspaper proprietors cannot complain if juries remember this in assessing damages'.[67]

Contempt of Court

By then, press attention was also being drawn to 'contempt of court' proceedings. Set loose by precedents such as the celebrated Tichborne Claimant trials of 1868–74,[68] and thereafter fuelled by the rise of 'sensation

---

[64] 'The Press and the Law of Libel', *Saturday Review*, 30 May 1857, 494, 493–94.
[65] 'Libel by Public Meeting', *Saturday Review*, 18 December 1888.
[66] See Whorlow letters to *The Times*, 19 February 1894, and *The Times*, 14 June 1894.
[67] Lord Justice Farwell, quoted in Paul Mitchell, *The Making of the Modern Law of Defamation*. Oxford: Hart, 2005, p. 119, see pp. 117–20.
[68] This was a sensational legal case in which the title to the Tichborne baronetcy was claimed by an Australian butcher on the grounds that he was the heir, Roger Tichborne, who had been presumed dead. His claim was rejected and the claimant was imprisoned for perjury, but the case became

journalism', contempt of court was a particularly broad and ill-defined misdemeanour dependent wholly on the decisions of each court and presiding judge as to procedure, punishment and even scope. Three broad types of 'contempt' can be distinguished: government-inspired proceedings designed to suppress criticism of legal institutions, attempts by individual judges to maintain their dignity and that of their courts, and motions by which one party sought to invoke contempt to further a private action.

As with libel, invocation of the law was the exception. But given the extent to which legal proceedings formed the raw material of journalism, the jeopardy of the press was potentially enormous. After 1830, instances of the first sort were confined to colonial contexts, deployed in defence of the imperial state (as in the cases of Alfred Moseley of the *Nassau Guardian* and Charles McLeod of the Grenada-based *Federalist*).[69] Instances of the second sort although also relatively infrequent did, when they flared up, illuminate the vulnerability of editors to arbitrary action. The case in 1851 of M. J. Whitty, who was pursued by a county court judge who took exception to an advertising placard for his paper the *Liverpool Journal*, and eventually imprisoned him in default of payment of fines for various 'offences' including contempt of court and resisting arrest, shows the wide prerogatives judges could assume.

From the later 1860s, it was cases arising out of private actions which rapidly proliferated. Financial journalism seems to have been especially prone to entanglements of this sort; but in the final decades of the century, contempt cast its net fairly indiscriminately. In most instance, editors found that abject contrition was enough to assuage the courts. Fines were usually token, although punishments could be substantial. In 1882, Edmund Dwyer, editor of the *Freeman's Journal*, was sentenced to three months and a £500 fine for reporting that the jury in a murder trial had been drunk the night before the verdict.[70] The broad discretion contempt procedures allowed made it the natural instrument for attempts in the later 1890s to provide for the prohibition of the publication of indecent evidence in the newspapers. Journalists were lukewarm, but press interests were vocal in their opposition. 'The whole of the jurisdiction claimed and exercised by the Judges is utterly inconsistent with the freedom of the

---

bound up in populist anti-aristocratic campaigns, including the publication of *The Englishman* newspaper.

[69] For the Mosley episode, see Martin J. Wiener, *An Empire on Trial: Race, Murder and Justice under British Rule, 1870–1935*. Cambridge University Press, 2009.

[70] *Western Daily Press*, 17 August 1882.

Press, and with the public interest in knowledge of the truth', trumpeted the *Daily News* in 1892.[71]

For a long time, there was little appetite to protect the press. The judiciary was more concerned that the newspapers should not, as Vice-Chancellor James expressed it in 1869, put themselves 'in the judgement seat' before the hearing of a case.[72] Even so, by the 1890s the prevalence of contempt cases, and indications that in some circumstances legal proceedings were being commenced with the ulterior motive of gagging newspapers, prompted the judiciary to differentiate between a technical offence and one with a clear tendency to prejudice a fair trial.[73] In 1896 in dismissing a case against the *Huntingdonshire Post*, Lord Chief Justice Russell regretted the growing frequency of applications for contempt: the power of committal might in some instances be necessary, he conceded, but should only be exercised in extreme cases.[74]

Copyright and the Press

The 1890s also saw a renewed attention to questions of newspaper copyright. The limitations of nineteenth-century copyright protection in respect of literature more generally are well known.[75] The position of the press was even more complex and uncertain. The key nineteenth-century statute, the 1842 Copyright Act, made no mention of newspapers at all, although it was generally accepted that newspapers could be considered a 'book' under the terms of the act.[76] But this only helped in respect to commentary because the vesting of rights in the literary rendition derived from and reinforced the principle that there could be no copyright in information itself, and thus none in news per se. Similarly, the clauses with which it dealt with transfer of copyright in serial works had little relevance for the press, where the established custom was that copyright in

---

[71] *Daily News*, 26 November 1892.
[72] *Economist*, quoted *Sheffield Independent*, 12 October 1869; see 'Contempt of Court', *Pall Mall Gazette*, 3 May 1875.
[73] J. Oswald, *Contempt of Court* (2nd ed., 1895), p. 64. For a sympathetic judicial view, see comments of Justice Kerkwitch [High Court, Chancery], *The Times*, 20 March 1897.
[74] Noted in *Pall Mall Gazette*, 15 April 1896.
[75] Catherine Seville, *The Internationalisation of the Copyright Law: Books, Buccaneers and the Black Flag in the Nineteenth Century*. Cambridge University Press, 2006.
[76] Fisher and Strahan, *Law of the Press*, p. 11; Isabella Alexander, *Copyright Law and the Public Interest in the Nineteenth Century*. Oxford: Hart, 2010, p. 206 provides evidence of contradictory judicial interpretations.

contributions continued to be the property of the author unless newspapers made specific indication of the contrary.[77]

Even copyright in the titles of newspapers was uncertain. Although legal commentaries suggested that a right analogous to a trademark protection, which prevented deliberately misleading titles, had been established by various legal precedents in the decades after 1842,[78] the ending of registration in 1869 rekindled anxieties. Proprietors were assured that copyright in title could be enforced by registration at Stationers Hall.[79]

More significant was the licence the absence of copyright in news afforded to the wholesale practice of cut and paste by which large swathes of newspaper copy were got up for much of the century. Few nineteenth-century newspapers could have survived long without the facility for unrestricted borrowings from their contemporaries, acknowledged and unacknowledged. Although the extent of this appropriation was an occasional grouse of the leading London dailies, particularly *The Times*, which incurred significant expenses in newsgathering and yet saw its material copied within hours by the evening papers,[80] the press generally had little interest in championing copyright in news.

This said, at the end of the century the appearance of newspapers composed almost entirely of extracts once again prompted calls for protection, led by the colonial press.[81] A number of Australian states recognised the costs of acquiring telegraphic news by granting forty-eight hours copyright in it. In Britain, in conjunction with the Society of Authors and a Copyright Association, some newspapers continued to press for amendment of the law. An abortive bill of 1891 proposed that a specific copyright reservation might be applied to parts of a newspaper; in 1892 in a case against the *St James' Gazette*, *The Times* argued that news was as much a manufactured article as was the form of words in which it was expressed.[82] The evidence to the Select Committee of 1898–99 showed the difficulty of balancing copyright in newsgathering against established

[77] As Sidney Low put it, 'A copyright which can only be safeguarded by special agreements and assignments applicable to every news paragraph is hardly worth having', 'Newspaper Copyright', *National Review*, 13 (July 1892), 648–55.

[78] For details, see 'Notes on Copyright in Titles of Magazines and Other Periodicals', *St James' Magazine* 4 (July 1880), 72–73.

[79] See comments of A. S. Ayrton, *Western Mail*, 19 August 1869.

[80] Evidence of Alexander Dobie, solicitor to *The Times*, to *Select Committee of the House of Lords on the Law of Libel and Defamation* (1843), Q747–69.

[81] South Australia and West Australia Acts of 1872, Tasmania 1884, Cape of Good Hope 1890 (124 hours), Natal 1895, see letter *The Times*, 11 July 1899, 8.

[82] Walter vs. Steinkopff, reported *Times Law Reports* 3 June 1892; discussed Alexander, *Copyright Law*, pp. 248–50.

borrowing practices. The Newspaper Society ultimately came out largely against any further tightening of the law, while the London press and the Institute of Journalists were more inclined to be in favour. In 1900, a proposal of an eighteen-hour copyright did not pass into law, but in a separate case the House of Lords judged that it was possible to assert copyright in reports of public speeches.[83]

Conclusion

The search for copyright in news serves as a reminder that the law could protect as well as constrain, just as the resulting tensions between proprietors and journalists remind us that at no point in the century was there a monolithic 'press' interest, any more than there was a one-dimensional relationship between newspapers and the law. As David Saunders has argued in relation to law and literature, to conceive of the press and law in entirely oppositional and negative terms is to miss the mutually constitutive nature of their relationship.[84] The nineteenth-century press enjoyed protections and freedoms denied to many of its continental and colonial counterparts, albeit via customary toleration rather than specific safeguards. At the same time, the legal system resisted the claims of the press to public good exclusions; pressmen and presswomen were as liable as any other citizen, more so, since they were implicated in the process of dissemination. The press might have complained, at times vehemently, at the uncertainty of its legal position, but this uncertainty was probably more beneficial than otherwise. The twentieth century was to bring greater clarity, but also more organised pressures for censorship: of indecent material in peacetime, and of reporting more generally in wartime.[85] As Lord Chief Justice Mansfield had declared in 1784, 'To be free, [was] to live under a government by law.'

---

[83] *Manchester Guardian*, 7 August 1900.

[84] David Saunders, 'Copyright, Obscenity and Literary History', *English Literary History* 57.2 (Summer 1990), 431–44, 441.

[85] A. Jones, *Press, Politics and Society: A History of Journalism in Wales.* Cardiff: University of Wales Press, 1993, p. 49; P. Towle, 'The Debate on Wartime Censorship in Britain, 1902–14', in Brian Bond and Ian Roy (eds.), *War and Society.* London: Croom Helm 1975, pp. 103–16.

CHAPTER 10

'Doing the Graphic': Victorian Special Correspondence

Catherine Waters

Readers of Victorian newspapers will be familiar with the range of common bylines used to refer to the journalist responsible for a news report before the introduction of the practice of signature later in the century. 'Our Special Commissioner', 'An Occasional Correspondent', 'Our Own Correspondent' and 'Our Special Correspondent' were all used imprecisely, if not interchangeably, in newspapers throughout the nineteenth century. But notwithstanding the employment of such seemingly generic bylines, the roles of the journalists so designated were not all the same – as an article in the *Leisure Hour* published on 1 January 1868 sought to explain. Entitled 'Our Own Correspondent', it begins: 'Who is the mysterious and apparently ubiquitous functionary that figures every morning under the above designation in the columns of the newspaper, few people comparatively have any very definite notion.'[1] The writer seeks to clarify two roles for 'our own correspondent':

> We are not speaking now of the regular correspondent, who, residing constantly in some foreign capital, gleans from the officials of the Government such information as they choose to impart, and as much more as he can; but of him who is the special messenger of the London press, and is ready to start to any quarter of the globe at a moment's notice.[2]

The article attempts to distinguish between the journalist now referred to as the foreign correspondent – based in one place and charged with keeping the public at home abreast of political affairs transpiring elsewhere – and the roving reporter who,

> when he has used up one place . . . gets orders to be off to another. Thus, he may be in Russia one day, shivering almost at zero, and after a brief interval,

---

[1] 'Our Own Correspondent', *Leisure Hour*, 1 January 1868, 53.   [2] 'Our Own Correspondent'.

sweltering under the hot sun of Spain or Italy; and a month later he may be bound for India, or on the voyage to China.[3]

However, the distinction drawn here – between those correspondents who were fixtures in various foreign capitals and the peripatetic 'special' – is at the same time obscured by the use of the common byline 'from Our Own Correspondent' for both of these journalists.

In her seminal study *Victorian News and Newspapers* (1985), Lucy Brown distinguishes the foreign correspondent from the war correspondent and argues that while 'the phrase "special correspondent" had no very precise meaning' in the nineteenth century, it nevertheless described someone who was working on a 'particular assignment' and who typically presented his investigations 'in a series of letters in successive issues' of the newspaper.[4] Thus war correspondence may be regarded as one form of special correspondence. In his 1871 survey of *The Newspaper Press*, James Grant argued as follows:

> 'The Special Correspondent' is an entirely different personage from the Correspondents regularly established in all the leading towns of Europe, or in America, India, or Australia. The latter are fixtures in the various capitals or important towns from which their communications are dated. These places are their spheres of duty all the year round. The Special Correspondent, on the contrary, so far from occupying a stationary position, is a gentleman whose vocation it is to go from place to place according to circumstances, and to record whatever matters of importance transpire in the different localities to which a sense of duty calls him.[5]

Having drawn this distinction, Grant says that the byline used to designate this journalist – as 'Our Own' or 'Our Special' – is merely a matter of editorial preference. However, two decades later in his 1890 account of *The Newspaper World*, Alfred Baker distinguished between these two bylines, explaining that the duties of the special 'are to deal with the especial event in hand, and he in no way supersedes or interferes with "our own correspondent," should the paper have a resident representative at or near the spot.'[6]

Despite this lack of clear definition of his role (they were mostly men at this time), the special correspondent played a significant part in the popularisation of news journalism from the 1850s onwards, not the least

---

[3] 'Our Own Correspondent', 54.
[4] Lucy Brown, *Victorian News and Newspapers*. Oxford: Clarendon Press, 1985, pp. 216–17.
[5] James Grant, *The Newspaper Press: Its Origin, Progress and Present Position*. London: Tinsley, 1871, p. 248.
[6] Alfred Baker, *The Newspaper World: Essays on Press History and Work, Past and Present*. London: Pittman, 1890, p. 56.

evidence of which may be deduced from the recurrent criticism directed towards him by conservative commentators who deplored what they saw as a commercially driven press deploying sensational reportage to sell newspapers. The specials were a bête noire of the *Saturday Review* (or 'Saturday Reviler' as this abrasive weekly was nicknamed by some for its slashing reviews), which criticised William Howard Russell's coverage of the Crimean campaign in *The Times*, for example, for

> mak[ing] his letters piquant by describing a general in his night-cap with a heavy cold, and the Commander-in-chief in a trench with a cloak up to his eyes ... [A]nd so the commander is drawn in this interesting attitude – caricatured and laughed at from one end of the kingdom to another. But no harm was meant – it was only a Special Correspondent in his vocation. He was getting up an interesting letter – showing off his style and his facility in composition. He was doing the graphic – that was all.[7]

'Doing the graphic' was indeed a hallmark of the special correspondent's work. This chapter briefly surveys the role as a mobile practice of journalism and explores some of the key features that distinguished the graphic writing associated with it.

While the employment of foreign correspondents for major metropolitan dailies like *The Times* dates from the early nineteenth century, and Henry Mayhew's reports on London labour and the London poor for the *Morning Chronicle* in 1849–50 carried the byline 'From our Special Correspondent', the peculiar role of the special as a roving journalist sent out to report upon particular events really begins in the 1850s, with Russell's famous Crimean War reports for *The Times*. Indeed, John Black Atkins's two-volume biography of Russell, published in 1911, identifies him in its subtitle as 'The First Special Correspondent'. But while reporting from the seat of war was undoubtedly the assignment that most tested the special correspondent's mettle, as Atkins notes, 'war correspondence is only the dramatic branch of special correspondence';[8] and when no war was in preparation or progress, specials had to turn their hand to cover all manner of events in any location at home or abroad as required by their newspaper.

As George Augustus Sala wryly described the multifarious demands placed upon the special correspondent in 1871, 'He must be Jack of all trades, and master of all – that are journalistic.' He continued:

---

[7] 'Our Own Correspondent', *Saturday Review*, 17 November 1855, 45.
[8] John Black Atkins, *The Life of Sir William Howard Russell: The First Special Correspondent*, 2 vols. London: John Murray, 1911, Vol. 2, p. 372.

> When there is no war afoot, he must be prepared to 'do' funerals as well as
> weddings, state-banquets, Volunteer reviews, Great Exhibitions, remark-
> able trials, christenings, coronations, ship-launches, agricultural shows,
> royal progresses, picture-shows, first-stone layings, horse-races, and
> hangings.[9]

Sala's heterogeneous inventory indicates that versatility was a key distinguishing attribute of the special correspondent. Mobility was another:

> It is expected from them that they should be able to start for the World's
> End at a moment's notice; to go to Russia in January and to India in July; to
> explore a district where typhus and small-pox are raging with the same
> equanimity as they displayed when they attended the marriage of the Prince
> of Wales, and which they have had an opportunity of airing at the wedding
> of the Princess Louise.[10]

As well as manifesting resourcefulness and versatility in this roving role, the
special correspondent needed to possess an unusual medley of skills and
some distinctive habits:

> It will be better for him to speak half-a-dozen languages with tolerable
> fluency; to have visited or resided in most parts of the habitable globe – if he
> knows something about the Rocky Mountains or the interior of Africa, so
> much the better; to be a good cook, a facile musician, a first-rate whist-
> player, a practised horseman, a tolerable shot, a ready conversationalist,
> a freemason, a philosopher, a moderate smoker – for tobacco is a very good
> buckler against the pangs of hunger – and a perfect master of the art of
> packing; that is to say, he should be able to compress a good-sized writing-
> case, a despatch-box, a pair of jack-boots, a Roget's *Thesaurus* and a Bible,
> a small keg of brandy, a change of linen, a waterproof sheet, a dark lantern,
> and a gridiron, into the area of a pair of saddle-bags.[11]

The comic miscellaneousness of the special's kit bespeaks the multi-
purpose nature of his work. Looking back over his career as a special –
from the days of the Crimean War to the Russo-Turkish conflict of
1877 – in an essay for the *Boy's Own Paper* in 1896, George A. Henty
provides a similar list of requirements but adds to those that Sala
mentions 'a stock of the few medicines absolutely necessary – quinine
against fevers, cholorodyne and Cockle's pills for general purposes,
ipecacuanha for dysentery; and if you add a bottle of essence of

[9] George Augustus Sala, 'The Special Correspondent: His Life and Crimes', *Belgravia: A London
Magazine*, 4 (1871), 220–21.
[10] Sala, 220–21.   [11] Sala, 220.

ginger and another of ammonia you are stocked for anything that may come'.[12]

Henty also highlights another distinctive feature of the role – the special's preparedness for departure at a moment's notice – giving examples of the kind of abrupt orders he received to cover an event overseas for the *Standard*: '"We are going to send out a man with this Ashanti expedition," or "You are to go with this Chitral expedition. One of the Castle line or a P. & O." as the case may be, "starts tomorrow; you had better go to the office at once and take your passage."'[13] Sala comically remarked in the preface to his re-published correspondence describing a tour from Waterloo to the Spanish Peninsula in 1866 that his long connection with the *Daily Telegraph* 'has converted me, into a kind of human teetotum, and given to my progression on this earth's surface a most fitful and erratic character'.[14] As he had been making preparations to leave Berlin for Königsberg late in 1864, Sala 'received a telegram containing only these words – "Revolution. Spain. Go there at once." The instructions were certainly vague', he writes, 'still I understood them at once, and thoroughly'.[15] The instructions given to W. J. C. Meighan of the *New York Herald* when he was sent by editor James Gordon Bennett to report on the Chicago fire of 1871 were similarly peremptory:

> Go to Chicago by the first train today; wire us simply the word 'Here' when you arrive there. Spare no expense. Go anywhere, and by any mode of travel, to get all the news. Picture graphically what you see, so that *Herald* readers will have as they read the burning city before their eyes. At the same time, bear in mind that while graphic picturing of scenes makes attractive reading, what the people all over the world want to know are *facts*, FACTS, FACTS.[16]

Finding the Chicago telegraph offices blocked by messages being sent to the East imploring help from relatives, Meighan took the initiative to send a message twice a day by engine to Cleveland, Ohio, 'whence his reports were telegraphed to New York'.[17] Set alongside the correspondence of Sala and Henty, his account suggests the similarities between the practice of

[12] G. A. Henty, 'The Life of a Special Correspondent, Part II', *Boy's Own Paper*, 20 June 1896, 599.

[13] Henty, 599.

[14] *From Waterloo to the Peninsula: Four Months' Hard Labour in Belgium, Holland, Germany, and Spain*. 2 vols. London: Tinsley, 1867, Vol. 1, p. ix.

[15] *The Life and Adventures of George Augustus Sala, Written by Himself*. London: Cassell, 1898, p. 422.

[16] Quoted in Michael MacDonagh, 'Our Special Correspondent', in *Mitchell's Newspaper Press Directory*. London: C. Mitchell and Co., 1903, p. 90.

[17] MacDonagh, 'Our Special Correspondent', p. 90.

special correspondence on both sides of the Atlantic and the way in which it was bound up with the new mobile technologies of the railroad and telegraph.

Arguably, however, the mobility and versatility of the Victorian special correspondent would have counted for nothing without the roving journalist's capacity to enter into the experiences of others so as to provide a vivid eyewitness report: an ability to observe and seize upon events wherever they happened, rendering them for the press in sufficiently graphic prose so as to transport readers imaginatively through vivid first-hand accounts. As Bennett's instruction to his special makes clear, his correspondence is to 'picture graphically' what he sees 'so that *Herald* readers will have as they read the burning city before their eyes'. Similarly, *Chambers's Journal* outlined the essential requirements of the 'modern Special Correspondent' in 1873 thus: 'he must be able, and that at a moment's notice, to put himself in the position of somebody else; to see with his eyes, to hear with his ears, and to express the results of another's experience in the first person'.[18] Special correspondence was, in effect, a new technology – like the railroad, the telegraph and the photograph, with all of which it was associated – that brought the world closer, shrinking space and time and conveying readers to distant places. Amongst other things, thinking about special correspondence as a mobile practice of journalism refocuses our attention upon its role in helping to produce the time-space compression we have been used to associating with the railroad and telegraph.

Notwithstanding the heterogeneous assortment of topics they covered, some specials came to be distinguished by particular aptitudes or associated with certain kinds of reporting. Alfred Baker identifies three 'varieties of the "special"': the 'travelling correspondent' who, he says, 'is in many cases merely the journalist on a holiday trip';[19] the 'special commissioner' who is charged 'by his editor to pursue some special line of inquiry on a matter of public moment';[20] and, 'most arduous' of all, the war correspondent. His categorisation provides a useful framework for my survey of special correspondence and its peculiar attributes here.

For an example of the 'travelling correspondent', we can do no better than turn again to Sala – the 'chief of travelled specials', according to Joseph Hatton[21] – who sent special correspondence to the *Daily Telegraph*

---

[18] 'A Versatile "Special"', *Chambers's Journal of Popular Literature, Science and Arts*, 20 September 1873, 597.
[19] Baker, *The Newspaper World*, p. 56.   [20] Baker, *The Newspaper World*, p. 57.
[21] Joseph Hatton, *Journalistic London: Being a Series of Sketches of Famous Pens and Papers of the Day*. London: Routledge, 1882, p. 169.

from many parts of the world, including Algeria, Australia, New Zealand, America and a number of European countries. Whether he was despatched to report upon a particular event or merely to provide a descriptive account of his travels, his special correspondence is marked by a colourful, loquacious style of 'word-painting' that was highly popular. As the *Athenaeum* remarked in a review of his re-published correspondence in *From Waterloo to the Peninsula*, 'Mr Sala cannot be otherwise than a droll and enlivening companion; and as we travelled with him from Belgium to Holland, from Amsterdam to Hamburg, and from Northern Germany to Madrid, he has provoked a good deal of merriment.'[22] Sala's letter to the *Daily Telegraph* of 9 December 1865, describing the depopulated aspect of Antwerp, encountered out of the tourist season in November, is a good example of his style as he eschews factual information about the city for fanciful reflection, ruminating upon the advantages and disadvantages of employing a local guide:

> I took one at Antwerp. After all, it was a new sensation. He plodded on before, like a horse on a towing-path. His tongue was the cable, and he drew me on leisurely, a lazy canal-boat. You get dazed and dreamy at last. You find yourself wondering what the *commissionaire* is like when he is at home; what he has for dinner; whether he rehearses to his family at supper-time that the Hotel de Ville is 'an elegant Gothic structure, built in 1377, the niches of which were formerly decorated with curious statues of the Counts of Flanders,' or puts his children through a course of chronology touching upon the dates of the erection of the cathedral and the fountain of Quentin Matsys.[23]

Playing with the role of the tourist, Sala's travelling correspondence is impressionistic, digressive and often whimsical. The move from the first- to the second-person pronoun in this passage is part of the beguiling effect. While used as a form of self-address by Sala, the repeated 'you' pulls the reader figuratively into the scene described here, creating a sense of jocular companionability with 'Our Special', whose correspondence remains centred incorrigibly upon himself.

The focus of the special correspondent upon his own role as eyewitness, while deplored by some critics as unwarrantable egotism,[24] was in fact a key

---

[22] Rev. of *From Waterloo to the Peninsula. Four Months' Hard Labour in Belgium, Holland, Germany and Spain by George Augustus Sala*, *Athenaeum*, 15 December 1866, p. 791.

[23] (From Our Special Correspondent), 'The Lions of Antwerp', *Daily Telegraph*, 9 December 1865, 7.

[24] For example, the *Saturday Review* complained again about William Howard Russell's reports, this time as *The Times*'s special correspondent on the American Civil War in 1861: 'It is evident that the great object for which a special correspondent is sent out is to report to admiring readers at home the

ingredient of his report, endowing it with its distinctive effects of immediacy and authenticity. As Judy McKenzie argues, public fascination with
adventurous specials, such as Sala or Russell, 'depended on their ability not
just to record events in an interesting and colourful fashion but to project
themselves into those events – to be there'.[25] Eyewitnessing was an important source of the verisimilitude of his report, as the example of special
correspondence sent by those journalists commissioned to cover the maiden voyage of the *Great Eastern* in September 1859 shows. Writing of 'the
profession of seeing and describing everything in the character of "our own
correspondent"' in *All the Year Round* on 1 October, John Hollingshead
sought to justify the publication of his account of the *Great Eastern*'s trial
journey almost a month after the event by arguing that his purpose was
'strictly to record what *I saw with my own eyes on board the ship*, and not
what was brought to me by well-meaning friends or well-instructed
messengers'.[26] Like Sala, Hollingshead had developed his skills as
a special correspondent in working for Dickens on *Household Words*, and
both journalists were included in the sizable press contingent that accompanied the *Great Eastern* when it left the Thames estuary for Weymouth on
Friday 9 September 1859.[27] Dickens had commissioned Hollingshead to
report on the voyage for *All the Year Round* and paid £10 for his passage.[28]
But neither editor nor contributor could have anticipated the dramatic
nature of the report that would be necessitated by the events of the journey.

Hollingshead's 'Great Eastern Postscript' provides a vivid account of the
tragic explosion that took place in a heater attached to one of the paddle
engine boilers just after the ship had passed Hastings. The eyewitness

thoughts, the actions, the comforts and discomforts, the honours and the slights of the special
correspondent himself . . . What are such trifles as the disposition of armies to him? He has far more
important matters to tell about. "Yesterday morning *I* left Mobile in the steamer *Florida*," and so he
goes on for well nigh a column, with all that Our Special Correspondent did, and thought, and saw,
and felt, in the steamer *Florida* – all in the highest flights of the high polite style.' 'Current History',
Saturday Review, 29 June 1861, 664.

[25] Judy McKenzie, 'Paper Heroes: Special Correspondents and their Narratives of Empire', in
Barbara Garlick and Margaret Harris (eds.), *Victorian Journalism: Exotic and Domestic*. Brisbane:
Queensland University Press, 1998, p. 125.

[26] [John Hollingshead], 'Great Eastern Postscript', *All the Year Round*, 1 October 1859, 546. Emphasis
in the original.

[27] Apart from his periodical contributions, Hollingshead was a special correspondent for the *Morning
Post* during the severe winter of 1860–61, and contributed a series of 'London Horrors', serialised
between 21 and 31 January, describing the distress of the working poor that was re-published as
Ragged London in 1861.

[28] Letter to Herbert Ingram, 13 September 1859. In Madeline House, Graham Storey and
Kathleen Tillotson, *The Letters of Charles Dickens* 12 vols. Oxford: Clarendon Press, 1965–2002,
Vol. 9, p. 122.

veracity of his narrative is conveyed by its being recounted from the perspective of his actual position in the dining room, 'between half-past five and six P.M.', where 'a dozen of "our own correspondents" had remained to congratulate a director of the company and a proprietor of newspapers [Herbert Ingram], upon the prospects of the great vessel in which they were seated.' Suddenly, he writes,

> death . . . stared us all in the face and spoke to us in a voice of thunder through a dull booming sound, a crash, another crash, and a fall of some heavy weight upon heavy wood. A number of shrieks upon deck, a distinct shock, a shower of broken glass which fell upon our table and about our heads, a smell of hot steam, and a sense of some awful danger, brought us all upon our feet.[29]

He goes on to describe the scene of devastation and initial panic on deck, the rescue of the captain's young daughter, the fatal injuries of the stokers who bore the brunt of the blast and the desperate efforts made to relieve their suffering with whatever materials were to hand. Despite the lapse of time between its publication and the accident it describes, Hollingshead's article shares the effect of immediacy that characterised the accounts of the special correspondents that appeared straight after the event in the metropolitan newspapers on Monday 12 September. In his report for the *Daily Telegraph* from 'on Board the Great Eastern, Portland Harbour, Saturday, 10.30am', for example, Sala describes the explosion and the reverberation that followed, as he too witnessed it from the dining saloon, in similarly vivid terms:

> Then came – to our ears, who were in the dining room – a tremendous crash, not hollow, as of thunder, but solid, as of objects that offered resistance. Then a sweeping, rolling, swooping, rumbling sound, as of cannon balls scudding along the deck above. Remember, I am only describing now my personal experience and sensations. The rumbling noise was followed by the smash of the dining room skylights, and the irruption of a mass of fragments of wood and iron, followed by a thick cloud of powdered glass, and then by coaldust. My garments are full of the first, my hair and eyebrows of the last, now.[30]

The surprising shift from past to present tense in the final sentence here helps convey the dramatic effect. Even more graphic is the description of the injured stokers: 'the face of one was utterly without human semblance, and looked simply like a mass of raw beefsteak. Another was so horribly scalded about the groin, that the two hands might be laid in the raw cavity,

---

[29] [Hollingshead], 'Great Eastern Postscript', 551
[30] (From Our Special Correspondent), 'The Trial Trip of the Great Eastern', *Daily Telegraph*, 12 September 1859, 5.

and scraps of his woollen undergarment were mixed up with hanks of boiled flesh.' According to his biographer, Ralph Straus, it was Sala's dispatches on this trial voyage of the *Great Eastern* that confirmed the proprietors of the *Daily Telegraph* 'in their belief that they had found a prince of special correspondents, and henceforth his status in their office was appreciably improved'.[31]

There is another less reputable feature of special correspondence, however, that Hollingshead's subsequent account of his involvement in reporting upon the trial run of the *Great Eastern* reveals. The practice of sham eyewitnessing or fabricating reports sometimes brought the specials into disrepute and in this case a journalist for the *Morning Post* was caught out. As Hollingshead later explained, upon his arrival at Weymouth he made straight for Fleet Street by train, arriving about midnight. He immediately wrote a third of a column about the explosion for the Sunday edition of the *Weekly Dispatch*, and the next morning he made for the office of the *Morning Post*, since he knew that its correspondent had left the *Great Eastern* at Gravesend: 'This representative had assumed that the voyage would be all "chicken and champagne," and he had written a paragraph for a "special edition" on the Saturday, stating that the vessel had arrived in Weymouth, after a most pleasant and successful voyage.'[32] Although the fabricated report as it appeared in the *Morning Post* was dated 'From Our Own Reporter on Board the Great Eastern, Weymouth, Saturday Morning', it said not a word of any accident and concealed its subterfuge with such spurious eyewitness claims as that 'we could distinctly see the crowds that were assembled in the beach at both [Hastings and Brighton]' and that 'we arrived about 10 o'clock this morning, pleased and gratified with the trip. The weather has been magnificent and the appearance of the sea by moonlight was sublime.'[33] Consulted as to how the *Morning Post* should deal with this false news in the Saturday special edition, Hollingshead 'advised utter silence' and 'reeled off three or four columns' which appeared under the byline 'From Our Own Correspondent' in the Monday edition.[34] What readers made of these contradictory reports in subsequent issues of the newspaper can only be conjectured. But it was

[31] Ralph Straus, *Sala: The Portrait of an Eminent Victorian*. London: Constable, 1942, p. 151. Straus is presumably echoing Carlyle's praise of George Henry Lewes as the 'prince of journalists'.
[32] John Hollingshead, *My Lifetime*, 2 vols. London: Sampson Low, Marston and Co, 1895, vol. 1, p. 109.
[33] (From Our Own Reporter), 'The Great Eastern', *Morning Post*, 10 September 1859, 5.
[34] Hollingshead notes that 'on Monday morning I reported myself to Charles Dickens, and told him what I had done. He quite approved of my action, and said our article, a fortnight hence, would not be affected by this special reporting.' Hollingshead, *My Lifetime*, p. 109.

episodes like this one that periodically fuelled suspicion regarding the authenticity of special correspondence throughout the second half of the nineteenth century.[35]

Against the tarnished image of the special correspondent associated with such subterfuge, Hollingshead opens his 'Great Eastern Postscript' with an account of the profession that emphasises its heroism:

> They are men who live only in action, who feed upon excitement. They belong to the same race who have wandered over parched deserts, who have sailed out into unknown seas who have thrown themselves amongst howling savages, who have sat over powder mines to gather information, and to spread it, when gathered, before an ever ravenous public.[36]

Sala was equally keen to promote the intrepidity of the special. 'His life!' he exclaims:

> It is to rise early or sit up late, completely as the exigencies of his situation compel him; to fear no peril, to shrink before no difficulty; to be able to recall the exordium of Burke's speech at the trial of Warren Hastings in the middle of a bombardment; to write his letters on a drum, on the deck of a steamboat during a gale, on horseback, in the garret of a house on fire, on the top of an omnibus, or on the top of Mont Blanc. Some Specials can write very well standing up in the coupe of an express train; others can indite their matter on mantelpieces; others in the dark; and others in bed.[37]

This elaboration of the seemingly endless flexibility and coolness in the face of danger required of the special correspondent may be hyperbolic. But the arduous demands of the role were real enough – even to the extent that the special sometimes became newsworthy in his own right, eclipsing the news he was delivering. Indeed, as Phillip Knightley argues, in his thrilling accounts from the field of battle, the war correspondent 'rapidly became the hero of his own story'.[38] Archibald Forbes's ride from the field of British victory at Ulundi to dispatch his report as special correspondent for the *Daily News* is a case in point.

---

[35] While the London papers appear to have turned a blind eye to the false report, it was noticed by some of the American papers – although their explanation for the mishap was different from Hollingshead's. Under the headline 'Danger of Drawing Upon the Imagination', the *Bangor Daily Whig and Courier* reported that the *Morning Post* 'writer had accidentally missed his passage and had accordingly invented a description, in total ignorance that anything of a momentous character had taken place', 30 September 1859, 2. See also the *Boston Daily Advertiser*, 28 September 1859, 2.

[36] [Hollingshead], 'Great Eastern Postscript', 546.   [37] Sala, 'The Special Correspondent', 220.

[38] Philip Knightley, *The First Casualty: The War Correspondent as Hero and Mythmaker from the Crimea to Kosovo*. London: Prion, 2000, p. 44.

Forbes first made his name as a special for the *Daily News* in covering the Franco-Prussian war of 1870–71, but the Anglo-Zulu war, fought between Britain and the Zulu kingdom in 1879, arguably secured his greatest fame. The battle of Ulundi brought the war to an end on 4 July, and to dispatch his report of the outcome, Forbes had to reach the nearest telegraph office at Landman's Drift some 110 miles distant. As the *Daily News* proclaimed on 24 July, 'His solitary and speedy ride . . . through a wild and hostile country, seamed with dongas, in any one of which cruel and exasperated enemies might be lurking, is an exploit much more spirited and stirring than that of the three who "brought the good news to Ghent."'[39] The same issue of the paper published Forbes's accounts of the battle, dated 3 and 4 July, and followed them with a report of the speech of Sir Michael Hicks-Beach to the House of Commons announcing the victory of her Majesty's forces under Lord Chelmsford: 'All arms reported to have done their duty admirably. Zulus slain estimated at eight hundred by Mr Archibald Forbes, who rode with the above news in fifteen hours to Landsman's Drift. (Cheers).'

The heroism of Forbes was lauded in the *Illustrated London News* with a front-page engraving representing the special correspondent as 'the bold, unwearied, dauntless, solitary horseman, "bloody with spurring, fiery red with haste"' (see **Figure 10.1**).[40] It was drawn by Richard Caton Woodville Jr., who worked for the *ILN* as a military artist for most of his life, thus underlining the extent to which Forbes's prowess as special correspondent was being merged with the heroism of the British army by the metropolitan press. Filling the entire front page, it shows Forbes looking determined but remarkably poised as his horse races across the Transvaal. The *ILN*'s call for him to be awarded a suitable honorary distinction at the request of the secretary of state for war in recognition of his performance of 'this valuable public service with such intrepid courage and so much personal address'[41] situates the special correspondent as hero of his own story – a position that Forbes clearly relished when he later wrote of this episode:

> To have held once and again in the hollow of my hand the exclusive power to thrill the nations; to have looked into the very heart of the turning points of nations and dynasties! What joy equal to the thrilling sense of personal force as obstacle after obstacle fell behind one conquered, as one galloped

---

[39] 'London, Thursday, July 24', *Daily News*, 24 July 1879, 5.
[40] 'Zulu War Illustrations', *Illustrated London News*, 9 August 1879, 125.
[41] 'Zulu War Illustrations', 126.

Figure 10.1 'Zulu War Illustrations', *Illustrated London News*, 9 August 1879, p. 125.

from the battle with tidings our people awaited hungeringly and tremblingly![42]

The story of Forbes's adventurous night ride was a thrilling narrative that received widespread publicity. But of more interest for my purposes is the way in which the episode highlights the function of special correspondence as a new technology associated with the 'annihilation of space and time' that is usually attributed to the railroad and telegraph in the nineteenth century. Reflecting upon the 'extraordinary' exploit of its special correspondent on 25 July, the *Daily News* argued that its 'novelty' lay neither in the 'boldness of the adventure' nor 'the manner of conveying the news', but in 'the character and occupation of our Special Correspondent himself' who was forced to report on the conflict 'under somewhat antiquated conditions' that recalled the circumstances and methods of the Crimean War correspondent of two decades earlier. As it explained, 'The Special Correspondent on the battlefield is a novelty altogether, but the rapid growth of the telegraphic system has brought out a newer development of this strictly modern innovation.'[43] Contrasting the task of the war correspondent of the present with that of his Crimean forebears, it observed: 'The telegraph wire follows him almost up to "the rough edge of battle". It was only by a curious chance that our Special Correspondent has now fallen upon a campaign which was cut off from the immediate companionship of the electric cord.'[44] As the trope of companionship here makes clear, like the telegraph, special correspondence was a technology whose development both cultivated and responded to the need for speed in the transmission of news. Their status as parallel technologies is similarly suggested by a writer in *Chambers's Journal* in 1873 who described them as compeers:

> There was an interval of competition between laconic telegrams recording bare facts, and the freer-handed 'descriptive' of the 'specials', and for a little it seems [sic] as if the telegraph system was discounting special correspondence. But the 'specials' rallied, and subdued their rival into being their slave.[45]

The development of the relationship between these 'rivals' was, however, uneven and specials such as Russell and Sala did not embrace the use of the cable in the same way that Forbes did. Nevertheless, as the cost of

---

[42] Quoted in Jennifer Crwys-Williams, *South-African Despatches: Two Centuries of the Best in South African Journalism*. Cape Town: Ashanti, 1989, p. 6.
[43] 'London, Friday, July 25', *Daily News*, 25 July 1879, 4.   [44] 'London, Friday, July 25', 5.
[45] 'The Special Staff', *Chambers Journal of Literature, Science and Art* (1873), 17.

telegraphy was reduced, and following Forbes's Franco-Prussian war success in arranging for his dispatches to reach the telegraph office with the least possible delay, an increasing premium was placed upon speed of transmission from the 1870s onwards.

This did not lessen the need for the special to provide a vivid discursive presentation of scene or event, but instead compounded the task. As a commentator in the *Newspaper Press Directory* in 1903 put it, 'He must wield a graphic pen, and a swift pen as well.' *Chambers's* noted that 'the price of the triumph' of the special correspondent over his rival, the telegraph, 'is costly':

> For [him] there is no longer dalliance over a late dinner, or a nap to refresh himself before commencing to write. His work is done now at the very acme of high-pressure speed. Eating, ease, or sleep alike must be disregarded by the 'special correspondent' who cares for his own credit and that of the journal which he represents. He must be able to write graphically faster than most clerks can copy, else he may as well retire from a profession for which he is unsuited. His bodily endurance and energy must keep pace with his mental vigour; he cannot afford to have a digestion, and the best preliminary training he can undergo is a full course of gymnastics, including equitation, and the ability to do without sleep.[46]

Thus what might have started out as a prosthetic relation between special correspondent and telegraph (the latter serving to overcome some of the limitations of distance encountered by the former) had begun, by the 1870s, to blur the boundary between human and machine. Like the factory worker compelled to work according to the rhythms of the steam-powered engine, the special correspondent had to adapt to the new time discipline associated with the telegraph: a process that accords with the industrial development of the press in other areas.

If the role of the special correspondent was being impacted by the rise of the telegraph in this way, what were the implications of these developments in technology for the Victorian newspaper reader? Combining swiftness of dispatch with the picturesque presentation of scene or event, special correspondence had from the beginning sought to transport readers imaginatively to the location described. As the writer in the *Leisure Hour* with which I began goes on to explain,

> We do not so much *hear* of the stirring events which take place abroad, as *see* them through the optics of the correspondent. We travel with him on his

---

[46] 'The Special Staff', 17–18.

devious round, and share the excitements of the way; while, knowing everything through his minute and faithful reports, we need not accept his
conclusions, because he furnishes us with the means of arriving at our own.[47]

To facilitate such virtual travel, special correspondence attempted to
reduce the imaginative distance between the positions of the correspondent
and reader, and the time and place of the events described, so as to generate
an effect of spatio-temporal immersion, of vividly evoking the presence of
temporally and spatially distant scenes. Russell set a high benchmark in this
regard, but other specials became equally adept. Consider, for example, the
account given by the special correspondent of the *Daily News* (probably
Hilary Skinner) of the field of battle the day after the surrender of the
French at Sedan in 1870:

> You must have been on several battle-fields to understand the signs of what
> has taken place by the look of the spot next morning. This group of dead
> horses, with a helmet or two and a dozen cuirasses with a broken trumpet and
> three dead cuirassiers, means serious work. The dark stains on the ground are
> where the wounded have lain and been removed. The little heap of swords
> under that hedge is where some dismounted troopers were forced to surren-
> der. Then we come to Prussian helmets crushed and trampled. Some are
> marked by shell or bullet, and have blood upon them. They tell of loss to the
> regiment to which they belonged. Others have no particular trace of violence,
> and may either be signs of wounded men, or of men who have simply thrown
> their helmets away in the heat of the action, and put on their forage caps to
> march more lightly. These dark stains, surrounded by knapsack and rifle, by
> greatcoat and cooking tin, are where men have lain who have been badly
> wounded, or even killed, but whose friends have made them as comfortable as
> could be under the difficulties of the time.[48]

The immersive quality of the representation of time and space in this
passage is palpable. As we saw in the earlier extract from Sala, pronoun
selection – 'you' and 'we' – is used as a boundary-crossing form of address
from the correspondent to the reader. Sharing his perspective, the reader is

---

[47] 'Our Own Correspondent', *Leisure Hour*, 55.
[48] (From Our Special Correspondent), 'War Letters. The Capitulation of the French Army', *Daily
News*, 6 September 1870, 6. The report is attributed to Archibald Forbes in John Fisher, *Eye-Witness:
An Anthology of British Reporting*. London: Cassell, 1960 and Jon E. Lewes, *The Mammoth Book of
Combat: Reports from the Frontline*. Philadelphia: Running Press, 2013. But Forbes joined
Robinson's staff on the *Daily News* only *after* the battle of Sedan. Skinner was attached to the
staff of the Crown Prince and carried his account to London, according to the *ODNB*, 'riding neck
and neck with W. H. Russell of The *Times*, and crossing from Ostend in the same boat; their
narratives appeared simultaneously on 6 September'. Thomas Seccombe, 'Skinner, John Edwin
Hilary (1839–1894)', rev. H. C. G. Matthew, *Oxford Dictionary of National Biography*, Oxford
University Press, 2004 [www.oxforddnb.com/view/article/25682, accessed 11 August 2015].

taken upon a forensic tour of the battlefield that is nonetheless artfully designed to draw us into the narrative scene. The miscellaneous itemisation of the debris scattered about – 'a helmet or two', 'a dozen Cuirasses', 'a broken trumpet', 'three dead cuirassiers' – is set in tension with the effort to make sense of this scene of carnage. While the time lag separating the moment of writing on 3 September 1870 and the moment of its publication on 6 September is an inevitable effect of transmission delay, the use of the present tense, combined with deictic demonstratives (such as 'this' and 'these'), seeks to create the illusion of simultaneity between the occurrence of these events and the act of their reading. The correspondent's retrospective construction of what took place here from the ghastly remnants of the preceding day's violence creates a complex layering of temporal reference in the passage that contributes to its haunting effect.

As the examples of Russell, Sala, Hollingshead and Forbes finally show then, special correspondence was a new mobile technology, characterised by the roving work of its practitioner whether as travelling correspondent, special commissioner or war correspondent. The journalists who worked in this role had to be versatile and resourceful, ready to cope with the peculiar exigencies of space and time that constrained the writing and dispatch of their letters. As the *Leisure Hour* noted, however,

> Even with all these rare qualities he will be nothing unless he have a faculty of observation rapid and comprehensive enough to seize upon everything that comes in its way, and sufficient volubility with the pen to chronicle all events as they take place, and pourtray [sic] all circumstances at once with a fidelity not to be impeached, and sufficient graphic effect to render the perusal of his despatches interesting and agreeable.[49]

Special correspondence was thus distinguished by the virtual mobility afforded readers who sought immersion in 'a vivid and dramatic presentation of scenes and events' that, as the *Newspaper Press Directory* put it, might 'surpass ... the enduring work of our leading novelists'.[50] Indeed, the very fact that so many of the special correspondents subsequently re-published their journalism, transferring their correspondence from the pages of newspapers to books, says something important about the ambiguous position of their writing – in between literature and journalism – in the print culture of their day.

[49] 'Our Own Correspondent', *Leisure Hour*, 53.
[50] MacDonagh, 'Our Special Correspondent', p. 90.

CHAPTER II

Reporting the Great Exhibition

Geoffrey Cantor

> One can scarcely take up a newspaper, read a periodical, listen to an
> address, or hold a conversation with a friend, but he finds reference is
> made to the well known building – the Crystal Palace.
>
> *Baptist Magazine*, September 1851[1]

As this contributor to the *Baptist Magazine* noted, during the summer of
1851 newspapers and periodicals were overflowing with reports and information concerning the Great Exhibition, which was currently attracting
large crowds to Hyde Park. Almost every daily, weekly and monthly carried
extensive descriptions of Paxton's innovative building and the numerous
exhibits it housed. Moreover, many periodicals published articles expressing their opinions of the Exhibition; it was frequently celebrated, although
some periodicals criticised the Exhibition or certain of its aspects. Not only
was the Exhibition extensively reported but, as I shall argue in this chapter,
it was, in a crucial sense, a creation of the periodical press.

The timing was fortuitous. With developments such as the reduction in
newspaper tax in 1836 (from 4d to 1d) and improvements in print technology, the price of newspapers and periodicals generally decreased and the
number of titles increased, and often too their circulation.[2] Thus during
the two decades prior to the Exhibition, a rise in the number of titles of
more than sixty per cent occurred, bringing the total number of titles
published in England to about 8,000.[3] The publisher Charles Knight
calculated that London alone published eighty-seven weekly periodicals

---

[1] S. Pearce, 'The Crystal Palace', *Baptist Magazine*, 43 (1851), 545–51, on 545.

[2] G. Dawson, R. Noakes and J. R. Topham, 'Introduction', in G. Cantor, G. Dawson, R. Noakes, S. Shuttleworth and J. R. Topham (eds.), *Science in the Nineteenth-Century Periodical*. Cambridge University Press, 2004, pp. 1–34, on pp. 16–17.

[3] The graph in Dawson, Noakes and Topham, 'Introduction', pp. 7–10, indicates that the number of English newspaper and periodical titles rose from slightly fewer than 5,000 in 1831 to approximately 8,000 in 1851. The authors, who drew on *The Waterloo Directory of English Newspapers and Periodicals: 1800–1900* (www.victorianperiodicals.com), also discuss the problems involved in ascertaining the numerical growth of periodicals in the nineteenth century. Scottish titles appear in the *Waterloo Directory* when an English, usually London, co-publisher is listed.

(not newspapers) in the week commencing 21 December 1850, with a circulation of 'fully 400,000'.[4] Thus an increased number and variety of newspapers and periodicals were poised to report and comment on this most prominent public event of the Victorian period. But one specific innovation was especially pertinent to the portrayal of the Exhibition in the press. Although written narratives of the Exhibition abound, the improved technology of rapidly reproducing large, good-quality wood engravings enabled illustrations of the building, the opening ceremony and many of the exhibits to be widely disseminated, particularly by such illustrated weeklies as *Illustrated London News* (hereafter *ILN*), founded in 1842, and the *Illustrated Exhibitor*, founded in 1851, which was published by John Cassell. In reporting the Exhibition, both titles achieved massive circulations; the first issue of the *Illustrated Exhibitor* is said to have sold 100,000 copies,[5] while the special issue of the *ILN* of 3 May 1851, which included a generously illustrated account of the opening ceremony, sold 200,000 copies.

Not only did the *ILN* thrive as a result of its extensive reportage of the Exhibition, but it was itself an exhibit in the Crystal Palace; visitors could watch it being produced on the vertical printing machine invented by Augustus Applegath and manufactured by Thomas Middleton of Southwark (Figure 11.1). This efficient steam-driven printing press had recently undergone significant improvements that enabled it to print 10,000 sheets an hour, an amazing rate that facilitated the rapid production of large numbers of this popular weekly.

The *ILN* was not the only illustrated periodical to include reports and also special supplements on the Exhibition. Another example is the *Art-Journal*, founded in 1839 as the *Art-Union*, and subtitled 'a monthly record of the fine arts, the industrial arts, and the arts of design and manufacture', which published four extensive supplements containing descriptions and copious illustrations of the fine art exhibits in the Crystal Palace. New illustrated periodicals were also established to satisfy the public's thirst for information about the Exhibition, including the *Illustrated Exhibitor* and the *Expositor: A Weekly Illustrated Recorder of Inventions, Designs, and Art-Manufactures*, which was first issued on 2 November 1850 and continued for more than four years (Figure 11.2). Published by Joseph Clayton, an avid proponent of

[4] *Knight's Cyclopaedia of the Industry of All Nations.* London: C. Knight, 1851, col. 404.
[5] S. Nowell-Smith, *The House of Cassell 1848–1958.* London: Cassell, 1958, p. 31; B. Maidment, 'Entrepreneurship and the Artisans: John Cassell, the Great Exhibition and the Periodical Idea', in L. Purbrick (ed.), *The Great Exhibition of 1851: New Interdisciplinary Studies.* Manchester University Press, 2001, pp. 79–113.

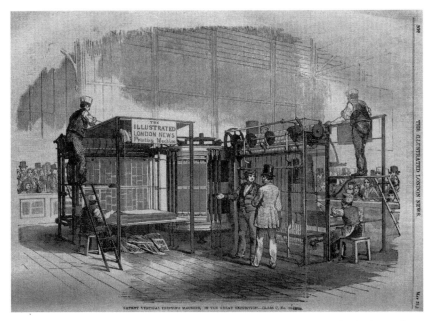

Figure 11.1 Visitors to the Crystal Palace watching Augustus Applegath's high-speed, steam-driven press printing the *Illustrated London News; Illustrated London News,* 31 May 1851, 502.

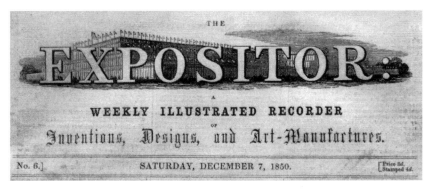

Figure 11.2 Masthead of the *Expositor,* 7 December 1850, 81.

free trade who also published the *Leader*, a radical weekly established in 1850, and several other titles, the *Expositor* was initially intended 'to prepare the public to visit the Great Exhibition with profit'. However, it also disseminated information about technological developments that were not directly linked to the Exhibition.[6] By contrast, the fortnightly *Journal of the Exhibition of 1851*, which rarely published illustrations, sought to provide a locus for comment on all aspects of the Exhibition; 'Its aim is *practical utility*; its purpose is *business*', asserted its editor.[7] However, it survived for less than a year.

Pre-Exhibition Publications

The early history of the Exhibition was marked by conflict, conducted mainly in newspapers and periodicals. The clamour against Prince Albert's vision of an international exhibition of industry was so strong that in late June and early July 1850 he was concerned that its opponents would wreck his plan and the House of Commons would vote to prevent the Exhibition building being erected in Hyde Park. Among his principal opponents, Albert identified *The Times*: 'The Exhibition is now attacked furiously by *The Times*', he complained to his mentor Baron von Stockmar.[8] Albert was reacting not only to the editorial published on 27 June against siting the Exhibition in Hyde Park[9] but also to the opposition expressed in its many other articles and in letters that it published. Although Albert singled out *The Times*, significant sections of the press had been ranged against his proposal since the plan for an exhibition was first made public in the autumn of 1849.

Among the newspapers that continually opposed the Exhibition was *John Bull*, a High Church, Tory, protectionist weekly. Characterised as 'admirably adapted to country gentlemen',[10] *John Bull* frequently portrayed the proposed Exhibition as 'the inaugural festival of Free-trade' and insisted that 'The Free Trade Bazaar in Hyde Park was devised for the purpose of exhibiting the operation of the system [of free trade] on a grand and showy scale.'[11] But *John Bull*'s antipathy extended to other concerns, including the Exhibition's alleged drain on the public purse and the fear

---

[6] Editorial, *Expositor*, 2 November 1850, 1.
[7] Editorial, *Journal of the Exhibition of 1851*, 9 November 1851, 3.
[8] Prince Albert to Baron von Stockmar, 28 June 1850: K. Jagow (ed.), *Letters of the Prince Consort 1831–1861*. London: J. Murray, 1938, p. 153.
[9] Editorial, *The Times*, 27 June 1850, 5.
[10] *Mitchell's Newspaper Press Directory*. London: C. Mitchell, 1851.
[11] *John Bull*, 23 March 1850, 185; 2 November 1850, 698.

that foreigners – especially revolutionaries – would use the Exhibition as an opportunity to invade Britain.

An intersecting range of concerns was articulated in some sections of the radical press. For example, Gracchus, a columnist on *Reynolds's Weekly Newspaper*, argued that only capitalists would benefit from the display of machinery, resulting in a further corrosion of the wages of factory workers and increased poverty. Opening the Exhibition to foreign competition would encourage foreign manufacturers to target the British market, thus further depressing the livelihoods of working people.[12] Although religious periodicals were divided on the wisdom of holding the Exhibition, some indeed shared the view of a contributor to the *British Millennial Harbinger*, an organ of Alexander Campbell's Primitive Christianity movement, who regarded 'this Exhibition with fear'. Describing himself as 'a pilgrim and stranger in this world, and a minister rude in speech in the kingdom of Christ', this writer expressed concern that the Exhibition, which would celebrate trade and physical luxuries, would drive the English yet further from the fundamental truths of biblical Christianity.[13]

Countering such criticisms of the proposed Exhibition were a number of general periodicals that enthusiastically supported Albert's proposals, including the *ILN*, *Punch*, the *Examiner*, *Morning Chronicle*, *Morning Post* and the *Athenæum*, as well as such specialised periodicals as the *Expositor*, the *Builder*, the *Art-Journal*, the *Artizan* and the *Journal of Design and Manufactures*. Although these periodicals articulated a range of arguments in support of the proposal for an industrial exhibition, two recurrent themes won wide applause. First was the boost it would give to manufacturing. It will 'raise the estimate of Industry amongst all classes', asserted the *Expositor*, which sought to advance the status of both industry and its workforce.[14] Second, as Albert made clear before the assembled civic representatives from across Britain and other dignitaries at a sumptuous banquet held at the Mansion House on 21 March 1850, the Exhibition would bring the nations together and thus lead to 'the realization of the unity of mankind'.[15] This vision was pertinent to the recent history of

---

[12] Gracchus, 'The monster bubble of 1851', *Reynolds's Weekly Newspaper: A Journal of Democratic Progress and General Intelligence*, 4 August 1850, 3. Gracchus was probably Edward Dowers Reynolds, the publisher's brother.

[13] A Watchman, 'The Great National Exhibition', *British Millennial Harbinger, Devoted to the Spread of Primitive Christianity*, 3rd ser., 4 (1851), 138–39. See also Geoffrey Cantor, *Religion and the Great Exhibition of 1851*. Oxford University Press, 2011.

[14] 'Influences of the Great Exhibition', *Expositor*, 8 February 1851, 226–27.

[15] 'Grand banquet at the Mansion House in honour of the Exhibition of 1851', *Morning Chronicle*, 22 March 1850, 5.

revolutions that had engulfed much of Europe and such wars as the one currently being fought over the control of the Duchies of Schleswig and Holstein.

While many periodicals endorsed Albert's overall plan, some of his supporters voiced pertinent criticisms. For example, the *Examiner*, a respected reformist weekly, contained a thoughtful editorial pointing out that as 'John Bull is terribly afraid of new ideas', the country had not adequately embraced the notion of an exhibition. The writer therefore urged the Commissioners to be far more vocal in encouraging the nation to back Albert's plan with enthusiasm. A very different kind of criticism was mounted in the April 1850 issue of the *Westminster Review* by the railway engineer William Bridges Adams who offered the Commissioners a number of constructive suggestions. For example, he pointed to the need to construct the Exhibition near a railway terminus (and not in Hyde Park which was far from a railway) to facilitate the transport of heavy equipment and exhibits. Also, some months before Paxton produced his celebrated plan for the building, Adams suggested that a large conservatory-like structure of iron and glass would be most appropriate for housing the Exhibition.[16]

As the public controversy over the proposed exhibition occurred principally in newspapers and the periodical press, it is significant that cuttings from such publications as *The Times, John Bull*, the *Economist*, some of which were highly critical of the Exhibition and of the Commissioners, were collected by Prince Albert and kept with his correspondence file relating to the Exhibition.[17] Thus, Albert and presumably the other Commissioners were aware of the criticisms mounted by these newspapers and periodicals. However, it is unclear how much influence the press exerted on the Commissioners' decisions, especially as the press was divided over many issues concerning the Exhibition. Nevertheless, some of the criticism and advice was adopted.

One example stemmed from the furore over the invitations to the official opening ceremony. In the light of previous attempts on the Queen's life – the latest on 27 June 1850 – the Commissioners announced on 16 April 1851, a fortnight before the opening, that only a select group, including the Commissioners, diplomats from foreign countries, aristocrats and the royal household, would be invited to the ceremony. This

---

[16] *Examiner*, 23 March 1850, 1–2; [William Bridges Adams], 'The Industrial Exhibition of 1851', *Westminster Review*, 53 (1850), 85–100.

[17] Held in the archive of the Royal Commission for the Great Exhibition of 1851, Imperial College, London.

group would then enjoy a private viewing before the public was admitted at
1 p.m.[18] However, a number of newspapers and periodicals expressed
outrage at this proposal to limit admission to the ceremony. They argued
that as the Exhibition had been promoted as a public event and funded by
public subscription, the ceremony should not be restricted to the social
elite but instead be open to all of the Queen's loyal citizens.[19] Only on
22 April 1851, just nine days before the opening, did the Commissioners
relent and a revised plan for the opening ceremony was promulgated. This
stated that the Queen had 'signified her Royal pleasure that arrangements
should be made . . . to gratify a wish very generally expressed on the part of
the public to be present at' the opening ceremony.[20] Season ticket holders
were now also admitted. However, the campaign by the *Expositor* to admit
exhibitors free of charge was unsuccessful.[21]

A second example of a successful campaign mounted in a periodical
arose from the justified fear of inventors and manufacturers that their
products were not adequately protected from rival entrepreneurs.
The forthcoming Exhibition thus provided a sharp focus for the prevailing
dissatisfaction over the inadequacy and expense of the existing patent laws.
The *Expositor* and the monthly *Engineer and Machinist*, in particular,
carried many articles on the need to reform the patent laws so that
British exhibitors would have some legal protection. In response to these
concerns, on 11 April, less than three weeks before the Exhibition opened,
Parliament passed the Protection of Inventions Act (14 & 15 Vict. c. 8),
which enabled an inventor to register an invention by submitting
a description of it, and also be granted a year in which to provide a full
petition for the patent.[22]

Although a number of newspapers and periodicals were embroiled in
arguments for or against the proposed Exhibition, many dailies and

[18] Minutes of 15 April 1851 in *Minutes of the Proceedings of Her Majesty's Commissioners for the Exhibition of 1851. 11th January 1850, to 24th April 1852* (London: William Clowes, printer, 1852), p. 330.

[19] For example, *Morning Chronicle*, 18 April 1851, 4; *Northern Star*, 19 April 1851, 4; *Manchester Examiner and Times*, 19 April 1851, 4.

[20] 'Opening of the Exhibition of 1851', *Standard*, 24 April 1851, [1]. The inclusion in the opening ceremony of a prayer by the Archbishop of Canterbury, John Bird Sumner, may also have resulted from pressure from religious periodicals.

[21] For example, editorial in *Expositor*, 24 May 1851, 57.

[22] For example, 'The patent laws, and projects for their amendment', *Expositor*, 28 June 1851, 142; F. W. Campin, 'Patent Law and the Great Exhibition', *Engineer and Machinist, and Engineering and Scientific Review*, 2 (1850–1), 315–17; L. Purbrick, 'Knowledge Is Property: Looking at Exhibits and Patents in 1851', *Oxford Art Journal*, 20 (1997), 53–60. While the Protection of Inventions Act was rushed through Parliament to address concerns raised specifically by the 1851 Exhibition, it paved the way for a far more extensive reform of the patent system in the 1852 Patent Law Amendment Act (15 & 16 Vict. c. 83).

weeklies provided readers with up-to-date factual information. Throughout the autumn of 1849 and the ensuing winter months, local newspapers carried accounts of the meetings between representatives of the Society of Arts[23] and local businessmen, manufacturers and civic leaders. Thus, the Exhibition was brought into the local domain and leading manufacturers committed themselves in public to support the project. Later, both local and national papers carried news bulletins about the meetings and decisions of the Commissioners, reproducing their circulars, and including official notices first published in the *London Gazette*. Likewise, much of the material published in the *Journal of the Exhibition of 1851* consisted of official notices and articles gleaned from newspapers.

Much Exhibition-related information was conveyed by, for example, the weekly *Athenæum*, which included accounts of the high-profile events at the Mansion House that were intended to advance the project and also regular reports on such issues as the receipt of donations to fund the Exhibition, the design of medals to be awarded to successful competitors, the fares to be charged by railway companies to transport visitors and the progress of the ongoing construction of the Crystal Palace.

The *ILN* adopted a particularly prominent role, which doubtless boosted its circulation, and it interceded on several occasions. For example, a competition had been held for the design of the Exhibition building, and the Building Committee received 245 submissions. However, this committee had adopted none of the submissions but rather advanced its own plan, which drew selectively on specific aspects of the submitted designs. In its issue of 22 June 1850, the *ILN* included a full-page illustration showing the design produced by the Building Committee and endorsed by the Commissioners for a building made principally of brick but with a large dome (Figure 11.3). Although the *Builder* and other periodicals had already voiced their dissatisfaction with the administration of the competition, this illustration in the *ILN* made clear to readers the size, shape and structure of the 'monster edifice' that the Building Committee intended to construct in Hyde Park. Quoting a letter that had appeared in the *Builder*, the *ILN* joined the chorus opposing the committee's handling of the competition and its cavalier treatment of the architects who had submitted plans.[24] While

---

[23] The Society for the Encouragement of Arts, Manufactures, and Commerce, generally known as the Society of Arts, had been founded in 1754 to 'embolden enterprise, enlarge science, refine art, improve our manufacturers and extend our commerce'. Although it had received its Royal Charter in 1847, it was not permitted to use the word 'Royal' in its name until 1908.

[24] 'Proposed building for the Great Industrial Exhibition of 1851', *ILN*, 22 June 1850, 445–46; *Builder*, 15 June 1850, 277–78.

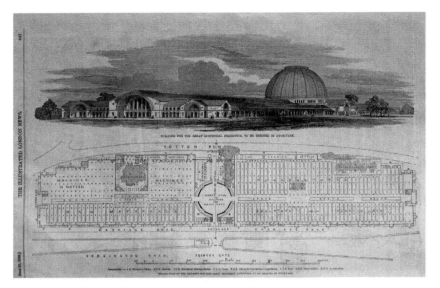

Figure 11.3 The Building Committee's proposal for a large domed brick structure to
house the 1851 Exhibition; *Illustrated London News*, 22 June 1850, 445.

criticising the committee's own design, the *ILN*'s publication of this illustration effectively disseminated the plan throughout the country and beyond,
and its appearance doubtless hardened the resolve of those who opposed
construction of the Exhibition in Hyde Park.

Two weeks later, the *ILN* published another illustration that was likewise to
play a prominent role in the Exhibition's early history. Speaking in the
parliamentary debate on 4 July concerning the use of Hyde Park for the
proposed Exhibition, the eminent Whig politician Thomas Spring Rice
mentioned that he had earlier that day seen 'a beautiful plan by
Mr. Paxton … which contemplated the use of iron, zinc, and glass only'.[25]
Two days later, the *ILN* published Paxton's innovative design for the
Exhibition hall (Figure 11.4).[26] A further five days elapsed before
the Building Committee submitted a report on this late entry, and the
Commissioners discussed Paxton's proposal, noting that its construction
would cost ten per cent more than the cost of erecting the committee's own
design.[27] (There were subsequent changes to Paxton's design including the

[25] *Morning Post*, 5 July 1850, 2.   [26] *ILN*, 6 July 1850, 13.
[27] Minutes of 11 July 1850 in *Minutes of the Proceedings*, p. 237.

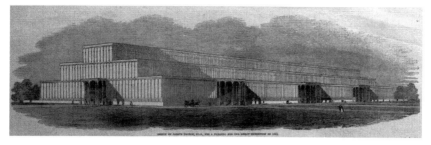

Figure 11.4 Paxton's design as presented in the *Illustrated London News*, 6 July 1850, 13.

addition of a circular transverse roof to enclose the trees.) Following the lead of the *ILN*, a number of dailies and weeklies offered enthusiastic written descriptions of Paxton's proposal and a variety of drawings of the building were also published. Over the next ten months, the *ILN* provided its readers with illustrations of the building's progress, starting with a view of the site on 17 August and continuing with a double-page view of the building (16 November), the raising of the ribs of the transept (14 December), the interior of the transept (25 January 1851), the view from the Serpentine (double-page, 8 February) and several other often reproduced illustrations.[28] Thus readers of the *ILN*, in London, elsewhere in the United Kingdom and even in foreign lands, could vicariously witness the building's construction. Moreover, it is doubtful whether Paxton's design would have achieved its widespread appeal without these impressive, widely distributed illustrations principally in the *ILN*.

During the weeks leading to the official opening, contemporary newspapers and periodicals conveyed, and also helped generate, the increasing excitement that swept through the country. 'The press vies in adding to the excitement', commented the *Expositor*.[29] Frequent notices appeared detailing the visits by the royal family, the arrival of goods and other arrangements. Even before the Exhibition opened, readers of the daily and weekly press would have learned much about it, and many would have been excited by the prospect of a visit.

[28] *ILN*, 7 August 1850, 125; 16 November 1850, 382–83; 14 December 1851, 453; 25 January 1851, 57 and 8 February 1851, 96–97.

[29] 'London Excitement', *Expositor*, 9 November 1850, 18.

Opening Ceremony

On 1 May, London celebrated the opening of the Exhibition as thousands of people converged on Hyde Park. The Queen's route from the palace was filled with cheering crowds. The opening ceremony itself was widely reported in the press, which also successfully conveyed the holiday atmosphere that pervaded London. The *Morning Post* proclaimed 1 May 'a memorable day in the history of England; – it marks, for all time, a great epoch in the annals of human history', while the *Standard* called it 'the great day of this century'.[30] Even *The Times*, Albert's old enemy, had changed its tune and published a eulogy that began: 'There was yesterday witnessed a sight the like of which has never happened before, and which, in the nature of things, can never be repeated.'[31] Many dailies and some weeklies contained full reports of the formal proceedings and also conveyed the excitement of the event. Soon the whole country and beyond could read about the appearance of the Crystal Palace, the arrival of the Royal party (including descriptions of the Queen's attire), the prominent guests, the unscheduled appearance of a 'Chinaman', the speeches, the accompanying music and the moment when the Queen declared 'the Exhibition opened!' The *ILN* took advantage of this lavish occasion by publishing on 3 May a special thirty-two-page issue, including a sixteen-page Exhibition supplement, for one shilling. Not only did it contain a full account of the proceedings but the double-page illustration showing Albert reading his address to the Queen on behalf of the Commissioners placed the reader at the very centre of this momentous event (Figure 11.5). The supplement included a double-page spread showing the south side and entrance of the Crystal Palace, together with the first two chapters of a history of industrial exhibitions, by W. Blanchard Jerrold, and a floor plan and guide to the Exhibition with illustrations of a number of exhibits.

Recording the Exhibition

Throughout the summer months of 1851, the *ILN* continued to publish Exhibition supplements containing views of the Crystal Palace and descriptions of many exhibits, often accompanied by illustrations. Other periodical publications also responded to the public appetite for information about the Exhibition. As noted earlier, from 7 June Cassell

[30] 'Royal inauguration of the Great Exhibition of 1851', *Morning Post*, 2 May 1851, 5; 'The opening of the Great Exhibition this day', *Standard*, 1 May 1851, [3].
[31] *The Times*, 2 May 1851, 4.

Figure 11.5 The double-page illustration of the opening of the Great Exhibition on
1 May 1851; *Illustrated London News*, 3 May 1851, 350–51.

issued each week his *Illustrated Exhibitor*, which contained twenty (later
sixteen) pages and cost 2d. A typical issue included a foldout plate
showing a section of the Exhibition and several short illustrated articles
examining a specific exhibit or type of exhibit, often designated by
country of origin, such as Italian or Indian contributions, or by class
(e.g. needlework, steam engines or sculpture). As Brian Maidment has
noted, the *Illustrated Exhibitor* not only presented the finished products
on display in the Crystal Palace but also demonstrated the manufacturing processes, with illustrations of artisans at work.[32]

The *Art-Journal* had taken a keen interest in Albert's project from the
start. Over a four-month period beginning with its May 1851 issue, each
issue included an extensive supplement with descriptions and copious
illustrations of the designs deployed by many of the exhibitors. These
supplements were subsequently collected together and issued
in September 1851 as the *Art-Journal Illustrated Catalogue*, priced at one
guinea, which also included further engravings and five essays by

---

[32] Maidment, 'Entrepreneurship and the Artisans'. See n. 5.

established experts on themes central to the Exhibition.[33] However, the financial outlay necessary to produce this lavishly illustrated work forced the editor, Samuel Carter Hall, to sell his share of the business to the publisher, George Virtue.

Although the illustrations of the Crystal Palace and its exhibits published in such periodicals as the *ILN, Art Journal, Expositor* and *Illustrated Exhibitor* were doubtless effective in conveying the Exhibition to their readers, there were also many unillustrated accounts in other periodicals; often they were written by visitors who recorded their personal narratives. For example, J. A. C. from Birmingham chronicled his visit in the *Sunday School Teachers' Magazine*, and the *Dundee Courier* carried a series of letters 'From "John" in London, to his friend "Peter" in the country' describing John's experiences visiting different parts of the Crystal Palace. A more didactic account of a visit was 'Mr. Merton's visit to the Crystal Palace' which was published in the Religious Tract Society's monthly *Visitor* over the signature 'E. V.' This chatty piece was intended to provide potential visitors with a safe perspective on the Exhibition that reflected the journal's evangelical principles.[34] Many other articles in the periodical press proved less personal and instead offered readers more objective descriptions of the Exhibition and the artefacts on display. Yet they all served as 'virtual' tours and could also be used by visitors to help navigate the building with its immense number and range of exhibits.

Descriptive accounts often concentrated on a specific section or sections of the Crystal Palace. For example, the *ILN* published a six-part 'A lady's glance at the Great Exhibition', which described exhibits considered to be of interest primarily to female visitors, such as the ornate parasols, fashionable gloves, attractive jewellery, fine fabrics, beautiful dresses and delicate embroidery. The well-informed and fashion-conscious author of this series also provided information about some of the production processes.[35] Two further examples are from the *Journal of Design and Manufactures*, which was edited by Henry Cole, who played a central role in creating the

---

[33] The *Athenæum* (6 September 1851, 942) doubted whether the Exhibition had generated 'any literary or pictorial record more interesting or attractive than this superb publication [the *Art-Journal Illustrated Catalogue*]'.

[34] J. A. C., 'A Sunday school teacher's visit to the Great Exhibition in the Crystal Palace', *Sunday School Teachers' Magazine and Journal of Education*, 4th ser., 2 (1851), 479–82; 'From "John" in London, to his friend "Peter" in the country', *Dundee Courier*, 20 August 1851, 2; 27 August 1851, 2; 3 September 1851, 2; 10 September 1851, 2; 1 October 1851, 2; 22 October 1851, 2; E. V., 'Mr. Merton's Visit to the Crystal Palace', *Visitor, or Monthly Instructor*, new ser. 1 (1851), 201–203.

[35] Z. M. W., 'A lady's glance at the Great Exhibition', *ILN*, 5 July 1851, 19; 19 July 1851, 98–99; 23 August 1851, 242–43; 6 September 1851, 291; 4 October 1851, 431; 25 October 1851, 530–31.

Exhibition. Apart from monthly reports on the Exhibition's progress, the *Journal* also reviewed specific classes of exhibits, such as 'Woollen and Mixed Goods in the Great Exhibition' and 'Printed Fabrics Exhibited at the Exhibition of 1851' (samples included).[36]

Reports often focused on particularly popular sections or exhibits, such as the Medieval Court, Applegath's high-speed press or the Koh-i-Noor diamond. Thus, *Eliza Cook's Journal*, which sought to encourage intellectual improvement, especially among women, carried an article describing the innovative revolver invented by Samuel Colt on display in the United States section. Yet the writer complained that this 'Exhibition of Peace is indeed teeming with the instruments of war'. An article followed on the widely feted Koh-i-Noor diamond, including a discussion of its turbulent history.[37] Religious periodicals frequently focused on the display of bibles mounted by the British and Foreign Bible Society. As 'Philo' writing in the *United Presbyterian Magazine* reported, 'There are the Bibles [in 150 languages] ranged against the wall. And a glorious sight it is. To the spiritual mind it is worth more than all the [other] treasures, of which this magnificent palace can boast.'[38] More technical periodicals concentrated on exhibits relating to their specialist topic. Thus, the *Expositor*, which was directed principally at skilled workmen, carried an extensive series entitled 'Walks among the machinery (British and Foreign) by a practical machinist and engineer'.[39]

Accounts of the Exhibition not only described the building and its contents but also frequently conveyed the excitement of a visit and the emotional impact on the visitor. One such example appeared in the *Morning Call*, a women's monthly miscellany edited by Sarah Stickney Ellis who, in describing a visit, expressed her admiration for the beautiful Crystal Palace adding: 'The sight is perfectly inspiriting. People start, and clap their hands, when they behold it.'[40] Many other visitors were likewise captivated by the building and sought poetic similes to express their reactions, such as the writer in a cheap religious monthly who described the Crystal Palace as 'this scene of Enchantment' which appeared 'chastely

---

[36] 'Woollen and mixed goods in the Great Exhibition', *Journal of Design and Manufactures*, 5 (1851), 119–24; 'Printed fabrics exhibited at the Exhibition of 1851', 137–42.

[37] *Eliza Cook's Journal*, 5 (1851), 200–202.

[38] 'Philo', 'The Great Exhibition', *United Presbyterian Magazine*, 5 (1851), 390–94.

[39] 'Walks among the machinery', *Expositor*, 24 May 1851, 66–67; *passim*. The *Magazine of Sciences* reprinted these articles without permission leading to a court case; *Morning Post*, 4 July 1851, 7.

[40] [S. S. Ellis], 'The Exhibition. Letter from a country visitor to her friend in the north', *Morning Call: A Table Book of Literature and Art*, 3 (1851), 515–28, on 518–19.

beautiful' and seemed 'less like a material reality, than a Creation of Fancy'.[41]

The Exhibition's aura of novelty and otherworldliness is conveyed by many poems, mostly celebratory. Some of these were published as individual items, such as Robert Franklin's *Wanderings in the Crystal Palace*.[42] However, a large number of short poems, many by women, appeared in newspapers and other periodical publications. One of the best known is William Makepeace Thackeray's euphoric 'May Day ode', published in *The Times* on 30 April. Less familiar is 'The Crystal Palace' in the July 1851 number of Ellis's *Morning Call*, which was probably written by her. Its opening lines convey the author's enthusiasm: 'A CRYSTAL PALACE!— princely thought and name! / The Poor Man's palace, where he finds his fame / Palace of Industry! more glorious still, / Worthy a nation's pride—a sovereign's will.' Even the *Church Sunday School Magazine* published a poem entitled 'A thought on the Crystal Palace' in which Eliza C. Green reflected on the biblical text: 'And the street of the city was pure gold, as it were transparent glass [Revelation 21:21]'.[43] The outpouring of poetry engendered by the Exhibition has not however attracted the study it deserves.

Reports in the periodical press often conveyed the excitement and sense of wonder felt by visitors as they examined the numerous artefacts on display. Thus, the Sunday school teacher encountered earlier remarked that 'Mingled feelings of wonder and admiration are roused at every gaze. You feel bewildered by the varied forms of beauty that invite inspection; at length some prominent one – perhaps the fountain – receives your attention.'[44] Writing in the *Expositor*, a German visitor reported that each new display rekindled his enthusiasm. During his perambulations, he repeatedly asserted that '"This must surely be the most beautiful!" until I enter the next department and find articles as wonderful and as tasteful.' Moreover, he noted that rather than becoming tired and apathetic 'my wonder and reverence only increase at each visit I pay to the Exhibition.'[45] Many other visitors reported that despite aching feet they were not

---

[41] Anon., 'Our last look at the Great Exhibition', *The Appeal; A Magazine for the People*, 6 (1851), 49–51, on 49.

[42] R. Franklin, *Wanderings in the Crystal Palace*. London: Houlston and Stoneman [1851].

[43] W. M. Thackeray, 'May Day ode', *The Times*, 30 April 1851, 5; S. S. Ellis, 'The Crystal Palace', *Morning Call: A Table Book of Literature and Art*, 3 (1851), 513–54; Eliza C. Green, 'A thought on the Crystal Palace', *Church Sunday School Magazine*, 6 (1851), 180–81.

[44] J. A. C., 'A Sunday school teacher's visit', 480.

[45] J. B., 'A German's letters from London to friends at home', *Expositor*, 10 May 1851, 31; 17 May 1851, 54.

oppressed and rendered apathetic; instead, they were constantly being challenged by more wonderful objects. Thus 'Philo' noted that even after 'the first fervour and flush of the feelings have passed away, and the various objects are contemplated with a calmer and less passionate eye, the intelligent expression of wonder, so far from being diminished, is perpetually upon the increase.'[46] The cumulative effect of seeing so many and such a variety of startling exhibits far transcended the visitors' normal experience.[47]

Not only did periodicals describe the Exhibition through the eyes of contributors, but potential visitors were also offered advice about how best to view the exhibits. For example, the *Family Economist*, a penny monthly directed at the self-improvement of the working classes, urged its readers, who were unlikely to spend more than a day or two at the site, to make profitable use of their time by planning their visit beforehand. The writer also urged working men to pay particular attention to exhibits relevant to their own trades.[48] By contrast, Ellis advised her friend – and her female readers – 'to pay your first visit to the Crystal Palace in company with someone who has been there before, and who knows the geography of the place; otherwise a whole day may be wasted in a kind of vague wandering inspection'. Her other principal piece of advice was 'by all means to go early', since the mornings were less crowded, more airy and pleasanter than the afternoons.[49]

The periodical press carried not only articles on the Exhibition but also a wide range of pertinent notices and advertisements. Thus, from the middle of 1850 the advertising columns of the *Athenæum*, which was owned by Charles Wentworth Dilke whose son served on the Exhibition's Executive Committee, carried such items as official notices advising potential exhibitors of the approaching deadline for making applications for space. Advertisements subsequently appeared for printed plans of the building, high-quality prints of the Crystal Palace and of many of the departments within the Exhibition and portraits of Victoria, Albert and Joseph Paxton. Readers were offered guidebooks to London (which were widely marketed) and such publications as the *Art-Journal Illustrated Catalogue*, the *Official Descriptive and Illustrated Catalogue* and Henry Mayhew's *1851 or, the Adventures of Mr. and Mrs. Sandboys*. Exhibition-

---

[46] 'Philo', 'The Great Exhibition', *United Presbyterian Magazine*, 5 (1851), 390–94, on 391.

[47] See also G. Cantor, 'Emotional Reactions to the Great Exhibition of 1851', *Journal of Victorian Culture* 20 (2015), 230–45.

[48] 'The Great Exhibition', *Family Economist*, 4 (1851), 122–24.

[49] [S. S. Ellis], 'The Exhibition. Letter from a country visitor to her friend in the north', pp. 82–83.

related lectures were advertised, including the series delivered by Edward Cowper, the professor of manufacturing art and mechanics at King's College, London. The *Athenæum* also carried reviews of some of the books that addressed the Exhibition, such as Charles Babbage's *Exposition of 1851* and Blanchard Jerrold's *How to see the Exhibition*.[50] Although these examples are taken from just one weekly publication, the Exhibition generated extensive advertisements and reviews in most newspapers and periodical publications. Thus even readers who were disinclined to read articles specifically on the Exhibition would nevertheless have encountered that ubiquitous event in the advertising sections of newspapers and in the endpapers of periodicals.

The celebration on 11 October, the final day of the Exhibition, and the formal closing ceremony four days later were widely reported in the periodical press, but they lacked the enthusiasm so evident in descriptions of the opening ceremony on 1 May. *The Times* even described the closing ceremony as 'a tame and awkward conclusion'.[51] For the press, the end of the Exhibition focused attention on two significant issues. The first, which had been under discussion for some months, was the fate of Paxton's widely admired Crystal Palace. Should it be dismantled, as the Commissioners had agreed when permission was first granted for its construction in Hyde Park? Or should it be turned into a winter garden, as Paxton and Cole had suggested? Second, the award of prizes was deemed unfair by a number of exhibitors who criticised the procedures adopted by the organisers, especially the Council of Chairmen, which consisted principally of the chairs of each of the thirty classes into which the exhibits had been divided. The *ILN*, which had previously championed most aspects of the Exhibition, was among the most critical voices on this issue.[52]

The closing of the Exhibition also initiated a flurry of periodical articles assessing its historical significance. The radical *Reynolds's Newspaper* asserted that the Exhibition had only benefited foreign manufacturers, leaving British industry depressed and exposed. It even suggested that the Exhibition had been an ego trip for Albert and his cronies. The ever-critical *John Bull* now looked forward to the return to normality after the disruption caused by the Exhibition; the editor resolutely insisted that its apparent success should not be taken 'as a triumph for Free Trade'.[53] Far more positive assessments were offered by many other periodical publications,

---

[50] *Athenæum*, 14 June 1851, 623–25; 21 June 1851, 657.   [51] *The Times*, 15 October 1851, 4.
[52] *ILN*, 25 October 1851, 529–30; 8 November 1851, 577–78; 15 October 1851, 586.
[53] Gracchus, 'Last words on the exhibition', *Reynolds's Newspaper: A Weekly Journal of Politics, History, Literature, and General Intelligence*, 12 October 1851, 7; *John Bull*, 18 October 1851, 668–69.

such as the *Wesleyan Methodist Association Magazine*, which claimed that the Exhibition – 'this wonder of this wondrous age' – 'has given a stimulus to the useful and ornamental arts; . . . expanded the views of multitudes, whose ideas of men and things were previously exceedingly circumscribed'. Likewise, the Whig *Edinburgh Review* proclaimed that 'all classes have increased their stock of knowledge, – enlarged the sphere of their enjoyments, cultivated new and instructive relations, exercised their national hospitality, [and] confirmed their loyalty'.[54] Just as the periodical press had earlier been deeply divided over Albert's proposal for an industrial exhibition, it now remained riven over the Exhibition's influence on the nation and its future.

Conclusion

Although a small proportion of periodicals, such as the *Latter-Day Saints Millennial Star*, snubbed the Exhibition by paying it scant attention, it provided the majority with extensive copy over a two-year period. As a writer in the November 1851 issue of the *Eclectic Review* noted, its readers had 'become familiar with the building . . . seen some of the beautiful engravings of this "Crystal Palace," [and] have read many descriptions of it in newspapers, magazines, pamphlets, and guides'.[55] Descriptions and analyses of the Crystal Palace and its contents filled many thousands of pages. The Exhibition was a media sensation. After the political and economic uncertainties of the 1840s, this immense, novel and exciting event was generally hailed as a cause for celebration. Some illustrated periodicals, such as the *ILN* and *Illustrated Exhibitor*, not only stoked public enthusiasm for the Exhibition but also benefited significantly from the extensive sales generated by their coverage of this extraordinary event.

Reports of the Exhibition were carried not only by British periodicals, some of which were distributed abroad, but also by newspapers and periodicals in almost every country. For example, foreign periodicals, such as the *Friend of India*, published in Calcutta, reprinted items about the Exhibition that had appeared in the British press. 'The description of the exhibition has formed a prominent topic in the newspapers and periodicals of the day, on both sides of the Atlantic' opined the

---

[54] Review of the *Official Catalogue, Edinburgh Review*, 94 (1851), 557–98, on 598; W. Reed, 'The year 1851', *Wesleyan Methodist Association Magazine*, 14 (1851), 570–73, on 571.

[55] Anon., 'Religious aspects of the Great Exhibition', *Eclectic Review*, n.s. 2 (1851), 623–41, on 627.

Cultivator, an agricultural monthly published in Albany, New York.[56] Accounts of the Exhibition were also generated by foreign visitors to London who sent reports to newspapers in their home countries; for example, Jules Janin forwarded regular copy to the *Journal des Débats* in Paris and Horace Greeley sent his chronicle to the *New York Tribune*.

As Brian Maidment has emphasised, the *Illustrated Exhibitor* offered a '"virtual" trip round the Exhibition for those unable to make the journey to London'.[57] However, his argument can be extended to include the *ILN* and the numerous other newspapers and periodicals that carried extensive and often illustrated accounts of the Exhibition. Their coverage of the Crystal Palace and its contents doubtless persuaded many to visit the Exhibition. Moreover, the extensive reports in the vast national and international network of newspapers and periodicals enabled many millions who were 'unable to make the journey to London' to undertake a 'virtual visit' to the Exhibition. Thus, the press enabled such readers to 'see' the Exhibition, thereby extending the number of 'visitors' far beyond the 2.5 million[58] who actually passed through the entrance booths at the Crystal Palace. For millions of readers, the Exhibition they encountered was the Exhibition created by the newspaper and periodical press. Moreover, as argued previously, the history of the Exhibition, from the first public announcements of Albert's proposals in the autumn of 1849 to accounts of the closing ceremony on 16 October 1851, is inseparable from its reportage and analysis in the contemporary press.

[56] 'Close of the Great Exhibition', *Cultivator*, n.s. 8 (1851), 393.
[57] B. Maidment, 'Illustrated Exhibitor', in L. Brake and M. Demoor (eds.), *The Dictionary of Nineteenth-Century Journalism*. Ghent and London: Academia Press and the British Library 2009, p. 301.
[58] Although more than 6 million people are recorded as having entered the Exhibition (First Report of the Commissioners for the Exhibition of 1851, to the Right Hon. Spencer Horatio Walpole. London: Her Majesty's Stationery Office, 1852, p. 88), many paid more than one visit. The number of individuals who visited the Exhibition is thus much smaller than 6 million, probably about 2.5 million.

PART III

The 'Globalisation'
of the Nineteenth-Century Press

Colonial Networks and the Periodical Marketplace

Mary L. Shannon

In Figure 12.1 from the periodical *Melbourne Punch* (1855–1925), the youthfulness of colonial Melbourne's up-and-coming commercial marketplace is emphasised through the figures of the Melbourne street boys. In this cartoon, settler barter culture is shown as dying out: the boy selling the periodical refuses to trade an issue for goods. *Melbourne Punch* itself stands for capital and modern commerce, not just culture. The street boys embody the energetic and possibly unruly forces of 'Young Australia'. However, in the background the sign 'PUNCH JUNIOR' reminds us that the new world has been born out of the old. Through its title, the periodical on sale advertises its imagined family relationship with the periodical which it imitates, the comic miscellany *Punch*, established in London in 1841. Such self-conscious references to the print culture of the imperial metropolis were not uncommon in the publishing world of mid-nineteenth-century colonial Australia's cultural capital. Writers, periodicals and newspapers from London found their way to Melbourne, and print culture networks based in London were reproduced by Melbourne immigrants such as R. H. Horne and William Howitt. Such complex relations between colonial and metropolitan print culture demand a more nuanced and careful scrutiny than is allowed by Benedict Anderson's somewhat generic idea of 'print capitalism'.[1]

This chapter will reveal the connections between the print culture and periodical networks of mid-nineteenth-century London and their counterparts in colonial Melbourne through the figure of writer and journalist R. H. Horne and the periodical *Melbourne Punch*. In so doing, it seeks to add to our knowledge of how, in Richard Scully's words, 'transnational press interactions . . . established and maintained complex webs of contact and communication that bound the British Empire – and the "British

---

[1] See Benedict Anderson, *Imagined Communities: Reflections on the Origin and Spread of Nationalism* (London: Verso, 1991). For a more transnational view of media, see John B. Thompson, *The Media and Modernity: A Social Theory of the Media*. Cambridge: Polity Press, 1995.

YOUNG AUSTRALIA COMMERCIAL OPERATIONS.

Fruit Merchant.—HERE, JEM, I'LL TRADE WITH YOU FOR SOME OF THEM PUNCHES FOR DATES. I AINT GOT NO CASH JUST NOW.

News Agent.—CAN'T SELL FOR NOTHING BUT CASH (RUNNING OFF). HERE YOU ARE, MELBOURNE PUNCH, ONLY SIXPENCE.

Figure 12.1 'Young Commercial Operations', *Melbourne Punch* I (1856), 22.
Institute of Historical Research Library, Senate House, University of London.

World" – together', particularly through numerous colonial imitations of *Punch* (one of the most imitated nineteenth-century periodicals, which became 'an important transcultural and transnational phenomenon').[2] R. H. Horne – Charles Dickens's friend and colleague – worked at the

[2] Richard Scully, 'A Comic Empire: The Global Expansion of *Punch* as a Model Publication, 1841–1936', *International Journal of Comic Art*, 15:2 (Fall 2013), 6–35, 10. See also Lurline Stuart,

Household Words office in London, socialised with staff members of *Punch* who also all worked nearby and exemplified the interconnected networks of editors, artists and journalists which operated in the metropolis and helped build Victorian London's formidable print culture. In 1852, Horne left London and sailed for the Melbourne gold fields. Three years later, he became a contributor to *Melbourne Punch*, which was started in 1855 in Collins Street and was presented as the 'child' of London *Punch*. The cultural capital of metropolitan print culture travelled with the body of its emigrants and was used to establish the periodical press of Melbourne. The first number of *Melbourne Punch* depicted writing and publishing as a personal business, with a cartoon of the anthropomorphised Punch family bidding farewell to Melbourne Punch Jnr as he leaves for Australia. In the cartoon, the embodied periodical emigrates just as London writers and booksellers emigrated; print culture itself is on the move, although its members remain connected in an imagined community. Horne's own body had cultural significance: his links to men such as Dickens and Douglas Jerrold made him the focus of literary gatherings which inspired the next generation of Melbourne writers.

This chapter reconstructs the overlapping print networks of *Household Words* and *Punch* in London and in Melbourne around mid-century to argue that because these networks were reinforced by strong ties of physical proximity, they had the background strength to sustain themselves when these networks became 'virtual' (to use Arjun Appadurai's term)[3] and transnational, and to be replicated abroad. It also glances briefly at connections between *Melbourne Punch* and its Sydney counterpart. Melbourne in the 1850s and 1860s was a city where emigrant writers like Horne wanted to replicate the energetic success of Dickens and his circle at *Household Words* and beyond. At the same time, they were troubled by the enormous cultural weight of those who belonged to those particular London networks. This ambivalence, what Andrew McCann calls 'the realities of cultural transportation and dislocation', was often approached through embodied images of a parent-child relationship.[4] It was not

---

Australian Periodicals With Literary Content 1821–1925: An Annotated Bibliography. Melbourne: Australian Scholarly Publishing, 2003.

[3] Arjun Appadurai, 'The Production of Locality', in *Modernity at Large: Cultural Dimensions of Globalisation* (Minneapolis: University of Minnesota Press, 1996), pp. 178–99.

[4] Andrew McCann, *Marcus Clarke's Bohemia: Literature and Modernity in Colonial Melbourne.* Carlton, Victoria: Melbourne University Press, 2004, p. 19. See Simon Sleight on British-Australian imperial relationships, 'Wavering between Virtue and Vice: Constructions of Youth in Australian Cartoons of the Late-Victorian Era', in Richard Scully and Marian Quartly (eds.), *Drawing the Line: Using Cartoons as Historical Evidence.* Melbourne: Monash University ePress,

a reactionary ambivalence; rather, it provided an enabling cultural tension. Writers and editors in colonial Melbourne used the cultural capital of the Old World to breathe vigorous life into the periodical marketplace of the New. In the space of two decades, Melbourne went from a small settlement to a lively literary hub. Much of this growth was driven by the presence of the gold fields. However, this chapter shows that the transplanting of brands like *Punch*, and of celebrities like Horne, played a significant role in this dramatic transformation.

Household Words and *Punch*: Emigration and Cultural Capital

Between 1850 and 1859, the *Household Words* office was located just off the Strand on Wellington Street, surrounded by the theatres, big newspaper offices and the Inns of Court. Wellington Street was full of newspaper and magazine offices: in the 1840s and 1850s it was home to more than twenty newspapers and periodicals, and thirteen booksellers or publishers.[5] Many of Horne's fellow-journalists on Wellington Street were part of networks of friends, colleagues and collaborators, who visited one another's houses, helped one another professionally and personally and were godparents to one another's children. These networks formed, fragmented and reformed over the 1840s and 1850s and were connected to two key locations: the *Punch* office, which was at 13 Wellington Street (South) until January 1844, and the office of *Household Words*, established at 16 Wellington Street North in 1850.[6] The original team of *Punch* included Mark Lemon and Henry Mayhew as co-editors, with Douglas Jerrold as a contributor and John Leech as illustrator. Other early members of the *Punch* team were W. H. Wills and Albert Smith. By 1850, the little building which housed *Household Words* was the regular workplace of Dickens, Wills (now Dickens's assistant editor), Horne and Dickens's father. A two-minute stroll away, at number 5 Wellington Street (South) was the office of the *Examiner*, edited by Dickens's close friend and literary advisor John Forster. At 17 Upper Wellington Street lived briefly one of the most famous contributors to *Household Words*, G. A. Sala, in the same building where

---

2009, 5.1–5.26, and Sleight, *Young People and the Shaping of Public Space in Melbourne, 1870–1914*. Farnham: Ashgate, 2013.

[5] See Mary L. Shannon, *Dickens, Reynolds and Mayhew on Wellington Street: The Print Culture of a Victorian Street*. Farnham: Ashgate, 2015, chap. 1.

[6] Shannon, Dickens, Reynolds and Mayhew on Wellington Street. See also Patrick Leary, *The Punch Brotherhood: Table Talk and Print Culture in Mid-Victorian Britain*. London: British Library, 2010, p. 147. The *Punch* office moved to 194 Strand in January 1844, before moving to the Bradbury & Evans office at 92 and finally 85 Fleet Street in 1845–6.

Jerrold had run *Douglas Jerrold's Weekly Newspaper* and next door to where Mayhew established the *London Labour and the London Poor* office in 1851. These writers and editors wrote for multiple publications, collaborated again and again in different combinations and helped one another through shared contacts and publishing ventures. *Punch*-ites Gilbert À Beckett and Jerrold both had plays or adaptations of their fiction performed at the Lyceum Theatre on Wellington Street; many of their circle visited the local coffee rooms and set up informal clubs in local taverns. London's publishing world in the Strand area in general, and in Wellington Street in particular, was made up of interconnected social and business networks.[7]

Horne's appointment to *Household Words* in 1850 as a staff writer brought him to the very heart of Dickens's network. He took part in the evening editorial staff meetings at the *Household Words* office and joined in the gatherings of Dickens's friends at the office and at dinners at Tavistock House. Horne had the distinction of being a member of Dickens's amateur dramatics troupe, and he performed before the Queen with John Forster, Mark Lemon and G. H. Lewes in 1851. Horne knew Forster in his own right in the 1830s and wrote for William Howitt in *Howitt's Journal*. In 1846, Horne joined the *Daily News* as Ireland correspondent under Dickens's editorship, along with a distinguished list of writers including *Punch* contributors Lemon and Jerrold. Horne collaborated with Jerrold and Angus B. Reach on their Whittington Club (a club and literary institute founded in 1847 on the Strand for the lower middle classes) and contributed to *Douglas Jerrold's Shilling Magazine*. Horne sailed to Melbourne with Howitt and his two sons on board the *Kent*; not only Howitt but also his wife and daughter were contributors to *Household Words*.[8] When Horne arrived in Melbourne, he carried with him immense cultural capital.[9]

In nineteenth-century Melbourne, Collins Street was the centre of the publishing trade; long, broad and fashionable, it was home to Melbourne's publishing heavyweights. In the 1850s and 1860s, *Melbourne Punch* was surrounded on Collins Street by the *Argus* (and its weekly the *Australasian*), the *Age* (and its weekly the *Leader*) and the *Herald*.[10] William Howitt's

[7] Shannon, chap. 1.

[8] Anne Blainey, *The Farthing Poet: A Biography of Richard Hengist Horne 1802–84, A Lesser Literary Lion*. London: Longmans Green & Co., 1968, p. 165.

[9] See Blainey, pp. 78, 165, 209; Cyril Pearl, *Always Morning: The Life of Richard Henry 'Orion' Horne*. Melbourne: F. W. Cheshire, 1960, p. 93; Monica Fryckstedt, 'Douglas Jerrold's Shilling Magazine', *Victorian Periodicals Review*, 19.1 (Spring, 1986), 5–6.

[10] Judith Buckrich, 'Collins Street', in *eMelbourne: The City Past and Present* (Encyclopedia of Melbourne Online), accessed 26 January, 2012. www.emelbourne.net.au.

brother Godfrey Howitt had a house at the east end of Collins Street, famous for its high walled garden.[11] There were structural as well as personal connections between the print culture of Collins Street and London's periodical publishing heartland around the Strand. In 1855, the following notice was published in the *Argus*, one of the two main Melbourne daily papers, published at 76 Collins Street East:

> MELBOURNE PUNCH, JN., Esq. begs to announce that having emigrated to the City which bears his name (both he and the city were named in compliment to a late illustrious Whig Nobleman), he has determined to issue a WEEKLY PERIODICAL of a highly interesting and instructive character. The first number will appear on or before Thursday, the 2nd of August.
>
> As it would ill become the modesty of youth to vaunt untested excellence, Mr. Punch, Junior, contents himself with observing that his Periodical will be in all respects superior to everything of the kind hitherto attempted in the universe. Printed and published (for the proprietors) by Edgar Ray, at the Auction Mart, Daily Advertiser Office, 66 Collins-street east, Melbourne. Price 6d. Subscriptions 6s. per quarter in advance.[12]

This mimicked the reports published in Melbourne's newspapers which marked the arrival of noteworthy emigrants. The first number of *Melbourne Punch* carried a cartoon of Mr Punch junior's triumphant arrival in Melbourne, as its founding editors worked to create a 'body' for their personified periodical (Figure 12.2). Here, *Melbourne Punch* trades on itself as a transplanting of London print culture.[13] Above the cartoon of Punch's arrival in Melbourne is the depiction of his departure; we see Melbourne Punch as a member of the Punch 'family', 'son of the celebrated Mr. Punch, of Fleet-street' (previously of Wellington Street). Note how the low-key, family scene of departure at the top becomes a grand state welcome at the bottom. The reader is asked to infer from the cartoon that Punch junior will go on to great things in the colony, even as they are asked to enjoy its mockery of the expectations of gold rush emigrants.[14] London print culture is used to bolster Melbourne's fledgling papers and periodicals, even to the extent of the spoof reports from *The Times* and the *Argus* (on Punch's departure and arrival, respectively) laid side by side and so given equal status and weight. A review in the *Argus* of this first number noted that 'the title-page represents Mr. Punch, Jun., as seated in

---

[11] Buckrich, 'Collins Street'.   [12] 'Miscellaneous', *Argus*, 9 July 1855, 7.
[13] *Punch*'s subtitle 'the London Charivari' is itself an allusion to early modern cultural antecedents: the charivari ritual.
[14] I am grateful to Ian Henderson for this point.

Figure 12.2 'Departure of Mr. Punch from Gravesend; Arrival of Mr. Punch in Australia', *Melbourne Punch* I (1856), 1.
Institute of Historical Research Library, Senate House, University of London.

his chair of office. The well-known features of his sire may be traced in his physiognomy ... The whole figure is significant of vigorous youth.'[15] This carries a dual meaning, as the 'well known features' of Mr Punch could be both the resemblance of the cartoon son to his cartoon father and the resemblance of the layout and typeface of *Melbourne Punch* to its London 'parent'. The body of the emigrant and the materiality of the printed page are linked; the 'vigorous youth' of the new venture is used both to connect *Melbourne Punch* to and to differentiate it from the London version.

The emigrant's body carried the print culture of the imperial metropolis with it, whether it was the personified body of Melbourne Punch junior on his fictional 'arrival' on board the 'Marco Polo', or the literal, physical bodies of Horne and Howitt upon their arrival on the 'Kent'. The notice in the Sydney *Empire* which announced the arrival of Horne and Howitt played up their 'Old World' connections, like the spoof report of the arrival of *Melbourne Punch*. It portrayed the two men as carriers of London print culture, although interestingly their contributions to *Household Words* are not thought worthy of mention:

> The ship Kent, which arrived at Melbourne two or three weeks ago, brought to that colony two gentlemen who have earned for themselves a distinguished rank in the world of literature ... We have not heard what are the ostensible objects of their voyage; but it may be fairly presumed, that the gentlemen to whom we now particularly allude have in contemplation literary works on the social state and mineral developments of Australia; and it is a gratifying circumstance, that talents of such high order and so peculiarly suited to such performances, should be employed in making this noble country better known to the people of England. The name of William Howitt, or of R.H. Horne, on the title page of a work descriptive of our Australian cities ... would ensure the attention of the British public ... As it may be safely calculated that these gentlemen will shortly visit our metropolis, we have extracted from a work, recently published in London, the following brief notices of their literary antecedents.[16]

There is a strange tension in evidence here between pride in the resources and energy of the youthful Australian cities (Melbourne was founded in 1835) and awed fetishisation of the 'literary world' of London and the 'Old Country'.[17] Horne's symbolic status as a literary celebrity in the *Argus*

---

[15] 'Melbourne Punch', *Argus*, 3 August 1855, 5.
[16] 'Our First Literary Arrivals', *Empire*, 8 October 1852, 1490.
[17] Arthur Angel Phillips, in a foundational text for Australian nationalist criticism, called this fetishisation 'The Cultural Cringe'. See Ian Henderson, 'Freud has a name for it': A. A. Phillips's 'The Cultural Cringe' (1950), *Southerly*, 69, 2 (2009), 127–47.

report comes not just from his 'talents of such high order' and the work of his own pen but also the fact of his perceived 'distinguished rank in the world of literature' (although Horne's autobiography admits that he was there purely to 'dig for gold' with no 'view to literature, science, art' or indeed journalism).[18] This sense of Horne's (and Howitt's) participation in a specific 'world' may have been bolstered by Horne's participation in the networks which operated on and around Wellington Street in the 1840s and 1850s.[19]

As a representative of the culture of the 'mother country', Horne's influence upon the younger literary arrivals to Melbourne was considerable, although not always, perhaps, because of the poetry which Horne persisted in producing.[20] Despite his many hardships along the way, and his eventual disenchantment with Australia and his return to England, what emigration allowed Horne to achieve in Melbourne was status as the kind of literary lion that he never managed to become in London. In Dwight's bookshop in Bourke Street, owned by Horne's colonial publisher, the young writers and journalists of Melbourne gathered for hard drinking and boisterous practical jokes. As the Scottish Australian educator and journalist Alexander Sutherland argued, Horne 'stirred up his young companions, who formed a little clique, to think of literature as an aim worth striving for, and in the midst of an utterly Bohemian life, he had a reckless devotion to art that had an unmistakeable influence'.[21] This clique included the immigrant journalist Marcus Clarke, immigrant poets George Gordon McCrae and Adam Lindsay Gordon and probably the Australian-born poet Henry Kendall.[22] Horne declared that 'I had many invitations, and received many kindnesses from persons to whom I had no other introduction than the knowledge of my literary position in the old country.'[23] Horne provided a physical link with the culture of 'home'; a conversation with Horne was one remove away from a conversation with

---

[18] R. H. Horne, *Australian Facts and Prospects: to which is prefixed The Author's Australian Autobiography*. London: Smith, Elder & Co, 1859, p. 2.

[19] A similar argument could be made about William Howitt; however, this chapter chooses to focus on Horne because of his impact on Melbourne literary life and his connection with *Melbourne Punch*. Horne stayed in Australia until 1869, much longer than Howitt, who left in 1854.

[20] Horne was best known as a poet, the author of *Orion*. See Pearl, and Anne Blainey, n. 9.

[21] Alexander Sutherland, *Victoria and Its Metropolis, Past and Present*, 2 vols. Melbourne: McCarron & Bird, 1888, 1:498. Compare Anne Blainey, p. 233: 'How far Horne influenced this earliest Australian literary movement is doubtful.'

[22] Anne Blainey, pp. 232–33; Pearl, p. 231. See also 'HORNE, R. H. (Richard Henry) (1802–84)', in William H. Wilde, Joy Hooton and Barry Andrews (eds.), *The Oxford Companion to Australian Literature*, 2nd edn. Melbourne and Oxford: Oxford University Press, 1994, p. 380.

[23] Horne, *Australian Facts*, p. 23.

Dickens, or with Jerrold. *Melbourne Punch*'s claim to status, however, came from its membership of the Punch 'family', and the way it hijacked the *Punch* brand. This form of plagiarism ('brandjacking', as Adrian Johns describes it) gave an air of both assurance and anxiety to the early numbers of *Melbourne Punch*.[24] Cultural capital was invested in the *Punch* name. The periodical made use of its London 'parent', while also aggressively asserting its own worth. It is 'Mr PUNCH,' – 'JUN.'

Periodical Networks in Colonial Melbourne

Despite Melbourne's physical separation from London (the voyage still took about four months at mid-century)[25] and the obvious differences between the two cities, London and Melbourne were mapped onto each other, and *Melbourne Punch* strove to use its 'parent' model to assert its continued place in the cultural conversation with London. This was particularly important in a period when Melbourne periodicals and newspapers competed with London imports for readers. This desire continued into the 1860s with the new generation of Melbourne writers and journalists, but it was already in evidence from the 1850s in the way Melbourne periodicals replicated the titles of their London forebears.[26] As well as *Melbourne Punch* (1855–), Melbourne titles such as the *Melbourne Illustrated News* (October–November 1853), the *Australian Builder* (1859–61), the *Spectator* (July 1865–March 1867), the *Melbourne Leader* (January 1856–June 1957; simply the *Leader* from January 1862) and the *Melbourne Examiner* (July 1857–September 1864) evoked, if they did not directly imitate, their London predecessors (of which the latter three were all published from Wellington Street).[27] More direct influences existed: the *Victorian Review* (1860–1), published out of the *Melbourne Punch* office by Edgar Ray, was

[24] Adrian Johns, *Piracy: The Intellectual Property Wars from Gutenberg to Gates*. University of Chicago Press, 2009, pp. 2–3. There was no business link between the two *Punches*; *Melbourne Punch* was an imitation, not a franchise. See Scully, p. 14.

[25] For sailing times, see J. R. McCulloch, *A Dictionary, Practical, Theoretical, and Historical, of Commerce and Commercial Navigation*. ed. Hugh G. Reid, rev. edn. London: Longmans, Green & Co., 1875. For a discussion of sailing times and conditions at mid-century, see Geoffrey Blainey, *The Tyranny of Distance: How Distance Shaped Australia's History*, 2nd edn. South Melbourne: Sun Books, 1983; first published 1966, pp. 161–64. For the effects of the gold rush, see pp. 178 and 197. On comparisons between London and Melbourne in nineteenth-century journalism and literature, see Kylie Mirmohamedi and Susan K. Martin, *Colonial Dickens: What Australians Made of the World's Favourite Writer*. Melbourne: Australian Scholarly Publishing, 2012, pp. 51–70.

[26] Lurline Stuart, *James Smith: The Making of a Colonial Culture*. Sydney: Allen & Unwin, 1989, p. 83.

[27] *Kelly's Post Office Directory* (1844), 156 and (1853), 555; imprint, *Leader*, 1 January 1853, 24; imprint, *Examiner*, 2 January 1848, 16.

modelled on the *Army and Navy Gazette*; the *Melbourne Monthly Magazine* (May–November 1855) was modelled on *Blackwood's*; the *Australian Journal* (Sept 1865–April 1962) was modelled on the *Family Herald* and the *Australasian Monthly Review* (March–April 1866) was modelled on the *Fortnightly Review*.[28] In the names of Melbourne's main dailies, the *Argus* and the *Age*, we hear the echoes of Wellington Street. In the Post Office Directory for 1844, 13 Wellington Street North (three doors down from the building which later contained *Household Words*) is listed as the office for the *Argus* weekly newspaper.[29] By 1844, this paper had already merged with its rival the *Age* to form the *Age and Argus*. Shirley Brooks was the editor of this short-lived paper (before it turned into *The English Gentleman* in 1845), around the same time as he first became involved with the *Punch* circle.[30]

Replication of metropolitan publishing practices can also be seen in the personal and professional connections between the networks established in and around the offices of *Household Words* and London *Punch*, and those which emerged in Melbourne with a focal point at the *Melbourne Punch* office in Collins Street. Of course, the strangeness of Melbourne upon arrival and the hardships to be faced by the unwary middle-class emigrant were emphasised in much emigration literature, including accounts by Howitt and Horne.[31] There is an emphasis on latent masculine aggression in descriptions of the streets of mid-century Melbourne, and the sanctum of the editor's office was represented as not safe from this violence. In 1855, the editor and the publisher of *Melbourne Punch* were attacked by the irate target of one of *Punch*'s cartoons:

> On Thursday afternoon Mr. Bernal, formerly a Gold Commissioner, and who figured rather prominently in a caricature in that morning's Punch, called at Punch's head-quarters, in Collins-street, where he met the reputed editor, Mr. Frederick Sinnett, and the publisher, Mr. Edgar Ray. After some conversation of a not over-amicable character ... Mr. Bernal proceeded to administer a dose of corporal chastisement ... assisted by a Mr. Candor ... The result was that the Punchites got well

---

[28] See Lurline Stuart, *James Smith*, pp. 89, 85, 90, 92. For details of nineteenth-century periodicals published in Melbourne, see Lurline Stuart, *Australian Periodicals*.

[29] *Kelly's Post Office Directory* (1844), 514.

[30] David Haldane Lawrence, 'Age (1825–1843)', in Laurel Brake and Marysa Demoor (eds.), *Dictionary of Nineteenth Century Journalism*. Ghent and London: Academia Press and British Library, 2009, p. 8; Patrick Leary, 'Brooks, Charles William Shirley (1816–1874)', *DNCJ*, p. 81.

[31] See William Howitt's *Land, Labour, and Gold or, Two Years in Victoria, with Visits to Sydney and Van Dieman's Land*, 2 vols. London: Longman, Brown, Green, and Longmans, 1855; and Horne's fictionalised accounts of his departure and journey to Melbourne and vignettes of Australian life published in *Household Words* 29 January–3 September 1853, as well as his *Australian Autobiography*.

'punched', and as is generally the case with those who come off 'second best' in such encounters, they have applied for and obtained summonses against their assailants. The double charge of assault will be heard in the City Court this morning, when Punch, Junior, will have the honour of making a personal acquaintance with his very particular friend the Right Worshipful and a bench of magistrates.[32]

This report first appeared in the *Melbourne Herald*; given that the *Herald*'s office was on Collins Street, the staff there may well have heard the commotion at number 66. The magistrate ruled against *Punch*, which responded with satire (Figures 12.3a and 12.3b). On hearing of these events, Horne could have been forgiven if he had decided that life as an editor and writer in Collins Street was far removed from life at the *Household Words* office.

However, responses to colonial life were more complicated than that: London and Melbourne were frequently aligned in language and rhetoric.[33] Andrew May positions late nineteenth-century Melbourne as 'a precinct of the global city', as part of what he sees as a growing transnational municipal community,[34] but in the 1850s and 1860s the neighbourhoods of Wellington Street and Collins Street were already linked through the personnel, content and practices of their respective periodicals by the 'transplanting of skills and of ready access to key networks in London'.[35] Despite the lure of a new start in a new country, Horne and his *Melbourne Punch* colleagues show that members of print networks in colonial Melbourne not only retained ties to London but considered themselves to be, in some way, still part of that London world.

London's print networks expanded into Melbourne and turned a local face-to-face community into a more virtual one that stretched the definition of what local might mean.[36] Horne brought with him a letter of introduction to Captain Chisholm at his office in Swanstone Street. Chisholm was the husband of the founder of the Family

---

[32] 'Punch in Trouble', *Empire*, 27 September 1855, 5. Reprinted from the *Melbourne Herald*, 22 September 1855.

[33] See Asa Briggs, *Victorian Cities*, 2nd edn. Harmondsworth: Penguin, 1968, p. 295.

[34] Andrew Brown-May, 'In the Precincts of the Global City: The Transnational Network of Municipal Affairs in Melbourne, Australia, at the End of the Nineteenth Century', in Pierre-Yves Saunier and Shane Ewen (eds.), *Another Global City: Historical Explorations into the Transnational Municipal Movement, 1850–2000*. Basingstoke: Palgrave Macmillan, 2008, pp. 19–34.

[35] Wallace Kirsop, 'Cole's Book Arcade', in John Hinks and Catherine Armstrong (eds.), *Worlds of Print: Diversity in the Book Trade*. New Castle, DE: Oak Knoll Press; London: British Library, 2006, p. 32.

[36] Appadurai, p. 189.

AN EDITOR'S ROOM IN MELBOURNE.

FURNISHED IN ACCORDANCE WITH A LATE MAGISTERIAL DECISION.

Figure 12.3a 'An Editor's Room in Melbourne'. *Melbourne Punch* I (1856), 69.
Institute of Historical Research Library, Senate House, University of London.

Colonisation Society Caroline Chisholm, who was widely considered
the model for Mrs Jellyby in *Bleak House*.[37] Caroline Chisholm's
Household Words article 'Pictures of Life in Australia' had been edited by

[37] *Australian Facts*, 178; Joanna Bogle, 'Chisholm, Caroline (1808–1877)', *Oxford Dictionary of National Biography*, accessed 11 August 2012, www.oxforddnb.com/.

(ADVERTISEMENT).

TO PUGILISTS AND OTHERS.

WANTED an Editor.—Literary qualifications not required, but he
must be up to anything under twelve stone.   Apply office of
this paper.

(ADVERTISEMENT).

TO EDITORS AND OTHERS.

THE recent decision of the Bench of Magistrates in the case of MR.
Bernal, emboldens Messrs. COLT and BOWIE to call renewed
attention to their very superior assortment of

REQUISITES FOR AN EDITORS ROOM.
These will be found to include

FIVE AND SIX BARRELLED REVOLVERS,
By the best English and American makers.

VERY SUPERIOR LIFE PRESERVERS,
Of extra size and weight, to suit heads of peculiar thickness.

SWORDSTICKS, BLUDGEONS, AND CANES,
In every Variety.

Messrs. C. and B. would call particular attention to their

EDITORS' INKSTANDS,
With compartments for Bullets, Caps, and Powder; also to their

RULER DIRKS AND AIR GUNS,
A very superior article, manufactured expressly for the Melbourne
market.

N.B.—A few very superior thorough-bred bull-dogs on sale.

Figure 12.3b 'To Editors and Others'. *Melbourne Punch* I (1856), 73.

Horne.[38] Horne's fellow-contributors to *Melbourne Punch* also had
connections to both *Punch* and Dickens's publishing ventures.[39] James
Smith, contributor and editor of *Melbourne Punch* from 1857 to 1863,
had once worked with Jerrold, according to Horne's biographer Anne

[38] Anne Lohrli, '*Household Words*' *A Weekly Journal 1850–1859 Conducted by Charles Dickens, Table of
Contents, List of Contributors and Their Contributions Based on the 'Household Words' Office Book.*
University of Toronto Press, 1973, p. 311.
[39] See Lurline Stuart, *Australian Periodicals*, pp. 84–85. See also Marguerite Mahood, *The Loaded Line:
Australian Political Caricature 1788–1901*. Carlton, Victoria: Melbourne University Press, 1973; and
Mahood, 'Melbourne Punch and Its Early Artists', *La Trobe Library Journal*, 4 (October 1969),
accessed 6 January 2014, www.slv.vic.gov.au/latrobejournal/issue/latrobe-04/t1-g-t1.html.

Blainey. Butler Cole Aspinall, another contributor, had been friends with G. H. Lewes in London, while James Stiffe was the originator of one of *Punch*'s most popular jokes, 'Advice to those about to marry – Don't'.[40] The unpaid contributor William À Beckett, later chief justice, was the elder brother of Gilbert À Beckett, a prolific contributor to *Punch*; Gilbert was also in Dickens's acting troupe and had written for the Lyceum.[41] In Melbourne, Horne came across the Irish politician and journalist Charles Gavan Duffy, also a contributor to *Melbourne Punch*, whom he had first met in Ireland when Horne was Dublin correspondent for the *Daily News* and Duffy edited the *Nation*. Duffy got Horne a job during one of Horne's frequent penniless states.[42] All of these members of the Melbourne print networks were emigrants, rather than Australian born.

As well as biographical links to the networks of London periodical publishing, Horne and his fellow-contributors to *Melbourne Punch* had a similar way of working to their metropolitan counterparts. Just as amongst Dickens's network in London, business and socialising went hand in hand. Along with *Melbourne Punch* artist Nicholas Chevalier, and fellow-contributors Archibald Michie and James Smith (all immigrants), Horne was a founding member of the Garrick Club (which never had enough money for permanent premises), set up in direct imitation of the London version. Horne was also a fellow-contributor to the same periodicals as key Garrick members and fellow gold-rush immigrants John Shillinglaw (a civil servant, journalist and historian) and theatrical critic James Nield.[43] A similar group, but which included younger writers, went on later to form the Yorick Club in the 1860s, with its premises in part of the *Melbourne Punch* building.[44] James Smith hosted gatherings at the Argus Hotel and Dining Rooms on Collins Street near the Argus office,[45] while round the corner at 71–81 Bourke Street the Theatre Royale was the favourite haunt of Marcus Clarke, immortalised in his sketch 'The Café Lutetia'.[46]

---

[40] Anne Blainey, p. 209; Mahood, *Loaded Line*, p, 44; Hugh McCrae, 'My Father and My Father's Friends', in *Story-Book Only*. Sydney and London: Angus and Robertson, 1948; first published 1935, pp. 1–56 (p. 33). The joke is also attributed to Henry Mayhew.

[41] See Arthur William à Beckett, *The à Becketts of 'Punch': Memories of Fathers and Sons*. Westminster: Archibald Constable, 1903, p. 22.

[42] Anne Blainey, p. 209; Pearl, p. 93.

[43] Lurline Stuart, *James Smith*, p. 45; Paul De Serville, 'Garrick Club', in *eMelbourne*, accessed 20 January 2012.

[44] McCrae, pp. 19–20.

[45] Advertisement inside front cover, *Melbourne Punch* 1 (1856); Lurline Stuart, *James Smith*, p. 7.

[46] McCann, p. 34. For a discussion of the fantastical elements of descriptions of this colonial Bohemia, see McCann, especially pp. 30–32, 46, and 51.

As in London, links of business, friendship and marriage became inter-woven. Frederick Sinnett, the first editor and co-publisher of *Melbourne Punch*, was a business partner of Horne's friend Archibald Michie; Michie's daughter Isabella married the nephew of William À Beckett.[47] Networks developed – as on Wellington Street – because writers frequently wrote for several publications, and such portfolio careers were assisted by the close physical proximity of Collins Street's newspaper offices, and also of the theatres. Of his fellow-contributors to *Melbourne Punch*, James Smith, William À Beckett, Charles Whitehead and Butler Cole Aspinall all wrote for other publications to which Horne also provided work.[48] Sinnett worked for both the *Argus* and *Melbourne Punch*.[49] Marcus Clarke started as theatre critic for the *Argus*, was a prolific playwright and married the actress Maria Dunn.[50] Furthermore, famous London figures were evoked and discussed through literary lectures, visits and obituaries: the assumption was that the Melbourne reader not only knew who these metropolitan people were but also cared.[51]

Colonial Australia and the Embodied Periodical

The culture of the 'mother country' provided competition for the periodical press of Collins Street, just as much as it was an essential reference point for their work. Imported books and periodicals from 'home' were big business in a colony with high literacy rates, as it cost at least twice as much to print a book in Australia as in England,[52] and English publications also carried the charm and *cachet* of 'home'.[53] A Melbourne writers like Horne in the 1850s and 1860s was much more likely to send their books to London for publica-tion than to launch them locally. But this cultural tension energised Melbourne's print culture. Conditions gradually changed over the 1850s and 1860s as men such as Smith and his contemporaries developed more

---

[47] 'Death of Sir Archibald Michie', *Argus*, 23 June 1899, 6.

[48] See Lurline Stuart, *Australian Periodicals*.

[49] Marjorie J. Tipping, 'Sinnett, Frederick (1830–1866)', *Australian Dictionary of Biography Online*, accessed 25 January 2012, http://adb.anu.edu.au/.

[50] Laurie Hergenhan, Ken Stewart and Michael Wilding, eds., *Cyril Hopkins' Marcus Clarke*. North Melbourne: Australian Scholarly Publishing, 2009, pp. 165–69; Michael Wilding, *Marcus Clarke*. Melbourne and Oxford: Oxford University Press, 1977, p. 7.

[51] See, for example, 'Lecture on Douglas Jerrold', *Argus*, 10 April 1858, 5.

[52] Elizabeth Webby, 'Writers, Printers, Readers', in Laurie Hergenhan (gen. ed.), *The Penguin New Literary History of Australia*. Ringwood, Victoria and Harmondsworth: Penguin, 1988, pp. 113–25 (114).

[53] Elizabeth Webby, 'Colonial Writers and Readers', in Webby (ed.), *The Cambridge Companion to Australian Literature*. Cambridge University Press, 2000, pp. 50–73 (50, 54).

of a local market for periodicals as well as books and newspapers.[54] Indeed, by the 1880s and 1890s the new generation of largely Australian-born writers and journalists was able to make a decent living from their writing, as 'a conscious attempt was being made in Australia to create a distinctively national culture', albeit one still engaged with European forms and traditions.[55] According to Lurline Stuart, 'close to 200 literary or partly-literary periodicals were produced in Melbourne in the nineteenth century'.[56] Working practices among the publishing networks of London and Melbourne helped develop Sydney's print culture, too, as a younger generation looked more to Sydney than to Melbourne as a cultural hub.[57] Edgar Ray, co-founder of *Melbourne Punch*, went on to found the third, and most enduring, incarnation of Sydney *Punch* (1864–88) with offices first in Pitt Street and then George Street.[58] Perhaps Ray's experience with *Melbourne Punch* was critical to the success of this periodical, the earlier versions of which had both lasted less than a year.[59] Certainly, Ray's second *Punch* enterprise drew on iconography of the embodied periodical similar to that of *Melbourne Punch*.

The first, failed attempt to found a *Punch* in Sydney was inspired, according to Richard Scully, by intercity rivalry; 'as a pretender to the title of pre-eminent metropolis of the Australasian colonies, then held by Melbourne ... it was unthinkable that Sydney should not possess a real British-and-London-style *Punch* when its rival did.'[60] As a spoof letter to Mr Punch in the opening pages of volume one put it, 'the sound of your advent is pleasant to the ears of New South Wales.'[61] This letter refers to the new Mr Punch as 'a hopeful representative of our old friend of Fleet-Street' who compares most favourably with 'a miserable prototype' that was last seen in the colony, 'a melancholy caricature' that 'wandered through the streets of Sydney'.[62] This failed *Punch* and its family 'plied

---

[54] Elizabeth Morrison shows that imported fiction from abroad was still hugely popular in the latter part of the century. See Morrison, 'Serial Fiction in Australian Colonial Newspapers', in John O. Jordan and Robert L. Patten (eds.), *Literature in the Marketplace: Nineteenth-Century British Publishing and Reading Practices*. Cambridge University Press, 1995, pp. 306–23.

[55] Richard White, *Inventing Australia: Images and Identity 1688–1980*. St. Leonards, NSW: Allen & Unwin, 1981, pp. 89, 85.

[56] Lurline Stuart, *James Smith*, pp. 83–84. See also D. H. Borchardt, 'Printing Comes to Australia', in Borchardt and Wallace Kirsop (eds.), *The Book in Australia*, p. 12.

[57] White, p. 87.   [58] Imprints, *Sydney Punch* vols. I and IV.

[59] Lurline Stuart, *Australian Periodicals*, p. 124.

[60] Scully, p. 15. For an older account of intercity rivalry which argues that Melbourne and Sydney developed very different literary traditions, see John Docker, *Australian Cultural Elites: Intellectual Traditions in Sydney and Melbourne*. Sydney: Angus and Robertson, 1974.

[61] 'Correspondence', Sydney *Punch*, May 27, 1864, 7.

[62] 'Correspondence', Sydney *Punch*, May 27, 1864, 7.

their performances with vigorous expectancy in George-street' then fell down the geographical scale of streets and places until they 'vanished into thin air, or perhaps Queensland'.[63] Ray's version, on the other hand, is lauded as 'a healthy offshoot from the real stock of the British Punch Family', able to provide the 'sagaciously critical' comments on Sydney society worthy of 'a true PUNCH'.[64] As in Melbourne, Edgar Ray's periodical is keen to establish its family tree.

Ray's successful version also seems understandably well aware of its Melbourne counterpart. Sydney *Punch* drew upon the parent-and-child imagery in its very first issues, too: the title page to the first volume showed Mr Punch the father offering his baby to the reader; given Edgar Ray's background, it was open to interpretation as to whether London *Punch* or *Melbourne Punch* was the depicted 'parent'. The title page for issues in volume four (1866) shows Mr Punch's triumphant arrival into Sydney Harbour (Figure 12.4), in an image reminiscent of the cartoon which depicted Melbourne Punch junior's own arrival in Victoria.[65] However, there are some significant differences. This title page looks only forward, not back; there is no Punch senior, no weeping family, no reference to the departure from England. This image places its emphasis wholly on arrival. There is a representation of the famous Punch profile on the medallion around the dog's neck, which reminds the reader of its London 'parent', as does the name of the periodical being read by the monocle-wearing kangaroo. The kangaroo, however, is significant: the suggestion is of course that this Australian reader is immersed in an Australian *Punch*, not the London version. Although Punch's ship is wafted in by figures loosely taken from Old World classical mythology, this scene of arrival emphasises the confidence and status of the new colony, so much so that the title of the periodical itself is given as *Punch*, not *Sydney Punch*. It is its own publication, not a derivative of London or of Melbourne, this implies. The adverts surrounding it – many of which are for businesses on the same street as the Sydney *Punch* office at 288 George Street – make a statement of commercial intent, and the fact that this is a title page rather than (in the case of the representation of Melbourne Punch junior's arrival) a one-off cartoon means that the reader would have been presented with this image week after week, issue after issue. Undoubtedly drawing on the same tropes of embodiment and emigrant arrival as *Melbourne Punch*, this image suggests

[63] 'Correspondence', Sydney *Punch*, May 27, 1864, 7.
[64] 'Correspondence', Sydney *Punch*, May 27, 1864, 7.
[65] The first issue of Sydney *Punch* also carried two cartoons depicting the arrival of Mr Punch to Sydney Cove (27 May 27 1864, 1–2).

Figure 12.4 Title page, Sydney *Punch* IV:87 (20 January 1866).
State Library of Victoria, http://handle.slv.vic.gov.au/10381/110000.

a desire to move beyond its brother-periodical in a more Australian-focused direction. However, the title page reveals the ways in which Sydney *Punch* was still very much in dialogue with both Melbourne and London periodicals and networks.

As with Melbourne and London, there were more than stylistic links between the periodical press of Melbourne and Sydney. Eugene Montagu

(Monty) Scott was a cartoonist and illustrator who, like Horne, migrated to Melbourne in the 1850s where he contributed work to *Melbourne Punch*. In 1866, he moved again, this time to Sydney, and became the chief cartoonist for Sydney *Punch*. He set up a photographic studio on George Street for a few years, not far from the Sydney *Punch* office.[66] Alfred Clint arrived in Melbourne in the 1860s, where he worked first as an assistant scene painter at the Theatre Royal. After a brief stint in Adelaide, he came to Sydney in 1869 employed on a production of Boucicault's *After Dark*. He was appointed scenic artist at the Prince of Wales Theatre, but he also joined the staff of Sydney *Punch* as a cartoonist and later contributed to the early issues of the *Bulletin*, an influential and long-running Sydney-based weekly. [67] Traffic between the publishing networks of Melbourne and Sydney also went the other way: Garnet Walch, author and dramatist, received his first full-time job as a journalist with Sydney *Punch*. He moved to Melbourne in 1872 where he developed a prolific career as a popular dramatist.[68] Henry Kendall had lived in Sydney before he joined Horne's clique of young admirers in Melbourne; in Sydney, he was befriended by William Bede Dalley, who wrote consistently for Sydney *Punch* as well as supporting it financially.[69]

The writers and editors of mid-century Melbourne, then, made clever use of their cultural double bind to develop Melbourne periodical publishing in ways which had an impact beyond their city. They were in dialogue with London's periodical marketplace, and they went on to develop connections with Sydney's periodical press, too. To compete with popular imported print, Melbourne's editors and journalists needed to show what was distinctive about their own work. Yet to assert the value of that work, they sought to show that they were linked to their London counterparts; they wanted to share the same virtual neighbourhood as Dickens, Jerrold, Lemon and Sala. They wanted to link Collins Street to Wellington Street. *Melbourne Punch* advertised itself as an embodiment of how print culture could use old forms to produce new versions, while Horne was valued because he was a living example of the old literary world. In using such a physical and material understanding of cultural capital, mid-century

---

[66] Suzanne Edgar, 'Scott, Eugene Montagu (Monty) (1835–1909)', *Australian Dictionary of Biography Online*, accessed 3 March 2015.

[67] Ailsa McPherson, 'Clint, Alfred', *Dictionary of Sydney*, 2012, accessed 4 March 2015, http://dictionaryofsydney.org/entry/clint_alfred.

[68] John Rickard, 'Walch, Garnet (1843–1913)', *Australian Dictionary of Biography Online*, accessed 3 March 2015.

[69] T. T. Reed, 'Kendall, Thomas Henry (1839–1882)', *Australian Dictionary of Biograph Online*, accessed 3 March 2015.

Melbourne print culture could not escape its European origins; nor did it wish to. The 'body' of the emigrant – whether the physical body of a person or the material form of a cartoon or publication – may have travelled the world, but the networks of periodical publishing made effective use of the links between colony and metropolis.

CHAPTER 13

Continental Currents: Paris and London

Juliette Atkinson

In 1839, the French critic Philarète Chasles declared of England and mainland Europe that the 'barriers have fallen, the isolation of the two great islands has been erased, popular prejudice has weakened, the speed of communication has thrown down a bridge across the strait.'[1] The foundations of these exchanges had been built more than a decade earlier, as periodicals with a cosmopolitan outlook flourished. The 1820s saw the creation in London of the *Westminster Review* (January 1824), the *Foreign Quarterly Review* (July 1827) and the *Athenaeum* (January 1828), while Paris welcomed the *Revue britannique* (June 1825), *Revue de Paris* (April 1829) and *Revue des deux mondes* (July 1829). All of these came to play major roles in increasing their readers' awareness of foreign literature through reviews, articles and translations.

This focus on foreign culture had an idealist dimension. French periodicals were particularly eager to trumpet their cosmopolitan contents as a sign of enlightenment at a time when Saint-Simonianism, the influential proto-socialist movement, was encouraging the spread of industrial and social progress across national boundaries. The weekly *Revue de Paris* (1829–1970) grandiosely promised that each issue would contain a section on foreign literature, as the 'fraternity of all idioms' should be 'exploited in the interests of the human spirit'.[2] For the monthly *Revue britannique* (1825–1901), erudition should turn from the study of antiquity to 'the movements and progress of the human mind, amongst all the nations participating in the improvement of modern civilisation'.[3] The early editor

---

[1] 'Les barrières sont tombées, l'isolement des deux grandes îles s'est effacé, le préjugé populaire a faibli, la rapidité des communications a jeté un pont sur le détroit', in P. Chasles, 'De la littérature anglaise actuelle', *Revue des deux mondes*, 17 (March 1839), 654–55.

[2] 'cette fraternité de tous les idiomes . . . [doit] être exploit[ée] au profit de l'esprit humain', L. Véron, 'Préface', *Revue de Paris* 1 (April 1829), iv.

[3] 'des mouvemens et des progrès de l'esprit humain, chez tous les peuples qui participent aux bienfaits de la civilisation moderne', in 'Préface', *Revue britannique, ou choix d'articles traduits des meilleurs écrits périodiques de la Grande-Bretagne*, 1 (June 1825), 7.

of the *Foreign Quarterly Review* (1827–46), John Cochrane, recalled in 1835 his hopes that the review would 'exercise a salutary influence in the propagation of sound and liberal ideas, in the inculcation of charity and toleration in matters of politics and religion, and in making the nations of Europe better acquainted with each other'; the prospectus for the *British and Foreign Review* (1835–44) expressed confidence that the 'human mind begins to be impatient of the trammels, which narrow policy, or ignorant prejudice, had imposed upon it'.[4] Although the *Westminster Review* (1824–1914) did not immediately give a central place to foreign thought, it too partook of the general optimism: in the months leading to its creation, Henry Southern hoped that 'every question will be discussed with a view to the interests and happiness of mankind at large.'[5]

Less disinterested motives were also at work. Parisian reviews bluntly admitted that France would benefit from keeping an eye on foreign political and industrial developments, with a view to importing those that appealed.[6] This also applied to literature; French critics in particular believed that national literature could be regenerated through contact with the foreign. On both sides of the channel, genuine curiosity and a desire to overcome insularity were coupled with more commercial instincts: attention to foreign literature could increase sales, as appears to have been the case for the *Athenaeum*.[7] Moreover, before the 1851 Anglo-French copyright treaty, borrowing material from abroad provided a cheap way of filling pages. Indeed, cosmopolitanism and profit continued to affect the circulation of foreign literature throughout much of the mid-nineteenth century.

Admiration and Imitation

Periodicals themselves were born out of intercultural exchanges. Publishers and editors monitored publications taking root across the English Channel, eager to adopt successful models. In the 1820s, British periodicals

[4] Prospectus to *Cochrane's Foreign Quarterly Review* (1835), quoted in W. Houghton, ed., *The Wellesley Index to Victorian Periodicals 1824–1900*. Vol. 2. London: Routledge & Kegan Paul, 1972, p. 131; 'Prospectus', *British and Foreign Review*, 1.1 (July 1835), 2. In 1835, Cochrane had left the *Foreign Quarterly Review* to found his own cosmopolitan periodical, *Cochrane's Foreign Quarterly Review*, which ended after only two numbers.

[5] Henry Southern, 5 May 1823, in *Wellesley Index . . . Vol. 3* (1979), 528.

[6] See, for example, 'Avertissement', *Revue des deux mondes*, 1 (1829), v; 'Préface', *Revue britannique*, 7–8.

[7] See L. Marchand, *The Athenaeum: A Mirror of Victorian Culture*. Chapel Hill: University of North Carolina Press, 1941, p. 46.

set the tone – Britain largely escaped the repressive censorship laws that occasionally crippled French publications and enjoyed a better railway infrastructure enabling rapid access to a wide readership. The current French wave of Anglomania also made Parisian men of letters particularly attentive to British trends. Publishers' attention, at first, was drawn not to London but Edinburgh: the *Edinburgh Review* (1802–1929) was an enormous source of envy. 'Je suis tout *Edinburgh Review*', declared Stendhal in 1818, and he was not the only one.[8] To French observers, the *Edinburgh* had given a new respectability to men of letters, thanks to its contributors' dazzling breadth of knowledge and what they saw as a comparative absence of puffery.[9] The *Revue de Paris* was one of many Parisian periodicals keen to replicate the formula: in 1829, Charles Nodier invited Lamartine to contribute to a new 'magazine' that a group of 'honourable men' had just created on the model of the *Edinburgh Review*.[10] The *Revue britannique*, a periodical devoted to translating British articles and fiction, plundered the *Edinburgh* above all publications.

One of the most significant illustrations of the transcultural forces shaping periodicals is undoubtedly that of the *Revue des deux mondes* (1829–present). The *Revue*, initially founded as a 'repository of politics, administrations and customs', was bought by the printer Auguste Auffray in January 1831, when François Buloz became its editor – a position he held until his death in 1877.[11] Buloz sought to emulate the best European periodicals, notably by devoting much greater space to literature. Following his appointment, he explained to readers that France was lagging behind England and Germany which, for the past thirty years, had been producing periodicals written by 'the highest intelligences, the most active and agile minds'. The *Revue des deux mondes*, he declared, would combine the erudition of German periodicals and the ability of publications such as the *Edinburgh Review* to move between discussions of

---

[8] Stendhal to A. de Mareste, 22 April 1818, in V. Del Litto (ed.), *Correspondance générale*. Paris: Honoré Champion, 1997–99, Vol. 3, p. 114.

[9] See D. Cooper-Richet, 'La presse britannique dans le Paris de la première moitié du XIXe siècle: modèle et vecteur de transferts culturels', in J-Y Mollier et al. (eds.), *La Production de l'immatériel: Théories, représentations et pratiques de la culture au XIXe siècle*. Saint-Etienne: Publications de l'Université de Saint-Etienne, 2008, pp. 126–27.

[10] Charles Nodier to Alphonse de Lamartine, 27 March 1829, in V. de Lamartine (ed.), *Lettres à Lamartine*. Paris: Calmann-Lévy, 1892, p. 62.

[11] In January 1830, the subtitle changed from 'Recueil de la politique, de l'administration et des mœurs' to 'Journal des voyages, de l'administration et des mœurs'. The monthly periodical also became a fortnightly in July 1831.

philosophical theories and literary criticism.[12] The contents over the following weeks demonstrate this range as well as the prestige of the *Revue*'s contributors: they included an article by Fenimore Cooper on the administration of the United States, a poem by Alfred de Vigny, a short story by Balzac, an article by Gustave Planche on Henry Fielding, one on Martin Luther by the historian Michelet, and Victor Hugo's thoughts on the destruction of national monuments. Managing the most important writers of nineteenth-century France was not a task for the faint-hearted, and Buloz's *Revue* was admired as fervently as Buloz himself was despised. In a merciless obituary, the novelist Edmond About recalled that Alexandre Dumas headed his letters 'Marseilles, 260 leagues from that imbecile Buloz' and smirked that most of those who attended his funeral did so 'in order to make sure that the grave was securely closed'.[13] Buloz's autocratic editorial style was also the source of his success: the *Revue*'s readership climbed steadily from 350 subscribers in 1831 to 1,000 in 1834 and 25,000 by 1868.[14]

In 1855, having accepted the role of editor of the *Edinburgh Review*, Henry Reeve wrote to François Buloz, stating that he would be overjoyed if he could give the older periodical the same status as that which the *Revue des deux mondes* was enjoying throughout Europe.[15] The letter neatly demonstrates how far the traffic of influence between Britain and France had changed direction in thirty years. By the 1840s, the *Revue*'s European reputation was firmly established. The journalist John Frazer Corkran, then working as Paris correspondent, notably for the *Morning Herald*, described the *Revue* as 'the great gun of French periodical literature', a work that was the '"Edinburgh", "Quarterly", and "Foreign Quarterly" combined ... to name its former contributors would be to set down every distinguished name in modern French literature'. By 1865, Margaret Oliphant assumed that the *Revue* was 'so familiar to many of our readers, that it may seem to them almost unnecessary to do more than mention its name'.[16]

---

[12] 'Prospectus', *Revue des deux mondes*, nouvelle série, 5 (January 1832), n.p. The declaration also serves as a useful reminder of the equal importance of German literature to French critics in the 1820s and 1830s.

[13] E. About, 'Notes from Paris', *Athenaeum*, 2569 (20 January 1877), 81–2.

[14] M.-L. Pailleron, *François Buloz et ses amis: La vie littéraire sous Louis-Philippe*. Paris: Calmann-Lévy, 1919, p. 20.

[15] Henry Reeve to François Buloz, 27 March 1855, Bibliothèque de l'Institut, Paris, MS. Lov H 1401–1417. Lettres adressées à François Buloz. Volume 13.

[16] [J. F. Corkran], 'The Newspaper Press of France', *Foreign Quarterly Review*, 30.60 (January 1843) 479–80; [M. Oliphant], 'French Periodical Literature', *Blackwood's*, 98.601 (November 1865), 604, rptd in V. Sanders and J. Wilkes (eds.), *Selected Works of Margaret Oliphant*, Vol. 14. London: Pickering & Chatto, pp. 33–50 (p. 36).

The prestige of the *Revue* was such that it was now British publishers who sought to learn from their French colleagues. A first serious attempt was made in May 1855, when Alexander Macmillan expressed a wish to 'make a thing like the *Revue des deux mondes*, and call it *The World of Letters*', a further nod to the current cosmopolitan mood.[17] The publication he eventually created, *Macmillan's Magazine* (1859–1907) was in fact a very different beast, following the advice that a periodical devoted to serialised fiction might be more profitable. Other publishers were more determined to follow in Buloz's footsteps. In November 1864, Matthew Arnold famously chose the *Revue* as an example of a publication that has 'for its main function to understand and utter the best that is known and thought in the world'.[18] The following month, Anthony Trollope and the publisher Frederic Chapman dined with George Eliot and George Henry Lewes to discuss the creation of an English periodical with similar ambitions. The resulting *Fortnightly Review* (1865–1954) echoed Arnold by explaining that 'it has often been regretted that England has no journal similar to the "Revue des deux mondes", treating of subjects which interest cultivated and thoughtful readers, and published at intervals which are neither too distant for influence on the passing questions, nor too brief for deliberation.'[19] As well as borrowing its publication schedule, the *Fortnightly* took from its French counterpart the policy of signing articles with contributors' names, its lack of affiliation with a political party and even the name of its regular column on public affairs – the 'Chronique'.[20] The *Fortnightly* also explicitly targeted the kind of educated readership that admired the *Revue*. At a time when France was so frequently associated with frivolity, Buloz's periodical impressed with its weightiness; Lewes contrasted it with the 'slighter' *Revue de Paris*, which was 'much more like our magazines', and Oliphant described valiantly grappling with articles on European foreign diplomacy and scientific studies on the brain on a 'broiling July afternoon'.[21] The *Fortnightly*'s first issue proposed similarly solemn fare on the English constitution (by Bagehot), on rationalism (by Eliot) and on the brain (by the editor himself, Lewes).

[17] Alexander Macmillan to Daniel Macmillan, 26 May 1855, in George A. Macmillan, *Brief Memoir of Alexander Macmillan*. Printed for private circulation, 1908, p. xxvi.

[18] M. Arnold, 'The Functions of Criticism at the Present Time', *National Review*, 19 (November 1864), 240.

[19] 'The Fortnightly Review', *Athenaeum*, no. 1952 (25 March 1865), 436.

[20] The *Fortnightly* began by announcing a liberal agenda, before stressing in a later advertisement that the periodical would 'become an organ for the unbiased expression of many and various minds on topics of general interest' [Advertisement], *Athenaeum*, no. 1957 (29 April 1865), 602; see also *Wellesley Index . . .* Vol. 2, pp. 173–74.

[21] [G. H. Lewes], 'French Literary Journals', *Foreign Quarterly Review*, 36.71 (October 1845): 70; [Oliphant], 'French Periodical Literature', 605, repr. *Selected Works of Margaret Oliphant*, Vol. 14, p. 36.

The prestigious periodical aimed at cultivated readers was one form developed through intercultural exchanges; the cheap periodical was another. While the former model tended to work slowly, as reviews built up their reputations, the latter was characterised by speed. Commercial success, rather than prestige, was at stake. In 1831, the savvy publisher Émile de Girardin created the Société nationale pour l'émancipation intellectuelle, in the image of Brougham's Society for the Diffusion of Useful Knowledge (SDUK). The Société was accompanied by the cheap periodical *Journal des connaissances utiles*, a thirty-two-page monthly to which readers could subscribe for an annual fee of four francs and which, Girardin proclaimed with suspect selflessness, had been created 'with the sole objective of improving the well-being of the poorer classes'.[22] (The first volume included a rather dense overview of the duties of public officers, observations on child care and health tips.) Four months later, William Chambers launched *Chamber's Edinburgh Journal* with Charles Knight following hard on his heels with the SDUK's *Penny Magazine* (1832–45). Knight gained an edge by adding wood engravings, a technique in which France lagged. France was also behind with steam-operated printing presses, which English periodicals would use to keep costs low.

French publishers had argued that one reason for disseminating articles on Britain was to keep abreast of industrial innovations: developments in publishing demonstrated this need. In 1823, the newspaper *Le Constitutionnel* spent 80,000 francs to purchase an English mechanical press.[23] Shortly after the launch of the *Penny Magazine*, the printer Alexandre Lachevardière returned from a visit to London determined to create a similar periodical, which Edouard Charton agreed to edit. In December 1832, Charton travelled to London to select English engravings for the French spin-off, which was launched in February 1833 as the *Magasin pittoresque*. Both the design and contents of the first issue closely mirrored its English model and, in December, the *Magasin* admitted that it was only after having witnessed the success of English periodicals, and Knight's in particular, that the project had been attempted.[24] Only eight months after the *Magasin*'s appearance, Girardin caught up by developing his own cheap and illustrated periodical, the *Musée des familles*. Jules Janin

---

[22] 'dans le seul but d'améliorer le bien-être général des classes pauvres', 'Société Nationale Pour L'Emancipation Intellectuelle', *Journal des connaissances utiles*, 1 (Octobre-Décembre 1831), 3.

[23] G. Feyel, *La Presse en France des origines à 1944* (Paris: Ellipses, 1999), p. 88.

[24] See M-L. Aurenche, *Edouard Charton et l'invention du Magasin Pittoresque (1833–1870)*. Paris: Honoré Champion, 2002; and J-P. Bacot, *La presse illustrée au XIXe siècle*. Limoges: Presses Universitaires de Limoges, 2005.

advertised the periodical's ambition to provide an educational and entertaining publication 'within everyone's reach, so cheap that it was almost
free, as was already being carried out in England by the best minds, united
with the most talented artists'. Moving quickly from homage to rivalry,
Janin trumpeted that 'we will therefore create a periodical costing *deux
sous*, a vast periodical which will combine in itself all the periodicals of
England.'[25]

Like founders of the major cosmopolitan periodicals, publishers of
cheap periodicals were motivated by both idealism and self-interest.
In a history of its creation, published in September 1833, the *Penny
Magazine* boasted of the moral but also financial benefits of working
with international partners:

> There is another advantage which stereotyping gives us, in allowing us to
> multiply casts to any extent. We can assist foreign nations in the production
> of 'Penny Magazines'; and we can thus not only obtain the high moral
> advantage of giving a tone to the popular literature of other nations, which
> shall be favourable to peace ... but we can improve our own 'Penny
> Magazine' out of the profit which accrues from the sale of these casts ...
> Further, the art of wood-cutting is imperfectly understood in France and
> Germany. We sell, therefore, to France and Germany many casts of our
> wood-cuts, at a tenth of what it would cost them to have them re-
> engraved.[26]

As the nineteenth century progressed, intellectual, commercial and industrial developments brought periodicals on both sides of the channel into
ever-closer relationships.

Reviewing Foreign Literature

'With us, the journal becomes celebrated, the individual writer is unheard
of; with the French, the individual writer is, comparatively speaking,
everything, and the journal merely the frame to the pictures which he
paints with it.'[27] The *Illustrated London News*'s distinction must be

[25] 'un cours d'instruction familière, amusante, variée, à la portée de tous, presque gratuite tant elle est à
bon marché, tel que le font en Angleterre les meilleurs esprits dans tous les genres, unis aux artistes les
plus habiles ... Nous allons donc faire un journal à *deux sous*, journal immense qui réunira à lui seul
tous les journaux de l'Angleterre', Jules Janin, 'Les Magasins Anglais', *Musée des familles: Lecture du
Soir*, 1 (Octobre 1833), 1.
[26] 'The Commercial History of a Penny Magazine', *Monthly Supplement of the Penny Magazine*
(October-November 1833), p. 471; see also Aurenche, *Edouard Charton*.
[27] [Unsigned] 'The 'Illustrated London News' en Français', *Exhibition Supplement to the Illustrated
London News*, 28 (17 May 1851), 436.

approached cautiously but nonetheless presents a helpful distinction. Although individual writers such as G. H. Lewes championed French literature in England, the fact that for much of the period most articles on French literature were unsigned meant that, unlike in France where knowledge of English literature was associated with a handful of critics, in England periodicals rather than individuals were often associated with Francophilia or Francophobia.

Indeed, the constant movement between Paris and London should not obscure the fact that, for much of the period, French literature was the subject of sustained attacks on its immorality – although the extent to which these dominated discussions has often been exaggerated. The most famous of these attacks are undoubtedly John Wilson Croker's 1834 and 1836 *Quarterly Review* articles on, respectively, French drama and fiction. The novels of Balzac, Sand and their contemporaries, he urged in his sixty-seven-page onslaught, 'pervert not only private but public morals – they deprave not only individuals but nations, and are alternately the cause and the consequence of a spirit which threatens the whole fabric of European society'. It was common to deplore French immorality, but many of Croker's contemporaries believed that he had overstepped the mark, and leapt to France's defence.[28]

Such defences were all the more politic given that English periodicals were not simply addressing a national audience but also an international one. In 1833, the *Edinburgh Review* had published a moderately less incendiary article asserting that 'the ties which form the cement of society' were being assailed through French novels. Whether out of mischief or with a sense of the publicity to be gained from controversy, the short-lived *Panorama littéraire de l'Europe* (1833–34) translated the piece, provoking furious responses in *L'Europe littéraire* (1833–34), which bitingly portrayed the *Edinburgh* as a periodical in decline, reduced to publishing inflammatory articles as a means of holding on to its dwindling readership.[29] A similar pattern occurred with Croker's article, which was translated by the *Revue britannique*, spurring Sainte-Beuve, in *La Revue des deux mondes*, to complain that it was 'impossible for people of common sense and

[28] [J. W. Croker], 'The State of French Drama', *Quarterly Review*, 51.101 (March 1834), 177–212; [J.W. Croker], 'French Novels', *Quarterly Review*, 56.111 (April 1836), 65–131 (p. 66). Amongst those articles that took issue with Croker was [G. Reynolds], 'The French Poets and Novelists', *Monthly Magazine*, 23.137 (May 1837), 524–32. See also n. 52.

[29] [Unsigned], 'French Literature – Recent Novelists', *Edinburgh Review*, 116 (July 1833), 330; 'Les Modernes Romanciers Français (Edinburgh review)', *Le Panorama Littéraire de l'Europe*, 1 (1833), 129–42; Cappot de Feuillide, 'De la Revue d'Edinbourg et de son article contre la littérature française: Deuxième article', *L'Europe littéraire* (20 October 1833), pp. 21–24.

taste . . . to keep quiet about the impression they received of such diatribes imported from abroad'.[30] In fact, the criticisms levelled at French novels were often not wildly different from those that disgruntled French reviewers wrote themselves, but receiving such judgements from abroad was a very different matter.

What is more striking about English periodicals than the attacks – which were often solitary outbursts published in periodicals that otherwise gave novels only occasional attention – is the frequency with which they reviewed and discussed French literature. The *Athenaeum* (1828–1921) was one of the most dedicated to the task: it offered occasional translations (including Victor Hugo's *Claude Gueux*, in 1834) as well as numerous reviews. Indeed, Marchand notes that 'so much attention did the magazine pay to foreign literature in the first years of Dilke's regime that some well-disposed English critics gave the editor a friendly warning'.[31] The *Westminster Review* played a similarly key role. While the Francophile John Stuart Mill was acting editor, it moved quickly to moderate the *Quarterly*'s views by questioning whether fiction could be used, as Croker had used it, to determine the moral health of a nation, and two years later boldly (and somewhat prematurely) insisted that 'the time has gone by, when French philosophy could be dismissed with a summary verdict of "irreligious," or French romance with that of "immoral"'.[32] The *Westminster* also benefited from Lewes's contributions, which included a long piece on French drama (September 1840) and, during Marian Evans's (later George Eliot's) tenure as assistant editor, seven articles on 'The Contemporary Literature of France' published between January 1852 and July 1853, which ranged from philosophy (the works of Comte in particular) to literature, with Sainte-Beuve's *Causeries du Lundi* receiving much praise, and Dumas's monumental memoirs rather tongue-in-cheek appreciation. In 1846, the *Westminster* had also absorbed the *Foreign Quarterly Review*, which since its creation in 1827 had included, as its title implied, countless reviews of French literature, including substantial coverage of Hugo, Sue, Sand, Balzac and their contemporaries. The periodical continued to produce sensitive, level-headed

---

[30] 'il est impossible aux gens d'humble sens et de goût, dont notre pays n'a pas jusqu'ici manqué, de taire l'impression qu'ils reçoivent de semblables diatribes importées de l'étranger', Sainte-Beuve, 'Des jugemens sur notre littérature contemporaine à l'étranger', *Revue des deux mondes*, 6 (June 1836), 750.

[31] Marchand, *The Athenaeum*, pp. 49–51.

[32] [A. Bisset], 'The Quarterly Review for April 1836, Article on French Novels', *London and Westminster Review* 25 (July 1836), 300–310; [F. B.], 'Balzac, Dumas, Soulié etc.; Philosophy of Fiction', *London and Westminster Review*, 29 (April 1838), 74.

criticism in later years, ranging from George Meredith's quiet defence of *Madame Bovary* to Justin McCarthy's thoughtful meditation on French licence and English prudery in 1864.[33] (They were joined in the later part of the 1850s by the weekly *Saturday Review* (1855–1938), which held a regular column on 'French Literature'.) Attention to French literature was neither scant nor relentlessly disapproving.

On the other side of the Channel, French readers were introduced to British authors mainly through the labours of a selection of prominent critics. Specialisation in foreign literature often conferred on these critics a professorial authority, and these periodical 'chairs' in literature often turned into genuine appointments.[34] Such was the case for Philarète Chasles, who inaugurated the chair of foreign literature at the Collège de France in 1841 and was, during the 1830s, the leading periodical writer on English literature. After being briefly imprisoned for his part in an anti-royalist plot, Chasles fled to London where he worked in a printing press off Chancery Lane. Upon his return to Paris, he made his name as a specialist on English topics at a time when demand for these was high: in 1821, he wrote an overview of English poetry for the *Revue encyclopédique* (1819–35), and in the 1830s he published articles on topics such as Fielding as well as reviews of Hemans, Dickens and Bulwer for the daily *Journal des débats* (1789–1944). In 1834, Chasles became a regular contributor to the *Revue des deux mondes*, for which he prepared articles on Walter Raleigh, Cowper and Keats, as well as surveys of recent novels. Like many French critics, he moved easily between newspapers and periodicals. The *British and Foreign Review* described Chasles in 1844 as 'remarkable for an acquaintance with our literature, quite unique in a Frenchman for its extent and accuracy ... His articles are conscientious, judicious, but dull' – a fair assessment.[35]

As Chasles's interest in English literature diminished in the 1840s, he was overtaken by a new generation of critics, the most enduring of which was Paul-Emile Daurand Forgues, whose contributions to French periodicals and newspapers lasted well into the 1860s. Forgues trained as a lawyer in Toulouse before moving to Paris to forge a literary career; in 1835, he began penning articles on English literature for the *Revue de Paris*, including

---

[33] See [George Meredith], 'Belles Lettres and Art' (October 1857); Justin McCarthy, 'Novels with a purpose' (July 1864).

[34] P. Régnier, 'Littérature étrangère et littérature nationale au XIXe siècle: la fonction de la *Revue des Deux Mondes*, 1829–1870', in M. Espagne and M. Werner (eds.), *Philologiques III. Qu'est-ce qu'une littérature nationale?* Paris: Editions de la Maison des Sciences de l'Homme, 1994, p. 293.

[35] G. H. Lewes, 'The State of Criticism in France', *British and Foreign Review*, 16.32 (February 1844), 331.

a critical piece on Bulwer, and articles on Southey, Burns and Coleridge. In 1838, he joined the liberal newspaper *Le Commerce* (1837–48) where he was put in charge of literary criticism and began signing his articles 'Old Nick'. He began providing articles on writers such as Browning and Tennyson to the *Revue des deux mondes* in 1846 and in the 1850s was instrumental in championing the works of Wilkie Collins, many of which he translated. (Collins dedicated *The Queen of Hearts* to him out of gratitude.) Other important Anglophile critics of the period include Eugène Forcade, who had an interest in essayists such as Jeffrey and Lamb and also wrote extensively on Charlotte Brontë; Emile Montégut, author of a number of articles on 'condition of England' fiction; and Joseph Milsand, who contributed articles to the *Revue des deux mondes* on English drama, Carlyle, Campbell as well as Browning and Tennyson.[36]

For many French critics, celebrating English literature was as much a means of resisting what they saw as worrying literary trends at home as it was about embracing the foreign. Both Chasles and Forgues, for example, were largely critical of French Romanticism, and English literature formed an appealing contrast to the worst excesses of the French writers of the 1830s. In fact, Chasles also grew disenchanted with the development of English literature, and he clung instead to Elizabethan drama, the eighteenth-century novel, and English Romantic poetry.[37] France was also host to discussions about the nascent concept of comparative literature. A series of anthologies entitled *Cours de littérature comparée* appeared in 1816; in the late 1820s François Villemain gave influential lectures on comparative medieval literature at the Sorbonne. These were followed by Jean-Jacques Ampère's 1830 lecture on comparative art and literature. Philarète Chasles added to the debates with an 1835 lecture entitled 'Littérature Etrangère et Comparée' which made it clear that, for him, attention to the foreign was a means of reinvigorating France, which he continued to see as the intellectual heart of Europe – 'the nature of France is to appropriate for herself what she touches, and to impress upon it an extraordinary magnetic force.'[38] Comparatists such as Chasles used the notion of

---

[36] Hippolyte Taine offered two important articles on Dickens and Thackeray in 1856–7, but his influential *Histoire de la littérature anglaise* (1863–64), which cemented his reputation as a critic of English literature, did not appear entirely in periodicals beforehand.

[37] See E. Margaret Phillips, *Philarète Chasles: critique et historien de la littérature anglaise*. Paris: E. Droz, 1933.

[38] 'Le propre de la France est de s'approprier ce qu'elle touche, et de lui imprimer une force magnétique extraordinaire', 'Cours de M. Philarète Chasles à l'Athénée: Littérature Etrangère Comparée', *Revue de Paris*, 13 (1835), 245.

comparative literature to reinforce rather than collapse the idea of distinct national characteristics.

However, the notion of French and English literature as distinct was complicated by the fact that critics frequently wrote for foreign periodicals. (Stendhal famously penned a large number of articles for periodicals such as the *New Monthly Magazine*.[39]) Contributions by French critics in British periodicals were occasionally signed, allowing editors to proclaim to their readers that they had gone out of their way to secure experts. Such was the case in 1836 when the *London and Westminster Review* (then simply *The London Review*) published a lengthy article on Hugo's poetry by Désiré Nisard, which appeared simultaneously in the *Revue de Paris* and was translated by John Stuart Mill. In a footnote, Mill noted that

> the following article is the first of a series of papers on contemporary French literature, with which we have been favoured by one of the first writers and critics in France. We state this, partly because the reader may be aided in understanding the article itself, if the fact of its French origin be previously known to him; and partly because, it being one of our objects to place before our readers a true picture of the present state of the French mind, this object is promoted by apprising them that the present article is itself a specimen, as well as in some degree a description, of that state.[40]

The following year, the *Athenaeum*, keen to secure its own authentic French critic, engaged Nisard's rival Jules Janin, who began a series on 'Literature of the Nineteenth Century. France' in April.

Nisard and Janin were identified, but that a number of such contributions remained anonymous meant that what English readers took to be English views on foreign literature were occasionally written by French writers and vice versa. Indeed, as periodicals liberally helped themselves to foreign articles to fill their pages, there were occasions when a French periodical translated an English article which was itself a translation from a French article. Buloz reeled off a number of such instances, such as a November 1833 issue of the *Revue britannique* which had reprinted a July 1833 *Revue encyclopédique* article and which the *Monthly Magazine*

---

[39] The *Wellesley Index*'s attributions for Stendhal's *New Monthly Magazine* include four 'Letters from Rome', published between September 1824 and 1825, a survey of 'Present French prose literature' (June 1825), and twenty-nine 'Sketches of Parisian society, politics, and literature', published between January 1826 and July 1829. See also K. McWatters, *Stendhal: Chroniques pour l'Angleterre. Contributions à la presse britannique*, 8 vols. Grenoble: Publications de l'Université des langues et lettres de Grenoble, 1980–95.

[40] D. N[isard], 'Victor Hugo', *London and Westminster Review*, 2.4 (January 1836), 389; see also D. Nisard, 'M. Victor Hugo en 1836', *Revue de Paris*, 25 (1836), 293–329.

had borrowed earlier in November – a movement which highlights the speed with which articles circulated, as well as the ease with which national differences could be erased.[41] Even without such confusions, anonymous contributions suggest the extent to which assumptions about British attacks on French literature must be made with caution: Philarète Chasles's unsigned review of George Sand's most controversial novel *Lélia*, for the *Athenaeum*, is as disapproving as any English-authored review, describing the work as 'a bold, brazen paradox, born, fostered, and nourished, in the very hot-bed of skepticism, in the whirl and turbulence of Parisian politics, manners, and questionable morality'.[42]

Relations between Paris and London involved the fluid exchange of reviewers as well as ideas and articles. Editors often travelled abroad to make contacts and encouraged their contributors to do the same. Charles Wentworth Dilke, who edited the *Athenaeum* between 1830 and 1846, sent his regular reviewer of French fiction Henry Chorley to Paris, from which Chorley reported back on the writers he had met, such as Janin, who had begun publishing his series of articles on nineteenth-century French literature for the *Athenaeum* (he was 'wilder and dirtier than ever') and Sue ('a fierce, black hearted fellow, who looked ready and willing to eat me up').[43] François Buloz left Paris for London on 21 June 1833 on a business trip that included meeting booksellers who disseminated his periodical.[44] (He had a close working relationship with Barthés and Lowell, who sold the *Revue*; indeed, foreign periodicals were available in Paris and London libraries and bookshops.) In May 1835, he sent Gustave Planche on his behalf, in what turned out to be a disappointing trip; he had more success with Montégut, who arrived in London in 1853 and was cordially received by the booksellers Baillière as well as the *Revue*'s faithful contact Barthés and Lowell. During his visit, he met with Carlyle (on whom he had published an article in 1849), who provided him with a letter of introduction to G. H. Lewes, who in turn introduced him to Thornton Hunt. Montégut also used the visit to take the pulse of English fiction; he was charmed by Gaskell's *Ruth*, bought a copy of *Mary Barton* and sent Buloz a copy of Collins's *Basil* to be forwarded to his fellow

---

[41] F. Buloz, 'Chronique de la quinzaine. 15 Juillet 1834: Deux mots à la Revue britannique', *Revue des deux mondes*, 3 (Juillet 1834), 251–52. See C. Didier, 'Les Samnites Anciens et les Samnites Modernes', *Revue encyclopédique*, 55 (July 1832) 74–86; 'The Brigands of Apulia', *Monthly Magazine*, 16.95 (November 1833), 559–63; 'Excursion dans les Abruzzes', *Revue britannique*, 6 (November 1833), 102–14.

[42] Unsigned, 'Lélia', *Athenaeum*, 309 (28 September 1833), 646.

[43] See R. T. Bledsoe, *Henry Fothergill Chorley: Victorian Journalist*. Aldershot: Ashgate, 1998, p. 29.

[44] T. Loué, *La Revue des deux mondes de Buloz à Brunetière*, 3 vols. Thèse, Université de Paris I, 1998, Vol. I, p. 76.

reviewer Forcade. Montégut's article on Gaskell's novels duly appeared in the *Revue*'s June 1853 issue.[45]

There is some truth to the common notion that French writers visited London for business, whereas British writers came to Paris for pleasure. In 1898, Yetta Blaze de Bury described the *Revue des deux mondes* as the '*salon* of Europe', and to a certain extent many of the more cosmopolitan periodicals functioned as printed 'salons'.[46] In Paris, this was literally the case. Philarète Chasles's wife held a salon on Wednesdays at the Palais de l'Institut at which eminent foreigners were always welcome; guests included Disraeli, Gladstone and Dickens.[47] Chasles was perfectly placed to serve as intermediary between French and English men of letters and, for example, introduced Matthew Arnold to Michelet in 1847. Corkran, who wrote for the *Foreign Quarterly Review*, arranged for Browning to meet the critic Joseph Milsand after the latter's laudatory review of Browning's poems had appeared in the *Revue des deux mondes* in August 1851. In turn, Milsand introduced Browning to the salon of his editor François Buloz, and the *Revue*'s critic Forgues visited the Brownings. In 1852, Carlyle proposed giving Emile Montégut an introduction to Browning as 'he might perhaps, if the acquaintance proved mutually pleasant, be of use to M. Montégut on various English subjects.'[48] French publishers eagerly fostered relations with British writers: Emile de Girardin famously hosted a banquet for Dickens, during which he was treated to an enormous plum pudding, accompanied by a gold-framed card describing it as an 'Hommage à l'illustre écrivain d'Angleterre'. Indeed, the world of cosmopolitan periodicals was often a remarkably intimate one.

Translating Foreign Literature

Periodical readers were also, of course, introduced to foreign literature through translations. One of the major French periodicals established in the 1820s made it its business to provide just that. *La Revue britannique* had no significant English equivalent. Before its creation in 1825, there had been a number of less successful attempts to create a periodical devoted to

---

[45] Emile Montégut to François Buloz, 4 January and 18 January 1853, Bibliothèque de l'Institut, Paris, MS. Lov H 1401–1417. Lettres adressées à François Buloz Vol. 11.

[46] Y. Blaze de Bury, 'Sixty Years of the *Revue des Deux Mondes*', *Cosmopolis*, 12.34 (Octobre 1898), 49.

[47] A. de Malarce, 'Quelques Salons de Paris: M. Philarète Chasles au Palais de l'Institut', *La Revue hebdomadaire*, 5 (Avril 1905), 61.

[48] Thomas Carlyle to François Buloz, 11 February 1852, Bibliothèque de l'Institut, Paris, MS. Lov H 1401–1417. Lettres adressées à François Buloz, Vol. 3.

reprinting foreign articles and fiction.[49] The *Revue encyclopédique* occasionally translated English articles, as did the *Revue des deux mondes*, but
this was not their *raison d'être*. In 1824, Amédée Pichot founded *L'Echo
britannique*, which managed to survive competition with the *Revue britannique* until 1835, when both it and Pichot became absorbed into its more
successful rival.

Louis-Sébastien Saulnier, Jean-Michel Berton and Dondey-Dupré, who
created the *Revue britannique*, deplored the poor foreign language skills of
the French, as well as the expense and difficulty of procuring English books
and periodicals in Paris. To compensate for this, they would publish 'the
translation of the most remarkable articles inserted in the different works
we have just indicated', but above all from the *Edinburgh Review*.[50]
Philarète Chasles's name quickly became attached to this project, and he
later claimed to have written (or translated) approximately a third of the
content until 1840.[51] Translations were often edited versions (sometimes
even loose adaptations) of the original article, the source was listed at the
end, and a footnote often contextualised the article or justified its
inclusion.

The *Revue britannique* did not at first display a strong interest in
literature, foreign or domestic, and when it did it was often to assess the
status of French rather than English culture. Indeed, the first literary article
it chose was a three-year-old article deprecating contemporary French
poetry. As Jones has considered, the *Revue* may have sought to use such
articles to gain publicity as well as to engage in the still lively debates
surrounding French Romanticism without bearing responsibility for the
views they chose to circulate. Both motivations may have determined the
decision to translate Croker's infamous attack on French novels, and,
whether out of a sense of fair play or out of a desire to keep the argument
alive, it also translated the *London and Westminster Review*'s riposte.[52]
Articles on British literature were scant in the 1820s and consisted to
a   large   extent   of   the   serialisation   between   November   1826
and February 1828 of Hazlitt's *Spirit of the Age*.

---

[49] See D. Cooper-Richet, 'La presse britannique dans le Paris de la première moitié du XIXe siècle',
pp. 115–30.
[50] 'la traduction des articles les plus remarquables insérés dans les différens receuils que nous venons
d'indiquer', 'Préface', *Revue britannique*, 7.
[51] See Phillips, *Philarète Chasles*.
[52] [A. Bisset], 'The Quarterly Review for April 1836, Article on French Novels', *London and
Westminster Review*, 3.2 (July 1836), 300–10. See also notes 28 and 32.

Amédée Pichot's arrival marked a change of emphasis. Pichot initially trained in medicine before turning to literature. Multilingual and an Anglophile, he produced the first French translation of Byron's complete works (1819–21) and was a passionate Shakespearean. Pichot contributed to a wide range of publications, working as editor of the *Revue de Paris* between 1831 and 1834 before joining the team of the *Revue britannique* in 1835; four years later, he became the periodical's editor and stayed on until his death in 1877.[53] Attention to British literature increased significantly in the 1830s, with articles on Coleridge (April 1835), overviews of Romantic poetry (February 1835), Scott and Hogg (September 1835), Goldsmith (May 1837) and Defoe (February 1840). More importantly, Pichot appears to have understood that one of the greatest appetites of the period was not for foreign articles, but for fiction.[54]

The presence of foreign fiction in mid-century English and French periodicals can very roughly be divided into three phases. In the 1840s, England looked to France for fiction. One reason may have been that it was cost effective, but publishers may also have been taking note of the phenomenal successes achieved in Paris with the *roman-feuilleton* since the late 1830s, when Girardin's *La Presse* (1836–1928) and Dutacq's *Le Siècle* (1836–1932) founded newspapers containing daily morsels of fiction at the bottom of the page.[55] Writers on both sides of the Channel regularly condemned this brazen quest for readers as crass, and in 1843 the *University Magazine* expressed its thankfulness that 'we have as yet no feuilleton in England. We do not draw a line across our newspaper columns; the upper portion devoted to the serious news ... the lower yielded up to a hasty criticism or scandalous story, making of the journal a very mermaid, with a fair head and foul termination.'[56] The phenomenal sales achieved by Girardin and Dutacq were, however, hard to ignore.

English readers never got to enjoy a slice of *The Three Musketeers* at the bottom of their copy of *The Times*, but periodicals directed at a mass

---

[53] See K. Jones, 'Chapitre 8. L'avènement d'Amédée Pichot en 1839', *La Revue britannique: son histoire et son action littéraire (1825–1840)*. Paris: Droz, 1939.

[54] As the focus of this article is on periodicals aimed at making foreign literature available to domestic readers, it has not focused on Galignani's publications, which were largely (although not exclusively) aimed at English expatriates. For more on English-language publications in Paris, see Diana Cooper-Richet, 'Les imprimés en langue anglaise en France au XIXe siècle: rayonnement intellectuel, circulation et modes de pénétration', in J. Michon and J-Y. Mollier (eds.), *Les mutations du livre et de l'édition dans le monde du XVIIIe siècle a l'an 2000*. Paris: L'Harmattan, 2002, pp. 122–40.

[55] See J-Y. Mollier 'Aux origines du feuilleton dans l'espace francophone', in M-F. Cachin et al. (eds.), *Au Bonheur du Feuilleton: Naissance et mutations d'un genre*. Paris: Creaphis, 2007, pp. 53–66.

[56] A. Holmes 'The Feuilletonists of France', *Dublin University Magazine*, 22.132 (December 1843), 701.

readership adapted the approach to English periodical styles by translating French bestsellers. As James has declared, 'from about 1844 the main outside influence on English lower-class fiction was from France ... French fiction formed the backbone of the *London Journal*, the *London Pioneer*, and the *Family Herald* between 1845 and 1849.'[57] The team behind the penny weekly *London Journal* (1845–1928) was committed to disseminating French literature for cultural as well as commercial reasons. Its first editor, G. W. M. Reynolds, was a committed Francophile who had lived in France between 1830 and 1836, produced his own fiction set in France and closely imitated French novels, such as his 1844–8 homage to Eugène Sue's phenomenon *Les Mystères de Paris, The Mysteries of London*. Reynolds had already played a significant role defending French novels from attacks such as Croker's in the *Monthly Magazine*, which he briefly edited. As the *London Journal*'s first editor, he gave readers serialised translations of works such as Dumas's *The Count of Monte Cristo*. John Wilson Ross took over from Reynolds in October 1846 but pursued his agenda with translations of Sue's *Martin the Foundling* and *Seven Deadly Sins*. Reynolds, meanwhile, added yet more French novels to the marketplace by launching the rival weekly *Reynolds' Miscellany* (1846–69). Part of these journals' appeal was the speed with which they could provide the latest Parisian hit: Sue's *Les Sept Péchés Capitaux* began to appear in the *Constitutionnel* on 9 November 1847 and kicked off in the *London Journal* eighteen days later.[58] Meanwhile, *Ainsworth's Magazine* (1842–54) sought to benefit from the current mania for French literature in a periodical aimed at middle-class readers, with the intended audience reflected in its choice of novelist: not Sue but George Sand, whose *Countess of Rudolstadt* was translated for the periodical by Matilda Hays.

Such serialisations dwindled in the 1850s, partly due to the introduction of the 1851 Anglo-French copyright treaty, to the perceived regained buoyancy of English fiction, and to the increasing attraction of fiction from America. In this decade, Parisian periodicals increasingly looked to Britain for inspiration. This new interest may have been caused by a number of factors: the novelty of the roman-feuilleton wearing off, a lassitude with home-grown novels expressed in such works as Caro's *Etudes morales sur le temps présent* (1855) and curiosity about the creation of British family periodicals such as *Household Words* (1850–59). 'The French say there is

---

[57] L. James, *Fiction for the Working Man, 1830–1850: A Study of the Literature produced for the Working Classes in Early Victorian Urban England*. London: Oxford University Press, 1963, p. 136.
[58] James, *Fiction for the Working Man*, p. 137.

a dearth of novels and romances', Kirwan smugly noted, before adding 'we cannot but rejoice, for our parts, to find our noble race of contemporary British novelists held up as examples worthy of being followed.'[59]

In the 1850s, Amédée Pichot (himself a prolific translator) hugely expanded the presence of British fiction, both as short stories and serialisations, in the *Revue britannique*. Dickens (whom Pichot had met in 1848) was the most frequently translated novelist; Pichot's own version of *David Copperfield* appeared between May 1849 and December 1851, and there was rarely a year when the *Revue* did not publish at least one Dickens short story. Bulwer Lytton and Charles Reade, however, were more often serialised: translations of *The Caxtons* (serialised in 1849), *What Will He Do With It?* (1858–9), *A Strange Story* (1861–2), and *It's Never Too Late to Mend* (1860), *Hard Cash* (1864) and *Put Yourself in His Place* (1869–71) meant that they were a constant presence for the *Revue*'s readers.[60]

The *Revue britannique* was far from the only Parisian publication to look towards England for fiction. The 1850s also saw the creation of the *Journal pour tous* by the printer Charles Lahure, who kept an eye on cheap British family magazines. The periodical's first issue, which appeared on 7 April 1855, declared that the *Journal* was 'a new creation': 'we did not have until the moment a truly popular periodical, such as has existed in England for a few years, which took the form of publishing, in a slim volume and for the smallest possible price, enough material to charm, for a week, the leisure of all the family' – a formula, Lahure added, which had achieved 'prodigious results' in England.[61] Readers were promised, in each issue, the serialisation of a new French novel or the translation of a foreign novel (and often both) as well as articles. Working with British novels post-1851 meant that Lahure had to travel to London to secure copyrights from novelists for the *Journal*, as well as for Hachette's *Bibliothèque des romans étrangers*, which he printed. Although Dickens did feature in the periodical (with *A Christmas Carol*, rather oddly published in the summer), the

[59] [A.V. Kirwan prob.], 'Decline of French Romantic Literature', *Fraser's Magazine*, 53.318 (June 1856), 711, 721.

[60] See the appendix of M. G. Devonshire, *The English Novel in France, 1830–1870*. London: University of London Press, 1929, for a longer list of short stories and novels serialised in French newspapers and periodicals.

[61] 'création nouvelle': 'nous n'avions pas jusqu'ici le journal populaire proprement dit, tel qu'il existe en Angleterre depuis quelques années, c'est-à-dire publiant, sous un mince volume et pour le prix le plus minime, assez de matière pour charmer, pendant une semaine, tous les loisirs de la famille'. 'cette nouvelle formule a obtenu en Angleterre des résultats qui tiennent du prodige', 'Avis au lecteur', *Journal pour tous*, in Jean-Yves Mollier, *Louis Hachette: Le Fondateur d'un Empire*. Paris: Fayard, 1999, p. 348.

Journal's choice was eclectic. It relied heavily on the Victorian stars of penny publications – now-forgotten writers such as John Frederick Smith, who Wheeler describes as 'the most popular novelist of the Victorian era', and who had helped massively to raise the circulation of the *London Journal* in 1849 with Stanfield Hall.[62] The *Journal pour tous* took note and serialised his *La Comtesse d'Arran* in 1860. It is hard to guess what a readership avid for Smith's novels would have made of a later choice, a translation of Byron's *Don Juan*, which readers were treated to through bi-weekly instalments lasting from 2 October to 18 December 1867.

Writing on developments in France such as the *Journal pour tous* in 1858, E. S. Dixon declared that 'the success of more than one low-priced journal is attributed in part to translations from the English. In this respect, the taste of the two nations is exactly opposite. French fictitious narrative, translated, is nearly unsaleable in England at the present date.'[63] Ironically, Dixon made this declaration shortly before the tide began to turn, as both French and British periodicals demonstrated an interest in each other's literature throughout the 1860s. In both cases, this resurgence may have been partly due to the desire to tap into the market for female readers. In Paris, the *Revue des deux mondes* regularly offered its readers highly condensed translations of English novels published in one or occasionally two lengthy instalments – all of them translated by Forgues. Forgues's choices reflect a sense of excitement about the developments of Victorian realism, and that of women writers in particular; his 'adaptations' included, in 1859, Ashford Owen's *Georgy Sandon or a Lost Love* (with its explicit homage to George Sand); Eliot's *The Mill on the Floss* (condensed into forty pages in June 1860); and Gaskell's *Cousin Phillis*, which appeared as *Cousine Philis* in April and May 1866). (Other novelists includes Ouida, Meredith and Trollope.)

Over in London, the repeal of the paper tax in 1861 provided a new impetus for British periodicals, and this coincided with the growing sense that with the excesses of French Romanticism now thirty years behind (and novelists such as Flaubert remaining a minority interest), a new generation of French novelists was not incompatible with family reading. The *Sixpenny Magazine: A Miscellany for All Classes and All Seasons*, launched by Ward and Lock in 1861, held some similarities with Lahure's *Journal pour tous* in its avowed intention to reach all sections of society. The first number began a serialised translation of *The King of*

---

[62] M. Wheeler, *English Fiction of the Victorian Period*. Abingdon: Routledge, 1999 (1985), p. 36.
[63] E. S. Dixon, 'Literary Small Change', *Household Words*, 18.446 (9 October 1858), 405.

the Mountains (*Le Roi des montagnes*, 1857) by Edmond About – considered 'safe' fare for women readers. The attempt must have been successful, since the periodical soon followed this up with a serialisation of Gustave Aimard's novel *Le Fils de la Tortue* (as *The Smuggler Chief*). Indeed, a number of periodicals targeting a female readership also drew on the renewed interest in French novels: *The Lady's Newspaper*, for example, chose the 1843 novel *Albino; or the Heir of Tremi* by Paul Féval, translated by Clara Sicard, and Charlotte Yonge's periodical *The Monthly Packet* opted for Féval's *Fairy of the Sands*.

Such an overview suggests the buoyancy of translation between 1830 and 1870, and the wealth of resources available to readers, but this picture comes with a caveat: very few of these translations were accurate. A substantial portion was condensed, to a larger or smaller extent. Often, periodicals clarified that they were meant as 'tasters', on a slightly larger scale than the lengthy extracts common to so many Victorian book reviews – Forgues followed an 1857 review of Whitty's *Friends of Bohemia* with a long excerpt four years later and stressed that the excerpt 'seemed to us to complete the analysis through which we previously sought to recommend the English work'. Translation, Forgues explained, provided a way of 'assisting criticism, enabling the study of certain foreign productions' in 'their original form'.[64] The phrase is curious, since excerpts and adaptations rarely provided access to the 'original form'. Authenticity was necessarily compromised by the attempt to reduce *The Mill on the Floss* to forty pages in the *Revue des deux mondes* (which leaps almost immediately to Maggie visiting her brother Tom at Stelling's school in Book II), or *The Count of Monte Cristo* to monthly instalments across five months, as *Ainsworth's Magazine* proposed in 1845–6.

Other interventions went beyond problems of space. Morality was a common factor – the *Mirror of Literature* reassured readers about to discover Sue's *The Wandering Jew* that it had taken pains 'to omit such passages and expressions as were not deemed in accordance with the taste of our readers'.[65] Some were stylistic: Amédée Pichot informed readers that he

---

[64] 'nous a paru compléter l'analyse par laquelle nous avons déjà essayé de recommander l'œuvre anglaise qui en a fourni la donnée. Nous usons encore ici d'un procédé qui, sans empêcher l'intervention de la critique, et lui venant au contraire en aide, permet d'étudier certaines productions étrangères dans leur mouvement et dans leurs formes originales', E. D. Forgues, 'La Fille du roi Bruce, Récit de la vie Bohème', *Revue des deux mondes*, deuxième période, 36 (1861), 892–913 (892).

[65] Eugène Sue, translated by David Mitchell Aird, 'The Wandering Jew', *Mirror of Literature*, 2.1 (6 July 1844), 1.

had polished Dickens's writing in *David Copperfield* to suit French tastes.[66] Other adaptations were altogether more bizarre: the *Revue britannique* devoted nine months to an extensive and often faithful translation of *Villette*, but, not content with changing names (so that Mrs Bretton becomes Mrs Graham) opened with an inserted musing on childhood memories. *Blackwood's* turned Balzac's *Père Goriot* into a five-page short story subtitled 'A True Parisian Tale of the Year 1830', which ends abruptly with the pensionnat's astonishment at Goriot's ungrateful daughters, and the narrator's hope that henceforth the father would gain the respect he deserved.[67] This constant interference points to the multiple and complex motivations lying behind the mid-nineteenth-century dissemination of foreign literature. Just as reviews imitated and adapted foreign periodical models and wrote reviews both out of cosmopolitan curiosity and a desire to take stock of the state of national literature, intercultural periodical exchanges in the period hovered constantly between a genuine attempt to engage with foreign culture, an impulse to silently absorb the foreign, and a recurrent wish to adapt rather than replicate the foreign for domestic use, so that foreign culture was both pervasive and filtered.

[66] For more on translation, as well as English novels in French periodicals more broadly, see M-F. Cachin, 'Victorian Novels in France', in L. Rodensky (ed.), *The Oxford Handbook of the Victorian Novel*. Oxford: Oxford University Press, 2013, pp. 185–205.

[67] 'La Maitresse d'Anglais ou le Pensionnat de Bruxelles. Premier Extrait', *Revue britannique*, 25 (March 1855), 185–224; [Arnout O'Donnell] 'Le Père Goriot: A True Parisian Tale of the Year 1830', *Blackwood's Edinburgh Magazine*, 37 (February 1835), 348–53.

CHAPTER 14

The Newspaper and the Periodical Press in Colonial India

Deeptanil Ray and Abhijit Gupta

The Troubled Legacy of James Augustus Hickey

Eastwards on the road to Esplanade from Raj Bhavan in Calcutta lies a narrow alley called Dacre's Lane. One can take the lane to go to the Dalhousie Square or Chandni Chowk market, but one has to walk carefully; the narrow passageway is packed with food stalls, honking cars and crowds of silent *babus* who walk by loud dance bars spewing Hindi film music. On the left, a crumbling Raj-era building bears testimony to the site of the first Bengali-language communist daily *Swadhinata* (Freedom), launched by the Communist Party of India in 1946 during the final collapse of the British Empire. A shop selling imported Chinese shoes now marks that building. An older building to its left dating back to the early days of the Empire, however, has disappeared. It was somewhere here, sixty-two years after the Mughal Emperor Farrukhsiyar granted a *firman* to the East India Company to pursue duty-free trading rights in all of Bengal, and ten years after the Great Bengal Famine of 1770, that an eccentric Irishman called James Augustus Hickey printed the first newspaper in the Indian subcontinent using moveable type.

Hickey's *Gazette*, the *Bengal Gazette, Or Original Calcutta Advertiser*, first appeared on a Saturday, 29 January 1780. It was a two-sheet newspaper

A note on the use of identifiers: the term 'India' is used here generally to identify the political territories in the Indian subcontinent under occupation by the British East India Company and, in the latter half of the nineteenth century, the Crown. Instead of 'Indian' (as in Indian-owned newspapers), we have chosen to use the term 'native' (as in native-owned newspapers): it reminds us of the coloniser's identification of Bengalis and Marathis and people of various ethnic and linguistic backgrounds residing in the Indian subcontinent who were clubbed under the common rubric of colonial discourse, and also referred to variously as 'subjects', 'Indians', 'gentoos', 'kala aadmis' and speakers of the 'vernacular'. While referring to newspapers owned by people of British origin in India, the term 'British' has been preferred over the problematic 'Anglo-Indian', which implies a sense of integration never realised in the field of newspapers and periodicals in nineteenth-century colonial India, as will become apparent later in this chapter.

with a print run of around 200 and had three columns printed on both sides with rough-faced type used for printing handbills and common advertisement posters that Hickey bought cheap and printed off a wooden flat-bed press constructed by unknown native craftsmen at Radha Bazar, Calcutta. Much of the newspaper was devoted to advertisements of property auctions, horse-stable charges, lottery schemes, advertisement of breads and sweet cakes, shoes, candle shades, clocks, pistols and regimental swords, cheap booze, requests for return of stolen books, rewards for capture of runaways slaves and the sale of young boys. The issue of the *Gazette* for 9–16 December 1780 carried an advertisement from Hickey himself: 'To be SOLD. A FINE Coffre Boy that understands the Business of a Butler, Kismutdar and Cooking. Price four hundred Sicca Rupees. Any Gentleman wanting such a Servant, may see him; and be informed of further particulars by applying to the printer'.[1] The *Gazette* also contained as 'news' all the gossip Hickey thought relevant to the British merchant community's pleasures in Calcutta: extracts from English newspapers shipped to the colonial metropolis from Britain; a 'Poet's Corner'; and Hickey's special comments on the private, scandalous affairs of the officials of the British East India Company – the 'scoops' mostly provided by Philip Francis, a dissatisfied member of the Council to then Governor-General of India Warren Hastings.

Hickey's monopoly was short lived. In November 1780, another publication supposedly approved by Warren Hastings and run by Peter Reed, a salt agent, and B. Messinck, a theatrical producer, hit the streets of Calcutta: the *India Gazette*. It offered four pages in a larger format, and with type bought from a Swedish missionary, John Zachariah Kiernander; its print was better than that in Hickey's newspaper. The appearance of a competitor so enraged Hickey that he vilified whoever he thought was encouraging the rival production: from its proprietors to Governor-General Hastings. Hickey's rage was subsequently the cause of his downfall. The *Bengal Gazette* was denied postal facilities, and losing everything to defamation charges, Hickey found himself in jail in June 1781. He continued his journalistic war from the prison in the form of lampoons against Hastings until and after March 1782, when Hastings had the press destroyed.

Although it did not last long, the *Gazette* catalysed the birth of a clutch of new newspapers. In February 1784, the *Calcutta Gazette* was launched as

---

[1] *Bengal Gazette*, December 9–16, 1780, 1; compiled in P. Thankappan Nair, *Hickey and his Gazette*. Kolkata: S. and T. Book Stall, 2001, p. 157.

an informal East India Company mouthpiece, and in the space of few years, a number of British-owned news periodicals appeared in Calcutta: the *Bengal Journal* (1785), the *Oriental Magazine or Calcutta Amusement* (1785), the *Calcutta Chronicle* (1786) and the *Bengal Hurkaru* (1798). The trend caught on in other Presidency towns: Madras had its first weekly the *Madras Courier* in 1785, followed by the *Madras Gazette* (1795) and the *India Herald* (1795); the *Bombay Herald* (1789) and the *Courier* (1790) appeared in Bombay. Unlike Hickey's *Gazette*, most of these periodicals were organs of local British opinion. They followed the military conquests of the Company with great enthusiasm and carried British news in the form of extracts from London newspapers, reports on parliamentary affairs, editorials and a compulsory 'Poet's Corner'. The periodicals' speculations on the fourth and final Anglo-Mysore War in 1798–9 between the East India Company and Tipu Sultan, the ruler of Mysore, prompted the Company to issue a set of press regulations (Wellesley regulations) in 1798 that effectively banned, under threat of deportation, the publication of any 'licentious' material relating to the Company's finances, military or naval preparations, shipping news, reprints from London newspapers that might affect the credit of British power in India and private scandals. This effectively put a check on the growth of the periodical business in India, and two decades were to pass before the Company relaxed its regulations on printing.[2] By that time, alongside European and British printers, native printers and editors had begun laying claim to Hickey's troubled legacy.

Why 'troubled'? Standing in front of Hickey's non-existent printing house in the Dacre's Lane of today, one is prompted to wonder on the fate of the 'Coffre Boy',[3] as well as on the profound nature of the technological shift in the making of newspapers and periodicals that was symbolically inaugurated by this Irish printer in a British colony. In pre-colonial India, manuscript newspaper cultures in India had existed for centuries. Following the introduction of paper manufacture in Delhi in the thirteenth century,[4] news dispatches, communiqués and the handwritten public newspapers (*akhbar*) were an integral part of the information networks of pre-colonial India, co-existing with the beautifully calligraphed

---

[2] S. Natarajan, *A History of the Press in India*. Bombay, Calcutta, New Delhi and Madras: Asia Publishing House, 1962, p. 13.

[3] 'Coffre' is a word of mixed meanings. Derived from the Arabic *kafir* (infidel), it was used in colonial India by Europeans as well as propertied natives to describe dark-skinned poorer natives, supposedly indicating African descent.

[4] For a historical overview of the use of paper in pre-colonial India, see Syed Ali Nadeem Rezavi, 'Paper Manufacture in Medieval India', *Studies in People's History* 1.1 (2014), 43–48.

and exquisitely ornamented manuscript books of the Buddhist, Hindu and Islamic traditions. A century after Hickey's *Gazette*, though, handwritten native newspapers had disappeared. This was not simply a battle won fair and square in the technological arena of print. In the social scale, this coincided with the total breakdown of pre-colonial societal structures, the subjugation of various peoples under colonialism, the devaluation and extermination of Arabic-, Persian-, Pali- and Sanskrit-based knowledge systems, and the championing of the imperial knowledge system in the Indian subcontinent, its superiority ensured through exercise of real and symbolic power.[5] This was indeed the 'the spectacle of the crumbling of an ancient world', as Marx had observed in 1853, which can only be observed with a particular shade of melancholy.[6]

Researchers of Indian print media are troubled that following Hickey's introduction of moveable type, the shift in focus to printed textual forms resulted in a complete loss of attention to the manuscript newspaper traditions. The progressivist model of press historiography in colonial India and later the nationalist model of press history have both ensured the general absence of reference to the native manuscript newspaper cultures. Colonial newspapers and periodicals were more ephemeral than books, and though some manuscript newspapers were in circulation during the first half of the nineteenth century, and even during the Uprising of 1857 when they were part of the information network of the rebels,[7] the fact remains that none of these have survived or were consciously archived.

---

[5] As Sudipta Kaviraj observes: 'Nyaya logic was supplanted by Western logic, not because it was rationally superior, but because it was aligned to colonial power. Ayurveda was replaced by modern Western medicine not because it was less effective, but because the colonial authorities and the modern elite abandoned and suppressed it . . . Sanskrit knowledge systems could die so comprehensively and so suddenly precisely because, in intellectual terms, it was no ordinary death. It was caused by instruments – not of superior techniques of knowledge but of power.' Sudipta Kaviraj, 'The Sudden Death of Sanskrit Knowledge', *Journal of Indian Philosophy* 33 (2005), 137.

[6] Karl Marx, 'The British Rule in India', *New-York Daily Tribune*, 25 June 25 1853; Marxist Internet Archive, www.marxists.org/archive/marx/works/1853/06/25.htm (accessed on 16 March 2015).

[7] After the capture of Delhi by British troops, documents of the rebel army were compiled with the express intent of bringing Muhammad Bahadur Shah Zafar, the last Mughal monarch of India, to trial. Of the 201 bundles of Urdu and Persian documents and correspondences seized at Delhi, and later press-listed by the Imperial Record Department of the Punjab Government in 1899, we briefly come across the names of some manuscript newspapers operating outside British control during 1857: the *Sirajul Akhbar* (17 issues, size 12" x 7¾", published in Persian from Delhi, 1 March–August 1857); *Delhi Urdu Akhbar* (17 issues, size 17½" x 11", published in Urdu from Delhi, 8 March–13 September 1857); *Tilism-i-Lakhnau* (one issue, size 12" x 7¾", published in Urdu from Lucknow, 16 January 1857); and *Sadiq-ul Akhbar* (12 issues, size 15" x 11", published in Urdu from Delhi, months not mentioned, 1857). *Press-List of 'Mutiny Papers' 1857, Being a Collection of the Correspondence of the Mutineers at Delhi, Reports of Spies to English Officials and Other Miscellaneous Papers*. Calcutta: Imperial Record Division and Superintendent Government Printing, India, 1921, p. 4.

This essay, then, proceeds with an awareness of that sense of incompleteness.

More trouble lies in wait when the history of the newspapers and periodicals in India is read solely in the light of the imperial blueprint for social control through newspapers. Printing in the Indian subcontinent was introduced by Portuguese missionaries; later, newspapers in the Indian languages were the preferred vehicles of the Christian missionaries for introducing the 'civilising mission' project to the native populations. The press policy of the East India Company, and later the Crown, was a mixture of pragmatic situational deterrents and a general view of newspapers and periodicals as natural appendages to imperial authority, culture and control in the colony, without the need for sustained intervention. As we will see, during the early half of the nineteenth century, the native newspapers and periodicals thrived under the Company's rule not because they zealously adhered to the 'mission' plan or the functional view of newspapers existing to naturalise imperial domination, but because they set about to pursue their own ethnocentric religious and social agenda with the tools borrowed from the European printers.

The Beginnings of Native News Periodicals

In the field of Bengali periodicals, the lead was provided not by Calcutta, but by Shrirampur (Serampore). In 1800, printing came to Shrirampur, a small Danish enclave about forty kilometres upriver from Calcutta. A group of Baptist missionaries led by William Carey set up a mission there, after being denied permission by the East India Company to operate in Company-controlled territory. Within a few years, Shrirampur became one of the most important centres of print in south and south-east Asia, publishing in nearly forty languages. Though Bibles comprised the bulk of the mission's output, Carey and his associates also published a wide range of dictionaries and grammars, as well as translations of Indian epics. But it was not till April 1818 that Joshua Marshman was able to launch the first-ever periodical in Bengali, in the form of the monthly *Dig-darshan*. This was to be followed shortly after by *Samachar Darpan*, arguably the first-ever Bengali newspaper.

Both *Dig-darshan* and *Samachar Darpan* were part of the larger missionary project but followed slightly different trajectories. Subtitled *A Magazine for Indian Youth*, *Dig-darshan* was distributed gratis in schools and was instrumental in dispensing Western knowledge. It is not an accident that the periodical appeared just one year after the formation of the Calcutta School-Book Society, and the setting up of the Hindu College in Calcutta, both in 1817. These had been the fruits of collaboration between the native intelligentsia, missionaries and some of the Company administrators, with similar initiatives to follow in the other Presidency cities of Madras and Bombay. *Dig-darshan* catered to the needs of the new curricula which had come into being, and Kopf speculates that 'it is likely that from its pages the Calcutta youth first learned of Western history, literature and science.'[8] The Calcutta School-Book Society, for instance, subscribed to 1,000 copies each of the first three numbers for classroom use, and by 1821 had purchased a total of 61,500 copies of the magazine.[9] But the *Dig-darshan* also served the purpose of testing the waters for a more ambitious publication, and 'copies of this little magazine were sent to the most influential members of government.' The magazine seems to have been welcomed alike by the government and 'wealthy natives', emboldening Marshman and William Ward 'to issue a prospectus for the publication of a weekly newspaper in the vernacular language' which was to be the *Samachar Darpan*.[10] Carey was alarmed at the prospect, no doubt owing to his previous run-ins with the Company, but the first issues of the *Samachar Darpan* invited no censure from the Hastings government. The *Darpan* came out as a weekly for more than a decade, but became a bi-weekly in January 1832. However, owing to rise in postage rates, it reverted to being a weekly in November 1834.[11]

Samachar Darpan found a ready readership among Calcutta readers, with the subscription list headed by the entrepreneur Dwarkanath Tagore, who was apparently so taken by the idea that from the 1820s, he began to buy as many newspapers as he could.[12] In the meantime, however, a new impulse came from a part of Calcutta which would later come to be known as the site of the Battala book trade. In 1818, an entrepreneur called Harachandra Roy informed the public that he had 'established a BENGALEE PRINTING PRESS, at No. 45 Chorebagaun Street, where he intends to publish a WEEKLY BENGALEE GAZETTE'.[13] In this he was joined by Gangakishore Bhattacharya, a Bengali printer

[8] David A. Kopf, *British Orientalism and the Bengal Renaissance: The Dynamics of Indian Modernization 1773–1835.* Berkeley and Los Angeles: University of California Press, 1969, p. 157.
[9] A. F. Salhauddin Ahmed, *Social Ideas and Social Change in Bengal 1818–1835.* Leiden: E. J. Brill, 1965, p. 80.
[10] John Clark Marshman, *The Life and Times of Carey, Marshman and Ward*, vol. II. London: Longman, Brown, Green, Longmans, & Roberts, 1859, p. 162.
[11] Brajendranath Bandyopadhyay, comp. *Sangbadpatre sekhaler katha* [Beng. The Past in Newspapers] vol. 1, 1818–30. Calcutta: Bangiya Sahitya Parishat, 2008, p. viii.
[12] Kopf, *British Orientalism*, p. 190.   [13] Ahmed, *Social Ideas*, p. 84n.

who had been trained in Carey's Mission Press at Shrirampur, and who, in the words of the *Friend of India* 'appears to have been the first who conceived the idea of printing works in the current language as a means of acquiring wealth'.[14] Gangakishore was likely trained as a printer at Carey's Mission Press in Shrirampur but soon left the establishment and emerged in the 1810s as the first-ever Bengali print entrepreneur, working in collaboration with the Ferris Press and issuing the first-ever illustrated book in Bengali in 1816 in the form of *Annada-Mangal*. Gangakishore's periodical, the *Bangal Gejeti*, existed for an uncertain period of time, possibly one year. Some early commentators of press history in Bengal have identified Gangakishore's *Bangal Gejeti* as the earliest native periodical in India, citing the year of its commencement as 1816 – two years prior to that of the *Samachar Darpan*.[15] Unfortunately, no copies of this periodical have survived to verify this claim.

Following the *Gejeti*, a number of Bengali newspapers were launched, with varying degrees of success and longevity. According to Bandyopadhyay, these were the *Sambad Kaumudi* (4 December 1821), the *Samachar Chandrika* (4 March 1822), the *Bamgadut* (10 May 1829), the *Sambad Prabhakar* (28 January 1831), the *Jnananeshwan* (18 June 1831), the *Sambad Purnochandroday* (10 June 1835) and the *Sambad Bhaskar* (March 1839). The bilingual *Kaumudi* was owned by the humanist-reformist Raja Rammohan Roy, who had earlier cut his teeth in the periodicals market by editing irregularly published journals such as the *Brahmanical Magazine* and the *Missionary and the Brahman*, devoted to religious polemics. *Kaumudi* was published under the name of Bhabanicharan Bandyopadhyay, who, however, found the contents of the *Kaumudi* too radical and parted ways to set up his own periodical, the *Samachar Chandrika*. According to Ahmed, *Kaumudi* elicited mixed responses: 'while it voiced reformist Hindu opinion, it antagonised the orthodox Hindus',[16] particularly on the subject of *sati* or the ritual immolation of Hindu widows, against which Rammohan was a campaigner.

At a close parallel stood the English-language periodical the *Calcutta Journal* (launched on 2 October 1818) of James Silk Buckingham – a free-

---

[14] 'Native Press', *The Friend of India*. Quarterly Series, September 1820, p. 123.
[15] P. N. Bose and H. W. B. Moreno, *A Hundred Years of The Bengali Press, Being a History of the Bengali Newspapers from Their Inception to the Present Day*. Calcutta: H. W. B. Moreno, Central Press, 1920, pp. 5–6. The authors identify Gangakishore Bhattacharya as Gangadhar Bhattacharji. This work is the possible source of Natarajan's problematic identification of Gangakishore as Gangadhar, and as the initiator of the 'first Indian newspaper in English' in 1816. See Natarajan, *History of the Press in India*, pp. 26, 60.
[16] Ahmed, *Social Ideas*, p. 86.

thinking mariner who had travelled extensively throughout the Arab world, advised the Egyptian monarch, resigned from the services of the Imam of Muscat in protest against the slave trade and appeared in Calcutta to become a liberal editor-publisher. Buckingham's *Calcutta Journal* held a strange attraction for English exiles in Calcutta as well as native readers. With a readership count at more than a thousand, it prioritised local reports and critiques of the postal services, the police and the Company bureaucracy over news of parliamentary affairs from England; published black-and-white plates highlighting the differences between elephant skulls and fossilised mammoth skulls, and illustrations tracing similarities in the facial lines of monkeys, natives, Europeans, Americans, Africans and ancient Greeks and Romans; and local reports focusing on the social life of Europeans and natives in and around Calcutta. The periodical's criticism of *sati* as well as of the government's disregard for social intervention in the lives of natives found strong support in reformers such as Raja Rammohan Roy. In the early nineteenth century, the *Calcutta Journal* is probably the only instance of a British news periodical sharing and enthusiastically exchanging views on social reform with the native press. Ironically, Rammohan's proximity to Buckingham, evidenced by the latter's *Calcutta Journal* carrying *Kaumudi* articles in translation, led to some degree of suspicion in official circles.[17] Faced with hostility on all fronts, the editorship changed hands several times, and *Kaumudi* was forced to stop publication for the first time in October 1822. Though it was able to resume publication in 1823 and even turned bi-weekly in January 1830, Rammohan's departure for the British Isles in the same year signalled the beginning of the end of the periodical, which finally ceased publication in 1836.

In the meantime, the anti-reformist *Samachar Chandrika* was going from strength to strength, turning into a bi-weekly by 1829 and reaching nearly 400 subscribers by 1836.[18] Its editor Bhabanicharan Bandyopadhyay was one of the most enterprising print entrepreneurs of his time, but his position in *Chandrika* was resolutely anti-reformist, especially on the subject of *sati*. Bhabanicharan's press also turned out some of the major Hindu texts in print for the first time, in a price and format targeted at the native Bengali reader. Swapan Chakravorty has discussed elsewhere how Bhabanicharan's initiatives may be considered to be the first systematic attempt to socialise the printed book in colonial Bengal.[19]

---

[17] Ahmed, *Social Ideas*, p. 87.   [18] Ahmed, *Social Ideas*, p. 89.
[19] Swapan Chakraborty, 'Purity and Print: A Note on Nineteenth Century Bengali Prose', in Abhijit Gupta and Swapan Chakraborty (eds.), *Print Areas: Book History in India*. New Delhi: Permanent Black, 2008.

The party of Rammohan meanwhile had not been idle either. Harihar Datta, one of the editors of the *Kaumudi* and a reformist, started the *Jam-i-Jahan-Numa* in March 1822. This was the first printed Urdu (or Hindusthani, as it was then called) newspaper in the subcontinent, though from the eighth number onwards, it began to be issued in both Urdu and Persian. Soon it became Persian-only and enjoyed a remarkably long lifetime by contemporary standards till 1845, chiefly owing to its pro-government stance and the consequent support it enjoyed from the government. Rammohan's Persian weekly, the *Mirat-ul-Akhbar* (estd. April 1822), on the other hand, raised the government's hackles on several occasions. According to Ahmed, James Silk Buckingham was closely associated with the journal and lavished high praise on it in the *Calcutta Journal*:

> Of all the papers that have appeared in the native languages, none has created a more favourable impression in our minds than the MIRAAT-OOL-UKHBAR ... The Editor, we are informed, is a Brahmin of high rank, a man of liberal sentiments, and by no means deficient in loyalty, well versed in the Persian language and possessing a competent knowledge of English ... The paper is besides under the superintendence of a person whose great experience ... cannot fail to be of great utility to the Editor.[20]

The person referred to in the last sentence was none other than Buckingham himself, and it was, therefore, not surprising that Rammohan was greatly distressed when Buckingham was deported in 1823. This was followed by the Press Regulation Act of 1823 which made licensing compulsory for periodicals and their printers. In protest, Rammohan discontinued publication of the *Mirat-ul-Akhbar*; the last issue of the periodical came out on 4 April 1823.

The Press Regulation Act resulted in the stagnation of newspapers in Calcutta till the 1830s, when the arrival of William Bentinck as the Company's governor-general led to the relaxation of the system of licensing and effected a growth in the number of newspapers and periodicals. As Natarajan notes, in 1828 there were only two British dailies (the *Bengal Hurkaru* and *John Bull*) whose cumulative print runs did not exceed 360 copies a day; one Persian weekly *Jami-i-Jehan-Numa*; and three Bengali periodicals (*Samachar Darpan*, *Samachar Chandrika* and *Sambad Kaumudi*); in the space of two years, there were thirty-three English newspapers (with a cumulative print run of 2,205) and sixteen Bengali newspapers and periodicals published from Calcutta.[21]

---

[20] Cited in Ahmed, *Social Ideas*, p. 91n.   [21] Natarajan, *History of the Press in India*, pp. 57–58.

Of the British-owned newspapers, the *Bengal Hurkaru* ruled the roost. Priced at seven annas, its daily print run was 800 copies. In the steeply hierarchical world of the East India Company–ruled India, the printing of a semi-official newspaper at the colonial capital and at the same site of production as the sensitive military newsletters of the Company had its perks: the *Hurkaru* enjoyed postal relief like no other newspaper and scored over its provincial competitors such as the *Madras Gazette* and *Madras Courier*, or the *Daily Gazette* and the *Courier* which were still functioning respectively from Madras and Bombay. Moreover, Bentinck's reduction and fixing of postal charges to two annas for sending newspapers to select cities resulted in a limited but steady circulation of the *Hurkaru* in other provincial capitals. The postage for a newspaper from Madras to Calcutta was one rupee and fourteen annas[22] – a considerable sum even for an East India Company officer hungry for 'Company-gossip' from other cities.

In general, the native newspapers were a poor, shabby lot. The English newspapers, on their part, denied the existence of the native newspapers, or if missionaries ran them argued for the importance of a free English press 'in awakening the slumbering energies of the natives of the soil'.[23] A review published in February 1840 in the *Calcutta Christian Observer* offers the following review of the native newspapers of Calcutta:

> These papers are printed mostly at native presses, conducted by native editors; and the greater number are issued weekly in small single or double folios, usually of three columns. Most are in Bengali only; a few in Bengali and English. Some of them, like those evanescent meteors called falling stars, have but just appeared and been extinguished even in their nascent coruscations; or, as abortive embryos, have existed but to die. Of their typographical execution little requires to be said; most of them are printed on indifferent paper, with indifferent and much worn types, are composed and worked off by native pressmen, and swarm with typographical errors. Some, however, of the larger ones especially, are both neatly and correctly executed, doing great credit to the enterprise and diligence of their conductors.[24]

The same could have been said of the British-owned press in Calcutta. Unlike the compositor for the British newspaper in Calcutta who worked with a thirty-odd character set in Roman type, the native compositor had

[22] Natarajan, *History of the Press in India*, p. 59.
[23] 'Miscellany–Native Press in Calcutta', *Calcutta Christian Observer*, February 1840; compiled in *Baptist Missionary Magazine*, Vol. 21. Boston: Press of John Putnam, 1841, 108.
[24] Miscellany–Native Press in Calcutta', pp. 108–9.

to address the additional hazard of arranging characters and glyphs ranging in the order of 300 to 350 – the typography-induced necessity of converting complex script-based Indian languages to recognisable type shapes had begun just then but was by no means complete. In the absence of standardisation and uniform font sizes, the font sets available in the market were often incompatible, and native printers had to make do with handcrafted fonts they had access to. Despite the later scholarly insistence on 'lineality' and uniformity enforced by moveable type, hands-on letter-press printing was always a chaotic affair.

In 1841, ten regular native news-periodicals were published in the Bengali language from Calcutta. By this time, the Press Regulation Act had been retracted and the Company had accepted the policy of Charles Metcalfe and his Law Councillor T. B. Macaulay to effect a uniform press law that relaxed licensing restrictions but maintained provisions against printing sedition and libel, a policy that was to last till 1856. The cumulative circulation of these periodicals in Calcutta was 2,231, and around 319 copies were dispatched (mostly by hand) to subscribers in other towns. An individual subscription for the bigger periodicals (*Sambad Prabhakar, Sambad Purnochandroday, Gyananweshan*) was one rupee a month; the others cost much less.[25] They struggled to find a way to meet expenses, mostly by soliciting funds from socio-religious societies and benevolent native compradors such as Dwarkanath, whose shipping profits from the opium trade in China found a small outlet in the patronising of these publications. Ramgopal Ghosh's *Bengal Spectator* (April 1842) was one such publication supported by Dwarkanath; it was one of the earliest native-run English newspapers, albeit short lived.

Reimagining the Public Sphere

For the East India Company, the deportation of people like Buckingham was an effective solution for checking editors critical of its policies, a solution that went back to the days of James Hickey. Like Buckingham, C. J. Fair, the editor of the *Bombay Gazette*, was deported in 1823. Fair had been instructed to publish reports by the Chief Justice of Bombay Presidency which were identified as falsifications by the Government of Bombay. There was a crack in the machinery though: the early prohibitory circulars for English editors failed to take into account the growth of the native press, and brown-skinned native editors who

---

[25] 'Miscellany–Native Press in Calcutta', p. 109.

could not be, against all reason, herded into ships departing for England. The Press Regulation Act was formulated to keep native editors in check: apart from enforcing a system of licenses, available to editors who had to file an affidavit in court before a magistrate, it prohibited the publication of all commentaries on all political and administrative affairs of the Company. The last provision effectively shifted the domain of 'news' solely to the British newspapers which, unlike their native counterparts, had access to officialdom through a system of special licenses issued only to British editors. But 'news' in colonial Bengal was not entirely about the Company bureaucracy, especially for the natives.

Following the reformist movement initiated by Rammohun Roy, there was a backlash among upper-class Hindus in Calcutta, who solicited funds from the Raja of Pathuriyaghata Gopimohan Thakur and, later, the Raja of Sovabajar Radhakanta Deb, to counter the rising Brahmo threat (Brahmoism was social and religious reform effected through a re-appraisal of ancient Vedic texts and new rituals focusing on a Supreme Mover 'Brahmo'). Iswar Gupta's *Sambad Prabhakar* was the vanguard of upper-class Hindu conservatism during this period. Launched as a daily, it stopped after publishing sixty-nine issues in 1832. It was revived in 1836 as a tri-weekly newspaper, and from 14 June 1839 regularly appeared as a daily.[26] The *Prabhakar* published polemical tracts upholding the sanctity of Hindu religious practices, scurrilous satires on reformers such as Ishwarchandra Vidyasagar who wanted to introduce women's education and reforms such as widow-remarriage, and literary essays by Jaygopal Tarkalankar, Prasannakumar Thakur, Rangalal Bandopadhyay, and Bankim Chandra Chattapadhyay. Of its authors, Bankim Chandra would later go on to launch the famous Bengali politico-literary periodical *Bangadarshan* (1872), which is credited with publishing the earliest Bengali novels by the same author and also laying the groundwork for his vision of a Hindu nation-state and a curious mishmash of the philosophies of Herbert Spencer, Comte and ancient Indian philosophy.

The Brahmo Samaj enthusiasts, organised around the Tattwabodhini Sabha or Society for Theoretical Understanding, initially found support in Rammohan's *Sambad Kaumudi*. After Rammohan's demise in England, the responsibilities for propagating the Brahmo ideal fell on Debendranath, the elder son of Prince Dwarkanath. Debendranath conducted a written test for appointing a full-time editor for the future

---

[26] Sandip Dutta, *Bangla samayikpatrer itibritta (1818–1899)* [Beng. An Outline of Bengali Periodicals, 1818–1899]. Kolkata: Gangchil, 2012, pp. 18–19.

mouthpiece of the Tattwabodhini Sabha and found a twenty-four-year-old agnostic best suited for the job. On 16 August 1843, the *Tattwabodhini Patrika* appeared as a four-page monthly folio newspaper under the editorship of Akkhaykumar Dutta.

Although the magazine bore affiliation to the Brahmo Samaj, Akkhaykumar had an agenda of his own: in a few years, the young free-thinker transformed the periodical into a socio-political journal focused on rational and scientific enquiry, much to the chagrin of Brahmo Samaj enthusiasts. Considered a philosophical radical, Akkhaykumar believed in the organic evaluation of Indian societies and culture and popularised a method of critical sociological enquiry which relied more on rational doubt than on various forms of political and religious dogma. He wrote extensively on topics of popular science and the need for women's education and universal secular education. He also ran a series of polemical articles against Brahminism, multiple marriages and compulsory child marriage, as well as the caste segregation of colonial societies which he considered reinforced by colonialism.[27] Akkhaykumar ran the *Tattwabodhini* for twelve years until Debendranath fired him for promoting irreligiosity – the magazine reverted back to its Brahmo ideals and continued for more than half a century, gradually losing its popularity.

The first native periodical to print in colour appeared in October 1851: the monthly *Bibidhartha-samgraha*, an organ of the Vernacular Literature Society and edited by Rajendralal Mitra. In terms of layout, it borrowed extensively from the penny magazines popular in England during that time; content-wise, it tried to 'Indianise' the contents of the British originals and was offered for sale at two annas (or a yearly subscription of one and a half rupees). Published in the quarto format, the early issues of this periodical ran to sixteen pages; from 1852 onwards, it published twenty-four pages per issue, with extensive use of wood-cut blocks Rajendralal imported from England.[28] *Bibidhartha-samgraha* published news-commentaries, tracts on archaeology, articles on comparative religion, travelogues describing visits to distant Hindu shrines, commercial information, historical novels and the occasional detective story, which was the staple reading of the propertied gentry of colonial Bengal. Much later,

---

[27] For an overview of Akkhaykumar Dutta's immense contributions to nineteenth-century colonial thought, see *Bigyan-buddhi Charchar Agrapathic Akkhaykumar Dutta O Bangali Samaj* [Beng. Bengali Society and Akshaykumar Dutta, the Pioneer of Scientific-Rational Enquiry], Muhammad Saiful Islam (ed.). Kolkata: Renaissance Publishers, 2006.

[28] Alok Ray, 'Sampadak Rajendralal Mitra', *Parikatha* 10.2 (May 2008), 37.

people such as Rabindranath Tagore would remember the magazine filling an important part of the imaginary landscapes of their childhood.[29]

Unconcerned with the Company's wars and expansion schemes, and in many ways unmindful of the lives of their native brethren in the villages, the native periodicals of early nineteenth century, with the exception of Akkhaykumar's *Tattwabodhini*, presented a strange inverted world of colonial imaginings: a public space where debate and discussion were shaped by religious affiliation. Rumour played an important role in this world, and print exacerbated the situation by fixing these rumours in print. The vitriolic rhetoric of *Sambad Kaumudi* and *Sambad Prabhakar*, perhaps, should be best seen as the confused outpourings of a world of journalism denied access to 'official' channels of news and facilities.

Postscript: The Mutiny and After

The Sepoy Uprising of 1857 led to further press regulations, in the form of the Act XV of 1857 according to which the 'liberty of the press of India [was] restricted for the period of one year'.[30] The uprising was also a test of loyalty for newspapers of the day. The Shrirampur paper *Friend of India*, for instance, was threatened with cancellation of its license under Act XV,[31] while the *Bengal Hurkaru*, the *Englishman* and the *Dacca News* were served warning notices.[32] Among Indian-run newspapers, the *Hindoo Patriot* under the editorship of the charismatic Harish Mukhopadhyay (Hurish Mookerjee) took such a strong anti-rebel line that Lord Canning reportedly used to send copies of the *Patriot* to the Home Office.[33] In Bengal, the mutiny was largely viewed as an uprising to re-establish Muslim rule in India and found little or no support among the upwardly mobile Bengali middle classes.

Following the assumption of power by the Crown in 1858, there was some degree of realignment as far as the periodical press was concerned, with older and newer interests coming into conflict. Nowhere was this more evident than in the battle between the notorious indigo farming lobby and the newly anointed Raj eager to distance itself from some of the

---

[29] Sandip Dutta, *Bangla samayikpatrer itibritta*, pp. 23–24.
[30] 'East India (Liberty of the Press)', *Accounts and Papers of the House of Commons*. Session 30 April–28 August 1857. Vol. XXIX, 147.
[31] Mrinal Kanti Chanda, *History of the English Press in India 1858–1880*. Calcutta: K. P. Bagchi, 2008, p. 1.
[32] Chanda, History of the English Press in India, p. 17.
[33] Chanda, *History of the English Press in India*, p. 17.

less savoury leftovers of the older dispensation. The oppressive practice of forced indigo cultivation in the lower delta of Bengal led to an unlikely coalition composed of the Bengali intelligentsia, the vernacular press, European missionaries and a section of the government against the indigo farmers, in which the lead was taken by the *Hindoo Patriot*. A series of peasant revolts broke out towards the end of the 1850s, in as many as nine districts of rural Bengal. But the planters' lobby was stoutly defended by a section of the British press, in particular the *Englishman* and the *Bengal Hurkaru*. Things came to a head when a Bengali play on the atrocities of the indigo planters, titled *Neel darpan* by Dinabandhu Mitra, was translated into English as *The Indigo-Planting Mirror* and paid for by the Bengal government. Copies of the play were also distributed to newspapers editors under government frank. This led to a libel case filed by the editors of the *Englishman* and the *Hurkaru* at the instance of the Landholders and Commercial Association, resulting in a prison sentence for the Reverend James Long who had facilitated the publication of the play.[34] But after the death of Harish Mukhopadhyay in 1861, the *Patriot* became steadily more pro-government, pulling its punches even during the promulgation of the Vernacular Press Act in 1877–8.

The 1860s saw a rapid increase in both book and periodical production, prompting the government to bring in the Press and Registration Act (Act XXV of 1867). This act may be regarded as a watershed in the history of print in South Asia, as it made it compulsory for all printers and publishers to register every publication in British India for a sum of two rupees. Some of the periodicals which began life during this period included the *Bamabodhini Patrika* (estd. 1863), one of the first periodicals in Bengali for women, and the *Grambarta Prakashika*, founded in the same year. The latter, edited by the legendary Harinath Majumder or 'Kangal' Harinanth, was particularly significant as it was printed from a remote village called Kumarkhali and devoted itself almost exclusively to rural issues, highlighting atrocities against the peasants by planters, zamindars and the administration. It was particularly critical of city-based periodicals which increasingly represented the interests of the landed gentry, such as the *Hindoo Patriot* and even the redoubtable *Amritabazar Patrika*.[35]

---

[34] For details about the *Neel darpan* case, see Ranajit Guha, 'Neel Darpan: The Image of a Peasant Revolt in a Liberal Mirror', *Journal of Peasant Studies*, 2.1 (1974), 1–46; Also see Nandi Bhatia, 'Censorship and the Politics of Nationalist Drama', in *Acts of Authority/Acts of Resistance: Theater and Politics*. Ann Arbor: University of Michigan Press, 2004, pp. 19–50.

[35] Dutta, *Bangla samayikpatrer itibritta*, pp. 27–28.

While the passing of Act XXV may not have been motivated by a spirit of surveillance, the same cannot be said of the Vernacular Press Act of 1878 (repealed in 1881), promulgated during the viceroyship of Lord Lytton. The act (modelled on the Irish Coercion Act of 1870) introduced a series of restrictions on the vernacular press but excluded the English-language press, much to the chagrin of the former. Opposition against the act, however, was muted. The likes of Bhudeb Mukhopadhyay, who edited the *Education Gazette*, maintained an acquiescent silence, while Dwarkanath Bidyabhushan of the influential *Somprakash* was silenced after a rap on his knuckles following a minor infraction.[36] But the periodical which remained steadfast in its opposition to the act was *Amritabazar Patrika*, founded in 1868 by Sisir Kumar Ghosh and his seven brothers as a weekly and then as a bilingual publication a year later. In a daring response to the act, the paper turned itself into an English-language periodical overnight and bypassed the jurisdiction of the act. In time, the paper would become a daily and gained its popularity among the 'liberal' Indian beneficiaries of the Permanent Settlement, the decaying Indian gentry, small businessmen and the emergent English-reading salaried classes of Calcutta for its championing of Bengali proto-nationalism.[37]

Many followed in the *Amritabazar*'s footsteps. In 1877, Surendranath Banerjee, a former Indian Civil Service officer, one of the earliest enthusiasts of Western-styled political organisations in India, the initiator of the Indian National Association and later president of the Indian National Congress, founded the Native Press Association, which unsuccessfully protested against the Vernacular Press Act before the viceroy during his Delhi *durbar*. In 1879, following the *Amritabazar*'s taking to English, Banerjee acquired a failing English weekly called the *Bengalee* for ten rupees and embarked on a journalistic career in English.[38] Spanning forty-six years, the *Bengalee* published Banerjee's social and political commentaries on the need for self-representation of natives under the Crown, his passionate championing of Western political ideas drawn from Burke and Mazzini, and his criticism of Bengali literature.[39]

---

[36] Asis Khastagir, 'Dwarkanath Bidyabhushan: ek birol pothik', *Parikatha* 10.2 (May 2008), 48–71, 63.

[37] See Deeptanil Ray, 'Speculating "National": Ownership and Transformation of the English-Language Press in India During the Collapse of the British Raj', *Media History Monographs* 16.2 (2013–2014), 5.

[38] Natarajan, *History of the Press in India*, p. 96.

[39] The tendency of the *Bengalee* to act as the arbiter of matters of native culture by virtue of its publication in English was satirised by Sukumar Ray, the Bengali poet and artist, in one of his short dramatic pieces, 'Chalachitta-Chanchari' in which Ishan, a self-proclaimed poet and author, proudly proclaims his worth because of a review of his poetry in the *Bengalee*, which he has

Even though the Vernacular Press Act was repealed a year after Lord Ripon became viceroy of India in 1880, the idea of having English-language newspapers as mouthpieces of native political opinion caught on in various provincial capitals and major cities of British India. In 1881, Sardar Dayal Singh Majithia, a Brahmo Samaj enthusiast from Punjab, founded the *Tribune* in Lahore. (A year later, a seventeen-year-old Rudyard Kipling was to return to this city to read and correct proofs in the office of Lahore's biggest British-owned daily, the *Civil and Military Gazette*; it would have caused him great heartbreak to know that the insignificant *Tribune* would outlive the imperial Lahore *Gazette* in the new century.) In 1878, two Tamil schoolteachers, G. Subramania Iyer and Veeraraghava Chari, and three law students protesting against the act launched the weekly *Hindu* in the city of Madras; by 1889, it had become a daily. In 1882, the Tamil-nationalist *Swadeshimitram* appeared as a Tamil weekly; it became a daily in 1889. In 1886, the first news weekly in the Telugu language, *Andhra Prakashika*, appeared in print.[40]

The chief among the native newspapers and periodicals of this period espousing ideas of political nationalism, democracy, and anti-colonialism were the Marathi-language *Kesari* and English-language *Mahratta* – published in two languages by the same editor and from different locations in Bombay Presidency and Pune to avoid police action. These were started in 1881 by the Maratha revivalist and activist-journalist Bal Gangadhar Tilak. By the turn of the century, the shift in focus from socio-cultural issues to political journalism (primarily in the English language) was clearly discernible in most native newspapers and periodicals. The 'Indian nation', as it increasingly came to be called, found new definitions drawn from Tilak's prose, Bankim Chandra's historical polemics in *Bamgadarshan*, Aurobindo Ghosh's militant nationalistic expositions in his English-language periodical *Bande Mataram* (1906) and Brahmabandhab Upadhyay's vitriolic anti-colonial outpourings in his Bengali-language periodical *Sandhya* (1904).

The 'nation', meanwhile, was also being imaginatively reconstructed by native political journalists from across the Arabian Sea: as Isabel Hofmeyr reminds us, Gandhi's early expositions of tenets of 'Hind Swaraj' [Self-Rule in Hindustan] first appeared as journalism in the pages of his South African news periodical *Indian Opinion* (1903).[41] The native newspapers

---

memorised. Sukumar Ray, 'Chalachitta-Chanchari', in Satyajit Ray and Partha Basu (eds.), *Samagra Shishusahitya*, 1976. Calcutta: Ananda, 1996, p. 85.

[40] Natarajan, *History of the Press in India*, p. 104.

[41] Isabel Hofmeyr, *Gandhi's Printing Press: Experiments in Slow Reading*. Cambridge, MA and London: Harvard University Press, 2013, p. 20.

and periodicals within the Indian subcontinent, and without, were fast
becoming instruments of politics, and the stage had been set for newer
reconceptualisations founded on an adherence or opposition to the Empire
on political grounds, and perhaps not so curiously, the use of English by
the native press as the predominant language of political journalism.

CHAPTER 15

British and American Newspaper Journalism in the Nineteenth Century

Joel H. Wiener

During the nineteenth century, near revolutionary changes occurred in both British and American newspaper journalism. Popular newspapers came increasingly to dominate the reading habits of millions of people in both countries. In Britain, these changes culminated in what is commonly referred to as the 'New Journalism', a phrase in use since 1887, when Matthew Arnold launched a ferocious attack against the 'feather-brained' journalism of W. T. Stead, the editor of the *Pall Mall Gazette*, in the pages of the *Nineteenth Century*.[1] In the United States, where the changes acquired an overtly sensationalist cast, the phrase 'Yellow Journalism' has been more generally applied. It dates from the circulation war of the 1890s in New York City between Joseph Pulitzer and William Randolph Hearst, the two leading newspaper proprietors.[2] Yet, in both countries, the striking transformations in newspaper journalism followed a broadly similar trajectory. In the early decades of the century, British and American papers were published mostly in a conventional six-column typographical format that emphasised parliamentary coverage and diplomatic news, addressed itself to a well-educated body of readers and by modern standards was predictably dull. A century later, as the circulation of individual newspapers expanded into the hundreds of thousands, they began to cater to a larger assortment of tastes. Their price was reduced from ten cents or more to a penny or less, and their content encompassed a much larger quantity of sports news, celebrity gossip and human-interest stories. Readers were able to choose among daily, evening and Sunday papers, which were published in almost every city of any size in Britain and the United States. Likewise, the visual side of print journalism became

---

[1] M. Arnold, 'Up to Easter', *Nineteenth Century*, 122 (1887), 638.
[2] See J. Wiener, ed., *Papers for the Millions: The New Journalism in Britain, 1850s to 1914*. New York: Greenwood Press, 1988; W. Campbell, *Yellow Journalism: Puncturing the Myths, Defining the Legacies*. Westport, CT: Praeger, 2001.

increasingly central, ranging from the publication of political cartoons and the early use of photographs to the development of the modern comic strip. As journalism slowly became professionalised, with reporters being hired on a regular basis (female as well as male), it featured by-lines and columns, as well as an energetically competitive approach to news stories that were increasingly dependent upon speed.

It is crucial to emphasise that this press revolution took place on both sides of the Atlantic and that the Anglo-American press was a product of a common culture and, as well, of a unified transatlantic sensibility. During the century, the contours of British and American society were steadily reconfigured by comparably broad social and political trends, including a burgeoning of commerce and industry, and a shift towards a more democratic polity. As the powerfully influential London *Times* (which was also read in nineteenth-century America) was dramatically overtaken in readership in late century by mass circulation newspapers such as Alfred Harmsworth's *Daily Mail* and Charles Pearson's *Daily Express*, so too was a well-respected newspaper such as James Webb's *Morning Courier and New-York Enquirer* supplanted by, among other papers, Pulitzer's *World* and Hearst's *New York Evening Journal*. But while a broad congruence between newspaper journalism in both countries is discernible, there were also significant differences. Cultural and economic factors, including the effects of speed, strength of class feeling, levels of education and the relative impact of technological developments, affected the degree of change. To the extent that both countries experienced similar changes in newspaper journalism, it is the case that many of these transformations developed more slowly in Britain. For example, American newspapers were initially more receptive to gossip columns, sports news, sensationalised crime stories and display advertising, which employed striking designs and bold layouts. Human-interest articles also were a feature of American popular journalism at an earlier period, as were several key elements of modern reporting, including aggressive interviewing and the use of the inverted pyramid (or summary news lead), a style of reporting that involved presenting the facts of a story in diminishing order of importance. Still, a discernible 'time lag' in America's favour was not always to be found. The interaction between the two national versions of newspaper journalism and their practitioners was reciprocal and fluid, and in a few areas the British press underwent change at an earlier period. For example, this was the case in regard to pictorial journalism, where the weekly *Illustrated London News*, which first appeared in 1842, and other illustrated newspapers such as the

Illustrated Times (1855), exercised a strong influence over American popular journalism throughout most of the century.

Cultural Factors

To better understand the interplay between the British and American newspaper press, it is necessary to bear in mind the respective positions of cultural authority in which each country was held. Between the two nations, the canon of critical literary judgement was almost uniformly conceded to Britain, at least until late in the century, when American writers such as Nathaniel Hawthorne, Henry Wadsworth Longfellow and Mark Twain began to gain a substantial following in British literary circles. Until then, the reputation of British writers almost uniformly prevailed. Charles Dickens, Anthony Trollope, Oscar Wilde and others were lionised during celebratory lecture tours in the United States. Their books and poems were reprinted and widely circulated – frequently without their consent – and it was assumed that almost anything they penned was worthy of consideration. Likewise, British parliamentary and financial news was of interest to educated American readers and copies of *The Times*, the *Morning Chronicle* and Britain's leading monthlies and quarterlies circulated in New York, Boston, Philadelphia and elsewhere. The very reverse was true of American newspapers, which were mostly castigated by British commentators. They were conceived (from a distance of several thousand miles) as being coarse, devoid of literary quality, prone to pander to vulgar tastes and rightly intended to be disposed of as soon as they were read. According to the art critic and journalist Theodore Child, writing in the *Fortnightly Review* (1885), newspapers in the United States emanated from a 'fidgety and purposeless civilization'.[3] In a powerful critique of cultural democracy, Matthew Arnold surpassed even Child's observation with his oft-quoted lamentation (written shortly after his visit to the United States in 1886): 'If one were searching for the best means to effect and kill in a whole nation the discipline of respect, the feeling for what is elevated, one could not do better than take the American newspapers.'[4]

The aversion to America's literary output (and its alleged debased standards) was a decisive factor in slowing the pace of journalistic change in Britain. Partly as a kind of holding operation for the maintenance

[3] T. Child, 'The American Newspaper Press', *Fortnightly Review*, new series, 38 (1885), 831.
[4] M. Arnold, *Civilization in the United States: First and Last Impressions of America*. Boston: Cupples and Hurd, 1888, pp. 177–78.

of values and in part as a way of erecting a barrier against a deluge
of American print, newspaper proprietors and journalists in Britain,
and their readers, resisted press innovations that appeared to have an
American label attached to them. This was especially true of changes
associated with the first successful popular transatlantic newspaper of the
century, the *New York Herald*, published and edited by James Gordon
Bennett, a transplanted Scotsman. The *Herald* first appeared in 1835 and
rapidly amassed a large circulation, derived primarily from its coverage of
sports, crime and 'society news', the latter signifying gossip about the
upper classes. Bennett did much to erect the parameters of modern
journalism, and he is arguably the most important individual to emerge
in transatlantic newspaper journalism during the nineteenth century.
Among other things, he pioneered the use of interviews, appointed a full-
time reporter to cover political and social news in the nation's capital and
gave unceasing publicity to one of the foremost crime stories of the age,
the Robinson-Jewett case of 1836, which involved the alleged murder of
a prostitute by an upstanding member of New York City's social set,
replete with salacious tidbits that Bennett doled out sparingly to his
readers each morning. On a number of occasions, he was also in the
vanguard of pictorial journalism, including the first sketches of crime
scenes.[5] Bennett is readily identifiable to readers of Dickens's *The Life and
Adventures of Martin Chuzzlewit* (1843-4), as the troublesome owner of
the 'New York Rowdy Journal', and as such he became a bogeyman of
popular journalism. During the 1830s and 1840s, a host of similar 'sensational' penny papers emerged in New York and other American cities,
including the *Baltimore Sun*; the *New York Tribune*, edited by Horace
Greeley, the idiosyncratic social and political reformer who was the
Democratic candidate for president in 1872; the Philadelphia *Public
Ledger*; and the New York *Sun*, which subsequently achieved transatlantic fame under the influence of its famous editor Charles A. Dana, who
constantly expounded the virtues of condensation and clarity in
journalism.[6] But it was Bennett's *Herald* that gained initial renown (of
a sort) on both sides of the Atlantic during these tumultuous decades in
American history and, notwithstanding legal and other barriers placed in

---

[5] The best analysis of the career of James Gordon Bennett (1795–1872) as a journalist is J. Crouthamel,
  Bennett's New York Herald and the Rise of the Popular Press. Syracuse University Press, 1989.
[6] There are many studies of both Greeley (1811–72) and Dana (1819–97), but the best are R. Williams,
  Horace Greeley: Champion of American Freedom. New York University Press, 2006; and J. Steele,
  The Sun Shines for All: Journalism and Ideology in the Life of Charles A. Dana. Syracuse University
  Press, 1993.

its path, exercised a pervasive influence on British as well as American journalism throughout much of the century.[7]

Popular and Sunday Press

The newspaper press in Britain underwent a different kind of popular transformation in the 1830s and 1840s, which also had lasting consequences. During America's 'democratic decades', when penny papers such as the *Herald* began to flourish, the foundation for a cheap mainstream commercial press was being laid based on the integration of popular reading tastes into traditional forms of journalism. Newspapers such as the *Tribune*, the *Herald* and both of the *Suns* segued into profitable undertakings that spoke to an expanding readership in its own demotic terms. On the other hand, in Britain hundreds of newly minted penny and halfpenny papers came into existence during these decades as byproducts of a fierce political and class struggle waged against a series of taxes on the press. Almost all of the cheap newspapers published during this 'War of the Unstamped', which was fought in the streets of London, Manchester, Birmingham and elsewhere between 1830 and 1836 (at which time the tax on newspapers was reduced to a penny), were illegal, and as such frontally opposed to the knowledge-stultifying effects of the 'taxes on knowledge'. Although they were widely circulated, and included such well-known publications as Henry Hetherington's *Poor Man's Guardian* (1831–5) and *Cleave's Weekly Police Gazette* (1834–6), for the most part they did not print news overtly, in the way that Bennett, Greeley, Benjamin Day of the New York *Sun* and other American journalists did. Instead many of the unstamped papers disseminated crime and sports news as a means of entertaining their readers and gaining political support, or they made use of pictorial devices to buttress their appeal. Others promoted popular fiction or exposed the alleged scandals of political or religious malefactors, which may be viewed retrospectively as a harbinger of modern investigative journalism. Yet because the political content of the unstamped campaign took precedence over everything else, this penny press had few if any ties to mainstream journalism and can in no sense be described as integrated into it. Instead these years of political protest in Britain witnessed a widening chasm between so-called 'respectable' and 'non-respectable' newspapers, or

---

[7] In New York City alone, thirty-four penny papers were launched in the six-year period ending in 1840. G. Barth, *City People: The Rise of Modern City Culture in Nineteenth Century America*. New York: Oxford University Press, 1980, pp. 70–71.

to employ modern terminology, between quality newspapers and their tabloid competitors.[8]

This gap was widened even further at mid-century by the emergence of cheap illustrated and Sunday papers in Britain. The Sunday newspaper has become a staple of modern journalism in both Britain and America and has acquired several different forms. For example, the *Observer* (dating from 1791) features political and literary analysis, while appealing primarily to an educated readership. Other Sunday newspapers, including the *News of the World*, which was terminated abruptly by Rupert Murdoch at the inception of the phone-hacking scandal in 2011, offer a hefty dose of sport and scandal. Still others, including Murdoch's *Sunday* Times, founded in 1821, or the *Sunday Telegraph*, are stuffed with miscellaneous news articles, feature stories and extended sections given over to travel, the arts and a mélange of business and domestic news. In both format and content, these latter newspapers resemble the American Sunday papers minus some of their populist content, including the bulging comic strips of the late nineteenth and early twentieth centuries. But while the Sunday press in Britain and America is mostly similar in format (and has been so since about the 1960s), the antecedents of each were markedly different. The Sunday press in Britain (minus the *Observer, Weekly Dispatch, Sunday Times* and several other newspapers already in circulation) came into existence in the immediate aftermath of the unstamped press campaign. It intermixed popular elements such as sports, crime and fiction with a radical perspective on political and social issues and a concentrated use of woodcuts. *Lloyd's Weekly Newspaper* (1842), the *News of the World* (1843) and *Reynolds's Newspaper* (1849) are the best examples from the period. All three survived well into the twentieth century and did much to attract large numbers of readers. They pushed back successfully against the denunciations of churchmen and others who believed the Sabbath was properly a day of rest and piety, and that neither the political sensibilities of workingmen nor their sensationalist tastes in journalism were properly stimulated on that day. Thus mid-century Sunday newspapers were, predictably, labelled 'non-respectable' and relegated to the same category as the cheap unstamped press. None of these Sunday papers was affiliated to a daily

---

[8] There are two major histories of the unstamped press campaign: J. Wiener, *The War of the Unstamped; The Movement to Repeal the British Newspaper Tax, 1830–1836*. Ithaca, NY: Cornell University Press, 1969; P. Hollis, *The Pauper Press: A Study in Working-Class Radicalism of the 1830's*. Oxford University Press, 1970. An important study of the subsequent parliamentary campaign against the taxes on knowledge is M. Hewitt, *The Dawn of the Cheap Press in Victorian Britain: The End of the 'Taxes on Knowledge', 1849–1869*. London: Bloomsbury Academic, 2014.

newspaper, as became the common practice in America. On the contrary, efforts by the *Daily Mail*, the *Daily Telegraph* and other newspapers to launch a Sunday publication in the late 1890s – in effect, to extend their six weekday editions to a seventh day – had to overcome formidable opposition.

The evolution of the American Sunday newspaper followed a different trajectory. Until the final decades of the century, Sunday papers played a limited role in American journalism, the major exception being Greeley's *Weekly Tribune* (founded in 1841 and actually published on Saturday), whose large national circulation was constructed around its literary highlights. As in Britain, newspapers that appeared on Sunday evoked a powerful strand of moral indignation. When these papers began to take root successfully in the 1890s as a seventh-day byproduct of Yellow Journalism, they rapidly became a central element of American mass circulation journalism. Under the aegis, notably, of Pulitzer and Hearst, they presented as much of a diet of sensationalism as their largely working-class and immigrant readers were prepared to ingest. They featured some non-respectable elements of the mid-century British Sunday papers with lots more added on: massive helpings of crime and sports, celebrity gossip, blaring headlines, the innovative use of pictures and humorous comic strip characters such as the 'Yellow Kid' – a slum child whose doings were accompanied by innovative word balloons and who became a retail advertising icon in late nineteenth-century America. Morrill Goddard and Arthur Brisbane, who both worked for Pulitzer before defecting to Hearst, created the two leading American Sunday papers of the period: Pulitzer's *The World on Sunday* (1898–1911) and the Sunday edition of Hearst's *New York Journal*, which began publication in 1895. Both newspapers incorporated a degree of sensationalism exceeding anything on offer in Britain until well into the twentieth century. In the words of a contemporary observer, they fused 'the characteristics of the circus poster and the patent medicine "ad"'.[9] Yet, and this is a seeming irony, they were integrated into American mainstream journalism in a way that was not the case in Britain. The explanation for this is that they drew organically upon the generalising popular developments of half a century earlier. They were also 'classless', as were their sister dailies, that is, subject to commercial pressures and moral opposition but not, it was widely agreed, operating in violation of a cultural red line.

[9] J. E. Rogers, *The American Newspaper*. University of Chicago Press, 1909, p. 56.

Evening Journalism

Similar developments occurred in evening journalism. Unlike the Sundays, which depended upon a relative degree of leisure among their readers, evening papers relied mostly on working-class readers who by late century had a small accretion of spending power. These papers were buffeted by commercial pressures and by such factors as the impact of speed on journalism, an improved technology that made possible the publication and distribution of a huge quantity of newspapers in much shorter periods of time, and the broad transatlantic social phenomenon referred to as 'suburbanisation'. Their objective was not to re-circulate news that had been printed earlier in the day but to provide intensified coverage of late-breaking developments, which frequently necessitated multiple editions. Evening papers employed any technology of speed that lay at hand and particularly became linked to the telegraph, telephone and typewriter. They developed a more competitive ethos than the morning press, with many fewer leaders and minimal coverage of foreign or parliamentary news. Their success was frequently tied to effective sports coverage: racing results, the latest baseball and cricket scores, round by round results of boxing matches. New positions were established in the newsroom to absorb and take advantage of these changes, especially the creation of rewrite men, who collected raw data from reporters and telegraph tapes and converted it into dramatic news stories. Evening newspapers also made use of striking headlines and simplified typography because their primary objectives were to attract by visual means the passing fancy of a worker or to extract a penny or two from middle-class commuters hurrying back to their suburban homes after a day at the office.

Not surprisingly, successful evening newspapers such as the New York *Evening Telegram*, which commenced publication in 1867, and the *Chicago Daily News*, which first appeared in 1876, gained traction earlier in America, in part because several of the factors alluded to earlier – speed, technological change and suburbanisation – were more firmly rooted in American society. For example, the electric telegraph, invented in the 1840s, was for several decades used more widely in American journalism, and this was true of the telephone and typewriter as well. By the late 1880s, all three inventions were ensconced in the newsrooms of evening papers, a bevy of rewrite men were employed to utilise them efficiently, and screaming headlines were routinely used to exploit the appeal of speed. As with the Sundays, the type of news featured in the evening press, sports, gossip and crime in particular, were integrated fully into the prevailing ethos of American journalism. Almost by definition evening (or afternoon) newspapers fared best in large cities because the sudden, unpredictable calamities and upheavals of a crowded urban space lent themselves more readily to competitive news stories. But while the sensationalised version of a classic evening paper established its roots earlier in America, Britain produced several notable, if relatively genteel, evening newspapers in the late nineteenth century, of a kind unmatched across the Atlantic. Foremost among these were the *Pall Mall Gazette* (1865–1923) and the *Westminster Gazette* (1893–1928). Both newspapers followed a conventional journalistic model and had tiny circulations by American standards. The *Westminster Gazette* was composed in an easily readable style, printed on green news-print and exceeded the bulk of its morning competitors in crime and sports coverage. And the *Pall Mall Gazette*, edited by the irascible, if brilliant, William T. Stead, from 1883 to 1889, provoked a storm of controversy with its uninhibited exposure of child prostitution in 1885 ('The Maiden Tribune of Modern Babylon'), its crossheads and other typographical innovations and its approbation of American society and its journalism.

Several key examples of evening newspapers can be used to elucidate some differences and similarities between the British and American press. The *Evening News*, published in London, comes as close as any news-paper of the period to emulating the 'classic' American evening format. Established as a halfpenny paper in 1881, it soon came to be regarded as a pioneer of early mass circulation journalism. Two years after its initial appearance, the Irish-born Frank Harris, best known for his provocative sexual memoir *My Life and Loves*, first published in 1931, became editor. Harris pursued a 'down-market' trajectory in line with his journalistic passion for 'kissing and fighting', and he supplemented this by a steady dosage of racing results and crime stories. When Kennedy Jones, an entrepreneurial Scottish journalist, purchased the paper in conjunction with Alfred Harmsworth (the future Viscount Northcliffe) in 1894, its sensationalising content was strengthened. It found itself in a fiercely competitive rivalry with the newly popularised *Evening Standard* (founded in 1859) and the penny *Star*, which appeared in 1888. The latter is, perhaps, the best known of late-nineteenth-century British evening newspapers because its editor Thomas Power O'Connor ('T. P.'), who wrote for and edited a number of newspapers and sat in the House of Commons for forty-nine years, was one of the foremost pioneers of the New Journalism. O'Connor championed a democratised press, that is, one offering his readers a diverse content appropriate to their varied interests, a venue in which 'everything that can be talked about can also be written about.'[10] At the outset, the *Star* gave extensive coverage to one of the leading crime stories of the age – the exploits of the East End assassin known as 'Jack the Ripper' – and this, to a degree, explains its successful breakthrough into mass circulation journalism. It accompanied its reporting of the Ripper's deeds with harrowing American-style headlines ('THE RIPPER SURPASSES HIMSELF IN FIENDISH MUTILATION'), producing an abundant combination of fear and titillation among its readers. It also featured a front-page political gossip column, written by O'Connor, and a large quantity of sports reporting, including regular contributions from Edward C. Mitchell ('Captain Coe'), who wrote one of the first popular columns on cricket.

Notwithstanding the crime, sports, gossip and occasionally ghoulish headlines propagated by the *Evening News*, the *Star*, Edward Hulton's *Manchester Evening Chronicle* (1897) and other British newspapers, all of this was distinctly mild when set next to the *New York Evening Journal*, the quintessential evening newspaper of the period. This Hearst paper, founded in 1896, fused all of the elements of Yellow and New Journalism and established itself as a self-generating conduit of sensationalism even in the absence of a complement of hard news. Hearst splashed headlines across the front page, putting into shade the six-column typography of the *Evening News* and the *Star*. His paper waxed ecstatic over crime stories, featured popular comic strips such as 'The Katzenjammer Kids', originated the modern occupation of sports reporter with its extensive coverage of baseball news (Charles Dryden, who wrote about baseball, was the best-paid sports writer in the United States at the time) and printed advice columns, which drew a large number of female readers to the paper. Much more can be written about the *Journal* and its teams of reporters (including women), who were assigned systematically to city beats and directed to cover them in a notably ruthless manner. The key point about Hearst and other American proprietors, such as Pulitzer, is that they surpassed British evening and morning papers in their ability to trumpet forms of sensationalism and entertainment. In doing so, they pointed the way towards a cutthroat tabloid sensibility that erupted on both sides of the Atlantic in the first half of the twentieth century.[11]

---

[10] T. P. O'Connor, 'The New Journalism', *The New Review*, 1 (1889), 430. O'Connor (1848–1929) lacks an up-to-date biographer but his memoirs are still a valuable source. T. O'Connor. *Memoirs of an Old Parliamentarian*, 2 vols. London: Ernest Benn, 1929.

[11] The best recent biographies of Hearst and Pulitzer are D. Nasaw, *The Chief: The Life of William Randolph Hearst*. Boston: Houghton Mifflin, 2000; and D. Brian, *Pulitzer: A Life*. New York: John Wiley & Sons, 2001.

Commercialism and Speed

Underlining many of the changes in popular journalism – in reporting, organisational structure and circulation that now began to climb precipitously – were two critical factors: commercialism and speed. The commercial ethic was deeply embedded in the structure of the press from the outset of the nineteenth century. Even idealistic printer-proprietors such as William Hone, who published a series of freethinking radical journals in London between 1817 and 1829 and was prosecuted on several occasions for seditious and blasphemous libel, were not averse to earning a profit through sales of their papers. In the 1830s and 1840s, commercialism became especially rife in American journalism as Bennett, Greeley and other newspaper owners eschewed customary ties to political parties and began to rely instead on large numbers of readers for financial support. And if the profit motive in British popular journalism was temporarily muted during the politically inspired War of the Unstamped, it nonetheless continued to resonate. Proprietors of newspapers sought to gain financial advantage by winning the custom of large numbers of new readers and attracting increased advertising. Their decisions as to content were driven by commercial motives, and these readers had little input into the final product. By the second half of the century, shareholding companies began to form and to invest large sums of money in newspapers. Their size was increased to accommodate a burgeoning quantity of news, while display advertising – which broke the column rule and featured an assortment of pictorial devices – was further developed. In the final decades of the century, powerful proprietors ('press lords') began to dominate the newspaper industry. By then advertising in particular had acquired a position of seminal importance in determining the profitability of a newspaper.

But if much nineteenth-century journalism on both sides of the Atlantic was self-evidently driven by a desire for profit and by the perception of news and advertising as exploitative commodities, the factor of increased speed was at least as critical to press innovation. And to a large degree, an obsession with speed and its application to journalism emanated from American culture. Speed was a phenomenon palpable to the many British writers and journalists who visited the United States during the nineteenth century and returned mostly with negative accounts of that country's rapid, if imbalanced, social pace. Not surprisingly, the telegraph, the first of the great 'speed' inventions of the century to directly impact and transform the nature of journalism, was integrated into the press in America both at an earlier period and with more sustained intensity than in Britain. News agencies began to make significant inroads in that country by mid-century, beginning with the New York Associated Press in 1848. During the Civil War of the 1860s, reporters representing both sides of the conflict transmitted many news accounts by telegraph. (The Press Association, a comparable British newsgathering organisation to the New York Associated Press, was not established until 1868.) London newspapers such as *The Times* and the *Daily News*, founded in 1846, relied on their correspondents to send wired stories from the battlefields, although these, admittedly, arrived several weeks late in London until 1866, when the successful laying of an Atlantic cable removed a critical barrier to transatlantic journalism. Even after the American conflict ended in 1865, the increased use of speed – for example, to report on the Franco-Prussian War of 1870–71 – had an American dimension. George Smalley, who headed the New York *Tribune*'s London office in the 1860s and 1870s (the first bureau of its kind to be opened in Europe by an American newspaper), maintained that 'whether we like it or not, the telegraph is our master.'[12] Smalley regularised and speeded up cabled dispatches from European cities to the *Tribune*'s New York office via London. These were then sent back to London newspapers including the *Daily News* often on the same day. In this way, Smalley and a growing number of journalists who joined him in making extensive use of the telegraph and cable became successful propagandists for a culture of speed.

From the late 1880s on, the typewriter and telephone complemented the telegraph in bringing about a dramatic reconfiguration of journalism constructed around speed. Typing bureaus sprang up in American cities (and subsequently in British cities) to assist reporters. Telephones were installed in newspaper offices, especially on evening newspapers, to facilitate the transmission of late breaking news, particularly sporting results. It is not surprising that American newspapers were initially more receptive to a culture of speed and that their proprietors demurred less frequently at the large expenses involved. For example, Bennett spent unprecedented sums of money during the Civil War to ensure that his *Herald* reporters were first with the news. They usually were although at times the competitive battle proved unnecessarily costly to him. For several decades, journalists and proprietors on both sides of the Atlantic reacted to the impact of speed in ways that were sometimes unpredictable. A compelling argument against speed, widely bruited about, was that it posed a threat to

---

[12] Quoted in J. Wiener, *The Americanization of the Press, 1830s-1914: Speed in the Age of Transatlantic Journalism*. London: Palgrave Macmillan, 2011, p. 93.

both creativity and accuracy in journalism. It was also asserted that the speeding up of print journalism by means of technology was an unnecessary diversion, a reaction that may perhaps be compared to the resistance to computer technology in the 1980s. Both Pulitzer and Hearst strongly encouraged the use of the typewriter and telephone, as did O'Connor, who made frequent personal use of both. O'Connor kept a typewriter in his private room in the House of Commons and employed it to write 'Mainly About People', his nightly column of political gossip that appeared in the *Star*. On the other hand, Harmsworth obsessed so favourably about the telephone that he kept one adjacent to his bedside until the day he died. Yet he stubbornly resisted the seeming advantages of the typewriter. Similar responses – positive and negative – were expressed on both sides of the Atlantic, as faster printing presses, the Linotype machine for setting type automatically and the halftone process for making newspaper photographs, all of which promoted the virtues of speed, were introduced in the final decades of the century. On the whole, American newspapers were more receptive to these innovations. Yet by 1900, the application of speed to journalism had mostly overcome resistance in both countries, and in this area at least there was relatively little to choose between the two versions of journalism.

The rise of paid reporting was a central development in the history of journalism. As a result of the increased emphasis on speed, a harshly competitive environment began to replace the earlier, more temperate days of newspaper work, when proprietors relied heavily on penny-a-liners to supply the news. This change also was particularly noticeable in America. Speed became the rival of quality and persistence, as proprietors and editors – many of the latter newly appointed to their jobs – insisted that their reporters outrace competitors to the finish line. An hour or two (sometimes less) seemed important to many of them if it meant a 'first past the post' story. Late-nineteenth-century memoirs of journalists, British as well as American, delineate this shift in intensity, as reporters began to cover assigned beats and were determined to gain scoops at the expense of their competitors. Pulitzer's *World*, headed by its brilliant managing editor Charles Chapin, was the first newspaper on either side of the Atlantic to systematically divide its newsroom into territorial and subject beats and to send forth reporters in pursuit of relevant stories.[13] And Pulitzer was

[13] A fine biography of Chapin (1858–1930), whose importance is often overlooked in the history of journalism, is J. Morris, *The Rose Man of Sing Sing: A True Tale of Life, Murder, and Redemption in the Age of Yellow Journalism*. New York: Fordham University Press, 2003.

restrained by comparison to Hearst, whose reporters (the 'attack squad') were known to forage for news stories in every possible corner, at times with more than a hint of desperation. They investigated and interviewed aggressively and dug ceaselessly for dirt, practices that won Hearst's approval, so long as their news stories gained first place for his papers. American reporters excelled at first at this competitive use of speed, but by the late nineteenth century the latter counted for almost as much among British journalists. When Ralph D. Blumenfeld, the American-born journalist who had been trained in Pulitzer press techniques in New York, took over the editorship of the *Daily Express* in 1902, he confronted a culture of apathy and inertia, notwithstanding that newspaper's credentials as a product of the New Journalism. Blumenthal quickly moved to give the *Daily Express* newsroom an 'American style' makeover, with speed and efficiency at its fore. The elderly, bearded subeditor sitting on a high stool holding on to his news story until the following day, or the day after (so the story went), was replaced by a rewrite man who quickly incorporated the latest news stories into the paper before putting it to bed. By 1900, the slogan, 'Get there first with the most news', which, predictably, was of American origin, was widely applied on both sides of the Atlantic, though still with an occasional stigma of non-respectability attached to it in Britain.

Transatlantic Interactions

Throughout the century, close transatlantic relationships and interactions developed among journalists and newspaper staff. For example, by mid-century, American illustrators had started to take their cue from abroad. Engravers looked with admiration to the pictorial work of Charles Knight and his influential Society for the Diffusion of Useful Knowledge in London, which published a number of cheap illustrated periodicals, including the *Penny Magazine* (1832–45).[14] In 1851, *Gleason's Pictorial Drawing-Room Companion*, published in Boston, became the first successful pictorial weekly in America. It drew inspiration from the *Illustrated London News*, though it provided more of a magazine format than the latter. Among the leading engravers and illustrators on the *Illustrated London News* was Henry Carter ('Frank Leslie'), who emigrated to America at the age of twenty-seven and subsequently founded a series of

---

[14] The most recent study of Knight is V. Gray, *Charles Knight: Educator, Publisher, Writer*. Aldershot: Ashgate, 2006.

illustrated newspapers including the celebrated *Frank Leslie's Illustrated Newspaper*, which published nearly 3,000 wood engravings during the Civil War. *Leslie's* competed vigorously for scoops with *Harper's Weekly* and helped transform the nature of transatlantic pictorial journalism. Under the aegis of Pulitzer and Hearst, American newspapers made striking use of engravings and early photographs and effectively invented illustrated comic strips during the 1890s. Yet visual journalism continued to emanate with greater energy and enthusiasm from Britain for much of the century. It was two outstanding London newspapers – the *Daily Graphic*, which began publication in 1890, and Harmsworth's *Daily Mirror* (1903) – that gave the most dynamic boost to pictorial journalism. Both papers made prodigious use of the halftone process to reproduce photographs, which by 1900 could be cleanly printed on high-speed rotary presses. The *Daily Mirror* gave a lot of space to crime and celebrity news, and before 1914 it was the most sensational pictorial newspaper to appear anywhere in the world. By virtue of its small size and populist content (shockingly so, in the view of many contemporaries), it may credibly be described as the most important of the early Anglo-American tabloid newspapers.

Other than in the visual department, transatlantic interactions continued to receive most of their stimuli from American sources. Many more British journalists flocked to the United States to observe its journalism than vice versa, especially during the third quarter of the century. Some came to condemn the American press; others returned to Britain with a more salutary or nuanced view. Among the latter was the celebrated George Augustus Sala, who was influenced by American journalism in a positive way during the Civil War. He initially worked as a correspondent for the *Daily Telegraph*, a newspaper founded in 1855 when the final penny duty on newspapers was repealed, and which rapidly transformed itself into one of the best of the numerous provincial and London newspapers established during the third quarter of the century. Sala imbibed some of the journalistic virtues of speed during his sojourn in America, where he became friendly with George Smalley. During a period of more than thirty years, he wrote an estimated 9,000 'social leaders' for the *Daily Telegraph*, helping transform that newspaper into a vehicle for the aspirations of an emergent middle- and lower-middle-class readership. Another key British journalist who learned much of his trade in America was Edmund Yates, the well-known gossip columnist and man about town. For a time in the 1870s, Yates worked as London Correspondent for the New York *Herald* (now owned by 'Commodore' Bennett, the son of the original owner), and he spent lengthy periods of time in New York, where he mingled with an influential coterie of literary journalists and reporters. As editor of the *World* in the 1870s, a controversial weekly society paper published in London, Yates helped establish both gossip and American-style interviewing as central modes of expression in the British press.[15]

During the final decades of the century, American journalists also began to work abroad in increasing numbers, and some exercised a considerable influence on the British press. In addition to Smalley and Blumenfeld, who did much to introduce American speed and competitive reporting techniques into the more quiescent environs of Fleet Street, the work of Chester Ives and Harold Frederic is worthy of citation. Ives reported for the *Herald* and the *Tribune* before settling in London in the late 1880s. He then established the *Morning*, a short-lived halfpenny daily newspaper, which was the first in Britain to put news on the front page, an American innovation. The bulk of this news was of the tabloid variety, in that it focused on sports, crime and entertainment. After its demise (and following a series of name changes), the *Morning* (1892) resurfaced as the *Daily Express* in 1900, and within a few years this quintessentially 'American' newspaper had become a staple of British popular journalism. Harold Frederic's contributions to transatlantic journalism are more muted and in some ways run counter to the rapid shift towards popularisation. Frederic was the London correspondent for the *New York Times* for fourteen years and a close friend of O'Connor and other British journalists. Instead of conveying the virtues of journalism as entertainment, he carried the torch for news objectivity and comprehensiveness that the *New York Times* ('All the News That's Fit to Print') came to represent under the ownership of Adolph Ochs, who took over the paper in 1896.[16] This important aspect of American newspaper history, still a minority taste for the most part today, had an influence on British journalism, though one that did not develop fully until the twentieth century.

A good portion of this chapter has focused on the press in London and New York, which tended to nurture influential journalists and produce most of the better-known newspapers. Throughout the century, 'Fleet Street' and

---

[15] The autobiographies of Sala and Yates are of considerable interest. See G. Sala, *The Life and Adventures of George Augustus Sala*, 2 vols. New York: Charles Scribner, 1895); and E. Yates, *Edmund Yates: His Recollections and Experiences*. London: Richard Bentley and Son, 1885. The best scholarly study of both men is P. D. Edwards, *Dickens's 'Young Men': George Augustus Sala, Edmund Yates and the World of Victorian Journalism*. Aldershot: Ashgate, 1997.

[16] The best study of Harold Fredric (1856–98), who was also a prominent novelist, is R. Myers, *Reluctant Expatriate: The Life of Harold Fredric*. Westport, CT: Greenwood Press, 1995.

'Newspaper Row' came to signify, respectively, the apex of journalist achievement in London and New York. Yet, it would be misleading to ignore the significant flowering of a regional and provincial press in both countries. Chicago and Manchester evolved as key centres of transatlantic journalism, as did other large metropolises, including St Louis, Birmingham, Boston, Liverpool, San Francisco and Leeds. Overall, the regional press in America took firmer root and established a more distinctive popular profile. This resulted primarily from the large size of the country, which made it unfeasible for New York (or another Eastern city) to service the daily reading needs of an expanding, westward-shifting population. The chief centres of regional journalism during the second half of the century were Chicago and St Louis, two of the fastest-growing cities in the country. Chicago in particular attracted many notable journalists in the second half of the century, including Melville Stone and Wilbur F. Storey, who established that city as a near rival to New York in news collecting and mass circulation journalism. Stone founded the *Chicago Daily News* in 1876 and subsequently pursued an editorial policy of 'sensational and intensely personal reporting'.[17] His specialty was 'detective journalism', which was shorthand for the exposure of public corruption and, from his aggressively anti-union perspective, the nefarious deeds of working-class agitators and anarchists. Storey, his arch competitor as editor of the *Chicago Times*, which commenced publication in 1854, had fewer journalistic scruples. He featured crime and sex-related stories, racy headlines and 'the juiciest and spiciest accounts of mayhem and scandal' he was able to acquire. Storey believed that all news was relevant so long as it held the attention of his readers. The following quote is generally ascribed to him (with an inevitable variation in the telling): 'Telegraph fully all news, and when there is no news, send rumors.'[18] To a degree, Manchester was analogous to Chicago. It was the major urban rival to London, and the *Manchester Guardian* (1821), its leading newspaper, was noted for its moderate liberalism, and under the editorship of C. P. Scott, from 1872 on, for its outstanding literary qualities. This placed it at the far end of the spectrum from the popularising trends dominant in Chicago (and in St Louis, where Pulitzer's *St Louis Post-Dispatch* prefigured the subsequent outpouring of Yellow Journalism). Manchester's chief importance in journalism at the time was as a distribution centre for the leading London newspapers, which served effectively as a national press.

---

[17] M. Stone, *Fifty Years a Journalist*. Garden City, NY: Doubleday, Page and Company, 1921, p. 78
[18] F. Wilkie, *Pen and Powder*. Boston: Ticknor and Company, 1888, p. 114. A good biography of Storey is J. Walsh, *To Print the News and Raise Hell: A Biography of Wilbur F. Storey*. Chapel Hill: University of North Carolina Press, 1968.

Telegraphic lines were placed directly in newspaper offices in Manchester, and local editions of several London papers were printed there. By 1900, a vigorous form of American-style popular journalism was also to be found in Manchester ('The Other Fleet Street'), led by Sir Edward Hulton's *Manchester Evening Chronicle* (1897), which soon had the largest circulation of any British evening newspaper outside London.

By the late 1890s, newspaper proprietors jostled for power and influence on both sides of the Atlantic. In the United States, Pulitzer and Hearst led the way in a cutthroat war for press supremacy that played out against a backdrop of jingoism and imperialist fervour. Both men represented extremes of the American press experience, hiring some of the best journalists available and paying large salaries to give sensationalist weight to their chief newspapers, the *World* and the *Journal*. Pulitzer articulated a firm sense of professionalism, but it was Hearst who more closely prefigured the tabloid experience of the twentieth century. Whether as a force for good or not, this experience encompassed a democratising cultural force and was to help transform popular daily journalism into a primary tool of working-class entertainment and aspiration. There is no precise equivalent to Hearst among Britain's late-nineteenth-century press barons, though Harmsworth comes closest. Like Hearst, he was a vital force in the development of mass circulation journalism, offering to British readers a slightly paler version of the American popular press experience, though one signifying a crucial moment of transition between the 'respectable' press of the mid to late nineteenth century and its unruly twentieth-century offshoot. Harmsworth's *Evening News* represented an important shift in this direction, as did his *Daily Mirror*. The third of his triumvirate of leading newspapers, the halfpenny *Daily Mail* (1896), was the first newspaper on either side of the Atlantic to reach a hitherto unattainable circulation of one million a day, and it did so by incorporating many of the striking press changes of the previous century. The paper had its proportionate share of speed, celebrity, gossip, xenophobia and sensationalism but also good news coverage, solid sports reporting, a decent amount of fiction and just about anything else that helped sustain the interests of its huge readership. It was an adequate measure of how far changes in transatlantic popular journalism had come by 1900. On both sides of the Atlantic, the web that underlay these powerful changes may appear difficult to penetrate at times. Yet its many interactions, together with the useful comparisons it offers between British and American journalism during the nineteenth century, make the effort worthwhile.

CHAPTER 16

Journalism and Empire in an English-reading World: *The* Review of Reviews

Simon J. Potter

Introduction

During the nineteenth century, print capitalism in Britain reached a pinnacle of sophistication. Never before had readers been able to access such a variety of newspapers and periodicals. New publications targeted a gradually increasing range of social classes, literary tastes and individual interests. In large part, the extraordinary vibrancy of the nineteenth-century British press reflected the economic, social and cultural vitality of the world's first industrial nation and of its capital city, London. Yet it was also a function of Britain's vast overseas empire and its links with a wider English-speaking – or, more accurately, English-reading – world. For the British newspaper and periodical press did not serve Britain alone. It was also the press of the wider British Empire and, more broadly, of all those who felt Britain's cultural influence. It served British settlers, within and beyond the borders of the formal empire, and a smaller but still influential readership of literate Asian, African and other non-white colonial subjects. British publications were also consumed by many who were neither British born nor British subjects, but who nevertheless used the British press to access a world-spanning culture. And all the while, the press went on informing readers back home in Britain about the empire and the world beyond its boundaries, about the diverse and far-flung places in which their own country and their own friends, colleagues and relations were becoming such a dominating presence. In many ways, the press thus acted as a 'transnational connector', simultaneously a part of and a conduit for larger worldwide flows of goods, ideas and people.[1] However, we also need to acknowledge the limitations of the nineteenth-century press as a means of global mass communication. Examining the case of the

---

[1] On transnational connectors, see Pierre-Yves Saunier, *Transnational History*. Basingstoke: Palgrave Macmillan, 2013, p. 57.

monthly *Review of Reviews*, the analysis that follows suggests both the achievements and the failures of the nineteenth-century press as a globalising force.

Periodicals circulated around the English-reading world through diverse channels. Copies of British newspapers, periodicals and books were routinely carried overseas by migrants and other travellers. Passengers also produced their own ships' journals, recording the experiences and expectations of millions of nineteenth-century British migrants. As formalised imperial mail services developed, publications were posted to overseas readers in increasing numbers by friends and family back 'home' in Britain, as well as to paying subscribers. By the mid-1840s, some 320,000 'printed sheets' – mainly newspapers – were mailed each year between Britain and the Canadas. Some readers received parcels of forty or fifty British newspapers at a time.[2] By the early 1860s, the state-subsidised Peninsular and Oriental Steam Boat Company was carrying around 176,000 British newspapers to the colonies in Australia and Zealand each month.[3] When in 1907 postage rates were reduced for periodicals mailed to Canada from Britain, the annual number of items sent increased by some 6 million.[4] This state-subsidised global traffic in British newspapers and periodicals served the interests of British publishers and advertisers and of publics around the empire. Some entrepreneurs took full advantage of the resulting commercial opportunities. From the 1840s onwards, 'steamship newspapers', published to coincide with the departure of each mail ship, were produced specifically to carry summaries of news to colonial readers.[5] Similarly, some periodicals were produced in the colonies with the intention that readers would post them to friends and family in Britain, to communicate something of settler life.[6] By 1912, a combined total of 140,000 newspapers a week were reaching Britain from India, Canada, South Africa, Australia and New Zealand.[7]

---

[2] *Report of Commission appointed to inquire into the state of the Canadian Post Office*, House of Commons Parliamentary Papers (henceforth HCPP), 1846 (721), pp. 34, 59, 69, 93.
[3] *Return of the Number of Letters and Newspapers which have been forwarded to and received from the Australian Colonies and New Zealand*, HCPP, 1864 (476), p. 1.
[4] Simon J. Potter, *News and the British World: The Emergence of an Imperial Press System, 1876–1922*. Oxford University Press, 2003, pp. 71–2.
[5] Peter Putnis, 'The British Transoceanic Steamship Press in Nineteenth Century India and Australia: An Overview', *Journal of Australian Studies*, 31 (2007), 69–79.
[6] Lurline Stuart, *Nineteenth Century Australian Periodicals: An Annotated Bibliography*. Sydney: Hale and Iremonger, 1979, pp. 40, 89, 90.
[7] Report by W. G. [Gates] on Inland Newspaper Rate, 19 November 1912, Royal Mail Archive, London, POST/30/3394, file 4.

The nineteenth century also saw British models of journalistic practice and enterprise spread around the English-reading world, as the empire expanded and coalesced and as settlers and indigenous peoples established their own newspapers and periodicals using British templates.[8] Meanwhile, news circulated around the empire through various channels. Throughout our period, editors routinely reprinted news and articles culled from newspapers and periodicals received from other parts of the empire. During the second half of the century, the construction of a network of undersea telegraph cables meant that 'raw' news could be transmitted almost instantaneously, around and beyond the empire. Reuters emerged as the 'news agency of the British empire', coordinating supplies of syndicated telegraphic news, and trading news with its counterpart agencies in Europe and the United States.[9] Reuters created a common pool of news for papers around the British Empire, which complemented, and also sometimes undermined, the networks of correspondents that many papers had established to gather bespoke supplies of overseas news and opinion. London became the news capital for the empire and for much of the world. Taken as a whole, this massive efflorescence and intermeshing of journalism in Britain and its colonies spread news and ideas not just about politics but also about the whole spectrum of modern life. The relationship between print capitalism and British imperial expansion was symbiotic. If the press acted to form an 'imagined community' in this period, then surely that community was imperial as well as national in scope.[10]

Of course, the English-reading world also encompassed the United States. Arguably, the nineteenth century saw the emergence of an 'Angloworld' in which the British Empire and the United States formed two similar and interconnected components in an overarching global structure of settlement, production and trade.[11] Applying this perspective to press history, we might see London and the major cities of the United States as the great publishing centres serving (or exploiting) a world-spanning market for the English printed word. Publishers in London, New York, Boston and Chicago could take advantage of advanced production facilities and large and easily accessible local markets that allowed

---

[8] Potter, *News and the British World*, pp. 16–27.
[9] Donald Read, *The Power of News: The History of Reuters*, 2nd edn. Oxford University Press, 1999.
[10] Benedict Anderson, *Imagined Communities: Reflections on the Origin and Spread of Nationalism*, 2nd edn. London: Verso, 1991. John B. Thompson, *The Media and Modernity: A Social Theory of the Media*. Cambridge: Polity, 1995.
[11] James Belich, *Replenishing the Earth: The Settler Revolution and the Rise of the Anglo-world, 1783–1939*. Oxford University Press, 2009.

substantial print runs and economies of scale.[12] These resources were simply not available in peripheral centres. British and American publishers were thus able to dominate the production of monthly and quarterly periodicals and of specialist publications for the world English-reading market, and also to control a substantial part of the book trade. Dynamic offshoots of print capitalism certainly existed on the periphery, but they generally had to focus on producing publications that met local tastes and requirements and the demand for topicality.

Should we interpret the transnational nature of print capitalism in the English-reading world as evidence for the existence of a globalised mass communications world order? Many imperial historians have recently followed the 'global turn', emphasising the role of the nineteenth-century British Empire in creating a much more densely interconnected world of migration, trade and finance. Some historians have even described this as 'imperial globalisation'.[13] Yet this label is misleadingly anachronistic. At most, the nineteenth century saw the development of a semi-globalised world order, characterised by an unprecedented degree of transnational interconnectivity, but falling far short of the near-total interdependence that many would see as the hallmark of the globalisation of today.[14] Even at the fin-de-siècle, inter-continental communication remained slow and imperfect, and the press a far from ideal transnational connector, as is illustrated by the case of the *Review of Reviews*.

The *Review of Reviews:* A Transnational Connector

During the late nineteenth and early twentieth centuries, a number of British periodical publishers sought directly to target colonial markets. From 1877, the London *Times* published a special weekly edition, composed of 'a careful Epitome of the events of interest during the week',

---

[12] On the links between the British and U.S. press, see Joel H. Wiener and Mark Hampton, eds., *Anglo-American Media Interactions, 1850–2000*. Basingstoke: Palgrave Macmillan, 2007; and Joel H. Wiener, *The Americanization of the British Press, 1830s-1914*. Basingstoke: Palgrave Macmillan, 2011.

[13] Tony Ballantyne, *Orientalism and Race: Aryanism in the British Empire*. Basingstoke: Palgrave, 2002, p. 195. Martin Thomas and Andrew Thompson, 'Empire and Globalisation: from "High Imperialism" to Decolonisation', *International History Review*, 36 (2014), 142–70.

[14] On semi-globalisation, see John Darwin, *After Tamerlane: The Global History of Empire since 1405*. London: Allen Lane, 2007, pp. 502–3. See also Simon J. Potter, 'Webs, Networks, and Systems: Globalization and the Mass Media in the Nineteenth- and Twentieth-Century British Empire', *Journal of British Studies*, 46 (2007), 621–46; and Simon J. Potter and Jonathan Saha, 'Global History, Imperial History and Connected Histories of Empire', *Journal of Colonialism and Colonial History*, 16 (2015), n.p.

a selection of leaders and articles from the paper and 'a serial story by a well-known and popular author'. A year's subscription cost eleven shillings in Britain, and thirteen shillings abroad.[15] Aiming more explicitly at colonial readers, in 1904 the *Daily Mail* established an 'Overseas Edition' to provide 'a message each week from the Heart of Empire'. Printed on special thin paper, a copy could be posted abroad for a halfpenny. In 1908, the London *Standard* started producing a special weekly edition, *The Standard of Empire*, priced at one penny and including four pages of selected 'Home News' for overseas readers.[16] The monthly *Empire Review*, founded in 1901, sold for one shilling to both British and overseas readers and sought to become 'an Imperial review in the true sense of the word, that is, a review common to the empire'.[17]

Some British periodicals also produced special editions in overseas centres, aimed at providing local readers with supplementary content that would seem more relevant and up-to-date.[18] One of the most ambitious and long-lived of these experiments in transnational publishing was W. T. Stead's *Review of Reviews*, based in London but with distinctive editions tailored for readers in North America, Australia and New Zealand. Stead was a well-known (indeed somewhat notorious) figure in British journalism, a radical Liberal who had made his reputation through a series of moral purity crusades and his forceful championing of British foreign and imperial interests. He was inspired by an intense enthusiasm for the closer union of Britain with its 'white settler' colonies in Canada, Australia, New Zealand and South Africa, and with the United States. This vision exerted a powerful influence over his plans for the *Review*. The magazine's mixed record of achievements and failures echoes the ambiguous nature of Stead's more general contribution to British politics and journalism.[19] A bold experiment, the *Review* pushed the fin-de-siècle periodical press

[15] Advertisement in *The Monthly Index to Periodicals – A Supplement to the Review of Reviews* (March 1895).
[16] Potter, *News and the British World*, pp. 126, 162.
[17] Sir Clement Kinloch Cooke to Fleming, 11 May 1901, Sir Sandford Fleming papers, Library and Archives Canada, Ottawa, file 11/73.
[18] Stuart, *Australian Periodicals*, pp. 2, 72, 87, 158.
[19] On Stead and his work, see Joseph O. Baylen, 'Stead, William Thomas (1849–1912)', *Oxford Dictionary of National Biography*. Oxford University Press, 2004; online edn, Sept 2010) www.oxforddnb.com/view/article/36258, accessed 27 April 2011. More recently, see Grace Eckley, *Maiden Tribute: A Life of W. T. Stead*. Philadelphia: Xlibris, 2007; W. Sydney Robinson, *Muckraker: The Scandalous Life and Times of W. T. Stead, Britain's First Investigative Journalist*. London: Robson Press, 2012; and Laurel Brake, Ed King, Roger Luckhurst and James Mussell, eds., *W. T. Stead: Newspaper Revolutionary*. London: British Library, 2012.

in new directions, not least as a transnational connector. Yet, while it achieved much, it never lived up to Stead's high hopes and grand dreams.

Stead presented the *Review* as a distinctive and ambitious type of publication: 'an index and a guide to all those [periodicals] already in existence'.[20] It would be an aggregator and disseminator of global knowledge, its purpose to 'democratise the best thought of the world' by monitoring, collating, summarising and republishing articles, leaders, illustrations and caricatures taken from periodicals published in Britain and around the world.[21] In various formats, evolving over time, it also provided indices of periodical articles and extensive lists of new books. Unlike syndicated news agencies such as Reuters, the *Review* did not pretend to present a politically neutral selection of material. What Stead republished reflected his own, sometimes eccentric, enthusiasms and allegiances. As we will see, this complicated his attempts to communicate with readers beyond Britain's shores.

Stead and others also contributed a significant amount of original material to the *Review*, often adopting a global perspective on current affairs. Each issue contained a long commentary on the previous month's events in Britain and overseas, immodestly but appropriately entitled 'The Progress of the World'. Stead generally wrote this essay, along with various articles on his favourite causes of the moment. He also usually contributed a monthly 'Character Sketch', which discussed 'some man or woman who has figured conspicuously before the world in the previous month' (later, the column would also feature profiles of institutions and countries).[22] New works of fiction by international authors were published or reprinted in condensed form in the *Review*, although the magazine focused on current affairs rather than literary topics.[23]

Stead's *Review* also had an explicitly transnational political agenda, reflecting his imperial enthusiasms: he proclaimed that the *Review* would educate the English-speaking world in its duties to humanity and work to

---

[20] 'Programme', *Review of Reviews* London edition, 1 (January 1890), 14. This format had previously been tried by some other British publications, and by American illustrated magazines.

[21] 'After Seven Years', *Review of Reviews* London edition, 15 (January 1897), 85–100, quote at 95. See also Laurel Brake, 'Stead Alone: Journalist, Proprietor, and Publisher 1890–1903', in Brake et al. (eds.), *W. T. Stead*, pp. 77–97; and Laurel Brake, 'Journalism and Modernism, Continued: The Case of W. T. Stead', in Ann Ardis and Patrick Collier (eds.), *Transatlantic Print Culture, 1880–1940: Emerging Media, Emerging Modernisms*. Basingstoke: Palgrave Macmillan, 2008, pp. 149–66, esp. p. 150.

[22] 'Programme', 14.

[23] J. O. Baylen, 'W. T. Stead as Publisher and Editor of the Review of Reviews', *Victorian Periodicals Review*, 12 (1979), 70–84. Brake, 'Stead Alone', p. 82.

encourage an alliance between the British Empire and the United States.[24] He pursued this latter objective by advocating three fundamental constitutional changes: 'home rule all round' to create a devolved, federal government for Britain and Ireland; imperial federation to link Britain and its settler colonies; and the eventual reunification of the British Empire with the United States. These causes were all idiosyncratic fantasies, yet they did reflect significant broader trends in British thinking about the country's long-term future as a world power. Stead also used the *Review* to advocate a wide-ranging, progressive civic revival throughout the English-speaking world, based on the promotion of lofty spiritual and moral values. He thought the *Review* could establish a 'civic church ... a great voice sounding out over seas and land the summons to all men to think seriously and soberly of the public life in which they are called to fill a part'.[25] Hence the bizarre, but characteristic, telegraphic address adopted by Stead for the *Review*'s offices: 'Vatican, London'.

Reaching a Global Readership

Stead wrote much about his own journalistic practices in the pages of the *Review*, turning the publication's innovative approach into a newsworthy story. This makes it a beguiling source for those seeking to understand how nineteenth-century periodicals were produced. However, we should not believe everything that Stead wrote about his venture: he sometimes offered a misleadingly self-aggrandising picture of his achievements. Despite his world-conquering rhetoric, he initially ran the *Review* on modest lines. This was by necessity rather than design: after the first few issues, he fell out with his publisher and had to produce and publish the *Review* himself. He recruited a small core staff and housed them in a makeshift office in a London flat. For a time, the *Review* was distributed to retailers and subscribers from a cellar in the same building, with Stead pitching in to help wrap issues for posting.[26]

Nevertheless, Stead worked hard to cultivate the worldwide readership that his global mission demanded. He claimed that a monthly magazine was particularly well suited to this role: daily and weekly papers were hopelessly out-of-date by the time they reached overseas readers.[27]

---

[24] 'To All English-Speaking Folk', *Review of Reviews* London edition, 1 (January 1890), 15–20.

[25] 'To All English-Speaking Folk' (January 1890).

[26] Grant Richards, *Memories of a Misspent Youth, 1872–1896*. London: William Heinemann, 1932, pp. 124–25.

[27] 'To All English-Speaking Folk' (January 1890), esp. 15.

The *Review* accepted subscriptions for delivery to any part of the world for a flat annual fee of 8s 6d.[28] Stead also claimed to distribute a thousand copies of the *Review* to missionaries around the world each month, free of charge.[29] The *Review* certainly did develop a significant readership outside Britain: one hostile critic described it as 'that remarkable publication, which, like the sun and the drum-tap of the British army, travels round the earth, and carries the name and fame of Stead into the remotest corners of the globe.'[30] By August 1890, 80,000 copies of the *Review* were being printed each month.[31] It is not clear what portion of the print run was shipped overseas, but Stead proudly reprinted extracts from letters received from readers around the world. Taking stock of his achievements in 1895, he claimed that the *Review* had 'helped many thousands scattered far and wide, over land and sea, to a deeper consciousness of the brotherhood of our English-speaking family'. He continued: 'At this moment in how many mission stations and dreary barracks, in how many lonely huts on boundless prairie or in densest bush, the pioneers of our race feel these familiar pages bring them with electric thrill into vitalising contact with the nerve-centres of the world!' He claimed the *Review* had also become 'an interpreter of the ideas and literature of our race to other races who do not speak our tongue', and offered evidence that it was read in Siberia, Tashkent and Bokhara and had subscribers in Iceland, St Helena, Newfoundland, the West Indies, Brazil, Argentina, India, New Guinea, Madagascar, Central Africa and the South African Karoo.[32]

As an aggregator of global news, the *Review* had particular appeal for a far-flung audience of isolated readers scattered in out-of-the-way places, who otherwise found it difficult to follow world affairs. However, to reach readers in the United States and promote his dream of Anglo-American unity, Stead needed a different marketing strategy. In the United States, he faced considerable competition from locally published papers that provided readers with more up-to-date information on current affairs than could a monthly produced in London. Initially, Stead sought to overcome this problem by printing copies of the London edition of the *Review* in New York, but this brought only a marginal improvement in terms of

---

[28] Advertised on the cover of *The Monthly Index to Periodicals – A Supplement to the Review of Reviews* (April 1895).
[29] 'After Seven Years', 90.
[30] Cyril Waters, '"Steadism" in Politics: A National Danger', *Westminster Review*, 137 (January 1892), 618–26, quote at 618.
[31] Baylen, 'Stead as Publisher', 75.
[32] 'After Five Years: To Our Readers', *Review of Reviews* London edition, 11 (January 1895), 3–5. For similar claims, see also 'After Seven Years'.

topicality. Stead thus decided to establish an American edition of the *Review*, compiled and printed in New York and containing up-to-date content adapted to local requirements.[33] As noted earlier, this strategy was not entirely unprecedented: other British periodicals had already tried to produce special editions in overseas centres. What made the *Review* unusual, and perhaps unique, was its combination of a global ideological purpose with a transnational publishing strategy.[34] This was surely one of the most significant attempts to harness the capabilities of the nineteenth-century periodical press as a transnational connector.

Stead appointed Dr Albert Shaw, an American, to edit the New York edition of the *Review*. He granted Shaw full control over local personnel and finances, a generous salary and an equal share in the profits.[35] He also provided advance proofs of the London edition each month: Shaw was given wide editorial discretion to cut, modify and insert material as he saw fit, as long as he conducted the *Review* 'in harmony with the broad general principles' laid down by Stead in print.[36] Shaw published his first New York edition of the *Review* in April 1891.[37] A comparison of the August 1891 New York edition and the July 1891 London edition (there remained a time lag of nearly a month between the appearance of material in London and its reprinting in New York) is instructive. Shaw's edition retained the general appearance of the London version, and many of his regular columns carried the same titles as Stead's. While Shaw added many supplementary pages, he also reprinted verbatim much of Stead's material.

Stead and Shaw shared similar religious and progressive political sensibilities, and they were both participants in an 'Atlantic era in social politics'.[38] Stead initially proclaimed Shaw 'an American editor after my own heart'.[39] However, Shaw was more circumspect and conservative in

---

[33] Lloyd J. Graybar, *Albert Shaw of the Review of Reviews*. Lexington: University Press of Kentucky, 1974, p. 47.

[34] A French 'imitation', *La Revue des Revues*, was a separate business concern, although Stead was in touch with the first editor. See 'The Revue des Revues', *Review of Reviews*, London edition 1 (May 1890), 429; and Ernest Smith, *Fields of Adventure: Some Recollections of Forty Years of Newspaper Life*. London: Hutchinson, 1923, p. 79.

[35] Graybar, *Albert Shaw*, esp. pp. 40, 45.

[36] W. T. Stead and Albert Shaw, co-signers, Memorandum of Agreement as to the Publication of the American Edition of the *Review of Reviews*, 26 December 1890, Albert Shaw papers, New York Public Library, quoted in Graybar, *Albert Shaw*, p. 45.

[37] This issue was vol. 3, no. 15 – reflecting the fact that runs of the first fourteen numbers of the London edition of the *Review* had been printed in New York.

[38] Daniel T. Rodgers, *Atlantic Crossings: Social Politics in a Progressive Age*. Cambridge, MA and London: Harvard University Press, 1998, quote at p. 4.

[39] 'To All English-Speaking Folk', *Review of Reviews*, London edition, 3 (January 1891), 1.

temperament than the volatile, radical Stead, and it soon became clear that they held quite different views on the specifics of social policy and foreign affairs, and on the nature of the relationship between the London and New York editions of the *Review*. Stead saw the two editions as part of a single enterprise under his overall control and thought that he might one day even relocate to New York himself:

> I feel as if the centre of the English-speaking world were shifting westward, and I feel this so strongly that, in discussing the question of the *Review of Reviews* with Dr. Albert Shaw, I specially reserved to myself the right to transfer the Central Office of the *Review of Reviews* from London to New York in case it should prove that the whole of the English-speaking race was destined to federate under the Stars and Stripes rather than under the Union Jack.[40]

However, Shaw had quite different plans for the development of the U.S. office. Initially, the New York edition incurred a financial loss. Stead covered the shortfall, but towards the end of 1891 Shaw offered to borrow additional funds himself, in return for a substantial proprietorial interest in the publication. Stead accepted, and in 1892 the New York *Review* was incorporated as a legal entity separate from the London business, Stead remaining a co-director. By 1893, the New York edition had achieved a substantial circulation of 85,000 (approaching the total for the London edition) and had begun to turn a profit. In London, Stead was meanwhile struggling to balance the books.[41] In terms both of readership and finance, Shaw's journal looked less and less like a subordinate offshoot of Stead's original.

Stead also made arrangements to publish an 'Australasian' edition of the *Review* for readers in Australia and New Zealand. The commercial rationale was not quite the same as for the American edition. In Australia and New Zealand, the *Review* did not face significant competition from locally produced, up-to-date monthly magazines. However, it did have to compete for colonial readers with other British monthlies, and with locally produced Australian and New Zealand weeklies. Stead thus had to find a way to convince readers to buy the *Review* in addition to their local weeklies and instead of any other overseas monthly. His solution was to combine copious British content with a broad Australasian perspective. A monthly supplement, produced in Melbourne and issued with the

---

[40] Stead to John Morley, c. 1890–91, quoted in Frederic Whyte, *The Life of W. T. Stead*, 2 vols. London: Jonathan Cape, 1925, vol. 2, p. 25. The original letter is now seemingly lost.
[41] Graybar, *Albert Shaw*, pp. 49, 52.

London edition, would offer a substantial element of Australian and New Zealand material missing from other British periodicals. Furthermore, unlike most colonial weeklies, which tended to stand for the interests of the particular colony in which they were published, the supplement would adopt an avowedly Australasian approach. It would present its coverage of current affairs so as to appeal to readers from all the different colonies, and to support the movement towards the unification of the colonies in a single federation (the federal Australian Commonwealth was eventually established in 1901, although it excluded New Zealand). The London edition that accompanied the supplement would meanwhile allow readers to 'breathe the air of the motherland'. In this best of both worlds, national and imperial identities and requirements would be catered to simultaneously. Reflecting his broader thinking about empire and English-speaking unity, Stead argued that this would not be a difficult task. For Stead, national and imperial interests were inherently compatible within a self-governing community of English-speaking peoples that included Britain, Australia, New Zealand and North America.[42]

Launched in July 1892 and composed of around thirty-two pages per issue, the Australasian supplement was edited by the Revd W. H. Fitchett. Born in England and brought up in Australia, Fitchett was the founding president of the Methodist Ladies' College, Hawthorn, Victoria (he edited the supplement in tandem with his work at the college), but he also had significant journalistic experience. Like Stead, he was a man of strong but not sectarian religious conviction, with a powerful faith in Britain's imperial mission. Fitchett subsequently gained some fame as the author of *Deeds that Won the Empire* (1897), one of a series of highly successful, patriotic history books that he wrote for children.[43] While he enjoyed the same degree of editorial independence as Shaw did in New York, he was neither co-proprietor in nor co-director of the Melbourne enterprise. Perhaps regretting the substantial stake he had granted to Shaw, this time Stead retained ultimate control.[44]

---

[42] W. T. Stead, 'To the English-Speaking Folk under the Southern Cross', *Review of Reviews Australasian Edition*, 1 (July 1892), 10–13, quote at 11. See also Meg Tasker, 'Two Versions of Colonial Nationalism: The Australasian "Review of Reviews" v. the Sydney "Bulletin"', *Victorian Periodicals Review*, 37 (2004), 111–22.

[43] A. G. Thomson Zainu'ddin, 'Fitchett, William Henry (1841–1928)', *Australian Dictionary of Biography*, adb.anu.edu.au/biography/fitchett-william-henry-6179/text10621, published first in hardcopy 1981, accessed online 4 February 2015. William Shum, typescript memoir RS78, W. H. Fitchett Papers, Methodist Ladies' College Archive, Hawthorn, Vic. I am grateful to the archivist for providing me with a copy of this document.

[44] 'After Seven Years', esp. 92–93.

Figure 16.1 Masthead, *Review of Reviews* London Edition, April 1893. Author's personal collection.

The supplement tapped a rich vein of Australasian advertisements and was priced affordably at nine pence an issue, including the London edition. The layout and format mirrored that of Stead's journal. Each issue included a small number of original articles: initially, many of these were profiles of Australian newspapers, journalists or caricaturists, complementing the role of the *Review* as an aggregator of press comment. Fitchett's monthly 'Progress of the Colonies' column discussed the previous month's events in Australia and New Zealand, echoing Stead's 'Progress of the World' column. As in the London edition, a 'Diary' chronicling significant events was included, focusing on Australian and New Zealand affairs but also using cable news reports to bring Stead's material up-to-date with more recent international events. Other regular features included brief Australian and New Zealand obituaries, notices of key debates in the different colonial parliaments and of significant government publications, selections of caricatures from Australian papers and a section on 'Books Relating to Australasia'. The adaptations were subtle. Fitchett borrowed the *Review of Reviews* masthead, but while in the London edition the female figure sat before a stylised globe, the Australasian version featured the Southern Cross in the background (see Figures 16.1 and 16.2).

Initially, Stead sent a bulk consignment of the London edition to Melbourne each month, composed of issues that had not yet been bound for publication. On arrival, the pages were stitched together with those of the Australasian supplement and distributed to subscribers and retailers. On the cover, the Australasian supplement was dated a month later than the London edition it accompanied. However, in reality it was printed almost two months after the London edition had gone to press. To reduce the time lag, in 1896 Stead started sending advance proofs of the London edition to Melbourne,

Figure 16.2 Masthead, *Review of Reviews* Australasian Edition, August 1893. Author's personal collection.

allowing the whole magazine to be printed in Australia.[45] In early 1897, Fitchett moved to mining Stead's proofs selectively for content and augmenting them with Australian and New Zealand material, perhaps in conscious imitation of Shaw's New York editorial practices. Instead of a supplement, Fitchett now published a distinct 158-page Melbourne edition, the *Review of Reviews for Australasia*.[46] Stead's writings were henceforth carefully merged with material produced by Fitchett and other local contributors.[47]

One *Review* or Three?

By 1897, Stead claimed that 100,000 copies of the London edition of the *Review* were being printed each month, with the New York and Melbourne editions bringing the combined circulation to between 200,000 and 220,000 copies. He argued that, assuming five readers per copy, this meant that one million people read the *Review* each month.[48] However, as already noted, we need to treat Stead's self-aggrandising propaganda with caution. By this time, the *Review* actually looked less like a single periodical, and more like three distinct editions carrying some common, and much disparate, content. As a transnational connector, this was perhaps initially its greatest strength. The *Review* developed a global audience for a body of shared material, by combining that material with

---

[45] 'After Seven Years', esp. 92–93.

[46] 'The "Review of Reviews" for Australasia', *Review of Reviews* London edition, 15 (April 1897), 380.

[47] Compare, for example, *Review of Reviews for Australasia*, 18 (20 March 1901) with *Review of Reviews* London edition, 23 (February 1901).

[48] 'After Seven Years'.

content adapted to local requirements. However, over time the amount of common material tended to diminish, ultimately undermining the ability of the *Review* to act as a coherent means of transnational communication. By the end of the century, the different editions were delivering quite varied, indeed even opposed, messages to their readers. As a result, Stead's global political and civic mission was less and less well served by his creation.

Many of the problems that a prospective transnational publication such as the *Review* faced in the 1890s derived from the slow or expensive nature of long-distance communication. Delays in getting the London proofs to New York occasioned numerous minor disagreements between Shaw and Stead. However, these conflicts also reflected significant differences of temperament and ideology. An open rift between the two men developed towards the end of 1893, precipitated by Stead's provocative campaign for civic and moral reform in Chicago. Shaw worried that Stead's American muckraking would damage the magazine's reputation, and he refused to market Stead's book *If Christ Came to Chicago* through the New York edition of the *Review*. He also resented Stead's tendency to advertise the New York magazine as a subordinate offshoot of the London edition.[49] By early 1895, Shaw was reprinting much less from Stead's advance proofs than had initially been the case. He wrote and commissioned an increasing amount of original content, covering not just American politics but also international affairs.[50] His approach to the latter topic differed significantly from that of Stead, and a climax of antagonism between the two editors was reached during the diplomatic crisis of 1895–6, when the U.S. government intervened in a confrontation between Venezuela and Britain over the disputed Venezuela–British Guiana boundary. During the crisis, Shaw continued to argue that Britain and the United States should be friends but stood firmly behind American diplomacy and against Britain's official stance. Privately, he told Stead that 'Anglo-Saxon civilisation would have a better chance if England were a little less greedy for territory.' Their relationship deteriorated still further when, in early 1897, Shaw pressed Stead to sell part of his share in the New York edition to the paper's business manager. Stead refused.[51]

---

[49] Graybar, *Albert Shaw*, pp. 50, 54–55. Joseph O. Baylen 'A Victorian's "Crusade" in Chicago, 1893–1894', *Journal of American History*, 51 (1964), 418–34, esp. 429.

[50] Compare, for example, the *Review of Reviews* London edition, 11 (January 1895) and the *Review of Reviews* New York edition, 11 (February 1895).

[51] Shaw to Stead, 27 November 1895 and Stead to Shaw, 14 July 1897, Shaw papers, quoted in Graybar, *Albert Shaw*, pp. 55–56. See also Whyte, *Life of Stead*, vol. 2, pp. 81–82. For an example of Shaw's writings about the dispute, see 'The Progress of the World', *Review of Reviews* New York edition, 13 (February 1896), 131–47. For Stead's view of the crisis, see Simon J. Potter, 'Jingoism, Public

That July, Shaw changed the title of the New York edition to the *American Monthly Review of Reviews*. On the new masthead, 'American Monthly' was set at twice the size of 'Review of Reviews'. In an editorial note, Shaw claimed that the new title had been adopted 'in order to distinguish it from Mr. Stead's English *Review of Reviews*'. He urged readers to refer to the magazine as the *American Monthly* and promised to present 'the great world movements … in terms which assume American ideals and standards as the basis of comparison'.[52] Shaw also further reduced the amount of material reproduced from Stead's advance proofs. His version of 'The Progress of the World' that month carried very little from Stead's column. This was unsurprising: Shaw's increased commitment to American interests would have jarred with Stead's extensive coverage of preparations for Queen Victoria's Diamond Jubilee, and with Stead's assertion that the celebrations had made London 'the centre of the world'.[53]

Hoping to resolve the dispute, Stead sailed for the United States that August. He confided to his friend, the Fourth Earl Grey, that 'my American editor has gone all wrong, having developed a violent Anglophobia' and was 'manifesting an unmistakeable determination to kick me out of my own magazine, neck and crop'.[54] Stead's trip did not heal the rift. In November, he drafted a letter to Shaw accusing him of having tricked his way into acquiring a majority share in the American edition during the negotiations of 1891–2, and threatening to refer the matter to his solicitor.[55] However, the surviving version of this letter in the Stead papers is incomplete, and marked 'not sent'. Stead presumably backed down, reflecting his reliance on his share of the profits of the New York *Review*, which subsidised the less commercially successful London edition and Stead's other journalistic activities.[56] Shaw's biographer admits that 'in a sense [Shaw] took advantage of Stead': Shaw was neither the first nor the last to do so.[57] While the two men eventually patched up their differences, their relationship thereafter was never close.[58]

Opinion, and the New Imperialism: Newspapers and Imperial Rivalries at the fin de siècle', *Media History*, 20 (2014), 34–50.

[52] *American Monthly Review of Reviews*, 16 (July 1897), 3.

[53] 'The Progress of the World', *Review of Reviews* London edition, 15 (June 1897), 519–28, quote at 519.

[54] Stead to Grey, 19 and 27 August 1897, Fourth Earl Grey papers, Durham University Archives, file 178/17.

[55] Stead to Shaw, 24 November 1897, W. T. Stead papers, Churchill College Cambridge, file STED 1/64.

[56] Baylen, 'Stead as Publisher', 76.   [57] Graybar, *Albert Shaw*, p. 69.

[58] Stead to Grey, 10 June 1908 and 27 February 1909, Grey papers, file 178/17.

In 1909, Stead confided to Grey (who was in Canada) that he did not even know how much of his work was being published in the American magazine:

> I pour copy into the yawning jaw of the monster, but how much of it ever sees the light on your side of the water I do not know . . . It is very odd that I should have picked out Shaw for the American Review when he is in the bottom of his soul so opposed by temperament and heredity to the rapprochement which I founded the Review in order to promote.[59]

As a transnational connector, the *Review* had proved a poor servant of Stead's dreams of Anglo-American unity.

While in the case of the New York *Review*, it was Shaw who had seemingly betrayed Stead's ideals, with the Australasian edition it was Stead who executed the *volte face*. Although Stead remained committed to English-speaking unity, during the late 1890s he became increasingly disillusioned with British diplomacy in South Africa. He believed that the British government had engineered a cynical, unjust confrontation with the Boer republic of the Transvaal and had then waged war in a shockingly inhumane fashion. Fitchett meanwhile continued to toe the pro-British line and carefully excluded Stead's anti-war comments from the pages of the Melbourne edition. He may have been concerned to protect the Melbourne edition's circulation: Stead's anti-war position had alienated many readers in Britain, bringing a significant decline in sales of the London edition, whereas Fitchett avoided offending the predominant pro-war sentiment in Australia and New Zealand. Yet it was also a matter of political convictions, and in November 1900 Stead published a scathingly sarcastic attack on his Australian collaborator's writings.[60] The two editors were unable to resolve their differences; at the end of 1903, Stead's son Henry moved from London to replace Fitchett in the editor's chair.[61] Fitchett wrote to John St Loe Strachey, editor of the London *Spectator*, that

> Mr Stead and I differ so profoundly on questions of imperial policy that the situation has grown impossible; and, by my own act, our literary partnership is ending. The Boer War has ended in South Africa, but it still rages in Mr Stead's mind; and the smoke of it fills the whole landscape of his writings.[62]

[59] Stead to Grey, 17 April 1909, Grey papers, file 178/17.
[60] 'The Evolution of a New God', *Review of Reviews* London edition, 22 (November 1900), 457–58.
[61] Whyte, *Life of Stead*, vol. 2, p. 231.
[62] Fitchett to Strachey, 25 November 1903, John St Loe Strachey papers, House of Lords Record Office, London, S/13/16/7. See also 'Review of Reviews for Australasia', *Review of Reviews* London edition, 29 (March 1904), 277.

Fitchett was appointed editor of a new Melbourne magazine, *Life*. He told Strachey that 'It will in fact be the one indigenous monthly in Australasia and will both reflect and influence opinion here; and, in the main, on your lines. For the "Spectator" is still my literary oracle and guide!'[63] Like the original plan for the Australasian supplement of the *Review*, Fitchett sought to combine an avowedly Australasian perspective with a British journalistic model. This was hardly a nationalist declaration of independence. Nevertheless, it was clear that, as in New York, divergent local editorial policies and viewpoints had undermined Stead's attempts to turn the *Review* into a reliable transnational disseminator of his political ideals.

Conclusion

Stead's failure to establish a close and lasting working relationship with either Shaw or Fitchett was partly due to conflicting personalities and opposing views about the correct balance between political principle and commercial self-interest. Fitchett could not support Stead's outspoken opposition to the South African War, fearing the impact this would have on circulation, and remaining certain of the virtues of British imperial policy. Shaw meanwhile disavowed Stead's cherished ideal of Anglo-American unity, while exploiting Stead's unworldly attitude to business to promote his own financial interests. The impact of all this on sales figures for the different editions was noticeable. By May 1901, the circulation of the London edition of the *Review* had dropped dramatically, to around 70,000, partly because of the unpopularity of Stead's anti-war stance. The Melbourne edition was meanwhile selling 40,000 copies, a healthy figure given the limited size of the Australian and New Zealand market, while the New York edition sold almost twice as many copies as the London and Melbourne editions combined, with a circulation of 200,000.[64] Meg Tasker has suggested that the London edition provided the Melbourne publication with 'economic security'.[65] However, it is more likely that the New York edition offered both the London and Melbourne enterprises a financial safety net. In commercial terms, Stead's prediction that the centre of the *Review*'s operations would one day shift from London to New York had come true. Indeed, when the London *Review of Reviews* was faltering after World War I, Shaw had the chance to purchase

[63] Fitchett to Strachey, 25 November 1903, Strachey papers, S/13/16/7.
[64] J. W. Robertson Scott, *The Life and Death of a Newspaper*. London: Methuen, 1952, p. 157. Graybar, *Albert Shaw*, p. 58, gives a somewhat lower circulation of 178,000 for the American edition in 1901.
[65] Tasker, 'Two Versions of Colonial Nationalism', 112.

it.[66] Had he done so, Stead's premonition that the head office of the *Review* would eventually cross the Atlantic, tracking the changing geopolitical centre of the English-reading world, would also have been fulfilled.

Stead's transnational publishing strategy was ahead of its time. In the 1890s, long-distance communication was either slow (by mail) or prohibitively expensive (by telegraph cable), and long-distance travel was both. It would simply not have been possible to coordinate the different editions of the *Review* closely, even if Stead had wished to do so. Moreover, to some extent such coordination would have been counterproductive. Autonomy allowed the Australasian and American editions to adapt to the requirements of local readers and to prosper. However, this autonomy also prevented Stead from using the overseas editions in the way that he had intended, to promote a coherent political message and set of ideals. His dream of using the *Review* to found a global civic church and to encourage the unification of the English-reading world may have been an unrealistic fantasy. Still, the uncoordinated nature of the *Review*'s overseas operations meant that even Stead came to recognise that, as a transnational connector, the *Review* was ultimately a poor means by which to achieve his goals. This leads us on to a larger point. While the nineteenth-century British press may have played a significant role in creating a semi-globalised world, we must beware of any facile attempt to draw a direct likeness with the role of the mass media in our own, hyper-connected age.

[66] Graybar, *Albert Shaw*, p. 57n.

PART IV

Journalists and Journalism

CHAPTER 17

Dickens and the Middle-class Weekly

John Drew

Between 30 March 1850 and his death on 9 June 1870, Charles Dickens was the editor and part owner, later also the publisher (1859–70), of two of the most prominent periodicals in the Anglophone world, *Household Words* and *All the Year Round*. Here were serialised many of the nineteenth century's most notable works of fiction – among them *Hard Times*, *North and South*, *Cranford*, *A Tale of Two Cities*, *The Woman in White*, *Great Expectations* and *The Moonstone* – together with well over seven thousand original short stories, poems, non-fiction articles, essays, reports and exposés, the majority of them commissioned, cajoled and copy-edited (at times, entirely rewritten) by Dickens and his trusty subeditor, W. H. Wills. To Lord Northcliffe of the *Daily Mail*, Dickens was, quite simply, 'the greatest magazine editor either of his own, or any other age'.[1] For the American intellectual and *Harper's Weekly* editor George W. Curtis, toasting Dickens's health in front of 200 other newspapermen in 1868, there was 'no doubt that among the most vigorous forces in the elevation of the character of the Weekly Press ha[ve] been *Household Words* and *All the Year Round*; and since the beginning of the publication of *Household Words*, the periodical literature of England has been born again.'[2] The founding of *Household Words* was itself the consummation of a desire to sit in the driver's cab (as Dickens liked to see it[3]) of a periodically issued publication that he had harboured since his first steps in journalism, but which found expression in a variety of abortive projects in the late 1830s and early 1840s. These can be briefly sketched.

---

[1] Arthur Bartlett Maurice, 'Dickens as an Editor', *Bookman* 30 (1909), 111.

[2] Cited in Frederic Hudson, *Journalism in the United States, from 1690 to 1872*. New York: Harper & Brothers, 1873, p. 664.

[3] For discussion of the railway metaphor in Dickens's editorial paradigms, see John Drew, 'Texts, Paratexts and "E –Texts": the Poetics of Communication in Dickens's Journalism', in Juliet John (ed.), *Dickens and Modernity* (*Essays and Studies*, 2012). Cambridge: D. S. Brewer, 2012, 61–93, 67–71.

As launch editor of *Bentley's Miscellany* (1837–9) Dickens had found himself working on a thoroughly sustainable literary monthly but believed that his power to shape and adapt it to his artistic vision was limited by the publisher's interference;[4] as launch editor and sole contributor to the weekly *Master Humphrey's Clock*, Dickens enjoyed this power to the utmost but found himself unable or unwilling to share it with co-contributors in such a way as to make the labour sustainable. The infrastructure of the journal and the whimsical concept of the multi-authored miscellany receded to little more than the packaging for the two serially published novels that the *Clock* carried, *The Old Curiosity Shop* (1840–41) and *Barnaby Rudge* (1841).[5] After travels in America and Italy, and the issuing of a further serial novel in monthly parts (*Martin Chuzzlewit*, 1843–4), Dickens's thoughts reverted strongly to the attractions of newspaper or magazine editing not only as a surer livelihood than novel writing and a powerful way of maintaining emotional bonds with his readers but also as a realisation of a genuine urge for some form of public service. In this he was encouraged by his new publishers, the former printers Bradbury and Evans, who were already enjoying success as proprietors of the satirical weekly *Punch*. We may be sure that table talk between Dickens and his circle during the mid-1840s canvassed many possibilities. Among them, hints have survived of an aborted periodical project of the kind Leigh Hunt (an important and underrated forbear) might have proposed, to be called *The Cricket*.[6] Vestiges of another grand scheme remain in the seventeen numbers of the *Daily News* (a new Liberal paper with strong backing among railway developers) which Dickens superintended as hands-on 'Literary Editor' in January-February 1846, before resigning and escaping what he privately – in a characteristic *volte face* – called the 'daily nooses' which the paper's other proprietors, including the hapless Bradbury and Evans, had prepared for him. His connection as a contributor, however, continued until

[4] For a profile, see 'Bentley's Miscellany, 1837–1868', in Walter E. Houghton and Jean H. Slingerland (eds.), *The Wellesley Index to Victorian Periodicals*, 5 vols. Toronto & London: University of Toronto Press/Routledge and Kegan Paul, 1966–89, Vol. 4, pp. 5–14; for Dickens's stormy relationship with its publisher, see 'Dickens and the Burlington Street Brigand', in R. Patten, *Dickens and his Publishers*. Oxford University Press, 1978, pp. 75–87.

[5] See Malcolm Andrews, 'Introducing Master Humphrey', *Dickensian*, 67 (1971), 70–86; and Kathryn Chittick, 'The Idea of a Miscellany: *Master Humphrey's Clock*', *Dickensian*, 78 (1982), 156–64.

[6] A lengthy letter to John Forster outlines the scheme; see Kathleen Tillotson and Nina Burgis, eds., *Letters of Charles Dickens: Vol. 4, 1844–1846*, 'Pilgrim' Edition. Oxford: Clarendon Press, 1977, pp. 327–29. Hereafter *Letters*.

later in the year,[7] by which time he had begun planning a new work of serial fiction in monthly parts (*Dealings with the Firm of Dombey & Son*, 1846–8); as this drew to a close in 1848, his journalistic interests were temporarily satisfied in a substantial if miscellaneous series of leaders, reviews and squibs in the pages of the *Examiner*, now somewhat staidly edited, in comparison with its adventurous youth under Leigh Hunt, by John Forster.[8]

The desire to 'found something' more enduring and personally driven remained strong, however. Thus, in late 1849, with *Dombey* concluded, and the first five monthly numbers of *David Copperfield* in print, Dickens reported that he had finally 'without a doubt, *got* the Periodical notion.'[9] His subsequent outlining to Forster of his ideas for the contents, as well as of a way of binding them all together conceptually under the rubric of 'The Shadow,' has often been discussed – as Forster himself remarks, 'hardly anything more characteristic survives him' in point of fanciful embellishment. Recent critics have fruitfully explored ways in which, respectively, the ideas of memory, the past and 'deep character' are subsequently evoked in the pages of the new periodical, in ways that can be clearly related to the kind of über-persona delineated in this remarkable prelude. The more sinister implications of a newsgathering entity represented as 'a certain SHADOW, which may go into any place, by sunlight, moonlight, starlight, firelight, candlelight, and be in all homes, and all nooks and corners, and be supposed to be cognisant of everything, and go everywhere' have not gone unnoticed.[10]

A blueprint for sustainability was also embodied (perhaps one should say, disembodied?) in 'The Shadow', a character 'which any of the writers may maintain without difficulty', concentrating 'into one focus all that is done in the paper'. Dickens's projection here of different contributors

---

[7] See John Drew and Michael Slater, 'What's in the Daily News? A re-evaluation, Part I', *Dickensian*, 106 (2010), 197–206; 'What's in the Daily News? A re-evaluation, Part II', *Dickensian*, 107 (2011), 22–39.

[8] For an overview of the *Examiner* contributions, see John Drew, *Dickens the Journalist*. Basingstoke: Palgrave, 2003, chap. 6.

[9] Both quotations from Dickens's letter to Forster, 22 and 23 November 1846, in *Letters* 4, pp. 658–60 (p. 660); *To* Forster, 30 September 1849, in *Letters* 5 (1847–9), ed. by Graham Storey and K. J. Fielding. Oxford: Clarendon Press, 1989, p. 619.

[10] *To* John Forster, *Letters* 5, pp. 622–23. For discussions of 'The Shadow' see Rosemarie Bodenheimer, *Knowing Dickens*. London and Ithaca, NY: Cornell University Press, 2007, pp. 55–56, 89; Jonathan V. Farina, '"A Certain Shadow": Personified Abstractions and the Form of *Household Words*', *Victorian Periodicals Review*, 42 (Winter 2009), 392–415; for its implications, see John Drew, 'An Uncommercial Proposition? At work on *Household Words* and *All the Year Round*', *Victorian Periodicals Review* 46.3 (Fall 2013) 291–316, 300–302.

collectively surrendering personality to take on the disguise of the nameless guiding spirit of the publication is not difficult to construe as an imaginative rendering of the process of writing anonymously for a publication. Anonymity was to be a distinguishing feature of Dickens's weekly journals from their inception; while a common enough feature of Victorian print culture at this time, their handling of it raises questions about the exercise of power, the communication of celebrity and the tension between authorial and corporate identity in a particularly acute fashion. In so far as these have been investigated as case studies of the relationship between Dickens as weekly magazine editor and specific contributors – Wilkie Collins, Elizabeth Gaskell, Harriet Martineau, Henry Morley – there has been a marked tendency to view the relationship in adversarial terms of oppressor versus oppressed.[11] More theoretical, generalised studies of anonymity, however, have found much evidence in Victorian debates about anonymity to suggest that actually 'Victorian readers and writers embraced a more flexible, collective notion of authorship' in which anonymity could provide strategic freedoms rather than uniformly equate to exclusion and lack of individual visibility. The practice and imaginative delineation of collective authorship in Dickens's journals and their challenge to constructions of the periodical 'author as an intentional, single-gendered agent in literary history' are research areas ripe for enquiry.[12]

For convenience *Household Words* and *All the Year Round* can be considered middle-class weeklies, but to do so begs a number of crucial questions about the relationship between the variables – known and unknowable – of frequency of publication, audience and aspiration. From the outset, Dickens and his publishers distributed the journals across three distinct frequencies, physical formats and price bands: as a 2d weekly, sold as an uncut, unstitched folding booklet of 24 pages; as a 9 or 11d

---

[11] See, respectively, Lillian Nayder, *Unequal Partners. Charles Dickens, Wilkie Collins, and Victorian Authorship*. Ithaca & London: Cornell University Press, 2002; Linda K. Hughes and Michael Lund, 'Textual/Sexual Pleasure and Serial Publication: North and South', chap. 4 of *Victorian Publishing and Mrs. Gaskell's Work*. Charlottesville and London: University Press of Virginia, 1999, pp. 96–123; Iain Crawford, '"Hunted and Harried by Pseudo-Philanthropists": Dickens, Martineau and *Household Words*' and Daragh Downes, 'Morley was alive: to begin with. The Curious Case of Dickens and his Principal Household Wordsmith', both in Hazel Mackenzie and Ben Winyard, eds., *Charles Dickens and the Mid-Victorian Press 1850–1870*. University of Buckingham Press, 2013, pp. 157–74, 185–200.
[12] See, respectively, Rachel Sagner Buurma, 'Anonymity, Corporate Authority, and the Archive: The Production of Authorship in Late-Victorian England', *Victorian Studies*, 50 (2007), 15; and Alexis Easley, *First-Person Anonymous: Women Writers and Victorian Print Media, 1830–70*. Aldershot: Ashgate, 2004, p. 188. Also Jasper Schelstraete, '"Literary Adventurers": Editorship, Non-Fiction Authorship and Anonymity', in Mackenzie and Winyard, *Mid-Victorian Press*, pp. 147–56.

monthly with green/blue wrapper, containing four or five weekly numbers, a table of contents and an increasingly substantial 'Advertiser' fore and aft; bi-annually, cloth-bound, with a title page and index, at 5s 6d. Although complete runs under Dickens's editorship only survive in the high-end volume form, enough instances of weekly and monthly formats remain as evidence to infer a deliberate hybridity of form, eloquent of an attempt to vertically integrate elements of the production and marketing, so as to maximise the publication's reach across different classes of purchasers.

As Lorna Huett has shown, in a groundbreaking essay on the significance of the physical format of Dickens's journals, if one takes into account such further factors as paper size and quality,

> a distinct ambiguity in the nature of Dickens's periodicals emerges ... In adopting the publishing and printing practices of the cheap educational magazines and the [penny] bloods, yet at the same time producing a journal which outwardly resembled the highbrow reviews, he deliberately trod a fine line between genres. The hybridity which characterised his journal's contents was also the defining characteristic of its structure and thus of its identity as a publication.[13]

At one level, positing hybridity as a definition of identity is little more than reiterating that *Household Words* and *All the Year Round* were miscellanies. However, the crossing of genre boundaries and the holding of different conventions in artful poise are characteristic Dickensian performances, which both journals clearly encouraged.[14] Timing is also crucial, for, with Newspaper Stamp duty still leviable until 1855, *Household Words* legally needed to steer clear of reporting hard news. Imaginative presentation of material, its translation into fictive scenarios – thinly or thickly disguised, obliquely or tangentially approached – was an early expedient which, drawing on a long-standing tradition of whimsicality in the British essay, was gradually cultivated into an aesthetic. On another level, the socio-cultural transitions and alertness implied by hybridity of form and content are arguably inscribed in a much more literal form on the cover and inner pages of every number of the magazine. The title '*Household Words*' and the legend 'Conducted by || Charles Dickens' running across every spread can be read as important complementary determinants of the journal's identity. Both deserve scrutiny.

---

[13] Lorna Huett, 'Among the Unknown Public: *Household Words, All the Year Round* and the Mass-Market Weekly Periodical in the Mid-Nineteenth Century', *Victorian Periodicals Review*, 38 (Spring 2005), 61–82 (78, 79).

[14] See Drew, 'An Uncommercial Proposition?' 306–7.

The hunt for a suitably versatile title dominated Dickens's thoughts in the new year of 1850, in a stream of letters to Forster. In mid-January, Dickens suggested 'The Robin. With this motto from Goldsmith. *The redbreast, celebrated for its affection to mankind, continues with us, the year round'.*[15] Then, before the month's end, came the suggestion 'Mankind', and next, as if to explain the underlying link between this ambitious circulation target and the editor who could successfully address such a readership, 'CHARLES DICKENS. A weekly journal designed for the instruction and entertainment of all classes of readers. CONDUCTED BY HIMSELF.' When this too failed to convince his advisor, Dickens peppered him with mixed shot:

> If there *be* anything wanting in the other name, . . . this is very pretty, and just supplies it[:] THE HOUSEHOLD VOICE. I have thought of many others, as – THE HOUSEHOLD GUEST. THE HOUSEHOLD FACE. THE COMRADE. THE MICROSCOPE. THE HIGHWAY OF LIFE. THE LEVER. THE ROLLING YEARS. THE HOLLY TREE . . . EVERYTHING.[16]

While each carries in nucleus a theme that can be detected in the journals as they unfolded over subsequent years, and the fertility of invention is remarkable, nevertheless the variety of ideas considered suggests a radical uncertainty as to the journal's purpose or angle on its material. The ideas of power and energy running through a number of these prototypes are developed in another suggestive title, again fitted out with its own epigraph, that brings the figures of Jo Gargery and the Blakean artist into unexpected communion:

THE FORGE: A WEEKLY JOURNAL,
CONDUCTED BY CHARLES DICKENS.

Thus at the glowing FORGE of Life our actions must be wrought,
Thus on the sounding anvil shaped
Each burning deed and thought. – *Longfellow*

Hitting at last in early February on 'HOUSEHOLD WORDS'[17] – a 'very pretty name' that pulled together earlier ideas about addressing familiarly

---

[15] As with the 1845 outline for *The Cricket*, the suggested quotation is from Goldsmith's *History of the Earth and Animated Nature* (1774). If Dickens thought this would induce Forster, author in 1848 of a biography of Goldsmith, to approve the title, he was mistaken.

[16] Letters to John Forster, ?mid-January, ?24–30 and ?31 January and ?1 February 1850, in *Letters 6* (1844–6), ed. by Graham Storey, Kathleen Tillotson and Nina Burgis. Oxford: Clarendon Press, 1988, pp. 11, 21, 25, 26.

[17] The full published title, strictly, was 'Household Words. / A Weekly Journal. / Conducted by Charles Dickens'; the fact that Dickens's name formed part of it would later prove legally decisive; see Drew, *Journalist*, pp. 135–36.

all ages and classes of readers in their own homes – Dickens ensured that its Shakespearean epigraph ('Familiar in their mouths as household words') would also sound a combative and aspirational note, recalling the famous 'St Crispin's Day' speech in Act IV of *Henry V*, with its projection of an elite minority and the promised conferral of social advancement. It functions as a suitably ambivalent, if not polyvalent, title for a journal that had as yet no fixed identity. Enough has been said to show that Dickens was brimming with imaginative hopes for what could be achieved with such a publication, but his notion of its precise contours was still understandably vague, as this outline, sent to a would-be contributor, of the kind of article that would be acceptable for submission suggests: 'It should be interesting, of course; if somewhat romantic, so much the better; we can't be too wise, but we must be very agreeable.'[18]

The adoption of what one hopes is the editorial (rather than the paternal) 'we' here leads naturally to consideration of the way in which Dickens's weekly journals figured the editorial role and persona, under the banner 'Conducted by Charles Dickens'.[19] For reasons already touched on, the persona has seldom been approached as representative of a genuine workers' collective but rather as a choric voice, reinforcing core Dickensian beliefs, and acting as a guarantor of good behaviour. The principal con-notation of 'Conducted by' can simply be taken then as part of its homage to *Chambers's Edinburgh Journal*, on which the layout and business model of *Household Words* was based and which, since 1832, had reassured readers that it was edited to impeccable moral standards by its two publishers-cum-educators, William and Robert Chambers.[20] However, in so far as con-ducting involves chaperoning, the strapline also implies movement on a shared journey, an already favoured editorial paradigm which Henry Morley plays with cheekily in beginning his 'Letter from a Highly Respectable Old Lady' with the ejaculation 'GRACIOUS Mr. Conductor (which is like an omnibus) what a nice new journal you have got!'[21] Omnibus conducting, train driving, electrical conduction, telegraphic signalling: all can become, in the *Household Words* and *All the Year Round* imaginary analogues for magazine editing, and form what

---

[18] Letter to Thomasina Ross, 21 January 1850, *Letters* 6, p. 13.

[19] For an extended meditation on Dickens's use of 'I' and 'we' in periodical publications, see Paul Schlicke's 'Our Hour: Dickens's Shifting Authorial Personae', in Mackenzie and Winyard (eds.), *Mid-Victorian Press*, pp. 261–76.

[20] For the debt to *Chambers's*, see Drew, *Journalist*, p. 110; and Laurel Brake, 'Second Life: *All the Year Round* and the New Generation of British Periodicals in the 1860s', in Mackenzie and Winyard (eds.), *Mid-Victorian Press*, pp. 11–34, 18–20.

[21] *HW* I, 186.

I have considered elsewhere as a widely dispersed 'poetics of communication' in Dickens's weekly journals, deriving from their strapline.[22]

In some ways, however, the musical connotations of 'Conducted by . . . ' have the most resonance for the kind of performance art to which the magazines aspired, week after week. At the outset of *Dickens, Journalism, Music*, Robert Bledsoe establishes 'the imaginative context for a consideration of the place of music in both journals,' observing how 'Dickens conducts the players in a journalistic orchestra who, under [his] direction, perform "home music" (one of the titles Dickens considered for the journal before settling on *Household Words*).'[23] Bledsoe also stresses music's repeated function in the journals as a catalyst for memory; memory's connection to shadow – of the past, of parting, of death – and the passage of time, has already been noted as a determining feature of Dickens's project in its early phase. According to an early-twentieth-century source, this was something he spoke of eloquently to Wilkie Collins, waxing lyrical over his desire, through a low-cost publication, to reach a mass audience:

> He told me . . . what faith he had in it; how he loved it; how honest he had found it; how quick to respond to the good and true; and how, when he had planned his periodical, he had felt like an organist who, touching a little keyboard, sets a mighty instrument quivering and throbbing, and filling the air with music.[24]

This beatific vision of Dickens as St Cecilia rather stretches the imagination, yet the idea of Dickens as editor orchestrating an ensemble and conducting from first violin is a helpful way of construing the function of the imprimatur which appears on every page.

Does the character and location of a journal's office have a bearing on its identity? If so, then the identities of *Household Words* and *All the Year Round* also owed something to mid-century Covent Garden, and a fancifully constructed building. A lease had been taken on premises at No. 16 Wellington-street North, on the eastern side of a busy thoroughfare leading south onto the Strand:

> The old, original *Household Words* office was a graceful, highly-inviting, *dainty* little structure. It really seemed in keeping with the brilliant owner,

[22] Drew, 'Paratexts', *passim*.

[23] Robert Terrell Bledsoe, *Dickens, Journalism, Music*. London: Continuum, 2012, pp. 8, 15.

[24] Hall Caine, 'Preface' to re-launch of *Household Words* (1902). Cited by Paul Lewis, '1902: *Household Words*' on the *Wilkie Collins Pages* www.web40571.clarahost.co.uk/wilkie/biography/Caine1902 .htm [accessed 27 March 2015].

and even with his genial, sympathetic character . . . It was but a miniature sort of building, but sufficed. Exceedingly pretty was the bowed front, the bow reaching up for one story, and a ground floor window, each giving a flood of light, quite necessary for literary work. It seemed more a residence suited, as the auctioneer would say, for 'a bachelor of position'.[25]

Bradbury & Evans's offices on Bouverie Street, Whitefriars, were less than five minutes' walk along Fleet Street to the east. Indeed, as Mary Shannon explores in detail, an astonishing network of editors and imprints can be pinpointed in the 1840s and 1850s to this short street and its environs.[26] For Dickens, it was a highly convenient set-up, and the living apartments on the upper floors proved a useful bivouac whenever – as was increasingly the case as the decade wore on – it suited him to stay in town, and not return to the marital home. The offices also functioned as a counting-house and a shop, with sales made direct to the public on the ground floor.

It was from here that the first number of *Household Words* was issued, inaugurating a weekly rhythm of editorial duties that would last, without break, until Dickens's death in June 1870. Friends and acquaintances, as usual, had personal perspectives on the promise of the early numbers. A good example is Henry Morley, a university-educated doctor who had written for the *Examiner* and who was just starting to contribute articles on sanitary matters to *Household Words*. Morley doubted strongly that 'Dickens was the right man to edit a journal of literary mark . . . he has not a sound literary taste.' Part of Morley's reservation concerned the writing style that he was asked to adopt, and the audience he was expected to entertain and educate:

> Dickens's journal does not seem my element . . . the readers are an undiscriminating mass to whom I'm not accustomed to imagine myself speaking . . . [P]oetry I write for cultivated tastes . . . in the *Examiner* I speak to people who are clever, liberal-minded, and love wit. *Household Words* has an audience which I cannot write for naturally.[27]

It is to Morley's credit, and Dickens's as his mentor, that he broadened his outlook and adapted his style so as to become the most prolific contributor to *Household Words* bar none. Nevertheless, this perception of – not to say prejudice against – the new readership Dickens was trying to reach was something of which commentators were acutely aware. After the first

[25] Percy H. Fitzgerald, *Memories of Charles Dickens*. Bristol: J. W. Arrowsmith, 1913, p. 125.
[26] See Mary Shannon, *Dickens, Reynolds, and Mayhew on Wellington Street. The Print Culture of a Victorian Street.* Aldershot: Ashgate, 2015.
[27] Cited in H. S. Solly, *Life of Henry Morley.* London: Arnold, 1898, p. 150.

number, the *Bradford Observer* reported Dickens's initiative as a bold stratagem to move down market to capture a vast but lowly readership whose support, unlike that of the middle-class devotees of his monthly serials, could not be counted on:

> Mr Dickens has started a new periodical ... Whether the effort will prove successful, time alone will tell: it is far from being a matter of course ... In that particular department hitherto selected by the author of 'Pickwick,' he has had few if any rivals ... Coming down however to the common battlefield of the pennies; forsaking the silver and cleaving to the copper, stepping out of the parlour, the drawing room, the boudoir and the club, to shake hands with miners and combers, with factory workers and 'horny palmed' artisans ... at the same time encountering the shock of some scores of rude competitors, who have pre-occupied the field and enlisted the sympathies of the multitude, – this is another matter.[28]

Predictably friendly puffs, in the form of extracts from Dickens's leading article in the first issue ('A Preliminary Word'), were offered by the *Daily News*, the *Morning Chronicle* and the *Examiner*[29] – but the sense that Dickens was taking a great gamble, albeit from philanthropic motives, was widespread.

Granted that part of Dickens's general intentions for his new work involved, as he saw it, stealing readers from sensational and incendiary publications at the cheaper end of the market, he cannot have expected a warm welcome from every quarter. Such publications were 'Bastards of the mountain ... Panders to the basest passions of the lowest natures', which *Household Words* considered it would be 'our highest service to displace' ('A Preliminary Word', p. 2). Unsurprisingly then, one of the papers that felt itself attacked, the recently launched *Reynolds's Newspaper*, made no bones about responding aggressively, with later editorial references to 'this drivelling, fawning, lickspittle Dickens ... that lickspittle hanger-on to the skirts of Aristocracy's robe ... originally a dinnerless penny-a-liner on the *Morning Chronicle*'.[30] With sales of his first issue estimated at more than 100,000, Dickens wrote to his wealthy Tory friend Angela Burdett Coutts that his new venture was 'playing havoc with the villainous literature'.[31]

---

[28] 'LITERARY NOTICES'. *The Bradford Observer* (Bradford, England), Thursday, 4 April 1850; p. 7 col. c.

[29] *The Daily News* (London, England), Thursday, 28 March 1850, Issue 1198, p. 5d; *The Morning Chronicle* (London, England), Friday, 29 March 1850, Issue 25099, p. 7b; 'THE LITERARY EXAMINER', *The Examiner* (London, England), Saturday, 30 March 1850, Issue 2200, p. 198b.

[30] 'Charles Dickens and the Democratic Movement', 8 June 1851, p. 7c.

[31] Fitzgerald, *Memories*, p. 135; and Philip Collins, 'The *All the Year Round* Letter Book', *Victorian Periodicals Newsletter*, 10 (1970), 23–29 (25); *Letters* 6, p. 83.

In the same letter, Dickens predicts that *Household Words* 'will become a *good property* ... and although the expences [sic] of such a venture are necessarily very great, the circulation much more than repays them'. The audited receipts ledger[32] shows that the total profits distributed amongst the magazine's four partners for its first six months of publication amounted to £526 5s 2d, or around £38,000 in terms of today's purchasing power.[33] Factoring in an estimate for start-up costs, as well as fixed and variable costs for the first semester, allows something like a total income figure to be projected, which in turn can be converted into an average number of copies sold weekly over the twenty-six weeks of the first half year: in this case, 34,500.[34] The first number was reported to have hit six figures; the sale seems to have steadied at just under 40,000; reports of sales for the 'Extra Numbers' for Christmas (1851–67), composed of inter-connected stories and poetry, plot a steep upward trajectory in the 1860s, from 191,000 (*Somebody's Luggage*, 1862) 'and ultimately reaching, Forster records, "before he died, to nearly three hundred thousand"'.[35] Dickens's decision, following an irreversible quarrel with his publishers Bradbury & Evans and fellow proprietors in *Household Words* to establish *All the Year Round* with an instalment of serial fiction as its leading article – a distinct break from its predecessor's custom of leading with a freshly researched, often satirical, non-fiction essay – was a modest publishing coup, and it led, so far as the UK circulation was concerned, to a doubling of regular circulation to something approaching 100,000. The break gave him 'the freedom,' as Laurel Brake argues, given the advent of a plethora of illustrated monthlies carrying high-quality fiction, 'to fashion a second life for his original plan, with relatively small changes, rather than to wholly rethink his project in light of the new generation of the magazine in the 1860s'.[36]

Yet circulation figures, even when accurate, are the most unidimensional of statistics, leaving us in the dark as to the numbers of readers countrywide who come into the sphere of influence of the distributed text after the

[32] Reproduced in Patten, *Dickens and his Publishers*, Appendix D, pp. 462–64.
[33] Figures calculated from *Inflation: The Value of the Pound, 1750–1998*, House of Commons Research paper 99/20 (23 February 1999); online at www.parliament.uk/documents/commons/lib/research/rp99/rp99-020.pdf. According to the magazine's articles of agreement, Dickens received a half, Bradbury & Evans a quarter, and Forster and Wills an eighth share respectively.
[34] See John Drew and Jonathan Buckmaster, '*Household Words*, Volume II 28 September 1850–22 March 1851: Nos 27–52', *Dickens Quarterly* 31.4 (2014), 312–33; 314–15&n.
[35] Drew, *Journalist*, 148&nn.
[36] Laurel Brake, 'Second Life'&c., in Mackenzie and Winyard (eds.), *Mid-Victorian Press*, pp. 11–33, 33.

census date, and ignorant of its extra-national journeying. The little that is known about the print runs and sales of Victorian periodicals within the British isles can only be augmented by suppositions and anecdotes about their impact overseas: in continental Europe, in the dependencies of the empire, and in the New World. The following nugget from *The Bury and Norwich Post*, however, indicates that Dickens's weeklies, like Magwitch and Micawber, were highly successful emigrants:

> Mr. Dickens's new story, 'A Tale of Two Cities,' seems to have secured a large circulation for the new periodical, *All The Year Round*. [I]t is in type at the present moment, and a thousand or two copies are now in the cabin of one of the Atlantic steamers, on their way to certain publishers at New York. This foreign branch of our periodical literature is increasingly lucrative. Although there is no copyright with America, yet arrangements are made by which early copies are forwarded, and a genuine sale obtained. But it is to the colonies that the chief export takes place. Every three weeks or so, you may see a van creeping heavily up Bouverie-street, laden with literature from the establishments of Messrs. Bradbury and Evans and others. Copies of *Punch* will greet the traveller's eye at the Cape, in the cities of Ind, in Melbourne, Sydney, Newzealand. I hardly know, indeed, what place to except.[37]

Dickens and W. H. Wills did not leave such matters to chance. At some point before 1854, arrangements were made with Bernard Tauchnitz in Leipzig to re-publish selections from *Household Words* in the publisher's pioneering pocket-size 'Collection of British and American Authors'. The ordering and presentation of material in these rare volumes are quite different from the date-stamped originals and seem partly designed to protect the continental copyright, in so far as this was possible, of the authors of the items deemed most likely to be pirated or translated without permission. That the European version of Dickens's journals had its own, substantial afterlife is attested in one of Percy Fitzgerald's recollections of his hero and mentor: 'Once at Aix-la-Chapelle the German attendant brought me a little book which he thought would please me, "Owzelverd von Dickens."'[38] The Tauchnitz editions do indeed announce *Household Words* as 'by Charles Dickens' (rather than 'conducted by'), leading, naturally enough, to confusion over authorship – including one embarrassing incident when a Swedish story by Fredrika Bremer ('Den Rätta') was translated into English and published in *Household Words* in 1851, then

---

[37] *The Bury and Norwich Post, and Suffolk Herald* (Bury Saint Edmunds, England), Tuesday 19 April 1859; Issue 4008, p. 2e.
[38] *Memories of Charles Dickens* (Bristol: J. Arrowsmith, 1911), p. 121n.

promptly translated back into Swedish and published in a newspaper under Dickens's name.[39]

It was in America, however, that Dickens and Wills made the greatest inroads, at a time when the development of a trans-federal rail network was beginning to integrate the market, encouraging publishers to advertise and pay for exclusive 'authorised' reprinting of British authors, well in advance of binding international copyright legislation. Dickens was 'a prize catch for such houses', and he and Wills rapidly established a series of profitable arrangements for the reprinting of material from the journals, often synchronously with their first British publication.[40] It was J. M. Emerson of Emerson & Co. who declared during his firm's serial-isation of *Great Expectations* that the journal they held in their hands 'has now the largest circulation of any similar publication in the world' and would 'find in this country alone more than three million readers'.[41] Americans thus encountered *All the Year Round* simultaneously with their Old World contemporaries and formed an important part of its community of readers. Inevitably, perhaps, the contents of the journal shifted to accommodate its new transatlantic and colonial readerships, helping account for what has often been noted as the increased interna-tionalism of its outlook, in comparison with *Household Words*.[42]

Such a shift is entirely consonant with twenty-first-century theorisation of the kind of cultural hybridity in which Dickens's journals knowingly participated. As new readerships developed, the columns of *All the Year Round* were permeable to submissions concerning and frequently sourced from distant contributors, according to the 'cultural logic of globalization', for, as Marwan Kraidy puts it, hybridity 'entails that traces of other cultures exist in every culture, thus offering foreign media and marketers transcul-tural wedges for forging affective links between their commodities and local communities'.[43] One does not have to look very far to find evidence of this kind of process at work in *All the Year Round*.[44] Its first number carried

[39] See H. K. Riikonen, 'Dickens's Reception in Finland', in Michael Hollington (ed.), *The Reception of Charles Dickens in Europe*, 2 vols. London: Bloomsbury, 2013, Vol. 2, p. 389. Riikonen does not identify the *HW* article; it is presumably Anna Mary Howitt's 'The Right One', *Household Words* III (9 August 1851), 473–77.

[40] Hazel Mackenzie, Ben Winyard and John Drew, 'Introduction to *All the Year Round Volume 1*' *Dickens Quarterly* 29.3 (2012): 251–77, 271. See also Drew, 'Paratexts', 72–73.

[41] U.S. edition of *All the Year Round*, Vol. 4 (12 January 1861), 336.

[42] See Drew, *Journalist*, pp. 148–51.

[43] Marwan M. Kraidy, *Hybridity, Or the Cultural Logic of Globalization*. Philadelphia: Temple University Press, 2005, p. 148.

[44] The process is analysed illuminatingly in Catherine Waters, *Commodity Culture in Dickens's Household Words: The Social Life of Goods*. Aldershot: Ashgate, 2008, pp. 118–19, and more widely

an article called 'A Piece of China', introducing the satirical recollections of the showman Albert Smith, following a lightning trip to Hong Kong, to gather material for his latest entertainment at Egyptian Hall – a show advertised prominently on p. 6 of the Advertiser for the first monthly part issue of the journal. Hannah Lewis-Bill argues that such critico-comical commodification of China in articles in Dickens's journals reveals 'an interest heightened by the threat [that] China ... a growing commodity superpower ... posed, albeit from afar, through its refusal to conform to British will'.[45] Indeed. The article itself suggests that readers were perhaps expected to be sufficiently savvy concerning the realities of globalisation not to feel too threatened either by cultural non-conformity or the limitations of cultural exchange:

> IT is a glowing, glaring morning at Hong Kong. I awake inside my net-muslin safe, wherein my boy, A-Pow has consigned me for security from the flies, like a jam tart under gauze in a pastrycook's window, during the dog-days ... A-Pow is about nine, of grave demeanour, and wearing a little pigtail.
> 'Gud morng,' he says.
> 'Chin-chin, A-Pow,' I reply.
> He thinks he is speaking English, and I imagine I am talking Chinese. We are both equally wrong. (*AYR* I [30 April 1859], 16)

Dickens and his co-writers in *Household Words* and *All the Year Round* were capable, in other words, of conducting a nuanced debate – encapsulated in the coverage of the Great Exhibition no less than in Harold Skimpole's nonchalant satisfaction with imperial exploration and American slavery – over the difference between cynical and 'virtuous cosmopolitanisms'.[46]

Two postscripts are perhaps required to complete this overview of Dickens's weekly magazines. The first is to point out that while, as Brake indicates, Dickens himself was 'a celebrity editor like very few others in nineteenth-century Britain', whose persona and 'presiding spirit' were crucial to the success of a stable of publications (32), the publications themselves outlived him by many more years than those during which he occupied the editorial chair. His son Charlie as 'Charles Dickens, Jun.' took over the baton and continued conducting *All the Year Round*

---

in Sabine Clemm, *Dickens, Journalism, and Nationhood: Mapping the World in Household Words.* London: Routledge, 2009.
[45] 'China, Commodities and Conflict in *Household Words*', in Mackenzie and Winyard (eds.), *Mid-Victorian Press*, pp. 123–32, 122.
[46] Tanya Agathocleous's wording, in *Urban Realism and the Cosmopolitan Imagination in the Nineteenth Century*. Cambridge University Press, 2011, p. 35.

successfully until 1895. Partway through his tenure (1881), he revived *Household Words* in a new larger format and ran both journals simultaneously for fourteen years, the latter continuing publication after his death, eventually being taken over by Manx novelist Hall Caine in 1902, as a project for his eighteen-year-old son Gordon to manage, which he appears to have done – as a penny magazine 'Founded by Charles Dickens' – until 1905.

A second, digital afterlife was inaugurated in March 2012, with the public launch of both *Household Words* and *All the Year Round* (1850–70) in an Open Access scholarly edition called *Dickens Journals Online*,[47] which combines full-page facsimiles with an accurate searchable transcript (corrected by more than 900 volunteers in a major crowdsourcing initiative) linked to tables of contents with authorship information from the two published indexes compiled by Anne Lohrli and E. A. Oppenlander, together with author biographies, subject and genre identifiers and various forms of contextual annotation. The project has been welcomed by academic reviewers in so far as its 'interactive approach – which encourages community moderation and correction – is the most innovative aspect of the site' and 'its role as a historical marker . . . promises a quantum leap in our understanding of Dickens and the Mid-Victorian Press.'[48] As well as invigorating debate about qualitative aspects of the journals under Dickens's editorship, the site offers the kind of real-time information about circulation, the location of readers, their favourite items and the amount of time they spend reading that is so conspicuously lacking from nineteenth-century records. Thus, for example, site statistics reveal that from launch to 29 March 2015, a period of three years, there was a total of 1,198,072 page views from users in 180 countries, averaging 10 minutes and 50s per reading session; the fourth most popular PDF download was Dickens's controversial meditation on 'The Noble Savage'.[49] However, lest we overestimate the value of such apparently rich quantitative data or the impact of such an apparently large online readership, it is worth converting the page view total into the readership of a 24-page issue, which produces a circulation of just under 50,000 for a single magazine, or of a mere 320 over a three-year publication run. Clearly the new digital readership is of a radically diminished kind, in comparison with the

---

[47] www.djo.org.uk hosted by the University of Buckingham.

[48] Respectively, Clare Horrocks, 'Advances in Digitization: The *Dickens Journals Online Project, 2012*' *Victorian Periodicals Review*, 45.3 (Fall 2012), 358–62, 359; Joseph McLaughlin, review, *Charles Dickens and the Mid-Victorian Press, 1850–1870, Nineteenth-Century Contexts* 37.1 (2015), 84–87, 87.

[49] *Household Words*, Vol. 2, 11 June 1853, 337–39.

journals' heyday in the nineteenth-century 'community of print'. That the online edition is also a diminished witness to the past, a shadow text not to be confused with the original, is a timely reminder articulated by Gillian Piggott in a late contribution to the *Tale of Two Cities* reading group blog, run in 2012 as a partnership between the Victorian Studies Centre at the University of Leicester and *Dickens Journals Online*:

> On opening the page, one is presented with a montage, heightening the fragmentariness of the serialized format. One is given ... the facsimile page of *All the Year Round*, cut off at the waist, montaged with part of the corrected modern text (a simple, clean font for greater reader clarity). This rather uncanny doubling of fragments can soon be resolved, with further mediation, through the use of scrolling tools ... With its old font and reproduced shadows and creases, the original facsimile is far more alluring to read than its modern double. Closer to the visual experience of the text the Victorians might have had, it is also, however, lying prostrate under the strange power of digitalization. Corpse-like, the page's shadows never vary and its creases do not move, which has an uncanny effect. Our experience of this historical text is very much determined by the present.[50]

Like a dead butterfly preserved under glass, never to flap its wings, the pages of the digitised journal embody a further paradoxical hybridity, teasing us out of thought: that of ephemera transfixed.

---

[50] See https://dickensataleoftwocities.wordpress.com/2012/11/09/narrative-and-time [accessed 29 March 2015].

CHAPTER 18

Harriet Martineau: Women, Work and Mid-Victorian Journalism

Iain Crawford

In *Becoming a Woman of Letters*, Linda Peterson explores the development of a whole new class of female professional authors during the
nineteenth century and examines the opportunities and challenges created for them by the emergence of a new literary marketplace.
Of particular interest to Peterson's study is Harriet Martineau, who
was one of the first of these new women authors and who resisted
conventional expectations that she remain within the domestic sphere
and the normative genre of feminine poetry; instead, Peterson notes, she
insisted upon writing 'on topics traditionally disallowed ... represents
a new style of woman writer [and] very much appears to be (what she was)
a professional woman of letters'.[1] Examining Martineau's emergence in
the early 1830s, Peterson and others have described the resistance she met
to her initial efforts to claim a new role for women authors, the intensity
of the attacks on her that followed the prominence she achieved with the
publication of *Illustrations of Political Economy* (1832–4), and her perse-
verance in consolidating her public role despite enduring hostility
towards her work from the major conservative figures and press outlets
of the 1830s.[2] However, although the disruptive effect of Martineau's
early publications has been recognised, much less attention has been paid
to the extent to which she continued to generate such responses in the
later phases of her career and the degree to which these attacks came from
more progressive quarters that might have been expected to be more

---

[1] Linda Peterson, *Becoming a Woman of Letters: Myths of Authorship and Facts of the Victorian Market*.
Princeton University Press, 2009, p. 30.
[2] See, for example, *The Times*'s comments – 'the parade of what is called philosophy in this book is
indeed one of the most preposterous and burlesque exhibitions that we have long met with', 'Society
in America by Harriet Martineau', 30 May 1837, 5; or *Fraser's* complaint that she proves that 'it is
possible for even a maiden lady to have as perfect an insight into the arcana of slave-state debauchery,
as the most free-thinking and free-acting bachelor', 'Practical Reasoning Versus Impracticable
Theories', May 1837, 567.

sympathetic to her. My focus in this chapter will be upon a conflict that has previously gone almost entirely unnoticed – one with William Makepeace Thackeray in and around the pages of the *Cornhill Magazine*. Examining this event, I argue, not only demonstrates the extent to which Martineau continued throughout her career to challenge masculine expectations for the role of a woman author in the Victorian press but, crucially, also reveals how, by the 1860s, she was able to serve as a model for the generation of women authors who followed her and who looked to claim an equal part in the Victorian world of letters.

The trigger and apparent explanation for Martineau's clash with Thackeray was an obituary she wrote in the *Daily News* following the death of the Whig historian and politician Thomas Babington Macaulay. Published on 31 December 1859, this piece was remarkably lacking in conventional generosity and amply demonstrated Martineau's characteristic readiness to put principle before sentiment as she unsparingly noted Macaulay's deficiencies as a writer of history. For her, Macaulay had repeatedly demonstrated the 'radical inaccuracy of his habit of thought'; was 'thoroughly deficient in moral earnestness'; and, above all else, 'cold and barren as regards the highest part of human nature', he 'wanted heart'.[3] Even though she did also praise his rhetorical and stylistic brilliance and commended the vital part he had played in saving the *Edinburgh Review* after Francis Jeffrey stepped down from the editorship, language such as this and the overall tone of her account of the late statesman made for anything but a valediction that would have given comfort to his grieving friends and family.

Precisely when the obituary appeared, one of those mourners found himself in an unusually opportune position to respond. Thackeray, a friend and intellectual ally of Macaulay since their time together at Trinity College, Cambridge, was in the thick of preparing copy for the second number of what had turned out to be his phenomenally successful new magazine, the *Cornhill*. He seized the moment and created a space both to reply to Martineau's charges and admonish her:

> The writer who said that Macaulay had no heart could not know him. Press writers should read a man well, and all over, and again; and hesitate, at least, before they speak of those αιδοια. Those who knew Lord Macaulay knew how admirably tender, and generous, and affectionate he was. It was not his business to bring his family before the theatre footlights, and call for bouquets from the gallery as he wept over them.[4]

---

[3] H. Martineau, 'Lord Macaulay', *Daily News*, 31 December 1859, 5.
[4] W. M. Thackeray, 'Nil Nisi Bonum', *Cornhill Magazine*, February 1860, 134.

As Thackeray's daughter recorded more than thirty years later, this was an account of the late historian that moved his family. Macaulay's brother Charles thus wrote to a friend that it was 'the outpouring of a tender, generous, noble nature' and went on to ask him to convey 'that the last book my brother read was the first number of "The Cornhill Magazine." It was open at Thackeray's story, on the table by the side of the chair in which he died.'[5]

Any satisfaction Thackeray may have felt at learning this, however, was to be short lived, for he soon discovered that, in his trenchant reply to Martineau, he had committed a faux pas of monumental proportions that quickly spread among London's literary circles. Late in March 1860, for example, it was discussed at one of the regular weekly dinners the senior staff of *Punch* held in the offices of Bradbury and Evans on Bouverie Street. Henry Silver, whose diary of these occasions provides a unique insight into the magazine and the literary world of which it was so central a part, recorded an exchange between Samuel Lucas, the editor of *Once a Week*, and John Leech, *Punch*'s best-known illustrator: 'Thackeray has not been seen since his αιδοια slip – no getting out of it, says Lucas, mistook it for private secrecies and thoughts. J. L. suggests that as it was Miss Martineau he was cutting up he used the Greek that she might enquire what it meant.'[6] Evidently, then, Thackeray was aware that Martineau had written the obituary and had intended to play upon her assumed lack of classical learning. Unfortunately, it was his own deficiencies as a classicist that were revealed, for what αιδοια actually meant was not 'private secrecies and thoughts' but, rather, 'the shameful parts', and it was the term that early Greek physicians had used to refer to the female genitalia.[7] Thackeray, an undistinguished scholar at Charterhouse who had gone on to university for just a single year, had clearly got it completely wrong. More significantly, the *Cornhill* had mapped itself on to the literary market place as a magazine intended to appeal to a broad and mixed audience, and Thackeray's own advertisement had described it as a 'social table' at which 'we shall suppose the ladies and children always present.'[8] Rather than adroitly putting Martineau in her place, then, his blunder threatened the very ethos of his

[5] Mrs R. Ritchie, 'The First Number of "The Cornhill,"' *Cornhill Magazine*, July 1896, 5.
[6] H. Silver, *Diary*, British Library, Add MS 88937/2/13. See P. Leary, *The Punch Brotherhood: Table Talk and Print Culture in Mid-Victorian London*. London: The British Library, 2010, for a full discussion of this group.
[7] S. B. Pomeroy, *Women in Hellenistic Egypt: From Alexander to Cleopatra*. New York: Schocken Books, 1984, p. 80.
[8] G. Smith, 'Our Birth and Parentage', *Cornhill Magazine*, January 1901, 7.

publication, and it was no wonder that he buried himself out of sight in the weeks that followed.

Although the incident clearly caused Thackeray considerable embarrassment in his circle, it was not a subject suitable for more public discussion, and it had no discernible impact upon the continuing success of the magazine. Similarly, his blunder has been recorded just once in modern scholarship and treated even there simply as matter for a passing footnote.[9] What I want to claim here, by contrast, is that this event reveals much more than Thackeray's linguistic ineptness and that the episode itself, the events that led up to it and its aftermath are richly indicative of Martineau's position in the world of the Victorian press; of the challenges she posed for the men who dominated that world; and, finally, of her role as an essential model and mentor to the next generation of Victorian women authors, women whose work and careers were made far easier by the pioneering model she provided.

Thackeray's mortifying error can also be seen as an extension of the kinds of attack Martineau was subjected to at the beginning of her career and the charges made against her for allegedly going beyond the boundaries appropriate for a woman writer. For, setting the mistake in the Greek aside, his larger claim in the response to Martineau is built on the conjoined assumptions that Macaulay had both a public and a private self and that his critic wronged him by focusing upon only the public self-representation evident through his writing and political oratory and judging him on his utterance alone. By contrast, Thackeray privileges his own position as Macaulay's friend and fellow writer, suggesting that this combination is what allows him to portray the man fully and truthfully. By requiring of Martineau a relationship with her subject that she did not have and that, as a Victorian woman, she could not have appropriately had or, if she had had, made public use of, he thus erases her writerly standing and, in the assumption that the private connection between men is what validates his authority to speak of the deceased, implies a more universal barrier to women's access to the public sphere.

Had the matter begun with Martineau's obituary of Macaulay and ended with Thackeray's response, it might have been simply a passing spat – one of some interest but perhaps not more broadly significant. However, placing this episode in the wider context of Martineau's entire relationship with the *Cornhill* reveals far more about her role in the mid-century press and the impact of her work upon other women writers. For, in fact, this was not her

[9] G. N. Ray, *Thackeray: The Age of Wisdom: 1847–1863*. New York: McGraw-Hill, 1959, p. 481.

and Thackeray's first connection over the magazine, nor would it be her final appearance in its pages, since she would publish three articles in it in 1865 and 1866, after Thackeray had left the editorship and, indeed, after his premature death.

By the 1850s, Martineau had become widely respected for her ability to write on an extraordinary range of issues and to command almost any genre. Recruited to the *Daily News* by Frederick Knight Hunt in 1852, she had established herself as one of its most authoritative leader writers, while she also continued to publish in the heavyweight quarterlies, most notably the *Edinburgh* and the *Westminster*. Meanwhile, across the Atlantic, she continued to write for the *Atlantic Monthly* and in the abolitionist press.[10] Her range made her clearly attractive to start-up ventures and, early in the decade, she had been sought after by editors of publications as diverse as the radical new weekly the *Leader* and Dickens's *Household Words* to lend her support to their start-up ventures. During these years, she also developed a cordial relationship with George Smith, the publisher who would launch the *Cornhill* and who brought out four of her books and, in 1858, a new edition of her early novel *Deerbrook*, first published in 1839. Indeed, Smith was to be literally her last publisher, since in addition to these books in the late fifties, it was also under his imprint that her posthumous *Autobiography* appeared in 1877, more than twenty years after she had completed it.

Given both her professional record and her history with the firm of Smith, Elder then, when Thackeray began looking for writers to supply the *Cornhill* with matter for its 'discussion and narrative of events interesting to the public',[11] it was natural for him to consider her as a prospective recruit. But, despite her ties to the firm and what she described as the 'noble terms' offered, she turned him down.[12] Her letters reveal that there were four factors to this decision: first, she was sceptical about the new model the *Cornhill* represented – as she cautiously continued in her letter to Smith, she distrusted 'Monthly Magazines set up all round in rivalship'. In this, events quickly proved that she was too conservative in her appraisal of the journalistic marketplace, and her distrust turned out to be wholly misplaced. Second, and rather more accurately, she doubted Thackeray's

---

[10] See the appendices to Deborah Anna Logan, ed., *The Collected Letters of Harriet Martineau*, 5 vols. London: Pickering and Chatto, 2007; and to Deborah A. Logan ed., *Harriet Martineau: Further Letters*. Bethlehem: Lehigh University Press, 2012, for the most comprehensive available listings of Martineau's periodical articles.

[11] Smith, 'Our Birth and Parentage', 7.

[12] *Collected Letters of Harriet Martineau*, vol. 4, p. 197.

'power of industry for *such* work', [13] echoing doubts his own publisher had about the editor's resilience and anticipating what indeed turned out to be his short-lived tenure. Third, with her health still poor, she claimed to be fully extended with her existing commitments to the *Daily News*, the *Edinburgh Review* and the *Anti-Slavery Standard*. Finally, she had also recently taken on another new commitment, again to an editor with whom she had a long relationship, when she agreed to write occasional pieces for Bradbury and Evans's new magazine *Once a Week*, and this, she claimed, left her neither time nor energy for an additional responsibility.

Examining her decision to work for *Once a Week* more closely, however, adds yet another layer to the narrative and further complicates the gender politics of Martineau's position and self-positioning in the world of journalism. For in accepting the invitation from its editor – the same Samuel Lucas who just a few months later would find himself at the *Punch* dinner where Thackeray's gaffe was the subject of discussion – she was motivated by something more than enthusiasm for his new project. What particularly drew her to it was her hostility towards Dickens and her readiness to seize the opportunity it provided to work against his interests. Just over three years earlier, that is, her long-standing personal and professional relationship with Dickens had ended with the ugly public quarrel in print that they had had over industrial safety at the end of 1855 and early in 1856.[14] Two years later, Martineau was further incensed by Dickens's public humiliation of his wife at the time of their separation and by the way he had retaliated against Bradbury and Evans for refusing to publish a self-serving account of his marital breakdown in the pages of *Punch*. Closing down *Household Words*, opening *All the Year Round*, and returning to Chapman and Hall as his publishers, Dickens had blended self-righteousness with an opportunistic move to strengthen his own economic position, much to Martineau's disgust.[15] As she wrote to Henry Reeve, her cousin and the editor of the *Edinburgh Review*, about Lucas's invitation: 'He asked me to write; & I was so indignant at Dickens's conduct to Bradbury and Evans, that I agreed – as have several other people with whom it is an honour to be associated.'[16] Clearly relishing a chance to support a rival to *All the Year*

---

[13] Elisabeth Sanders Arbuckle, ed., *Harriet Martineau's Letters to Fanny Wedgwood*. Stanford University Press, 1983, p. 182.

[14] See I. Crawford, 'Harriet Martineau, Charles Dickens, and the Rise of the Victorian Woman of Letters,' *Nineteenth-Century Literature* 68.4 (2014), 449–83.

[15] See Michael Slater, *Charles Dickens*. New Haven and London: Yale University Press, 2009, pp. 432–60, for a full discussion of this episode.

[16] *Collected Letters*, vol. 4, p. 177.

Round and reluctant to venture on to the uncertain ground of a new kind of shilling monthly, especially under Thackeray's leadership, she concentrated her efforts on *Once a Week* and passed up the *Cornhill*'s offer.

If a variety of factors thus contributed to her turning Thackeray down, his blundering comment in the second issue can only have confirmed her in the decision. Her letters reveal that she did follow the *Cornhill*, so it seems reasonable to assume that she knew all about Thackeray's faux pas. Moreover, despite his assumption that she would have had to 'enquire what it meant', shortly before his article appeared she had coincidentally written to a correspondent that she 'had . . . a sound classical education'[17] and so certainly had the tools to find out for herself what he had said, if not the opportunity to discern what he had intended by it. While she was aware of the magazine's remarkable success, then, there clearly could have been no possibility of her contributing as long as he was its editor. Instead, she continued to work for a wide variety of other outlets and, with her reluctance to write for the new, and very successful, monthly magazines evidently overcome, appeared in *Macmillan's* in June 1862.

By then Thackeray had fulfilled her expectations and given up his editorship. His death eighteen months later removed any remaining obstacle between her and the *Cornhill* and, even though she was now in the final two years of her active career, she would go on to appear in its pages three times in 1864 and 1865.[18] By contrast with 1859, when she had been solicited by Thackeray, the initiative to write for the magazine now appears to have come from her, judging by a letter from George Smith to her in July 1864.[19]

If the combination of personal relationships and abundant other opportunities to write on issues of importance to her had kept Martineau away from the *Cornhill* in 1859, similar factors apparently played into reversing her decision in 1864. She had become keenly engaged in two issues that were drawing wide public interest at the time: the nature of the education required for the successful advancement of the middle class and the need for trained nurses to support improvements in public health. Her longstanding friendship with the Arnold family, and especially with Matthew Arnold, was relevant to the first of these, while her connection with Florence Nightingale played an important part in the second. And, in both cases, her advocacy of the issue was inseparable from a concern with

---

[17] *Collected Letters*, vol. 4, p. 213.

[18] 'Middle Class Education: Boys', *Cornhill Magazine*, October 1864, 409–26; 'Middle Class Education: Girls', *Cornhill Magazine*, November 1864, 549–68; 'Nurses Wanted', *Cornhill Magazine*, April 1865, 409–25.

[19] Harriet Martineau Papers, University of Birmingham, HM 819.

the ways in which women could be prepared for and provided with a growing range of professional opportunities to work and support themselves – a theme at the heart of her entire career. In the mid-1860s, she wrote extensively on both topics, taking advantage, as it were, of all the platforms open to her as she made use of a wide range of daily, weekly and monthly venues, but for my purposes here, I focus only upon the two essays that addressed education, since they can be seen as her final response to Thackeray's attempt to silence her journalistic voice.

Martineau's *Cornhill* articles 'Middle Class Education: Boys', which appeared in October 1864, and 'Middle Class Education: Girls', which came out the following month, both spoke into an ongoing wider national conversation. Interest in the state of education in Britain had been stimulated by the appearance earlier in the year of the report of the Clarendon Commission, which had been set up in 1861 to examine the condition of the public schools and which had now produced a devastating analysis of the deficiencies of nine elite institutions. In the aftermath of the report's publication, Martineau had used her position as a leader writer for the *Daily News* to add her support to calls for a similar study of the education available to middle-class families. During the same year, Matthew Arnold had contributed his voice to the conversation with the publication of his book *A French Eton; or, Middle Class Education and the State*, as well as with his essay on the role of the French Academy in the April issue of the *Cornhill*. When Martineau wrote her two articles, then, she accomplished several related goals: first, she engaged in a large and ongoing cultural conversation on a topic of special importance to her. Second, as she did so, she responded to the views of a longtime friend whom she fundamentally supported but with whom she had some disagreement over the role of the state in providing education. Finally, by appearing in the *Cornhill* she both made use of its highly influential venue to expand her audience on this topic and was able to put behind her any awkwardness that may have lingered from the former editor's mishap. Characteristically, however, even as she created the occasion to move forwards, she found a way to embed within her contributions to the magazine one final response to that now late editor.

Martineau had apparently originally conceived of the two essays as a single piece, since in his July letter to her Smith refers to the need to break them up into smaller sections, and they share both a common stress upon the need to clarify the agenda for middle-class education and an emphasis upon the centrality of classical learning to that agenda. Although the essay on boys focuses more upon the role of the state in organising education and that on girls more upon the processes of cultural formation, both work from an assumption that 'we are in a perfect chaos as to the objects and materials of school instruction.'[20] But, while the two essays examine different sectors of the education currently offered – that on boys paying particular attention to the broad spectrum of school types and that on girls inevitably having much to say about ladies' academies and other 'genteel' schools – they share a view of the nature of curriculum that takes on a fresh significance in light of the earlier episode with Thackeray.

For, despite acknowledging the new kinds of knowledge that had become essential to Britain's youth, Martineau emphasises that classical learning is still 'an instrument for the training and cultivation of thought, by which other kinds of knowledge are to be obtained' and is 'the best, for the middle class, in all its gradations, if it is the best for any other'.[21] Even more telling is a lengthy section in the second essay in which she praises the expansion of access for girls to classical training and connects it to economic changes that have been 'familiarising the mind of society with the idea of women becoming self-dependent' and to 'a radical change in the principle and conduct of the intellectual culture of the educators of the next generation'.[22] Martineau does not, of course, mention Thackeray's hapless attempt to make use of his own classical education to assail a woman who had modelled the life of self-dependence and whose entire career had been devoted to shaping the intellectual culture of her times, but our awareness of his blunder makes her concluding language even more resonant:

> Not all the ignorance, the jealousy, the meanness, the prudery, or the profligate selfishness which is to be found from end to end of the middle class, can now reverse the destiny of the English girl, or retard that ennobling of the sex which is a natural consequence of its becoming wiser and more independent, while more accomplished, gracious, and companionable. The briars and brambles are cleared away from the women's avenue to the temple of knowledge. Now they have only to knock, and it will be opened to them.[23]

Though she nods in the direction of conventional expectations of femininity with 'accomplished, gracious, and companionable', Martineau's larger point is that classical learning is foundational to the education of the girls of the period and that those, such as Thackeray, who simply assume it to be a masculine preserve, misunderstand the historical forces that are leading these girls to grow up to become women who will both continue to shape Victorian culture and take on an increasingly important role in its professional life.

[20] 'Boys', 417. [21] 'Boys', 415. [22] 'Girls', 554. [23] 'Girls', 567.

The two essays in the *Cornhill* were among the very last works Martineau published during her lifetime, but they were clearly not the end of her influence upon the generation of younger women writers that was emerging by the 1860s. For, even though her own extraordinary contribution to nineteenth-century letters was almost complete, a larger transition had begun to take hold in the environment for aspiring women writers. As Linda Peterson has noted, 'a new discourse of women's work' had developed and been given specific voice by Martineau's contemporary Anna Jameson in her 1856 *The Communion of Labour.* Jameson, and this discourse, challenged traditional binary distinctions between male and female work by arguing that 'the duties of both men and women emerge from the home and radiate out into the public sphere.'[24] The new understanding of labour and intellectual activity allowed female authors to claim their right to literary work and professional lives with a freedom unimaginable thirty years earlier when Martineau was beginning her own career, and it was the essential context in which a younger generation rose to prominence during the 1860s. As they did so, however, it is clear that these women authors recognised the debt they owed their predecessor, even as she was in the process of withdrawing from public life.

Among the many examples of this recognition, the most poignant perhaps is offered by one of the new writers who began to establish herself in the 1860s, a woman who could hardly have had a closer connection to both Martineau and the *Cornhill.* For among the emerging women writers of the decade was Thackeray's own daughter, his beloved Annie, who had entered the 'temple of knowledge' with her father's encouragement and began her long literary career with a first contribution to the *Cornhill* while he was still its editor. If Thackeray was one formative influence, however, he might well have been disconcerted to know just how important to his daughter's professional growth Harriet Martineau had been. Citing Martineau's *Deerbrook* in a letter to a friend when she was just eighteen, Annie Thackeray anticipated the need she would face to make her own way through life as she referred to her father's chronically precarious finances: 'Papa says in a few years, we shall have only 200£ a year to live on & as my favourite Miss Martineau says it is far nobler to earn than to save.'[25] Some years later, when she had gone on to construct a modestly successful literary career of her own, she paid tribute to the role Martineau had played in inspiring her. For left among Martineau's papers after her death was a letter from Annie Thackeray to friend and one-time

---

[24] *Becoming a Woman of Letters*, p. 46.
[25] A. T. Ritchie, *Anne Thackeray Ritchie: Journals and Letters*, ed. Abigail Burnham Bloom and John Maynard. Columbus: Ohio State University Press, 1994, p. 43.

collaborator Henry Atkinson in which she describes the impact of Martineau's praise for her 1867 novel *The Village on the Cliff:*

Dear Mr. Atkinson

I am so touched and so grateful and glad and proud that I don't quite know in what words to write about it; & I do think it is so kind of you to have thought how glad I should be! I only could wish as I looked at the little scrap of paper that was so much to me that I could have shown it to my father, and that is the most grateful thing I can say to you and to the writer of those kindest words. There is nobody whose praise now, could be to me what Miss Martineau's is . . . I know I first came to life over a brown watered book called the Settlers at Home, walking up the Champs Elysées at Paris twenty years ago, when I was 8 or 9 years old. Her books haven't been books but friends & counsellors & comforters; & that she of all people should make me and my sister so glad by her praise seems like a delightful miracle on purpose to make us happy.[26]

Annie Thackeray's literary career was a modest one, but its very ordinariness is itself a testimony to the shift in the world of letters to which Martineau had contributed so much by helping to make it possible for women authors to work in both literature and journalism and to have professional lives of their own. Martineau could certainly be a difficult character, the male writers who dominated early and mid-Victorian letters often found her exasperating, and it was indeed her own bluntness about Macaulay that prompted Thackeray's blunder. In the example of her own extraordinary career and her tireless advocacy of expanding women's access to education and enlarging their professional opportunities, she was nevertheless a pioneering model for the young writers who would become mid-Victorian women of letters. Even so, and as her entire engagement with the *Cornhill* reveals, she also knew only too well how difficult it was to negotiate the uncertain boundaries between public writing and private selves, especially for women seeking to have their voices heard in new ways in the journalism of the middle decades of the nineteenth century. That her connection with the *Cornhill* should have ended on such a different note from that with which it began, then, may indeed be a 'delightful miracle' and was certainly one of the unlikelier conclusions to this revealing episode in the world of nineteenth-century letters.

[26] Letter to Henry Atkinson, n.d., Harriet Martineau Papers, University of Birmingham, HM 886.

CHAPTER 19

Wilkie Collins and the Discovery of an 'Unknown Public'

Graham Law

I began to stop ... and look attentively at these all-pervading specimens of what was to me a new species of literary production ... From
looking in at the windows of the shops, I got on to entering the shops
themselves, to buying specimens of this locust-flight of small publications, to making strict examination of them from the first page to
the last, and finally, to instituting inquiries about them in all sorts of
well-informed quarters. The result – the astonishing result – has been
the discovery of an Unknown Public; a public to be counted by
millions; the mysterious, the unfathomable, the universal public of
the penny-novel Journals.[1]

'The Unknown Public', Collins's most widely cited piece of journalism,
first appeared anonymously as a leader in Dickens's two-penny weekly
miscellany *Household Words* in summer 1858. This was during a period of
rapid expansion for the periodical press, in large part because of the
gradual removal of the fiscal constraints known to their radical enemies
as the 'taxes on knowledge', the main steps being the abolition by
Parliament of the advertisement duty in 1853, the newspaper stamp in
1855, and the paper tax in 1861, following the formation of the Association
for the Repeal of the Taxes on Knowledge (ARTK) in 1849 and
a provocative report from a House of Commons Select Committee in
1851.[2] As the opening quotation suggests, Collins's article on the emergence of a common reading public avoids such an objective approach
reflecting the insights of contemporary political science, instead taking
the form of a personalised, dramatic narrative. This develops in three
stages, the first two marked by a comic tone mocking the immaturity of

---

[1] [Wilkie Collins], 'The Unknown Public', *Household Words* (21 August 1858), 217–22, 217.
[2] For the pioneering account of this campaign, see C. D. Collet, *History of the Taxes on Knowledge*, 2
vols. (London: T. Fisher Unwin, 1899). For the most comprehensive analysis, see Martin Hewitt,
The Dawn of the Cheap Press in Victorian Britain: The End of the 'Taxes on Knowledge', 1849–1869.
London: Bloomsbury, 2014.

lower-class readers, in contrast to the sophistication of the known reading public following journals such as *Household Words*. The piece thus opens with the journalist as natural historian, first tracking down the 'locust-flight' of penny entertainment papers in unsavoury shops up and down the land, and then dissecting a representative set of five of the best selling for their chief contents. These are sensational fiction in the form of short tales or lengthy serials, and the 'Answers to Correspondents' columns replying to requests for information and advice from anxious readers. However, the intent to amuse gives way in the final stage to a visionary vein where, triumphantly driven by a 'universal law of progress',[3] the common readership is envisaged as being sentimentally educated over time to appreciate the quality of fine literature and thus provide a mass audience for the best writers.

The predominantly ironic, personalised style of 'The Unknown Public' was by no means untypical within Collins's early output as a journalist, or indeed among the non-fiction material more generally featured in Dickens's weekly magazines. The lion's share of Collins's journalistic contributions to *Household Words* and *All the Year Round* took the form of humorous monologues or dialogues on contemporary social issues.[4] Along with Collins, George Sala and Edmund Yates were among the 'young men' that Dickens gathered round him to provide a steady supply of such material for his journals, and it is no coincidence that both were to become influential proponents of a more personalised style of periodical writing, later known as the 'New Journalism'.[5] Though the New Journalism could be robustly political when later wielded by firebrands such as W. T. Stead,[6] in Dickens's editorial hands at least, the personalised style served to restrain his editorial assistants from crossing the line between reformism and radicalism. As one of his less submissive contributors put it, in his political views Dickens was 'swayed by every breath of feeling and sentiment. He was a Liberal by impulse, and what the "Dryasdust" school [Carlyle's derisive term for utilitarian] would have called a "wobbler"'.[7] Indeed, much the same could be said of Collins himself. This helps explain why the lengthy political campaign led by the ARTK is overlooked not

---

[3] Collins, 'The Unknown Public', 222.

[4] The fullest digital archive of these journals is *Dickens Journals Online (DJO)*, dir. John Drew, www.djo.org.uk.

[5] See P. D. Edwards, *Dickens's 'Young Men'*. Aldershot: Ashgate, 1997.

[6] See his pair of manifestos: W. T. Stead, 'Government by Journalism', *Contemporary Review* 49 (May 1886), 653–74, and 'The Future of Journalism', *Contemporary Review* 50 (November 1886), 663–79.

[7] John Hollingshead, *My Lifetime*, 2 vols. London: Sampson Low, Marston, 1895, Vol. I, pp. 99–100.

only in 'The Unknown Public' itself but indeed in *Household Words* throughout its decade of publication.

The correspondence of both Dickens and Collins shows how little sympathy the two had for the movement to remove the fiscal constraints on the press. Corresponding with W. C. Macready, Dickens gave his reasons for declining to sign a petition for the removal of the newspaper stamp, calling it a 'fair tax enough' that left the press 'extremely accessible to the poor man', and offering the duty on soap as a more worthy target of protest.[8] This although *Household Narrative* (1850–5), his monthly supplement offering a summary of public affairs, had recently been the subject of an unsuccessful prosecution by the Board of Inland Revenue for refusing to pay the stamp duty.[9] In turn, Collins wrote in 1861 to C. D. Collet, secretary of the ARTK, refusing to lend his support for the final repeal of the paper duty, since he did not consider it 'one of the urgent public wants of the present time'.[10] Back in March 1855, while Parliament was debating the abolition of the newspaper stamp, Collins had privileged the profits of authors and publishers above the need for information among common readers, suggesting to the painter E. M. Ward that such a move would 'enable any scoundrel who starts a low paper to steal articles from good papers'.[11] The form chosen for Collins's article on the emergence of a common reading public was thus hardly an innocent one.

Something similar is true of the anthropological trope of the 'discovery' of a new species of reader, which indeed already carried revisionist overtones. Just a couple of weeks before 'The Unknown Public', Margaret Oliphant's 'The Byways of Literature: Reading for the Million' had appeared unsigned in the conservative monthly *Blackwood's Magazine*. There, Oliphant also adopted the form of the personalised monologue, though, with the use of the editorial first person plural, the tone was more sombre, the style more elevated and the analysis of popular publications more specific. Implicitly breaking her own rule of concealing her gender identity in her journalism, Oliphant's narrative device is that of a guardian of a restless female child on a business visit to a cathedral town, who thus resorts to purchasing six named penny journals as a distraction. The detailed perusal of these paltry papers

[8] To W. C. Macready, 31 January 1852, *The Letters of Charles Dickens*, ed. Madeline House et al., Pilgrim edition, 12 vols. Oxford: Clarendon Press, 1965–2000, Vol. 6, pp. 586–87.
[9] See Unsigned, 'Newspapers – and the Stamp Question', *British Quarterly Review* (February 1852), 135–62, 136–38.
[10] To C. D. Collet, 16 February 1861, *The Collected Letters of Wilkie Collins: Addenda and Corrigenda (4)*, ed. William Baker et al. London: Wilkie Collins Society, 2008, p. 3.
[11] To E. M. Ward, 20 March 1855, *The Letters of Wilkie Collins*, ed. William Baker and William M. Clarke, 2 vols. Basingstoke: Macmillan, 1999, Vol. 1 p. 139.

leads the writer to lament the decline of working-class aspirations. In exposing the modern fallacy of 'imagining that the laws of progress are universal',[12] she challenges Victor Hugo's famous dictum in his mediaeval romance *Notre Dame de Paris* that the printing press will destroy the church.[13] Two decades earlier, shortly after Parliament had acted to reduce the burden of the taxes on knowledge, Thackeray was perhaps the first Victorian author to make use of the 'discovery' trope. This was in the Tory monthly *Fraser's Magazine*, which carried his 'Half-a-crown's Worth of Cheap Knowledge' in March 1838. There, in preference to risking personal injury by visiting on their own territory 'the aborigines of The Seven Dials or the natives of Wapping',[14] the author simply calls at Paternoster Square to purchase a selection of the latest popular serials which amply reveal the nature of the tribe. The larger sum expended is a sign not only of the remaining fiscal constraints but also of the wider generic range of papers purchased, including radical, sporting and pornographic journals in addition to those purveying popular fiction. The judgement regarding the poverty and perversity of 'the literary wants and tastes of the poorer classes', however, is even more stark.[15] In between came the most unrelenting anthropological journey of 'discovery', William Hepworth Dixon's eight-part exposé of 'The Literature of the Lower Orders' in the *Daily News* of late 1847. There, Hepworth Dixon consistently adopts the metaphor of the popular press as a danger to public welfare akin to a contaminated water supply, imagining his own role as that of a health inspector set to watch the 'springs of that literature' and to take 'every possible means ... to keep them unpolluted'.[16] The *Daily News* was, of course, the new liberal paper founded by Dickens and his publishers Bradbury and Evans to combat the continuing threat of the Chartist movement. Though Dickens had resigned as editor well before Dixon's investigations, the fact that his friend John Forster then still had a hand on the editorial reins of the daily suggests that Dixon's articles would have met with Boz's approval.[17]

[12] [Margaret Oliphant], 'The Byways of Literature', *Blackwood's Magazine* 84 (August 1858), 200–16, 201; reprinted in *Selected Works of Margaret Oliphant*, ed. Joanne Shattock. London: Pickering & Chatto, 2011, Vol. I, pp. 179–202, 182.

[13] '*Ceci tuera cela ... La presse tuera l'église.*': Victor Hugo, *Notre Dame de Paris*, 5 vols. Paris: Charles Gosselin, 1831, Vol. 5, pp. 31–32.

[14] [W. M. Thackeray], 'Half-a-crown's Worth of Cheap Knowledge', *Fraser's Magazine* 17 (March 1838), 279–90, 280.

[15] Thackeray, 'Half-a-crown's Worth', 280.

[16] [William Hepworth Dixon], 'The Literature of the Lower Orders', *Daily News*, 8 parts (26 October; 2, 9, 25, 29 November; 16, 27, 30 December 1847), 3, 3, 2–3, 3, 3, 3, 3, 3 (I, 3).

[17] The likelihood is increased by the fact that extracts from Hepworth Dixon's articles were reprinted approvingly in the weekly *Examiner*, by then formally under the editorship of Forster, on

Moreover, the broader investigations of Thackeray and Hepworth Dixon remind us that those of Oliphant and Collins were unjustified in limiting their selection of popular reading matter to the penny fiction journals. Led by the *Family Herald* (1842–), *London Journal* (1845–) and *Reynolds's Miscellany* (1846–), this genre of popular print entertainment had already flourished for more than a decade when 'The Unknown Public' made its startled discovery. Following the abolition of the stamp duty, along with penny daily newspapers in both the metropolis and the major provincial cities, a wide range of new forms of cheap weekly publications had begun to emerge which for the first time were able freely to combine information on current affairs with literary material. Though overlooked by Collins and Oliphant, these newer 'species of literary production' were soon to be surveyed by more sympathetic commentators adopting a sociological rather than a natural historical perspective. Most notable here was the far-seeing pair of articles on 'The Periodical Press' by E. S. Dallas, appearing in *Blackwood's* in early 1859. In drawing attention to serial publication as 'the great event of modern history',[18] Dallas concentrated less on the older generation of journals of mass consumption symbolised by the *Family Herald*, than on the recent proliferation of class journals, that is, periodicals targeting those finely differentiated categories of readers affiliated to specific religious, political, professional, social, regional and cultural communities. Inevitably, Dallas in turn remained unaware of a development in popular print culture then only beginning to emerge in both the provinces and the metropolis, that is, the cheap weekly news miscellany, pioneered by the *People's Journal* in Dundee (1858–), which was to prove such an important venue for popular literature in the later Victorian decades.

In the light of the foregoing description of the discursive context of Collins's landmark essay, I now provide an overview of the author's career in journalism. In the process, I need to distinguish between the narrower use of that term employed hitherto, that is, the contribution of articles on public affairs to the press, and a broader conception that includes the writing of shorter fiction for periodical publication. I thus largely overlook Collins's output of around twenty full-length serial novels. These included compositions for monthly and weekly literary miscellanies, as well as metropolitan and provincial newspapers, beginning with 'The Dead

30 October ('The Moral Epidemic', 690–1) and 6 November 1847 ('The Literature of the Lower Order', 709).
[18] [E. S. Dallas], 'Popular Literature: The Periodical Press', *Blackwood's Edinburgh Magazine* 85, 2 parts (January-February 1859), 96–112, 180–95; I, 100.

Secret' in *Household Words* in early 1857 and continuing for more than thirty years until his death when the uncompleted 'Blind Love' was still running in the *Illustrated London News*.[19]

Articles

Collins began to write non-fiction pieces regularly from 1851–2, when he became a frequent contributor not only to *Household Words* but also to *Bentley's Miscellany* (1837–68) and the *Leader* (1850–60). The *Leader* was the exception in more than one sense. Unlike *Household Words*, *Bentley's*, selling for half-a-crown, was the illustrated house monthly of a book publisher, though both had the format of a magazine with miscellaneous contents, including a good deal of fiction, but excluding news. The *Leader*, in contrast, was a weekly newspaper and thus paid the stamp tax until its abolition: it gave most of its space to the 'News of the Week', together with commentary on it by editors and readers in the 'Public Affairs' and 'Open Council' columns, respectively.[20] There were substantial review sections on 'Literature' and 'The Arts', plus a regular 'Portfolio' of poetry, literary essays and (occasionally) fiction. Moreover, with Thornton Hunt and G. H. Lewes as its leading lights, the *Leader* was a radical organ, committed to socialism, secularism and rationalism. Priced at sixpence, the paper was beyond the economic reach of working-class readers, though there was a regular column expressing solidarity with 'Organizations of the People', including those opposing the taxes on knowledge. On the other hand, like *Household Words*, *Bentley's Miscellany* was never more extreme than liberal reformist. Indeed, Richard Bentley's financial difficulties in the early 1850s meant that to avoid alienating potential conservative readers, his house magazine exhibited even more political soft-pedal than usual.[21]

Collins seems never to have written for the *Leader*'s political department, and all his early contributions were in the 'Portfolio'. Even his first essay, 'A Plea for Sunday Reform', was less sympathetic to secularism than the title suggests; its demand was for enlightened entertainment for the poor on the Sabbath, whether open public galleries in the afternoon or free sacred concerts in the evening, with the aim of cultivating 'fit tastes for

[19] See Graham Law, 'The Serial Publication in Britain of the Novels of Wilkie Collins (Waseda University Law Society) *Humanitas* 33 (February 1995), 1–29.

[20] A comprehensive digital archive for the *Leader* can be found at *Nineteenth-Century Serials Edition (NCSE)*, www.ncse.ac.uk/index.html.

[21] On Bentley's economic situation, see Royal A. Gettmann, *A Victorian Publisher: A Study of the Bentley Papers*. Cambridge: Cambridge University Press, 1960, pp. 119–52.

God's day'.[22] Collins then produced 'Magnetic Evenings at Home', a series of sensational accounts of the powers of mesmerism addressed to Lewes himself, and based on experiments personally witnessed in Somerset.[23] A convinced Comtean, Lewes responded with marked scepticism; the two men were clearly separated by a gulf at once social, temperamental and philosophical. The tensions came to a head in February 1852 in correspondence with the new owner Edward Pigott, in which Collins objected strongly to the 'license of religious expression' in the paper, as evidenced by contributions by Hunt and others which he judged to be blasphemous.[24] Although Collins remained on friendly terms with Pigott – the two were to become keen sailing companions – for a period of around two years he seems to have submitted nothing at all to the *Leader*.

In mid-1854, the *Leader* office was shaken by rumours, soon to be confirmed, that Hunt had long been the sexual partner of Lewes's wife Agnes with the husband's sanction, and that Lewes himself was now cohabiting with Marian Evans, the subeditor of the *Westminster Review* soon to become famous as the novelist 'George Eliot'. Despite his own unconventional liaison formed only a few years later, Collins was indignant with Lewes in particular, advising Pigott to extricate himself as soon as possible from such 'a dangerous and degrading connection'.[25] When Lewes and Evans escaped from the scandal to Germany, Pigott, who came from a wealthy Somerset family and had had financial control of the paper since late 1851, was left not only to deal with the fallout but also to find a replacement for his most active contributor. Collins immediately stepped in out of sympathy for Pigott. He began to act as regular reviewer for the paper, covering not only literature and the theatre but also the visual arts. This was a task which he had already performed at *Bentley's Miscellany* for a few months in the summer of 1851. In late 1854 when Pigott was away in Paris on business, Collins even seems temporarily to have taken on editorial responsibility, just as he was to do with *All the Year Round* in late 1867 while Dickens was on his reading tour of America. At the *Leader*, the role of reviewer lasted something over a year, ending only after Lewes returned and resumed his duties. This period of journeyman work at the paper – once more covering the Royal Academy Exhibition in a series of weekly

---

[22] [Wilkie Collins], 'A Plea for Sunday Reform', *Leader* (27 September 1851), 925–26, 926.
[23] See Catherine Peters, *The King of Inventors: A Life of Wilkie Collins*. London: Secker & Warburg, 1991, pp. 109–10.
[24] To Edward Pigott, [20 February 1852], *Letters of Wilkie Collins*, Vol. I, pp. 83–86.
[25] To Edward Pigott, [4/11/18 July 1854], *The Collected Letters of Wilkie Collins*, ed. William Baker et al., 4 vols. London: Pickering & Chatto, 2005, Vol. I, pp. 106–7.

reports, and frequently 'doing' a batch of books, or two or three theatrical performances – clearly stood the author in good stead when he joined the editorial staff of *Household Words* in the autumn of 1856.[26]

By the mid-1850s, Collins's offerings to Dickens's miscellany had shifted from the initial short tales to a predominance of non-fiction, a pattern which continued until he resigned from the *All the Year Round* editorial staff at the beginning of 1862. Thereafter, he probably contributed only a handful, the last identified piece being 'The Dead Lock in Italy', a report on the progress towards Italian unification, sent home during the course of a continental tour with Pigott, which takes the form of a letter to an Italian exile in London from an Englishman visiting Rome. Indeed, few of Collins's more than fifty contributions take the conventional form of the discursive essay of review or criticism, rare examples being 'Portrait of an Author, Painted by his Publisher' (reviewing Edmond Werdet's *Portrait Intime de Balzac*) and 'To Think or be Thought For' (a critique of British art history), both reprinted in his only collected volume of journalistic pieces, *My Miscellanies* (1863). More typically, themes previously treated conventionally, such as the notice of an exhibition or the record of a journey, reappear in parodic form as humorous personal anecdotes, as in 'The Royal Academy in Bed' or 'My Black Mirror'. Even serious literary subjects, such as the debased state of English drama (in 'Dramatic Grub Street'), are dealt with ironically in the first person. Most typical, however, are the dramatic comic monologues that Collins creates to draw 'Sketches of Character', evoke 'Fragments of Personal Experience' or air 'Social Grievances'. Representative cases are 'Pray Employ Major Namby' (a cry from the heart of a single lady besieged by a noisy military neighbour), 'Laid Up in Lodgings' (an autobiographical account of encounters with female servants in Paris and London) and 'A Petition to the Novel Writers' (an elderly gentleman's complaint against the man-hating heroines of contemporary fiction). Though the form of the comic monologue clearly owes something to Boz, Collins had made earlier experiments with 'The New Dragon of Wantley' (*Leader*, 20 December 1851) and 'Passage in the Life of Perugino Potts' (*Bentley's Miscellany*, February 1852). The former is a recently identified anecdote narrated by an eccentric amateur naturalist in a rural parish, where the inhabitants have been terrorised by his escaped reptile. However, the butt of the humour is less the mediaeval fears of the villagers than the modernising obsession of the

---

[26] For a more detailed analysis of Collins's relations with the *Leader*, see Graham Law and Andrew Maunder, *Wilkie Collins: A Literary Life*. Basingstoke: Palgrave, 2008, pp. 49–52.

narrator, so that the story comes close to parodying the radical earnestness of the *Leader* in its call 'for an immediate supply of Missionaries of the Brotherhood of Common Sense to convert Stoke Muddleton'.[27]

A further point concerning Collins's role in Dickens's weeklies is that there is little evidence of tensions with editorial policy. The only Collins piece to be rejected by Dickens seems to have been the melodramatic tale 'Mad Monkton' in 1853, because its theme of hereditary insanity had the potential to offend 'those numerous families in which there is such a taint'. At the same time, Dickens let Collins know that there were 'many things, both in the inventive and descriptive way, that he could do for us if he would like to work in our direction'.[28] The audience imagined throughout Collins's articles seems consistent with the paper's 'known' readership as evoked in 'The Unknown Public'. The social grievances which obsess Collins's comic monologists are also a far cry from the democratic reforms demanded in the People's Charter of 1838.[29] A typical example is 'Strike!', a piece from February 1858 never reprinted by the author. Speaking for and to 'Englishmen of the middle classes', the narrator complains that, while they have fought hard for 'the promotion of religious and political reforms', they put up too easily with social grievances.[30] Beginning with an anecdote about how the residents of a small English town combined to defeat the exorbitance of a monopolistic fishmonger, he demands similar actions to have communication cords installed in trains, to improve the comfort of both the London omnibus and the London theatre and to reduce the costs of private education. Given the frequency with which these calls are repeated in Dickens's papers by both Collins and others, it is clear that the irony works with rather than against the speaker.

Overall, we must conclude that investment in the genre of the comic monologue in Collins's early articles tends to work against concerted participation in projects of political change. This is especially noticeable in comparison with the tone of Collins's later journalism. While it is true that the author contributed relatively few articles to periodicals after the mid-1860s, and of those several take the amiable form of personal recollections (e.g. 'Reminiscences of a Story Teller' in the *Universal Review* of June 1888), there are also a number of pieces on the rights of authors

---

[27] [Wilkie Collins], 'The New Dragon of Wantley', *Leader* (20 December 1851), 1213–14 (1214); on the identification of the narrative, see Wilkie Collins, *'The New Dragon of Wantley': A Lost Tale*, ed. Graham Law. London: Wilkie Collins Society, 2007, pp. 1–12.

[28] To W. H. Wills, 8 February 1853, *Letters of Charles Dickens*, Vol. 7, p. 23.

[29] See Malcolm Chase, *Chartism: A New History*. Manchester University Press, 2007.

[30] [Wilkie Collins], 'Strike!', *Household Words* (6 February 1858), 169–72, 169.

in which the humour is more bitter. Notable here are 'A National Wrong' (with James Payn in *Chambers' Journal*, 12 February 1870) and 'Considerations on the Copyright Question' (in the New York *International Review*, June 1880), a pair of aggressive attacks on the 'piracy' of American publishers in the absence of relevant international copyright agreements.

Shorter Fiction

More than fifty works of shorter fiction by Collins published during his lifetime have now been identified, from the recently recovered 'Volpurno' from mid-1843,[31] to 'The First Officer's Confession' from late 1887. Almost all were issued first in periodicals of one kind or another, with the majority appearing during the 1850s and 1860s in Dickens's family miscellanies, while more than a dozen remained uncollected at the author's death, including the examples just mentioned. Short tales were not uncommon in the mid-Victorian period, especially in periodicals aimed at a family audience, where they served as filler between the runs of full-length serial novels, though they were given pride of place in the special numbers and annuals that flourished at Christmas. Such stories typically mimicked a traditional mode of oral delivery with narrator and audience both personalised, combining a gothic fear of the uncanny with the consolations of hearth and home. With more than twenty tales issued around the winter holiday season, and even more dealing with the uncanny, Collins's output of shorter fiction certainly follows these general trends.

Though none of his earliest tales is associated with the Christmas season, many are in the gothic vein. 'The Twin Sisters', appearing in *Bentley's Miscellany* in March 1851, remained among the stories uncollected during the author's lifetime. Though untypical in its contemporary setting and third-person narration, it announces one of Collins's most consistent gothic themes, that of the *doppelgänger* or double, represented here by the wrong identical twin to whom the hero at first proposes. As Catherine Peters notes, Collins prefigures Stevenson in using 'the double in investigations of the shadow-self: the underside of a personality which compensates for inadequacies in the external persona, or, suppressed or denied full expression, takes revenge in unexpected ways'.[32] Another example is

---

[31] See Daniel Hacks, 'Volpurno – or the Student: A Forgotten Tale of Madness by Wilkie Collins', *Times Literary Supplement* (2 January 2009), 14–15.
[32] Peters, *King of Inventors*, p. 92.

'The Siege of the Black Cottage', first issued in February 1857 in New York in *Harper's New Monthly Magazine*. This is the short, dramatic story of the bravery of a poor stonemason's daughter, narrated by the woman herself. The main events take place when the teenage Bessie is left alone at night in an isolated cottage, and acts with unexpected courage and ingenuity to protect a large sum of money, left in her care by a wealthy neighbour, from a violent gang of ruffians. But there is also a frame narrative, where the adult Bessie, now married to a rich gentlemen-farmer, explains to a young visitor how her social advancement came about as an indirect reward for her energetic performance under siege. The tale's questioning of conventionally assigned class and gender roles is thus distinctly circumscribed.

Another group is composed of narratives taking the form of fiction but constructed from historical materials, for which it is tempting to employ the anachronistic terms 'faction' or 'infotainment'. Under the heading 'Cases Worth Looking At', *My Miscellanies* includes three such tales, of which the author comments: 'while the facts of each narrative exist in print, the form in which the narrative is cast is of my own devising.'[33] Each derives from pre-revolutionary French court records and was initially published by Dickens in his weekly papers, with 'Memoirs of an Adopted Son' perhaps the best. Near the end of his life, Collins was to repeat the experiment with three anecdotes illustrating miscarriages of justice entitled 'The Victims of Circumstances'. These were commissioned in late 1884 by the Boston juvenile paper *Youth's Companion*, though only published intermittently in 1886–7.[34]

The special Christmas numbers of Dickens's weekly miscellanies, generally devoted to a group of tales, appeared consecutively from 1851 to 1867. In the first couple of years, there was no unifying theme other than Yuletide itself, but thereafter Dickens worked to construct a specific narrative device as a frame on each occasion. Collins appeared in nine in all, each with a strong conceptual framework, including eight consecutively from 1854–61, and in two cases – *The Perils of Certain English Prisoners* (1857) and *No Thoroughfare* (1867) – the work was co-authored by Dickens and Collins alone.[35] In *A House to Let* (1858), to which Elizabeth Gaskell contributed her widely anthologised 'Manchester Marriage', Collins not only worked with Dickens to compose the dénouement, 'Let at Last', but

---

[33] Wilkie Collins, *My Miscellanies*, 2 vols. London: Sampson Law, 1863, Vol. 2, p. 1.
[34] See Wilkie Collins, *The Victims of Circumstances*, ed. Graham Law. London: Wilkie Collins Society, 2002, pp. 1–6.
[35] Collaboration between the two authors is analysed in Lillian Nayder, *Unequal Partners*. New York: Cornell University Press, 2002.

his two sole contributions, 'Over the Way' and 'Trottle's Report', with their focus on the loss and restoration of the young boy, not only reinforce Dickens's chosen theme of the gift of the Christ child but are so committed to the narrative frame that they can hardly stand as independent tales.

The influence of Dickens's method of interlinking tales is readily apparent in Collins's early collections of short fiction. Composed of five stories from *Household Words* plus one new composition ('The Lady of Glenwith Grange', also centred on relations between sisters), the first is constructed as by the wife of a travelling portrait-painter from tales told by her husband's sitters, but it also declares its gothic leanings in its title, *After Dark* (1856). The second, *The Queen of Hearts* (1859), makes use of the Scheherazade-like conceit of an elderly lawyer spinning stories with his two brothers to detain his beautiful young ward, so that his absent son will have time to return from the Crimean War to claim her heart. Among the ten reprinted tales were 'Mad Monkton' and 'The Black Cottage', though in the latter case the original frame of Bessie's address to the young visitor had to be stripped away. Collins was outraged when the *Athenaeum* reviewer dismissed his latest volumes as merely a reprint from *Household Words*, stoutly defending the new narrative framework which took up nearly a fifth of the allotted pages: 'If the critic in question will be so obliging as to open the book, he may make acquaintance with three stories ... which he has not met with before in Household Words, or in any other English period-ical whatever; and he will, moreover, find the whole collection of stories connected by an entirely new thread of interest.'[36]

After Dickens's death in 1870, in his work for the periodical press Collins devoted a good deal more time to composing serial fiction than complete tales, though the reduced output was even more concentrated on Christmas fare. For twelve consecutive years from 1876 to 1887, Collins faithfully composed a seasonal tale specifically for the popular New York sports and theatre paper *The Spirit of the Times*, with whose editor (Edward Buck) Collins had become intimate during his six-month reading tour of North America from late 1873. These stories, typically lighter in tone and more comic in mood than those for Dickens's Christmas special numbers, not only formed the core of Collins's final collection of shorter fiction *Little Novels* (1888) but had also served as seasonal offerings for a wide range of English periodicals. These included many of the outlets that vied for Collins's later serial novels, including not only middle-class monthly literary miscellanies such as *Temple Bar* and *Belgravia* but also such popular

---

[36] To the editor of the *Athenaeum*, 26 October 1859, *Collected Letters of Wilkie Collins*, Vol. i, p. 181.

weekly venues as the provincial newspaper syndicates operated by
W. F. Tillotson of Bolton; illustrated metropolitan papers including the
Graphic; and even *Bow Bells*, the penny novel journal that succeeded
Reynolds's Miscellany. Nevertheless, these developments can hardly be
interpreted simply as a fulfilment of Collins's 'unparalleled prospect' of
a universal audience with the power to discriminate.[37]

Conclusion

In the end, one struggles to draw a clear line dividing Collins's shorter
contributions to the periodical press into fiction and non-fiction. Rather,
his journalistic preference for dramatisation produces a grey zone between
articles and stories, with pieces such as 'The New Dragon of Wantley' or
'Memoirs of an Adopted Son' especially difficult to position. If it is naive to
take Collins at his word as the 'discoverer' of a new mass audience, it is
nevertheless the case that his work for the periodical press over several
decades played a significant role in establishing and extending a new mode
of personalised journalism. This innovation, wide reaching in its socio-
political consequences, has been described critically by Jürgen Habermas as
an important aspect of the historical transition from a 'culture-debating'
to a 'culture-consuming' public.[38] Though driven ultimately by changes
in the economic foundations of the press as an industry, according to
Habermas this transformation was also marked by the gradual integration
of 'the once separate domains of journalism and literature' and the eventual
abandonment of 'the rigorous distinction between fact and fiction'.[39]

---

[37] Collins, 'The Unknown Public', p. 222.
[38] Jürgen Habermas, *The Structural Transformation of the Public Sphere*, trans. Thomas Burger.
Oxford: Polity Press, 1989, pp. 159–75.
[39] Habermas, *The Structural Formation*, p. 170.

CHAPTER 20

Margaret Oliphant and the Blackwood 'Brand'

Joanne Shattock

Margaret Oliphant's long service to the firm of William Blackwood & Sons, and to *Blackwood's Magazine* in particular, was acknowledged in obituaries and posthumous assessments of her career. Her forty-five-year association with the publishing house was brought into sharp focus in her own mind in 1895 as she read through boxes of the firm's correspondence in preparation for her official history, *Annals of a Publishing House*, which was published after her death in 1897. Reading through letters from the 1850s, she recalled being asked to write an article at very short notice, prompting the reflection: 'I suppose I must have become by this time a sort of general utility woman in the Magazine.'[1] She went on to describe writing her article in the midst of a house removal, on a temporary desk in a dusty room with the carpets rolled up, a picture which nicely conveyed one popular perception of Oliphant, ever industrious, able to write quickly and to order, constantly juggling her professional and domestic commitments.

In this chapter, I argue that Margaret Oliphant was not merely, as she self-deprecatingly presented herself, a willing servant of the magazine, but rather that her reviewing and the writing of articles were as creatively satisfying as her novel writing, and in the eyes of one of the magazine's editors, as important. I want then to examine William Blackwood & Sons' relationship with one of its longest-serving authors in the second half of the nineteenth century.

Reading, Writing and Reviewing

The contract to write reviews and articles was struck in 1854, two years after *Katie Stewart*, Oliphant's first novel for Blackwoods was serialised in *Blackwood's Magazine*. She wrote to John Blackwood, the editor, suggesting

---

[1] Mrs Oliphant, *Annals of a Publishing House. William Blackwood and his Sons. Their Magazine and Friends.* 2 vols. Edinburgh and London: William Blackwood and Sons. 1897, Vol. 2, p. 475.

that she be paid a regular sum in return for which she would supply 'essays and reviews of a lighter sort'. 'Keep your own councils as to these reviews', he advised her. 'I shall let no one know that you are the author. You will feel much more at liberty when writing incog [sic] under the Magazine's broad banner.'[2] Later he wrote: 'Your mind also will be much refreshed by a release from the constant strain of writing original works of fiction.'[3]

The implication of that remark and of Oliphant's request for regular reviewing was that her 'miscellaneous papers', as they both referred to them, would occupy a secondary position in her work schedule, giving relief from the pressures of novel writing. In his obituary forty-three years later, John Blackwood's successor William Blackwood III noted her position 'in the first rank of our domestic novelists' but also pronounced her 'the most accomplished periodical writer of her day'. Periodical writing was, he suggested, 'the medium she loved best'. It was as an essayist and a 'fearless critic' that she attained 'perhaps her highest felicity of style'.[4]

That view was not shared by other obituarists, nor by later reassessments of Oliphant, most notably Henry James's often quoted comment in his obituary that no one had had a 'personal say' so 'publicly and irresponsibly'[5] and Virginia Woolf's depiction of her in *Three Guineas* as a literary drudge who wrote 'innumerable faded articles, reviews, sketches of one kind and another which she contributed to literary papers'.[6] Up to a point Oliphant could be said to have subscribed to Woolf's view of some of her literary production, in her resistance to collecting her articles and reviews into books, a practice in which many of her contemporaries were engaged from the 1870s onwards.[7] In her 'New Books' column for July 1879, she accused Matthew Arnold of 'a total absence of that critical faculty in respect to his own productions which he exercises so unhesitatingly in respect to others' by including some of his book reviews in his *Mixed Essays* (1879). She acknowledged that some literary essays 'of a high order' deserved to be reprinted, some of Arnold's among them, but 'the ordinary level of clever reviews'[8] did

2   Blackwood Papers, National Library of Scotland, MS 30357, letter of 28 November 1854.
3   MS 4106, 28 March [1854]; MS 30357, Blackwood Letterbook, copy of a letter of 26 December 1854.
4   [William Blackwood and J. H. Lobban], 'Mrs Oliphant', *Blackwood's Magazine* 162 (July 1897), 161–4, 162.
5   Henry James, *London Notes* (August 1897), rptd *Notes on Novelists*. London, 1914, pp. 357–60.
6   Virginia Woolf, *Three Guineas*. London: Hogarth Press, 1938, p. 166.
7   See Joanne Shattock, 'The Culture of Criticism', in J. Shattock (ed.), *Cambridge Companion to English Literature 1830–1914*. Cambridge University Press, 2010, pp. 71–90.
8   [M. Oliphant]. 'New Books', *Blackwood's Magazine* 126 (July 1879), 88–107. See *Selected Works of Margaret Oliphant*, ed. Joanne Shattock and Elisabeth Jay, 25 vols. London: Pickering & Chatto, 2011–16. Vol. 3, ed. Valerie Sanders (2011), pp. 192–93. Hereafter *Selected Works*.

not warrant preserving. She went on in later articles to criticise Grant Allen, Andrew Lang and Robert Buchanan for their propensity, as she saw it, for self-important and unnecessary 'book making'.

Oliphant subscribed to Blackwood's view that anonymity was the best policy as regards the magazine, so that the extent of her contributions, apart from the novels and short stories re-published under her name, went unnoticed by the public. At least that was the theory. The *Athenaeum's* obituary of John Blackwood, who died in 1879, gave one of the first indications of her position in the magazine's inner circle, noting that 'Mrs Oliphant, whose ability he encouraged at a time when she was almost unknown in the literary world has also, it is understood, been one of the mainstays of the magazine during the last ten or fifteen years.'[9]

By 1879, this was in fact true. Over the course of fifteen years, she had developed a close working relationship with John Blackwood, which turned into a much valued friendship. As was the case with her more illustrious fellow novelist and Blackwood author George Eliot, Blackwood was not an obvious confidante or mentor, but both came to rely on him and valued his friendship. Blackwood was ten years older than Oliphant, humorous, intelligent but not an intellectual, and very much at home in male company. She by her own admission was excessively shy, in awe of the Blackwood tradition, forthright in her dealings with him but also vulnerable. She became more vulnerable in 1859 when she was suddenly widowed and forced to support her two young children by her writing. Blackwood and his brother Major William Blackwood were sympathetic and generous, offering her books for review, and also work as a translator.[10] She benefited from George Eliot's temporary defection to George Smith's *Cornhill Magazine* in 1862–3 for the serialisation of *Romola*. John Blackwood encouraged her in the writing of her 'Carlingford' novels between 1862 and 1866.[11] He also encouraged her articles and reviews, scrutinising them as he did her fiction, trusting her judgement when it came to contemporary novels, but giving her a steer in regards to a particular argument she might take when she moved into unfamiliar territory, supplying background information and correcting errors as he saw them. He agreed with her that biography was her particular

---

[9] *Athenaeum*, 1 November 1879, 1974.

[10] She translated the Comte de Montalembert's seven-volume *The Monks of the West*, published by Blackwood between 1861 and 1879, although her work was not acknowledged. She reviewed the first two volumes in *Blackwood's Magazine* 89 (June 1861), 665–81.

[11] The series began in *Blackwood's* with her stories 'The Executor' (May 1861), 'The Rector' (September 1861) and 'The Doctor's Family' (October-January 1862). *Salem Chapel* (1863), *The Perpetual Curate* (1864) and *Miss Marjoribanks* (1866), followed, all serialised in the magazine before publication in volume format.

'forte' and encouraged her writing of biographical sketches for the magazine.[12] He sent articles back when he thought them too long or too 'flat', and at other times accepted them gratefully without comment to fill a gap in an issue. When he was particularly pleased with one, he placed it first in a number, a sign of editorial approval.

He used her unashamedly to promote Blackwood books, sending her the unbound sheets of the first two volumes of John Hill Burton's 1867 *History of Scotland* so that her two reviews in the magazine would coincide with the book's publication.[13] He asked her to review the poems of a protégé, David Wingate, a Glasgow miner turned poet. He cajoled her into reviewing the Queen's *Leaves from a Journal of our Life in the Highlands*, and the first volumes of Theodore Martin's biography of Prince Albert (neither of them published by his firm) at a time when she was frantically busy with other projects.[14] As a sign of appreciation, he sent her several brace of grouse from his country estate that summer.

There were other more professionally orientated rewards, including a generous article on 'The Novels of Mrs Oliphant' in June 1873 written by the Reverend W. Lucas Collins, another *Blackwood's* stalwart, and before that a review of her *Life of Edward Irving* (1862) also by Collins.[15] *Blackwood Magazine*'s practice of promoting and publicising the work of its own contributors as well as Blackwood authors would become apparent later in Oliphant's career. John Blackwood also suggested she use her insider status to hit back at William Hepworth Dixon of the *Athenaeum*, whom they both thought had written the one unfavourable review of *The Perpetual Curate* (1864), her second Carlingford novel. He proposed that she should savage his latest book on the Holy Land, and that they would keep her authorship secret.[16] Interestingly, she declined his offer.

There were more direct benefits in a writing life that combined prolific reviewing with the writing of novels, biography and literary histories. That pattern was becoming familiar in the second half of the nineteenth

---

[12] Blackwood to Oliphant MS 30362, 22 March 1867. The most notable of these sketches were her *Historical Sketches of the Reign of George II*, which were initially published in the magazine and re-published in two volumes in 1869. The series was Blackwood's idea, and the only one of her various series in the magazine that he agreed to re-publish in book form.

[13] 'The History of Scotland', *Blackwood's Magazine* 101 (March 1867) 317–38; and 'Elizabeth and Mary', 101 (April 1867), 389–414.

[14] 'David Wingate', *Blackwood's Magazine* 92 (July 1862), 48–61. See *Selected Works*, Vol. 1, ed. Joanne Shattock, pp. 269–89; 'A Royal Idyll', 102 (September 1867), 375–84; 'The Queen of the Highlands', 103 (February 1868), 242–50; *Selected Works*, Vol. 13 (2013), ed. Joanne Shattock, pp. 125–40.

[15] 'Mrs Oliphant's Novels', *Blackwood's Magazine* 113 (June 1873) 722–39; 'The Life of Edward Irving', *Blackwood's Magazine* 91 (June 1862), 737–57.

[16] See *Selected Works*, Vol. 17, *The Perpetual Curate*, ed. Joanne Shattock, pp. xxii–xxiii.

century, making Oliphant a quintessential example of what Linda Peterson has called a Victorian 'woman of letters', a phenomenon which was part of the professionalisation of authorship in the period.[17] Elisabeth Jay in her *Mrs Oliphant: A Fiction to Herself* (1995) suggests that Oliphant's voracious reading and reviewing fuelled her creativity,[18] a point I have explored elsewhere in relation to *The Perpetual Curate*. Reading her reviews of fiction in *Blackwood's* between 1861 and 1863, the period leading up to the novel's composition, it is clear that the novels of the little-known Frederick William Robinson (1830–1901), notably *High Church* (1860), *No Church* (1861) and *Church and Chapel* (1863), all of which she had either read or reviewed, influenced her creation of the church- and chapel-centred community of Carlingford. It is also possible that she adapted a subplot from Wilkie Collins's *No Name* (1862), which she was known to have been reading at the same time she was writing *The Perpetual Curate*.[19]

There were also certain economies in a regime of constant reading and reviewing. Trev Broughton notes how she 'tuned up' for the *Life of Edward Irving* (1862) by writing reviews of religious memoirs and sermons, and also a biographical sketch of Irving for *Blackwood's*.[20] Oliphant followed her practice of writing a preliminary sketch in the magazine with her later biographies of John Tulloch and Laurence Oliphant.[21] Both David Finkelstein and Broughton have noted how a review of the Scottish theologian E. B. Ramsay's *Reminiscences of Scottish Life and Character*, commissioned by Blackwood to tide her over financially in the dark winter of 1860, opened a seam of writing on Scottish nationhood, Scottish culture and the Scottish church.[22]

Moving from Henry Colburn, a metropolitan-based publisher of cheap fiction to William Blackwood & Sons, one of the seven major publishers of

---

[17] See Linda H. Peterson, *Becoming a Woman of Letters. Myths of Authorship and Facts of the Victorian Market.* Princeton University Press, 2009, chap. 1.

[18] Elisabeth Jay, *Mrs Oliphant. A Fiction to Herself. A Literary Life.* Oxford: Clarendon Press, 1995, chap. 7.

[19] See my Introduction to *The Perpetual Curate, Selected Works*, Vol. 17, 2014, pp. xv–xx. The usual comparison made with the Carlingford series is Trollope's Barchester novels.

[20] Trev Broughton, Introduction, *Selected Works*, Vol. 7 (2012), pp. xiii–xciii, xv; 'Edward Irving', *Blackwood's Magazine* 84 (November 1858), 567–86.

[21] 'Principal Tulloch', *Blackwood's Magazine* 139 (April 1886), 415–81, and 'Laurence Oliphant', p. 145 (February 1889). For edited extracts from both full-length biographies, see *Selected Works*, Vol. 8 (2012), ed. David Jasper.

[22] Broughton, Introduction to *Selected Works*, Vol. 7, p. xv; David Finkelstein, '"Long and Intimate Connections": Constructing a Scottish Identity for Blackwood's Magazine', in Laurel Brake, Bill Bell and David Finkelstein (eds.), *Nineteenth-Century Media and the Construction of Identities.* Basingstoke: Palgrave, 2000, pp. 326–38, 327 ff.

fiction in the country,[23] Oliphant knew she had made an advantageous career move. She was also aware that she had received an entrée into the Scottish literary establishment.[24] Whatever insecurity she may have felt at the beginning – she made several references to her femininity in what she observed was the ultra-masculine Blackwood ethos[25] – she bought into that Blackwood ethos, and into the traditions and history of the firm and its magazine. She would add Macmillan, Longman, Smith Elder, Tinsley and others to her list, but Blackwood remained her publisher of choice.

Oliphant's relationship with John Blackwood became more personal as the years went on, cemented initially by their both having young families, and encouraged by his unfeigned belief in her ability. Their letters are full of family news, current politics and gossip as well as the business at hand. She received regular invitations to his country house, Strathtyrum, near St Andrews, and she in turn invited him and his wife to visit her in Windsor during his annual trips to London. Like George Eliot, Oliphant respected his judgement: 'Few better or bolder critics ever existed', she wrote of him in her review of J. W. Cross's *George Eliot's Life* in 1885.[26] He knew how to get the best from her, reacting tolerantly to her bad time keeping and responding practically to her bad handwriting (he routinely had her articles set up in type before reading them). He was generous in his financial dealings with her, quick to praise and not afraid to tell her when her work was not up to standard. She in turn respected his prejudices, which included Carlyle, Browning and John Stuart Mill, tactfully placing reviews and articles on all three elsewhere.[27]

The New Generation

Oliphant's relationship with John Blackwood's successor, his nephew William, was quite different. She had known 'Willie', as he was called by

---

[23] According to J. A. Sutherland, *Victorian Novelists and Publishers*. London: Athlone Press, 1976, pp. 2–5.

[24] She had been introduced to Major William Blackwood, John Blackwood's brother, by David Macbeth Moir, the famous 'Delta' of the early years of *Blackwood's Magazine*, who was a friend of her mother. *The Autobiography of Margaret Oliphant*, Elisabeth Jay (ed.). Oxford University Press, 1990, p. 34.

[25] 'A feminine critic must find but a limited orbit open to her', she wrote to John Blackwood, Blackwood MS 4103, f. 252 [1854]. The following year she commented, 'I am sometimes doubtful whether in your most manly and masculine of magazines a womanish story-teller like myself may not become wearisome.' *Autobiography and Letters of Mrs M.O.W. Oliphant*, Mrs Harry Coghill (ed.). Edinburgh and London: William Blackwood and Sons, 1899, p. 160. Hereafter Coghill.

[26] 'The Life and Letters of George Eliot', *Edinburgh Review* 161 (April 1885), 514–53. See *Selected Works*, Vol. 3, ed. Valerie Sanders, 2011, p. 449.

[27] See J. S. Clarke, *Margaret Oliphant: Non-Fictional Writings. A Bibliography*. Victorian Fiction Research Guide 26. St Lucia: University of Queensland, 1997.

his family and close colleagues, since 1857, when he acted as an assistant to his uncle and his father, Major William Blackwood. Even after he was made a partner following his father's death in 1861, he was in her eyes the junior partner. She negotiated the change at the top with varying strata-gems, alternately seeking to ingratiate herself or subtly emphasising her seniority. She sought to bolster his confidence by commenting positively on the latest number of the magazine or by repeating the good reports of it she had heard or read elsewhere. She addressed her letters to 'Mr Blackwood', and she made a fuss about his health – he was a bachelor and prone to sporting injuries.

William Blackwood was respectful and cautious in his dealings with her, relying on the advice of Joseph Langford, the London office manager, on her articles as on most editorial matters in the early years of his editorship. He used his uncle's tactic of hospitality to advance their relationship, inviting her and her elder son for a weekend at his family home in Colinton. He occasionally resorted to flattery. He had spent his apprentice years in the firm chasing up her late proofs and her eleventh-hour serial instalments; while recognising her seniority, he was not always fully appreciative of her talents. But like his uncle, he was sympathetic to her financial problems. Also like John Blackwood, he enlisted her reviewing skills to promote the Blackwood brand. He persuaded her to place a review of T. P. Chesney's *The Private Secretary*, serialised in *Blackwood's* in 1880–1 in John Morley's *Pall Mall Gazette*, an episode that seems to have soured her relationship with Morley. He asked her to review John Hill Burton's *A History of the Reign of Queen Anne* (1880) in the magazine so as to follow on the heels of its publication.[28]

In return for these favours, Blackwood asked John Skelton, another regular reviewer, to write an appreciation of her *Literary History of England* (1882), published by Macmillan. Skelton's article, 'A Little Chat about Mrs Oliphant in a Letter from an Island' (January 1883) was a whimsical and at times self-indulgent tribute, celebrating her 'unwearied and facile pen' that had been at work for more than thirty years, and the versatility and fertility of her intellect. He did not suppose, he went on, that 'Mrs Oliphant is one of the writers who consciously entertain or profess, what is called in the jargon of the day, "high views of the literary *calling*"', but it could be said of her that she had 'never written a page which she would wish unwritten, and which is not perfectly sweet and clean and wholesome'. He disagreed with some of her views of individual writers in her history but concluded that it

---

[28] 'The Reign of Queen Anne', *Blackwood's Magazine* 127 (February 1880), 139–62.

contained 'admirable criticism as well as sound sense and true feeling' and would stand up well when compared with the work of 'the magnificent young lions of the London press', who were inclined to patronise her by inferring that her work was really very fair 'for a woman'.[29] Oliphant, unsurprisingly, was not pleased by the article.

Her relationship with William Blackwood in contrast to her equable relationship with John Blackwood was tested on a number of occasions. One involved a row over a second edition of her biography of Tulloch. Another was a sharp exchange about her column 'The Old Saloon', which ran in *Blackwood's* between January 1887 and December 1892. The latter altercation turned on whose authority was paramount, the author's or the editor's, and was triggered by Blackwood's irritation over what he interpreted as her promotion of her protégés in the column. Oliphant could have responded that she had learned the art of puffing from a good teacher but refrained. She did, though, raise the issue of intellectual property and editorial control:

> In respect to the tone of your letter you must permit me to say that though I have done much work for the Magazine and received pay for it yet we do not stand exactly in the relation of Master and servant and that it has never been one of the rights of an editor to rate a contributor as he might do a shopman – the Saloon in George Street is unquestionably yours – but the Old Saloon as a sort of criticism was not invented or thought of by you but by me. You did not make and cannot own it nor is it any necessary part of Maga, any more than Ambrose's Tavern was.[30]

Her reference to Ambrose's Tavern, the location of the *Noctes Ambrosianae*, the celebrated series of imaginary conversations that ran in *Blackwood's Magazine* between 1822 and 1835 was proleptic. She would soon become immersed in the early years of William Blackwood & Sons and the founding of their famous magazine. For the moment, the editor and his increasingly assertive contributor agreed to differ and she resumed her work for the magazine.

Writing the History of the House of Blackwood

Blackwood's proposal in August 1894 that she should write the history of the House of Blackwood was a spur of the moment proposition, prompted

[29] [John Skelton], 'A Little Chat about Mrs Oliphant in a letter from an Island', *Blackwood's Magazine* 133 (January 1883) 73–91. See 73, 76, 81, 82, 88.
[30] Blackwood MS 4592, 9 November [1892].

in part by yet another request for regular employment as opposed to the hand-to-mouth existence offered by reviewing. His uncle had once thought of the project, he explained, and he now saw his way to implement it. He proposed an annual fee of 500 pounds for each year she spent on the project. She responded immediately, professing enthusiasm, and declaring, somewhat disingenuously, that it was 'the kind of work I prefer to any other'.[31] She estimated that the book would take two years.

The death of her last surviving child Francis or 'Cecco' in October of that year plunged her into despair, for which the writing of the history proved to be a lifeline. 'I can think of nothing better, if I must go on with this weary life so long, as to conclude everything with this book', she wrote to Blackwood in the midst of her grief.[32] That too was proleptic. The research began in January 1895. She found the task of reading through boxes of letters and documents, which were given a preliminary sorting in the Edinburgh office, alternately tedious and fascinating. Having begun as an act of homage on both their parts to the firm they had served for so long, Blackwood and Oliphant found themselves in a dispute with Mary Porter, John Blackwood's daughter, who had conceived the idea of writing a memoir of her father. David Finkelstein has described the battle which ensued, which had its origins in the uneasy relations between John Blackwood's widow and the rest of the Blackwood family.[33] The negotiations with Mary Porter, who had collected many of her father's letters, had the beneficial effect of uniting Oliphant and Blackwood, both now determined to prevent a competing memoir by an inexperienced and partisan family member. In the end, Oliphant's failing health determined the outcome. She completed the first two volumes of the history, which took the story up to 1861 with the death of Major William Blackwood, shortly before her death in June 1897. They were published the same year. Mary Porter completed the third volume, with the subtitle *John Blackwood*, in 1898.

Blackwood and Sons' Farewell to Mrs Oliphant

The first volume of *Annals of a Publishing House: William Blackwood and his Sons: Their Magazine and Friends* contained the inscription: 'I dedicate these volumes to the memory of my old and valued friend, Mrs Oliphant.

[31] Letter of 26 August [1894], reprinted in Coghill p. 405.
[32] Letter of 3 November [1894], reprinted in Coghill, p. 414.
[33] See David Finkelstein, *The House of Blackwood. Author Publisher Relations in the Victorian Era.* Pennsylvania State University Press, 2002, chap. 6, pp. 113–28.

[signed] William Blackwood.' In his 'Prefatory Note', he presented the *Annals* as a fitting culmination of Oliphant's forty-five-year association with the firm:

> A few years ago, when I was talking with Mrs Oliphant over some new outlet for her ceaseless literary activity, the happy thought struck me of asking her to carry out my uncle's idea and to become the historian of the firm in whose service she was already an honoured veteran. For forty years she had worked incessantly for the 'Magazine', intimate with its history, thoroughly imbued with all its traditions, and very loyal to its past. Mrs Oliphant eagerly accepted the trust, entered into its fulfilment with even more than her wonted enthusiasm, and, with a pathetic prescience of what was to come, regarded the work as a fitting completion of her long and strenuous literary life.[34]

More significantly, he utilised the coincidence of her death with the completion of the first two volumes of the *Annals* to maximise publicity for the firm and to give Oliphant an impressive send off. The firm took the obituaries of its major authors and the choice of obituarist seriously.[35] William Blackwood III contributed to only two in his first twenty-one years as editor. One was a fourteen-page memoir of George Eliot, which was largely written by his assistant Alexander Allardyce; the other was of Oliphant. His co-author for that was J. H. Lobban, a recent recruit to the Blackwood staff, who would become assistant to the next editor. It was unlikely that he knew Oliphant well. The obituary was followed in September 1897 by an article on 'Mrs Oliphant as a Novelist' by J. H. Millar, an Edinburgh lawyer who had been a *Blackwood's* contributor for only eighteen months. In December 1897, a review of the *Annals*, entitled 'Maga and her Publishers', was written by Lobban and in April 1898, an article 'Mrs Oliphant as a Biographer' by Millar. In February 1899, a double number of the magazine celebrated its 1000th issue. This contained a spoof 'Noctes', co-written by Millar, as a reminder of the celebrated series, and it included a reference to Oliphant. Finally in May 1899, Millar reviewed Oliphant's posthumously published *Autobiography and Letters* (1899), which had been compiled by her cousin and secretary Annie Coghill and published by Blackwood.

---

[34] *Annals*, Vol. 1, p. viii.
[35] Oliphant wrote an obituary of Thackeray which she sent to John Blackwood in 1863. He politely declined it and wrote the magazine's brief tribute himself. William Blackwood refused her offer of an obituary of Carlyle. She was not considered as a possible author for Blackwood's obituary of either George Eliot or Trollope.

It is difficult not to see this as a plan devised in house to publicise the *Annals*, while marking the passing of a long-serving member of the Blackwood team. Capitalising on the Queen's Diamond Jubilee in June 1897 shortly before Oliphant's death, Blackwood and Lobban's unsigned obituary reprised a point made by Skelton in his 1883 article that 'in high and lofty example of perfect womanliness Mrs Oliphant has been to the England of letters what the Queen has been to our society as a whole.'[36] The articles that followed eschewed hyperbole, but they gave Oliphant a good press. Millar's article on her novels singled out the Carlingford series, *The Wizard's Son*, *The Ladies Lindores* and *Kirsteen*, plus early Scottish novels such as *Katie Stewart* and *Passages in the Life of Margaret Maitland*, the beginning of an Oliphant 'canon'.[37] The focus of Millar's article on her biographies (April 1898) was the three major ones, Irving, Tulloch and Laurence Oliphant, but he singled out her short biography of Thomas Chalmers for special praise and ended the article with the *Annals*, which he treated as a biography, complimenting Oliphant on her balance of narrative and correspondence; in other words, he saw it as a Victorian 'Life and Letters'.[38]

Lobban's review of the *Annals* in the December 1897 number ended with a fulsome tribute to Oliphant:

> It is her profound regret that Mrs Oliphant did not live to know that 'Maga' was more than satisfied with the brilliant performance of this final task … we must go back to the days of Wilson and Lockhart and Aytoun for any parallel to the brilliancy and loyalty and unwavering devotion of Margaret Oliphant.[39]

The section on Oliphant in the spoof 'Noctes' followed the general line of praise:

> Mistress Oliphant! Ah, sirs, yon wis a gran' wumman, a fine writer, an' a stench freen' o' the hoose o' Blackwood. Her awnals o' the firm's a fair maisterpiece. No' that I wis a' thegither satisfeed wi' her accoont o' James Hogg. But death clears a' scores, an' sin we forgathered on this side o' the Styx, mony a pleasant hoor hae I passed in her company, an' mony's the

---

[36] 'Mrs Oliphant', *Blackwood's Magazine* 162 (July 1897) 163. Skelton had written: 'The value of such an example [the wholesomeness of Oliphant's writing] is incalculable, – it is to the England of letters what Queen Victoria (might I not add Lord Beaconsfield?) has been to that other England which, in spite of craven counsels and infatuation in high places is still strong and of good courage.' *Blackwood's Magazine* 133 (January 1883), 77.

[37] [J. H. Millar], 'Mrs Oliphant as a Novelist', *Blackwood's Magazine* 162 (September 1897), 305–19.

[38] [J.H. Millar], 'Mrs Oliphant as a Biographer', *Blackwood's Magazine* 163 (April 1898), 501–12.

[39] [J. H. Lobban], 'Maga and her Publishers', *Blackwood's Magazine* 162 (December 1897), 860–72, 872.

time I had thocht hoo muckle better oor Scots writers o'novelles an'
romances micht dae gin they wad condeshend to tak' a gude few leaves
oot o' *her* byuck.[40]

There was one final tribute: the review of Oliphant's posthumously
published *Autobiography and Letters* by J. H. Millar in May 1899. Linda
Peterson's edition of that text provides some revealing insights into the
behind-the-scenes rumblings that preceded its publication.[41] The review,
by someone who had not known her long, but who no doubt had heard
much about her, was affectionate and knowledgeable. It had one muted
point of criticism. On her propensity always to be 'behindhand' with her
finances, constantly working off her debts to her publishers who acted as
her bankers, Millar made the point that in no other calling would she have
been as fortunate: 'We know of no other "profession" other than letters in
which remuneration can be anticipated to the same amount and on the
same terms.'[42] It might have been William Blackwood III speaking.

It is difficult not to see the trajectory of Oliphant's career as aligned with
the fate of the House of Blackwood and its famous magazine, joining them
as she did at mid-century when the firm was at the height of its prestige and
the magazine was still a nationally significant monthly, and following both
into a gradual decline from the late 1870s, as the firm failed to keep abreast
of new developments in publishing, and the magazine was overtaken first
by rival metropolitan 'shilling' monthlies and then by new weeklies and the
New Journalism. The 'general utility woman' did well by her association
with *Blackwood's Magazine*. Amidst the self-congratulation and the celebration of *'Maga's'* place in the cultural history of the nineteenth century,
William Blackwood & Sons, in the person of William Blackwood III, for
the moment forgot their differences and seemed genuinely to show its
appreciation.

---

[40] [J. H. Millar and G. S. Street], 'Noctes Ambrosianae No. LXXII', *Blackwood's Magazine* 165
(February 1899), 167–92, 190.
[41] Linda H. Peterson, 'Introduction', *The Autobiography of Mrs M.O.W. Oliphant, Selected Works of
Margaret Oliphant*, Vol. 6. London: Pickering & Chatto, 2012, pp. xi–xxiv.
[42] [J. H. Millar], 'The Record of a Life', *Blackwood's Magazine* 165 (May 1899), 895–904, 901.

CHAPTER 21

Marian Evans the Reviewer

Fionnuala Dillane

Marian Evans's stepson and executor of her estate, Charles Lee Lewes, introduced George Eliot's posthumously published collection of periodical writings *Essays and Leaves from a Notebook* (1884)[1] with a series of disclaimers that reinforce impressions of the novelist's ambivalence about her journalism, impressions given weight not least by Evans's own negative statements in her letters about the debased state of the medium with its 'hodge-podge of conceited incompetence, hackneyed phrases, unscrupulous praise and unscrupulous blame'.[2] In his preface, Lewes explains that requests from her readers 'that articles known to have been written by George Eliot in the *Westminster Review* before she had become famous under that pseudonym, should be republished' persuaded the writer to put together a revised selection of such work before her death. The 'wishes' of her readers are 'now gratified' Lewes observes, adding a cautionary clause, 'as far, at any rate as it is possible to gratify them. For it was not George Eliot's desire that the whole of those articles should be rescued from oblivion.'[3] This authorised edition of her journalism contained seven articles from her 'fugitive writings' that she considered 'deserving of a permanent form', the running order was specified, some pieces were revised and the manuscript was accompanied by a 'written injunction that no other pieces written by her, of date prior to 1857, should be republished'.[4]

---

[1] *Essays and Leaves from a Notebook*, Vol. 21, with a Preface by Charles Lee Lewes in *The Works of George Eliot*. London: Blackwood and Sons, 1884. The volume also included the previously unpublished series of 'working notes' including 'Notes on Form in Art', written in 1868, perhaps a more overt statement of a literary aesthetic than anything found in her published journalism.

[2] See, for example, *George Eliot Letters*, 9 vols., Gordon S. Haight (ed.). New Haven: Yale University Press, 1954–78, henceforth, *GEL*, Vol. 8, p. 437. See also, Vol. 2, p. 305; Vol. 3, pp. 148, 302; Vol. 4, p. 197.

[3] Lewes, Preface, *The Works of George Eliot*, p. v.

[4] Lewes, Preface, *The Works of George Eliot*, p. v.

With this explicit burial of most of her so-called fugitive writings and the expressed sanction against making such work part of the legacy of George Eliot, considerations of which were so pressing during George Henry Lewes's final illness and in the aftermath of his death in 1878, Evans was carefully cultivating a particularised image of the writer and the writing life, a lifelong practice once her fiction brought her to public attention. From the success of her early stories published first anonymously and then pseudonymously,[5] Evans persistently and quite effectively controlled information about her biography, her unconventional private life and the circulation of her image always striving to ensure a definite distance was maintained between the literary persona 'George Eliot' and the writer Marian Evans.[6] After her death, it was impossible for even the devoted Charles Lee Lewes to sustain that bifurcation: the first unauthorised edition of her journalism appeared in New York in 1883 amidst a range of biographical and critical studies, negative and positive personal reminiscences, as well as images of her various homes in the increasingly celebrity-driven periodical press that then, as now, sought to cultivate a sense of intimacy between readers and their idols, a type of intimacy inimical in so many ways to the critical detachment cultivated in so much of Evans's journalism.[7]

In 1919, George Redway reproduced Evans's hitherto unknown earliest writings emphasising their role in helping establish a natural history of 'George Eliot': while acknowledging most authors understandably may wish the early 'scaffolding' for later masterpieces should remain unseen, 'the student of literature . . . has other views', he observes, and a justifiable interest in tracing the 'development of literary power'.[8] It was eighty-three

---

[5] Her clerical stories appeared anonymously in *Blackwood's Edinburgh Magazine* in 1857; they were republished in volume format as *Scenes of Clerical Life* in 1858 under the pseudonym 'George Eliot'.

[6] On the success of Evans's cultivation of a separate literary persona, see, for example, K. K. Collins, 'Introduction', in K. K. Collins (ed.), *George Eliot: Interviews and Recollections*. Palgrave Macmillan, 2010, p. xvi. Collins notes that extensive searching has revealed no printed sources before 1870 specifically linking George Eliot to 'Marian Evans'; see K. K. Collins, *Identifying the Remains, George Eliot's Death in the London Religious Press*. Victoria, BC: ELS Editions, 2006, p. 79, n.3.

[7] The unsigned preface to this collection complied by Nathan Sheppard cites a newspaper articulating the general sentiment that George Eliot's 'series of striking essays ought to be collected and reprinted, both because of substantive worth and because of the light they throw on the author's literary canons and predilections'. See *The Essays of George Eliot*, Complete. Collected and Arranged with an Introduction on her 'Analysis of Motives' by Nathan Sheppard. New York: Funk and Wagnalls, 1883. Far from 'complete', as this edition erroneously claimed, it only includes material from the *Westminster Review, Fortnightly Review* and *Blackwood's Edinburgh Magazine* (p. 5).

[8] George Redway, ed., *Early Essays of George Eliot*. Westminster, 1919, p. 7. The short volume reprints the five pieces that comprise the 'Poetry and Prose from the notebook of an Eccentric' published in the *Coventry Herald and Observer* in 1846 and 1847.

years after her death before anything approaching a comprehensive (though still not complete) edition of Evans's journalism appeared to feed that interest further. In his introduction to that still invaluable collection, Thomas Pinney, its editor, drew attention to the 1884 volume, complaining that it 'gives a very imperfect idea of the extent and variety of her periodical writings.'[9] Despite Pinney's reservations, I suggest that it is worth returning to Evans's own edition to see what this carefully authorised version of the writer as journalist constructed in her later life might tell us about that career in its own terms rather than covering again the well-worn ground that parses the journalism for its signposts to the work of the novelist.

Most obviously, *Essays and Leaves from a Notebook* is a partial selection: her journalism is represented by a mere seven articles from more than ten times that number of essays and reviews identified to date as written by Marian Evans. She eschews all of her work in the *Leader, Saturday Review* and *Pall Mall Gazette* in favour of the longer periodical writings, a pattern repeated by many of her critics since, who emphasise, sometimes exclusively, her handful of *Westminster* essays only. She consigns to oblivion the shorter pieces for the weeklies and dailies, smacking too much of the ephemeral, it is presumed, for the long dureé of legacy but which are amongst her liveliest and most diverse in terms of subject matter and style, ranging from a barrister-like attack on the madcap writer of a pamphlet suggesting that the novels of Walter Scott were in fact written by Scott's brother and sister-in-law, to a moving consideration of the intractable conflict of equally legitimate but opposing claims at the heart of Sophocles' *Antigone* (and, by inference, all tragedy).[10]

But despite these omissions, Evans's selection still gestures towards the range and variety of her journalism so often overlooked. She includes work from four periodicals – the quarterly *Westminster Review*, monthlies *Fraser's Magazine* and *Blackwood's Edinburgh Magazine* and the bi-monthly *Fortnightly Review* – in what could be described broadly as four journalistic sub-genres. There is one chatty and rather informal travel piece that discusses personal experiences of contemporary art, music, food and leisure

---

[9] Thomas Pinney, ed., *Essays of George Eliot*. London: Routledge and Kegan Paul, 1963, p. vii. He added 'even those she chose for reprinting have lost some of their liveliness through revision'. Pinney's edition reproduces the original version of Evans's work, with Evans's revisions, mostly consisting of toned down critique or deleted paragraphs, signalled in the main text via footnotes. The essay 'Three Months in Weimar' is an amalgamation of two essays, 'Three Months in Weimar' and 'Liszt, Wagner and Weimar' published in *Fraser's Magazine* in June and July 1855, respectively.

[10] See 'Who wrote the Waverly novels?' *Leader* (19 April 1856), 375–76 and 'The *Antigone* and its morals', *Leader* (29 March 1856), 306.

activities in Germany. Four of her longer *Westminster* articles are included, representing different periodical essay styles: the 'slashing' articles on the eighteenth-century poet Edward Young ('it would hardly be possible to find a more typical instance than Young's poetry, of the mistake which substitutes interested obedience for sympathetic emotion and baptises egoism as religion') and the popular Evangelical preacher John Cumming (with his 'unscrupulosity of statement . . . argumentative white lies . . . and flagrant unveracity');[11] a mostly paraphrased account on the pioneering work of the German social historian W. H. von Riehl, 'The Natural History of German Life' that includes an extravagantly lively polarisation of city and country inhabitants to amuse her metropolitan readers; and a championing of Heinrich Heine's writings in the much practiced mid-century 'life and works' essay mode.[12] Continuing the variety of forms, she includes a long review from the *Fortnightly* on William Lecky's history of rationalism in Europe where she marshals a trenchant attack on the perceived soft approach to witchcraft and superstition in Lecky's study along with asides on the inadequacies of pitching work down to an audience constructed as passive and unreflecting.[13]

The selection concludes with the layered political polemic that is Felix Holt's 'Address to Working Men', written expressly for her loyal editor John Blackwood in 1868 in response to his repeated requests that 'Felix' should speak again about new realities of the franchise in the wake of the 1867 Reform Act. It is an odd piece: Felix Holt is clearly a fictional character, but there is no explanatory paratextual material acknowledging this fact and in this blankness, it draws attention to the deflecting layers that make it so difficult to be definitive about the politics and personal positioning in Evans's periodical work.[14] It is worth noting that only two

---

[11] Lewes (ed.), *Essays and Leaves from a Notebook*, p. 32 and pp. 129–30.

[12] Rosemary Ashton uses this term to describe George Henry Lewes's 1866 essay on Comte for the *Fortnightly Review* in 1866; see Rosemary Ashton, 'Introduction', in Rosemary Ashton (ed.), *Versatile Victorian: Selected Critical Writings of George Henry Lewes*. Bristol: Bristol Classical Press, 1992, p. 7.

[13] The Lecky article, 'The Influence of Rationalism' along with the 'The Grammar of Ornament', a review of a source book on design written by her friend, the architect Owen Jones, were her only non-anonymous reviews, both published in the first number of the *Fortnightly Review* in 1865. The *Fortnightly*, edited by Lewes had a policy of signed reviews. Evans no doubt contributed these two pieces to help Lewes's venture with the prestige of her name; see *GEL* 4, p. 193.

[14] For Blackwood's conception of this piece, which he requested from Evans having heard Disraeli address an Edinburgh audience in 1867 that included printers who worked for Blackwood, for subsequent correspondence about the shape and purpose of the 'Address', and the decision not to include a framing introduction, see *GEL* 6, pp. 394, 397–406; 414–15, 418. Avrom Fleishman's summary fully captures the layered ambiguities of this puzzling work: 'We are dealing with a fictive statement by a fictional worker, ostensibly to real workers, made by an authoress operating under

articles deal with what might be termed 'literary' writings (the essays on Young and Heine), and even in these, considerable space is given to the life rather than the works.

Her selection, I suggest, gives little sense that she saw her journalism as constituting some type of literary manifesto for the fiction to come, a case that is often made about her periodical writings. However 'edited', this authorised volume offers a fair representation of the career of a writer interested in addressing culture from diverse perspectives, foregrounding concerns that are consistent across all of her journalism. We witness an unwavering promotion of philosophically radical, heterodox positions; regular interventions on questions of theology that contest comfortable pieties and moral frameworks that have been undermined, it is repeatedly asserted, by the indisputable revelations of then current biblical scholarship; and the related advocacy of developmental (and interdependent) theories of science and other cultures of knowledge. Altogether, this body of work sets out an explicitly secularist agenda. Finally, the collection accurately registers her lifelong attention to biography as much as fiction and poetry, and to writings by European (mostly German) as much as by British authors.

It is worth noting too that missing from this selection, along with those lively shorter works noted earlier, is any sense of her contribution to debates about women's writing, though this aspect of her work is central to her non-fiction prose legacy in the late twentieth-century. Debates about gender and literary culture are explicit in the widely anthologised 'Silly novels by lady novelists' (also, by far, her most genuinely and consistently droll article), and unsurprisingly, in shorter pieces on Margaret Fuller and Mary Wollstonecraft. The role of women in the production and promotion of literatures is the main subject matter of her other much-discussed essay, the uneven, though amusing 'Woman in France: Madame de Sablé' (her first long article for the *Westminster*). Less expansive though still pointed claims about authorship and female perspectives feature too in a range of less-well-known reviews of mid-century women novelists and poets, including Harriet Beecher Stowe, Geraldine Jewsbury and Elizabeth Barrett Browning.[15]

---

a double pseudonym and actually addressing people of a quite different class', see Avrom Fleishman, *George Eliot's Intellectual Life*. Cambridge University Press, 2010, p. 156.

[15] See for instance, 'Woman in France: Madame de Sable', *Westminster Review* (October 1854), pp. 448–73; 'Silly Novels by Lady Novelists', *Westminster Review* (October 1856), pp. 442–61; 'Margaret Fuller and Mary Wollstonecraft', *Leader* (13 October 1855), 988–89, all reprinted in A. S. Byatt and Nicholas Warren, eds., *George Eliot: Selected Essays, Poems and Other Writings*. London: Penguin, 1989.

But as any survey of the range of critical and biographical material on this much studied novelist demonstrates, we each find our own 'George Eliot' in Evans's journalistic *oeuvre*, just as she did: the literary critic, the humanist, the feminist, the conservative, the radical, the meliorist, the realist, the nationalist, the cosmopolitan, the atheist, the sceptic, the believer, the humourist, the scientist, the sympathetic sage and the harsh satirist are all there amongst the various speaking positions she occupied writing in different styles for a range of different journals. I do not mean to imply that she simply ventriloquised editorial positions or gratified different audiences by telling them what they wanted to hear or that there is no Marian Evans in the various purposefully shaped publications of this anonymous periodical journalist. Rather, given that she was a canny and adaptable professional as well as an evolving, restless thinker, a self-made intellectual and experimental writer, I suggest that she was well suited to the dynamic and differentiated platforms offered by the periodical press, that such platforms allowed for the possibility 'to write out of one's own varying unfolding self'.[16]

The various distinct phases of her journalistic career give just one sense of that 'varying unfolding self'. Her first journalism, 'Poetry and Prose from the Notebook of an Eccentric', a series of loosely connected sketches, was published between December 1846 and February 1847 in the broadsheet owned by her friend, ribbon manufacturer, radical and occasional man of letters Charles Bray, who played a significant role in ushering the writer into print.[17] Through Bray, she also met John Chapman, radical publisher and future owner of the *Westminster Review*. Chapman had already published her translation of Strauss's *Life of Jesus* (1846) and was instrumental in paving the way for Evans's move from Coventry to London and to her new life as a full-time journalist. This initial testing

[16] George Eliot to Sara Hennell, 14 July 1862, in a letter about her ambitions with *Romola* to move beyond the sort of pastoral realist fiction that had made her such a popular novelist only five years into her fiction-writing career; see *GEL* 4, p. 49. On her constant re-inventions of her personae across all of her writings, see Rosemarie Bodenheimer, *The Real Life of Mary Ann Evans: George Eliot, Her Letters and Her Fiction*. Ithaca: Cornell University Press, 1994.

[17] Given the focus in this volume on journalism, I will not address either the fiction or the poetry Evans published first in the periodical press. For details of that periodical poetry, see Antoine Gerard van den Broek, ed., *The Complete Shorter Poetry of George Eliot*, 2 vols. London: Pickering and Chatto, 2005. For suggestive models that consider the significance of the implications for poetry publication in the periodical press, see Kathryn Ledbetter, *Tennyson and Victorian Periodicals: Commodities in Contex*. Aldershot: Ashgate, 2007. On Evans's periodical fiction, see Carol Martin, *George Eliot's Serial Fiction*. Columbus: Ohio State University Press, 1994; Fionnuala Dillane, *Marian Evans and the Periodical Press*. Cambridge University Press, 2013; and Kathleen McCormack, 'George Eliot's First Fiction: Targeting *Blackwood's*', *The Bibliotheck*, 21 (1996), 69–80.

of journalistic modes includes reviews of works on church history in France in the *Coventry Herald and Observer* in 1849 and her first metropolitan publications: a review of Greg's *Creed of Christendom* in the *Leader* in 1851 (the liberal socialist newspaper founded and edited by George Henry Lewes and Thornton Hunt, and of Mackay's *Progress of the Intellect* in the *Westminster* that same year – these two periodicals remained central to her life as a professional journalist.

The next distinctive phase of Evans's career is characterised by her total absorption in the world of metropolitan periodical journalism as (unpaid) co-editor of the *Westminster Review* with Chapman from October 1851 to April 1854. During this time, she wrote very little but accumulated extensive and varied publishing experience, as her letters to *Westminster* contributors and colleagues testify. There is a clear sense of her awareness of how to shape material to suit specific audiences; how to calibrate the relationship between entertainment and instruction in any given article; and, not least, how to get work done to immoveable deadlines. While Chapman busied himself with other aspects of his precarious publishing business, Evans took a direct role in the day-to-day running of the periodical in its early years, helping successfully reshape its material format, intellectual reach and public standing.[18]

Her letters give a lively sense of her confident assertion of what was required of effective periodical journalism, replete as they are with opinions on the style and substance of work by the *Westminster* contributors she is employing and editing, and on the range and value of material in rival journals. She voices her concern about one writer, for instance, unsure about his alertness to the need for all journalism to entertain and instruct, even in the weighty *Westminster*: 'the greatest danger with respect to him would be the tendency occasionally rather to exhibit his own information than to instruct the reader and so produce a striking article, instead of a popular and useful one.'[19]

She quit her unpaid editorial role at the *Westminster* in 1854 for a range of intersecting reasons: her business relationship with Chapman had become increasingly fractious; she needed to earn more money to help support her recently widowed sister; and, most significantly, she had already made the decision to spend her life with Lewes, one of the reasons, we presume, she left her home (and workplace) at 142 Strand to find her own lodgings

---

[18] See, for example *Athenaeum* No. 1276 (10 April 1852), 413, where the Contemporary Literature section is singled out as a specific selling point of the *Review* and *Leader*, 3 (10 January 1852), 37–38.

[19] *GEL* 8, p. 55.

in October 1853. She needed to find new ways of making a living. Evans travelled to Germany with Lewes in July 1854, returning in March the following year and, during this time, apparently resolved to supplement her annual stipend from her father's legacy (approximately £90) by the most obvious and practical means available to an highly educated woman, with a number of years of experience in metropolitan journalism who would now be a social outcast because of her unconventional personal relationship.

From the second half of 1854 until January 1857, Evans worked full time as an anonymous freelance journalist writing predominantly for the *Leader* (more than thirty articles are acknowledged) and the *Westminster Review*.[20] This work registers in particular the influence of her immersion in European culture reinforced no doubt by her extended stay in Germany.[21] More than two-thirds of her entire journalistic output appeared between July 1855 and January 1857. It is unsurprising, given the volume of material covered and the speed with which the writing must have been executed, that Evans was queasy about the re-publication of such writings. Stylistically, however, she was at her most inventive: she began to develop a more pliable and mercurial reviewing voice, ventriloquising male and female positions, often within the same review.

She opens her first essay that explicitly addresses the role of women in literary culture, 'Woman in France,' with the famously brazen character-isation of women who unsuccessfully ape intellectual men: 'when not feeble imitation, they are usually absurd exaggeration of the masculine style, like the swaggering gait of a bad actress in male attire.'[22] Her filling in for Lewes's lively and distinctive 'Vivian' persona in the *Leader* in 1854 offers her own version of this dressing up[23] and so convincing are her 'performances' at times, that one writer, bruised by a negative review written by Evans in the *Westminster*, directed her response to her critic in terms that made it clear that she thought the *Westminster*'s 'Belles Lettres'

---

[20] Her translation of Feuerbach's *The Essence of Christianity* was published by Chapman in 1854. Kerry McSweeney provides a compact summary of the influence of Feuerbach's thinking on Evans and in particular on her reviews in his *George Eliot (Marian Evans): A Literary Life*. London: Macmillan, 1991. See especially pp. 32–40. She also worked on a translation of Spinoza's *Ethics* during this time, and though it was completed in 1856, it was not published until 1981.

[21] On this period of Evans's life, see Gerlinde Röder-Bolton, *George Eliot in Germany, 1854–55, 'Cherished Memories'*. Aldershot. Ashgate, 2006.

[22] 'Woman in France', in Byatt and Warren, *Selected Essays*, p. 8.

[23] See, for instance, the exaggeratedly self-reflecting opening to 'The Romantic School of Music', *Leader* (October 1854), 1027–28, which for the most part is merely a rehearsal of Liszt's criticism of Meyerbeer.

reviewer was Lewes.[24] She stopped review work to devote her energies to the less precarious business of fiction writing in January 1857, but there was a brief return to periodical publication when as the established writer George Eliot, she adopted a range of different and intriguing personae, sometimes gendered distinctly male, sometimes distinctly female, in four short pieces in the *Pall Mall Gazette* 1865.[25] These include two 'letters' as 'Saccharissa', her only overt female persona invented for the often very jocular and entertaining 'correspondence' section of the *PMG*. It must have amused her that so authoritative were her interventions on the ongoing debates in the correspondence pages about household finances and women's fashion that included her tongue-in-cheek asides on the dynamics of political economy, a fellow correspondent insisted that letters were clearly written by a man, in drag, as it were.[26]

The main reason why the work of Evans the journalist is considered at all, of course, is the ongoing significance of her novels: as her early editors, Sheppard, Lewes, Redway and Pinney all note, readers want to trace the development (and it is always cast as a development) from Evans's journalism to George Eliot's fiction. This tracing has taken two dominant forms: the first seeks continuities and patterns of coherence between the journalism and the fiction, what Avrom Fleishman, speaking more generally, has called the 'extractive approach', where a position espoused in a piece of literary writing is taken as a direct representation of a writer's views.[27]

---

[24] See Evans's evisceration of the extravagant rhetoric in the pamphlet by the wounded poet in 'Belles Lettres', *Westminster Review* (January 1857), 312–14. On the feminist dynamics of these male personae, see Catherine Sherri Smith, 'George Eliot, Straight Drag and the Masculine Investments of Feminism', *Women's Writing*, 3.2 (1996), 97–111.

[25] As well as her signed work as 'George Eliot' for the *Fortnightly* and Felix Holt's 'Address' that are also part of this final phase of her journalistic career, I would add her 'Leaves from a Notebook' and *Impressions of Theophrastus Such* (1879), not because they appear in periodicals but precisely for their return to some of the personae marshalled in her periodical work and not least for the attack on journalism and the business of reviewing in particular that is everywhere apparent in these writings.

[26] 'Futile Falsehoods' *Pall Mall Gazette* (3 April 1865), pp. 2–3; 'Modern Housekeeping', *Pall Mall Gazette* (13 May 1865), p. 4. See 'Dress', *Pall Mall Gazette* (20 May 1865), p. 3 for the letter that questions the veracity and gender pose of 'Saccharissa'. On the *Pall Mall* work, see Kathleen McCormack, 'The Saccharissa Essays: George Eliot's Only Woman Persona', *Nineteenth-Century Studies* 4 (1990), 41–59; and Bruce Robbins, 'The Butler Did It: On Agency in the Novel', *Representations*, 6 (Spring 1984), - 85–97. On the Lecky review in the *Fortnightly*, see Sarah Nash, 'What's in a Name?: Signature, Criticism, and Authority in the *Fortnightly Review*', *Victorian Periodicals Review* 43.1 (Spring 2010), 57–82, especially 64–66.

[27] See Fleishman, *George Eliot's Intellectual Life*, p. x. Rather than considering the journalism as an aesthetic blueprint or transparent handout for the fiction, Fleishman takes a third way by selecting her most philosophical essays and reviews as indicative of the mind of cultured intellectual working out philosophical positions (p. 11; see also pp. 44–92). Michael Wolff, 'Marian Evans to George Eliot: The Intellectual Foundations of Her Career', Ph.D dissertation, Princeton University, 1958, is a foundational work for this type of philosophical consideration of the journalism. The majority of

The second, conversely, claims a distinct rupture in stylistic and aesthetic terms between the pre- and post-fiction work, a purposeful break in mode, that is, if not necessarily in message.[28] Dallas Liddle, for instance, emphatically rejecting the arguments for a continuity between the rhetorical styles of Evans the journalist and George Eliot the fiction writer, recasts the relationship as confrontational.[29] In this reading, Marian Evans's journalism displays the strained torsions of a wise, moral and sympathetic writer, struggling to articulate her beliefs from within the brutally monologic, restrictive format that is the mid-century periodical review. Her magnanimous moral philosophy, it is argued, is so much more suitably matched to the flexible, expansive polyphony of literary fiction.

A body of more recent work that considers Evans's journalism from a variety of feminist, class, philosophical and biographical perspectives is more attentive to the poly-vocal layering and diversity of genres that are a feature of Victorian periodical journalism more generally and of Evans's writing (as indicated already) more particularly; as such, it overcomes these continuity/rupture models that have long dominated studies of Evans's journalism.[30] As these more recent accounts make clear, Evans's periodical writings compel attention on their own terms as rich, wide-ranging mid-

critical and biographical studies on George Eliot's fiction follow the thematic or formal continuities approach. Of the articles predominantly centred on George Eliot the journalist, Richard Stang, 'The Literary Criticism of George Eliot', *PMLA*, 72 (1957), 952–61 offers the best overview of consistent intellectual and aesthetic theories in both the journalism and the fiction with a judicious and representative sampling of concerns that recur in her periodical work.

[28] See, for instance, Dallas Liddle, *The Dynamics of Genre: Journalism and the Practice of Literature in Mid-Victorian Britain*. Charlottesville: University of Virginia Press, 2009; Kyriaki Hadjiafxendi, '"George Eliot", the Literary Market-place and Sympathy', in Kyriaki Hadjiafxendi and Polina Mackay (eds.), *Authorship in Context: From the Theoretical to the Material*. Basingstoke: Palgrave Macmillan, 2007, pp. 33–55. Jeff Nunokawa, 'Essays: Essay v. Novel (Eliot, Aloof), in Amanda Anderson and Harry E. Shaw (eds.), *A Companion to George Eliot*. Oxford: Wiley-Blackwell, 2013), pp. 192–203.

[29] Liddle, *Dynamics of* Genre, p. 102.

[30] See, for instance, Alexis Easley, *First-Person Anonymous: Women Writers and Victorian Print Media, 1830–1870*. Aldershot: Ashgate, 2004, which historicises Evans's vocalising of a range of class and gendered perspectives in another of the 'slashing' essays so regularly characterised as discursively monological in content and tone, 'Silly Novels by Lady Novelists'; Joanne Shattock, 'The "Orbit" of the Feminine Critic: Gaskell and Eliot', *Nineteenth-Century Gender Studies* 6.2 (2010) available at www.ncgsjournal.com/issue62/issue62.htm, which addresses the impact of genre, biographical and personal experiences shaping Evans's 'Woman of France'; David Goslee, 'Ethical Discord and Resolution in George Eliot's Essays', *Prose Studies*, 25.3 (December 2002), 58–81, suggests Evans's *Westminster* essays contain a series of complex gendered personae negotiating social and traditional structures from a flexible secularist stance; Kimberley J. Stern, 'A Common Fund', *Prose Studies: History, Theory, Criticism*, 30.1 (April 2008), 45–62, argues Evans's journalism constitutes an important intervention in literary history by disrupting the entrenched and limited masculine conventions of mid-Victorian journalism with its more inclusive, enriched, less rigidly gendered and interdisciplinary perspectives.

century journalism written in a variety of formats in particular circumstances by an exceptionally erudite and interestingly pragmatic woman who sometimes wrote on the same material for different publications, recasting her work to suit particular target audiences and editorial constraints and who was not above promoting the work of her friends.[31]

Her work offers an understanding of the play between forms and formats that characterised the transitional period in journalistic reviewing at mid-century as Evans moves between traditional quarterlies and newly dynamic weeklies; between long essay and shorter, punchier review; from arts-page fillers in the *Leader* to re-vamped and extended dedicated book review sections in the *Westminster*. In its anonymity, which facilitated those 'double-jobbing' reviews, as has been argued even more importantly, her work exemplifies, along with that of her fellow women journalists, the opportunities for purposeful if veiled contributions to critical and public debate via the performance of gendered authorship: both that collective masculine 'we' that dominates mid-century review conventions, which she replicated with ease, and the sometimes self-conscious, sometimes subversive play with that gendered authority that emerges more overtly in her later journalism from the mid-1850s outlined earlier. In these terms, Marian Evans's journalism is in many ways a representative of its time and place.[32]

She was by no means the most typical nor the most prolific of mid-Victorian journalists when compared with Geraldine Jewsbury, Margaret Oliphant, Charles Dickens or George Henry Lewes, for instance, because she gave up full-time essay and review writing once her fiction career took off in 1857. But she deserves our attention as a journalist, not least, as Liddle has put it straightforwardly, because she produced 'undeniably *good* journalism' that still entertains and informs: 'the reviews are well-researched and written with craft, and the "slashing" satires of mid-Victorian "lady novelists" and Evangelical preachers remain wickedly witty even for

---

[31] See, for instance, her reviews about Milton in the *Leader* (August 1855), 750 and in the *Westminster Review* (October 1855), 603–4 and on Alfred Stahr's work in *Saturday Review* (31 May 1856), 109–10 and in the *Leader* (17 March 1855), 257–58. She had met Stahr in Germany; he was one of many writers known to her whose work she reviewed. She gives an early plug for Lewes's Goethe biography in her spirited defence of the enlarged ethical vision of Goethe's controversial novel in 'The Morality of Wilhelm Meister', *Leader* (July 1855), 703, and 'reviews' the biography later that year in the *Leader* (November 1855), 1058–61 in a piece that acknowledges vested interest and so quotes rather than critiques the work.

[32] See Easley, *First-Person Anonymous*; and Joanne Wilkes, *Women Reviewing Women in Nineteenth-Century Britain: The Critical Reception of Jane Austen, Charlotte Brontë and George Eliot*. Aldershot: Ashgate, 2010, for extended considerations of gendered performances in reviewer mode by women writers.

a generation less familiar with their particular subjects.'[33] In terms of her distinctive style, Rosemary Ashton observes that her journalism registers 'above all, that quality so striking also in the novels, the power of analogy'.[34] Even in the shortest review, she adds colour and dimension and interest with the sturdily concrete comparative frames that encompass the communicative potential as well as the entertainment value of these pieces. She cuts through the complicated layers of scholarship to introduce a French study of the Greek playwright Menander, known predominantly because of German classical scholarship, with the purposefully prosaic analogy that includes populist references to Dickens's *Dombey and Son* and national stereotypes:

> The Germans are the purveyors of the raw material of learning for all of Europe; but as Mr Toots suggests, raw materials require to be cooked, and in this kind of cookery, as well as the other, the French are supreme. To have the Latin work of a German writer boiled down to a portable bulk and served up in that delicate crystal vessel, the French language, is a benefit that will be appreciated by those who are at all acquainted with the works of Germans, and still more by those who are not acquainted with Latin.[35]

As has been pointed out in all overviews of her journalism, many of her assessments have stood the test of time. She offered (not unqualified) defences of Tennyson and more controversially of Browning and Arnold, when others saw little to recommend them.[36] Here she is on Browning's contentious 1855 collection *Men and Women*, which she reviewed in the *Westminster*:

> To read poems is often to substitute for thought: fine-sounding conventional phrases and the sing-song of verse demand no co-operation in the reader; they glide over his mind with the agreeable unmeaningness of 'the compliments of the season', or a speaker's exoridium on 'feelings too deep for expression'. But let him expect no such drowsy passivity in reading Browning. Here he will find no conventionality, no melodious commonplace, but freshness, originality, sometimes eccentricity of expression; no

---

[33] Liddle, *Dynamics of Genre*, pp. 100–1.

[34] Rosemary Ashton, 'Introduction', in Rosemary Ashton (ed.), *George Eliot: Selected Critical Writing*. Oxford University Press, 1992, p. x.

[35] 'Menander and the Greek Comedy', *Leader* (16 June 1855), 578.

[36] Richard Stang was amongst the first to register the significance of her assessments in the context of the journalism of her peers; see his pioneering article, Stang, 'Literary Criticism of George Eliot', p. 958. Contrast her views, for instance, with those of Margaret Oliphant who had little time for contemporary poetry, see Joanne Shattock, 'Introduction', in Joanne Shattock (ed.), *The Selected Works of Margaret Oliphant, Vol. 1 Literary Criticism 1854–69*. London: Pickering and Chatto, 2011, p. xxvii.

didactic laying-out of a subject, but dramatic indication, which requires the reader to trace by his own mental activity the underground stream of thought that jets out in elliptical and pithy verse. To read Browning, he must exert himself, but he will exert himself to some purpose. If he finds the meaning difficult of access, it is always worth his effort ... Indeed, in Browning's best poems he makes us feel that what we took for obscurity in him was superficiality in ourselves.[37]

This sense of the confrontation with otherness, which Browning's challenging poetry represents, is a feature in Evans's reviews of works that she admires, and its inverse, that gliding, melodious, 'feeling too-deep-for-expression' vagueness is persistently exposed for its affective emptiness at best and for its amoral and insincere play on emotions in her vehement but reasoned critique of influential writers such as Young and Cumming. Kimberly Stern, in her illuminating analysis of Evans's writings on women, points up Evans's advocacy of the 'really cultured woman' as one who 'admits the limits of her own knowledge, engaging in a perpetual, recursive interrogation of her history and worldview'.[38] In counter-distinction to seductions of the affective, of the too readily sympathetic that abjure the challenge of otherness and suspend the potential for continuous learning and new knowledge formation, this characterisation of Evans's reviewing, in content and in purpose, as writing and as reading, also offers different ways of thinking about what has been diagnosed as her demanding or unsympathetic critical voice. It has the potential to recast the developmental views of individual, social and spiritual life that recur throughout her reviews as part of those widely recognised ever-evolving issues of her writing life, as Helen Small puts it in 'her growing concern with the relation between the pursuit of human commonality and a proper ethical partiality' and 'her overarching concern with the right relation between claims of partiality and claims of impartiality'.[39]

It is worth considering how much this cultivated, critical individualist improvement is part of the *Westminster*'s agenda, that organ of radical opinion that proclaimed in its 1852 prospectus co-written by Evans and

---

[37] Byatt and Warren, *Selected Essays*, p. 349. Originally published in 'Belles Lettres', *Westminster Review* (January 1856), 290–96.

[38] Stern, 'Common Fund', 56. Stern relates this practice of self-conscious critical scrutiny to recent work on the ethics of cosmopolitanism and critical distancing, citing, for instance, Amanda Anderson's influential and compelling study, *The Powers of Distance: Cosmopolitanism and the Cultivation of Detachment*. Princeton University Press, 2001, see Stern, 'Common Fund', pp. 56, 58

[39] Helen Small, 'George Eliot and the Cosmopolitan Cynic', *Victorian Studies*, 55.1 (Autumn 2012), 85–105, 88.

Chapman a commitment to 'fearlessness of investigation and criticism'.[40]
A comparison of the review of *Men and Women* in the *Westminster* with an
article on German culture for a very different magazine is illuminating in
this regard. Evans's description of the trial to melodically inclined English
ears of Wagner's music in an informal, variety piece for the literary,
middle-class monthly *Fraser's Magazine* six months earlier works well
with the Browning article because the reviewer in both cases articulates
a similar understanding of the aesthetic challenge presented by the English
poet and the German composer, neither of whom courts conventional
platitudes, easy popularity or familiar emotional engagement (and, Evans
suggests, neither poet nor composer has a sense for melodic line).

In the *Fraser's* article, the writer intimates that Wagner's music, new to
England in 1855, and causing much controversy, would find in some future
audience fuller understanding and recognition but does not suggest that
the onus is on the English listener to 'exert himself to some purpose' as
a worthwhile extension of the self as in the Browning piece. In this more
reader friendly of magazines and in this more personable, meandering
occasional mode, the writer, in the role of general listener for her general
readership, is instead honestly upfront about the limitations of her 'purely
individual assessment', her lack of technical understanding and the relative
immaturity of her ear and is resigned to never understanding the value of
Wagner's works. Crucially, she makes her readers comfortable in their
rejection of Wagner by identifying entirely with them, though the double-
edged natural history analogy is significant: 'We are but in "the morning of
the times"', she writes 'and must learn to think of ourselves as tadpoles
unprescient of the future frog. Still the tadpole is limited to tadpole
pleasures; and so, in our state of development, we are swayed by
melody.'[41] Unlike the Browning piece in the more progressive
Westminster, there is a complacent and reassuring acceptance of the fact
that this generation of listeners will never 'get' Wagner, because he can
never be comprehended by mid-nineteenth-century English ears. But there
is also the acknowledgement, that recursive, self-critical, self-questioning
realisation, that such complacency is related to a type of musical immaturity, to the less sophisticated sensory organism that is the mid-Victorian
concert goer in its basic stage of development. The insistent undertone is
more fully, if still gently unpacked in the anecdote that follows explaining

[40] 'Prospectus', *Westminster and Foreign Quarterly Review* (January 1852), reprinted in Byatt and
Warren, *Selected Essays*, pp. 3–7, 5.
[41] 'Liszt, Wagner, and Weimar', *Fraser's Magazine* (July 1855), 48–62, reprinted in Ashton, *Selected
Critical Writings*, pp. 83–109, 87.

that the first performance of a symphony by the now revered and so familiar Beethoven produced 'a general titter among the musicians in the orchestra . . . at the idea of sitting seriously to execute such music!'[42]

It is worth contrasting this recognition of the need to acknowledge the value of exceptional otherness by accepting the limitations of both the self and the social with Margaret Oliphant's review of Browning's *Men and Women* that was part of a survey of mid-century poets for *Blackwood's Magazine*. Oliphant writes vividly and amusingly with a type of stunned bafflement that pitches Browning in terms that do not demand the exertion of our faculties but, contrarily, depicts him in the 'tadpole' stage of development as it were, though the metaphors are mixed as the analogy progresses:

> Robert Browning is the wild boy of the household – the boisterous noisy shouting voice which the elder people shake their heads to hear. It is very hard to make out what he would be at with those marvellous convolutions of words; but, after all, he really seems to mean something, which is a comfort in its way . . . sometimes he works like the old primitive painters with little command of his tools, but something genuine in his mind, under which comes out in spite of the stubborn brushes and pigments, marvellous ugly, yet somehow true. Only a few of his *Men and Women* is it possible to make out.[43]

The problem is with the potential child genius, even with all of his marvellous truths; it is the poet who is in his infancy, not his readers. And though there may be self-reflexive undercutting of her own opinion in the form of those perplexed elders, the reverse analogy gives no sense of continuous unfolding and some potential future meeting or maturing of minds on the part of the reader.

Pinney emphasises the attractions of this self-questioning, lively, reflexive pre–George Eliot writings that constitute the bulk of her journalism as exemplifying an unfettered radical enthusiasm: 'George Eliot wrote most of her articles in the 1850s, after she had outgrown the self-conscious awkwardness of her provincial days and before she took on the new self-consciousness of her fame. They have in consequence the freedom and

---

[42] 'Liszt, Wagner, and Weimar', p. 88. Evans met Wagner and his wife Cosima (Liszt's daughter) a number of time in 1877, attending concerts and social gatherings with them. For a fascinating argument on the temporal and elongated artistic form in Wagner and George Eliot's longer fiction, see Nicholas Dames, *The Physiology of the Novel: Reading Neural Science, and the Form of Victorian Fiction.* Oxford University Press, 2007.

[43] Originally published in 'Modern Light Literature – Poetry', *Blackwood's Magazine* 79 (February 1856), 125–38; see Shattock, *Selected Works of Margaret Oliphant*, Vol. 1, p. 119.

occasional raciness typical of her mind in those years.'[44] A. S. Byatt takes
a similar line: 'It is worth remarking . . . how much of her writing at this
time drew its life from a kind of ferocious, witty and energetic rejection',
fuelled by a buoyant sense of possibility.[45] Apart from the appealing (no
matter how old-fashioned) notion implied by both Pinney and Byatt
that the journalist might be closer to a 'real' Marian Evans, uncon-
strained as she was by the burden of a successful pseudonym, not yet
invested in the need to maintain a rigid division between a private and
public self to protect both her unconventional partnership with the
already married Lewes and the capital of her new name, it is impossible
to imagine, had she not become the famous George Eliot, that the
journalism would never be of interest. Already, by the time she stopped
working as a full-time journalist in January 1857, she had accumulated
a body of articles championing European contributions to literary culture, biblical criticism, comparative history, music and art that sought to
counter what she viewed as an overly habituated, insular English mind-
set, articulating views on the value of comparative culture she shared, not
coincidentally, with the two journals with which she was most associated, the *Leader* and the *Westminster* in their early 1850s incarnations at
least.

If there is a dominant concern in her journalism, it is its advanced
heterodoxy, grounded in what Goslee has described as the 'militantly
secular' stance of her essays and reviews.[46] Had her first fictional efforts
failed, as many critics have observed, her strategic invention of the elusive
new fiction-writing persona 'George Eliot' protected her expanding and
increasingly busy journalistic career against reputational damage. That she
managed to succeed so immediately as a fiction writer, financially comfortable within one year of publishing her first story, is hardly grounds to
dismiss the various phases of her time as a journalist as dalliance, apprenticeship or necessity only, to question the good faith in which that journalism was written, or to assume that in turning from periodical reviewing to
the much more lucrative business of fiction writing that the journalism had
no value to her, to her contemporaries or to us.

---

[44] Pinney, *Essays*, p. 1.
[45] Byatt, 'Introduction', in Byatt and Warren, *Selected Essays*, pp. ix–xxxiv, xiii.
[46] Goslee, 'Ethical Discord', p, 59. This more evidently and consistently secularist agenda of her
journalism could be contrasted productively with her fiction, which, as K. K. Collins has demonstrated in his scrupulous analysis of the conflicting views about her role as a Christian model that
were registered in George Eliot's obituaries, offered contemporary readers little clear sense of the
precise nature of her heterodoxy. See Collins, *Identifying the Remains*.

As James Benson has expertly shown, Marian Evans's antipathy was not towards periodicals or periodical writing but towards bad journalism, over-simplified journalism, ill-informed journalism,[47] just as her reviews rail against bad logic, opportunistic poetry, false preaching, ill-informed theological history and misdirected didacticism in imaginative writing. It is precisely this concern for the state of literary reviewing that sees her return to the essay form at the end of her life in *Impressions of Theophrastus Such* for a destructive exposé of the limits of such bad journalism, which, naturally, she had to publish in volume format rather than in the periodical press, which she was attacking. The luxury of a successful literary career meant she could stay outside the fray in ways the younger, grafting professional could not. Marian Evans read periodicals for all of her life, Margaret Harris noting that her reading material in her final days included the *Cornhill*. Suitably distracting end-of-life stuff, let's infer, for the militant secularist.[48]

---

[47] James D. Benson, '"Sympathetic" Criticism: George Eliot's Response to Contemporary Reviewing', *Nineteenth-Century Fiction*, 29.4 (March 1975), 428–40.

[48] Margaret Harris, 'George Eliot as Journalist', in John Rignall (ed.), *Oxford's Reader's Companion to George Eliot*. Oxford University Press, 2000, pp. 186–89, 189.

CHAPTER 22

Oscar Wilde, New Journalist

John Stokes and Mark W. Turner

'I write only on questions of literature and art – am hardly a journalist', Oscar Wilde told an unknown correspondent in the mid-1880s.[1] This was either disingenuous or an attempt to distance himself from the more disreputable aspects of the profession as he had, in fact, been writing for journals and newspapers for several years. It was true, however, that he wrote mainly on 'questions of literature and art'. His earliest forays into authorship had been in Irish periodicals to which he offered long treatments of the highly aesthetic Grosvenor Gallery in London as early as 1877; on leaving Oxford, he had written for the *Athenaeum* and sent poems to the *World*; he went on to contribute to various theatrical and society papers as well as to the progressive *Nineteenth Century* and the *Fortnightly Review*, among others. He was editor of the *Woman's World* from 1887 to 1889 and took that occasion to refashion, not altogether successfully, what a popular woman's monthly magazine might look like. Although almost all of Wilde's reviews and similar short journalism appeared in the 1880s and very little in the 1890s – nothing after 1890 – he was not a jobbing journalist exactly, even during that period. Apart from his stint as an editor, he was not a salaried journalist either, labouring away for a single title, at least not at first; rather, he was a professional author who continually wrote articles and reviews on literature, drama and art.[2] In fact, he was among a large group of literary figures who, in addition to pursuing their careers as 'authors' of fiction, drama, poetry and non-fiction, also reviewed regularly, or semi-regularly, for the periodical press – for monthlies, weeklies and dailies. Like many others, Wilde thought of himself as a member of an admittedly factional literary community.

---

[1] *The Complete Letters of Oscar Wilde*, Merlin Holland and Rupert Hart-Davis (eds.). London: Fourth Estate, 2000, p. 293.

[2] See Josephine M. Guy and Ian Small, *Oscar Wilde's Profession: Writing and the Culture Industry in the Late 19th Century*. Oxford University Press, 2000.

His writing for the *Pall Mall Gazette*, which sits squarely in the middle of his career as a regular contributor to the press, is particularly significant.[3] Beginning in 1885, he provided at least eighty-five reviews, all of them anonymous, for a radical evening newspaper which by that point had, under the editorship of W. T. Stead, established itself firmly as the paper most closely associated with the so-called New Journalism.[4] It is generally acknowledged, as it was at the time, that Stead 'conceived the editor's role as marshalling the public, and drew upon techniques from American dailies, such as cross heads, interviews, bold headlines, illustrations, indices and specials' (or special correspondents) to capture the public's imagination (and their pennies).[5] A hallmark of his editorial style was campaign journalism, most famously in the 'Maiden Tribute of Modern Babylon' scandal of 1885, in which he unveiled the depth and breadth of child prostitution across London. For Stead, such robust, or sensational, campaigning was part of the supposedly 'democratic' mission of the press, to engage the public in direct and immediate ways. He wrote passionately for the notion of 'government by journalism' and he and the *Pall Mall Gazette* were at the heart of social and political debates about the status of a shifting journalistic culture.[6] An emphasis on more digestible paragraphs and shorter columns came to replace extended court and parliamentary reporting and 'entertainment' in a variety of forms (serial and other fiction, widespread use of illustration, human interest narratives, eventually games and puzzles, etc.) put pressure on the amount of space that could be allocated to 'news'. Critical opinion in press history suggests that the role of the press as an important democratic force was cheapened even as it was championed. Indeed, the emphasis on personality obviously apparent in interviews, biographical notes and sketches and gossip columns has been said to reflect or, at least, to have developed alongside the theatricalisation of the world of politics itself as meetings became increasingly well

---

[3] See *The Complete Works of Oscar Wilde*, John Stokes and Mark W. Turner (eds.), Vols. 6 and 7, Journalism, Parts I and II. Oxford University Press, 2013. This edition also contains an appendix of 'dubia', texts of a number of anonymous items of journalism possibly written by Wilde. Also see Mark W. Turner, 'Journalism', in Kerry Powell and Peter Raby (eds.), *Oscar Wilde in Context*. Cambridge University Press, 2013, pp. 270–77.

[4] See *W. T. Stead: Newspaper Revolutionary*, Roger Luckhurst, Laurel Brake and James Mussell King (eds.). London: British Library, 2012.

[5] See James Mussell's entry on the 'New Journalism', in Laurel Brake and Marysa Demoor (eds.), *Dictionary of Nineteenth Century Journalism*. Gent: Academia Press; London: British Library, 2009, p. 443.

[6] W. T. Stead, 'Government by Journalism', *Contemporary Review*, XLIX (May, 1886), 653–74; and W. T. Stead, 'The Future of Journalism', *Contemporary Review* (November 1886), 663–79.

organised and individuals picked out for their 'charisma'.[7] This is the moment when the word 'celebrity' starts to refer to a person and not to a quality. Theatre, politics and journalism, it has been argued, were now mutually entwined.

However, as Laurel Brake has shown, there were precedents for some of Stead's techniques which developed out of the quality evening press and monthly and weekly periodicals.[8] The *Fortnightly Review* had introduced signature into the higher journalism in 1865, and Edmund Yates's *World* had made a feature of celebrity interviews in the 1870s, to name only two examples of the ways 'personality' was being introduced across a number of decades. Moreover, other papers responded to the demands of technology and readership in similar ways: the *Daily Chronicle* (1876), for example, exploited the possibilities of orchestrated controversy together with generous use of the correspondence column. The transformations afoot would continue to reshape the look and feel of print culture well into the 1890s: later to come were papers clearly influenced by Stead's approach such as the *Westminster Gazette* (1893), which took over as the mouthpiece of liberalism when the *Pall Mall* was bought up by conservative interests, and the evening paper the *Star* (1888). By the mid-1890s, when titles such as the *Daily Mail* (1896) reached astonishing circulations of more than a million, the New Journalism had clearly come to shape and perhaps even define the mass daily press.

Given such dramatic changes in the periodical press, it is not surprising that historians have long worried about the origins of the term 'New Journalism', although Matthew Arnold's dismissive application in 1887 to describe the claims made by Stead remains the most famous.[9] This comes at the end of an essay otherwise given over to the Irish situation, specifically to Gladstone's policy of Home Rule – which Arnold was passionately against and Stead equally passionately for. Although Arnold ostensibly recognised that 'the new voters, the democracy, as people are fond of calling them' had every right to vote on the issue, he remained

---

[7] See Kate Campbell, 'W. E. Gladstone, W. T. Stead, Matthew Arnold and a New Journalism: Cultural Politics in the 1880s', *Victorian Periodicals Review*, 36.1 (Spring 2003), 20–40.

[8] Laurel Brake, 'The Old Journalism and the New: Forms of Cultural Production in London in the 1880s', in *Subjugated Knowledges. Journalism, Gender and Literature*. Houndmills: Macmillan, 1994, pp. 83–103.

[9] It may well be that W. T. Stead, the object of Arnold's attack, had actually preempted him in its use. It certainly was the case that immediately after Arnold's article Stead was proud to describe his paper as 'new journalism'. See Owen Mulpetre, *W. T. Stead and the New Journalism*, unpublished master's thesis, University of Teeside, 2010, www.attackingthedevil.co.uk/pdfs/W.T_Stead_and_the_New_Journalism.pdf.

sceptical about the value of popular opinion since the people 'have many merits, but among them is not that of being, in general, reasonable persons who think fairly and seriously'. This is where 'the new journalism' came in, almost as an addendum:

> We have had opportunities of observing a new journalism which a clever and energetic man has lately invented. It has much to recommend it; it is full of ability, novelty, variety, sensation, sympathy, generous instincts; its one great fault is that it is feather-brained. It throws out assertions at a venture because it wishes them true; does not correct either them or itself, if they are false; and to get at the state of things as they truly are seems to feel no concern whatever.[10]

On 3 May 1887, the *Pall Mall Gazette* responded with a couple of anonymous paragraphs, presumably composed by Stead, in its 'Occasional Notes' column. The first summarised in seemingly generous spirit Arnold's complaints:

> Mr. Mathew Arnold is a very pleasant gentleman and the apostle of a new kind of religion, which is the outcome of a laudable attempt to extract all the grave and sweet reasonableness of the Christian faith without any of the grim ruggedness of Hebrew morality. We could have wished, however, that in practice this eminent apostle of sweetness and light had condescended to remember one ancient Hebraic mandate which runs 'Thou shalt not bear false witness against thy neighbour.' In describing Democracy at the present day in the *Nineteenth Century* he does us the honour of describing the New Journalism which, he says, we have invented, as being eminently typical of the democratic spirit of modern England.[11]

The ingenuity of this riposte lay in the way it threw back at Arnold a number of his own most lapidary phrases, implying that not only was the newspaper literate and culturally informed but that it was guided by Arnold's own high-minded critical principles. 'Sweet reasonableness' comes from *Literature and Dogma* (1873), 'sweetness and light' from *Culture and Anarchy* (1869). The repetition of Arnold's praise is tactical and betrays no hint of recognising the derogatory possibilities present in his combination of words. Those virtues might seem slight when compared with the high ideals set down in Arnold's essay 'The Function of Criticism at the Present Time' which exhorted criticism to be 'sincere, simple,

---

[10] Matthew Arnold, 'Up to Easter', *Nineteenth Century*, 21 (May 1887), 629–43, p. 638. Repr. in *The Last Word, The Complete Prose Works of Matthew Arnold*. Vol. 11, R. H. Super (ed.). Ann Arbor: University of Michigan Press, 1977, pp. 190–209, p. 202.

[11] *Pall Mall Gazette*, 3 May 1887, p. 3.

flexible, ardent, ever widening its knowledge',[12] although in the minds of
Stead and his colleagues there would have been no contradictions hidden
among Arnold's mixed bag of compliments. 'Ability, novelty, variety,
sensation, sympathy, generous instincts' were precisely the qualities that
they might feel justified in claiming for their paper – and for its contributors. In practical terms, this meant being *au fait* with the contemporary
world, versatile, capable of making a stir and yet sparing with harsh
dismissals of the popular mood. Of course, no one could demonstrate
these virtues all the time, but they did remain in place as professional
requirements. And this was as true for literary journalists, including critics,
as it was for writers on political or social matters. Oscar Wilde, no less than
anyone else, was subject to the same pressures; indeed, he seems at first to
have welcomed them.

The range of topics and books Wilde discusses in his *Pall Mall Gazette*
reviews was extensive, and it provided him scope to share his impressive
learning and intellectual engagements. Writing for a strongly liberal paper,
he was free to honour his heritage by reviewing books on Celtic archaeology and by protesting against the anti–Home Rule conservatism of his
old Trinity College tutor J. P. Mahaffy. He could demonstrate his
resources as a classical scholar by critiquing recent translations from the
Greek; he could pursue his interest in radical writers whether French
(Béranger, George Sand) or English (William Morris, Edward
Carpenter); he could display his passion for Balzac. Direct experience of
America and its poets – some renowned such as Whitman, but others far
less well known in England – gave him unusual authority when writing on
work from across the Atlantic. The range may have been wide, but it was
no less personal for all that.

Yet, the review columns remained anonymous. While anonymity had
been challenged since the mid-1860s, convention varied according to the
periodical genre. In the monthly magazines, there was both anonymity and
signature, of fiction and non-fiction, although often authorship was something like an open secret, and individual authors were named in reviews,
monthly round-ups of the magazines, and even in advertisements. In the
weekly press, the practice varied, although a periodical such as the *Saturday
Review* partly staked its reputation for robust criticism on the freedom its
anonymous critics had to speak directly and even cuttingly. In the daily

---

[12] Matthew Arnold 'The Function of Criticism at the Present Time', *National Review*, 2:1 (November
1864), 280–307. Repr. in *Lectures and Essays in Criticism. The Complete Prose Works of Matthew
Arnold*, Vol. 3, R. H. Super (ed.). Ann Arbor: University of Michigan Press, 1962, pp. 258–85.

newspaper press, the long-standing assumption was that anonymity supported the power of the editorial 'we', the voice of the leaders that defined the politics of the paper. 'The system which came into vogue, when newspapers first of all made their appearance, is still generally in form', one commentator noted in 1888. 'The Press-man', he continues, 'writes day after day, year after year, and dies making no sign'.[13] Nevertheless, in a two-part article on anonymity, published in the *New Review* in 1889 and 1890, Tighe Hopkins acknowledges that different sectors of the press act in different ways: 'nowhere, save in the connection with the newspaper Press, do we hear this remarkable talk about the tremendous power and dignity of anonymous writing. Publishers and magazine editors know well enough the value that attaches to a reputed and reputable man.'[14]

What is interesting about Wilde, by the middle of the 1880s, is that he was already established as a 'name'. He was not yet the Oscar Wilde who wrote the brilliant plays of the 1890s, but he was still a celebrity, a figure whose movements were reported in the society pages and whose lectures and tours received widespread coverage in the press. It was in part because of his renown that he was invited to edit the *Woman's World* for Cassell in 1887. When he contributed two reviews on single volumes to the *Speaker*[15] in 1890, they both bore his signature even though the convention for book reviews in that newly launched periodical was anonymity. Clearly at this stage, the policy was mixed and probably depended on the particular combination of reviewer and book.

It is noticeable, then, that Wilde's *Pall Mall Gazette* book reviews are all anonymous; the newspaper did not seek to trade on his name, which it could easily have done, given Wilde's prominence as a public figure by this time. To explain this fact, it may be that we need to distinguish between the deliberate use of anonymity (i.e. privileging the collective 'we' of the journal instead of the individual writer) and the growth of personality journalism (i.e. providing content about celebrities). These are not necessarily contradictory practices, and they both operated at the *Pall Mall*

---

[13] Anonymous, 'Reflections on Anonymous Journalism v. Personal Journalism', *Sell's Dictionary of the World's Press*, 1888, Vol. 1, p. 86. Laurel Brake suggests 'that while the periodical press was moving, with reservations, toward signature and fragmented authority, the newspaper press came to occupy the middle ground between blanket anonymity and the vulgarity of named contributors: a kind of acknowledged collectivity that indicated the individuality of journalist by generic bylines (From our own Correspondent).' (Brake, 'The Old Journalism and the New', p. 91.)

[14] Tighe Hopkins, 'Anonymity?' *The New Review*, 1 (October 1889), 523. The second part of Hopkins's article appears in the *New Review*, 2 (March, 1890), 265–76.

[15] For information on this new liberal periodical which although not a financial success attracted many distinguished contributors, see *Dictionary of Nineteenth Century Journalism*, p. 587.

Gazette. However, the overall situation among the press was, as John Mullan has described it, very mixed: 'By the 1880s, previously obdurate journals had begun to use signatures for reviews, though some weeklies kept to anonymous reviewing: the "Spectator" and "Athenaeum" stayed anonymous to the end of the century, while the "Saturday Review" only began regularly attributing reviews in the 1890s.'[16] The *Nineteenth Century*, which launched in 1877, made a virtue of signature, following the lead of the *Fortnightly* and others. The policy here was designed to ensure an open forum, to encourage dialogue and even disagreement, although, in the end, it remained pretty solidly liberal in its discourse. In fact, it was probably the weekly *Saturday Review* that the evening daily *Pall Mall Gazette* most resembled in its approach to the issue,[17] and the two anonymous portmanteau reviews Wilde published in the former in 1887 are not especially different in tone from those he was writing for the latter, though the political resonances are more obvious.

Wilde began his professional career at a moment when the responsibilities of the press, which include the matter of anonymity, were much debated and when journalism was becoming ever more professionalised, when entering the world of newspapers could hold its own again other career paths, especially for men. In one of the first 'guide books' for budding journalists, John Dawson's *Practical Journalism, How to Enter Thereon and Succeed* (1885), we are told that 'a hint of Bohemianism still clings to journalism,' but that 'Every year . . . the Press is drawing to itself a better class of men. The overcrowding of other professions has something to do with this, and it is further influenced by the fact that the pecuniary rewards of journalism are now greater than they were.'[18]

Furthermore, according to Dawson, journalism was a particularly useful route for those with literary skills: 'no profession, perhaps, offers to a young man who is possessed of literary ability so ready and speedy a means of earning money as journalism.'[19] Exactly how much Wilde (or others like him) earned as a freelance reviewer is not known. Dawson suggests that 'a guinea is the lowest sum that is paid for an article of the orthodox column in length, on the London daily press', and Arthur Reade, author of another 1885 guide for journalists, says that £3 10s was what might be paid by

---

[16] John Mullan, *Anonymity*. London: Faber and Faber, 2007, p. 210.
[17] See *Dictionary of Nineteenth Century Journalism*, p. 478: 'In many respects it resembled a daily version of the *Saturday Review* or the *Cornhill Magazine*.'
[18] John Dawson, *Practical Journalism, How to Enter Thereon and Succeed*. London: L. Upcott Gill, 1885, pp. 2, 3.
[19] Dawson, p. 4.

a newspaper for a review. 'As a rule,' Reade tells us, 'reviewing is not a well-paid branch of newspaper work' because it was a more considered form of journalism, requiring more time to write, in order to consult other books and consider the subject closely.[20] Still, Wilde came from a family accustomed to earning money from journalism – his mother had written for nationalist Irish publications and his brother Willie was a jobbing journalist for the *Daily Telegraph* and others – so he was familiar with writing for the press at various levels. And, of course, he would have welcomed the income from his articles and reviews, however modest.

The exact status of the literary review is hard to determine, in the context of a shifting New Journalistic culture. According to Reade,

> The real requisite of a review is that it shall be a candid opinion, by a competent man, of the value of the book under notice to those who may be inclined to purchase it. No display of the learning of the writer of the review is necessary. He must be competent to detect errors in the work he is reviewing. His duty is to be the friend (i.e. advisor) of the intending purchaser.[21]

Good reviewing requires some specialist knowledge if the opinion is to matter to the reader, although he concludes that 'no book-buyer now trusts the judgment of a critic.'[22] Dawson agrees that specialist authors make the best reviewers – they are most able to take on the ideas in any given book – but he looks back nostalgically to the tradition of Hazlitt and concludes that 'we are not without our clever critics nowadays, though, as a rule, most of the so-called criticism written in the newspapers is of the flimsiest possible character, and either marked by abuse or fulsome flattery.'[23] The newspaper and weekly review (less so the monthly) is an occasion for some learned (or, learned enough) critic to express an opinion on a recently published work. This opinion is informed partly through knowledge, partly through a subjective judgement about quality, intended to inform the reader who may wish to purchase or who may wish simply to know what is being published and discussed popularly. In other words, reviews may be as important for keeping readers up-to-date culturally as they are for actually helping sell copies.

The question to ask of Wilde is, what qualities did his writing possess that made it so suitable for the new modes of presentation? What did the New Journalism require of a book review? As Laurel Brake's chapter in this

---

[20] See Dawson, pp. 112–13. Arthur Reade, *Literary Success: A Guide to Practical Journalism*. London: Wyman and Sons, 1885, p. 67.
[21] Reade, p. 6. [22] Reade, p. 63. [23] Dawson, p. 47.

volume makes clear, the 'review' had been a mainstay for periodicals throughout the nineteenth century. Indeed, the lengthy 'review article' was the foundation of the intellectually weighty quarterlies, although reviews of various kinds could be found at all levels of the periodical press – quarterly reviews, but also monthly magazines, weekly reviews and papers, weekend or Sunday newspapers and dailies, both morning and evening. In short, there were many kinds of 'review' by the last decades of the nineteenth century, but the hefty review article which so dominated review culture earlier in the century had been eclipsed by shorter forms. Among the casualties of the shorter review were extended passages of quotations from the book under consideration, which had long been a mainstay. Shorter reviews became less an occasion to quote, less an opportunity for a wide range of discussion and more a chance to engage readers in ways that were informative but also entertaining. In that way, the review was but one element in a publication determined to involve the reader in every respect.

Take, for example, Wilde's anonymous 'Batch of Books'[24] of 2 May 1887, the moment of Arnold's attack, which appears in the middle of a paper packed with a mélange of information, political opinion and sheer gossip. Fittingly, it is a portmanteau piece dealing with seven novels. Although we have little idea if Wilde himself selected the books under consideration, by writing about them he makes them his own, especially the first, a translation of Dostoevsky's *Injury and Insult* which is given by far the longest treatment. This is not the only time that Wilde reviewed a Russian novel in the *Pall Mall Gazette*,[25] and it may be relevant that Stead as editor took a great interest in Russian politics, advised by the expatriate journalist Olga Novikoff. Wilde opens by comparing the great Russian novelists – Turgenev, Tolstoy, Dostoevsky – one with another, bringing to the task a potently romantic vocabulary reinforced by aestheticism. Turgenev is praised for 'taking existence at its most fiery-coloured moments, he can distil into a few pages of perfect prose the moods and passions of many lives' and the review goes to apply a favourite critical formula – 'unity of impression'. Arriving at Dostoevsky, Wilde hails 'a realism that is pitiless in its fidelity, and terrible because it is true', a tacit rebuke to the definitions of Zolaesque realism that were currently going the rounds of literary debate. There are references both biblical and classical.

[24] 'A Batch of Novels', *Pall Mall Gazette*, 2 May 1887, II, repr. in *The Complete Works of Oscar Wilde*, Vol. 6 Journalism, Part I, pp. 165–67.

[25] For reviews of Russian novels, see *The Complete Works of Oscar Wilde*, Vols. 6 and 7; Journalism, Parts I and II, nos. 34, 67, 69, 75, 151, 153, 154, 157, 158.

Dostoevsky's heroine is 'like one of the noble victims of Greek tragedy. She is Antigone with the passion of Phaedra.' His hero is compared with a leading character in George Eliot's *Romola*. There are epigrams: the hero 'never thinks evil, he only does it'; there's paradox such as he has 'enthusiasm for all that life cannot give'. Throughout this long opening paragraph, all the polymathic brilliance that we now associate with 'Oscar Wilde' is on display, although few presumably could have attributed the review to him at the time.

Following *Injury and Insult*, Wilde turns to two novels, both of which with hindsight we can speculate would have carried a particular interest. The first is by William Hardinge, who had been sent down from Oxford in the 1870s for exchanging homoerotic letters with Walter Pater. Wilde sums up the plot like this: 'A girl of high birth falls passionately in love with a young farm-bailiff, who is a sort of Arcadian Antinous and a very Ganymede in gaiters. Social difficulties naturally intervene, so she drowns her handsome rustic in a convenient pond.' It is surely inconceivable that Wilde would not have heard about the Hardinge affair during his time at Oxford;[26] both Antinous and Ganymede feature in the coded homosexual language of the period. (Of course, what proportion of his immediate readership would have picked up on the hints is once again another matter.) It is hard, even now, to be confident about the tone of his final words of praise: 'the book is a delightful combination of romance and satire, and the heroine's crime is treated in the most picturesque manner possible.' The irony here seems to be directed at outdated melodramatic ways, the wit shifting from the crypto-homoerotic to matters of literary form. The next novel to be judged, in a week when Home Rule politics was major news, 'tells of modern Ireland': Rosa Mulholland's *Marcella Grace*. Rather surprisingly perhaps, given his normal preference for art over nature, Wilde finds much to praise in Mulholland's treatment of landscape: 'She never shrieks over scenery like a tourist, nor wearies us with sunsets like the Scotch school; but all through her book there is a subtle atmosphere of purple hills and silent moorland; she makes us live with nature, and not merely look at it.' While the adjective 'shrieking' may carry associations to do with gender (compare Eliza Lynn Linton's condemnation of the 'shrieking sisterhood' in 1870),[27] it certainly distinguishes Mulholland's approach from English appropriation of Irish beauty.

---

[26] Richard Ellmann, *Oscar Wilde*. London: Hamish Hamilton, 1987, pp. 58–59.
[27] [Eliza Lynn Linton,] 'The Shrieking Sisterhood', *Saturday Review* (12 March 1870).

Wilde's fidelity to the Irish cultural heritage recovered and celebrated by his parents is present even in his anonymous writings.

George Eliot returns in the penultimate paragraph by a back-door route. She is quoted in praise of the authoress of the novel under review: *Soap* by Constance MacEwen. Wilde's source for Eliot's opinion, like a similar passage from Carlyle, is a publisher's advertisement on the back cover of the volume – an economical way of suggesting literary knowledge that he was to employ on other occasions. But economy of means is best illustrated by the final paragraph, which manages to package together three obviously inferior novels: 'the first shows some power of description and treatment, but is sadly incomplete, the second is quite unworthy of any man of letters. And the third is absolutely silly.' The first, *A Marked Man* is by Faucet Streets, whose one novel this seems to have been. The second, *That Winter Night*, is by Robert Buchanan, well-known journalist and author of the notorious 1871 attack on the 'Fleshly School' of Dante Gabriel Rossetti and the Pre-Raphaelites,[28] a movement that Wilde admired greatly. For the reviewer to deny Buchanan the status of 'man of letters' is precise in its offensiveness. The third novel is by a woman, Evelyn Owen, and the choice of epithet 'silly' is perhaps designed to evoke George Eliot's essay 'Silly Novels by Lady Novelists' (1856). The review concludes with a warning to publishers by a reviewer who has clearly studied the trade: 'we sincerely hope that a few more novels like these will be published, as the public will then find out that a bad book is very dear at a shilling.'

This review – and Wilde was to compose many similar pieces – treats subjects of intense personal interest in a manner accessible to most of its readers – if, that is, they had kept up with the press, specifically with the *Pall Mall Gazette*. It fulfils ideals conceded by Arnold and championed by Stead being full of 'ability, novelty, variety, sensation, sympathy, generous instincts' – the only doubtful quality there being 'sensation'. As a survey of current trends, it is both concise and dense; it manages to be highly individual but is by no means aimed at a coterie. It is designed rather for the broadly culturally aware and thereby achieves the avowed aim of the New Journalism for a widening, or 'democratisation', of the reading public. The greater the range of topics and texts the more condensed the style. Hence the paradox, the epigram, succinct parallelism, catchy alliteration – all tricks and twists of style that we now think of as typically Wildean. In fact, if we think that we can now observe here the seeds of

---

[28] Thomas Maitland [Robert Buchanan], 'The Fleshly School of Poetry', *Contemporary Review* 18 (1871).

Wilde's later work – in genres other than criticism – that may only confirm the part the New Journalism played in determining the kind of popular writer that he was already on the way to becoming.

Consider a sentence that comes at the end of Wilde's 1888 review of six slim volumes of verse, most of it clearly inferior. The final book under consideration was an obviously doomed attempt to turn the Gospels into devotional poetry. Wilde concludes: 'It is a curious fact that the worst work is always done with the best intentions, and that people are never so trivial as when they take themselves very seriously.' Looking back now, we may well be struck by the fact that within this sentence lay, potentially, the subtitle to *The Importance of Being Earnest* and the title of the 1891 volume of essays, *Intentions*. Neither future use could have been apparent in 1888, not to the reader of the *Pall Mall Gazette*, not to Wilde himself. At the time, the sentence was simply a clever and thoroughly appropriate comment on the work under consideration. Its inherent paradoxes brilliantly fulfilled the requirements of the moment, which was enough. In such ways, the demands of the New Journalism to be full of 'ability, novelty, variety, sensation, sympathy . . . ' were a spur to wit. In fact, whole sentences in the journalism could be extracted and put into the mouths of Lord Henry Wotton or Lord Darlington – and in a few instances they were. But that does not mean that Wilde's reviews were merely a trial run for other genres of supposedly greater cultural value and that they were inferior to what came later or what was going on alongside: such 'literary' activities as short stories, poems, fairy stories.

What becomes clear when we look closely at Wilde's reviews in the *Pall Mall Gazette* is that the need for compression in no way reduced either precision of meaning or expansiveness of ideas. This was despite the fact that the New Journalism could be seen as evidence of the changing patterns of everyday life and the increasingly frantic pace of modernity. In 1889, *Sell's Press Directory* put it this way:

> One of the most obvious demands of the times, to be noticed by the most superficial observer, is that concession to the continual hurrying, the necessity for getting the most done in the least possible time, to which the great mass of the population is subject, shall be made by all the purveyors of what is to be read, be the work newspapers, novels, or histories . . . The demand rises on all hands for succinctness, for forceful terseness, for information in compendiums, encyclopaedic handbooks and primers, for blue-book facts in precis form, for the gist of things, for extracts and cuttings, tit-bits and boilings-down.[29]

[29] J. W. Robertson-Scott, 'The "New Journalism",' *Sell's Dictionary of the World's Press*, 1889, Vol.i, p. 49.

In Wilde's hands, the 'continual hurrying', which defined much of the New Journalism and which some equated to bad writing, became a virtue. Far from simply 'boiling down', he distilled, throughout his reviewing career and with typical aplomb, the flood of print into refined paragraphs. Indeed, it is that quickly delivered message – the wry apercu, the effortless dismissal, the insouciant paradox – which defines Wilde's modern way of thinking. The New Journalism did not create this mode for Wilde – we see that developing throughout his writing career – but it did give him the space in which to sharpen his aphoristic points.

Guide to Further Reading

Reference Works and Online Resources

Asterisked titles are available online by subscription. Other URLs indicate resources that are available on open access as of March 2016.

Brake, Laurel and Marysa Demoor, eds., *Dictionary of Nineteenth-Century Journalism in Great Britain and Ireland*. Brussels and London: Academia Press and the British Library, 2009. Also available online from ProQuest.

*British Periodicals. ProQuest. Available on subscription: http://search.proquest.com

*Nineteenth-Century British Newspapers. Gale Cengage. Available on subscription: http://find.galegroup.com

Dickens Journals Online (DJO) www.djo.org.uk

King, Andrew, Alexis Easley and John Morton, eds. *The Routledge Handbook to Nineteenth-Century British Periodicals and Newspapers*. Abingdon: Routledge, 2016.

Nineteenth-Century Serials Edition (NCSE) www.ncse.ac.uk

*Nineteenth-Century UK Periodicals Online. Gale Cengage. Available on subscription: http://find.galegroup.com

Periodical Poetry Index www.periodicalpoetry.org

*Victorian Periodicals Review, ed. Alexis Easley. Baltimore: Johns Hopkins University Press, 1968 – Contains an annual bibliography.

*The Waterloo Directory of English Newspapers and Periodicals, 1800–1900, ed. John S. North. Waterloo, ON: North Waterloo Academic Press, 1997, 2003. Also available online on subscription: www.victorianperiodicals.com

The Waterloo Directory of Irish Newspapers and Periodicals, 1800–1900. Waterloo, ON: North Waterloo Academic Press, 1986.

The Waterloo Directory of Scottish Newspapers and Periodicals, 1800–1900. Waterloo, ON: North Waterloo Academic Press, 1989.

*The Wellesley Index to Victorian Periodicals, 1824–1900, eds. W. E. Houghton et al. 5 vols. Toronto: University of Toronto Press, 1966–89. Available online from Pro Quest: http://wellesley.chadwyck.co.uk

The Yellow Nineties Online www.1890s.ca

Part I   Periodicals, Genres and the Production of Print

2   *Beyond the 'Great Index': Digital Resources and Actual Copies*

Brake, Laurel, 'London Letter: Researching the Historical Press, Now and Here', *Victorian Periodicals Review*, 48 (2015), 245–53.

Fyfe, Paul, 'Technologies of Serendipity', *Victorian Periodicals Review*, 48 (2015), 261–66.

Hayles, N. Katherine, *Writing Machines*. Cambridge, MA: MIT Press, 2002.
  'Translating Media: Why We Should Rethink Textuality', *The Yale Journal of Criticism*, 16 (2003), 263–90.

Hughes, Linda K., 'SIDEWAYS!: Navigating the Material(ity) of Print Culture', *Victorian Periodicals Review*, 47 (2014), 1–30.

Leary, Patrick, 'Googling the Victorians', *Journal of Victorian Culture*, 10 (2005), 72–86.

Mussell, James, *The Nineteenth-Century Press in the Digital Age*. Basingstoke: Palgrave, 2012.

Nicholson, Bob, 'Counting Culture; Or, How to Read Victorian Newspapers from a Distance', *Journal of Victorian Culture*, 17 (2012), 238–46.

Robson, Catherine, 'How We Search Now: New Ways of Digging Up Wolfe's "Sir John Moore"', in Veronica Alfano and Andrew Stauffer, eds., *Virtual Victorians*. Basingstoke: Palgrave Macmillan, 2015, 11–28.

Turner, Mark W., 'Time, Periodicals, and Literary Studies', *Victorian Periodicals Review*, 39:4 (2006), 309–16.

Wolff, Michael, 'Charting the Golden Stream: Thoughts on a Directory of Victorian Periodicals', *Victorian Periodicals Newsletter*, 4 (1971), 23–38.

3   *The Magazine and Literary Culture*

Cronin, Richard, *Paper Pellets: British Literary Culture After Waterloo*. Oxford University Press, 2010.

Dart, Gregory, *Metropolitan Art and Literature 1810–1840: Cockney Adventures*. Cambridge University Press, 2012.

Fang, Karen, *Romantic Writing and the Empire of Signs: Periodical Culture and Post-Napoleonic Authorship*. Charlottesville and London: University of Virginia Press, 2010.

Higgins, David, *Romantic Genius and the Literary Magazine: Biography, Celebrity, Politics*. London: Routledge, 2005.

Hull, Simon P., *Charles Lamb, Elia and the London Magazine: Metropolitan Muse*. London: Pickering and Chatto, 2010.

Morrison, Robert and Daniel S. Roberts, eds., *Romanticism and Blackwood's Magazine: 'An Unprecedented Phenomenon'*. Basingstoke: Palgrave Macmillan, 2013.

Parker, Mark, *Literary Magazines and British Romanticism*. Cambridge University Press, 2000.

Schoenfield, Mark, *British Periodicals and Romantic Identity: The 'Literary Lower Empire'*. New York: Palgrave Macmillan, 2009.

Stewart, David, *Romantic Magazines and Metropolitan Literary Culture*. Basingstoke: Palgrave Macmillan, 2011.

Wheatley, Kim, *Romantic Feuds: Transcending the 'Age of Personality'*. Farnham: Ashgate, 2013.

4 Periodical Formats: The Changing Review

Bakhtin, M. M., *The Dialogic Imagination. Four Essays*, ed. Michael Holquist. Austin: University of Texas Press, 1981.

Bolter, Jay David and Richard Grusin, *Remediation: Understanding New Media*. Cambridge, MA: MIT Press, 1999.

Garrison, Laurie, *Science, Sexuality and Sensation Novels*. Basingstoke: Palgrave Macmillan, 2011.

Law, Graham, *Serializing Fiction in the Victorian Press*. Basingstoke: Palgrave Macmillan, 2000.

Liddle, Dallas, *The Dynamics of Genre. Journalism and the Practice of Literature in Mid-Victorian Britain*. Charlottesville and London: University of Virginia Press, 2009.

Roper, Derek, *Reviewing Before the Edinburgh 1788–1802*. Newark: University of Delaware Press, 1978.

Shattock, Joanne, 'Contexts and Conditions of Criticism 1830–1914', in M. A. R. Habib, ed., *The Cambridge History of Literary Criticism*. Vol. 6. *The Nineteenth Century*. Cambridge University Press, 2013, pp. 21–45.

Politics and Reviewers: The Edinburgh *and the* Quarterly *in the Early Victorian Age*. Leicester University Press, 1989.

'Reviews' and 'Reviewing', in Laurel Brake and Marysa Demoor, eds., *Dictionary of Nineteenth Century Journalism*. London and Brussels: British Library and Academia Press, 2009, pp. 538–39.

5   *Gendered Production: Annuals and Gift Books*

Boyle, Andrew, *An Index to the Annuals Vol. 1 the Authors (1820–1850)*. Worcester: Andrew Boyle (Booksellers) Ltd. Worcester, 1967.

Faxon, Frederick W., *Literary Annuals and Gift Books: A Bibliography 1923–1903*. 1912.

Harris, Katherine D., *Forget Me Not: The Rise of the British Literary Annual, 1823–1835*. Athens: Ohio University Press, 2015.

Hunnisett, Basil, *Steel-Engraved Book Illustration in England*. London: Scolar Press, 1980.

Houfe, Simon, *Dictionary of British Book Illustrators and Caricaturists 1800–1914*. Woodbridge: Antique Collectors' Club, 1978.

Kooistra, Lorraine Janzen, *Poetry, Pictures, and Popular Publishing: The Illustrated Gift Book and Victorian Visual Culture 1855–75*. Athens: Ohio University Press, 2011.

Ledbetter, Kathryn, *British Victorian Women's Periodicals: Beauty, Civilization, and Poetry*. London: Palgrave Macmillan, 2009.

Onslow, Barbara, *Women of the Press in Nineteenth Century Britain*. Basingstoke and London: Macmillan, 2000.

6   *Graphic Satire, Caricature, Comic Illustration and the Radical Press 1820–1845*

Fox, Celina, *Graphic Journalism in England During the 1830s and 1840s*. New York and London: Garland Publishing, 1988.

Gatrell, Vic, *City of Laughter: Sex and Satire in Eighteenth-Century London*. London: Atlantic Books, 2006.

   The First Bohemians: Life and Art in London's Golden Age. London: Allen Lane, 2013.

George, M. D., *Hogarth to Cruikshank: Social Change in Graphic Satire*, revised edn. London: Viking, 1987.

Hollis, Patricia, *The Pauper Press*. Oxford University Press, 1970.

James, Louis, *Print and the People*. London: Allen Lane, 1976.

Klancher, Jon P., *The Making of the English Reading Audience 1790–1832*. Madison: University of Wisconsin Press, 1987.

Kunzle, D., *The History of Comic Strip – the Nineteenth Century*. Berkeley: University of California Press, 1990.

Maidment, Brian, *Comedy, Caricature and the Social Order*. Manchester: Manchester University Press, 2013.

   'Dinners or Desserts? – Miscellaneity, Knowledge and Illustration in Magazines of the 1820s and 1830s', *Victorian Periodicals Review*, 43. 4 (Winter 2010), 353–87.

Marriott, J., ed., *Unknown London: Early Modernist Visions of the Metropolis, 1815–1845*, 6 vols. London: Pickering and Chatto, 2000.

7 Illustration

Altick, Richard, *The English Common Reader: A Social History of the Mass Reading Public 1800–1900*. Chicago and London: University of Chicago Press, 1957.

Anderson, Patricia, *The Printed Image and the Transformation of Popular Culture 1790–1860*. Oxford: Clarendon Press, 1991.

Beegan, Gerry, *The Mass Image: A Social History of Photomechanical Reproduction in Victorian London*. Houndmills, Basingstoke: Palgrave Macmillan, 2008.

Brake, Laurel, and Marysa Demoor, eds., *The Lure of Illustration in the Nineteenth Century: Picture and Press*. Basingstoke: Palgrave Macmillan, 2009.

Carlisle, Janice, *Picturing Reform in Great Britain*. Cambridge University Press, 2012.

Cooke, Simon, *Illustrated Periodicals of the 1860s: Contexts and Collaborations*. New Castle, DE: Oak Knoll Press, 2010.

Hughes, Linda K., 'Inventing Poetry and Pictorialism in *Once a Week*: A Magazine of Visual Effects', *Victorian Poetry* 48.1 (Spring 2010), 41–72

Jackson, Mason, *The Pictorial Press: Its Origin and Progress*. London: Hurst and Blackett, 1885.

Leary, Patrick, *The Punch Brotherhood: Table Talk and Print Culture in Mid-Victorian England*. London: British Library, 2010.

Kooistra, Lorraine Janzen, '"Making Poetry" in *Good Words*: Why Illustration Matters to Periodical Poetry Studies', *Victorian Poetry* 52.1 (Spring 2014), 111–39.

Maidment, Brian, *Reading Popular Prints 1790–1870*. 2nd ed. Manchester: Manchester University Press, 2001.

Martin, Michèle. 2006. *Images at War: Illustrated Periodicals and Constructed Nations*. Toronto: University of Toronto Press, 2006.

Sinnema, Peter. *Dynamics of the Pictured Page: Representing the Nation in the Illustrated London News*. Aldershot: Ashgate, 1998.

8 Periodical Poetry

Blair, Kirstie, '"A Very Poetical Town": Newspaper Poetry and the Working-Class Poet in Victorian Dundee,' *Victorian Poetry* 52.1 (Spring 2014), 89–109.

Erickson, Lee, 'The Market', in Richard Cronin, Alison Chapman and Antony H. Harrison, eds., *A Companion to Victorian Poetry*. Oxford: Blackwell, 2002, pp. 345–60.

Feldman, Paula R., 'The Poet and the Profits: Felicia Hemans', in Isobel Armstrong and Virginia Blain, eds., *Women's Poetry, Late Romantic to Late Victorian*. London: Macmillan, 1999.

Hobbs, Andrew and Claire Januszewski, 'How Local Newspapers Came to Dominate Victorian Poetry Publishing', *Victorian Poetry*, 52.1 (Spring 2014), 65–87.

Houston, Natalie M., 'Newspaper Poems: Material Texts in the Public Sphere', *Victorian Studies*, 50.2 (Winter 2008), pp. 233–42.

Hughes, Linda K., 'What the *Wellesley Index* Left Out: Why Poetry Matters to Periodical Studies', *Victorian Periodicals Review*, 40 (Summer 2007), 91–125.

  '"Between Politics and Deer-Stalking": Browning's Periodical Poetry', *Victorian Poetry*, 52.1 (Spring 2014), 161–82.

Ledbetter, Kathryn, *Tennyson and Victorian Periodicals: Commodities in Context*. Aldershot: Ashgate, 2007.

Peterson, Linda H., *Becoming a Woman of Letters: Myths of Authorship and Facts of the Victorian Market*. Princeton University Press, 2009.

Part II   The Press and the Public

9   *The Press and the Law*

Alexander, Isabella, *Copyright Law and the Public Interest in the Nineteenth Century*. Oxford: Hart, 2010.

Fisher, J., and J. A. Strahan, *The Law of the Press. A Digest of the Law Specially Affecting Newspapers*. London: W. Clowes & Son, 1891.

Gilmartin, Kevin, *Print Politics. The Press and Radical Opposition in Early Nineteenth Century England*. Cambridge University Press, 1996.

Goldstein, R. J., *Political Censorship of the Arts and the Press in Nineteenth Century Europe*. Basingstoke: Macmillan, 1989.

Harling, Philip, 'The Law of Libel and the Limits of Repression, 1790–1832', *Historical Journal*, 44.1 (2001), 107–34.

Hewitt, Martin, *The Dawn of the Cheap Press in Victorian Britain: The End of the 'Taxes on Knowledge', 1849–69*. London:Bloomsbury Academic, 2014.

Jones, Aled, *Powers of the Press. Newspapers, Power and the Public in Nineteenth Century England*. Aldershot: Ashgate, 1996.

Kent, Christopher, 'The Editor and the Law', in Joel Wiener, ed., *Innovators and Preachers. The Role of the Editor in Victorian England*. Westport, CT: Greenwood Press, 1985, pp. 99–119.

Marsh, Joss, *Word Crimes: Blasphemy, Culture and Literature in Nineteenth Century England*. University of Chicago Press, 1998.

Pease, Allison, *Modernism, Mass Culture and the Aesthetics of Obscenity*. Cambridge University Press, 2000.

10 'Doing the Graphic': Victorian Special Correspondence

Baker, Alfred, *The Newspaper World: Essays on Press History and Work, Past and Present* London: Pitman, 1890.

Blake, Peter, *George Augustus Sala and the Nineteenth-Century Periodical Press: The Personal Style of a Public Writer*. Farnham: Ashgate, 2015.

Brown, Lucy. *Victorian News and Newspapers*. Oxford: Oxford University Press, 1985.

Donovan, Stephen and Matthew Rubery, *Secret Commissions: An Anthology of Victorian Investigative Journalism*. Peterborough: Broadview, 2012.

Garlick, Barbara and Margaret Harris, eds., *Victorian Journalism: Exotic and Domestic*. Brisbane: Queensland University Press, 1998.

Grant, James, *The Newspaper Press: Its Origin, Progress and Present Position*. 2 vols. London: Tinsley, 1871.

Griffiths, Andrew, *The New Journalism, the New Imperialism and the Fiction of Empire, 1870–1900*. Basingstoke: Palgrave Macmillan, 2015.

Hatton, Joseph, *Journalistic London: Being a Series of Sketches of Famous Pens and Papers of the Day*. London: Routledge, 1882.

Knightley, Philip, *The First Casualty: The War Correspondent as Hero and Mythmaker from the Crimea to Kosovo*. London: Prion, 2000.

McKenzie, Judy. 'Paper Heroes: Special Correspondents and Their Narratives of Empire'. In Garlick and Harris, 124–40.

Sala, George Augustus. 'The Special Correspondent: His Life and Crimes', *Belgravia: A London Magazine*, 4 (1871), 211–22.

Waters, Catherine. 'Dickens's "Young Men", *Household Words* and the Development of the Victorian "Special Correspondent",' In Ewa Kujawska-Lis and Anna Krawczyk-Laskarzewska, eds., *Reflections on/of Dickens*. Newcastle upon Tyne: Cambridge Scholars Publishing, 2014, pp. 18–31.

'"Much of Sala, and but Little of Russia": "A Journey Due North", *Household Words*, and the Birth of a Special Correspondent', *Victorian Periodicals Review*, 42.4 (Winter 2009), 305–23.

11 Reporting the Great Exhibition

Cantor, Geoffrey, *Religion and the Great Exhibition of 1851*. Oxford University Press, 2011.

Cantor, Geoffrey, ed., *The Great Exhibition: A Documentary History*, 4 vols. London: Pickering & Chatto, 2013.

Cantor, Geoffrey, Gowan Dawson, Richard Noakes and Jonathan R. Topham, eds., *Science in the Nineteenth-Century Periodical: Reading the Magazine of Nature*. Cambridge University Press, 2004.

Part III   The 'Globalisation' of the Nineteenth-Century Press

12   Colonial Networks and the Periodical Marketplace

Anderson, Benedict, *Imagined Communities: Reflections on the Origin and Spread of Nationalism*. London: Verso, 1991.

Appadurai, Arjun, *Modernity at Large: Cultural Dimensions of Globalisation*. Minneapolis: University of Minnesota Press, 1996.

Johns, Adrian, *Piracy: The Intellectual Property Wars from Gutenberg to Gates*. University of Chicago Press, 2009.

Lohrli, Anne, *'Household Words' A Weekly Journal 1850–1859, Conducted by Charles Dickens, Table of Contents, List of Contributors and Their Contributions Based on the 'Household Words' Office Book*. University of Toronto Press, 1973.

Morrison, Elizabeth, 'Serial Fiction in Australian Colonial Newspapers', in John O. Jordan and Robert L. Patten, eds., *Literature in the Marketplace: Nineteenth-Century British Publishing and Reading Practices*. Cambridge University Press, 1995, pp. 306–23.

Shannon, Mary L., *Dickens, Reynolds and Mayhew on Wellington Street: The Print Culture of a Victorian Street*. Farnham: Ashgate, 2015.

Stuart, Lurline, *Australian Periodicals with Literary Content 1821–1925: An Annotated Bibliography*. Melbourne: Australian Scholarly Publishing, 2003.

Thompson, John B., *The Media and Modernity: A Social Theory of the Media*. Cambridge: Polity Press, 1995.

13   Continental Currents: Paris and London

Aurenche, Marie-Laure, *Edouard Charton et l'invention du Magasine Pittoresque (1833–1870)*. Paris: Honoré Champion, 2002.

Cachin, Marie-Françoise, 'Victorian Novels in France', in Lisa Rodensky, ed., *The Oxford Handbook of the Victorian Novel*. Oxford University Press, 2013, pp. 185–205.

Cachin, Marie-Françoise, Diana Cooper-Richet, Jean-Yves Mollier and Claire Parfait, eds., *Au bonheur du feuilleton: Naissance et mutations d'un genre (Etats-Unis, Grande-Bretagne, France, XVIIIe-XXe siècles)*. Paris: Créaphis, 2007.

Chartier, Roger and Henry-Jean Martin, eds., *Histoire de l'Edition Française, Tome III: Le Temps des éditeurs*. Paris: Fayard-Cercle de la Librairie, 1990.

Cooper-Richet, Diana, 'Les imprimés en langue anglaise en France au XIXe siècle: rayonnement intellectuel, circulation et modes de pénétration', in Jacques Michon and Jean-Yves Mollier, eds., *Les mutations du livre et de l'édition dans le monde du XVIIIe siècle a l'an 2000*. Paris: L'Harmattan, 2002, pp. 122–40.

Devonshire, M. G., *The English Novel in France, 1830–1870*. London: University of London Press, 1929.

James, Louis, *Fiction for the Working Man, 1830–1850: A Study of the Literature Produced for the Working Classes in Early Victorian Urban England*. London: Oxford University Press, 1963.

Jones, Katheryn, *La revue britannique, son histoire et son action littéraire (1825–1840)*. Paris: Droz, 1939.

King, Andrew, *The London Journal 1845–83: Periodical, Production, and Gender*. Aldershot: Ashgate, 2004.

Zdraveva, Blanche Vassileva, *Les Origines de la Revue des Deux Mondes et les littératures européennes (1831–1842)* Thèse: Université de Fribourg, Suisse, 1930.

14   The Newspaper and the Periodical Press in Colonial India

Ahmed, A. F. Salhauddin, *Social Ideas and Social Change in Bengal 1818–1835*. Leiden: E. J. Brill, 1965.

Bose P. N., and H. W. B. Moreno, *A Hundred Years of The Bengali Press, Being a History of the Bengali Newspapers from Their Inception to the Present Day*. Calcutta: H. W. B. Moreno, Central Press, 1920.

Chanda, Mrinal Kanti, *History of the English Press in India 1858–1880*. Calcutta: K. P. Bagchi, 2008.

Gupta, Abhijit, and Swapan Chakraborty, eds., *Print Areas: Book History in India*. New Delhi: Permanent Black, 2008.

Hofmeyr, Isabel, *Gandhi's Printing Press: Experiments in Slow Reading*. Cambridge, MA and London: Harvard University Press, 2013.

Kopf, David A., *British Orientalism and the Bengal Renaissance: The Dynamics of Indian Modernization 1773–1835*. Berkeley and Los Angeles: University of California Press, 1969.

Natarajan, S., *A History of the Press in India*. Bombay, Calcutta, New Delhi and Madras: Asia Publishing House, 1962.

Ray, Deeptanil, 'Speculating "National": Ownership and Transformation of the English-Language Press in India during the Collapse of the British Raj', *Media History Monographs*, 16.2 (2013–2014).

15   British and American Newspaper Journalism in the Nineteenth Century

Baldasty, G. *The Commercialization of News in the Nineteenth Century*. Madison: University of Wisconsin Press, 1992.

Chalaby, J. *The Invention of Journalism*. London: Macmillan, 1998.

Conboy, M. *The Press and Popular Culture.* London: Sage, 2002.

Edwards, P. D., *Dickens's 'Young Men': George Augustus Sala, Edmund Yates and the World of Victorian Journalism.* Aldershot: Ashgate, 1997.

Mulvey, C., *Transatlantic Manners: Social Patterns in Nineteenth-Century Anglo-American Travel Literature.* Cambridge University Press, 1990.

Palmegiano, E. *Perceptions of the Press in Nineteenth-Century British Periodicals.* London: Anthem Press, 2012.

Schudson, M., *The Power of News.* Cambridge, MA: Harvard University Press, 1995.

Smythe, T. *The Gilded Age Press, 1865–1900.* Westport, CT: Praeger, 2003.

Stevens, J. *Sensationalism and the New York Press.* New York: Columbia University Press, 1991.

Wiener, Joel H., *The Americanization of the British Press, 1830s-1914.* Basingstoke: Palgrave Macmillan, 2011.

   ed., *Papers for the Millions: The New Journalism in Britain, 1850s to 1914.* New York: Greenwood Press, 1988.

Williams, K. *Get Me a Murder a Day! A History of Media and Communication in Britain.* London: Bloomsbury Academic, 2010.

16   Journalism and Empire in an English-reading World: The Review of Reviews

Laurel Brake, Ed King, Roger Luckhurst and James Mussell, eds., *W. T. Stead: Newspaper Revolutionary.* London: British Library, 2012.

Palmegiano, E. M., *The British Empire in the Victorian Press, 1832–1867: A Bibliography.* New York and London: Garland Publishing, 1987.

Potter, Simon J., *News and the British World: The Emergence of an Imperial Press System, 1876–1922.* Oxford University Press, 2003.

   ed., *Newspapers and Empire in Ireland and Britain: Reporting the British Empire, c. 1857–1921.* Dublin: Four Courts Press, 2004.

   'Webs, Networks, and Systems: Globalization and the Mass Media in the Nineteenth- and Twentieth-century British Empire', *Journal of British Studies,* 46 (2007), 621–46.

   'Jingoism, Public Opinion, and the New Imperialism: Newspapers and Imperial Rivalries at the *fin de siècle*', *Media History,* 20 (2014), 34–50.

Putnis, Peter, 'The British Transoceanic Steamship Press in Nineteenth Century India and Australia: An Overview', *Journal of Australian Studies,* 31 (2007), 69–79.

Read, Donald, *The Power of News: the History of Reuters,* 2nd edn. Oxford University Press, 1999.

Vann, J. Don and Rosemary T. VanArsdel, eds., *Victorian Periodicals and Victorian Society.* Toronto and Buffalo: University of Toronto Press, 1994.

Part IV Journalists and Journalism

17 Dickens and the Middle-class Weekly

Bledsoe, Robert Terrell, *Dickens, Journalism, Music*. London: Continuum, 2012.

Clemm, Sabine, *Dickens, Journalism, and Nationhood: Mapping the World in Household Words*. London: Routledge, 2009.

Drew, John, *Dickens the Journalist*. Basingstoke: Palgrave, 2003.

'Texts, Paratexts and "E –Texts": The Poetics of Communication in Dickens's Journalism', in Juliet John, ed., *Dickens and Modernity (Essays and Studies)*. Cambridge: D. S. Brewer, 2012, pp. 61–93.

'An Uncommercial Proposition? At Work on *Household Words* and *All the Year Round*', *Victorian Periodicals Review*, 46.3 (Fall 2013), 291–316.

Farina, Jonathan V., '"A Certain Shadow": Personified Abstractions and the Form of *Household Words*', *Victorian Periodicals Review*, 42.4 (Winter 2009), 392–415.

Huett, Lorna, 'Among the Unknown Public: *Household Words, All the Year Round* and the Mass-Market Weekly Periodical in the Mid-Nineteenth Century', *Victorian Periodicals Review*, 38.1 (Spring 2005), 61–82.

Mackenzie, Hazel, and Ben Winyard, eds., *Charles Dickens and the Mid-Victorian Press 1850–1870*. University of Buckingham Press, 2013.

Nayder, Lillian, *Unequal Partners. Charles Dickens, Wilkie Collins, and Victorian Authorship*. Ithaca and London: Cornell University Press, 2002.

Waters, Catherine, *Commodity Culture in Dickens's* Household Words*: The Social Life of Goods*. Aldershot: Ashgate, 2008.

18 Harriet Martineau: Women, Work and Mid-Victorian Journalism

Crawford, Iain, 'Harriet Martineau, Charles Dickens, and the Rise of the Victorian Woman of Letters', *Nineteenth-Century Literature*, 68.4 (2014), 449–83.

Martineau, Harriet, *Harriet Martineau's Letters to Fanny Wedgwood*, ed. Elisabeth Sanders Arbuckle. Stanford University Press, 1983.

The Collected Letters of Harriet Martineau, 5 vols., ed. Deborah Anna Logan. London: Pickering and Chatto, 2007.

Harriet Martineau: Further Letters, ed. Deborah A. Logan. Bethlehem: Lehigh University Press, 2012.

19 Wilkie Collins and the Discovery of an 'Unknown Public'

Collins, Wilkie. *The Letters of Wilkie Collins*, ed. William Baker and William M. Clarke, 2 vols. Basingstoke: Macmillan, 1999.

The Collected Letters of Wilkie Collins, ed. William Baker et al., 4 vols. London: Pickering & Chatto, 2005.

The Collected Letters of Wilkie Collins: Addenda and Corrigenda (4), ed.
William Baker et al. London: Wilkie Collins Society, 2008.

Habermas, Jürgen, *The Structural Transformation of the Public Sphere*, trans. by
Thomas Burger. Oxford: Polity Press, 1989.

Law, Graham and Andrew Maunder, *Wilkie Collins: A Literary Life*. Basingstoke:
Palgrave, 2008.

Nayder, Lillian, *Unequal Partners*. Ithaca, NY: Cornell University Press, 2002.

Peters, Catherine, *The King of Inventors: A Life of Wilkie Collins*. London: Secker &
Warburg, 1991.

20 *Margaret Oliphant and the Blackwood 'Brand'*

Clarke, J. S., ed., *Margaret Oliphant: Non-Fictional Writings. A Bibliography*.
Victorian Fiction Research Guide 26. St Lucia: University of Queensland,
1997.

Finkelstein, David, '"Long and Intimate Connections": Constructing a Scottish
Identity for *Blackwood's Magazine*', in Laurel Brake, Bill Bell,
David Finkelstein, eds. *Nineteenth-Century Media and the Construction of
Identities*. Basingstoke: Palgrave, 2000, pp. 326–38.

The House of Blackwood. Author Publisher Relations in the Victorian Era.
Pennsylvania State University Press, 2002.

Jay, Elisabeth, *Mrs Oliphant. A Fiction to Herself. A Literary Life*. Oxford:
Clarendon Press, 1995.

Oliphant, Margaret, *Autobiography and Letters of Mrs M.O.W. Oliphant*. ed.
by Mrs Harry Coghill. Edinburgh and London: William Blackwood and
Sons, 1899, rptd Leicester University Press, 1974, ed. Linda H. Peterson,
Selected Works of Margaret Oliphant, Vol. 6, London: Pickering & Chatto,
2012.

The Autobiography of Margaret Oliphant, Elisabeth Jay ed. Oxford University
Press, 1990.

Selected Works of Margaret Oliphant, Joanne Shattock and Elisabeth Jay eds., 25
vols. London: Pickering & Chatto Routledge, 2011–16.

Shattock, Joanne, 'The Culture of Criticism', in Joanne Shattock, ed., *Cambridge
Companion to English Literature 1830–1914*. Cambridge University Press,
2010, pp. 71–90.

'Becoming a Professional Writer', in Linda H. Peterson, ed., *Cambridge
Companion to Victorian Women's Writing*. Cambridge University Press,
2015 pp. 29–42.

21   Marian Evans the Reviewer

Armstrong, Isobel. *Victorian Scrutinies: Reviews of Poetry 1830–1870*. London: Athlone Press, 1972.

Ashton, Rosemary. *142 Strand: A Radical Address in Victorian London*. London: Chatto and Windus, 2006.

Dames, Nicholas. 'On Not Close Reading: The Prolonged Excerpt as Victorian Critical Protocol', in Rachel Ablow, ed., *The Feeling of Reading: Affective Experience and Victorian Literature*. Ann Arbor: University of Michigan Press, 2010, pp. 11–26.

Dillane, Fionnuala. *Before George Eliot: Marian Evans and the Periodical Press*. Cambridge University Press, 2013.

Easley, Alexis, 'Authorship, Gender and Identity: George Eliot in the 1850s', *Women's Writing*, 3.2 (1996), 145–60.

Eliot, George, *George Eliot A Writer's Notebook 1854–1879, and Uncollected Writings*, ed. Joseph Wiesenfarth. Charlottesville: University Press of Virginia, 1981.
  The Journals of George Eliot, eds. Margaret Harris and Judith Johnston. Cambridge University Press, 1998.

Gray, Beryl. 'George Eliot and the *Westminster Review*', *Victorian Periodicals Review* 33.3 (Fall 2000), 212–24.

Hadjiafxendi, Kyriaki. 'Profession, Vocation, Trade: Marian Evans and the Making of the Woman Professional Writer', *Nineteenth-Century Gender Studies* 5.2 (Summer 2009), available at http://ncgsjournal.com/issue52/had.htm.

Harris, Margaret, ed., *George Eliot in Context*. Cambridge University Press, 2013.

Stange, G. Robert, 'The Voices of the Essayist', *Nineteenth-Century Fiction* 35.3 (1980), 312–30.

22   Oscar Wilde: New Journalist

Brake, Laurel, 'The Old Journalism and the New: Forms of Cultural Production in London in the 1880s', in *Subjugated Knowledges. Journalism, Gender and Literature*. Basingstoke: Macmillan, 1994, pp. 83–103.

Stokes, John, 'Wilde the Journalist', in Peter Raby, ed., *The Cambridge Companion to Oscar Wilde*. Cambridge University Press, 1997, pp. 69–79.

Turner, Mark W., 'Journalism', in Kerry Powell and Peter Raby, eds., *Oscar Wilde in Context*. Cambridge University Press, 2013, pp. 270–77.

Wilde, Oscar, *The Complete Works of Oscar Wilde*, eds. John Stokes and Mark W. Turner, Vols. vi and vii, Journalism, Parts I and II. Oxford University Press, 2013.

Index

Printed in Great Britain
by Amazon

42458386R00244